COMMERCIAL LAW OF THE EUROPEAN UNION

IUS GENTIUM

Comparative Perspectives on Law and Justice

VOLUME 4

COMMERCIAL LAW OF THE EUROPEAN UNION

By

GABRIËL MOENS

and

JOHN TRONE

Springer

Gabriël Moens
School of Law
Murdoch University
South Street, Murdoch
Western Australia 6150
Australia
g.moens@murdoch.edu.au

John Trone
School of Law
Murdoch University
South Street, Murdoch
Western Australia 6150
Australia
j.trone@murdoch.edu.au

ISBN 978-90-481-8773-7 e-ISBN 978-90-481-8774-4
DOI 10.1007/978-90-481-8774-4
Springer Dordrecht Heidelberg London New York

Library of Congress Control Number: 2010924627

Printed on acid-free paper

Springer is part of Springer Science+Business Media (www.springer.com)

Foreword

The Hon. Michael Kirby AC CMG*

This splendid book performs the heroic task of introducing readers to the large canvas of the commercial law of the European Union (EU). The EU began as an economic community of six nations but has grown into 27 member states, sharing a significant political, social and legal cohesion and serving almost 500 million citizens. It generates approximately 30% of the nominal gross world product. The EU is a remarkable achievement of trans-national co-operation, given the history (including recent history) of national, racial, ethnic and religious hatred and conflict preceding its creation.

Although, as the book recounts, the institutions of the EU grew directly out of those of the European Economic Community, created in 1957 [1.20], the genesis of the EU can be traced to the sufferings of the Second World War and to the disclosure of the barbarous atrocities of the Holocaust. Out of the chaos and ruins of historical enmities and the shattered cities and peoples that survived those terrible events, arose an astonishing pan-European Movement.

At first, this movement was focused on a shared desire for a Charter of Human Rights for Europe, if not for the wider world.[1] In February 1949, the International Council of the European Movement approved a "Declaration of Principles of the European Union". Those principles observed that "no state should be admitted to the European Union which does not accept the fundamental principles of a Charter of Human Rights and which does not declare itself willing and bound to ensure their application".[2]

---

*Justice of the High Court of Australia (1996–2009); President of the Institute of Arbitrators & Mediators Australia (2009–).

[1] Hersch Lauterpacht, *An International Bill of Rights of Man* (New York: Columbia University Press, 1945); Hersch Lauterpacht, *International Law and Human Rights* (New York: F A Praeger, 1950).

[2] A H Robertson, "Introduction" in *Collected Edition of the Travaux Préparatoires of the European Convention on Human Rights* (The Hague: Martinus Nijhoff, 1975), I: xxiii,

If the urgent challenge in Europe 60 years ago was to expiate events shocking to humanity, the ultimate objective was, as stated, to create a "European Union". Whilst economic progress was a pre-condition to healing the wounds of conflict, the founders of the European Movement recognised that something more than economic progress or even human rights institutions was required. The message of the "Congress of Europe" at The Hague in The Netherlands in May 1948 was addressed, over the heads of nation states, to the peoples of Europe. It recognised that intense practical, as well as moral, principles pointed toward a resolution of past history in the shape of a "European Union". Such a Union would be founded on economics; but it would be enlarged in popular imagination, by acceptance of friendship amongst the peoples of traditional enemies and by the creation of legal, economic, governmental, social and cultural links so that the cycle of war and inhumanity would be broken forever.

One of the key actors in the earlier movement that brought together the federation of the British colonies of Australia in 1901 was Alfred Deakin. He declared that, to achieve the objective of a national constitution in Australia, a "series of miracles" was required.[3] Such were the rivalries between the isolated communities of settlers who had taken control of continental Australia from the indigenous peoples. A series of constitutional conventions of those settlers followed in the 1890s. At one stage, they even envisaged expansion of the new Commonwealth to embrace New Zealand as part of an Australasian nation. Although the New Zealand politicians eventually opted out, somehow, the warring Australian factions clung together. Presumably, every now and again, their disputes over free trade and protectionism and the carve-up of revenues and taxes were subjected to a reality check. In this way, a trans-continental antipodean nation was born.

If we compare the way the three English-speaking settler federations of the United States of America, Canada and Australia were created, it must be acknowledged that their paths to political union were infinitely simpler than those that confronted the founders of the EU. Although the USA was born in a rebellion against the British Crown, which had denied its settlers the rights that Englishmen enjoyed at home, and although all three federations continued to face conflicts (mainly with their indigenous peoples, and in the US, the Civil War over slavery and secession), the ties that bound the peoples in each of these nations were so much stronger than existed in Europe in 1945. The English language predominated both in official and domestic communications. Legal traditions of representative

---

cited in Lord Lester of Herne Hill, Lord Pannick and Javan Herberg, *Human Rights Law and Practice* (3rd ed, London: LexisNexis, 2009), 6 [1.16].

[3] Alfred Deakin quoted in David Headon and John Williams (eds), *Makers of Miracles: The Cast of the Federation Story* (Carlton, Vic: Melbourne University Press, 2000), v, xiii, 141.

democracy, uncorrupted officials and independent courts afforded stable institutions on which to build national unity. Commonalities of religion and features of culture and history bound the several peoples of the USA, Canada and Australia together. These elements eventually helped to forge a strong national identity. Trade and commerce grew rapidly as an attribute of federal nationhood and flourished in an environment in which the law upheld contracts and protected competition.

In the Australian case, the creation of a continental common market was guaranteed by the express inclusion in the 1901 constitution of Section 92. In uncompromising language, this provision guaranteed that "trade, commerce and intercourse among the States . . . shall be absolutely free". Those words presented difficulties to the courts which tried to accommodate the unbending language to the felt necessities of governmental regulation to advance reasonable social objectives. In time, the constitutional words were given a clearer explanation by the Australian courts.[4] Interestingly, recent judicial elaborations have concerned local attempts to regulate online gambling,[5] a subject that has also arisen in the EU [3.120].

However, the circumstances in which these homogeneous settler communities came together in federal political and economic unions were easily distinguishable from the circumstances that occasioned, and accompanied, the evolution of the EU. In this respect, the EU's development to its present economic strength and support in popular imagination, depended on larger miracles, more frequently manifesting themselves.

This book is a story of how the institutions of the EU emerged, changed, adapted and developed. If it does nothing else but to reveal the complexity of the EU's institutional, legal, social and regulatory arrangements, that achievement will itself be notable. Many experts in Europe spend their busy days making, interpreting, applying, publicising and criticising the laws that are described in this book. However, most ordinary citizens of the EU probably get by with almost as little knowledge of EU law as do citizens in the countries that enjoy the strongest trading links with the EU. This work is principally addressed to readers outside the EU. Most especially to the practising lawyers, judges and regulators in advanced economies whose work brings them into contact with a question involving (directly or by analogy) EU law.

It is impossible, in any of those countries, for a busy practitioner to master the entire network of legal regulations that govern economic, political and social activities at home. But it is the fate of the present generation of legal practitioners to live and work in a profession that is increasingly required to know the laws of other places. In my youth, this was truly exceptional. Indeed, most lawyers and judges could survive with

[4] *Cole v Whitfield* (1988) 165 CLR 360 at 408; 78 ALR 42.

[5] *Betfair Pty Ltd v Western Australia* (2008) 234 CLR 418; [2008] HCA 11.

knowledge of their own sub-national legislation, to which were added the broad principles of the common law and an occasional federal statute or two. Now, that is changing. Contemporary practitioners of law (and especially those who must deal with international trade and commerce) need to be aware of trans-national legal regimes and the growing body of international law itself.

This explosion in the law makes, at once, for a more demanding life in achieving familiarity with legal systems that may be different in important respects from one's own. Yet, the positive side of this development is that it opens up employment and other opportunities that did not exist in earlier generations. The Internet has come just in time to afford access to the vast and growing body of EU law, whose basic rules many modern non-EU legal practitioners will need to familiarise themselves with.

This book has many merits. Amongst the chief of them is that:

- It allows a non-expert, from outside the EU, to see the broad contours of EU commercial law, and to understand its categories and taxonomies;
- It affords copious references (many of them online) to permit the reader to dig more deeply and to explore aspects of EU law that may be relevant or interesting for particular purposes;
- It presents the material in the English language and with a proper mixture of broad concepts and fastidious detail. It also affords convenient summaries and conclusions in every chapter; collects questions for discussion in academic classes; and presents the whole in a style that brings home to the reader the frequent similarities of the economic, social and other problems with which the EU is grappling at the same time as such issues are arising at home; and
- For a reader from within the EU, the book has a double merit. It affords those who use it the same broad overview as is provided to those looking from outside the EU into the engine room of its legal system. It also provides, to some extent, a perspective of EU law, involving the special advantage of being written from the outside, not specifically from inside the citadel. It was the Scottish poet Rabbie Burns who prayed that we should all be given the gift "to see oursels as others see us".[6] For the EU lawyer, this book has such a merit.

There is an occasional hint in this text of impatience, even possibly exasperation, at the detail of European law when it reaches down to the *minutiae* of tiny problems of great specificity:

- Is the Swedish ban on alcohol advertising compatible with the free trade objectives of the EU? [2.100]

[6] Robert Burns, *To a Louse*, verse 8 in *Works of Robert Burns* (London: Henry G Bohn, 1842), 241.

- Is a prohibition in Mrs Thatcher's UK on the importation of inflatable German love dolls based on a "morality" exception or is it really an impermissible burden on trade and competition? [2.100]
- Is the provision of abortion for patients a "service" protected by EU rules? [3.160]
- How may the UK's disapproval of Scientology impinge upon the free movement of persons within the EU? [3.55]
- May an Italian plumber set up a shingle in Germany? [3.90]; Problem Question 10
- Should a British national, like his French partner, be allowed to sue for the death of their child outside France, and can the restriction of recovery to nationals be justified? [3.300]

In every chapter the authors plunge with unflagging energy into the vast collection of case law that the EU has produced, based on the ever-expanding collection of EU Treaty provisions, Regulations, Directives and Decisions. The enormity of the regulations is borne out by nothing more than a glance at the table of legislation at the front of the book. Yet, the authors are not distracted by the sheer detail: far from it. On every page, they illustrate their taxonomies with countless instances. They never let the detail get them down.

The plain fact is that regulating a large and ever-growing economic market for such a substantial portion of the world's population, was never going to be a broad-brush enterprise. Especially was this so because of the predominance within the EU of the civil law tradition. That tradition, from the time of Napoleon's codifiers, tended to favour detailed regulation on all manner of subjects on the footing that the discretion of judges and other decision-makers was a form of tyranny. The codifiers' tradition grew out of the mistrust of the judiciary in royal France. The English judiciary, chosen in their maturity from senior members of the independent Bar, had often, historically, stood up for the liberties of the people. The common law system was therefore more content to enhance judicial powers and to trust such decision-makers with large leeways for choice. As parliamentary legislation has lately come to predominate in the countries of the common law, we have perhaps moved more closely to the civilian approach, with its tendency to great detail. The object is always to reduce the decision-maker to the "mouth of the law", as Montesquieu expressed it.

To anyone who complains about the detail of EU law, as described in this work, the answer that the authors inferentially give is: consider the alternative. We are dealing, after all, with regulations that will govern, in various degrees of detail, huge populations, countless corporations, all concentrated in a relatively small portion of the world's surface and in 27 member states. If the EU did not exist, the result would be an enormous cacophony of inconsistent legal regimes applied throughout Europe, with 27 different ways of tackling the same issue. This book, accordingly, portrays a most telling point. It may describe a complex network of laws for economic and social regulation. But, to a large extent, EU law in the areas examined has replaced national regimes that previously existed. The book may be concerned with a broad outline of legal rules of great particularity. Yet, in another sense, the creation of a single legal regime has substantially reduced disparities and inconsistencies in the law. It has done so with the acceptance of the over-arching principles of the primacy of EU law [12.65]; of the principle of subsidiarity [1.135]; and of the rule of proportionality [1.140], [2.125], [4.30].

I realise that the issue of federalism is still a highly sensitive one in the EU. One can master the details collected in this book without ever allowing that fateful word to cross one's mind (or if it does, to cross one's tongue). Yet, standing back from the detail collected here and looking at it from the outside and from above, as it were, there can be little doubt that a federation of sorts is emerging within the EU. The difficulty of getting politicians and people to address that fact candidly cannot be denied. The rejection in some countries of the common currency (*Euro*) [1.15] is an indication of the resistance that still exists in parts of Europe to the displacement of the "sovereignty" of nation states and their parliaments. Likewise, the much publicised rejection of popular referenda, held to approve the ill-fated European Constitution of 2004, [1.50] reflected the lingering anxiety that exists about handing more power over to Brussels, or for that matter, to the EU's principal judicial organ, the European Court of Justice in Luxembourg.

For all of these hesitations, the features of a kind of federation seem clear enough in these pages. They include shared institutions, reflecting the traditional branches of government. They extend to organs for making EU-wide law, in a field assigned to the Union. They are reflected in the common economic market that has been created. And, as well, there is a growing popular appreciation, in many EU countries, about the social advances that must come in the train of economic ones.

In every acknowledged federation, there are debates and conflicts over the powers that should be ceded to the centre and those that should be retained by the constituent parts. In keeping with most federations in the modern world, the tendency in Europe has been towards the accretion of more power to the centre.[7] Arguments of efficiency, economy and rationality are commonly advanced in favour of this centripetal movement. Yet there remain strong voices defending the merits, on some topics at least, of retaining local regulation of specific subjects about which local people feel most strongly. So it is in Europe.

Until the EU, its institutions and peoples, feel confident enough and sure enough of their Union to discuss the unmentionable "F" word, there will

---

[7] *New South Wales v Commonwealth (Work Choices Case)* (2006) 229 CLR 1 at 224 [611]; [2006] HCA 52.

remain constitutional deficiencies in Europe that are hinted at throughout this book. The enormous detail of the EU regulations described here will then be recognised as far from the chief problem which the EU "federation" presents to the peoples living within its borders. In the member states, there are regular elections. Periodically the electors throw out their national governments. They elect new leaders. They thereby impose the cleansing effect of democracy that reaches down into the civil service and keeps it on its toes.

There are elections for the European Parliament. However, the larger a political unit becomes, the greater is the risk of a democratic deficit.[8] That risk is clearest of all in the context of the United Nations Organisation. Although the *Charter* of the UN is expressed to be made in the name of the "Peoples of the United Nations", in truth it is, as its name suggests, a collection of Nations. The democratic accountability of those who make its treaties and other laws is, at most, highly indirect.

The democratic checks and controls that exist in the EU are less developed than those that operate in the member states, however, imperfect these may be. In part, this deficit may have been tolerated until now because of the pretence that the EU was nothing more than a technical body, looking after the economy. However, when one reads this book, even an otherwise unfamiliar reader will come quickly to the conclusion that what began in economics now expands into many attributes of social regulation. To some extent, this expansion is overt, as in the adoption of rules against immaterial discrimination [10.55], [10.85]. In other cases, it is simply a consequence of the operation of economic facts upon notions of the way in which a contemporary and just society should operate [10.120].

The issues of the future of the emerging European federation may still be too sensitive for open popular and political debate in the diverse societies that constitute the EU. Still, the day will come when that debate will arrive. The ever-expanding detail of the EU regulations, described in this book, make that day inevitable. So does the growing role played by the EU in international affairs, not least in matters of world trade.

Eventually too, the present division between the functions of the European Court of Justice and of the European Court of Human Rights will require rationalisation. The Court of Justice has improved the persuasive force of its reasoning in recent decades by embracing the less "cryptic", conclusory style of explaining its opinions and by utilising the more rhetorical and discursive style familiar to the common law [11.20]. The logical extension of this reform is the provision to the judges of the Luxemburg court of the facility, enjoyed at Strasbourg, to publish dissenting opinions when this is considered relevant and appropriate. Transparency should be

---

8 Alfred C Aman Jr, *The Democracy Deficit: Taming Globalization through Law Reform* (New York: New York University Press, 2004), 162.

the watchword of modern governmental institutions, particularly in the courts. The civil law prohibition on this liberty is just one of the institutional changes needed to improve democratic accountability within the EU. Yet it may not come about until a substantial popular discussion is commenced concerning the democratic deficit and the ways in which the EU institutions can be made more immediately accountable to the people whom they govern in the detailed ways described in these pages.

These are large politico-philosophical questions. Perhaps prudently, the authors steer around them. Yet to anyone living in a federation, such questions are the stuff of daily political debates. To anyone living in a federation, the EU looks like one; but it is a federation that, as yet, dares not speak its name.

The authors are to be congratulated for assembling and organising this compilation of information on EU law. Their work will be precious to practitioners who take their first steps into the unknown territory of EU law. It will be useful to scholars and teachers, because younger lawyers today are increasingly engaged with the world about them and they need to be instructed intensively in regional and international law. As this book shows, the EU has often been an important source of global stimulus to new perceptions of basic rights, as in the field of human sexuality [10.120] or in the growing debates over the protection of animal and plant life and biodiversity [2.100].

That so much has been achieved for the governance of so many living in societies of so much historical animosity is remarkable. The fact that it has occurred in such a short time constitutes a mighty human achievement. That the EU has evolved with a high level of acceptance by the people, parliaments and societies of Europe is undoubtedly a kind of miracle, given the many languages that are spoken [11.70]; the differing stages of economic development reached; and the distinct religious, cultural and social traditions observed. By collecting the material; organising it so skilfully; presenting it so clearly; and summarising it so succinctly, the authors have also worked a kind of miracle. Their efforts will be appreciated by legal practitioners, judges, scholars and teachers within and outside the EU because they have made the essence of EU commercial law available in a single book.

It is my hope that this book will also enhance the utilisation of EU law in other countries and legal traditions, including my own. On every page, we have an explanation of how the EU tackles questions that are coming before the courts, officials and judges of other countries at the same time. As the authors show, there is much wisdom to be gleaned from the way the EU tackles such problems. We who are outside Europe should be more aware of that wisdom. This book provides a key to unlock what has, until now, largely been unknown and unused save for a few experts in the field.

Sharing the wisdom of law from other places is itself a contribution to peace and justice in the world, which I take to have been amongst the original objectives as a result of which the EU emerged from the ashes of war and the horrors of genocide. When law replaces war for such a large portion of humanity, we need to know it, to admire it and to learn from it.

Sydney, Australia
18 March 2010

Michael Kirby

Preface

I am delighted to write the Preface to this book. The European Union (EU) is an economic trading bloc of 27 nations. As its membership already extends to most European nations, the EU is one of the world's most important trading entities.

The volume of EU legal acts is enormous. For example, in 2009 alone, there were 353 issues of the legislation series of the EU's Official Journal. The decisions of the two sections of the Court of Justice in 2007 take over 17,000 pages in the official law reports. What is even more daunting is that the volume of this legislation and case law is matched by its complexity.

This book is aimed at legal practitioners who practise outside of the EU and business people from outside the Union. Legal practitioners who have not been trained in EU law face considerable obstacles in dealing effectively with the avalanche of complex legal acts adopted by EU institutions. Hence, it is essential to find a clear path through this morass of legal material.

This book certainly fills the need for a book about EU business law written from a non-EU perspective. It provides a lucid and concise overview of the most important areas of European Union commercial law that are relevant for those from non-Member States such as the United States, Canada, Australia, Asia and Latin America. Mercifully, this work avoids those academically fascinating complex theoretical discussions which are likely to confuse, rather than to enlighten readers. Such matters are best left to further and advanced studies in the academy.

This book deals with the latest jurisprudence of the European Court of Justice and legislation issued by EU institutions. Each chapter contains extensive references to other books and articles for further reading. Useful websites are referred to throughout each chapter. Although this book is mainly aimed at the practitioners' market, the book is also capable of being used as a student text. The review problems set out in Appendix A will greatly assist the use of the book for teaching purposes.

I commend this book to a wide readership. It constitutes an excellent and stimulating discussion of the business law of the European Union. Practitioners, business people, law students, as well as those in government will derive substantial benefit from this book in their respective work.

Sydney, Australia
February 2009

David Flint

Acknowledgements

Many people helped us in the writing of this book. Most importantly, we must thank our loyal and patient families for their constant support and encouragement. We are very grateful to Justice Kirby for generously writing such an impressive Foreword at short notice. We must also thank the publishing editor at Springer, Neil Olivier and his assistant Diana Nijenhuijzen for their patience and constant assistance throughout the publication process. Serena Zhang printed out a very large number of cases and statutes. Poornima Purushothaman, Project Manager at Integra Software Services Pvt Ltd, diligently and skilfully incorporated revisions to the proofs. We would also like to thank the anonymous reviewers for making valuable suggestions. John Trone would like to thank Clive Turner and Peter Butler.

Perth, Australia — Gabriël Moens
Perth, Australia — John Trone
18 January 2010

Contents

Foreword v

Preface xv

Acknowledgements xvii

Abbreviations xxxiii

Table of Cases xxxv

Table of EU Founding Treaties lxxvii

Table of International Agreements lxxxv

Table of Legislation xci

1 The Political Institutions of the European Union 1

[1.05] Introduction 1
[1.10] Outline of This Chapter 1
[1.15] Basic Policies of the European Union 2
[1.20] Development of the European Union 4
[1.25] Single European Act 6
[1.30] Maastricht Treaty 6
[1.35] Treaty of Amsterdam 7
[1.40] Charter of Fundamental Rights 7
[1.45] Treaty of Nice 8
[1.50] European Constitution 8
[1.55] Treaty of Lisbon 9
[1.60] Relations Between the EU and the United States 10
[1.65] Relations Between the EU and Australia 12
[1.70] Relations Between the EU and Canada 14

[1.75] Relations Between the EU and New Zealand 15
[1.80] Relations Between the EU and South Africa 16
[1.81] Relations Between the EU and Other Common Law Jurisdictions 17
[1.85] Political Institutions of the European Union 18
[1.90] Commission 18
[1.95] Council 20
[1.100] Parliament 20
[1.105] European Council 22
[1.110] EU Courts 22
[1.115] European Central Bank 23
[1.120] EU Committees 24
[1.125] Other Officials 25
[1.130] Distribution of Powers Between the EU and the Member States 26
[1.135] Subsidiarity 27
[1.140] Proportionality 28
[1.145] Cooperation Between and Secession of Member States 30
[1.150] EU Legislation 31
[1.155] Public Availability of EU Legal Acts 33
[1.160] Conclusion 34
Further Reading 35

2 Free Movement of Goods 39
[2.05] Introduction 39
[2.10] Customs Union 39
[2.15] Common Customs Tariff 41
[2.20] Rules of Origin 42
[2.25] Added Value 43
[2.30] Elimination of Quantitative Restrictions Between Member States 44
[2.35] Measures with an Equivalent Effect 45
[2.40] Import Authorisation 46
[2.45] Production Quotas 46
[2.50] Transport Restrictions 46
[2.55] Maximum Prices 46
[2.60] Packaging, Labeling and Product Description Rules 47
[2.65] Indications of Origin 48
[2.70] Advertising Restrictions 48
[2.75] Prohibition of Prize Competitions 49
[2.80] Censorship Classification 49
[2.85] Sunday Closing Laws 49
[2.90] Creation of Individual Rights 50

[2.95] Arts 120 and 121 TFEU 50
[2.100] Treaty Exceptions to Art 34 TFEU 50
[2.105] Rule of Reason 55
[2.110] Permissible Grounds for Limitation of Free Movement of Goods 57
[2.115] Restriction of Selling Arrangements 59
[2.120] Necessity Principle 61
[2.125] Proportionality 63
[2.130] Private Action Threatening Interstate Trade 65
[2.135] Harmonisation 66
[2.140] Technical Standards 67
[2.145] Mutual Acceptance of Goods 68
[2.150] European Economic Area (EEA) Agreement 69
[2.155] Conclusion 70
Further Reading 71

3 Free Movement of Persons and Services 73
[3.05] Introduction 73
[3.10] Freedom of Movement for Workers 73
[3.15] Application of Art 45 TFEU 74
[3.20] Concept of "Worker" in Art 45 TFEU 74
[3.25] "Worker" Is Defined in EU Law Not National Law 75
[3.30] Workers with Low Incomes 76
[3.35] Right of Residence 76
[3.40] Discrimination Based on Nationality of Worker 77
[3.45] Obstacles to Freedom of Movement 78
[3.50] Exceptions to Free Movement of Workers 79
[3.55] Public Policy 79
[3.60] Public Service Employment 81
[3.65] Secondary Legislation Regarding Free Movement of Workers 83
[3.70] Freedom of Establishment 85
[3.75] Establishment by Professionals 86
[3.80] Establishment by Companies 88
[3.85] Establishment of Subsidiaries 88
[3.90] Removal of Discrimination 90
[3.95] When the Protection Applies 91
[3.100] Limitations upon Freedom of Establishment 92
[3.105] Exercise of Official Authority 92
[3.110] Public Policy Exception 92
[3.115] Consumer Protection 93
[3.120] Prevention of Crime 93
[3.125] Prevention of Tax Avoidance 94
[3.130] Collective Action 95

[3.135] Abuse of Freedom of Establishment 96
[3.140] Establishment of Service Providers 96
[3.145] EU Company Law 97
[3.150] Freedom to Provide Services 99
[3.155] Services Defined 100
[3.160] Broad Interpretation of "Services" 100
[3.165] Scope of Protection 101
[3.170] Discrimination Based on Nationality of Service Provider 102
[3.175] Obstacles to Provision of Services 103
[3.180] Limitations to Freedom to Provide Services 104
[3.185] Consumer Protection 105
[3.190] Protection of Fundamental Rights 106
[3.195] EU Secondary Legislation Regarding Provision of Services 106
[3.200] Services in the Internal Market 106
[3.205] Professional Services 107
[3.210] Transport Services 108
[3.215] Rail Transport 109
[3.220] Air Transport 109
[3.225] Inland Waterways and Maritime Transport 110
[3.230] Road Transport 111
[3.235] Electronic Commerce and Communications 111
[3.240] Postal Services 113
[3.245] Insurance and Investment Services 113
[3.250] Payment Services 114
[3.255] Cross-Border Mediation 114
[3.256] International Commercial Arbitration 115
[3.260] Provision of Services by Non-EU Citizens 116
[3.265] Freedom of Movement and Residence for EU Citizens Within the Union 116
[3.270] Secondary Legislation 117
[3.275] Right of Entry 117
[3.280] Right of Residence 118
[3.285] Restrictions upon Free Movement of EU Citizens 118
[3.290] Schengen Agreement 120
[3.295] Non-EU Citizens 122
[3.300] Non-discrimination on the Ground of Nationality 124
[3.305] Conclusion 125
Further Reading 127

4 Free Movement of Capital 131
[4.05] Introduction 131
[4.10] Movement of Capital Defined 132

[4.15] Restrictions upon the Movement of Capital 134
[4.20] Justifications for Restrictive Measures 136
[4.25] Overriding Requirements 137
[4.30] Proportionality 140
[4.35] Protective Measures 141
[4.40] Money Laundering 141
[4.45] Banking 142
[4.50] Securities 144
[4.55] Insurance 146
[4.60] Conclusion 146
Further Reading 147

5 Commercial Law and Policy 149
[5.05] Introduction 149
[5.06] Common Commercial Policy 149
[5.10] Broad Interpretation of Art 207 150
[5.15] Treaty-Making by the European Union 151
[5.20] Scope of the EU's Treaty-Making Power 152
[5.25] Express or Implied Treaty-Making Powers? 153
[5.30] Implied Powers Recognised 154
[5.31] Common Rules on Imports and Exports 156
[5.35] Anti-dumping and Subsidies 157
[5.40] WTO Obligations 157
[5.45] Anti-dumping Legislation 159
[5.50] Dumping 159
[5.55] Normal Value 160
[5.60] Constructing the Normal Value 160
[5.65] Constructed Value Includes Sales Costs 161
[5.70] Constructed Value Includes Profit 162
[5.75] Constructed Value Where No Sale in the Ordinary Course of Trade 162
[5.80] Export Price 163
[5.85] Comparison of the Export Price and Normal Value 164
[5.90] Dumping Margin 164
[5.95] Subsidies Legislation 165
[5.100] Subsidy 165
[5.105] Countervailable Subsidies 166
[5.110] Amount of the Subsidy 167
[5.115] Material Injury 167
[5.120] Injury Calculated as a Whole 167
[5.125] Each Determination of Injury Is Independent 168
[5.130] Finding of Injury Gives Rise to a Discretion 169
[5.135] Threat of Injury 170
[5.140] Community Industry 170

[5.145] Community Interest 171
[5.150] Investigation of Complaints 172
[5.155] Termination of the Investigation and the Proceeding 173
[5.160] Undertakings 174
[5.165] Anti-dumping and Countervailing Duties 175
[5.170] Provisional Duty 176
[5.175] Definitive Duty 176
[5.180] Duty Applies Prospectively 177
[5.185] Duty Applied Generally 177
[5.190] Refund of Duty 177
[5.195] Review by the Council 178
[5.200] Judicial Review of Findings 178
[5.205] Conclusion 180
Further Reading 181

6 **Competition Law** 183
[6.05] Introduction 183
[6.10] Direct Effect of the Competition Rules 184
[6.15] Art 101 TFEU 184
[6.20] Voidness of Prohibited Agreements 185
[6.25] Concept of an "Undertaking" 185
[6.30] Single Economic Unit 187
[6.35] Associations of Undertakings 187
[6.40] Undertakings Situated Outside the EU 188
[6.45] Concept of "Agreement" 189
[6.50] Unilateral Acts 190
[6.55] Types of Prohibited Agreements 191
[6.60] Exclusive Purchasing Agreements 192
[6.65] Object of the Agreement 192
[6.70] Prevention, Restriction or Distortion 193
[6.75] Effect upon Trade Between Member States 193
[6.80] De Minimis Effect 195
[6.85] Justification for Limitations 196
[6.90] Declaration of Inapplicability 197
[6.95] Block Exemptions 197
[6.100] Concerted Practices 198
[6.105] Abuse of a Dominant Position 199
[6.110] Dominant Position 200
[6.115] Concept of Abuse 200
[6.120] Special Responsibility of Dominant Undertakings 202
[6.125] Substantial Part of the Internal Market 203
[6.130] Relevant Market 203
[6.135] Exercise of Industrial Property Rights 204
[6.140] Effect upon Trade 205

[6.145] No Exemptions for Abuses ... 206
[6.150] Merger Control Under the TFEU ... 206
[6.155] Merger Control Under the EU Regulation ... 207
[6.160] State Aid ... 208
[6.165] Application of the Competition Rules ... 210
[6.170] Agriculture ... 210
[6.175] Transport ... 211
[6.180] Undertakings with Exclusive Rights ... 212
[6.185] Services of General Economic Interest ... 212
[6.190] Enforcement of the Competition Rules ... 213
[6.195] Regulation 1/2003 ... 213
[6.200] Investigation by the Commission ... 214
[6.205] Imposition of Fines ... 214
[6.210] Limitation Periods ... 215
[6.215] Judicial Review of Commission Assessments ... 216
[6.220] Researching Commission Documents ... 216
[6.225] Enforcement by National Competition Authorities ... 217
[6.230] Interaction of EU and National Competition Law ... 217
[6.235] Cooperation with Non-member States ... 218
[6.240] Conclusion ... 220
Further Reading ... 221

7 Removal of Taxation Barriers to Trade ... 229
[7.05] Introduction ... 229
[7.10] Customs Duties ... 229
[7.15] Internal Taxation ... 230
[7.20] Customs Duty or an Internal Tax? ... 231
[7.25] Indirect Taxation ... 233
[7.30] Similar Domestic Products ... 234
[7.35] Harmonization of Indirect Taxation ... 236
[7.40] Value Added Tax (VAT) ... 237
[7.45] Capital Taxation ... 238
[7.50] Excise Duties ... 239
[7.55] Harmonization of Direct Taxes ... 240
[7.60] Mergers Directive ... 240
[7.65] Parent/Subsidiary Directive ... 242
[7.70] Arbitration Convention ... 243
[7.75] Interest and Royalties Directive ... 244
[7.80] Taxation of Individuals ... 244
[7.85] Conclusion ... 245
Further Reading ... 246

8 Public Procurement ... 247
[8.05] Introduction ... 247

[8.10] Public Works, Supplies and Services Directive 248
[8.15] Exclusions from the Directive 248
[8.20] Contracting Authorities Regulated by the Directive 248
[8.25] Threshold Amounts 248
[8.30] Definitions of Public Contracts 249
[8.35] Requirements Applicable to Annex II A Services 249
[8.40] Non-discrimination Obligations of Contracting Authorities 249
[8.45] Requirements as to Technical Specifications 250
[8.50] Procedures for the Award of Public Contracts 250
[8.55] Publicity of Contracting Opportunities 251
[8.60] Award of Public Contracts 251
[8.65] Requirements Applicable to Annex II B Services....... 251
[8.70] Qualification and Disqualification of Bidders 252
[8.75] Excluded Sectors 252
[8.80] Enforcement of the Procurement Rules 253
[8.85] General Provisions of the TFEU 254
[8.90] Quantitative Restrictions 254
[8.95] Competition Law Rules 255
[8.100] WTO Agreement on Public Procurement 256
[8.105] Conclusion 256
Further Reading 257

9 **Industrial and Commercial Property Rights** 259
[9.05] Introduction 259
[9.10] Compatibility of National Law with EU Law 259
[9.15] Industrial and Commercial Property 260
[9.20] Protection of Packaging 261
[9.25] Art 36 TFEU Derogates from Free Movement of Goods 262
[9.30] Exhaustion of Rights: Copyright 262
[9.35] Exhaustion of Rights: Patents 263
[9.40] Exhaustion of Patent Rights: Compulsory Licences 264
[9.45] Exhaustion of Rights: Trade Marks................... 265
[9.50] Exhaustion of Other Rights 267
[9.55] Prevention of Deception of Consumers 267
[9.60] Relationship with Competition Law 268
[9.65] Relationship Between Arts 36 and 101 TFEU.......... 268
[9.70] Exemptions 270
[9.75] Systems of Property Ownership 271
[9.80] Harmonisation of Copyright 271
[9.85] Copyright in the Information Society 272
[9.90] Copyright in Computer Programs..................... 273
[9.95] Copyright in Databases............................. 273

[9.100] International Treaties Relating to Copyright 274
[9.105] Patents 274
[9.110] Trade Marks 276
[9.115] Harmonisation of Trade Marks 277
[9.120] Graphical Representation 277
[9.125] Distinctive Character 278
[9.130] Prohibited Uses of Marks 279
[9.135] Exhaustion of Trade Marks Rights 280
[9.140] Violation of a Licensing Agreement 281
[9.145] Revocation of a Trade Mark 282
[9.150] Community Trade Marks 282
[9.155] International Registration of Trade Marks 283
[9.160] Designs 283
[9.165] Plant Variety Rights 285
[9.170] Semi-conductors 285
[9.175] Geographical Indications 286
[9.180] Enforcement Measures 288
[9.185] Counterfeit Goods 289
[9.190] Conclusion 290
Further Reading 291

10 Social Dimension of the European Union 295
[10.05] Introduction 295
[10.10] Equal Pay for Equal Work 295
[10.15] Equal Pay and the Elimination of Sex Discrimination 296
[10.20] Defrenne (No 2) Litigation 296
[10.25] Equal Work Carried Out in the Same Establishment 297
[10.30] Application of Art 157 TFEU to Indirect Discrimination 298
[10.35] Further Indirect Discrimination Rulings 300
[10.40] Concept of "Pay" 301
[10.45] Equal Pay Under EU Directives 302
[10.50] Job Classification Schemes 303
[10.55] Concept of "Sex" Discrimination 303
[10.60] Equal Opportunities Directive 304
[10.65] Genuine and Determining Occupational Requirements 305
[10.70] Discrimination in the Supply of Goods and Services 305
[10.75] Discrimination Against Pregnant Workers 306
[10.80] Maternity Leave 307
[10.85] Prohibited Forms of Affirmative Action 308
[10.90] Permissible Forms of Affirmative Action 309
[10.95] Affirmative Action Under the Current Directive 310

[10.100] Other Forms of Discrimination 311
[10.105] Racial Discrimination 312
[10.110] Age Discrimination 313
[10.115] Disability Discrimination 314
[10.120] Sexual Orientation Discrimination 314
[10.125] Other Social Provisions: Arts 151 and 153 TFEU 315
[10.130] Charter of Fundamental Rights 315
[10.135] Vocational Training 316
[10.140] Data Protection: Personal Information 316
[10.145] Transfer of Personal Data to Non-member States 318
[10.150] Data Protection: Electronic Communications 319
[10.155] Consumer Protection 321
[10.160] Unfair Commercial Practices 321
[10.165] Sale of Consumer Goods 322
[10.170] Advertising Restrictions 324
[10.175] Unfair Terms 325
[10.180] Unit Pricing 325
[10.185] Product Labelling 325
[10.190] Distance Contracts 326
[10.195] Doorstep Selling 327
[10.200] Consumer Credit 328
[10.205] Timeshare Contracts 329
[10.210] Air and Rail Passengers 329
[10.215] Product Liability 329
[10.220] Product Safety 330
[10.225] Implementation by Member States 331
[10.230] Conclusion 332
Further Reading 333

11 Judicial Review and the European Court of Justice 337
[11.05] Introduction 337
[11.10] Composition of the Court 337
[11.15] Independence of the Judges 338
[11.20] Judgments of the Court 338
[11.25] Advocates-General 339
[11.30] Advice of the Advocates-General 339
[11.35] Role of the Advocate-General 340
[11.40] General Court 341
[11.45] Methods of Interpretation 341
[11.50] Literal Interpretation 342
[11.55] Historical Interpretation 342
[11.60] Contextual Interpretation 343
[11.65] Teleological Interpretation 344
[11.70] All Language Versions Considered 345

[11.75] Jurisdiction of the Court 346
[11.80] Causes of Actions 346
[11.85] Action for Annulment 347
[11.90] Characteristic of a Reviewable Act 349
[11.95] Substance Not Form 349
[11.100] Review Is Not Limited to Regulations, Decisions or Directives 349
[11.105] Reviewability of "Acts" of the Institutions and Other Bodies 350
[11.106] Grounds of Review 351
[11.110] Action for Failure to Act 351
[11.115] Action for Failure to Fulfil a Treaty Obligation 352
[11.120] Indirect Actions 353
[11.125] Preliminary Rulings 354
[11.130] Concept of "Court or Tribunal" in Art 267 TFEU 357
[11.135] Scope of Art 267 TFEU 359
[11.140] Obligatory References 361
[11.145] Acts of the Institutions 362
[11.150] Judicial Policy-Making and Retroactivity 363
[11.155] Blaizot Case 364
[11.160] Conclusion 365
Further Reading 366

12 The Effect of EU Law upon National Law 367
[12.05] Introduction 367
[12.10] van Gend en Loos Case 367
[12.15] Test for Direct Effect 369
[12.20] When Are Treaty Provisions Directly Effective? 370
[12.25] Vertical and Horizontal Direct Effect 370
[12.30] Direct Applicability Versus Direct Effect 371
[12.35] Direct Effect of Regulations 372
[12.40] Direct Effect of Directives 373
[12.45] Vertical Versus Horizontal Direct Effect of Directives 375
[12.50] Indirect Effect of Directives 376
[12.55] Direct Effect of Decisions 378
[12.60] Compensation for Breaches of EU Law 378
[12.65] Supremacy of EU Law Over National Law 381
[12.70] Supremacy Over National Constitutional Law 382
[12.75] Reassertion of the Supremacy of EU Law 384
[12.80] Duty of the National Authorities 384
[12.85] Factortame Litigation 385
[12.90] Fundamental Rights as General Principles of EU Law 386
[12.95] Protection of Fundamental Rights Expanded 387

[12.100] Broad Range of Fundamental Rights Protected 389
[12.105] Textual Basis for Fundamental Rights Protection 390
[12.110] Relationship with the European Convention on Human Rights 391
[12.115] Conclusion 393
Further Reading 394

13 The European Union and the World Trading System 397
[13.05] Introduction 397
[13.10] Three-Track Trading System 397
[13.15] Multilateral Approach: GATT 1994 398
[13.20] Dispute Resolution System 398
[13.25] Most-Favoured Nation 399
[13.30] Non-discrimination 399
[13.35] Gradual Reduction of Tariff Barriers 400
[13.40] Elimination of Import Quotas 400
[13.45] Safeguards 400
[13.50] Uniform Administration of Customs 400
[13.55] Protection of Health 401
[13.60] The EU and GATT 401
[13.65] GATT and Preliminary Rulings 403
[13.70] Position of GATT Under EU Law 403
[13.75] Position of the WTO Agreement Under EU Law 404
[13.80] WTO Agreement 405
[13.85] Agricultural Products 405
[13.90] Sanitary Measures 406
[13.95] Technical Barriers 406
[13.100] Preshipment Inspection 407
[13.105] Rules of Origin 407
[13.110] Import Licensing 407
[13.115] Services 408
[13.120] Intellectual Property 408
[13.125] Continuing Negotiations Through the WTO 409
[13.130] Regional Free Trade Agreements 409
[13.135] Bilateral Free Trade Agreements 411
[13.140] International Sale of Goods 413
[13.145] Domestic Implementation 414
[13.150] Application of the CISG 416
[13.155] Formation of the Contract 417
[13.160] Performance of the Contract 417
[13.165] Breach of Contract and Remedies 418
[13.170] Conclusion 419
Further Reading 419

Appendix A Problem Questions ... 423

Appendix B Table of Equivalence: EEC Treaty Version – Treaty of Amsterdam Version ... 439

Appendix C Table of Equivalence: Treaty of Amsterdam Version – Treaty of Lisbon Version ... 455

Index ... 475

Abbreviations

AC	Law Reports, Appeal Cases.
All ER (EC)	All England Law Reports. European Cases.
ATNIF	Australian Treaties (Not Yet In Force).
ATS	Australian Treaty Series.
BFSP	British and Foreign State Papers.
BISD 26S/290	GATT, Basic Instruments and Selected Documents, 26th Supplement, p 290.
Can TS	Canadian Treaty Series.
CEC	European Community Cases.
Ch	Law Reports, Chancery Division.
CLR	Commonwealth Law Reports.
Cm	Command Paper (1986-) [United Kingdom].
CMLR	Common Market Law Reports.
Cth	Commonwealth of Australia.
DSR	Dispute Settlement Reports.
DSU	Understanding on Rules and Procedures governing the Settlement of Disputes.
EC	European Community/Treaty Establishing the European Community.
ECHR	European Court of Human Rights, Reports of Judgments and Decisions.
ECR	European Court Reports.
ECR-SC	Reports of European Community Staff Cases.
ECSC	European Coal and Steel Community.
EEA	European Economic Area.
EEC	European Economic Community.
EFTA	European Free Trade Association.
EFTA Ct Rep	Report of the EFTA Court.
EHRR	European Human Rights Reports.
Env LR	Environmental Law Reports.
ETMR	European Trade Mark Reports.
ETS	European Treaty Series [Council of Europe].
EU	European Union.

F 3d	Federal Reporter, Third Series.
F Supp 2d	Federal Supplement, Second Series.
Fed Reg	Federal Register.
HR Doc	House of Representatives Document [United States].
ILM	International Legal Materials.
NZTS	New Zealand Treaty Series.
OJ C	Official Journal of the European Union. Information and Notices.
OJ EPO	Official Journal of the European Patent Office.
OJ L	Official Journal of the European Union. Legislation.
Qd R	Queensland Reports.
S Ct	Supreme Court Reporter.
SEA	Single European Act.
State Dept No	State Department Treaty Number [United States].
Statute	Protocol on the Statute of the Court of Justice.
TEU	Treaty on European Union.
TFEU	Treaty on the Functioning of the European Union.
TIAS	Treaties and Other International Acts Series.
Treaty Doc	Senate Treaty Doc [United States].
UKTS	United Kingdom Treaty Series.
UNTS	United Nations Treaty Series.
US	United States Reports.
USC	United States Code.
UST	United States Treaties and Other International Agreements.
WTAM	World Trade and Arbitration Materials.
WTO	World Trade Organization.

Table of Cases

International Courts and Tribunals

European Court of Justice Decisions

Aalborg Portland A/S v Commission (C-204/00 P) [2004] ECR I-123; [2005] 4 CMLR 4 (p 251) . . . [6.45], [6.205], [6.215]

Aannemersbedrijf P K Kraaijeveld BV ea v Gedeputeerde Staten van Zuid-Holland (C-72/95) [1996] ECR I-5403; [1997] 3 CMLR 1 . . . [11.70]

Abdoulaye v Regie nationale des usines Renault SA (C-218/98) [1999] ECR I-5723; [2001] 2 CMLR 372 . . . [10.40], [10.80]

Abrahamsson v Fogelqvist (C-407/98) [2000] ECR I-5539 . . . [10.85], [11.130]

Accession by the Community to the European Convention on Human Rights, Re (Opinion 2/94) [1996] ECR I-1759; [1996] 2 CMLR 265 . . . [5.15]

Acme Industry & Co Ltd v Council (T-48/96) [1999] ECR II-3089; [1999] 3 CMLR 823 . . . [5.60], [5.150]

Adeneler v Ellinikos Organismos Galaktos (C-212/04) [2006] ECR I-6057; [2006] 3 CMLR 30 (p 867) . . . [1.150], [12.50]

Administration des douanes et droits indirects v Rioglass SA (C-115/02) [2003] ECR I-12705; [2006] 1 CMLR 12 (p 273) . . . [9.10]

Adoption of Decision 2006/1016, Re: Parliament v Council (C-155/07) [2009] 1 CMLR 23 (p 632) . . . [1.100]

Adoui v Belgium (115/81) [1982] ECR 1665; [1982] 3 CMLR 631 . . . [3.55]

Advocaten voor de Wereld VZW v Leden van de Ministerraad (C-303/05) [2007] ECR I-3633; [2007] 3 CMLR 1 (p 1) . . . [12.100], [12.105]

Ahokainen v Virallinen syyttäjä (C-434/04) [2006] ECR I-9171; [2007] 1 CMLR 11 (p 345) . . . [2.100]

Aid to Seleco, Re: Italy v Commission (C-328/99) [2003] ECR I-4035; [2005] 2 CMLR 48 (p 1169) . . . [6.160]

Air Liquide Industries Belgium SA v Ville de Seraing (C-393/04) [2006] ECR I-5293; [2006] 3 CMLR 23 (p 667) . . . [7.15]

Ajinomoto Co Inc v Council (C-76/98 P) [2001] ECR I-3223; [2001] 2 CMLR 40 (p 989) ... [5.55]
AKZO Chemie BV v Commission (5/85) [1986] ECR 2585; [1987] 3 CMLR 716 ... [1.90]
AKZO Chemie BV v Commission (C-62/86) [1991] ECR I-3359; [1993] 5 CMLR 215 ... [6.115], [6.130]
Akzo Nobel Chemicals Ltd v Commission (T-125/03) [2007] ECR II-3523; [2008] 4 CMLR 3 (p 97), under appeal C-550/07 ... [12.100]
Alabaster v Woolwich plc (C-147/02) [2004] ECR I-3101; [2004] 2 CMLR 9 (p 186) ... [10.15], [10.40], [11.125]
Albany International BV v Stichting Bedrijfspensioenfonds Textielindustrie (C-67/96) [1999] ECR I-5751; [2000] 4 CMLR 446 ... [6.85], [6.180]
Alessandrini Srl v Commission (C-295/03 P) [2005] ECR I-5673 ... [12.100]
Alevizos v Ipourgos Ikonomikon (C-392/05) [2007] ECR I-3505; [2007] 2 CMLR 51 (p 1404) ... [3.20], [3.60], [11.135]
Alfons Lütticke GmbH v Hauptzollamt Saarlouis (57/65) [1966] ECR 205; [1971] CMLR 674 ... [12.15]
Algemene Transport- en Expeditie Onderneming van Gend en Loos (NV) v Nederlandse Administratie der Belastingen (26/62) [1963] ECR 1; [1963] CMLR 105 ... [12.10], [12.15], [12.30], [12.65]
Allianz SpA v West Tankers Inc (C-185/07) [2009] All ER (EC) 491; 48 ILM 485 ... [3.256]
Allied Corporation v Commission (239/82) [1984] ECR 1005; [1985] 3 CMLR 572 ... [5.200]
Allied Corporation v Council of Ministers (53/83) [1985] ECR 1621; [1986] 3 CMLR 605 ... [5.200]
Altair Chimica SpA v ENEL Distribuzione SpA (C-207/01) [2003] ECR I-8875; [2003] 5 CMLR 17 (p 867) ... [6.05]
Altmark Trans GmbH v Nahverkehrsgesellschaft Altmark GmbH (C-280/00) [2003] ECR I-7747; [2003] 3 CMLR 12 (p 339) ... [6.160]
Allué v Università degli studi di Venezia (33/88) [1989] ECR 1591; [1991] 1 CMLR 283 ... [3.60]
Alpine Investments BV v Minister Van Financiën (C-384/93) [1995] ECR I-1141; [1995] 2 CMLR 209 ... [3.165], [3.185]
Ambulanz Glöckner v Landkreis Südwestpfalz (C-475/99) [2001] ECR I-8089; [2002] 4 CMLR 21 (p 726) ... [6.75], [6.130]
Amministrazione delle Finanze dello Stato v Chiquita Italia SpA (C-469/93) [1995] ECR I-4533 ... [13.70]
Amministrazione delle Finanze dello Stato v Simmenthal SpA (No 2) (106/77) [1978] ECR 629; [1978] 3 CMLR 263 ... [12.75], [12.80]
Amministrazione delle Finanze dello Stato v Societa Petrolifera Italiana SpA (267/81) [1983] ECR 801; [1984] 1 CMLR 354 ... [13.65]
Ampafrance SA v Directeur des Services Fiscaux de Maine-et-Loire (C-177/99) [2000] ECR I-7013 ... [11.85]

AM & S Europe Ltd v Commission (155/79) [1982] ECR 1575; [1982] 2 CMLR 264 . . . [12.100]
Amurta v Belastingdienst (C-379/05) [2007] ECR I-9569; [2008] 1 CMLR 33 (p 851) . . . [1.130], [4.20], [4.25], [11.135]
Andersson v Sweden (C-321/97) [1999] ECR I-3551; [2000] 2 CMLR 191 . . . [11.145]
Angelidaki v Organismos Nomarkhiaki Aftodiikisi Rethimnis (C-378/07) [2009] 3 CMLR 15 (p 571) . . . [12.50]
Angonese v Cassa di Risparmio di Blozano SpA (C-281/98) [2000] ECR I-4139; [2000] 2 CMLR 1120 . . . [3.15], [12.25]
Anker v Germany (C-47/02) [2003] ECR I-10447; [2004] 2 CMLR 35 (p 845) . . . [3.60]
Antonio Munoz Y Cia SA v Frumar Ltd (C-253/00) [2002] ECR I-7289; [2002] 3 CMLR 26 (p 734) . . . [12.35]
AOK Bundesverband v Ichthyol-Gesellschaft Cordes (C-264/01) [2004] ECR I-2493; [2004] 4 CMLR 22 (p 1261) . . . [6.25]
Apothekerkammer des Saarlandes v Saarland (C-171/07) [2009] 3 CMLR 31 (p 1133) . . . [3.110]
A-Punkt Schmuckhandels GmbH v Schmidt (C-441/04) [2006] ECR I-2093; [2006] 2 CMLR 33 (p 873) . . . [2.110]
Arcaro, Criminal Proceedings Against (C-168/95) [1996] ECR I-4705; [1997] 1 CMLR 179 . . . [12.45]
Archer Daniels Midland Co v Commission (C-510/06 P) [2009] 4 CMLR 20 (p 889) . . . [6.45]
Arduino v Compagnia Assicuratrice RAS SpA (C-35/99) [2002] ECR I-1529; [2002] 4 CMLR 25 (p 866) . . . [6.05], [11.135]
Arens-Sikken v Staatssecretaris van Financiën (C-43/07) [2008] ECR I-6887; [2008] 3 CMLR 43 (p 1303) . . . [4.10], [4.15], [4.20]
Arne Mathisen AS v Council (T-340/99) [2002] ECR II-2905 . . . [5.120], [5.160], [5.200]
Arsenal Football Club plc v Reed (C-206/01) [2002] ECR I-10273; [2003] 1 CMLR 12 (p 345) . . . [9.110], [9.130]
Asjes, Criminal Proceedings Against (209/84) [1986] ECR I-1425; [1986] 3 CMLR 173 . . . [6.05]
ASML Netherlands BV v Semiconductor Industry Services GmbH (C-283/05) [2006] ECR I-12041 . . . [12.110]
Asnef-Equifax, Servicios de Información sobre Solvencia y Crédito, SL v Asociación de Usuarios de Servicios Bancarios (Ausbanc) (C-238/05) [2006] ECR I-11125; [2007] 4 CMLR 6 (p 224) . . . [6.75], [6.80]
Asscher v Staatssecretaris van Financiën (C-107/94) [1996] ECR I-3089; [1996] 3 CMLR 61 . . . [3.95]
Assedic Pas-de-Calais AGS v Dumon (C-235/95) [1998] ECR I-4531; [1999] 2 CMLR 113 . . . [11.135]

Associação Nacional de Operadores de Máquinas Recreativas (Anomar) v Portugal (C-6/01) [2003] ECR I-8621; [2004] 1 CMLR 43 (p 1357)... [3.160]
Association des Centres distributeurs Édouard Leclerc v SARL "Au blé vert" (229/83) [1985] ECR 1; [1985] 2 CMLR 286... [2.35]
Association Greenpeace France v Ministère de l'Agriculture et de la Pêche (C-6/99) [2000] ECR I-1651; [2001] 2 CMLR 45 (p 1129)... [11.125]
Associazione Nazionale Autotrasporto Viaggiatori (ANAV) v Comune di Bari (C-410/04) [2006] ECR I-3303; [2006] 2 CMLR 63 (p 1544)... [8.85]
Atlantic Container Line AB v Commission (T-395/94) [2002] ECR II-875... [6.40]
Atlantic Container Line AB v Commission (T-191/98) [2003] ECR II-3275; [2005] 4 CMLR 20 (p 1283)... [6.120]
Audiolux SA v Groupe Bruxelles Lambert SA (C-101/08) [2010] Bus LR 197... [12.90]
Austria v Council (C-445/00) [2003] ECR I-8549... [11.105]
Autorità Garante della Concorrenza e del Mercato v Ente Tabacchi Italiani – ETI SpA (C-280/06) [2007] ECR I-10893; [2008] 4 CMLR 11 (p 277)... [6.25]
Autotrasporti Librandi Snc di Librandi F & C v Cuttica Spedizioni e Servizi Internazionali Srl (C-38/97) [1998] ECR I-5955; [1998] 5 CMLR 966... [6.110]
Azienda Nazionale Autonoma delle Strade (C-192/98) [1999] ECR I-8583... [11.130]
Badeck, Proceedings for a Review of Legality by (C-158/97) [2000] ECR I-1875; [2001] 2 CMLR 6 (p 79)... [10.90]
Bagnasco v Banca Popolare di Novara soc coop arl (BNP) (C-215/96) [1999] ECR I-135; [1999] 4 CMLR 624... [6.75]
Baldinger v Pensionsversicherungsanstalt der Arbeiter (C-386/02) [2004] ECR I-8411; [2005] 1 CMLR 20 (p 499)... [3.65]
Ban on British Beef, Re: Commission v France (C-1/00) [2001] ECR I-9989; [2002] 1 CMLR 22 (p 627)... [1.90]
Ban on Night Lorry Traffic, Re: Commission v Austria (C-320/03) [2005] ECR I-9871; [2006] 2 CMLR 12 (p 337)... [2.50], [2.110]
Barber v Guardian Royal Exchange Assurance Group (C-262/88) [1990] ECR I-1889; [1990] 2 CMLR 513... [10.40]
BASF AG v Commission (T-4/89) [1991] ECR II-1523... [6.45]
BAT Cigaretten-Fabriken GmbH v Commission (35/83) [1985] ECR 363; [1985] 2 CMLR 470... [6.45]
Bayer AG v Commission (C-2/01 P) [2004] ECR I-23; [2004] 4 CMLR 13 (p 653)... [6.50]
Bayerische Hypo- und Vereinsbank AG v Commission (T-56/02) [2004] ECR II-3495; [2004] 5 CMLR 29 (p 1592)... [6.45]
Bayerische Hypotheken- und Wechselbank AG v Dietzinger (C-45/96) [1998] ECR I-1199; [1998] 2 CMLR 499... [10.195]

Bayerische Motorenwerke AG v Deenik (C-63/97) [1999] ECR I-905; [1999] 1 CMLR 1099 . . . [9.135]
Becker v Finanzamt Münster-Innenstadt (8/81) [1982] ECR 53; [1982] 1 CMLR 499 . . . [12.40]
Beguelin Import Co v SA GL Import-Export (22/71) [1971] ECR 949; [1972] CMLR 81 . . . [6.20], [6.40]
Belgische Radio en Televisie v SV Sabam (127/73) [1974] ECR 51 and 313; [1974] 2 CMLR 238 . . . [6.10], [8.95], [12.25]
Belgium v Commission (C-142/87) [1990] ECR I-959; [1991] 3 CMLR 213 . . . [6.160]
Belgium v Humbel (263/86) [1988] ECR 5365; [1989] 1 CMLR 393 . . . [3.160]
Belgium v Motte (247/84) [1985] ECR 3887; [1987] 1 CMLR 663 . . . [2.100]
Belgium v Spain (C-388/95) [2000] ECR I-3123 . . . [9.15], [11.115]
Bernini v Minister van Onderwijs en Wetenschappen (C-3/90) [1992] ECR I-1071 . . . [3.30]
Bertelsmann AG v Independent Music Publishers and Labels Association (C-413/06 P) [2008] ECR I-4951; [2008] 5 CMLR 17 (p 1073) . . . [1.150], [6.215]
Bestuur van het Algemeen Burgerlijk Pensioenfonds v Beune (C-7/93) [1994] ECR I-4471; [1995] 3 CMLR 30 . . . [10.40]
Bettati v Safety Hi-Tech Srl (C-341/95) [1998] ECR I-4355 . . . [11.45]
Bilka-Kaufhaus GmbH v Von Hartz (170/84) [1986] ECR 1607; [1986] 2 CMLR 701 . . . [10.30]
Biret International Council SA v Council [2003] ECR I-10497; [2006] 1 CMLR 17 (p 436) . . . [13.75]
Blaizot v University of Liège (24/86) [1988] ECR 379; [1989] 1 CMLR 57 . . . [11.150], [11.155]
Blanckaert v Inspecteur van de Belastingdienst/Particulieren/Ondernemingen Buitenland te Heerlen (C-512/03) [2005] ECR I-7685; [2005] 3 CMLR 39 (p 1097) . . . [4.10], [4.15]
Bleis v Ministère de l'Education Nationale (C-4/91) [1991] ECR I-5627; [1994] 1 CMLR 793 . . . [3.60]
Block v Finanzamt Kaufbeuren (C-67/08) [2009] 2 CMLR 39 (p 1015) . . . [4.10]
Bluhme, Criminal Proceedings Against (C-67/97) [1998] ECR I-8033; [1999] 1 CMLR 612 . . . [2.100]
Bodson v SA Pompes funèbres des régions libérées (30/87) [1988] ECR 2479; [1989] 4 CMLR 984 . . . [6.40]
Boehringer Ingelheim KG v Swingward Ltd (C-143/00) [2002] ECR I-3759; [2002] 3 CMLR 26 (p 623) . . . [9.45]
Boehringer Ingelheim KG v Swingward Ltd (C-348/04) [2007] ECR I-3391; [2007] 2 CMLR 52 (p 1445) . . . [1.150], [9.135]
Boehringer Mannheim GmbH v Commission (7/72) [1972] ECR 1281; [1973] CMLR 864 . . . [6.230]

Booker Aquaculture Ltd v Scottish Ministers (C-20/00) [2003] ECR I-7411; [2003] 3 CMLR 6 (p 133) ... [12.100]
Borawitz v Landesversicherungsanstalt Westfalen (C-124/99) [2000] ECR I-7293 ... [3.40]
Bordessa, Criminal Proceedings Against (C-358/93) [1995] ECR I-361; [1996] 2 CMLR 13 ... [2.10]
Bossi v Commission (346/87) [1989] ECR 303 ... [11.85]
Bouchoucha, Criminal Proceedings Against (C-61/89) [1990] ECR I-3551; [1992] 1 CMLR 1033 ... [3.135]
Bowden v Tuffnell Parcels Express Ltd (C-133/00) [2001] ECR I-7031; [2001] 3 CMLR 52 (p 1342) ... [11.55]
BPB plc v Commission (T-53/03) [2008] ECR II-1333 ... [6.45]
BP Soupergaz Anonimos Etairia Geniki Emporiki-Viomichaniki kai Antiprossopeion v Greece (C-62/93) [1995] ECR I-1883 ... [12.60]
Brasserie du Pecheur SA v Germany (C-46/93) [1996] ECR I-1029; [1996] 1 CMLR 889 ... [2.90], [12.60]
Brasserie Nationale SA v Commission (T-49/02) [2005] ECR II-3033 ... [6.45]
Brentjens' Handelsonderneming BV v Stichting Bedrijfspensioenfonds voor de Handel in Bouwmaterialen (C-115/97) [1999] ECR I-6025; [2000] 4 CMLR 566 ... [6.85]
Bristol-Myers Squibb v Paranova A/S (C-427/93) [1996] ECR I-3457; [1997] 1 CMLR 1151 ... [9.45]
Britannia Alloys & Chemicals Ltd v Commission (C-76/06 P) [2007] ECR I-4405; [2007] 5 CMLR 3 (p 251) ... [6.205], [11.60]
British Airways plc v Commission (T-219/99) [2003] ECR II-5917; [2004] 4 CMLR 19 (p 1008) ... [1.90]
British Airways plc v Commission (C-95/04 P) [2007] ECR I-2331; [2007] 4 CMLR 22 (p 982) ... [6.115]
British American Tobacco Co Ltd v Commission (142/84) [1987] ECR 4487; [1988] 4 CMLR 24 ... [6.150]
British Shoe Corporation Footwear Supplies Ltd v Council (T-598/97) [2002] ECR II-1155; [2002] 2 CMLR 7 (p 110) ... [5.200]
British Sugar plc v Commission (C-359/01 P) [2004] ECR I-4933; [2004] 5 CMLR 8 (p 329) ... [6.75]
Broede v Sandker (C-3/95) [1996] ECR I-6511; [1997] 1 CMLR 224 ... [3.150]
Broekmeulen v Huisarts Registratie Commissie (246/80) [1981] ECR 2311; [1982] 1 CMLR 91 ... [11.130]
Brother International GmbH v Hauptzollamt Giessen (26/88) [1989] ECR 4253; [1990] 3 CMLR 658 ... [2.25]
Brother Industries Ltd v Council (250/85) [1988] ECR 5683; [1990] 1 CMLR 792 ... [5.75], [5.85], [5.130]
Brzeziński v Dyrektor Izby Celnej w Warszawie (C-313/05) [2007] ECR I-513; [2007] 4 CMLR 4 (p 121) ... [2.10], [7.15], [7.30], [11.155]

Buet v Ministere Public (C-382/87) [1989] ECR 1235; [1993] 3 CMLR 659 . . . [2.70]
Burbaud v Ministère de l'Emploi et de la Solidarité (C-285/01) [2003] ECR I-8219; [2003] 3 CMLR 21 (p 635) . . . [3.60]
Burtscher v Stauderer (C-213/04) [2005] ECR I-10309; [2006] 2 CMLR 13 (p 382) . . . [4.15]
"Buy Irish" Campaign, Re: Commission v Ireland (249/81) [1982] ECR 4005; [1983] 2 CMLR 104 . . . [11.115]
Cadbury Schweppes plc v Commissioners of Inland Revenue (C-196/04) [2006] ECR I-7995; [2007] 1 CMLR 2 (p 43) . . . [1.130], [3.70], [3.135]
Caisse Nationale d'Assurance Vieillesse des Travailleurs Salaries (Cnavts) v Thibault (C-136/95) [1998] ECR I-2011; [1998] 2 CMLR 516 . . . [10.80]
Canon Inc v Council (277/85) [1988] ECR 5731; [1989] 1 CMLR 915 . . . [5.70], [5.75], [5.125], [5.200]
Carbotermo SpA v Comune di Busto Arsizio (C-340/04) [2006] ECR I-4137; [2006] 3 CMLR 7 (p 195) . . . [8.05]
Carp Snc di L Moleri e V Corsi v Ecorad Srl (C-80/06) [2007] ECR I-4473 . . . [12.55]
Cartagena Protocol on Biosafety, Re (Opinion 2/00) [2001] ECR I-9713; [2002] 1 CMLR 28 (p 809) . . . [5.15]
Cartesio Oktató és Szolgáltató bt, Proceedings re (C-210/06) [2008] ECR I-9641; [2009] 1 CMLR 50 (p 1394) . . . [3.80]
Casati, Re (203/80) [1981] ECR 2595; [1982] 1 CMLR 365 . . . [4.05]
Celozzi v Innungskrankenkasse Baden-Württemberg (C-332/05) [2007] ECR I-563 . . . [3.40]
Centrafarm BV v Sterling Drug Inc (15/74) [1974] ECR 1147; [1974] 2 CMLR 480 . . . [6.30], [9.35]
Centrafarm BV v Winthrop BV (16/74) [1974] ECR 1183, [1974] 2 CMLR 480 . . . [9.45]
Centre Belge D'études de Marche Tele-Marketing SA v Compagnie Luxembourgeoise de Télediffusion SA (311/84) [1985] ECR 3261; [1986] 2 CMLR 558 . . . [8.95]
Centro di Musicologia Walter Stauffer v Finanzamt München für Körperschaften (C-386/04) [2006] ECR I-8203; [2009] 2 CMLR 31 (p 777) . . . [3.70], [4.10], [4.25]
Centros Ltd v Erhvervs- og Selskabsstyrelsen (C-212/97) [1999] ECR I-1459; [1999] 2 CMLR 551 . . . [3.135]
Centrum voor gelijkheid van kansen en voor racismbestrijding v Firma Feryn NV (C-54/07) [2008] ECR I-5187; [2008] 3 CMLR 22 (p 695) . . . [10.105], [11.125]
CEPSA Estaciones de Servicio SA v LV Tobar e Hijos SL (C-279/06) [2008] ECR I-6681; [2008] 5 CMLR 19 (p 1327) . . . [6.20]
Chacón Navas v Eurest Colectividades SA (C-13/05) [2006] ECR I-6467; [2006] 3 CMLR 40 (p 1123) . . . [10.115], [11.135], [12.100]

Chateignier v Office national de l'emploi (C-346/05) [2006] ECR I-10951; [2007] 1 CMLR 20 (p 618) . . . [11.135]
Chemial Farmaceutici v DAF SpA (140/79) [1981] ECR 1; [1981] 3 CMLR 350 . . . [7.15]
Chen v Secretary of State for the Home Department (C-200/02) [2004] ECR I-9925; [2004] 3 CMLR 48 (p 1060) . . . [3.165]
Chevassus-Marche v Conseil régional de la Réunion (C-212/96) [1998] ECR I-743; [1998] 2 CMLR 330 . . . [7.30]
Chronopost SA v Union française de l'express (Ufex) (C-83/01 P) [2003] ECR I-6993; [2003] 3 CMLR 11 (p 303) . . . [6.160]
Cidrerie Ruwet SA v Cidre Stassen SA (C-3/99) [2000] ECR I-8749; [2000] 3 CMLR 1390 . . . [2.110]
CILFIT Srl v Ministro della Sanita (283/81) [1982] ECR 3415; [1983] 1 CMLR 472 . . . [11.60], [11.70], [11.125], [11.140]
Ciola v Land Vorarlberg (C-224/97) [1999] ECR I-2517; [1999] 2 CMLR 1220 . . . [3.40], [3.165], [12.65]
Cipolla v Fazari (C-94/04) [2006] ECR I-11421; [2007] 4 CMLR 8 (p 286) . . . [3.175], [3.180], [3.185], [6.05], [11.135]
Clean Car Autoservice GmbH v Landeshauptmann von Wien (C-350/96) [1998] ECR I-2521; [1998] 2 CMLR 637 . . . [3.15], [3.40], [3.55]
Climax Paper Converters Ltd v Council (T-155/94) [1996] ECR II-873; [1996] 3 CMLR 1031 . . . [5.165]
CNL-SUCAL (SA) NV v HAG GF AG (C-10/89) [1990] ECR I-3711; [1990] 3 CMLR 571 . . . [11.20]
Coditel Brabant SA v Commune d'Uccle (C-324/07) [2009] 1 CMLR 29 (p 789) . . . [8.85]
Colegio de Oficiales de la Marina Mercante Española v Administración del Estado (C-405/01) [2003] ECR I-10391; [2005] 2 CMLR 13 (p 279) . . . [3.60]
Coleman v Attridge Law (C-303/06) [2008] ECR I-5603; [2008] 3 CMLR 27 (p 777) . . . [10.115]
Colim NV v Bigg's Continent Noord NV (C-33/97) [1999] ECR I-3175; [2000] 2 CMLR 135 . . . [2.35]
College van burgemeester en wethouders van Rotterdam v Rijkeboer (C-553/07) [2009] 3 CMLR 28 (p 1041) . . . [10.140]
Collins v Imtrat Handelsgesellschaft mbH (C-92/92) [1993] ECR I-5145; [1993] 3 CMLR 773 . . . [9.10]
Collins v Secretary of State for Work and Pensions (C-138/02) [2004] ECR I-2703; [2004] 2 CMLR 8 (p 147) . . . [3.20], [3.35], [3.40], [11.20]
Columbus Container Services BVBA & Co v Finanzamt Bielefeld-Innenstadt (C-298/05) [2007] ECR I-10451; [2009] 1 CMLR 8 (p 241) . . . [1.130], [3.85], [11.125]
Commission v Anic Partecipazioni (C-49/92) [1999] ECR I-4125; [2001] 4 CMLR 17 (p 602) . . . [6.45], [6.65], [6.100], [6.205]

Commission v AssiDomän Kraft Products AB (C-310/97 P) [1999] ECR I-5363; [1999] 5 CMLR 1253 . . . [11.85]
Commission v BASF AG (C-137/92 P) [1994] ECR I-2555 . . . [1.90]
Commission v Belgium (C-2/90) [1992] ECR I-4431; [1993] 1 CMLR 365 . . . [2.10], [7.30]
Commission v Belgium (C-173/94) [1996] ECR I-3265 . . . [3.60]
Commission v Belgium (C-319/01) [2002] ECR I-10779 . . . [12.65]
Commission v Council (C-25/94) [1996] ECR I-1469 . . . [1.95]
Commission v Council (C-27/04) [2004] ECR I-6649 . . . [11.100]
Commission v Denmark (171/78) [1980] ECR 447; [1981] 2 CMLR 688 . . . [7.15], [7.30]
Commission v European Investment Bank (C-15/00) [2003] ECR I-7281 . . . [1.15]
Commission v Ferriere Nord SpA (C-516/06 P) [2007] ECR I-10685; [2008] 4 CMLR 10 (p 267) . . . [11.85]
Commission v France (167/73) [1974] ECR 359; [1974] 2 CMLR 216 . . . [12.80]
Commission v France (168/78) [1980] ECR 347; [1981] 2 CMLR 631 . . . [7.30]
Commission v France (90/79) [1981] ECR 283; [1981] 3 CMLR 1 . . . [7.15], [7.20]
Commission v France (270/83) [1986] ECR 273; [1987] 1 CMLR 401 . . . [3.85]
Commission v France (96/85) [1986] ECR 1475; [1986] 3 CMLR 57 . . . [3.75]
Commission v France (318/86) [1988] ECR 3559; [1989] 3 CMLR 663 . . . [10.65]
Commission v France (C-366/88) [1990] ECR I-3571; [1992] 1 CMLR 205 . . . [11.100]
Commission v France (C-265/95) [1997] ECR I-6959 . . . [2.130]
Commission v France (C-23/99) [2000] ECR I-7653 . . . [9.10]
Commission v France (C-302/00) [2002] ECR I-2055 . . . [7.30]
Commission v France (C-304/02) [2005] ECR I-6263; [2005] 3 CMLR 13 (p 275) . . . [11.115]
Commission v France (C-121/07) [2008] ECR I-9159 . . . [12.65]
Commission v Germany (C-298/95) [1996] ECR I-6747 . . . [12.65]
Commission v Germany (C-191/95) [1998] ECR I-5449; [1999] 2 CMLR 1265 . . . [1.90]
Commission v Germany (C-20/01) [2003] ECR I-3609 . . . [1.90], [11.115]
Commission v Germany (C-103/01) [2003] ECR I-5369 . . . [3.60]
Commission v Germany (C-441/02) [2006] ECR I-3449 . . . [3.55]
Commission v Germany (C-490/04) [2007] ECR I-6095 . . . [3.170], [3.175]
Commission v Germany (C-318/05) [2007] ECR I-6957 . . . [3.45]
Commission v Greece (C-306/89) [1991] ECR I-5863; [1994] 1 CMLR 803 . . . [11.55]

Commission v Greece (C-391/92) [1995] ECR I-1621; [1996] 1 CMLR 359 . . . [2.115]
Commission v Greece (C-185/96) [1998] ECR I-6601; [2001] 1 CMLR 28 (p 744) . . . [3.65]
Commission v Greece (C-387/97) [2000] ECR I-5047 . . . [11.115], [12.65]
Commission v Greece (C-394/02) [2005] ECR I-4713 . . . [11.115]
Commission v Greece (C-568/07) [2009] ECR . . . [11.115]
Commission v Ireland (55/79) [1980] ECR 481; [1980] 1 CMLR 734 . . . [7.25]
Commission v Ireland (C-235/91) [1992] ECR I-5917; [1993] 1 CMLR 325 . . . [2.100]
Commission v Italy (7/61) [1961] ECR 317; [1962] CMLR 39 . . . [11.115]
Commission v Italy (7/68) [1968] ECR 423; [1969] CMLR 1 . . . [2.10], [11.60]
Commission v Italy (24/68) [1969] ECR 193; [1971] CMLR 611 . . . [2.10]
Commission v Italy (73/79) [1980] ECR 1533 . . . [7.20]
Commission v Italy (319/81) [1983] ECR 601; [1983] 2 CMLR 517 . . . [7.15]
Commission v Italy (C-235/89) [1992] ECR I-777 . . . [9.75]
Commission v Italy (C-283/99) [2001] ECR I-4363 . . . [3.60]
Commission v Italy (C-456/03) [2005] ECR I-5335 . . . [1.150]
Commission v Italy (C-173/05) [2007] ECR I-4917 . . . [2.10], [2.15]
Commission v Italy (C-110/05) [2009] 2 CMLR 34 (p 876) . . . [2.110], [2.120]
Commission v Ladbroke Racing Ltd (C-359/95 P) [1997] ECR I-6265; [1998] 4 CMLR 27 . . . [6.05]
Commission v Luxembourg (2/62) [1962] ECR 425; [1963] CMLR 199 . . . [7.15]
Commission v Luxembourg (C-32/05) [2006] ECR I-11323 . . . [1.150]
Commission v Netherlands (C-144/99) [2001] ECR I-3541 . . . [1.150]
Commission v NTN Corporation (C-245/95 P) [1998] ECR I-401 . . . [5.125], [5.150], [5.195]
Commission v Parliament (C-378/00) [2003] ECR I-937 . . . [1.90]
Commission v Spain (C-298/97) [1998] ECR I-3301 . . . [12.65]
Commission v Spain (C-274/98) [2000] ECR I-2823 . . . [12.65]
Commission v Spain (C-278/01) [2003] ECR I-14141 . . . [11.115]
Commission v Spain (C-514/03) [2006] ECR I-963 . . . [3.175]
Commission v Spain (C-503/03) [2006] ECR I-1097 . . . [3.55], [3.290]
Commission v Spain (C-154/08) [2009] ECR . . . [11.115]
Commission v Tetra Laval BV (C-12/03) [2005] ECR I-987; [2005] 4 CMLR 8 (p 573) . . . [6.215]
Commission v United Kingdom (170/78) [1980] ECR 417 and [1983] ECR 2265 . . . [7.30]
Commission v United Kingdom (165/82) [1983] ECR 3431; [1984] 1 CMLR 44 . . . [10.65]

Commission v United Kingdom (C-65/04) [2006] ECR I-2239 . . . [1.20]
Commission v Volkswagen AG (C-74/04 P) [2006] ECR I-6585; [2008] 4 CMLR 16 (p 1297) . . . [6.50]
Compagnie Maritime Belge Transports SA v Commission (C-395/96 P) [2000] ECR I-1365; [2000] 4 CMLR 1076 . . . [6.40], [6.105], [6.110], [6.115], [6.120], [6.145]
Compulsory Patent Licences, Re: Commission v United Kingdom (C-30/90) [1992] ECR I-829; [1992] 2 CMLR 709 . . . [9.40], [9.75]
Concordia Bus Finland Oy AB v Helsingin Kaupunki (C-513/99) [2002] ECR I-7213; [2003] 3 CMLR 20 (p 589) . . . [8.40], [8.60]
Conegate Ltd v Customs and Excise Commissioners (121/85) [1986] ECR 1007; [1986] 1 CMLR 739 . . . [2.100]
Connect Austria Gesellschaft für Telekommunikation GmbH v Telekom-Control-Kommission (C-462/99) [2003] ECR I-5197; [2005] 5 CMLR 6 (p 302) . . . [12.50]
Consorzio Aziende Metano v Comune di Cingia de' Botti (C-231/03) [2005] ECR I-7287; [2006] 1 CMLR 2 (p 17) . . . [8.85]
Consorzio del Prosciutto di Parma v Asda Stores Ltd (C-108/01) [2003] ECR I-5121; [2003] 2 CMLR 21 (p 639) . . . [9.15]
Consorzio Industrie Fiammiferi v Autorità Garante della Concorrenza e del Mercato (C-198/01) [2003] ECR I-8055; [2003] 5 CMLR 16 (p 829) . . . [12.65]
Consorzio italiano della componentistica di ricambio per autoveicoli and Maxicar v Régie nationale des usines Renault (53/87) [1988] ECR 6039; [1990] 4 CMLR 265 . . . [9.10]
Coöperatieve Stremsel-en Kleurselfabriek v Commission (61/80) [1981] ECR 851; [1982] 1 CMLR 240 . . . [6.75]
Cöoperatieve Vereniging "Suiker Unie" UA v Commission (40/73) [1975] ECR 1663; [1976] 1 CMLR 295 . . . [6.80]
Coote v Granada Hospitality Ltd (C-185/97) [1998] ECR I-5199; [1998] 3 CMLR 958 . . . [12.45], [12.50]
Copad SA v Christian Dior couture SA (C-59/08) [2009] ETMR 40 (p 683) . . . [9.110], [9.140]
Corbeau, Criminal Proceedings Against (C-320/91) [1993] ECR I-2533; [1995] 4 CMLR 621 . . . [6.05], [6.185]
Corsica Ferries France SA v Gruppo Antichi Ormeggiatori del Porto di Genova Coop arl (C-266/96) [1998] ECR I-3949; [1998] 5 CMLR 402 . . . [6.180]
Cosmetic Products Directive, Re: France v Parliament (C-244/03) [2005] ECR I-4021; [2005] 3 CMLR 6 (p 118) . . . [11.85]
Costa v ENEL (6/64) [1964] ECR 585; [1964] CMLR 425 . . . [12.65]
Courage Ltd v Crehan (C-453/99) [2001] ECR I-6297; [2001] 5 CMLR 28 (p 1058) . . . [6.10], [6.20]
Cousin, Criminal Proceedings Against (162/82) [1983] ECR 1101; [1984] 2 CMLR 780 . . . [2.25]

Cowan v Tresor Public (186/87) [1989] ECR 195; [1990] 2 CMLR 613 . . . [3.165]
Crailsheimer Volksbank eG v Conrads (C-229/04) [2005] ECR I-9273; [2006] 1 CMLR 21 (p 563) . . . [10.195]
Cristini v Sociéte Nationale des Chemins de fer Français (32/75) [1975] ECR 1085; [1976] 1 CMLR 573 . . . [3.65]
Cullet v Centre Leclerc à Toulouse (231/81) [1985] ECR 305; [1985] 2 CMLR 524 . . . [8.95]
Customs Agents, Re: Commission v Italy (C-35/96) [1998] ECR I-3851; [1998] 5 CMLR 889 . . . [6.25]
D v Inspecteur van de Belastingdienst/Particulieren/Ondernemingen Buitenland te Heerlen (C-376/03) [2005] ECR I-5821; [2005] 3 CMLR 19 (p 515) . . . [4.10], [4.20]
Dalmine SpA v Commission (C-407/04 P) [2007] ECR I-829 . . . [11.106]
Dansk Rørindustri A/S v Commission (C-189/02) [2005] ECR I-5425; [2005] 5 CMLR 17 (p 796) . . . [6.40], [6.45], [6.205], [8.95], [12.110]
Dansk Supermarked A/S v A/S Imerco (58/80) [1981] ECR 181; [1981] 3 CMLR 590 . . . [9.30]
De Coster v Collège des bourgmestre et échevins de Watermael-Boitsfort (C-17/00) [2001] ECR I-9445; [2002] 1 CMLR 12 (p 285) . . . [3.160], [11.130]
De Danske Bilimportører v Skatteministeriet, Told- og Skattestyrelsen (C-383/01) [2003] ECR I-6065; [2003] 2 CMLR 41 (p 1265) . . . [7.15], [7.30]
De Groot en Slot Allium BV v Ministere de l'Economie, des Finances et de l'Industrie (C-147/04) [2006] ECR I-245; [2009] 1 CMLR 22 (p 603) . . . [2.60], [2.110]
de Jaeck v Staatssecretaris van Financiën (C-340/94) [1997] ECR I-461; [1997] 2 CMLR 779 . . . [3.25]
De Landtsheer Emmanuel SA v Comité Interprofessionnel du Vin de Champagne (C-381/05) [2007] ECR I-3115; [2007] 2 CMLR 43 (p 1146) . . . [10.170]
de Vos v Stadt Bielefeld (C-315/94) [1996] ECR I-1417 . . . [3.65]
Defrenne v Belgium (No 1) (8/70) [1971] ECR 445; [1974] 1 CMLR 494 . . . [10.40]
Defrenne v SABENA (No 2) (43/75) [1976] ECR 455; [1976] 2 CMLR 98 . . . [10.20], [10.25], [11.150]
Defrenne v SABENA (No 3) (149/77) [1978] ECR 1365; [1978] 3 CMLR 312 . . . [10.15]
Dekker v Stichting Vormingscentrum voor Jonge Volwassenen Plus (C-177/88) [1990] ECR I-3941 . . . [10.75]
Delimitis v Henninger Brau AG (C-234/89) [1991] ECR I-935; [1992] 5 CMLR 210 . . . [6.20], [6.90], [6.95]
Demirel v City of Schwäbisch (12/86) [1987] ECR 3719; [1989] 1 CMLR 421 . . . [11.145]

Denkavit Futtermittel GmbH v Minister für Ernährung (251/78) [1979] ECR 3369; [1980] 3 CMLR 513 . . . [2.100]
Denkavit Loire SARL v France (132/78) [1979] ECR 1923; [1979] 3 CMLR 605 . . . [7.20]
Denmark v Commission (C-233/96) [1998] ECR I-5759 . . . [11.50]
Denuit v Transorient-Mosaïque Voyages and Culture SA (C-125/04) [2005] ECR I-923; [2005] 1 CMLR 48 (p 1291) . . . [11.130]
Deutsche Bakels GmbH v Oberfinanzdirektion Münich (14/70) [1970] ECR 1001; [1971] CMLR 188 . . . [11.55]
Deutsche Grammophon Gesellschaft GmbH v Metro SB Großmärkte GmbH & Co KG (78/70) [1971] ECR 487; [1971] CMLR 631 . . . [9.30]
Deutsche Lufthansa AG v ANA Aeroportos de Portugal SA (C-181/06) [2007] ECR I-5903 . . . [11.135]
Deutsche Telekom AG v Schröder (C-50/96) [2000] ECR I-743; [2002] 2 CMLR 25 (p 583) . . . [10.15]
Deutscher Apothekerverband EV v 0800 Docmorris NV (C-322/01) [2003] ECR I-14887; [2005] 1 CMLR 46 (p 1205) . . . [2.35], [2.135]
Dias v Director da Alfândega do Porto (C-343/90) [1992] ECR I-4673 . . . [11.135]
Diego Calì & Figli Srl v Servizi Ecologici Porto di Genova (SEPG) (C-343/95) [1997] ECR I-1547; [1997] 5 CMLR 484 . . . [6.25]
Dillenkofer v Germany (C-178/94) [1996] ECR I-4845; [1996] 3 CMLR 469 . . . [12.60]
Directmedia Publishing GmbH v Albert-Ludwigs-Universität Freiburg (C-304/07) [2008] ECR I-7565; [2009] 1 CMLR 7 (p 213) . . . [9.95]
Disposable Beer Cans, Re: Commission v Denmark (302/86) [1988] ECR 4607; [1989] 1 CMLR 619 . . . [2.105], [2.110]
Dispute over Mox Plant, Re: Commission v United Kingdom (C-459/03) [2006] ECR I-4635; [2006] 2 CMLR 59 (p 1429) . . . [5.15]
Ditta Fratelli Cucchi v Avez SpA (77/76) [1977] ECR 987 . . . [7.20]
Donà v Mantero (13/76) [1976] ECR 1333; [1976] 2 CMLR 578 . . . [3.20]
Donatella Calfa, Criminal Proceedings Against (C-348/96) [1999] ECR I-11; [1999] 2 CMLR 1138 . . . [3.160], [3.285]
Dorsch Consult Ingenieurgesellschaft mbH v Bundesbaugesellschaft Berlin mbH (C-54/96) [1997] ECR I-4961; [1998] 2 CMLR 237 . . . [11.130]
Dow Chemical Ibérica SA v Commission (97/87) [1989] ECR 3165 . . . [12.70]
Draft Agreement establishing a European Laying-up Fund for Inland Waterway Vessels (Opinion 1/76) [1977] ECR 741; [1977] 2 CMLR 279 . . . [5.30]
Draft Treaty on a European Economic Area, Re (No 1) (Opinion 1/91) [1991] ECR I-6079; [1992] 1 CMLR 245 . . . [1.15], [5.15]
Draft Treaty on a European Economic Area, Re (No 2) (Opinion 1/92) [1992] ECR I-2821; [1992] 2 CMLR 217 . . . [5.15]

Dundalk Water Supply Scheme, Re: Commission v Ireland (45/87) [1988] ECR 4929; [1989] 1 CMLR 225 . . . [8.90]

Dunlop Slazenger International Ltd v Commission (T-43/92) [1994] ECR II-441 . . . [6.45]

Dutch Air Transport Agreement, Re: Commission v Netherlands (C-523/04) [2007] ECR I-3267; [2007] 2 CMLR 48 (p 1299) . . . [5.30]

Dynamic Medien Vertriebs GmbH v Avides Media AG (C-244/06) [2008] ECR I-505; [2008] 2 CMLR 23 (p 651) . . . [2.35], [2.80], [2.110], [2.115], [12.110]

Dzodzi v Belgium (C-197/89) [1990] ECR I-3763 . . . [12.110]

Echternach v Minister van Onderwijs en Wetenschappen (389/87) [1989] ECR 723; [1990] 2 CMLR 305 . . . [3.60]

Eckelkamp v Belgium (C-11/07) [2008] ECR I-6845; [2008] 3 CMLR 44 (p 1137) . . . [4.10], [4.15], [4.20], [4.25], [11.125], [11.135]

Edilizia Industriale Siderurgica Srl (Edis) v Ministerio delle Finanze (C-231/96) [1998] ECR I-4951; [1999] 2 CMLR 995 . . . [12.60]

Édouard Dubois et Fils SA v Garoner Exploration SA (C-16/94) [1995] ECR I-2421; [1995] 2 CMLR 771 . . . [2.10]

EEC Seed Crushers' and Oil Processors' Federation (FEDIOL) v Commission (191/82) [1983] ECR 2913; [1984] 3 CMLR 244 . . . [5.200]

Église de Scientologie de Paris v Prime Minister (C-54/99) [2000] ECR I-1335 . . . [4.15], [4.20], [4.30]

Elsner-Lakeberg v Land Nordrhein-Westfalen (C-285/02) [2004] ECR I-5861; [2004] 2 CMLR 36 (p 874) . . . [10.30]

El-Yassini v Secretary of State for the Home Department (C-416/96) [1999] ECR I-1209; [1999] 2 CMLR 32 . . . [11.130]

Emesa Sugar (Free Zone) NV v Aruba (C-17/98) [2000] ECR I-665 . . . [11.25]

EMI Electrola GmbH v Patricia im-und Export Verwaltungsgesellschaft mbH (C-341/87) [1989] ECR 79; [1989] 2 CMLR 413 . . . [9.15]

EMI Records v CBS Schallplatten GmbH (96/75) [1976] ECR 913; [1976] 2 CMLR 235 . . . [9.65]

Employees of the Consiglio Nazionale delle Ricerche (National Research Council), Re: Commission v Italy (225/85) [1987] ECR 2625; [1988] 3 CMLR 635 . . . [3.60]

Entreprenørforeningens Affalds/Miljøsektion (FFAD) v Københavns Kommune (C-209/98) [2000] ECR I-3743; [2001] 2 CMLR 39 (p 936) . . . [6.180]

Epichirisseon Metalleftikon Viomichanikon Kai Naftiliakon AE v Council (C-121/86) [1989] ECR 3919 . . . [5.50], [5.175]

Erasun v Instituto Nacional de Empleo (C-422/93) [1995] ECR I-1567; [1996] 1 CMLR 861 . . . [11.135]

Essent Netwerk Noord BV v Aluminium Delfzijl BV (C-206/06) [2008] ECR I-5497; [2008] 3 CMLR 32 (p 895) . . . [6.160]

Établissements Consten SàRL v Commission (56/64) [1966] ECR 299; [1966] CMLR 418 . . . [6.65], [6.75], [9.65]

Eugen Schmidberger, Internationale Transporte und Planzüge v Austria (C-112/00) [2003] ECR I-5659; [2003] 2 CMLR 34 (p 1043) . . . [2.130]

Euroalliages v Commission (T-132/01) [2003] ECR II-2359 . . . [5.200]

Euromin v Council (T-597/97) [2000] ECR II-2419 . . . [5.200]

European Night Services Ltd v Commission (T-374/94) [1998] ECR II-3141 . . . [6.80]

European Road Transport Agreement, Re: Commission v Council (22/70) [1971] ECR 263; [1971] CMLR 335 . . . [5.30], [11.100]

Europeenne et Luxembourgeoise D'investissements SA (Elisa) v Directeur General des Impots (C-451/05) [2007] ECR I-8251; [2008] 1 CMLR 13 (p 276) . . . [4.10], [4.25]

Europemballage Corporation v Commission (6/72) [1973] ECR 215; [1973] CMLR 199 . . . [6.40], [6.115], [6.150]

EVN AG v Austria (C-448/01) [2003] ECR I-14527; [2004] 1 CMLR 22 (p 739) . . . [11.135]

Export Tax on Art Treasures, Re (No 2) (48/71) [1972] ECR 529; [1972] CMLR 283 . . . [12.70]

Expulsion of Foreign Nationals, Re: Commission v Netherlands (C-50/06) [2007] ECR I-4383; [2007] 3 CMLR 8 (p 168) . . . [3.265]

Extramet Industrie SA v Council (C-358/89) [1991] ECR I-2501; [1993] 2 CMLR 619 . . . [5.125]

Fabbrica italiana accumulatori motocarri Montecchio SpA v Council (C-120/06 P) [2008] ECR I-6513 . . . [12.100], [13.70], [13.75]

Faccini Dori v Recreb Srl (C-91/92) [1994] ECR I-3325; [1994] 1 CMLR 665 . . . [11.35], [12.45], [12.50]

Fachverband der Buch- und Medienwirtschaft v LIBRO Handelsgesellschaft mbH (C-531/07) [2009] 3 CMLR 26 (p 972) . . . [2.110]

Fahmi v Bestuur van de Sociale Verzekeringsbank (C-33/99) [2001] ECR I-2415; [2003] 1 CMLR 45 (p 1280) . . . [3.65]

Federación Española de Empresas de Tecnología Sanitaria (FENIN) v Commission (C-205/03 P) [2006] ECR I-6295; [2006] 5 CMLR 7 (p 559) . . . [6.25]

Fédération nationale de la coopération bétail and viande (FNCBV) v Commission (T-217/03) [2006] ECR II-4987; [2005] 5 CMLR 12 (p 465), appeal dismissed sub nom Coop de France bétail et viande v Commission (C-101/07 P) [2008] ECR I-10193; [2009] 4 CMLR 15 (p 743) . . . [6.35]

Federconsumatori v Comune di Milano (C-463/04) [2007] ECR I-10419; [2008] 1 CMLR 46 (p 1187) . . . [4.10], [4.15], [4.20], [4.25], [4.30]

Ferrero SpA v Office for Harmonisation in the Internal Market (T-140/08) [2009] ECR . . . [9.150]

Ferriere Nord SpA v Commission (C-219/95 P) [1997] ECR I-4411; [1997] 5 CMLR 575 . . . [6.75], [11.70]

Fidium Finanz AG v Bundesanstalt für Finanzdienstleistungsaufsicht (C-452/04) [2006] ECR I-9521; [2007] 1 CMLR 15 (p 489) . . . [3.150], [3.260], [4.10]

Finanzamt Dinslaken v Meindl (C-329/05) [2007] ECR I-1107; [2007] 2 CMLR 12 (p 255) . . . [3.90]
Firma August Stier v Hauptzollamt Hamburg-Ericus (31/67) [1968] ECR 235 . . . [7.25]
Firma Fink-Frucht GmbH v Hauptzollamt München-Landsbergerstrasse (27/67) [1968] ECR 223 . . . [7.25]
FKP Scorpio Konzertproduktionen GmbH v Finanzamt Hamburg-Eimsbüttel (C-290/04) [2006] ECR I-9461; [2007] 1 CMLR 33 (p 937) . . . [3.165]
Flugreisen v Zentrale zur Bekämpfung unlauteren Wettbewerbs eV (66/86) [1989] ECR 803; [1990] 4 CMLR 102 . . . [6.105], [6.145]
Foglia v Novello (No 1) (104/79) [1980] ECR 745; [1981] 1 CMLR 45 . . . [11.135]
Foglia v Novello (No 2) (244/80) [1981] ECR 3045; [1981] 1 CMLR 585 . . . [11.135]
Foreningen AF Danske Videogramdistributorer v Laserdisken (C-61/97) [1998] ECR I-5171; [1999] 1 CMLR 1297 . . . [9.30]
Foselev Sud-Ouest SARL v Administration des douanes et droits indirects (C-18/08) [2009] 1 CMLR 30 (p 827) . . . [12.55]
Foto-Frost v Hauptzollamt Lubeck-Ost (314/85) [1987] ECR 4199; [1988] 3 CMLR 571 . . . [11.125]
France v Commission (C-332/98) [2000] ECR I-4833 . . . [6.160]
France v Commission (C-233/02) [2004] ECR I-2759 . . . [5.15]
France Télécom SA v Commission (C-202/07 P) [2009] 4 CMLR 25 (p 1149) . . . [6.110], [6.115], [6.120]
Francovich v Italy (C-6/90) [1991] ECR 5357; [1993] 2 CMLR 66 . . . [12.40], [12.60]
Franz Egenberger GmbH Molkerei und Trockenwerk v Bundesanstalt für Landwirtschaft und Ernährung (C-313/04) [2006] ECR I-6331 . . . [1.75]
Fratelli Graffione SNC v Ditta Fransa (C-313/94) [1996] ECR I-6039; [1997] 1 CMLR 925 . . . [2.110]
Fratelli Variola Spa v Amministrazione Italiana delle Finanze (34/73) [1973] ECR 981 . . . [12.35]
Freistaat Bayern v Eurim-Pharm GmbH (C-347/89) [1991] ECR I-1747; [1993] 1 CMLR 616 . . . [2.40]
French Nurses, Re: Commission v France (307/84) [1986] ECR 1725; [1987] 3 CMLR 555 . . . [3.60]
Gabalfrisa SL v Agencia Estatal de Administración Tributaria (C-110/98) [2000] ECR I-1577; [2002] 1 CMLR 13 (p 343) . . . [11.130]
Gambelli, Criminal Proceedings Against (C-243/01) [2003] ECR I-13031; [2006] 1 CMLR 35 (p 913) . . . [3.160], [3.165]
García v Delegado del Gobierno en la Región de Murcia (C-261/08) [2009] ECR . . . [11.70]
Garland v British Rail Engineering Ltd (12/81) [1982] ECR 359; [1982] 1 CMLR 696 . . . [10.40]

Garlic Preparations in Capsule Form, Re: Commission v Germany (C-319/05) [2007] ECR I-9811; [2008] 1 CMLR 36 (p 943) . . . [2.100]
Garofalo v Ministero della Sanita (C-69/96) [1997] ECR I-5603; [1998] 1 CMLR 1087 . . . [11.130]
Gaston Schul BV v Inspecteur der Invoerrechten en Accijnzen (15/81) [1982] ECR 1409; [1982] 3 CMLR 229 . . . [7.40]
Gaston Schul Douane-expediteur BV v Minister van Landbouw, Natuur en Voedselkwaliteit (C-461/03) [2005] ECR I-10513 . . . [11.125], [11.140]
GB-INNO-BM NV v Conféderation du Commerce Luxembourgeois ASBL (362/88) [1990] ECR I-667; [1991] 2 CMLR 801 . . . [2.70]
Gebhard v Consiglio dell'Ordine degli Avvocati e Procuratori di Milano (C-55/94) [1995] ECR I-4165; [1996] 1 CMLR 603 . . . [3.70], [3.150]
Gebruder Knauf Westdeutsche Gipswerke v Hauptzollamt Hamburg-Jonas (118/79) [1980] ECR 1183 . . . [11.55]
Geddo v Ente Nazionale Risi (2/73) [1973] ECR 865; [1974] 1 CMLR 13 . . . [2.30]
Geffroy, Criminal Proceedings Against (C-366/98) [2000] ECR I-6579; [2001] 2 CMLR 25 (p 525) . . . [2.60]
General Motors BV v Commission (C-551/03 P) [2006] ECR I-3173; [2006] 5 CMLR 1 (p 1) . . . [6.65]
Generalised Tariff Preferences, Re: Commission v Council (45/86) [1987] ECR 1493; [1988] 2 CMLR 131 . . . [11.106]
Generics (UK) Ltd v Smith Kline & French Laboratories Ltd (C-191/90) [1992] ECR I-5335; [1993] 1 CMLR 89 . . . [9.15]
Germany v Commission (C-245/97) [2000] ECR I-11261 . . . [11.50]
Germany v Commission (C-239/01) [2003] ECR I-10333 . . . [11.85]
Germany v Commission (C-465/02) [2005] ECR I-9115 . . . [1.150]
Germany v Commission (T-374/04) [2007] ECR II-4431 . . . [11.45]
Germany v Commission (T-349/06) [2008] ECR II-2181 . . . [11.45]
Germany v Parliament (C-380/03) [2006] ECR I-11573; [2007] 2 CMLR 1 (p 1) . . . [12.100]
Gervais, Criminal Proceedings Against (C-17/94) [1995] ECR I-4353 . . . [3.95]
Gesellschaft fur Überseehandel mbH v Handelskammer Hamburg (49/76) [1977] ECR 41 . . . [2.20]
Gesellschaft zur Verwertung von Leistungsschutzrechten mbH (GVL) v Commission (7/82) [1983] ECR 483; [1983] 3 CMLR 645 . . . [8.95]
Gestetner Holdings Plc v Council of Ministers (C-156/87) [1990] ECR I-781; [1990] 1 CMLR 820 . . . [5.130], [5.140], [5.160], [5.200]
Geurts v Administratie van de BTW, registratie en domeinen (C-464/05) [2007] ECR I-9325; [2008] 1 CMLR 29 (p 755) . . . [3.90]
Gibraltar European Elections, Re: Spain v United Kingdom (C-145/04) [2006] ECR I-7917; [2007] 1 CMLR 3 (p 87) . . . [11.115]
Gillespie v Northern Health and Social Services Board (C-342/93) [1996] ECR I-475; [1996] 2 CMLR 969 . . . [10.15], [10.40], [10.80]

Gillette Co v LA-Laboratories Ltd Oy (C-228/03) [2005] ECR I-2337; [2005] 2 CMLR 62 (p 1539) . . . [9.110]
Giuffrida v Council (105-75) [1976] ECR 1395 . . . [11.106]
Giuffrida v Council (64/80) [1981] ECR 693 . . . [1.150]
Givane v Secretary of State for the Home Department (C-257/00) [2003] ECR I-345; [2003] 1 CMLR 17 (p 587) . . . [11.70]
Glocken GmbH v Unita Sanitaria Locale Centro-Sud (407/85) [1988] ECR 4233 . . . [2.125]
Golden Shares, Re: Commission v Portugal (C-367/98) [2002] ECR I-4731; [2002] 2 CMLR 1213 . . . [4.10], [4.15], [4.20], [4.25]
Golden Shares, Re: Commission v Spain (C-463/00) [2003] ECR I-4581; [2003] 2 CMLR 18 (p 557) . . . [4.10]
Golden Shares, Re: Commission v United Kingdom (C-98/01) [2003] ECR I-4641; [2003] 2 CMLR 19 (p 598) . . . [4.10]
Goldstar Co Ltd v Council (C-105/90) [1992] ECR I-677; [1992] 1 CMLR 996 . . . [5.55]
Gøttrup-Klim ea Grovvareforeninger v Dansk Landbrugs Grovvareselskab AmbA (C-250/92) [1994] ECR I-5641; [1996] 4 CMLR 191 . . . [6.110]
Government of the French Community v Flemish Government (C-212/06) [2008] ECR I-1683; [2008] 2 CMLR 31 (p 859) . . . [1.130], [12.70]
Grad v Finanzamt Traunstein (9/70) [1970] ECR 825; [1971] CMLR 1 . . . [12.40], [12.55]
Graf v Filzmoser Maschinenbau GmbH (C-190/98) [2000] ECR I-493; [2000] 1 CMLR 741 . . . [3.40], [3.45]
Grant v South-west Trains Ltd (C-249/96) [1998] ECR I-621; [1998] 1 CMLR 993 . . . [10.40], [10.55], [12.110]
Graphite Electrodes Cartel Appeal, Re: Commission v SGL Carbon AG (C-301/04 P) [2006] ECR I-5915; [2006] 5 CMLR 15 (p 877) . . . [12.110]
Gravier v City of Liège (293/83) [1985] ECR 593; [1985] 3 CMLR 1 . . . [10.135]
Grundig Italiana SpA v Ministero Delle Finanze (C-255/00) [2002] ECR I-8003; [2003] 1 CMLR 36 (p 1065) . . . [12.60]
Guérin Automobiles v Commission (C-282/95 P) [1997] ECR I-1503; [1997] 5 CMLR 447 . . . [6.10]
Guimont, Criminal Proceedings Against (C-448/98) [2000] ECR I-10663; [2003] 1 CMLR 3 (p 52) . . . [2.110], [2.135]
Gullung v Conseil de L'ordre des Avocats (292/86) [1988] ECR 111; [1988] 2 CMLR 57 . . . [3.75]
Gysbrechts, Criminal Proceedings Against (C-205/07) [2008] ECR I-9947; [2009] 2 CMLR 2 (p 45) . . . [2.125]
Habermann-Beltermann v Arbeiterwohlfahrt Bezirksverband (C-421/92) [1994] ECR I-1657; [1994] 2 CMLR 681 . . . [10.75]
Haegeman (R & V) Sprl v Belgium (181/73) [1974] ECR 449; [1975] 1 CMLR 515 . . . [11.145]

Halifax plc v Customs and Excise Commissioners (C-255/02) [2006] ECR I-1609; [2006] 2 CMLR 36 (p 943) . . . [7.40]

Halliburton Services BV v Staatssecretaris van Financiën (C-1/93) [1994] ECR I-1137; [1994] 3 CMLR 377 . . . . . . [3.90]

Handels-Og Kontorfunktionaerernes Forbund v Dansk Arbejdsgiverforening (109/88) [1989] ECR 3199; [1991] 1 CMLR 8 . . . [10.50]

Hansa Fleisch Ernst Mundt GmbH & Co KG v Landrat des Kreises Schleswig-Flensburg (C-156/91) [1992] ECR I-5567 . . . [12.55]

Hansen (H) Jun v Hauptzollamt Flensburg (148/77) [1978] ECR 1787; [1979] 1 CMLR 604 . . . [7.30]

Harz v Deutsche Tradax GmbH (79/83) [1984] ECR 1921; [1986] 2 CMLR 430 . . . [12.50]

Hasselblad (GB) Ltd v Commission (86/82) [1984] ECR 883; [1984] 1 CMLR 559 . . . [6.100]

Hauer v Land Rheinland-Pfalz (44/79) [1979] ECR 3727; [1980] 3 CMLR 42 . . . [12.95]

Heinrich, Proceedings brought by (C-345/06) [2009] 3 CMLR 7 (p 219) . . . [1.155]

Heintz van Landewijck Sarl v Commission (209/78) [1980] ECR 3125; [1981] 3 CMLR 134 . . . [6.45]

Heirs of Barbier v Inspecteur van de Belastingdienst Particulieren/Ondernemingen Buitenland te Heerlen (C-364/01) [2003] ECR I-15013; [2004] 1 CMLR 40 (p 1283) . . . [4.10]

Hercules (SA) Chemicals NV v Commission (T-7/89) [1991] ECR II-1711; appeal dismissed (C-51/92 P) [1999] ECR I-4235; [1999] 5 CMLR 976 . . . [6.45]

HFB Holding für Fernwärmetechnik Beteiligungsgesellschaft mbH & Co KG v Commission (T-9/99) [2002] ECR II-1487; appeal dismissed (C-189/02 P) [2005] ECR I-5425; [2005] 5 CMLR 17 (p 796) . . . [6.45]

Hill v Revenue Commissioners (C-243/95) [1998] ECR I-3739; [1998] 3 CMLR 81 . . . [10.15]

Hlozek v Roche Austria Gesellschaft mbH (C-19/02) [2004] ECR I-11491; [2005] 1 CMLR 28 (p 702) . . . [10.20]

H M Customs and Excise v Schindler (C-275/92) [1994] ECR I-1039; [1995] 1 CMLR 4 . . . [2.10], [3.160], [3.175], [3.185]

Hoekstra v Bestuur der Bedrijfsvereniging voor Detailhandel en Ambachten (75/63) [1964] ECR 177; [1964] CMLR 319 . . . [3.25]

Hoffman-La Roche & Co AG v Centrafarm Vertriebsgesellschaft Pharmazeutischer Erzeugnisse mbH (102/77) [1978] ECR 1139; [1978] 3 CMLR 217 . . . [6.135], [9.45]

Hofmann v Barmer Ersatzkasse (184/83) [1984] ECR 3047; [1986] 1 CMLR 242 . . . [10.75]

Höfner v Macrotron GmbH (C-41/90) [1991] ECR I-1979; [1993] 4 CMLR 306 . . . [6.25]

Hollmann v Fazenda Pública (C-443/06) [2007] ECR I-8491; [2008] 1 CMLR 10 (p 216) . . . [4.10], [4.15]
Huber v Germany (C-524/06) [2008] ECR I-9705; [2009] 1 CMLR 49 (p 1360) . . . [10.140]
Hugin Kassaregister AB v Commission (22/78) [1979] ECR 1869; [1979] 3 CMLR 345 . . . [6.75]
Hüls AG v Commission (C-199/92 P) [1999] ECR I-4287; [1999] 5 CMLR 1016 . . . [6.65], [6.100], [11.125], [12.100]
Humblet v Belgium (6/60) [1960] ECR 559 . . . [11.50]
Iannelli & Volpi SpA v Ditta Paolo Meroni (74/76) [1977] ECR 557; [1977] 2 CMLR 688 . . . [2.90]
IAZ International Belgium SA (NV) v Commission (96/82) [1983] ECR 3369; [1984] 3 CMLR 276 . . . [6.35]
IKEA Wholesale Ltd v Commissioners of Customs & Excise (C-351/04) [2007] ECR I-7723 . . . [13.75]
ILO Convention No 170 concerning Safety in the Use of Chemicals at Work, Re (Opinion 2/91) [1993] ECR I-1061; [1993] 3 CMLR 800 . . . [5.15], [5.30]
Impact v Minister for Agriculture and Food (C-268/06) [2008] ECR I-2483; [2008] 2 CMLR 47 (p 1265) . . . [12.40], [12.50], [12.60]
Imperial Chemical Industries Ltd v Commission (48/69) [1972] ECR 619; [1972] CMLR 557 . . . [6.40]
Imperial Chemical Industries plc v Colmer (C-264/96) [1998] ECR I-4695; [1998] 3 CMLR 293 . . . [3.85], [11.135]
IMS Health GmbH & Co OHG v NDC Health GmbH & Co KG (C-418/01) [2004] ECR I-5039; [2004] 4 CMLR 28 (p 1543) . . . [6.135]
Industrie des Poudres Sphériques v Council (C-458/98) [2000] ECR I-8147 . . . [5.45], [5.50]
Inspection of Organic Produce by Private Bodies, Re: Commission v Austria (C-393/05) [2007] ECR I-10195; [2008] 1 CMLR 42 (p 1121) . . . [3.105], [3.175]
Inspection of Organic Produce by Private Bodies, Re: Commission v Germany (C-404/05) [2007] ECR I-10239; [2008] 1 CMLR 43 (p 1148) . . . [3.105], [3.185]
Instituto Chemioterapico Italiano Spa v Commission (6/73) [1974] ECR 223; [1974] 1 CMLR 309 . . . [8.95]
Inter-Environnement Wallonie ASBL v Region Wallonie (C-129/96) [1997] ECR I-7411; [1998] 1 CMLR 1057 . . . [12.40]
International Agreement on Natural Rubber, Re (Opinion 1/78) [1979] ECR 2871; [1979] 3 CMLR 639 . . . [5.10]
International Fruit Co NV v Produktschap voor Groenten en Fruit (No 3) (21-24/72) [1972] ECR 1219; [1975] 2 CMLR 1 . . . [13.60], [13.70]
International Potash Co v Council (T-87/98) [2000] ECR II-3179 . . . [5.165]
International Transport Workers' Federation v Viking Line ABP (C-438/05) [2007] ECR I-10779; [2008] 1 CMLR 51 (p 1372) . . . [1.130], [3.130], [12.100]

Internationale Handelsgesellschaft mbH v Einfuhr-und Vorratsstelle für Getreide und Futtermittel (11/70) [1970] ECR 1125; [1972] CMLR 255 . . . [12.70], [12.90]
Internationaler Hilsfonds eV v Commission (T-294/04) [2005] ECR II-2719 . . . [1.125]
Irish Creamery Milk Suppliers Association v Ireland (36/80) [1981] ECR 735; [1981] 2 CMLR 455 . . . [11.135]
Irish Sugar plc v Commission (T-228/97) [1999] ECR II-2969; [1999] 5 CMLR 1300 . . . [6.120]
Italy v Commission (41/83) [1985] ECR 873; [1985] 2 CMLR 368 . . . [6.75]
Italy v Commission (C-298/00 P) [2004] ECR I-4087 . . . [6.160]
Italy v Commission (C-301/03) [2005] ECR I-10217 . . . [11.100]
Italy v Sacchi (155/73) [1974] ECR 409; [1974] 2 CMLR 177 . . . [8.95]
Italy v Watson (118/75) [1976] ECR 1185; [1976] 2 CMLR 552 . . . [3.270]
ITC Innovative Technology Center GmbH v Bundesagentur für Arbeit (C-208/05) [2007] ECR I-181; [2008] 1 CMLR 15 (p 343) . . . [3.45], [3.150], [3.165]
Jäger v Finanzamt Kusel-Landstuhl (C-256/06) [2008] ECR I-123; [2008] 2 CMLR 10 (p 268) . . . [4.10], [4.15]
Jägerskiöld v Gustafsson (C-97/98) [1999] ECR I-7319; [2000] 1 CMLR 235 . . . [2.10], [4.10]
Jany v Staatssecretaris van Justitie (C-268/99) [2001] ECR I-8615; [2003] 2 CMLR 1 (p 1) . . . [3.30], [3.70]
Jenkins v Kingsgate (Clothing Productions) Ltd (96/80) [1981] ECR 911; [1981] 2 CMLR 24 . . . [10.30]
Jersey Produce Marketing Organisation Ltd v States of Jersey (C-293/02) [2005] ECR I-9543; [2006] 1 CMLR 29 (p 738) . . . [2.10]
John Deere Ltd v Commission (C-7/95 P) [1998] ECR I-3111; [1998] 5 CMLR 311 . . . [6.65], [6.80], [6.100]
Jokela and Pitkäranta (C-9/97) [1998] ECR I-6267 . . . [11.130]
Jundt v Finanzamt Offenburg (C-281/06) [2007] ECR I-12231 . . . [3.105]
Kaba v Secretary of State for the Home Department (C-356/98) [2000] ECR I-2623; [2003] 1 CMLR 39 (p 1150) . . . [3.65]
Kachelmann v Bankhaus Hermann Lampe KG (C-322/98) [2000] ECR I-7505; [2002] 1 CMLR 7 (p 155) . . . [11.135]
Kadi v Commission (C-402/05 P) [2008] ECR I-6351; [2008] 3 CMLR 41 (p 1207) . . . [1.15], [5.30], [12.100], [12.110]
Kalanke v Freie Handestadt Bremen (C-450/93) [1995] ECR I-3051; [1996] 1 CMLR 175 . . . [10.85]
Kali und Salz AG v Commission (19/74) [1975] ECR 499; [1975] 2 CMLR 154 . . . [6.130]
Kamer van Koophandel en Fabrieken voor Amsterdam v Inspire Art Ltd (C-167/01) [2003] ECR I-10155; [2005] 3 CMLR 34 (p 937) . . . [3.135], [11.125], [11.135]

Kanal 5 Ltd v Föreningen Svenska Tonsättares Internationella Musikbyrå (STIM) upa (C-52/07) [2008] ECR I-9275; [2009] 5 CMLR 18 (p 2175) . . . [6.120]
Karlsson, Proceedings brought by (C-292/97) [2000] ECR I-2737 . . . [12.100]
Kauppatalo Hansel Oy v Imatran Kaupunki (C-244/02) [2003] ECR I-12139; [2004] 3 CMLR 17 (p 366) . . . [8.40]
Keck, Criminal Proceedings Against (C-267/91) [1993] ECR I-6097; [1995] 1 CMLR 101 . . . [2.35], [2.115], [11.20]
Keller v Instituto Nacional de la Seguridad Social (C-145/03) [2005] ECR I-2529 . . . [11.135]
Kemikalieinspektionen v Toolex Alpha AB (C-473/98) [2000] ECR I-5681 . . . [2.100]
Kempf v Staatssecretaris van Justitie (139/85) [1986] ECR 1741; [1987] 1 CMLR 764 . . . [3.25]
Keurkoop BV v Nancy Kean Gifts BV (144/81) [1982] ECR 2853; [1983] 2 CMLR 47 . . . [9.10], [9.15]
Klöppel v Tiroler Gebietskrankenkasse (C-507/06) [2008] ECR I-943 . . . [3.40]
Köbler v Austria (C-224/01) [2003] ECR I-10239; [2003] 3 CMLR 28 (p 1003) . . . [12.60]
Kofoed v Skatteministeriet (C-321/05) [2007] ECR I-5795; [2007] 3 CMLR 33 (p 875) . . . [1.150]
Koninklijke Philips Electronics NV v Remington Consumer Products Ltd (C-299/99) [2002] ECR I-5475; [2002] 2 CMLR 52 (p 1329) . . . [9.110], [9.120], [9.125]
Konsumentombudsmannen (KO) v De Agostini (Svenska) Förlag AB (C-34/95) [1997] ECR I-3843; [1998] 1 CMLR 32 . . . [2.110], [2.115], [3.185]
Konsumentombudsmannen (KO) v Gourmet International Products AB (C-405/98) [2001] ECR I-1795; [2001] 2 CMLR 31 (p 672) . . . [2.100], [2.115], [3.175]
Koyo Seiko Co Ltd v Council (256/84) [1987] ECR 1899; [1989] 2 CMLR 76 . . . [5.60]
Kranemann v Land Nordrhein-Westfalen (C-109/04) [2005] ECR I-2421; [2005] 2 CMLR 15 (p 341) . . . [3.25], [3.60]
Krawczynski v Dyrektor Izby Celnej w Bialymstoku (C-426/07) [2008] ECR I-6021 . . . [7.30]
Kremzow v Austria (C-299/95) [1997] ECR I-2629; [1997] 3 CMLR 1289 . . . [11.125]
Krüger GmbH & Co KG v Hauptzollamt Hamburg-Jonas [1997] ECR I-4517; [1998] 1 CMLR 520 . . . [11.125]
Kurz v Land Baden-Württemberg (C-188/00) [2002] ECR I-10691 . . . [3.30]
Kutz-Bauer v Freie und Hansestadt Hamburg (C-187/00) [2003] ECR I-2741; [2005] 2 CMLR 35 (p 862) . . . [12.65]
Kuwait Petroleum (GB) Ltd v Customs and Excise Commissioners (C-48/97) [1999] ECR I-2323; [1999] 2 CMLR 651 . . . [11.55]

Kyocera Electronics Europe GmbH v Hauptzollamt Krefeld (C-152/01) [2003] ECR I-13821 . . . [11.70]
Kyowa Hakko Kogyo Co Ltd v Commission (T-223/00) [2003] ECR II-2553 . . . [6.230]
Läärä v Kihlakunnansyyttäjä (C-124/97) [1999] ECR I-6067; [2001] 2 CMLR 14 (p 257) . . . [2.10]
Laboratoires Pharmaceutiques Bergaderm SA v Commission (C-352/98 P) [2000] ECR I-5291 . . . [12.60]
Laguillaumie, Re (C-116/00) [2000] ECR I-4979 . . . [11.135]
Lamaire NV v Nationale Dienst voor Afzet van Land- en Tuinbouwprodukten (C-130/93) [1994] ECR I-3215; [1995] 3 CMLR 534 . . . [2.10]
Lamberts v European Mediator (T-209/00) [2002] ECR II-2203; [2003] 1 CMLR 32 (p 942) . . . [1.125]
Land Brandenburg v Sass (C-284/02) [2004] ECR I-11143; [2005] 1 CMLR 27 (p 681) . . . [10.20]
Land Nordrhein-Westfalen v Uecker (C-64/96) [1997] ECR I-3171; [1997] 3 CMLR 963 . . . [3.15]
Land Rheinland-Pfalz v Alcan Deutschland GmbH [1997] ECR I-1591; [1997] 2 CMLR 1034 . . . [6.160]
Laserdisken ApS v Kulturministeriet (C-479/04) [2006] ECR I-8089; [2007] 1 CMLR 6 (p 187) . . . [12.110]
Laval un Partneri Ltd v Svenska Byggnadsarbetareförbundet (C-341/05) [2007] ECR I-11767; [2008] 2 CMLR 9 (p 177) . . . [3.150], [3.170], [3.180], [3.190], [12.100]
Law on Privatisation of Equity in Volkswagenwerk GmbH, Re: Commission v Germany (C-112/05) [2007] ECR I-8995; [2008] 1 CMLR 25 (p 643) . . . [4.10], [4.15], [4.20], [4.25], [4.30]
Lawrence v Regent Office Care Ltd (C-320/00) [2002] ECR I-7325; [2002] 3 CMLR 27 (p 761) . . . [10.20]
Lenz v Finanzlandesdirektion für Tirol (C-315/02) [2004] ECR I-7063; [2004] 3 CMLR 13 (p 274) . . . [4.15]
Leonesio v Italian Ministry of Agriculture and Forestry (93/71) [1972] ECR 287; [1973] CMLR 343 . . . [12.35]
Léon van Parys NV v Belgisch Interventie- en Restitutiebureau [2005] ECR I-1465 . . . [13.75]
Leur-Bloem v Inspecteur der Belastingdienst (C-28/95) [1997] ECR I-4161; [1998] 1 CMLR 157 . . . [11.135]
Levin v Secretary of State for Justice (53/81) [1982] ECR 1035; [1982] 2 CMLR 454 . . . [3.25], [3.30]
Lewen v Denda (C-333/97) [1999] ECR I-7243; [2000] 2 CMLR 38 . . . [10.15], [10.40]
Libertel Groep BV v Benelux-Merkenbureau (C-104/01) [2003] ECR I-3793; [2005] 2 CMLR 45 (p 1097) . . . [9.120], [11.55]
Lidl Belgium GmbH & Co KG v Etablissementen Franz Colruyt NV (C-356/04) [2006] ECR I-8501; [2007] 1 CMLR 9 (p 269) . . . [10.170]

Liga Portuguesa de Futebol Profissional v Departamento de Jogos da Santa Casa da Misericórdia de Lisboa (C-42/07) [2010] 1 CMLR 1 (p 1)... [3.120]

Limburgse Vinyl Maatschappij v Commission (C-238/99 P) [2002] ECR I-8375; [2003] 4 CMLR 10 (p 397)... [6.65]

Lindqvist, Criminal Proceedings Against (C-101/01) [2003] ECR I-12971; [2004] 1 CMLR 20 (p 673)... [10.140]

"Loi Evin", Re: Commission v France (C-262/02) [2004] ECR I-6569; [2004] 3 CMLR 1 (p 1)... [2.120]

L'Oréal SA v Bellure NV (C-487/07) [2009] ETMR 55 (p 987)... [9.130]

Lugano Convention, Re (Opinion 1/03) [2006] ECR I-1145... [5.15], [5.30]

Luisi v Ministero del Tesoro (286/82) [1984] ECR 377; [1985] 3 CMLR 52... [3.165]

Macarthys Ltd v Smith (129/79) [1980] ECR 1275; [1980] 2 CMLR 205... [10.25]

Manfredi v Lloyd Adriatico Assicurazioni SpA (C-295/04) [2006] ECR I-6619; [2006] 5 CMLR 17 (p 980)... [6.10], [6.20], [6.75], [6.230], [12.65]

Mangold v Helm (C-144/04) [2005] ECR I-9981; [2006] 1 CMLR 43 (p 1132)... [10.100], [10.110], [11.135], [12.40], [12.100]

Manninen, Proceedings brought by (C-319/02) [2004] ECR I-7477; [2004] 3 CMLR 40 (p 881)... [4.15], [4.20], [4.25]

Marketing of Chocolate, Re: Commission v Spain (C-12/00) [2003] ECR I-459; [2005] 2 CMLR 33 (p 799)... [2.60], [2.110], [2.115]

Marks & Spencer plc v Halsey (C-446/03) [2005] ECR I-10837; [2006] 1 CMLR 18 (p 480)... [1.130], [3.125]

Marleasing SA v La Comercial Internacional de Alimentación SA (C-106/89) [1990] ECR 1; [1992] 1 CMLR 305... [12.50]

Marschall v Land Nordrhein Westfalen (C-409/95) [1997] ECR I-6363; [1998] 1 CMLR 547... [10.90]

Marshall v Southampton and South West Hampshire Area Health Authority (152/84) [1986] ECR 723; [1986] 1 CMLR 688... [12.45]

Marshall v Southampton and South West Hampshire Area Health Authority (No 2) (C-271/91) [1993] ECR I-4367; [1993] 3 CMLR 293... [12.40], [12.50]

Martinez v Parliament (T-222/99 R) [1999] ECR II-3397; [2002] 1 CMLR 31 (p 893)... [11.85]

Martínez Sala v Freistaat Bayern (C-85/96) [1998] ECR I-2691... [3.65]

Maruko v Versorgungsanstalt der Deutschen Bühnen (C-267/06) [2008] ECR I-1757; [2008] 2 CMLR 32 (p 914)... [10.40], [10.120]

Masterfoods Ltd v HB Ice Cream Ltd (C-344/98) [2000] ECR I-11369; [2001] 4 CMLR 14 (p 449)... [6.10]

Mattern v Ministre du Travail et de l'Emploi (C-10/05) [2006] ECR I-3145; [2006] 2 CMLR 42 (p 1080)... [3.30]

Maurin, Criminal Proceedings Against (C-144/95) [1996] ECR I-2909 ... [11.125]
Mayr v Bäckerei und Konditorei Gerhard Flöckner OHG (C-506/06) [2008] ECR I-1017; [2008] 2 CMLR 27 (p 759) ... [10.75], [11.135]
Meca-Medina v Commission (C-519/04 P) [2006] ECR I-6991; [2006] 5 CMLR 18 (p 1023) ... [3.20], [6.85]
Medicinal Product Certificate, Re: Spain v Council (C-350/92) [1995] ECR I-1985; [1996] 1 CMLR 415 ... [9.75]
Meeusen v Hoofddirectie van de Informatie Beheer Groep (C-337/97) [1999] ECR I-3289; [2000] 2 CMLR 659 ... [3.65]
Megner v Innungskrankenkasse Vorderpfalz (C-444/93) [1995] ECR I-4741 ... [3.30]
Meilicke v ADV/ORGA (C-83/91) [1992] ECR I-4871 ... [11.135]
Meilicke v Finanzamt Bonn-Innenstadt (C-292/04) [2007] ECR I-1835; [2007] 2 CMLR 19 (p 469) ... [4.25]
Meints v Minister van Landbouw, Natuurbeheer en Visserij (C-57/96) [1997] ECR I-6689; [1998] 1 CMLR 1159 ... [3.65]
Merck Genéricos Produtos Farmacêuticos Lda v Merck & Co Inc (C-431/05) [2007] ECR I-7001; [2007] 3 CMLR 49 (p 1339) ... [5.15]
Merino García v Bundesanstalt für Arbeit (C-266/95) [1997] ECR I-3279 ... [3.40]
Messner v Firma Stefan Krüger (C-489/07) [2009] ECR ... [10.190]
Metock v Minister for Justice, Equality and Law Reform (C-127/08) [2008] ECR I-6241; [2008] 3 CMLR 39 (p 1167) ... [3.265], [11.20]
Metronome Musik GmbH v Music Point Hokamp GmbH (C-200/96) [1998] ECR I-1953; [1998] 3 CMLR 919 ... [9.30]
Metsä-Serla Oyj v Commission (C-294/98 P) [2000] ECR I-10065 ... [6.40]
Meyhui NV v Schott Zwiesel Glaswerke AG (C-51/93) [1994] ECR I-3879 ... [2.35]
Micro Leader Business v Commission (T-198/98) [1999] ECR II-3989 ... [6.30]
Microsoft Corporation v Commission (T-201/04) [2007] ECR II-3601; [2007] 5 CMLR 11 (p 846) ... [6.135]
Milk Marketing Board of England and Wales v Cricket St Thomas Estate (C 372/88) [1990] ECR I-1345; [1990] 2 CMLR 800 ... [11.70]
Miller International Schallplatten Gmbh v Commission (19/77) [1978] ECR 131; [1978] 2 CMLR 334 ... [6.75]
Minebea Co Ltd v Council (260/84) [1987] ECR 1975; [1989] 2 CMLR 76 ... [5.60]
Ministère Public v Gauchard (20/87) [1987] ECR 4879; [1989] 2 CMLR 489 ... [3.95]
Ministero dell'Industria, del Commercio e dell'Artigianato v Lucchini SpA (C-119/05) [2007] ECR I-6199; [2009] 1 CMLR 18 (p 501) ... [11.135], [12.65]

Ministerul Administraţiei şi Internelor – Direcţia Generală de Paşapoarte Bucureşti v Jipa (C-33/07) [2008] ECR I-5157; [2008] 3 CMLR 23 (p 715) . . . [3.285]
Ministre de l'Intérieur v Olazabal (C-100/01) [2002] ECR I-10981; [2005] 1 CMLR 49 (p 1297) . . . [3.55]
Miwon Co Ltd v Council (T-51/96) [2000] ECR II-1841 . . . [5.160], [5.200]
Molkerei-Zentrale Westfalen Lippe GmbH v Hauptzollamt Paderborn (28/67) [1968] ECR 143; [1968] CMLR 187 . . . [7.25]
Montecatini SpA v Commission (C-235/92 P) [1999] ECR I-4539; [2001] 4 CMLR 18 (p 691) . . . [6.65], [6.100], [11.125]
Morais, Criminal Proceedings Against (C-60/91) [1992] ECR I-2085; [1992] 2 CMLR 533 . . . [6.75]
Morgan v Bezirksregierung Köln (C-11/06) [2007] ECR I-9161; [2009] 1 CMLR 1 (p 1) . . . [1.130]
Moser v Land Baden-Württemberg (180/83) [1984] ECR 2539; [1984] 3 CMLR 720 . . . [3.15]
Motosykletistiki Omospondia Ellados NPID (MOTOE) v Dimosio (C-49/07) [2008] ECR I-4863; [2008] 5 CMLR 11 (p 790) . . . [6.25], [6.110], [6.180]
Mukand Ltd v Council (T-58/99) [2001] ECR II-2521; [2002] 3 CMLR 13 (p 336) . . . [5.125], [5.200]
Muller, Criminal Proceedings Against (304/84) [1986] ECR 1511 . . . [2.100]
Müller-Fauré v Onderlinge Waarborgmaatschappij OZ Zorgverzekeringen UA (C-385/99) [2003] ECR I-4509; [2004] 2 CMLR 33 (p 777) . . . [3.160], [3.180]
Municipality of Almelo v NV Energiebedrijf Ijsselmij (C-393/92) [1994] ECR I-1477 . . . [11.130]
Musik-Vertrieb Membran GmbH v Gema (55/80) [1981] ECR 147; [1981] 2 CMLR 44 . . . [9.15]
Musique Diffusion Française SA v Commission (100/80) [1983] ECR 1825; [1983] 3 CMLR 221 . . . [6.80]
My v Office National des Pensions (C-293/03) [2004] ECR I-12013; [2005] 1 CMLR 37 (p 937) . . . [3.15]
N v Inspecteur van de Belastingdienst Oost/kantoor Almelo (C-470/04) [2006] ECR I-7409; [2006] 3 CMLR 49 (p 1249) . . . [12.60]
Nachi Europe GmbH v Hauptzollamt Krefeld (C-239/99) [2001] ECR I-1197 . . . [5.200], [11.125]
Nachi Fujikoshi Corporation v Council (255/84) [1987] ECR 1861; [1989] 2 CMLR 76 . . . [5.60], [5.120]
Nádasdi v Vám- és Pénzügyőrség Észak-Alföldi Regionális Parancsnoksága (C-290/05) [2006] ECR I-10115; [2007] 1 CMLR 21 (p 627) . . . [7.15], [7.25]
Nadin, Criminal Proceedings Against (C-151/04) [2005] ECR I-11203; [2006] 2 CMLR 15 (p 435) . . . [3.70]
Nashua Corporation v Council (C-133/87) [1990] ECR I-719; [1990] 2 CMLR 6 . . . [5.75], [5.160], [5.200]

Natural Sweet Wines, Re: Commission v France (196/85) [1987] ECR 1597; [1988] 2 CMLR 851 . . . [7.30]
Neste Markkinointi Oy v Yötuuli Ky (C-214/99) [2000] ECR I-11121; [2001] 4 CMLR 27 (p 993) . . . [6.60]
Netherlands v Commission (C-452/00) [2005] ECR I-6645 . . . [11.106]
Netherlands v Parliament (C-377/98) [2001] ECR I-7079; [2001] 3 CMLR 49 (p 1173) . . . [12.100]
Netherlands v Reed (59/85) [1986] ECR 1283; [1987] 2 CMLR 448 . . . [3.65]
New Cotton Support Scheme, Re: Spain v Council (C-310/04) [2006] ECR I-7285; [2006] 3 CMLR 47 (p 1277) . . . [11.106]
New Holland Ford Ltd v Commission (C-8/95 P) [1998] ECR I-3175 . . . [6.65], [6.80]
Nijman, Criminal Proceedings Against (125/88) [1989] ECR 3533; [1991] 1 CMLR 92 . . . [2.100]
Ninni-Orasche v Bundesminister für Wissenschaft, Verkehr und Kunst (C-413/01) [2003] ECR I-13187; [2004] 1 CMLR 19 (p 638) . . . [3.20], [3.25]
Nippon Seiko KK v Council (258/84) [1987] ECR 1923; [1989] 2 CMLR 76 . . . [5.60]
Nold Kohlen- und Baustoffgrosshandlung v Commission (4/73) [1974] ECR 491; [1974] 2 CMLR 338 . . . [12.95], [12.100]
Nolte v Landesversicherungsanstalt Hannover (C-317/93) [1995] ECR I-4625 . . . [3.30]
Noordwijks Cement Accoord, Re (8/66) [1967] ECR 75; [1967] CMLR 77 . . . [11.95]
Nordsee Deutsche Hochseefischerei GmbH v Reederei Mond Hochseefischerei Nordstern AG & Co Ltd (102/81) [1982] ECR 1095 . . . [11.130]
North Western Health Board v McKenna (C-191/03) [2005] ECR I-7631; [2006] 1 CMLR 6 (p 121) . . . [10.40], [10.80]
NTN Toyo Bearing Co Ltd v Council (240/84) [1987] ECR 1809; [1989] 2 CMLR 76 . . . [5.60], [5.200]
Nygård v Svineafgiftsfonden (C-234/99) [2002] ECR I-3657 . . . [2.10], [7.15]
O2 Holdings Ltd v Hutchison 3G UK Ltd (C-533/06) [2008] ECR I-4231; [2008] 3 CMLR 14 (p 397) . . . [9.130], [10.170]
Oberkreisdirector des Kreises Borken v Handelsonderneming Moormann BV (190/87) [1988] ECR 4689; [1990] 1 CMLR 656 . . . [12.40]
O'Byrne v Sanofi Pasteur MSD Ltd (C-127/04) [2006] ECR I-1313; [2006] 2 CMLR 24 (p 656) . . . [10.215]
Office national de l'emploi v Ioannidis (C-258/04) [2005] ECR I-8275; [2005] 3 CMLR 47 (p 1285) . . . [3.65]
Officier van Justitie v De Peijper (104/75) [1976] ECR 613; [1976] 2 CMLR 271 . . . [2.125]
Officier van Justitie v Kolpinghuis Nijmegen BV (80/86) [1987] ECR 3969; [1989] 2 CMLR 18 . . . [12.45]

Officier van Justitie v Kramer (3/76) [1976] ECR 1279; [1976] 2 CMLR 440 . . . [5.30]

Officier van Justitie v van Haaster (190/73) [1974] ECR 1123; [1974] 2 CMLR 521 . . . [2.45]

O'Flynn v Adjudication Officer (C-237/94) [1996] ECR I-2617; [1996] 3 CMLR 103 . . . [3.40], [3.65]

Oliehandel Koeweit BV v Minister van Volkshuisvesting (C-307/00) [2003] ECR I-1821; [2003] 2 CMLR 9 (p 273) . . . [11.135]

Omega Spielhallen- und Automatenaufstellungs-GmbH v Oberbürgermeisterin der Bundesstadt Bonn (C-36/02) [2004] ECR I-9609; [2005] 1 CMLR 5 (p 91) . . . [3.190]

Ordre des Advocats au Barreau de Paris v Klopp (107/83) [1984] ECR 2971; [1985] 1 CMLR 99 . . . [3.75]

Ordre des Barreaux Francophones et Germanophones v Conseil des Ministres (C-305/05) [2007] ECR I-5305; [2007] 3 CMLR 28 (p 731) . . . [12.100], [12.110]

Orfanopoulos v Land Baden-Württemberg (C-482/01) [2004] ECR I-5257; [2005] 1 CMLR 18 (p 433) . . . [3.55]

Origin Marking of Retail Goods, Re: Commission v United Kingdom (207/83) [1985] ECR 1201; [1985] 2 CMLR 259 . . . [2.65]

Oscar Bronner GmbH & Co KG v Mediaprint Zeitungs- und Zeitschriftenverlag GmbH & Co KG (C-7/97) [1998] ECR I-7791; [1999] 4 CMLR 112 . . . [6.115], [6.130], [6.135]

Ospelt v Schlossle Weissenberg Familienstiftung (C-452/01) [2003] ECR I-9743; [2005] 3 CMLR 40 (p 1125) . . . [2.150], [4.15]

Österreichischer Gewerkschaftsbund v Austria (C-195/98) [2000] ECR I-10497; [2002] 1 CMLR 14 (p 375) . . . [3.60], [11.130]

OTO SpA v Ministero delle Finanze (C-130/92) [1994] ECR I-3281; [1995] 1 CMLR 84 . . . [5.10]

Oude Luttikhuis v Verenigde Coöperatieve Melkindustrie Coberco BA (C-399/93) [1995] ECR I-4515 . . . [6.75]

Oulane v Minister voor Vreemdelingenzaken en Integratie (C-215/03) [2005] ECR I-1215 . . . [3.160], [3.170], [3.270]

P v S (C-13/94) [1996] ECR I-2143; [1996] 2 CMLR 247 . . . [10.15], [10.55], [12.100]

Palacios de la Villa v Cortefiel Servicios SA (C-411/05) [2007] ECR I-8531; [2008] 1 CMLR 16 (p 385) . . . [10.110]

Parfums Christian Dior SA v Evora BV (C-337/95) [1997] ECR I-6013; [1998] 1 CMLR 737 . . . [9.15]

Parke, Davis & Co v Probel (24/67) [1968] ECR 55; [1968] CMLR 47 . . . [9.75]

Parliament v Council (13/83) [1985] ECR 1513; [1986] 1 CMLR 138 . . . [11.110]

Parliament v Council (C-181/91) [1993] ECR I-3685; [1994] 3 CMLR 317 . . . [11.100]

Parliament v Council (C-392/95) [1997] ECR I-3213; [1997] 3 CMLR 896 . . . [1.100]
Paul Reber GmbH & Co KG v Office for Harmonisation in the Internal Market (T-304/06) [2008] ECR II-1927 . . . [9.150]
Peak Holding AB v Axolin-Elinor AB (C-16/03) [2004] ECR I-11313; [2005] 1 CMLR 45 (p 1182) . . . [9.135]
Persche v Finanzamt Lüdenscheid (C-318/07) [2009] ECR I-359; [2009] 2 CMLR 32 (p 819) . . . [4.10], [4.15], [4.20], [4.25]
Petersen v Arbeitsmarktservice Niederösterreich (C-228/07) [2008] ECR I-6989; [2009] 1 CMLR 2 (p 43) . . . [3.25]
Petrie v Università degli Studi di Verona (C-90/96) [1997] ECR I-6527; [1998] 1 CMLR 711 . . . [3.60]
Petrotub SA v Council (C-76/00 P) [2003] ECR I-79 . . . [1.150], [5.45], [5.90], [11.45], [13.75]
Pfeiffer v Deutsches Rotes Kreuz, Kreisverband Waldshut eV (C-397/01) [2004] ECR I-8835; [2005] 1 CMLR 44 (p 1123) . . . [12.50]
Pfizer Inc v Eurim-Pharm GmbH (1/81) [1981] ECR 2913; [1982] 1 CMLR 406 . . . [9.45]
Pharmacia & Upjohn SA v Paranova A/S (C-379/97) [1999] ECR I-6927; [2000] 1 CMLR 51 . . . [2.100]
Pharmon BV v Hoechst AG (19/84) [1985] ECR 2281; [1985] 3 CMLR 775 . . . [9.40], [9.75]
PIAGEME v BVBA Peeters (C-369/89) [1991] ECR I-2971; [1993] 3 CMLR 725 . . . [2.60]
Piau v Commission (T-193/02) [2005] ECR II-209; appeal dismissed (C-171/05 P) [2006] ECR I-37* . . . [6.35]
Pigs Marketing Board (Northern Ireland) v Redmond (83/78) [1978] ECR 2347; [1979] 1 CMLR 177 . . . [2.90], [11.135]
Pippig Augenoptik GmbH & Co KG v Hartlauer Handelsgesellschaft mbH (C-44/01) [2003] ECR I-3095; [2004] 1 CMLR 39 (p 1244) . . . [10.170]
Placanica, Criminal Proceedings Against (C-338/04) [2007] ECR I-1891; [2007] 2 CMLR 25 (p 607) . . . [3.115], [3.120], [3.185]
Politi Sis v Ministry for Finance (43/71) [1971] ECR 1039; [1973] CMLR 60 . . . [12.30], [12.35]
Portugal v Commission (C-249/02) [2004] ECR I-10717 . . . [11.85]
Portugal v Council (C-149/96) [1999] ECR I-8395 . . . [13.75]
Poucet v Assurances Générales de France (C-159/91) [1993] ECR I-637 . . . [6.25]
Prantl, Criminal Proceedings Against (16/83) [1984] ECR 1299; [1985] 2 CMLR 238 . . . [9.20]
Presidente del Consiglio dei Ministri v Regione Sardegna (C-169/08) [2009] ECR . . . [3.165]
PreussenElektra AG v Schleswag AG (C-379/98) [2001] ECR I-2099; [2001] 2 CMLR 36 (p 833) . . . [11.135]

Private Teaching, Re: Commission v Greece (147/86) [1988] ECR 1637; [1989] 2 CMLR 845 . . . [3.105]
Procter & Gamble Co v Office for Harmonisation in the Internal Market (C-383/99 P) [2001] ECR I-6297; [2001] 5 CMLR 28 (p 1058) . . . [9.125]
Procureur de la République v Association de Défense des Brûleurs D'huiles Usagées (240/83) [1985] ECR 531 . . . [2.110]
Procureur de la République v Giry (253/78) [1980] ECR 2327; [1981] 2 CMLR 99 . . . [2.110]
Procureur du Roi v Dassonville (8/74) [1974] ECR 837; [1974] 2 CMLR 436 . . . [2.35], [2.65], [2.105]
Procureur Général v Buys (5/79) [1979] ECR 3203; [1980] 2 CMLR 493 . . . [8.95]
Productores de Musica de España (Promusicae) v Telefonica de España SAU (C-275/06) [2008] ECR I-271; [2008] 2 CMLR 17 (p 465) . . . [10.150], [11.125], [12.100]
Pubblico Ministero v Ratti (148/78) [1979] ECR 1629; [1980] 1 CMLR 96 . . . [12.40]
Public Employees (No 2), Re: Commission v Belgium (149/79) [1982] ECR 1845; [1982] 3 CMLR 539 . . . [3.60]
Public Service Employment, Re: Commission v Luxembourg (C-473/93) [1996] ECR I-3207; [1996] 3 CMLR 981 . . . [3.60]
Pupino, Criminal Proceedings Against (C-105/03) [2005] ECR I-5285; [2005] 2 CMLR 63 (p 1569) . . . [11.135]
Purity Requirements for Beer, Re: Commission v Germany (178/84) [1987] ECR 1227; [1988] 1 CMLR 780 . . . [2.120]
Pyres v Commission (T-256/01) [2005] ECR-SC II-99 . . . [1.40]
Quelle AG v Bundesverband der Verbraucherzentralen und Verbraucherverbände (C-404/06) [2008] ECR I-2685; [2008] 2 CMLR 49 (p 1347) . . . [10.165]
Quietlynn Ltd v Southend Borough Council (C-23/89) [1990] ECR I-3059; [1990] 3 CMLR 55 . . . [2.100]
R v Bouchereau (30/77) [1977] ECR 1999; [1977] 2 CMLR 800 . . . [3.55], [11.70]
R v Commissioners of Customs and Excise; Ex parte EMU Tabac Sarl (C-296/95) [1998] ECR I-1604; [1998] 2 CMLR 1205 . . . [11.70]
R v Competition Commission; Ex parte Milk Marque Ltd (C-137/00) [2003] ECR I-7975; [2004] 4 CMLR 6 (p 293) . . . [2.35], [6.230]
R v H M Treasury; Ex parte British Telecommunications plc (C-392/93) [1996] ECR I-1631; [1996] 2 CMLR 217 . . . [12.60]
R v H M Treasury; Ex parte Centro-COM Srl (C-124/95) [1997] ECR I-81; [1997] 1 CMLR 555 . . . [1.130], [5.06]
R v Inland Revenue Commissioners; Ex parte Commerzbank AG (C-330/91) [1993] ECR I-4017; [1993] 3 CMLR 457 . . . [3.90]
R v Medicines Control Agency; Ex parte Rhône-Poulenc Rorer Ltd (C-94/98) [1999] ECR I-8789; [2000] 1 CMLR 409 . . . [2.100]

R v Ministry of Agriculture, Fisheries and Food; Ex parte Hedley Lomas (C-5/94) [1996] ECR I-2553; [1996] 2 CMLR 391 . . . [12.60]
R v Secretary of State for Employment; Ex parte Seymour-Smith (C-167/97) [1999] ECR I-623; [1999] 2 CMLR 273 . . . [10.30], [10.35], [10.40], [12.45]
R v Secretary of State for Health; Ex parte British American Tobacco (Investments) Ltd (C-491/01) [2002] ECR I-11453; [2003] 1 CMLR 14 (p 395) . . . [1.135], [1.140], [12.100], [13.75]
R v Secretary of State for Health; Ex parte Richardson (C-137/94) [1995] ECR I-3407; [1995] 3 CMLR 376 . . . [11.155]
R v Secretary of State for Transport; Ex parte Factortame Ltd (No 2) (C-213/89) [1990] ECR 2433; [1990] 3 CMLR 1 . . . [12.85]
R (on the Application of ABNA Ltd) v Secretary of State for Health (C-453/03) [2005] ECR I-10423; [2006] 1 CMLR 48 (p 1290) . . . [1.140], [12.100]
R (on the Application of Alliance for Natural Health) v Secretary of State for Health (C-154/04) [2005] ECR I-6451; [2005] 2 CMLR 61 (p 1490) . . . [12.100]
R (on the Application of Bidar) v London Borough of Ealing (C-209/03) [2005] ECR I-2119; [2005] 2 CMLR 3 (p 56) . . . [11.155]
R (on the Application of International Air Transport Association) v Department for Transport (C-344/04) [2006] ECR I-403; [2006] 2 CMLR 20 (p 557) . . . [1.140], [1.150], [11.125], [11.135], [11.140]
R (on the Application of International Association of Independent Tanker Owners) v Secretary of State for Transport (C-308/06) [2008] ECR I-4057; [2008] 3 CMLR 9 (p 203) . . . [5.15]
R (on the Application of Teleos Plc) v Commissioners of Customs and Excise (C-409/04) [2007] ECR I-7797; [2008] 1 CMLR 6 (p 98) . . . [1.140], [11.60]
R (on the Application of Wells) v Secretary of State for Transport, Local Government and the Regions (C-201/02) [2004] ECR I-723; [2004] 1 CMLR 31 (p 1027) . . . [12.45]
Raccanelli v Max-Planck-Gesellschaft zur Förderung der Wissenschaften eV (C 94/07) [2008] ECR I-5939; [2008] 3 CMLR 25 (p 751) . . . [3.15]
Racke v Hauptzollamt Mainz (98/78) [1979] ECR 69 . . . [1.155]
Racke (A) GmbH & Co v Hauptzollamt Mainz (C-162/96) [1998] ECR I-3655; [1998] 3 CMLR 219 . . . [5.15]
Radio Telefis Eireann v Commission (C-241/91 P) [1995] ECR I-743; [1995] 4 CMLR 718 . . . [6.135], [6.140], [9.10]
Radiosistemi Srl v Prefetto di Genova (C-388/00) [2002] ECR I-5845 . . . [2.135]
Raulin v Minister van Onderwijs en Wetenschappen (C-357/89) [1992] ECR I-1027; [1994] 1 CMLR 227 . . . [3.20]
Ravil SARL v Bellon import SARL (C-469/00) [2003] ECR I-5053 . . . [9.15]

Rechnungshof v Österreichischer Rundfunk (C-465/00) [2003] ECR I-4989; [2003] 3 CMLR 10 (p 265) . . . [10.140]
Région Wallonne v Commission (C-95/97) [1997] ECR I-1787 . . . [11.85]
Regione Siciliana v Commission (C-417/04 P) [2006] ECR I-3881; [2006] 2 CMLR 64 (p 1557) . . . [11.85]
Reisch v Bürgermeister der Landeshauptstadt Salzburg (C-515/99) [2002] ECR I-2157; [2004] 1 CMLR 44 (p 1394) . . . [4.10]
Reliance Industries Ltd v Council (T-45/06) [2008] ECR II-2399 . . . [5.45], [5.95]
Rendo NV v Commission (T-16/91) [1992] ECR II-2417 . . . [5.200]
Rewe-Zentral AG v Bundesmonopolverwalting für Branntwein (120/78) [1979] ECR 649; [1979] 3 CMLR 494 . . . [2.105], [2.110]
Rewe Zentralfinanz eG v Finanzamt Köln-Mitte (C-347/04) [2007] ECR I-2647; [2007] 2 CMLR 42 (p 1111) . . . [1.130], [3.85]
Reyners v Belgium (2/74) [1974] ECR 631; [1974] 2 CMLR 305 . . . [12.20]
Reynolds (R J) Tobacco Holdings Inc v Commission (C-131/03 P) [2006] ECR I-7795; [2007] 1 CMLR 1 (p 1) . . . [11.85], [11.100]
Rheinmühlen-Düsseldorf v Einfuhr- und Vorratsstelle für Getreide und Futtermittel (166/73) [1974] ECR 33; [1974] 1 CMLR 523 . . . [11.125]
Richards v Secretary of State for Work and Pensions (C-423/04) [2006] ECR I-3585; [2006] 2 CMLR 49 (p 1242) . . . [1.130], [10.15], [10.55], [11.155], [12.100]
Rima Eletrometalurgia SA v Council (C-216/91) [1993] ECR I-6303 . . . [5.150]
Rinke v Ärztekammer Hamburg (C-25/02) [2003] ECR I-8349 . . . [10.15]
Ritek Corporation v Council (T-274/02) [2006] ECR II-4305 . . . [5.60]
Robert Bosch GmbH v Kleding Verkoopbedrijf de Geus en Uitdenbogerd (13/61) [1962] ECR 45; [1962] CMLR 1 . . . [11.135]
Robins v Secretary of State for Work and Pensions (C-278/05) [2007] ECR I-1053; [2007] 2 CMLR 13 (p 269) . . . [12.60]
Roders (F G) BV v Inspecteur der Invoerrechten en Accijnzen (C-367/93) [1995] ECR I-2229 . . . [7.30]
Roquette Frères SA v Hauptzollamt Geldern (C-228/92) [1994] ECR I-1445 . . . [11.85]
Roquette Frères SA v Tax Office of Pas-de-Calais (C-88/99) [2000] ECR I-10465 . . . [12.60]
Rosengren v Riksåklagaren (C-170/04) [2007] ECR I-4071; [2007] 3 CMLR 10 (p 239) . . . [2.30], [2.35], [2.100], [2.125]
Rotexchemie v Hauptzollamt Hamburg-Waltershof (C-26/96) [1997] ECR I-2817 . . . [5.200]
Rothley v Parliament (T-17/00 R) [2000] ECR II-2085; [2002] 2 CMLR 29 (p 737) . . . [11.85]
Roudolff, Criminal Proceedings Against (803/79) [1980] ECR 2015 . . . [11.65]
Rummler v Dato-Druck GmbH (237/85) [1986] ECR 2101; [1987] 3 CMLR 127 . . . [10.50]

Rutili v Minister for the Interior (36/75) [1975] ECR 1219; [1976] 1 CMLR 140 . . . [3.55]
Sadam Zuccherifici v Council (C-41/99) [2001] ECR I-4239 . . . [1.150]
Säger v Dennemeyer & Co Ltd (C-76/90) [1991] ECR 4221; [1993] 3 CMLR 639 . . . [3.170]
Salerno v Commission (87/77) [1985] ECR 2523 . . . [1.150]
Salzmann, Re (C-300/01) [2003] ECR I-4899; [2004] 1 CMLR 29 (p 959) . . . [4.15]
Sandoz v Finanzlandesdirektion für Wien, Niederösterreich und Burgenland (C-439/97) [1999] ECR I-7041; [2001] 3 CMLR 63 (p 1639) . . . [4.15]
Sanz de Lera, Criminal Proceedings Against (C-163/94) [1995] ECR I-4821; [1996] 1 CMLR 361 . . . [4.05], [4.15], [4.20], [4.30]
Scandinavian Airlines System AB v Commission (T-241/01) [2005] ECR II-2917; [2005] 5 CMLR 18 (p 922) . . . [6.125]
Schempp v Finanzamt München V (C-403/03) [2005] ECR I-6421; [2005] 3 CMLR 37 (p 1051) . . . [3.300]
Schmid v Belgium (C-310/91) [1993] ECR I-3011; [1995] 2 CMLR 803 . . . [3.65]
Scholz v Opera Universitaria di Cagliari (C-419/92) [1994] ECR I-505; [1994] 1 CMLR 873 . . . [3.90]
Schöning-Kougebetopoulou v Freie und Hansestadt Hamburg (C-15/96) [1998] ECR I-47; [1998] 1 CMLR 931 . . . [3.40], [3.60], [12.65]
Schreiber, Criminal Proceedings Against (C-443/02) [2004] ECR I-7275; [2004] 3 CMLR 10 (p 211) . . . [2.120]
Schutzverband Gegen Unwesen in der Wirtschaft v Weinvertriebs GmbH (59/82) [1983] ECR 1217; [1984] 1 CMLR 319 . . . [2.125]
Schwarz v Finanzamt Bergisch Gladbach (C-76/05) [2007] ECR I-1721; [2007] 3 CMLR 47 (p 1283) . . . [3.160], [3.165], [3.175]
Schwierung v Court of Auditors (142/85) [1986] ECR 3177 . . . [11.106]
SECAP SpA v Comune di Torino (C-147/06) [2008] ECR I-3565; [2008] 2 CMLR 56 (p 1558) . . . [8.85]
Servizi Ausiliari Dottori Commercialisti v Calafiori (C-451/03) [2006] ECR I-2941; [2006] 2 CMLR 45 (p 1135) . . . [3.180]
Sevince v Staatssecretaris van Justitie (C-192/89) [1990] ECR I-3461; [1992] 2 CMLR 57 . . . [11.145]
SGL Carbon AG v Commission (C-308/04) [2006] ECR I-5977; [2006] 5 CMLR 16 (p 922) . . . [6.235]
Shanghai Bicycle Corporation v Council (T-170/94) [1997] ECR II-1383 . . . [5.165], [5.200]
Shanghai Teraoka Electronic Co Ltd v Council (T-35/01) [2004] ECR II-3663 . . . [5.120]
Sharp Corporation v Council (301/85) [1988] ECR 5813; [1989] 1 CMLR 381 . . . [5.65], [5.85]
Shield Mark BV v Kist (C-283/01) [2003] ECR I-14313; [2005] 1 CMLR 41 (p 1046) . . . [11.135]

Showa Denko KK v Commission (C-289/04 P) [2006] ECR I-5859; [2006] 5 CMLR 14 (p 840) . . . [6.235]

Siderúrgica Aristrain Madrid SL v Commission (C-196/99 P) [2003] ECR I-11005 . . . [6.40], [8.95]

Sieckmann v Deutsches Patent-und Markenamt (C-273/00) [2002] ECR I-11737; [2005] 1 CMLR 40 (p 1021) . . . [9.110], [9.120]

Silberquelle GmbH v Maselli-Strickmode GmbH (C-495/07) [2009] ECR I-137 . . . [9.145]

Silhouette International Schmied GmbH & Co KG v Hartlauer Handelsgesellschaft MBH (C-355/96) [1998] ECR I-4799; [1998] 2 CMLR 953 . . . [12.50]

Silver Seiko Ltd v Council (273/85) [1988] ECR 5927; [1989] 1 CMLR 249 . . . [5.80], [5.125], [5.165]

Sinochem Heilongjiang v Council (T-161/94) [1996] ECR II-695; [1997] 3 CMLR 214 . . . [5.200]

Sinochem National Chemicals Import & Export Corporation v Council (T-97/95) [1998] ECR II-85 . . . [5.130]

Sirdar v Secretary of State for Defence (C-273/97) [1999] ECR I-7403; [1999] 3 CMLR 559 . . . [10.65]

Skatteministeriet v Codan (C-236/97) [1998] ECR I-8679; [2001] 1 CMLR 36 (p 941) . . . [11.70]

Skatteverket v A (C-101/05) [2007] ECR I-11531; [2009] 1 CMLR 35 (p 975) . . . [1.130], [4.05], [4.15], [4.20], [4.30]

Skoma-Lux sro v Celní ředitelství Olomouc (C-161/06) [2007] ECR I-10841; [2008] 1 CMLR 50 (p 1336) . . . [1.155]

Snellers Auto's BV v Algemeen Directeur van de Dienst Wegverkeer (C-314/98) [2000] ECR I-8633; [2000] 3 CMLR 1275 . . . [2.110]

Sociaal Fonds voor de Diamantarbeiders v Indiamex NV (37/73) [1973] ECR 1609; [1976] 2 CMLR 222 . . . [2.15]

Sociedad General de Autores y Editores de España (SGAE) v Rafael Hoteles SA (C-306/05) [2006] ECR I-11519 . . . [9.85], [11.45]

Società Italiana per l'Oleodotto Transalpino v Ministero delle Finanze (266/81) [1983] ECR 731; [1984] 2 CMLR 231 . . . [5.10]

Società SADAM v Comitato Interministeriale dei Prezzi (88-90/75) [1976] ECR 323; [1977] 2 CMLR 183 . . . [2.55], [2.95]

Société Cadi Surgelés v Ministre des Finances (C-126/94) [1996] ECR I-5647; [1997] 1 CMLR 795 . . . [2.15]

Société Civile Immobilière Parodi v Banque H Albert de Bary et Cie (C-222/95) [1997] ECR I-3899; [1998] 1 CMLR 115 . . . [3.175]

Société d'Importation Edouard Leclerc-Siplec v TF1 Publicité SA [1995] ECR I-179; [1995] 3 CMLR 422 . . . [2.115]

Société de Vente de Ciments et Betons de L'Est SA v Kerpen & Kerpen GmbH (319/82) [1983] ECR 4173; [1985] 1 CMLR 511 . . . [6.20], [6.70]

Société Technique Miniére v Maschinenbau Ulm GmbH (56/65) [1966] ECR 235; [1966] CMLR 357 . . . [6.65]

Society for the Protection of Unborn Children v Grogan (C-159/90) [1991] ECR I-4685; [1991] 3 CMLR 849 . . . [3.160]
Sodemare SA v Regione Lombardia [1997] ECR I-3395; [1997] 3 CMLR 591 . . . [3.165]
Sotgiu v Deutsche Bundespost (152/73) [1974] ECR 153 . . . [3.60]
Sot Lelos kai Sia EE v GlaxoSmithKline AEVE Farmakeftikon Proionton (C-468/06) [2008] ECR I-7139; [2008] 5 CMLR 20 (p 1382) . . . [6.120]
Sotralentz SA v Commission (T-149/89) [1995] ECR II-1127 . . . [6.230]
Spain v Lenzing AG (C-525/04 P) [2007] ECR I-9947; [2008] 1 CMLR 40 (p 1068) . . . [6.215]
Specialarbejderforbundet i Danmark v Dansk Industri (C-400/93) [1995] ECR I-1275; [1996] 1 CMLR 515 . . . [10.10], [10.20], [10.35]
Staatsanwaltschaft Freiburg v Keller (234/85) [1986] ECR 2897; [1987] 1 CMLR 875 . . . [12.70]
Stadt Halle, RPL Recyclingpark Lochau GmbH v Arbeitsgemeinschaft Thermische Restabfall- und Energieverwertungsanlage TREA Leuna (C-26/03) [2005] ECR I-1; [2006] 1 CMLR 39 (p 1027) . . . [8.05]
Stadtgemeinde Frohnleiten v Bundesminister für Land- und Forstwirtschaft, Umwelt und Wasserwirtschaft (C-221/06) [2007] ECR I-9643; [2008] 1 CMLR 30 (p 779) . . . [2.10], [7.15], [7.30]
Stamatelaki v NPDD Organismos Asfaliseos Eleftheron Epangelmation (C-444/05) [2007] ECR I-3185; [2007] 2 CMLR 44 (p 1185) . . . [3.175]
Standesamt Stadt Niebüll, Proceedings brought by (C-96/04) [2006] ECR I-3561; [2006] 2 CMLR 58 (p 1414) . . . [11.130]
Stauder v City of Ulm (29/69) [1969] ECR 419; [1970] CMLR 112 . . . [11.55], [11.70], [12.90]
Steen v Deutsche Bundespost (C-332/90) [1992] ECR I-341; [1992] 2 CMLR 406 . . . [3.95]
Steinhauser v City of Biarritz (197/84) [1985] ECR 1819; [1986] 1 CMLR 53 . . . [3.95]
Steymann v Staatssecretaris van Justitie (196/87) [1988] ECR 6159; [1989] 1 CMLR 449 . . . [3.30]
Stoke-on-Trent City Council v B & Q plc (C-169/91) [1992] ECR I-6635; [1993] 1 CMLR 426 . . . [2.85], [2.125]
Stora Kopparbergs Bergslags AB v Commission (C-286/98 P) [2000] ECR I-9925; [2001] 4 CMLR 12 (p 370) . . . [6.40]
Stradasfalti Srl v Agenzia delle Entrate Ufficio di Trento (C-228/05) [2006] ECR I-8391 . . . [11.85]
Sumitomo Chemical Co Ltd v Commission (T-23/02) [2005] ECR II-4065 . . . [11.45]
Supply of Medicines by Pharmacies to Nearby Hospitals, Re: Commission v Germany (C-141/07) [2008] ECR I-6935; [2008] 3 CMLR 48 (p 1479) . . . [1.130], [2.100], [2.120]
Svensson v Ministre du Logement et de l'Urbanisme (C-484/93) [1995] ECR I-3955 . . . [4.15]

Swedish Match Philippines Inc v Council (T-171/97) [1999] ECR II-3241 . . . [5.125]
Syndicat français de l'Express international (SFEI) v La Poste (C-39/94) [1996] ECR I-3547; [1996] 3 CMLR 369 . . . [6.160]
Synetairismos Farmakopoion Aitolias & Akarnanias (Syfait) v GlaxoSmithKline plc (C-53/03) [2005] ECR I-4609; [2005] 5 CMLR 1 (p 1) . . . [11.130]
Tariff Preferences for Canned Tuna Imports, Re: Spain v Council (C-342/03) [2005] ECR I-1975; [2006] 1 CMLR 8 (p 173) . . . [1.150]
Technointorg v Commission (294/86) [1988] ECR 6077; [1989] 1 CMLR 281 . . . [5.125]
Teckal Srl v Comune di Viano (C-107/98) [1999] ECR I-8121 . . . [11.135]
Tele Danmark A/S v Handels-og Kontorfunktionoerernes Forbund I Danmark (HK) (C-109/00) [2001] ECR I-6993; [2002] 1 CMLR 5 (p 105) . . . [10.75]
Telemarsicabruzzo SpA v Circostel (C-320/90) [1993] ECR I-393 . . . [11.135]
Tepea BV v Commission (28/77) [1978] ECR 1391; [1978] 3 CMLR 392 . . . [6.45], [6.100]
Terrapin (Overseas) Ltd v Terranova Industrie CA Kapferer & Co (119/75) [1976] ECR 1039; [1976] 2 CMLR 482 . . . [9.55], [9.65]
Test Claimants in the CFC and Dividend Group Litigation v Inland Revenue Commissioners (C-201/05) [2008] ECR I-2875; [2008] 2 CMLR 53 (p 1482) . . . [4.15]
Test Claimants in the FII Group Litigation v Commissioners of Inland Revenue (C-446/04) [2006] ECR I-11753; [2007] 1 CMLR 35 (p 1021) . . . [4.05], [4.10], [4.15], [12.60]
Test Claimants in the Thin Cap Group Litigation v Commissioners of Inland Revenue (C-524/04) [2007] ECR I-2107; [2007] 2 CMLR 31 (p 765) . . . [12.60]
Tetra Pak International SA v Commission (C-333/94 P) [1996] ECR I-5951; [1997] 4 CMLR 662 . . . [6.115], [6.130]
Thai Bicycle Industry & Co Ltd v Council (T-118/96) [1998] ECR II-2991 . . . [5.55], [5.200]
Thetford Corporation v Fiamma SpA (35/87) [1988] ECR 3585; [1988] 3 CMLR 549 . . . [9.10]
Thieffry v Paris Bar Council (71/76) [1977] ECR 765; [1977] 2 CMLR 373 . . . [3.75]
Thijssen v Controledienst voor de verzekeringen (C-42/92) [1993] ECR I-4047 . . . [3.105]
Thyssen Stahl AG v Commission (C-194/99 P) [2003] ECR I-10821 . . . [6.100]
Timex Corporation v Council (264/82) [1985] ECR 849; [1985] 3 CMLR 550 . . . [5.150], [5.200]
T-Mobile Netherlands BV v Raad van bestuur van de Nederlandse Mededingingsautoriteit (C-8/08) [2009] 5 CMLR 11 (p 1701) . . . [6.100]

Tobacco Advertising Directive 2003/33, Re: Germany v Council (C-380/03) [2006] ECR I-11573; [2007] 2 CMLR 1 (p 1) . . . [1.140], [1.150]
Tokyo Electric Co Ltd v Council (260/85) [1988] ECR 5855; [1989] 1 CMLR 169 . . . [5.65], [5.70], [5.130]
Toshiba Europe GmbH v Katun Germany GmbH (C-112/99) [2001] ECR I-7945; [2002] 3 CMLR 7 (p 164) . . . [10.170], [11.50]
Transocean Marine Paint Association v Commission (17/74) [1974] ECR 1063; [1974] 2 CMLR 459 . . . [11.30]
Travel-Vac SL v Sanchís (C-423/97) [1999] ECR I-2195; [1999] 2 CMLR 1111 . . . [10.195]
Tréfileurope Sales SARL v Commission (T-141/89) [1995] ECR II-791 . . . [6.45], [6.230]
Trojani v Centre public d'aide sociale de Bruxelles (C-456/02) [2004] ECR I-7573; [2004] 3 CMLR 38 (p 820) . . . [3.20], [3.25], [3.30], [3.265]
Trummer, Proceedings brought by (C-22/97) [1999] ECR I-1661; [2000] 3 CMLR 1143 . . . [4.10], [4.15]
Turpeinen, Proceedings brought by (C-520/04) [2006] ECR I-10685; [2007] 1 CMLR 28 (p 783) . . . [3.45]
TWD Textilwerke Deggendorf GmbH v Germany (C-188/92) [1994] ECR I-833; [1995] 2 CMLR 145 . . . [11.85], [11.125]
Unilever Bestfoods (Ireland) Ltd v Commission (C-552/03 P) [2006] ECR I-9091; [2006] 5 CMLR 27 (p 1494) . . . [6.65]
Unilever Italia SpA v Central Food SpA (C-443/98) [2000] ECR I-7535; [2001] 1 CMLR 21 (p 566) . . . [12.45]
Union Royale Belge des Sociétés de Football Association ASBL v Bosman (C-415/93) [1995] ECR I-4921; [1996] 1 CMLR 645 . . . [3.15], [3.20], [3.45], [3.150], [11.125], [12.100]
Unión de Televisiones Comerciales Asociadas v Administración General del Estado (C-222/07) [2009] 3 CMLR 2 (p 34) . . . [4.25]
Unità Socio-Sanitaria Locale n° 47 di Biella v Istituto nazionale per l'assicurazione contro gli infortuni sul lavoro (C-134/95) [1997] ECR I-195 . . . [3.150]
United Brands Co v Commission (27/76) [1978] ECR 207; [1978] 1 CMLR 429 . . . [6.130]
United Foods NV v Belgium (132/80) [1981] ECR 995; [1982] 1 CMLR 273 . . . [7.20]
United Kingdom v Council (C-84/94) [1996] ECR I-5755; [1996] 2 CMLR 671 . . . [1.140]
United Pan-Europe Communications Belgium SA v Belgium (C-250/06) [2007] ECR I-11135; [2008] 2 CMLR 2 (p 45) . . . [3.160], [3.165], [3.175], [3.190], [4.25], [12.100]
University Fees, Re: Commission v Belgium (C-47/93) [1994] ECR I-1593; [1994] 3 CMLR 723 . . . [10.135]
Uruguay Round Treaties, Re (Opinion 1/94) [1994] ECR I-5267; [1995] 1 CMLR 205 . . . [5.15], [5.30], [13.60]

VAG France SA v Établissements Magne SA (10/86) [1986] ECR 4071; [1988] 4 CMLR 98 . . . [6.20]
Vajnai, Criminal Proceedings Against (C-328/04) [2005] ECR I-8577 . . . [11.125]
Validity of Directive 2003/86, Re: Parliament v Council (C-540/03) [2006] ECR I-5769; [2006] 3 CMLR 28 (p 779) . . . [1.40], [12.100], [12.110]
Validity of Decisions 2004/496 and 2004/535, Re: Parliament v Council (C-317/04) [2006] ECR I-4721; [2006] 3 CMLR 9 (p 251) . . . [10.140]
van Buynder, Criminal Proceedings Against (C-152/94) [1995] ECR I-3981 . . . [3.95]
van Duyn v Home Office (41/74) [1974] ECR 1337; [1975] 1 CMLR 1 . . . [3.55], [12.15], [12.40]
van Gend en Loos – see Algemene Transport- en Expeditie Onderneming van Gend en Loos (NV) v Nederlandse Administratie der Belastingen
van Hilten-van der Heijden v Inspecteur van de Belastingdienst (C-513/03) [2006] ECR I-1957 . . . [4.10]
VAT Rates on Wine, Re: Commission v Belgium (356/85) [1987] ECR 3299; [1988] 3 CMLR 277 . . . [7.30]
Vatsouras v Arbeitsgemeinschaft (ARGE) Nürnberg 900 (C-22/08) [2009] All ER (EC) 747 . . . [3.20], [3.30]
Velvet & Steel Immobilien und Handels GmbH v Finanzamt Hamburg-Eimsbüttel (C-455/05) [2007] ECR I-3225 . . . [11.60], [11.70]
Vereinigte Familiapress Zeitungsverlags- und Vertriebs GmbH v Heinrich Bauer Verlag (C-368/95) [1997] ECR I-3689; [1997] 3 CMLR 1329 . . . [2.35], [2.75], [2.110]
Vereniging ter Bevordering van het Vlaamse Boekwezen (VBVB) v Commission (43/82) [1984] ECR 19; [1985] 1 CMLR 27 . . . [6.45]
Vereniging voor Energie, Milieu en Water v Directeur van de Dienst uitvoering en toezicht Energie (C-17/03) [2005] ECR I-4983; [2005] 5 CMLR 8 (p 361) . . . [11.60], [11.135]
Vereniging van Vlaamse Reisbureaus v Sociale Dienst van de Plaatselijke en Gewestelijke Overheidsdiensten (311/85) [1987] ECR 3801; [1989] 4 CMLR 213 . . . [6.05]
Viho Europe BV v Commission (C-73/95 P) [1996] ECR I-5457; [1997] 4 CMLR 419 . . . [6.30]
Vlassopoulou v Ministerium für Justiz (C-340/89) [1991] ECR I-2357; [1993] 2 CMLR 221 . . . [3.75]
Völk v Etablissements J Vervaecke SPRL (5/69) [1969] ECR 295; [1969] CMLR 273 . . . [6.80]
Von Colson v Land Nordrhein-Westfalen (14/83) [1984] ECR 1891; [1986] 2 CMLR 430 . . . [12.50]
Voss v Land Berlin (C-300/06) [2007] ECR I-10573; [2008] 1 CMLR 49 (p 1313) . . . [10.30], [10.35]
VTB-VAB NV v Total Belgium NV (C-261/07) [2009] 3 CMLR 17 (p 697) . . . [12.40]

Walrave v Association Union Cycliste Internationale (36/74) [1974] ECR 1405; [1975] 1 CMLR 320 . . . [3.20], [12.25]
Walter Rau Lebensmittelwerke v de Smedt PVBA (261/81) [1982] ECR 3961; [1983] 2 CMLR 496 . . . [2.60]
Webb v EMO Air Cargo (UK) Ltd (C-32/93) [1994] ECR I-3567; [1994] 2 CMLR 729 . . . [10.75]
Weber v Parliament (C-314/91) [1993] ECR I-1093 . . . [1.15]
Weigel v Finanzlandesdirektion für Vorarlberg (C-387/01) [2004] ECR I-4981; [2004] 3 CMLR 42 (p 931) . . . [7.15], [7.30]
Wilhelm v Bundeskartellamt (14/68) [1969] ECR 1; [1969] CMLR 100 . . . [6.230]
Wiljo NV v Belgium (C-178/95) [1997] ECR I-585; [1997] 1 CMLR 627 . . . [11.85], [11.125]
Willy Kempter AG v Hauptzollamt Hamburg-Jonas (C-2/06) [2008] ECR I-411; [2008] 2 CMLR 21 (p 586) . . . [11.125]
Wilson v Ordre des avocats du barreau de Luxembourg (C-506/04) [2006] ECR I-8613; [2007] 1 CMLR 7 (p 217) . . . [3.205], [11.55], [11.125], [11.130]
Wirth v Landeshauptstadt Hannover (C-109/92) [1993] ECR I-6447 . . . [3.160]
Wood v Fonds de Garantie des Victimes des Actes de Terrorisme et d'Autres Infractions (C-164/07) [2008] ECR I-4143; [2008] 3 CMLR 11 (p 265) . . . [3.300]
Wood Pulp Cartel, Re: A Ahlström Osakeyhtiö v Commission (89/85) [1988] ECR 5193; [1988] 4 CMLR 901 . . . [6.40]
Woodspring District Council v Bakers of Nailsea Ltd (C-27/95) [1997] ECR I-1847; [1997] 2 CMLR 266 . . . [11.125]
Working Time Directive, Re: United Kingdom v Council (C-84/94) [1996] ECR I-5755; [1996] 2 CMLR 671 . . . [1.150]
Work Visa Regime, Re: Commission v Germany (C-244/04) [2006] ECR I-885; [2006] 2 CMLR 23 (p 631) . . . [3.175]
Worringham v Lloyds Bank Ltd (69/80) [1981] ECR 767; [1981] 2 CMLR 1 . . . [10.40]
Wouters v Algemene Raad van de Nederlandse Orde van Advocaten (C-309/99) [2002] ECR I-1577; [2002] 4 CMLR 27 (p 913) . . . [6.25]
X, Criminal Proceedings Against (C-74/95) [1996] ECR I-6609 . . . [11.130]
X v Staatssecretaris van Financiën (C-155/08) [2009] All ER (EC) 888 . . . [4.25]
Yoshida Nederland BV v Kamer van Koophandel en Fabrieken voor Friesland (34/78) [1979] ECR 115; [1979] 2 CMLR 747 . . . [2.20]
Yusuf v Council (T-306/01) [2005] ECR II-3533; [2005] 3 CMLR 49 (p 1335) . . . [1.150]
Zino Davidoff SA v Tesco Stores Ltd (C-414/99) [2001] ECR I-8691; [2002] 1 CMLR 1 (p 1) . . . [9.135]
Zoni, Criminal Proceedings Against (90/86) [1988] ECR 4285 . . . [2.125]

Züchner v Bayerische Vereinsbank AG (172/80) [1981] ECR 2021; [1982] 1 CMLR 313 . . . [6.75], [6.100]
Zuckerfabrik Watenstedt GmbH v Council (6/68) [1968] ECR 409; [1969] CMLR 26 . . . [1.150]
Zurstrassen v Administration des Contributions Directes (C-87/99) [2000] ECR I-3337; [2001] 3 CMLR 66 (p 1715) . . . [3.65]

European Commission

Decision 82/861 Telespeed Services Ltd v United Kingdom Post Office OJ L 360, 21.12.1982, p 36; [1983] 1 CMLR 457 . . . [8.95]
Decision 85/75 Re Fire Insurance OJ L 35, 7.2.1985, p 20; [1985] 3 CMLR 246 . . . [6.75]
Decision COMP/A.37.507/F3 AstraZeneca, 15 June 2005 . . . [6.75]

European Court of Human Rights

Bosphorus Hava Yollari Turizm Ve Ticaret Anonim Sirketi v Ireland (45036/98) ECHR 2005-VI, 42 EHRR 1 (p 1) . . . [12.110]
Cooperatieve Producentenorganisatie van de Nederlandse Kokkelvisserij UA v Netherlands, No 13645/05, 20 January 2009 . . . [12.110]

European Free Trade Association Court

Criminal Proceedings Against A (E-1/07) [2007] EFTA Ct Rep 246; [2008] 1 CMLR 37 (p 982) . . . [2.150]
Karlsson v Iceland (E-4/01) [2002] EFTA Ct Rep 240 . . . [2.150]
L'Oréal Norge AS v Per Aarskog AS (E-9/07) [2008] EFTA Ct Rep 259; [2008] ETMR 60 (p 943) . . . [2.150]

GATT Panels

European Communities – Refunds on Exports of Sugar, GATT Panel Report, L/4833, adopted 6 November 1979, BISD 26S/290; 20 ILM 862 . . . [1.65]

World Trade Organization Dispute Resolution Bodies

European Communities – Measures affecting Asbestos and Asbestos-containing Products, Report of the Appellate Body, DS135, 12 March 2001, DSR 2001: VII, 3243; 40 ILM 1193 . . . [13.30], [13.55]

European Communities – Measures Concerning Meat and Meat Products (Hormones), Report of the Appellate Body, DS26, DS48, 13 February 1998, DSR 1998: I, 135 . . . [13.60], [13.90]
European Communities – Regime for the Importation, Sale and Distribution of Bananas, Report of the Appellate Body, DS27, 25 September 1997, DSR 1997: II, 589 . . . [1.60], [13.85], [13.115]
European Communities – Selected Customs Matters, Report of the Appellate Body, DS315, 13 November 2006, DSR 2006: IX, 3791; 18 no 6 WTAM 3 . . . [13.50]
European Communities – Trade Description of Sardines, Report of the Appellate Body, DS231, 26 September 2002, DSR 2002: VII, 3359 . . . [13.95]
United States – Continued Dumping and Subsidy Offset Act of 2000, Decision by the Arbitrator under Art 22.6 of the DSU, DS217, 31 August 2004, DSR 2004: IX, 4591 . . . [1.60]
United States – Continued Dumping and Subsidy Offset Act of 2000, Report of the Appellate Body, DS217, 16 January 2003, DSR 2003: I, 375; 42 ILM 427 . . . [1.60]
United States – Continued Suspension of Obligations in the EC-Hormones Dispute, Report of the Appellate Body, DS320, 16 October 2008, DSR 2008: IX to XI . . . [13.60]
United States – Tax Treatment for "Foreign Sales Corporations", Recourse to Art 22.6 Arbitration Report, DS108, 30 August 2002, DSR 2002: VI, 2517; 41 ILM 1400 . . . [1.60]

National Courts

Australia

Downs Investments Pty Ltd (in liq) v Perwaja Steel Sdn Bhd [2002] 2 Qd R 462 . . . [13.165]
Hannaford v Australian Farmlink Pty Ltd [2008] FCA 1591 . . . [13.140]

Czech Republic

Treaty of Lisbon Case I, Constitutional Court, Pl US 19/08, 26 November 2008 . . . [1.55]
Treaty of Lisbon Case II, Constitutional Court, Pl US 29/09, 3 November 2009 . . . [1.55]

Germany

Treaty of Lisbon Case, Constitutional Court, 2 BvE 2/08 & 5/08; 2 BvR 1010/08, 1022/08, 1259/08 & 182/09, 30 June 2009 . . . [1.55]

United Kingdom

Bulmer (H P) Ltd v J Bollinger SA [1974] Ch 401; [1974] 2 CMLR 91 . . . [11.65]
R v Secretary of State for Transport; Ex parte Factortame Ltd (No 1) [1990] 2 AC 85; [1989] 3 CMLR 1 . . . [12.85]
R v Secretary of State for Transport; Ex parte Factortame Ltd (No 2) [1991] AC 603; [1990] 3 CMLR 375 . . . [12.85]

United States

Asante Technologies Inc v PMC-Sierra Inc 164 F Supp 2d 1142 (ND Cal 2001) . . . [13.145]
BP Oil International Ltd v Empresa Estatal Petoleos de Ecuador 332 F 3d 333 (5th Cir 2003) . . . [13.145]
Caterpillar Inc v Usinor Industeel 305 F Supp 2d 659 (ND Ill 2005) . . . [13.145]
Delchi Carrier v Rotorex Corporation 71 F 3d 1024 (2d Cir 1995) . . . [13.145]
Filanto SpA v Chilewich International Corporation 789 F Supp 1229 (SD NY 1992) . . . [13.145]
Genpharm Inc v Pliva-Lachema AS 361 F Supp 2d 49 (ED NY 2005) . . . [13.145]
Intel Corporation v Advanced Micro Devices Inc 542 US 241 (2004) . . . [6.235]
Medellin v Texas 552 US 491; 128 S Ct 1346 (2008) . . . [13.145]
Usinor Industeel v Leeco Steel Products Inc 209 F Supp 2d 880 (ND Ill 2002) . . . [13.145]

Table of EU Founding Treaties

Current Founding Treaties

Treaty on European Union

Art 1 . . . [1.55]
Art 3(1) . . . [1.130], [6.05]
Art 3(2) . . . [3.265]
Art 3(3) . . . [1.15]
Art 3(4) . . . [1.15]
Art 4(1) . . . [1.130]
Art 4(3) . . . [12.40], [12.50]
Art 5(1) . . . [1.135]
Art 5(2) . . . [1.130]
Art 5(3) . . . [1.135]
Art 5(4) . . . [1.140]
Art 6(1) . . . [1.40], [10.130], [12.105]
Art 6(2) . . . [12.110]
Art 9 . . . [1.15]
Art 10(2) . . . [1.100], [1.105]
Art 11 . . . [2.110]
Art 13(1) . . . [1.85], [1.120], [11.135]
Art 14(1) . . . [1.90], [1.100]
Art 14(2) . . . [1.100]
Art 14(3) . . . [1.100]
Art 15(1) . . . [1.105]
Art 15(2) . . . [1.105]
Art 15(3) . . . [1.155]
Art 15(4) . . . [1.105]
Art 15(5) . . . [1.105]
Art 16(1) . . . [1.95]
Art 16(3) . . . [1.95]
Art 16(4) . . . [1.95]

Art 16(7) . . . [1.95]
Art 16(9) . . . [1.95]
Art 17(1) . . . [1.90]
Art 17(3) . . . [1.90]
Art 17(4) . . . [1.90]
Art 17(5) . . . [1.90]
Art 19(1) . . . [11.45]
Art 19(2) . . . [11.10]
Art 20 . . . [1.145]
Art 20(4) . . . [1.145]
Art 21 . . . [5.20]
Art 24(2) . . . [1.55]
Art 28 . . . [12.70]
Art 37 . . . [5.20]
Art 47 . . . [5.20]
Art 48(4) . . . [1.145]
Art 48(6) . . . [1.145]
Art 49 . . . [1.20], [1.100]
Art 50 . . . [1.145]
Art 53 . . . [1.145]

Treaty on the Functioning of the European Union

Art 2 . . . [1.130]
Art 4(2) . . . [1.130]
Art 4(3) . . . [12.80]
Art 6 . . . [1.130]
Art 8 . . . [10.15]
Art 10 . . . [10.55]
Art 12 . . . [10.155]
Art 15(2) . . . [1.100]
Art 18 . . . [1.15], [3.300], [10.135]
Art 19(1) . . . [10.55], [10.100]
Art 20(1) . . . [1.15]
Art 21(1) . . . [1.15], [3.265]
Art 25 . . . [7.10], [7.20], [7.25]
Art 26 . . . [7.05]
Art 26(1) . . . [1.15]
Art 26(2) . . . [1.15], [3.265], [4.05], [13.05]
Art 28 . . . [1.15], [7.10], [7.20], [7.25]
Art 28(1) . . . [1.15], [2.10], [2.15]
Art 28(2) . . . [2.15]
Art 29 . . . [2.15]

Art 30 . . . [1.15], [2.10], [7,15]
Art 34 . . . [1.15], [2.30], [2.35], [2.65], [2.70], [2.85], [2.90], [2.100], [2.105], [2.110], [2.115], [2.120], [2.130], [8.90], [9.05], [9.10], [9.20], [9.25], [9.30], [9.45], [9.55], [9.65]
Art 35 . . . [1.15], [2.30], [9.10], [9.25], [9.55], [9.65]
Art 36 . . . [2.100], [2.120], [2.125], [6.135], [9.05], [9.10], [9.15], [9.20], [9.25], [9.30], [9.35], [9.40], [9.45], [9.60], [9.65]
Art 38 . . . [1.15]
Art 39 . . . [6.170]
Art 42 . . . [6.170]
Art 45 . . . [1.15], [3.10], [3.15], [3.20], [3.25], [3.30], [3.35], [3.40], [3.55]
Art 45(2) . . . [3.40]
Art 45(3) . . . [3.55]
Art 48 . . . [3.65]
Art 49 . . . [1.15], [3.70], [3.75], [3.85], [3.90], [3.95], [3.205], [12.20]
Art 51 . . . [3.105], [3.180]
Art 52(1) . . . [3.110], [3.180]
Art 54 . . . [3.70], [3.80], [3.85], [4.45]
Art 56 . . . [1.15], [3.150], [3.165], [3.170], [3.175], [3.205]
Art 57 . . . [3.155], [3.160]
Art 58(1) . . . [3.210]
Art 62 . . . [3.180]
Art 63 . . . [1.15], [5.10]
Art 63(1) . . . [4.05], [4.15]
Art 63(2) . . . [4.05]
Art 64 . . . [4.20], [5.10]
Art 65 . . . [5.10]
Art 65(1) . . . [4.20], [4.25]
Art 65(3) . . . [4.20]
Art 66 . . . [4.35], [5.10]
Art 67 . . . [1.55]
Art 67(2) . . . [1.15]
Art 75 . . . [4.35]
Art 77(1) . . . [1.15], [3.290]
Art 79(3) . . . [5.20]
Art 90 . . . [1.15], [3.210]
Art 91 . . . [1.120]
Art 95(1) . . . [3.210]
Art 101 . . . [5.45], [6.25], [6.30], [6.35], [6.40], [6.45], [6.55], [6.105], [6.150], [6.225], [6.230], [9.05], [9.65], [11.30]
Art 101(1) . . . [6.10], [6.15], [6.20], [6.30], [6.60], [6.65], [6.70], [6.75], [6.80], [6.85], [6.90], [6.100], [6.170], [6.175], [6.195], [6.230], [9.60], [12.25]
Art 101(2) . . . [6.20], [6.90], [6.95], [9.60]
Art 101(3) . . . [6.90], [6.195], [6.230], [9.60], [9.70], [11.30]

Art 102 . . . [5.45], [6.10], [6.30], [6.105], [6.115], [6.125], [6.130], [6.135], [6.140], [6.150], [6.180], [6.195], [6.225], [6.230], [8.95], [9.05], [12.25]
Art 103(1) . . . [6.195]
Art 105 . . . [6.190]
Art 106(1) . . . [6.180], [8.95]
Art 106(2) . . . [6.185]
Art 107 . . . [1.15], [6.160]
Art 108 . . . [6.160]
Art 110 . . . [7.05], [7.15], [7.20], [7.25], [7.30], [7.40], [12.15]
Art 111 . . . [7.15], [7.20]
Art 113 . . . [1.15], [7.35]
Art 114 . . . [1.15]
Art 115 . . . [7.55]
Art 116 . . . [7.55]
Art 118 . . . [9.05]
Art 120 . . . [1.15], [2.95]
Art 121(1) . . . [2.95]
Art 126 . . . [1.15]
Art 127 . . . [1.115]
Art 128(1) . . . [1.115]
Art 130 . . . [1.115]
Art 148(2) . . . [1.120]
Art 151 . . . [10.125]
Art 153 . . . [10.125]
Art 157 . . . [1.15], [10.10], [10.20], [10.25], [10.30], [10.35], [10.40], [10.55], [10.80], [11.150]
Art 157(4) . . . [10.95]
Art 165(4) . . . [1.120]
Art 166(1) . . . [10.135]
Art 167(5) . . . [1.120]
Art 168(4) . . . [1.120]
Art 168(5) . . . [1.120]
Art 169(1) . . . [10.155]
Art 172 . . . [1.120]
Art 175 . . . [1.120]
Art 191(2) . . . [2.110]
Art 191(4) . . . [5.20]
Art 192(1) . . . [1.120]
Art 194(2) . . . [1.120]
Art 206 . . . [5.06]
Art 207 . . . [1.15], [5.06], [5.10], [5.15], [5.20], [5.35], [13.60]
Art 209(2) . . . [5.20]
Art 212(3) . . . [5.20]
Art 214(4) . . . [5.20]

Art 215 . . . [4.35], [5.10]
Art 216(1) . . . [5.15], [5.20], [5.25]
Art 217 . . . [5.20]
Art 218 . . . [5.15], [11.75]
Art 228(1) . . . [1.125]
Art 230 . . . [1.100]
Art 234 . . . [1.90]
Art 238 . . . [1.95]
Art 240(1) . . . [1.95]
Art 244 . . . [1.90]
Art 251 . . . [11.10]
Art 252 . . . [11.25]
Art 253 . . . [11.10]
Art 256 . . . [11.40], [11.75]
Art 257 . . . [11.40]
Art 258 . . . [8.90], [11.115]
Art 259 . . . [11.115]
Art 260 . . . [11.115]
Art 263 . . . [1.120], [1.150], [11.75], [11.85], [11.90], [11.100], [11.105], [11.106], [11.120], [11.125]
Art 264 . . . [11.85]
Art 265 . . . [11.110]
Art 266 . . . [11.110]
Art 267 . . . [11.75], [11.125], [11.130], [11.135], [11.140], [11.145], [12.40]
Art 277 . . . [11.120]
Art 278 . . . [11.85]
Art 279 . . . [11.85]
Art 282 . . . [1.110], [1.115]
Art 285 . . . [1.110]
Art 287 . . . [1.110]
Art 288 . . . [1.150], [11.90], [11.100], [12.30], [12.35], [12.40]
Art 291(1) . . . [1.145]
Art 294 . . . [1.100]
Art 296 . . . [1.150], [5.90], [11.106]
Art 297 . . . [1.155]
Art 299 . . . [1.150]
Art 300 . . . [1.120]
Art 304 . . . [1.120]
Art 307 . . . [1.120]
Art 311 . . . [7.40]
Art 314 . . . [1.100]
Art 315 . . . [1.100]
Art 326 . . . [1.145]
Art 345 . . . [9.05], [9.75]

Art 352 . . . [1.130]
Art 356 . . . [1.145]
Annex I . . . [9.175]

Declaration (No 17) concerning Primacy . . . [12.85]
Declaration (No 24) concerning the Legal Personality of the European Union . . . [5.20]
Protocol (No 2) on the Application of the Principles of Subsidiarity and Proportionality . . . [1.120], [1.135]
Protocol (No 3) on the Statute of the Court of Justice . . . [11.10], [11.15], [11.20], [11.40], [11.125]
Protocol (No 8) relating to Article 6(2) of the Treaty on European Union on the Accession of the Union to the European Convention on the Protection of Human Rights and Fundamental Freedoms . . . [12.110]
Protocol (No 12) on the Excessive Deficit Procedure . . . [1.15]
Protocol (No 19) on the Schengen Acquis Integrated into the Framework of the European Union . . . [3.290]
Protocol (No 27) on the Internal Market and Competition . . . [6.05]
Protocol (No 30) on the Application of the Charter of Fundamental Rights of the European Union to Poland and to the United Kingdom . . . [1.40]

Historical Founding Treaties

Treaty Instituting the European Coal and Steel Community, Paris, 18 April 1951, 261 UNTS 140; 158 BFSP 630 . . . [1.20]
Treaty Establishing the European Atomic Energy Community, Rome, 25 March 1957, 298 UNTS 167; 163 BFSP 206 . . . [1.20]
Treaty Establishing the European Economic Community, Rome, 25 March 1957, 298 UNTS 11; 163 BFSP 206 . . . [1.20]
Treaty Establishing a Single Council and a Single Commission of the European Communities, Brussels, 8 April 1965, 1348 UNTS 81; 4 ILM 776; OJ 152, 13.7.1967, p 1 . . . [1.20]
Single European Act, Luxembourg, 17 February 1986, The Hague, 28 February 1986, 1754 UNTS 3; 25 ILM 506; OJ L 169, 29.6.1987, p 1 . . . [1.25]
Treaty on European Union, Maastricht, 7 February 1992, 1757 UNTS 3; 31 ILM 247; OJ C 191, 29.7.1992, p 1 . . . [1.30], [4.05]
Treaty of Amsterdam, Amsterdam, 2 October 1997, 37 ILM 56; OJ C 340, 10.11.1997, p 1 . . . [1.35]
Treaty of Nice, Nice, 26 February 2001, OJ C 80, 10.3.2001, p 1; UKTS 2003 No 22 (Cm 5879) . . . [1.45]
Treaty Establishing a Constitution for Europe, Rome, 29 October 2004, OJ C 310, 16.12.2004, p 1; EC 2004 No 8 (Cm 6429) . . . [1.50]

Treaty of Lisbon, Lisbon, 13 December 2007, OJ C 306, 17.12.2007, p 1; EC 2007 No 13 (Cm 7294) . . . [1.55]

Accession Treaties

Treaty of Accession of the United Kingdom, Ireland and Denmark, Brussels, 22 January 1972, 1375 UNTS 2; OJ L 73, 27.3.1972, p 5 . . . [1.20]

Treaty of Accession of Greece, Athens, 28 May 1979, 1382 UNTS 2; OJ L 291, 19.11.1979, p 9 . . . [1.20]

Treaty of Accession of Spain and Portugal, Madrid, 12 June 1985, OJ L 302, 15.11.1985, p 9 . . . [1.20]

Treaty of Accession of Finland and Sweden, Corfu, 24 June 1994, OJ C 241, 29.8.1994, p 9; UKTS 1995 No 43 (Cm 2887) . . . [1.20]

Treaty of Accession of Czech Republic, Estonia, Cyprus, Latvia, Lithuania, Hungary, Malta, Poland, Slovak Republic and Slovenia, Athens, 16 April 2003, OJ L 236, 23.9.2003, p 17; UKTS 2004 No 32 (Cm 6312) . . . [1.20]

Treaty of Accession of Bulgaria and Romania, Luxembourg, 25 April 2005, OJ L 157, 21.6.2005, p 11; EC 2005 No 2 (Cm 6657) . . . [1.20]

Table of International Agreements

Paris Convention for the Protection of Industrial Property, Paris, 20 March 1883, as revised at Stockholm, 14 July 1967, 828 UNTS 305; 24 UST 2140; TIAS 6923; [1972] ATS 12 . . . [9.105]

Statute of the Council of Europe, London, 5 May 1949, 87 UNTS 103; ETS no 1 . . . [1.15]

Convention for the Protection of Human Rights and Fundamental Freedoms, Rome, 4 November 1950, as amended by Protocol No 11, Strasbourg, 11 May 1994, 2061 UNTS 7; ETS No 155 . . . [12.95], [12.110]

International Covenant on Civil and Political Rights, New York, 16 December 1966, 999 UNTS 171 . . . [12.110]

Agreement on Andean Subregional Integration (Cartagena Agreement), Bogotá, 26 May 1969, 8 ILM 910 . . . [13.130]

Patent Cooperation Treaty, Washington, 19 June 1970, 1160 UNTS 231; 28 UST 7645; TIAS 8733; [1980] ATS 6 . . . [9.105]

Convention on the Grant of European Patents, Munich, 5 October 1973, 1065 UNTS 199; 13 ILM 268 . . . [9.105]

United Nations Convention on Contracts for the International Sale of Goods, Vienna, 11 April 1980, 1489 UNTS 3; 19 ILM 671; [1988] ATS 32 . . . [13.140]–[13.165]

Exchange of Notes between the European Community and New Zealand comprising an Agreement on Trade in Mutton, Lamb and Goatmeat, Brussels, 17 October 1980, 1324 UNTS 239; OJ L 275, 18.10.1980, p 28; NZTS 1980 No 13 . . . [1.75]

Agreement between the European Community and Australia concerning Trade in Mutton, Lamb and Goatmeat, Brussels, 14 November 1980, 1641 UNTS 287; [1980] ATS 32; OJ, L 275, 18.10.1980, p 20 . . . [1.65]

Australia-New Zealand Closer Economic Relations – Trade Agreement, Canberra, 28 March 1983, 1329 UNTS 175; [1983] ATS 2 . . . [13.135]

International Convention on the Harmonized Commodity Description and Coding System, Brussels, 14 June 1983, 1503 UNTS 3; [1988] ATS 30; OJ L 198, 20.7.1987, p 3 . . . [2.15]

Agreement on the Future of Hong Kong (Joint Declaration between the United Kingdom and China), Peking, 19 December 1984, 1399 UNTS 33; 23 ILM 1366 . . . [1.81]

Agreement between the United States and Israel on the Establishment of a Free Trade Area, Washington, 22 April 1985, 24 ILM 653 . . . [13.135]

Agreement between the States of the Benelux Economic Union, Germany and France on the Gradual Abolition of Checks at their Common Frontiers, Schengen, Luxembourg, 14 June 1985, OJ L 239, 22.9.2000, p 13; 30 ILM 73 . . . [3.290]

Protocol Relating to the Madrid Agreement Concerning the International Registration of Marks, Madrid, 27 June 1989, OJ L 296, 14.11.2003, p 22; [2001] ATS 7; Treaty Doc 106-41 . . . [9.155]

Convention on the Rights of the Child, New York, 20 November 1989, 1577 UNTS 3 . . . [12.110]

Fourth ACP-EEC Convention (Lomé Convention), Lomé, 15 December 1989, 1924 UNTS 3; 29 ILM 783; OJ L 229, 17.8.1991, p 3 . . . [13.85]

Agreement Relating to Community Patents, Luxembourg, 15 December 1989, OJ L 401, 30.12.1989, p 1; EC 1991 No 22 (Cm 1452) . . . [9.105]

Convention Applying the Schengen Agreement, Schengen, Luxembourg, 19 June 1990, OJ L 239, 22.9.2000, p 19; 30 ILM 84 . . . [3.290]

Convention on the Elimination of Double Taxation in connection with the Adjustment of Profits of Associated Enterprises, Brussels, 23 July 1990, 1847 UNTS 3; OJ L 225, 20.8.1990, p 10 . . . [7.70]

International Convention for the Protection of New Varieties of Plants of 2 December 1961, as Revised at Geneva on 10 November 1972, 23 October 1978 and 19 March 1991, OJ L 192, 22.7.2005, p 64; [2000] ATS 5; Treaty Doc 104-17 . . . [9.165]

Treaty Establishing a Common Market (Treaty of Asuncion), Asunción, 26 March 1991, 30 ILM 1041 . . . [13.130]

Agreement between the European Community and the United States regarding the Application of Competition Laws, Washington, 23 September 1991, OJ L 95, 27.4.1995, p 47; 30 ILM 1487; [1991] 4 CMLR 823 . . . [1.60], [6.235]

Agreement on the Common Effective Preferential Tariff Scheme for the ASEAN Free Trade Area, Singapore, 28 January 1992, 31 ILM 513, as amended at Bangkok, 15 December 1995, 35 ILM 1084 and on 31 January 2003 . . . [13.130]

Agreement on the European Economic Area, Porto, 2 May 1992, 1801 UNTS 3; OJ L 1, 3.1.1994, p 3 . . . [2.150]

North American Free Trade Agreement, Washington, Ottawa, Mexico, 8, 11, 14, 17 December 1992, 32 ILM 296, 605 . . . [13.130]

North American Agreement on Labor Cooperation, Mexico, Washington, Ottawa, 8, 9, 12, 14 September 1993, 32 ILM 1499 . . . [13.130]

North American Agreement on Environmental Cooperation, Mexico, Washington, Ottawa, 8, 9, 12, 14 September 1993, 32 ILM 1480 . . . [13.130]

Marrakesh Agreement establishing the World Trade Organization, Marrakesh, 15 April 1994, 1867 UNTS 3; OJ L 336, 23.12.1994, p 3; [1995] ATS 8 p 1 . . . [5.40], [13.10], [13.60], [13.75], [13.80]

- General Agreement on Tariffs and Trade 1994, defined in Annex 1A to the WTO Agreement, 1867 UNTS 190; OJ L 336, 23.12.1994, p 20; [1995] ATS 8 p 14 . . . [5.40], [5.100], [13.15], [13.20], [13.25], [13.30], [13.35], [13.40], [13.45], [13.50], [13.55], [13.60], [13.65], [13.70], [13.80], [13.85], [13.130]
- Understanding on the Interpretation of Art XXIV, 1867 UNTS 219; OJ L 336, 23.12.1994, p 16; [1995] ATS 8 p 25 . . . [13.130]
- Agreement on Agriculture, 1867 UNTS 410; OJ L 336, 23.12.1994, p 22; [1995] ATS 8 p 34 . . . [13.85]
- Agreement on the Application of Sanitary and Phytosanitary Measures, 1867 UNTS 493; OJ L 336, 23.12.1994, p 40; [1995] ATS 8 p 65 . . . [13.60], [13.90]
- Agreement on Technical Barriers to Trade, 1868 UNTS 120; OJ L 336, 23.12.1994, p 86; [1995] ATS 8 p 114 . . . [13.95]
- Agreement on Implementation of Art VI of GATT 1994, 1868 UNTS 201; OJ L 336, 23.12.1994, p 103; [1995] ATS 8 p 143 . . . [5.40], [5.90]
- Agreement on Preshipment Inspection, 1868 UNTS 368; OJ L 336, 23.12.1994, p 138; [1995] ATS 8 p 205 . . . [13.100]
- Agreement on Rules of Origin, 1868 UNTS 397; OJ L 336, 23.12.1994, p 138; [1995] ATS 8 p 215 . . . [13.105]
- Agreement on Import Licensing Procedures, 1868 UNTS 436; OJ L 336, 23.12.1994, p 151; [1995] ATS 8 p 229 . . . [13.110]
- Agreement on Subsidies and Countervailing Measures, 1869 UNTS 14; OJ L 336, 23.12.1994, p 156; [1995] ATS 8 p 238 . . . [5.40]
- Agreement on Safeguards, 1869 UNTS 154; OJ L 336, 23.12.1994, p 184; [1995] ATS 8 p 289 . . . [13.45]
- General Agreement on Trade in Services (GATS), 1869 UNTS 183; OJ L 336, 23.12.1994, p 190; [1995] ATS 8 p 299 . . . [5.30], [13.115]
- Agreement on Trade-related Aspects of Intellectual Property Rights (TRIPS), 1869 UNTS 299; OJ L 336, 23.12.1994, p 214; [1995] ATS 8 p 341 . . . [9.100], [5.30], [13.120]
- Understanding on Rules and Procedures governing the Settlement of Disputes, 1869 UNTS 401; OJ L 336, 23.12.1994, p 234; [1995] ATS 8 p 375 . . . [13.20]
- Agreement on Government Procurement, 1915 UNTS 103; OJ L 336, 23.12.1994, p 273; OJ C 256, 3.9.1996, p 1 . . . [8.100]

Free Trade Agreement between Canada and Israel, Toronto, 31 July 1996, Can TS 1997 No 49 . . . [13.135]

Free Trade Agreement between Canada and Chile, Santiago, 4 December 1996, 36 ILM 1067, Can TS 1997 No 50 . . . [13.135]

WIPO Copyright Treaty, Geneva, 20 December 1996, 2186 UNTS 121; 36 ILM 65; OJ L 89, 11.4.2000, p 8 . . . [9.100]

WIPO Performances and Phonograms Treaty, Geneva, 20 December 1996, 2186 UNTS 203; 36 ILM 76; OJ L 89, 11.4.2000, p 15 . . . [9.100]

Agreement between the European Community and Canada on Mutual Recognition, London, 14 May 1998, OJ L 280, 16.10.1998, p 3; Can TS 1998 No 40 . . . [1.70]

Agreement between the European Community and the United States on Mutual Recognition, London, 18 May 1998, OJ L 31, 4.2.1999, p 3; State Dept No 99-53 . . . [1.60]

Agreement between the European Community and the United States on the Application of Positive Comity Principles in the Enforcement of their Competition Laws, Brussels-Washington, 3–4 June 1998, OJ L 173, 18.6.1998, p 28; TIAS 12958; 37 ILM 1070 . . . [1.60], [6.235]

Agreement between the European Community and Australia on Mutual Recognition in relation to Conformity Assessment, Canberra, 24 June 1998, 2076 UNTS 245; [1999] ATS 2; OJ L 229, 17.8.1998, p 3 . . . [1.65]

Agreement between the European Community and New Zealand on Mutual Recognition in relation to Conformity Assessment, Wellington, 25 June 1998, 2071 UNTS 429; OJ L 229, 17.8.1998, p 62; NZTS 1998 No 4 . . . [1.75]

Agreement between the European Community and Hong Kong, China on Cooperation and Mutual Administrative Assistance in Customs Matters, Hong Kong, 13 May 1999, OJ L 151, 18.6.1999, p 21 . . . [1.81]

Agreement between the European Community and Canada regarding the Application of Competition Laws, Bonn, 17 June 1999, 2101 UNTS 23; OJ L 175, 10.7.1999, p 50; Can TS 1999 No 38 . . . [1.70], [6.235]

Geneva Act of the Hague Agreement Concerning the International Registration of Industrial Designs, Geneva, 2 July 1999, 2279 UNTS 3; OJ L 386, 29.12.2006, p 30 . . . [9.160]

Agreement between the European Community and South Africa on Trade, Development and Cooperation, Pretoria, 11 October 1999, OJ L 311, 4.12.1999, p 3 . . . [1.80]

Agreement between the United States and Jordan on the Establishment of a Free Trade Area, Washington, 24 October 2000, 41 ILM 63 . . . [13.135]

Free Trade Agreement between Canada and Costa Rica, Ottawa, 23 April 2001 . . . [13.135]

Agreement between the European Community and India for Scientific and Technological Cooperation, New Delhi, 23 November 2001, OJ L 213, 9.8.2002, p 30 . . . [1.81]

Agreement between the European Community and South Africa on Trade in Wine, Paarl, 28 January 2002, OJ L 28, 30.1.2002, p 4 . . . [1.80], [9.175]

Agreement between the European Community and South Africa on Trade in Spirits, Paarl, 28 January 2002, OJ L 28, 30.1.2002, p 113 . . . [1.80], [9.175]

Singapore-Australia Free Trade Agreement, Singapore, 17 February 2003, 2257 UNTS 103; [2003] ATS 16 . . . [13.135]

US–Singapore Free Trade Agreement, Washington, 6 May 2003, HR Doc No 108-100 . . . [13.135]

US–Chile Free Trade Agreement, Miami, 6 June 2003, HR Doc No 108-101 . . . [13.135]

Agreement between the European Community and Canada on Trade in Wines and Spirit Drinks, Niagara-on-the-Lake, 16 September 2003, OJ L 35, 6.2.2004, p 3 . . . [1.70], [9.175]

Agreement between the European Community and India on Customs Cooperation and Mutual Administrative Assistance in Customs Matters, Brussels, 28 April 2004, OJ L 304, 30.9.2004, p 25 . . . [1.81]

Protocol No 14 to the Convention for the Protection of Human Rights and Fundamental Freedoms, amending the Control System of the Convention, Strasbourg, 13 May 2004, ETS No 194 . . . [12.110]

Australia-US Free Trade Agreement, Washington, 18 May 2004, [2005] ATS 1; HR Doc No 108-199 . . . [13.135]

US–Morocco Free Trade Agreement, Washington, 15 June 2004, HR Doc No 108-201 . . . [13.135]

Australia-Thailand Free Trade Agreement, Canberra, 5 July 2004, [2005] ATS 2 . . . [13.135]

Dominican Republic-Central America-United States Free Trade Agreement, Washington, 5 August 2004, HR Doc 109-36 . . . [13.135]

Agreement between the United States and Bahrain on the Establishment of a Free Trade Area, Washington, 14 September 2004, HR Doc No 109-71 . . . [13.135]

Agreement between the European Community and the United States on Trade in Wine, London, 10 March 2006, OJ L 87, 24.3.2006, p 2; State Dept No 06-127 . . . [1.60], [9.175]

Agreement between the United States and Oman on the Establishment of a Free Trade Area, Washington, 19 January 2006, HR Doc 109-118 . . . [13.135]

Air Transport Agreement between the European Community and the United States, Washington, 30 April 2007, OJ L 134, 25.5.2007, p 4; 46 ILM 470 . . . [3.220]

Agreement between the European Union and the United States on the Processing and Transfer of Passenger Name Record (PNR) Data by Air Carriers to the United States Department of Homeland Security, Brussels, 23 July 2007-Washington, 26 July 2007, OJ L 204, 4.8.2007, p 18 . . . [10.145]

Free Trade Agreement between Canada and the States of the European Free Trade Association, Davos, Switzerland, 26 January 2008 . . . [1.70]

New Zealand-China Free Trade Agreement, Beijing, 7 April 2008 . . . [13.135]

Free Trade Agreement between Canada and Peru, Lima, 29 May 2008 . . . [13.135]

Australia-Chile Free Trade Agreement, Canberra, 30 July 2008, [2009] ATS 6 . . . [13.135]

Free Trade Agreement between Canada and Colombia, Lima, Peru, 21 November 2008 . . . [13.135]

Agreement between the European Community and Australia on Trade in Wine, Brussels, 1 December 2008, [2008] ATNIF 20; OJ L 28, 30.1.2009, p 3 . . . [1.65], [9.175]

Agreement Establishing the Association of Southeast Asian Nations (ASEAN)–Australia–New Zealand Free Trade Area, Cha-am, Thailand, 27 February 2009, [2010] ATS 1 . . . [13.135]

Free Trade Agreement between Canada and Jordan, Amman, 28 June 2009 . . . [13.135]

Malaysia-New Zealand Free Trade Agreement, Kuala Lumpur, 26 October 2009 . . . [13.135]

Table of Legislation

European Union

Regulations

Council Regulation 19/65 of 2 March 1965 on the application of Article 81(3) (formerly Article 85(3)) of the Treaty to certain categories of agreements and concerted practices (OJ P 36, 6.3.1965, p 533)... [9.70]

Council Regulation 802/68 of 27 June 1968 on the common definition of the concept of the origin of goods (OJ L 148, 28.6.1968, p 1)... [2.20]

Regulation 1612/68 of the Council of 15 October 1968 on freedom of movement for workers within the Community (OJ L 257, 19.10.1968, p 2)... [3.65]

Regulation 2988/74 of the Council of 26 November 1974 concerning limitation periods in proceedings and the enforcement of sanctions under the rules of the European Economic Community relating to transport and competition (OJ L 319, 29.11.1974, p 1)... [6.210]

Council Regulation 2137/85 of 25 July 1985 on the European Economic Interest Grouping (EEIG) (OJ L 199, 31.7.1985, p 1)... [3.145]

Council Regulation 4055/86 of 22 December 1986 applying the principle of freedom to provide services to maritime transport between Member States and between Member States and third countries (OJ L 378, 31.12.1986, p 1)... [3.225]

Council Regulation 2658/87 on the tariff and statistical nomenclature and on the Common Customs Tariff (OJ L 256, 7.9.1987, p 1)... [2.15]

Council Regulation 3976/87 of 14 December 1987 on the application of Article 85(3) of the Treaty to certain categories of agreements and concerted practices in the air transport sector (OJ L 374, 31.12.1987, p 9)... [3.220], [6.175]

Council Regulation 2299/89 of 24 July 1989 on a code of conduct for computerized reservation systems (OJ L 220, 29.7.1989, p 1)... [10.210]

Council Regulation 3916/90 of 21 December 1990 on measures to be taken in the event of a crisis in the market in the carriage of goods by road (OJ L 375, 30.12.1990, p 10) . . . [3.230]

Council Regulation 3921/91 of 16 December 1991 laying down the conditions under which non-resident carriers may transport goods or passengers by inland waterway within a Member State (OJ L 373, 31.12.1991, p 1) . . . [3.225]

Council Regulation 3922/91 of 16 December 1991 on the harmonization of technical requirements and administrative procedures in the field of civil aviation (OJ L 373, 31.12.1991, p 4) . . . [3.220]

Council Regulation 684/92 of 16 March 1992 on common rules for the international carriage of passengers by coach and bus (OJ L 74, 20.3.1992, p 1) . . . [3.230]

Council Regulation 881/92 of 26 March 1992 on access to the market in the carriage of goods by road within the Community to or from the territory of a Member State or passing across the territory of one or more Member States (OJ L 95, 9.4.1992, p 1) . . . [3.230]

Council Regulation 2407/92 of 23 July 1992 on licensing of air carriers (OJ L 240, 24.8.1992, p 1) . . . [3.220]

Council Regulation 2408/92 of 23 July 1992 on access for Community air carriers to intra-Community air routes (OJ L 240, 24.8.1992, p 8) . . . [3.220]

Council Regulation 2913/92 of 12 October 1992 establishing the Community Customs Code (OJ L 302, 19.10.1992, p 1) . . . [2.20]

Council Regulation 3577/92 of 7 December 1992 applying the principle of freedom to provide services to maritime transport within Member States (maritime cabotage) (OJ L 364, 12.12.1992, p 7) . . . [3.225]

Council Regulation 95/93 on common rules for the allocation of slots at EU airports (OJ L 14, 21.2.1993, p 1) . . . [3.220]

Commission Regulation 1617/93 of 25 June 1993 on the application of Article 85(3) of the Treaty to certain categories of agreements and concerted practices concerning joint planning and coordination of schedules, joint operations, consultations on passenger and cargo tariffs on scheduled air services and slot allocation at airports (OJ L 155, 26.6, 1993, p 18) . . . [6.175]

Council Regulation 3118/93 of 25 October 1993 laying down the conditions under which non-resident carriers may operate national road haulage services within a Member State (OJ L 279, 12.11.1993, p 1) . . . [3.230]

Council Regulation 2100/94 of 27 July 1994 on Community plant variety rights (OJ L 227, 1.9.1994, p 1) . . . [9.50], [9.165]

Council Regulation 3286/94 of 22 December 1994 laying down Community procedures in the field of the common commercial policy in order to ensure the exercise of the Community's rights under international trade rules, in particular those established under the auspices of the World Trade Organization (OJ L 349, 31.12.1994, p 71) . . . [13.60]

Council Regulation 1356/96 of 8 July 1996 on common rules applicable to the transport of goods or passengers by inland waterway between Member States with a view to establishing freedom to provide such transport services (OJ L 175, 13.7.96, p 7) . . . [3.225]

Council Regulation 12/98 of 11 December 1997 laying down the conditions under which non-resident carriers may operate national road passenger transport services within a Member State (OJ L 4, 8.1.1998, p 10) . . . [3.230]

Council Regulation 974/98 of 3 May 1998 on the introduction of the euro (OJ L 139, 11.5.1998, p 1) . . . [1.15]

Council Regulation 2679/98 of 7 December 1998 on the functioning of the internal market in relation to the free movement of goods among the Member States (OJ L 337, 12.12.1998, p 8) . . . [2.130]

Council Regulation 659/1999 of 22 March 1999 laying down detailed rules for the application of Article 93 of the EC Treaty (OJ L 83, 27.3.1999, p 1) . . . [6.160]

Commission Regulation 2790/1999 of 22 December 1999 on the application of Article 81(3) of the Treaty to categories of vertical agreements and concerted practices (OJ L 336, 29.12.1999, p 21) . . . [6.95]

Council Regulation 1346/2000 of 29 May 2000 on insolvency proceedings (OJ L 160, 30.6.2000, p 1) . . . [3.145]

Commission Regulation 2658/2000 of 29 November 2000 on the application of Article 81(3) of the Treaty to categories of specialisation agreements (OJ L 304, 5.12.2000, p 3) . . . [6.95]

Commission Regulation 2659/2000 of 29 November 2000 on the application of Article 81(3) of the Treaty to categories of research and development agreements (OJ L 304, 5.12.2000, p 7) . . . [6.95], [9.70]

Council Regulation 44/2001 of 22 December 2000 on jurisdiction and the recognition and enforcement of judgments in civil and commercial matters (OJ L 12, 16.1.2001, p 1) . . . [3.256]

Regulation 1049/2001 of the European Parliament and of the Council of 30 May 2001 regarding Public Access to European Parliament, Council and Commission documents (OJ L 145, 31.5.2001, p 43) . . . [1.155]

Council Regulation 2157/2001 of 8 October 2001 on the Statute for a European company (SE) (OJ L 294, 10.11.2001, p 1) . . . [3.145]

Council Regulation 6/2002 of 12 December 2001 on Community designs (OJ L 3, 5.1.2002, p 1) . . . [9.50], [9.160]

Commission Regulation 1400/2002 of 31 July 2002 on the application of Article 81(3) of the Treaty to categories of vertical agreements and concerted practices in the motor vehicle sector (OJ L 203, 1.8.2002, p 30) . . . [6.95]

Regulation 1406/2002 of the European Parliament and of the Council of 27 June 2002 establishing a European Maritime Safety Agency (OJ L 208, 5.8.2002, p 1) . . . [3.225]

Regulation 1592/2002 of the European Parliament and of the Council of 15 July 2002 on common rules in the field of civil aviation and establishing a European Aviation Safety Agency (OJ L 240, 7.9.2002, p 1) . . . [3.220]
Regulation 1606/2002 of the European Parliament and of the Council of 19 July 2002 on the application of international accounting standards (OJ L 243, 11.9.2002, p 1) . . . [3.145]
Council Regulation 1/2003 of 16 December 2002 on the implementation of the rules on competition laid down in Articles 81 and 82 of the Treaty (OJ L 1, 4.1.2003, p 1) . . . [6.195], [6.200], [6.205], [6.210], [6.225], [6.230]
Commission Regulation 358/2003 of 27 February 2003 on the application of Article 81(3) of the Treaty to certain categories of agreements, decisions and concerted practices in the insurance sector (OJ L 53, 28.2.2003, p 8) . . . [6.95]
Council Regulation 1383/2003 of 22 July 2003 concerning customs action against goods suspected of infringing certain intellectual property rights and the measures to be taken against goods found to have infringed such rights (OJ L 196, 2.8.2003, p 7) . . . [9.185]
Council Regulation 1435/2003 of 22 July 2003 on the Statute for a European Cooperative Society (SCE) (OJ L 207, 18.8.2003, p 1) . . . [3.145]
Council Regulation 139/2004 of 20 January 2004 on the control of concentrations between undertakings (OJ L 24, 29.1.2004, p 1) . . . [6.155]
Regulation 261/2004 of the European Parliament and of the Council of 11 February 2004 establishing common rules on compensation and assistance to passengers in the event of denied boarding and of cancellation or long delay of flights (OJ L 46, 17.2.2004, p 1) . . . [10.210]
Regulation 549/2004 of the European Parliament and of the Council of 10 March 2004 laying down the framework for the creation of the Single European Sky (OJ L 96, 31.3.2004, p 1) . . . [3.220]
Commission Regulation 772/2004 of 27 April 2004 on the application of Article 81(3) of the Treaty to categories of technology transfer agreements (OJ L 123, 27.4.2004, p 11) . . . [6.95], [9.70]
Commission Regulation 773/2004 of 7 April 2004 relating to the conduct of proceedings by the Commission pursuant to Articles 81 and 82 of the EC Treaty (OJ L 123, 27.4.2004, p 18) . . . [6.200]
Regulation 847/2004 of the European Parliament and of the Council of 29 April 2004 on the negotiation and implementation of air service agreements between Member States and third countries (OJ L 195, 2.6.2004, p 3) . . . [5.30]
Regulation 852/2004 of the European Parliament and of the Council on the hygiene of foodstuffs (OJ L 139, 30.4.2004, p 1) . . . [10.220]
Regulation 881/2004 of the European Parliament and of the Council of 29 April 2004 establishing a European Railway Agency (OJ L 220, 21.6.2004, p 3) . . . [3.215]

Regulation 883/2004 of the European Parliament and of the Council of 29 April 2004 on the coordination of social security systems (OJ L 200, 7.6.2004, p 1) . . . [3.65]

Council Regulation 2007/2004 of 26 October 2004 establishing a European Agency for the Management of Operational Cooperation at the External Borders of the Member States of the European Union (OJ L 349, 25.11.2004, p 1) . . . [3.295]

Council Regulation 673/2005 of 25 April 2005 establishing additional customs duties on imports of certain products originating in the United States of America (OJ L 110, 30.4.2005, p 1) . . . [1.60]

Regulation 1889/2005 of the European Parliament and of the Council of 26 October 2005 on controls of cash entering or leaving the Community (OJ L 309, 25.11.2005, p 9) . . . [4.40]

Regulation 2111/2005 of the European Parliament and of the Council of 14 December 2005 on the establishment of a Community list of air carriers subject to an operating ban within the Community and on informing air transport passengers of the identity of the operating air carrier (OJ L 344, 27.12.2005, p 15) . . . [10.210]

Council Regulation 510/2006 of 20 March 2006 on the protection of geographical indications and designations of origin for agricultural products and foodstuffs (OJ L 93, 31.3.2006, p 12) . . . [9.175]

Regulation 562/2006 of the European Parliament and of the Council of 15 March 2006 establishing a Community Code on the rules governing the movement of persons across borders (Schengen Borders Code) (OJ L 105, 13.4.2006, p 1) . . . [3.290]

Regulation 1107/2006 of the Parliament and of the Council of 5 July 2006 concerning the rights of disabled persons and persons with reduced mobility when travelling by air (OJ L 204, 26.7.2006, p 1) . . . [10.210]

Council Regulation 1184/2006 of 24 July 2006 applying certain rules of competition to the production of and trade in certain agricultural products (OJ L 214, 4.8.2006, p 7) . . . [6.170]

Regulation 1924/2006 of the European Parliament and of the Council of 20 December 2006 on nutrition and health claims made on foods (OJ L 404, 30.12.2006, p 9) . . . [10.185]

Commission Regulation 1998/2006 of 15 December 2006 on the application of Articles 87 and 88 of the Treaty to de minimis aid (OJ L 379, 28.12.2006, p 5) . . . [6.160]

Regulation 2006/2004 of the European Parliament and of the Council of 27 October 2004 on cooperation between national authorities responsible for the enforcement of consumer protection laws (OJ L 364, 9.12.2004, p 1) . . . [10.225]

Regulation 1371/2007 of the European Parliament and of the Council of 23 October 2007 on rail passengers' rights and obligations (OJ L 315, 3.12.2007, p 14) . . . [10.210]

Regulation 450/2008 of the European Parliament and of the Council of 23 April 2008 laying down the Community Customs Code (OJ L 145, 4.6.2008, p 1)... [2.15], [2.20]

Commission Regulation 800/2008 of 6 August 2008 declaring certain categories of aid compatible with the common market in application of Articles 87 and 88 of the Treaty (OJ L 214, 9.8.2008, p 3)... [6.160]

Regulation 1331/2008 of the European Parliament and of the Council of 16 December 2008 establishing a common authorisation procedure for food additives, food enzymes and food flavourings (OJ L 354, 31.12.2008, p 1)... [10.220]

Regulation 1332/2008 of the European Parliament and of the Council of 16 December 2008 on food enzymes (OJ L 354, 31.12.2008, p 7)... [10.220]

Regulation 1333/2008 of the European Parliament and of the Council of 16 December 2008 on food additives (OJ L 354, 31.12.2008, p 16)... [10.220]

Regulation 1334/2008 of the European Parliament and of the Council of 16 December 2008 on flavourings and certain food ingredients with flavouring properties for use in and on foods (OJ L 354, 31.12.2008, p 34)... [10.220]

Commission Regulation 41/2009 of 20 January 2009 concerning the composition and labelling of foodstuffs suitable for people intolerant to gluten (OJ L 16, 21.1.2009, p 3)... [10.220]

Council Regulation 169/2009 of 26 February 2009 applying rules of competition to transport by rail, road and inland waterway (OJ L 61, 5.3.2009, p 1)... [6.175]

Council Regulation 207/2009 of 26 February 2009 on the Community trade mark (OJ L 78, 24.3.2009, p 1)... [9.45], [9.150], [9.155]

Council Regulation 260/2009 of 26 February 2009 on the common rules for imports (OJ L 84, 31.3.2009, p 1)... [5.31]

Council Regulation 597/2009 of 11 June 2009 on protection against subsidised imports from countries not members of the European Community (OJ L 188, 18.7.2009, p 93)... [5.95]

Art 1(1)... [5.100], [5.165]
Art 2(d)... [5.115]
Art 3... [5.100]
Art 4... [5.105]
Art 5... [5.105]
Art 6... [5.100]
Art 7... [5.100]
Art 8... [5.115], [5.125], [5.135]
Art 9... [5.140], [5.185]
Art 10... [5.150]
Art 11(9)... [5.155]
Art 12... [5.165], [5.170]

Art 13 . . . [5.160]
Art 14(2) . . . [5.155]
Art 15 . . . [5.145], [5.165], [5.175], [5.185]
Art 16 . . . [5.180]
Art 18 . . . [5.160]
Art 19 . . . [5.155], [5.160], [5.195]
Art 21 . . . [5.190]
Art 23 . . . [5.165]
Art 24 . . . [5.165], [5.185]
Art 26 . . . [5.150]
Art 27 . . . [5.150]
Art 28 . . . [5.150]
Art 29(3) . . . [5.150]
Art 31 . . . [5.145]

Council Regulation 599/2009 of 7 July 2009 imposing a definitive anti-dumping duty and collecting definitively the provisional duty imposed on imports of biodiesel originating in the United States of America (OJ L 179, 10.7.2009, p 26) . . . [5.165]

Council Regulation 1061/2009 of 19 October 2009 establishing common rules for exports (OJ L 291, 7.11.2009, p 1) . . . [5.31]

Council Regulation 1225/2009 of 30 November 2009 on protection against dumped imports from countries not members of the European Community (OJ L 343, 22.12.2009, p 51)

Art 1(1) . . . [5.45], [5.50], [5.165]
Art 1(4) . . . [5.55]
Art 2(1) . . . [5.50], [5.55], [5.60]
Art 2(2) . . . [5.50]
Art 2(3) . . . [5.60], [5.70]
Art 2(8) . . . [5.50], [5.80]
Art 2(9) . . . [5.80]
Art 2(10) . . . [5.50], [5.85]
Art 2(11) . . . [5.90]
Art 2(12) . . . [5.50], [5.90]
Art 3 . . . [5.50], [5.115], [5.135]
Art 4(1) . . . [5.140]
Art 4(3) . . . [5.185]
Art 5 . . . [5.150]
Art 6(1) . . . [5.45], [5.50]
Art 6(9) . . . [5.155]
Art 7 . . . [5.165], [5.170]
Art 8 . . . [5.155], [5.160]
Art 9(2) . . . [5.155]
Art 9(4) . . . [5.145], [5.165], [5.175]
Art 9(5) . . . [5.185]
Art 10 . . . [5.180]

Art 11(2) . . . [5.160]
Art 11(3) . . . [5.155], [5.160], [5.190]
Art 11(8) . . . [5.190]
Art 13 . . . [5.165]
Art 14 . . . [5.165], [5.185]
Art 16 . . . [5.150]
Art 17 . . . [5.150]
Art 18 . . . [5.150]
Art 19(3) . . . [5.150]
Art 21 . . . [5.145]

Directives

Council Directive 64/221 of 25 February 1964 on the co-ordination of special measures concerning the movement and residence of foreign nationals which are justified on grounds of public policy, public security or public health (OJ 56, 4.4.1964, p 850) . . . [3.55], [3.285]

First Council Directive 67/227 on the harmonisation of legislation of Member States concerning turnover taxes (OJ L 71, 14.4.1967, p 1301) . . . [7.40]

Council Directive 76/207 of 9 February 1976 on the implementation of the principle of equal treatment for men and women as regards access to employment, vocational training and promotion, and working conditions (OJ L 39, 14.2.1976, p 40) . . . [10.75], [10.85], [10.90], [12.50]

Council Directive 76/211 of 20 January 1976 on the approximation of the laws of the Member States relating to the making-up by weight or by volume of certain prepackaged products (OJ L 46, 21.2.1976, p 1) . . . [10.185]

Second Council Directive 77/91 of 13 December 1976 on coordination of safeguards which, for the protection of the interests of members and others, are required by Member States of companies, in respect of the formation of public limited liability companies and the maintenance and alteration of their capital, with a view to making such safeguards equivalent (OJ L 26, 31.1.1977, p 1) . . . [3.145]

Council Directive 77/249 of 22 March 1977 to facilitate the effective exercise by lawyers of freedom to provide services (OJ L 78, 26.3.1977, p 17) . . . [3.205]

Sixth Council Directive 77/388 of 17 May 1977 on the harmonization of the laws of the Member States relating to turnover taxes – Common system of value added tax: uniform basis of assessment (OJ L 145, 13.6.1977, p 1) . . . [7.40]

Fourth Council Directive 78/660 of 25 July 1978 on the annual accounts of certain types of companies (OJ L 222, 14.8.1978, p 11) . . . [3.145]

Third Council Directive 78/855 of 9 October 1978 concerning mergers of public limited liability companies (OJ L 295, 20.10.1978, p 36)... [3.145]
Sixth Council Directive 82/891 of 17 December 1982 concerning the division of public limited liability companies (OJ L 378, 31.12.1982, p 47)... [3.145]
Seventh Council Directive 83/349 of 13 June 1983 on consolidated accounts (OJ L 193, 18.7.1983, p 1)... [3.145]
Council Directive 85/374 of 25 July 1985 on the approximation of the laws, regulations and administrative provisions of the Member States concerning liability for defective products (OJ L 210, 7.8.1985, p 29)... [10.215]
Council Directive 85/577 of 20 December 1985 to protect the consumer in respect of contracts negotiated away from business premises (OJ L 372, 31.12.1985, p 31)... [10.195]
Council Directive 87/54 of 16 December 1986 on the legal protection of topographies of semiconductor products (OJ L 24, 27.1.1987, p 36)... [9.170]
Council Directive 87/102 of 22 December 1986 for the approximation of the laws, regulations and administrative provisions of the Member States concerning consumer credit (OJ L 42, 12.2.1987, p 48)... [4.45]
Council Directive 88/361 of 24 June 1988 for the implementation of Article 67 of the Treaty (OJ L 178, 8.7.1988, p 5)... [4.10]
Directive 89/552 of 3 October 1989 of the European Parliament and of the Council on the coordination of certain provisions laid down by law, regulation or administrative action in Member States concerning the provision of audiovisual media services (OJ L 298, 17.10.1989, p 23)... [10.170]
Council Directive 89/665 on the coordination of the laws, regulations and administrative provisions relating to the application of review procedures to the award of public supply and public works contracts (OJ 1989 L 395, 30.12.1989, p 33)... [8.80]
Eleventh Council Directive 89/666 of 21 December 1989 concerning disclosure requirements in respect of branches opened in a Member State by certain types of company governed by the law of another State (OJ L 395, 30.12.1989, p 36)... [3.145]
Council Directive 90/434 of 23 July 1990 on the common system of taxation applicable to mergers, divisions, partial divisions, transfers of assets and exchanges of shares concerning companies of different Member States and to the transfer of the registered office, of an SE or SCE, between Member States (OJ L 225, 20.8.1990, p 1)... [7.60]
Council Directive 90/435 of 23 July 1990 on the common system of taxation applicable in the case of parent companies and subsidiaries of different Member States (OJ L 225, 20.8.1990, p 6)... [7.65]
Council Directive 90/496 of 24 September 1990 on nutrition labelling for foodstuffs (OJ L 276, 6.10.1990, p 40)... [10.185]

Council Directive 91/440 of 29 July 1991 on the development of the Community's railways (OJ L 237, 24.8.1991, p 25) . . . [3.215]
Council Directive 91/670 of 16 December 1991 on the mutual acceptance of licences for persons working in civil aviation (OJ L 373, 31.12.1991, p 21) . . . [3.220]
Council Directive 92/13 coordinating the laws, regulations and administrative provisions relating to the application of Community rules on the procurement procedures of entities operating in the water, energy, transport and telecommunications sectors (OJ L 76, 23.3.1992, p 14) . . . [8.80]
Council Directive 92/75 of 22 September 1992 on the indication by labelling and standard product information of the consumption of energy and other resources by household appliances (OJ L 297, 13.10.1992, p 16) . . . [10.185]
Council Directive 92/79 of 19 October 1992 on the approximation of taxes on cigarettes (OJ L 316, 31.10.1992, p 8) . . . [7.50]
Council Directive 92/80 of 19 October 1992 on the approximation of taxes on manufactured tobacco other than cigarettes (OJ L 316, 31.10.1992, p 10) . . . [7.50]
Council Directive 92/83 of 19 October 1992 on the harmonisation of the structures of excise duties on alcohol and alcoholic beverages (OJ L 316, 31.10.1992, p 21) . . . [7.50]
Council Directive 92/84 of 19 October 1992 on approximation of the rates of excise duty on alcohol and alcoholic beverages (OJ L 316, 31.10.1992, p 29) . . . [7.50]
Council Directive 92/85 of 19 October 1992 concerning the implementation of measures to encourage improvements in the safety and health of pregnant workers, workers who have recently given birth and women who are breastfeeding (OJ L 348, 28.11.1992, p 1) . . . [10.75], [10.80]
Council Directive 93/13 of 5 April 1993 on unfair terms in consumer contracts (OJ L 95, 21.4.1993, p 29) . . . [10.175]
Council Directive 93/22 of 10 May 1993 on investment services in the securities field (OJ L 141, 11.6.1993, p 27) . . . [4.50]
Council Directive 93/83 of 27 September 1993 on the coordination of certain rules concerning copyright and rights related to copyright applicable to satellite broadcasting and cable retransmission (OJ L 248, 6.10.1993, p 15) . . . [9.95]
Directive 94/11 of the European Parliament and of the Council of 23 March 1994 on the approximation of the laws, regulations and administrative provisions of the Member States relating to labelling of the materials used in the main components of footwear for sale to the consumer (OJ L 100, 19.4.1994, p 37) . . . [10.185]
Directive 94/19 of the European Parliament and of the Council of 30 May 1994 on deposit-guarantee schemes (OJ L 135, 31.5.1994, p 5) . . . [4.45]

Directive 95/46 of the European Parliament and of the Council of 24 October 1995 on the protection of individuals with regard to the processing of personal data and on the free movement of such data (OJ L 281, 23.11.1995, p 31)... [10.140], [10.145]

Council Directive 95/59 of 27 November 1995 on taxes other than turnover taxes which affect the consumption of manufactured tobacco (OJ L 291, 6.12.1995, p 40)... [7.50]

Directive 96/9 of the European Parliament and of the Council of 11 March 1996 on the legal protection of databases (OJ L 77, 27.3.1996, p 20)... [9.95]

Council Directive 96/48 of 23 July 1996 on the interoperability of the trans-European high-speed rail system (OJ L 235, 17.9.1996, p 6)... [3.215]

Directive 97/5 of 27 January 1997 of the European Parliament and of the Council on cross-border credit transfers (OJ L 43, 14.2.1997, p 25)... [4.45]

Directive 97/7 of the European Parliament and of the Council of 20 May 1997 on the protection of consumers in respect of distance contracts (OJ L 144, 4.6.1997, p 19)... [10.190]

Directive 97/9 of the European Parliament and of the Council of 3 March 1997 on investor-compensation schemes (OJ L 84, 26.3.1997, p 22)... [4.50]

Directive 97/67 of the European Parliament and of the Council of 15 December 1997 on common rules for the development of the internal market of Community postal services and the improvement of quality of service (OJ L 15, 21.1.1998, p 14)... [3.240]

Directive 98/5 of the European Parliament and of the Council of 16 February 1998 to facilitate practice of the profession of lawyer on a permanent basis in a Member State other than that in which the qualification was obtained (OJ L 77, 14.3.1998, p 36)... [3.205]

Directive 98/6 of the European Parliament and of the Council of 16 February 1998 on consumer protection in the indication of the prices of products offered to consumers (OJ L 80, 18.3.1998, p 27)... [10.180]

Directive 98/27 of the European Parliament and of the Council of 19 May 1998 on injunctions for the protection of consumers' interests (OJ L 166, 11.6.1998, p 51)... [10.225]

Directive 98/34 of the European Parliament and of the Council of 22 June 1998 laying down a procedure for the provision of information in the field of technical standards and regulations and of rules on Information Society services (OJ L 24, 21.7.1998, p 37)... [2.140]

Directive 98/44 of the European Parliament and of the Council of 6 July 1998 on the legal protection of biotechnological inventions (OJ L 213, 30.7.98, p 13)... [9.105]

Council Directive 98/49 of 29 June 1998 on safeguarding the supplementary pension rights of employed and self-employed persons moving within the Community (OJ L 209, 25.7.1998, p 46)... [3.65]

Directive 98/71 of the European Parliament and of the Council of 13 October 1998 on the legal protection of designs (OJ L 289, 28.10.1998, p 28)... [9.50], [9.160]

Directive 1999/44 of the European Parliament and of the Council of 25 May 1999 on certain aspects of the sale of consumer goods and associated guarantees (OJ L 171, 7.7.1999, p 12)... [10.165]

Directive 1999/93 of the European Parliament and of the Council of 13 December 1999 on a Community framework for electronic signatures (OJ L 13, 19.1.2000, p 12)... [2.135]

Directive 1999/94 of the European Parliament and of the Council of 13 December 1999 relating to the availability of consumer information on fuel economy and CO2 emissions in respect of the marketing of new passenger cars (OJ L 12, 18.1.2000, p 16)... [10.185]

Directive 2000/13 of the European Parliament and of the Council on the approximation of the laws of the Member States relating to the labeling, presentation and advertising of foodstuffs (OJ L 109, 6.5.2000, p 29)... [2.135], [10.185]

Directive 2000/31 of the European Parliament and of the Council of 8 June 2000 on certain legal aspects of information society services, in particular electronic commerce, in the Internal Market (OJ L 178, 17.2.2000, p 1)... [3.235]

Directive 2000/35 of the European Parliament and of the Council of 29 June 2000 on combating late payment in commercial transactions (OJ L 200, 8.8.2000, p 35)... [2.135]

Council Directive 2000/43 of 29 June 2000 implementing the principle of equal treatment between persons irrespective of racial or ethnic origin (OJ L 180, 19.7.2000, p 22)... [10.105]

Council Directive 2000/78 of 27 November 2000 establishing a general framework for equal treatment in employment and occupation (OJ L 303, 2.12.2000, p 16)... [10.100], [10.110], [10.115], [10.120]

Directive 2001/14 of the European Parliament and of the Council of 26 February 2001 on the allocation of railway infrastructure capacity and the levying of charges for the use of railway infrastructure and safety certification (OJ L 75, 15.3.2001, p 29)... [3.215]

Directive 2001/16 of the European Parliament and of the Council of 19 March 2001 on the interoperability of the conventional rail system (OJ L 110, 20.4.2001, p 1)... [3.215]

Council Directive 2001/23 of 12 March 2001 on the approximation of the laws of the Member States relating to the safeguarding of employees' rights in the event of transfers of undertakings, businesses or parts of undertakings or businesses (OJ L 82, 22.3.2001, p 16)... [10.125]

Directive 2001/24 of the European Parliament and of the Council on the reorganisation and winding-up of credit institutions (OJ L 125, 5.5.2001, p 15)... [4.45]

Directive 2001/29 of the European Parliament and of the Council of 22 May 2001 on the harmonisation of certain aspects of copyright and related rights in the information society (OJ L 167, 22.6.2001, p 10) . . . [9.85]

Directive 2001/34 of the European Parliament and of the Council on the admission of securities to official stock exchange listings and on information to be published on those securities (OJ L 184, 6.7.2001, p 1) . . . [4.50]

Directive 2001/84 of the European Parliament and of the Council of 27 September 2001 on the resale right for the benefit of the author of an original work of art (OJ L 272, 13.10.2001, p 32) . . . [9.80]

Council Directive 2001/86 of 8 October 2001 supplementing the Statute for a European company with regard to the involvement of employees (OJ L 294, 10.11.2001, p 22) . . . [3.145]

Directive 2001/95 of the European Parliament and of the Council of 3 December 2001 on general product safety (OJ L 11, 15.1.2002, p 4) . . . [10.220]

Directive 2002/6 of the European Parliament and of the Council of 18 February 2002 on reporting formalities for ships arriving in and/or departing from ports of the Member States of the Community (OJ L 67, 9.3.2002, p 31) . . . [3.225]

Directive 2002/20 of the European Parliament and of the Council of 7 March 2002 on the authorisation of electronic communications networks and services (Authorisation Directive) (OJ L 108, 24.4.2002, p 21) . . . [3.235]

Directive 2002/21 of the European Parliament and of the Council of 7 March 2002 on a common regulatory framework for electronic communications networks and services (Framework Directive) (OJ L 108, 24.4.2002, p 33) . . . [3.235]

Directive 2002/22 of the European Parliament and of the Council of 7 March 2002 on universal service and users' rights relating to electronic communications networks and services (Universal Service Directive) (OJ L 108, 24.4.2002, p 51) . . . [3.235]

Directive 2002/47 of the European Parliament and of the Council of 6 June 2002 on financial collateral arrangements (OJ L 168, 27.6.2002, p 43) . . . [4.45]

Directive 2002/58 of the European Parliament and of the Council of 12 July 2002 concerning the processing of personal data and the protection of privacy in the electronic communications sector (OJ L 201, 31.7.2002, p 37) . . . [10.150]

Directive 2002/65 of the European Parliament and of the Council of 23 September 2002 concerning the distance marketing of consumer financial services (OJ L 271, 9.10.2002, p 16) . . . [10.190]

Directive 2002/87 of the European Parliament and of the Council of 16 December 2002 on the supplementary supervision of credit institutions, insurance undertakings and investment firms in a financial conglomerate (OJ L 35, 11.2.2003, p 1)... [4.45]

Directive 2003/6 of the European Parliament and of the Council of 28 January 2003 on insider dealing and market manipulation (market abuse) (OJ L 96, 12.4.2003, p 16)... [4.50]

Directive 2003/33 of the European Parliament and of the Council of 26 May 2003 on the approximation of the laws, regulations and administrative provisions of the Member States relating to the advertising and sponsorship of tobacco products (OJ L 152, 20.6.2003, p 16)... [10.170]

Council Directive 2003/48 of 3 June 2003 on taxation of savings income in the form of interest payments (OJ L 157, 26.6.2003, p 38)... [7.80]

Council Directive 2003/49 of 3 June 2003 on a common system of taxation applicable to interest and royalty payments made between associated companies of different Member States (OJ L 157, 26.6.2003, p 49)... [7.75]

Directive 2003/71 of the European Parliament and of the Council of 4 November 2003 on the prospectus to be published when securities are offered to the public or admitted to trading (OJ L 345, 31.12.2003, p 64)... [4.50]

Directive 2003/74 of the European Parliament and of the Council of 22 September 2003 amending Council Directive 96/22 concerning the prohibition on the use in stockfarming of certain substances having a hormonal or thyrostatic action and of beta-agonists (OJ L 262, 14.10.2003, p 17)... [13.60]

Council Directive 2003/86 of 22 September 2003 on the right to family reunification (OJ L 251, 3.10.2003, p 12)... [3.295]

Council Directive 2003/96 of 27 October 2003 restructuring the Community framework for the taxation of energy products and electricity (OJ L 283, 31.10.2003, p 51)... [7.50]

Council Directive 2003/109 of 25 November 2003 concerning the status of third-country nationals who are long-term residents (OJ L 16, 23.1.2004, p 44)... [3.295]

Directive 2004/17 coordinating the procurement procedures of entities operating in the water, energy, transport and postal services sectors (OJ L 134, 30.4.2004, p 1)... [8.75]

Directive 2004/18 on the coordination of procedures for the award of public works contracts, public supply contracts and public service contracts (OJ L 134, 30.4.2004, p 114)... [8.10], [8.15], [8.20], [8.25], [8.30], [8.35], [8.40], [8.45], [8.50], [8.55], [8.60], [8.65], [8.70], [8.80], [8.100]

Directive 2004/25 of the European Parliament and of the Council of 21 April 2004 on takeover bids (OJ L 142, 30.4.2004, p 12)... [3.145]

Directive 2004/38 of the European Parliament and of the Council of 29 April 2004 on the right of citizens of the Union and their family members to move and reside freely within the territory of the Member States (OJ L 229, 29.6.2004, p 35) . . . [3.55], [3.270], [3.275], [3.280], [3.285]

Directive 2004/39 of the European Parliament and of the Council of 21 April 2004 on markets in financial instruments (OJ L 145, 30.4.2004, p 1) . . . [3.85], [3.245], [4.50]

Directive 2004/48 of the European Parliament and of the Council of 29 April 2004 on the enforcement of intellectual property rights (OJ L 157, 30.4.2004, p 45) . . . [9.180]

Directive 2004/109 of the European Parliament and of the Council of 15 December 2004 on the harmonisation of transparency requirements in relation to information about issuers whose securities are admitted to trading on a regulated market (OJ L 390, 31.12.2004, p 38) . . . [4.50]

Council Directive 2004/113 implementing the principle of equal treatment between men and women in the access to and supply of goods and services (OJ L 373, 21.12.2004, p 37) . . . [10.70]

Directive 2005/29 of the European Parliament and of the Council of 11 May 2005 concerning unfair business-to-consumer commercial practices in the internal market (OJ L 149, 11.6.2005, p 22) . . . [10.160]

Directive 2005/36 of the European Parliament and of the Council of 7 September 2005 on the recognition of professional qualifications (OJ L 255, 30.9.2005, p 22) . . . [3.205]

Directive 2005/56 of the European Parliament and of the Council of 26 October 2005 on cross-border mergers of limited liability companies (OJ L 310, 25.11.2005, p 1) . . . [3.145]

Directive 2005/60 of the European Parliament and of the Council of 26 October 2005 on the prevention of the use of the financial system for the purpose of money laundering and terrorist financing (OJ L 309, 25.11.2005, p 15) . . . [4.35], [4.40]

Directive 2006/24 of the European Parliament and of the Council of 15 March 2006 on the retention of data generated or processed in connection with the provision of publicly available electronic communications services or of public communications networks (OJ L 105, 13.4.2006, p 54) . . . [10.150]

Directive 2006/43 of the European Parliament and of the Council of 17 May 2006 on statutory audits of annual accounts and consolidated accounts (OJ L 157, 9.6.2006, p 87) . . . [3.145]

Directive 2006/48 of the European Parliament and of the Council of 14 June 2006 relating to the taking up and pursuit of the business of credit institutions (OJ L 177, 30.6.2006, p 1) . . . [3.85], [4.45]

Directive 2006/49 of the European Parliament and of the Council of 14 June 2006 on the capital adequacy of investment firms and credit institutions (recast) (OJ L 177, 30.6.2006, p 201) . . . [4.45]

Directive 2006/54 of the European Parliament and of the Council of 5 July 2006 on the implementation of the principle of equal opportunities and equal treatment of men and women in matters of employment and occupation (recast) (OJ L 204, 26.7.2006, p 23) . . . [10.45], [10.60], [10.65], [10.80], [10.95]

Council Directive 2006/112 of 28 November 2006 on the common system of value added tax (OJ L 347, 11.12.2006, p 1) . . . [7.40]

Directive 2006/114 of the European Parliament and of the Council of 12 December 2006 concerning misleading and comparative advertising (codified version) (OJ L 376, 27.12.2006, p 21) . . . [10.170]

Directive 2006/115 of the European Parliament and of the Council of 12 December 2006 on rental right and lending right and on certain rights related to copyright in the field of intellectual property (OJ L 376, 27.12.2006, p 28) . . . [9.80]

Directive 2006/116 of the European Parliament and of the Council of 12 December 2006 on the term of protection of copyright and certain related rights (OJ L 372, 27.12.2006, p 12) . . . [9.80]

Directive 2006/123 of the European Parliament and of the Council of 12 December 2006 on services in the internal market (OJ L 376, 27.12.2006, p 36) . . . [3.140], [3.200]

Directive 2007/23 of the European Parliament and of the Council of 23 May 2007 on the placing on the market of pyrotechnic articles (OJ L 154, 14.6.2007, p 1) . . . [10.220]

Directive 2007/64 of the European Parliament and of the Council of 13 November 2007 on payment services in the internal market (OJ L 319, 5.12.2007, p 1) . . . [3.250], [4.45]

Council Directive 2008/7 of 12 February 2008 concerning indirect taxes on the raising of capital (OJ L 46, 21.2.2008, p 11) . . . [7.45]

Directive 2008/48 of the European Parliament and of the Council of 23 April 2008 on credit agreements for consumers (OJ L 133, 22.5.2008, p 66) . . . [10.200]

Directive 2008/52 of the European Parliament and of the Council of 21 May 2008 on certain aspects of mediation in civil and commercial matters (OJ L 136, 45.5.2008, p 3) . . . [3.255]

Commission Directive 2008/84 of 27 August 2008 laying down specific purity criteria on food additives other than colours and sweeteners (OJ L 253, 20.9.2008, p 1) . . . [10.220]

Directive 2008/95 of the European Parliament and of the Council of 22 October 2008 to approximate the laws of the Member States relating to trade marks (OJ L 299, 8.11.2008, p 25)

Art 1 . . . [9.115]
Art 2 . . . [9.120]
Art 3(1) . . . [9.125]
Art 4(1) . . . [9.125]
Art 5(1) . . . [9.130]
Art 5(2) . . . [9.130]
Art 7 . . . [9.45]

Art 7(1) . . . [9.135]
Art 7(2) . . . [9.135]
Art 8(2) . . . [9.140]
Art 12(1) . . . [9.145]

Council Directive 2008/118 of 16 December 2008 concerning the general arrangements for excise duty (OJ L 9, 14.1.2009, p 12) . . . [1.150], [7.50]

Directive 2008/122 of the European Parliament and of the Council of 14 January 2009 on the protection of consumers in respect of certain aspects of timeshare, long-term holiday product, resale and exchange contracts (OJ L 33, 3.2.2009, p 10) . . . [10.205]

Directive 2009/24 of the European Parliament and of the Council of 23 April 2009 on the legal protection of computer programs (OJ L 111, 5.5.2009, p 16) . . . [9.30], [9.90]

Directive 2009/45 of the European Parliament and of the Council of 6 May 2009 on safety rules and standards for passenger ships (Recast) (OJ L 163, 25.6.2009, p 1) . . . [3.225]

Directive 2009/48 of the European Parliament and of the Council of 18 June 2009 on the safety of toys (OJ L 170, 30.6.2009, p 1) . . . [10.220]

Council Directive 2009/50 of 25 May 2009 on the conditions of entry and residence of third-country nationals for the purposes of highly qualified employment (OJ L 155, 18.6.2009, p 17) . . . [3.295]

Directive 2009/52 of the European Parliament and of the Council of 18 June 2009 providing for minimum standards on sanctions and measures against employers of illegally staying third-country nationals (OJ L 168, 30.6.2009, p 24) . . . [3.295]

Directive 2009/65 of the European Parliament and of the Council of 13 July 2009 on the coordination of laws, regulations and administrative provisions relating to undertakings for collective investment in transferable securities (UCITS) (OJ L 302, 17.11.2009, p 32) . . . [4.50]

Directive 2009/81 of the European Parliament and of the Council of 13 July 2009 on the coordination of procedures for the award of certain works contracts, supply contracts and service contracts by contracting authorities or entities in the fields of defence and security (OJ L 216, 20.8.2009, p 76) . . . [8.75]

Directive 2009/101 of the European Parliament and of the Council of 16 September 2009 on coordination of safeguards which, for the protection of the interests of members and third parties, are required by Member States of companies within the meaning of the second paragraph of Article 48 of the Treaty, with a view to making such safeguards equivalent (OJ L 258, 1.10.2009, p 11) . . . [3.145]

Directive 2009/102 of the European Parliament and of the Council of 16 September 2009 in the area of company law on single-member private limited liability companies (OJ L 258, 1.10.2009, p 20) . . . [3.145]

Directive 2009/110 of the European Parliament and of the Council of 16 September 2009 on the taking up, pursuit and prudential supervision of the business of electronic money institutions (OJ L 267, 10.10.2009, p 7) . . . [4.45]

Directive 2009/138 of the European Parliament and of the Council of 25 November 2009 on the taking-up and pursuit of the business of Insurance and Reinsurance (Solvency II) (recast) (OJ L 335, 17.12.2009, p 1) . . . [3.85], [3.245], [3.260], [4.55]

Other Instruments

Charter of Fundamental Rights, Nice, 7 December 2000, OJ C 364, 18.12. 2000, p 1, as amended at Strasbourg, 12 December 2007, OJ C 303, 14.12.2007, p 1 . . . [1.40], [10.95], [10.130], [10.135], [10.140], [12.105]

Council Decision 70/243 of 21 April 1970 on the replacement of financial contributions from Member States by the Communities' own resources (OJ L 94, 28.4.1970, p 19) . . . [7.40]

Council Decision 93/16 of 21 December 1992 on the extension of the legal protection of topographies of semiconductor products to persons from the United States of America and certain territories (OJ L 11, 19.1.1993, p 20) . . . [9.170]

Council Decision 94/700 of 24 October 1994 on the extension of the legal protection of topographies of semiconductor products to persons from Canada (OJ L 284, 1.11.1994, p 61) . . . [9.170]

Council Decision 94/824 of 22 December 1994 on the extension of the legal protection of topographies of semiconductor products to persons from a Member of the World Trade Organization (OJ L 349, 31.12.1994, p 201) . . . [9.170]

Council Decision 1999/468 laying down the Procedures for the Exercise of Implementing Powers Conferred on the Commission (OJ L 184, 17.7.1999, p 23) . . . [1.90]

Council Decision 2000/365 of 29 May 2000 concerning the request of the United Kingdom of Great Britain and Northern Ireland to take part in some of the provisions of the Schengen acquis (OJ L 131, 1.6.2000, p 43) . . . [3.290]

Commission Decision 2000/518 of 26 July 2000 on the adequate protection of personal data provided in Switzerland (OJ L 215, 25.8.2000, p 1) . . . [10.145]

Commission Decision 2000/520 of 26 July 2000 on the adequacy of the protection provided by the safe harbour privacy principles and related frequently asked questions issued by the US Department of Commerce (OJ L 215, 25.8.2000, p 7) . . . [10.145]

Commission Notice on agreements of minor importance which do not appreciably restrict competition under Article 81(1) of the Treaty establishing the European Community (de minimis) (OJ C 368, 22.12.2001, p 13) . . . [6.80]

Commission Decision 2002/2 of 20 December 2001 on the adequate protection of personal data provided by the Canadian Personal Information Protection and Electronic Documents Act (OJ L 2, 4.1.2002, p 13)... [10.145]

Council Decision 2002/192 of 28 February 2002 concerning Ireland's request to take part in some of the provisions of the Schengen acquis (OJ L 64, 7.3.2002, p 20)... [3.290]

Commission Decision 2003/490 of 30 June 2003 on the adequate protection of personal data in Argentina (OJ L 168, 5.7.2003, p 19)... [10.145]

Guidelines on the assessment of horizontal mergers under the Council Regulation on the control of concentrations between undertakings (OJ C 31, 5.2.2004, p 5)... [6.155]

Commission Notice: Guidelines on the application of Article 81 of the EC Treaty to technology transfer agreements (OJ C 101, 27.4.2004, p 2)... [6.95]

Commission Notice on the co-operation between the Commission and the courts of the EU Member States in the application of Articles 81 and 82 EC (OJ C 101, 27.4.2004, p 54)... [6.225]

Commission Notice: Guidelines on the effect on trade concept contained in Articles 81 and 82 of the Treaty (OJ C 101, 27.4.2004, p 81)... [6.80]

Commission Notice: Guidelines on the application of Article 81(3) of the Treaty (OJ C 101, 27.4.2004, p 97)... [6.90]

Decision 2241/2004 of the European Parliament and of the Council of 15 December 2004 on a single Community framework for the transparency of qualifications and competences (Europass) (OJ L 390, 31.12.2004, p 6)... [3.65]

Council Decision 2004/926 of 22 December 2004 on the putting into effect of parts of the Schengen acquis by the United Kingdom of Great Britain and Northern Ireland (OJ L 395, 31.12.2004, p 70)... [3.290]

Commission Interpretative Communication (OJ C 179, 1.8.2006, p 2)... [8.85]

Commission Notice on Immunity from fines and reduction of fines in cartel cases (OJ C 298, 8.12.2006, p 17)... [6.205]

Council Decision 2006/954 of 18 December 2006 approving the accession of the European Community to the Geneva Act of the Hague Agreement concerning the international registration of industrial designs (OJ L 386, 29.12.2006, p 28)... [9.160]

Council Decision 2007/436 of 7 June 2007 on the system of the European Communities' own resources (OJ L 163, 23.6.2007, p 17)... [7.40]

Decision 70/2008 of the European Parliament and of the Council of 15 January 2008 on a paperless environment for customs and trade (OJ L 23, 26.1.2008, p 21)... [2.15]

Guidelines on the assessment of non-horizontal mergers under the Council Regulation on the control of concentrations between undertakings (OJ C 265, 18.10.2008, p 6)... [6.155]

National Jurisdictions

Australia

Patents Act 1990 . . . [9.105]
Therapeutic Goods Act 1989 (Cth) . . . [1.65]
Sale of Goods (Vienna Convention) Act 1987 (ACT) . . . [13.145]
Sale of Goods (Vienna Convention) Act 1986 (NSW) . . . [13.145]
Sale of Goods (Vienna Convention) Act 1987 (NT) . . . [13.145]
Sale of Goods (Vienna Convention) Act 1986 (Qld) . . . [13.145]
Sale of Goods (Vienna Convention) Act 1986 (SA) . . . [13.145]
Sale of Goods (Vienna Convention) Act 1987 (Tas) . . . [13.145]
Sale of Goods (Vienna Convention) Act 1987 (Vic) . . . [13.145]
Sale of Goods (Vienna Convention) Act 1986 (WA) . . . [13.145]

Austria

Bundesgesetzblatt 96/1988, p 1530 . . . [13.145]

Belgium

Law of 4 September 1996, Belgisch Staatsblad, 7 January 1997, p 17471 . . . [13.145]

Canada

Act Respecting the United Nations Convention on Contracts for the International Sale of Goods (RSQ, c C-67.01) . . . [13.145]
Canada-EFTA Free Trade Agreement Implementation Act (SC 2009 c 6) . . . [1.70]
International Conventions Implementation Act (RSA, c I-6.8) . . . [13.145]
International Sale of Goods Act (RSBC 1996, c 236) . . . [13.145]
International Sale of Goods Act (CCSM, c S11) . . . [13.145]
International Sale of Goods Act (RSNB, c I-12.21) . . . [13.145]
International Sale of Goods Act (RSNL 1990, c I-16) . . . [13.145]
International Sale of Goods Act (RSNWT 1988, c I-7) . . . [13.145]
International Sale of Goods Act (SNS 1988, c 13) . . . [13.145]
International Sale of Goods Act (RSO 1990, c I.10) . . . [13.145]
International Sale of Goods Act (RSPEI, c I-6) . . . [13.145]
International Sale of Goods Act (SS 1990-91, c I-10.3) . . . [13.145]

International Sale of Goods Act (SY 1992, c 7) . . . [13.145]
International Sale of Goods Contracts Convention Act (RS, c I-20.4) . . . [13.145]
International Sales Conventions Act (SNu 2003, c 9) . . . [13.145]
Patent Rules (SOR/96-423) . . . [9.105]

China

Basic Law of Hong Kong Special Administrative Region (1990) . . . [1.81]

France

Law 82-842 of 10 June 1982, Journal Officiel de la République Française, 11.6.1982, p 1840 . . . [13.145]

Germany

Bundesgesetzblatt 1989 II 588 . . . [13.145]

India

Patents Act 1970 . . . [9.105]

Ireland

Patents Act 1992 . . . [9.105]

Italy

Law No 765 of 11 December 1985 . . . [13.145]

Luxembourg

Law of 26 November 1996, Mémorial A, no 86 of 10.12.1996, p 2441 . . . [13.145]

Malaysia

Patents Act 1983 (Act 291) . . . [9.105]

New Zealand

Patents Act 1958 . . . [9.105]
Sale of Goods (United Nations Convention) Act 1994 . . . [13.145]

Singapore

Patents Act (Chapter 221) . . . [9.105]
Sale of Goods (United Nations Convention) Act (Chapter 283A) . . . [13.145]

South Africa

Patents Act 1978 . . . [9.105]

United Kingdom

Patents Act 1977 . . . [9.105]

United States

19 USC 2411 . . . [1.60]
22 USC 6021 . . . [1.60]
28 USC 1782(a) . . . [6.235]
35 USC 351 to 376 . . . [9.105]

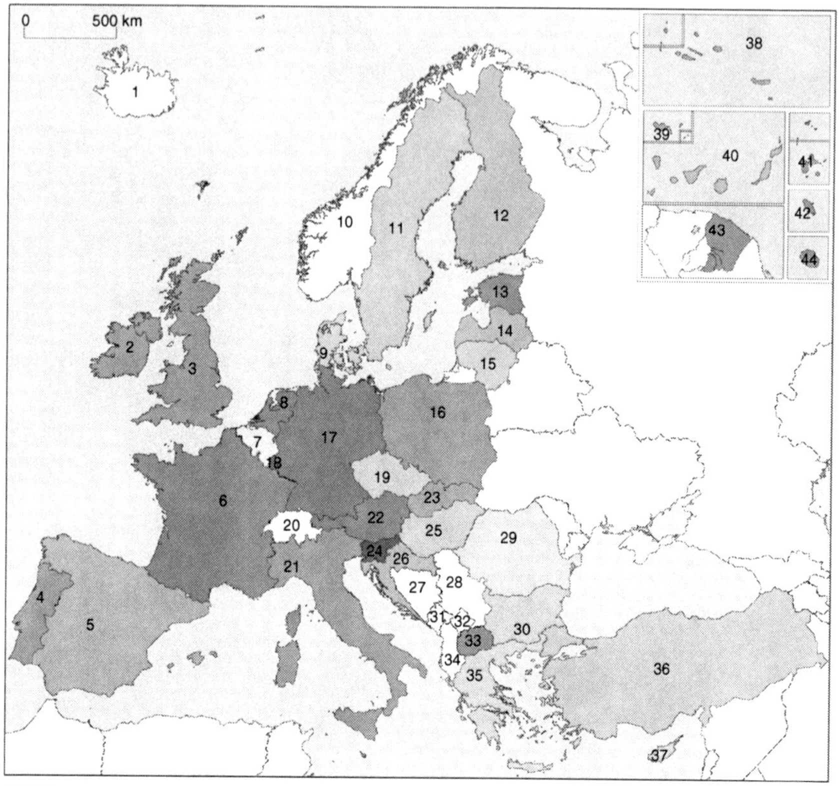

Member states of the European Union (2008)

Candidate countries (Croatia, FYR Macedonia and Turkey)

Adapted from a map supplied by the Delegation of the European Union to Australia.

1. Iceland
2. Ireland
3. United Kingdom
4. Portugal
5. Spain
6. France
7. Belgium
8. Netherlands
9. Denmark
10. Norway
11. Sweden
12. Finland
13. Estonia
14. Latvia
15. Lithuania
16. Poland
17. Germany
18. Luxembourg
19. Czech Republic
20. Switzerland
21. Italy
22. Austria
23. Slovak Republic
24. Slovenia
25. Hungary
26. Croatia
27. Bosnia Herzegovina
28. Serbia
29. Romania
30. Bulgaria
31. Montenegro
32. Kosovo
33. FYR Macedonia
34. Albania
35. Greece
36. Turkey
37. Cyprus
38. Azores (P)
39. Madeira (P)
40. Canary Islands (S)
41. Guadeloupe (F)
42. Martinique (F)
43. French Guiana
44. Reunion (F)

Chapter 1
The Political Institutions of the European Union

[1.05] Introduction

The European Union (EU) is an economic trading bloc comprising 27 nations. The Member States are (in order of accession): Belgium, the Netherlands, Luxembourg, France, Germany, Italy, the United Kingdom, Ireland, Denmark, Greece, Spain, Portugal, Austria, Finland, Sweden, Czech Republic, Estonia, Cyprus, Latvia, Lithuania, Hungary, Malta, Poland, Slovenia, Slovak Republic, Bulgaria and Romania. Given its membership, the EU is one of the world's most important trading entities.

European Union Law is of considerable interest to international trade lawyers and businesspeople in non-member States such as the United States, Australia, Canada, New Zealand and South Africa. First, the EU is a major trading and investment partner. Secondly, the EU is one of the great powers in the world's economic affairs. Thirdly, the future regional development of other regions of the world will at some stage need a reference point. The EU is a viable model of regional economic integration.

It is a fallacy to assume that lawyers and businesspeople who have not been trained in EU law would be able to deal efficiently with the avalanche of complex legal acts adopted by the European Union. While it is practically impossible to keep up with all of the legislation and case law issued by EU legislators and the European Court of Justice, an understanding of the EU legal system as a whole substantially facilitates the work of lawyers and businesspeople involved in trade with the European Union. This book thus gives an account of the most important areas of European Union business law. It has been written from the viewpoint of legal practitioners, businesspeople and law students from non-member States.

[1.10] Outline of This Chapter

This chapter discusses the development of the EU, the trading relationship between the EU and a number of common law nations, the EU's

G. Moens, J. Trone, *Commercial Law of the European Union*,
Ius Gentium: Comparative Perspectives on Law and Justice 4,
DOI 10.1007/978-90-481-8774-4_1, © Springer Science+Business Media B.V. 2010

political institutions and the legal acts which they may adopt. In subsequent chapters, specific trade-related topics will be discussed in order to provide a comprehensive overview of the EU's legal system so far as it is relevant to the development of trading opportunities.

[1.15] Basic Policies of the European Union

The Treaty on European Union (TEU) and the Treaty on the Functioning of the European Union (TFEU) are the founding Treaties of the European Union. The Court has described the TFEU as the "constitutional charter" of the Community. See *Re Draft Treaty on a European Economic Area (No 1)* (Opinion 1/91) [1991] ECR I-6079 at [21]; [1992] 1 CMLR 245; *Weber v Parliament* (C-314/91) [1993] ECR I-1093 at [8]; *Commission v European Investment Bank* (C-15/00) [2003] ECR I-7281 at [75]; *Kadi v Commission* (C-402/05 P) [2008] ECR I-6351 at [81]; [2008] 3 CMLR 41 (p 1207).

The founding Treaties detail the specific economic policies by which the EU pursues its aims. The EU is described as "a highly competitive social market economy, aiming at full employment and social progress" (Art 3(3) TEU). The Treaties require that Member States operate in conformity with the principle of "an open market economy with free competition" (Art 120 TFEU).

The EU constitutes an internal market (Art 3(3) TEU). The internal market comprises "an area without internal frontiers in which the free movement of goods, persons, services and capital is ensured" (Art 26(2) TFEU). The EU is empowered to adopt measures which have as their object the establishment and functioning of the internal market (Art 26(1) TFEU). See generally, Rodolphe Munoz, "The Development of the Ex-ante Control Mechanism Regarding Implementation of the Internal Market" in Takis Tridimas and Paolisa Nebbia (eds), *European Union Law for the Twenty-First Century* (Oxford: Hart, 2004), II: 103; Niamh Nic Shuibhne (ed), *Regulating the Internal Market* (Cheltenham, UK: Edward Elgar, 2006).

The TFEU requires the implementation of four fundamental freedoms, namely abolition as between the Member States of obstacles to the freedom of movement of goods, persons, services and capital (Arts 21(1), 28, 45, 56, 63 TFEU). The freedom of EU nationals to establish a business in another Member State is also guaranteed (Art 49 TFEU).

Some characteristics of the single market should be noted. There are no border controls concerning goods at the internal frontiers between EU Member States. There are also no controls on persons at these internal frontiers (Arts 67(2), 77(1) TFEU). There is mutual recognition of the various national laws regarding goods, so that a good that may be sold under the law of one Member State may be sold in the other Member States. The EU seeks to harmonise indirect taxation between the Member States so far as is required for the operation of the internal market (Art 113 TFEU).

Certain anti-competitive actions are prohibited as incompatible with the internal market. Anti-competitive undertakings are void (Art 102 TFEU). Abuse of a dominant market position within the internal market is similarly prohibited (Art 102 TFEU). State aid that distorts or threatens to distort competition in trade between the Member States is also prohibited (Art 107 TFEU).

The EU is also a customs union (Art 28(1) TFEU). The EU achieves this task through the elimination of customs duties and quantitative restrictions on imports and exports between the Member States (Arts 30, 34–35 TFEU), the establishment of a common external customs tariff applicable to trade with non-member states (Art 28(1) TFEU) and a common commercial policy towards non-member countries (Art 207 TFEU).

The Union adopts common policies on agriculture, fisheries and transport (Arts 38, 90 TFEU). The economic policies of the Member States are coordinated and, to that end, national laws are approximated (Art 114 TFEU). The Treaty contains general principles of non-discrimination on the ground of nationality (Art 18 TFEU) and equal pay for equal work (Art 157 TFEU).

The EU is a monetary union (Art 3(4) TEU). The EU has adopted the Euro (€) as its common currency (Art 3(4) TEU). It came into use for financial transactions in 1999. On 1 January 2002 Euro banknotes and coins went into circulation.

The Euro has replaced the national currencies of sixteen EU Member States. These states are: Austria, Belgium, Cyprus, Finland, France, Germany, Greece, Ireland, Italy, Luxembourg, Malta, Netherlands, Portugal, Slovak Republic, Slovenia and Spain. See Art 1(a) and Annex, Council Regulation 974/98 of 3 May 1998 on the introduction of the euro (OJ L 139, 11.5.1998, p 1).

Eleven Member States have not adopted the Euro: Bulgaria, Czech Republic, Denmark, Estonia, Hungary, Latvia, Lithuania, Poland, Romania, Sweden and the United Kingdom. Most of these Member States will adopt the Euro following a transition period. However, the United Kingdom, Denmark and Sweden have opted out of the single currency.

States adopting the Euro must satisfy requirements as to inflation, interest rates, budget deficits, public debt and exchange rate stability. All Member States are under a duty not to run excessive budget deficits (Art 126 TFEU; elaborated upon in Art 1, Protocol (No 12) on the Excessive Deficit Procedure). See generally, Charles Proctor, *The Euro and the Financial Markets: The Legal Impact of EMU* (Bristol: Jordans, 1999); Paul Beaumont and Neil Walker (eds), *Legal Framework of the Single European Currency* (Oxford: Hart, 1999).

There is a common citizenship of the European Union. The citizens of each Member State are also citizens of the Union. EU citizenship does not replace citizenship of the Member States (Art 9 TEU; Art 20(1) TFEU). See generally, Matthew J Elsmore and Peter Starup, "Union Citizenship—

Background, Jurisprudence, and Perspective: The Past, Present, and Future of Law and Policy" (2007) 26 *Yearbook of European Law* 57; Paul O'Neill and Susan R Sandler, "The EU Citizenship Acquis and the Court of Justice: Citizenship Vigilant or Merely Vigilant Treaty Guardian?" (2008) 7 *Richmond Journal of Global Law and Business* 205; Dimitry Kochenov, "Ius Tractum of Many Faces: European Citizenship and the Difficult Relationship between Status and Rights" (2009) 15 *Columbia Journal of European Law* 169; Markus Kotzur, "A European Glance on the Notion of Citizenship" (2009) 1 *City University of Hong Kong Law Review* 91.

The European Union should be distinguished from the Council of Europe, which is a separate international organization that is also devoted to European integration. The Council was established in 1949. See *Statute of the Council of Europe*, London, 5 May 1949, 87 UNTS 103; ETS no 1. This treaty is available at http://conventions.coe.int. The Council's website is at http://www.coe.int. See generally, Tony Joris and Jan Vandenberghe, "The Council of Europe and the European Union: Natural Partners or Uneasy Bedfellows?" (2009) 15 *Columbia Journal of European Law* 1. The European Court of Human Rights is a body of the Council of Europe.

[1.20] Development of the European Union

This section traces the historical development of the European Union. Much detailed material relating to the history of the EU may be found at the following website: http://aei.pitt.edu/ [Archive of European Integration].

The origins of the European Union lie in the formation of the European Economic Community (EEC) in 1957. See *Treaty Establishing the European Economic Community*, Rome, 25 March 1957, 298 UNTS 11; 163 BFSP 206. Through a series of amending treaties the EEC became the European Community (EC) and eventually the European Union.

The members of the EU are also members of the European Atomic Energy Community (Euratom), a separate international organisation also established in 1957. See *Treaty Establishing the European Atomic Energy Community*, Rome, 25 March 1957, 298 UNTS 167; 163 BFSP 206. This organisation promotes the joint development of nuclear energy for peaceful purposes. The Treaty does not apply to the employment of atomic energy for military purposes. See *Commission v United Kingdom* (C-65/04) [2006] ECR I-2239 at [26]. See generally, Thomas F Cusack, "A Tale of Two Treaties: An Assessment of the Euratom Treaty in Relation to the EC Treaty" (2003) 40 *Common Market Law Review* 117. Euratom's website is at http://www.euratom.org.

Before July 2002 there was a third European Community, the European Coal and Steel Community (ECSC). However, the founding Treaty for that Community (the Treaty of Paris) expired on 23 July 2002. See OJ L 194,

23.7.2002, pp 35–36; Art 97, *Treaty Instituting the European Coal and Steel Community*, Paris, 18 April 1951, 261 UNTS 140; 158 BFSP 630. The ECSC has thus ceased to function. The ECSC formerly directed and controlled output, markets, supply and demand for coal and steel.

The original EEC, Euratom and European Coal and Steel Community Treaties each provided for separate Commissions and Councils of Ministers. In 1965 the Member States adopted a Treaty that merged the three Commissions into a single Commission and merged the three Councils into a single Council. See *Treaty Establishing a Single Council and a Single Commission of the European Communities*, Brussels, 8 April 1965, 1348 UNTS 81; 4 ILM 776; OJ 152, 13.7.1967, p 1.

The original members of the EEC were Belgium, Netherlands, Luxembourg, France, Germany and Italy. The membership of the EEC gradually expanded through a series of accession treaties. The EEC was first enlarged on 1 January 1973 with the accession of the United Kingdom, Ireland and Denmark. See *Treaty of Accession*, Brussels, 22 January 1972, 1375 UNTS 2; OJ L 73, 27.3.1972, p 5.

Greece became a Member State on 1 January 1981. See *Treaty of Accession*, Athens, 28 May 1979, 1382 UNTS 2; OJ L 291, 19.11.1979, p 9. Spain and Portugal joined the EC on 1 January 1986. See *Treaty of Accession*, Madrid, 12 June 1985, OJ L 302, 15.11.1985, p 9. Austria, Finland and Sweden became members on 1 January 1995. See *Treaty of Accession*, Corfu, 24 June 1994, OJ C 241, 29.8.1994, p 9; UKTS 1995 No 43 (Cm 2887).

The largest enlargement took place on 1 May 2004, when EU membership expanded to include the Czech Republic, Estonia, Cyprus, Latvia, Lithuania, Hungary, Malta, Poland, the Slovak Republic and Slovenia. See *Treaty of Accession*, Athens, 16 April 2003, OJ L 236, 23.9.2003, p 17; UKTS 2004 No 32 (Cm 6312); Christophe Hillion, "The European Union is Dead. Long Live the European Union ... A Commentary on the Treaty of Accession 2003" (2004) 29 *European Law Review* 583; Kirstyn Inglis, "The Union's Fifth Accession Treaty: New Means to make Enlargement Possible" (2004) 41 *Common Market Law Review* 937.

Finally, Bulgaria and Romania became members on 1 January 2007. See *Treaty of Accession*, Luxembourg, 25 April 2005, OJ L 157, 21.6.2005, p 11; EC 2005 No 2 (Cm 6657); Adam Lazowski, "And Then They Were Twenty-seven ... A Legal Appraisal of the Sixth Accession Treaty" (2007) 44 *Common Market Law Review* 401.

Any European state that respects certain fundamental values may apply for membership of the EU (Art 49 TEU). Croatia, the Former Yugoslav Republic of Macedonia and Turkey have been accepted as candidates for EU membership. Applications for membership have been lodged by Albania (28 April 2009) and Iceland (23 July 2009). Bosnia and Herzegovina, Montenegro, Serbia and Kosovo (under UN Security Council Resolution 1244/99) are potential candidates. EU Membership is limited to European nations. On 20

July 1987 Morocco applied for membership but was rejected on the ground that it was not a European nation. Information about the enlargement process is available at http://ec.europa.eu/enlargement/countries/index_en.htm

[1.25] Single European Act

By the 1980s many non-tariff barriers continued to impede the free flow of goods within the Community. These barriers included quantitative restrictions and measures having equivalent effect, including physical, technical and fiscal barriers. In 1985 the European Commission published a landmark White Paper. See Commission of the European Communities, *Completing the Internal Market* (COM (85) 310 Final). This White Paper was destined to become the blueprint for the creation of the "internal market" by the end of 1992.

The Single European Act (SEA) was the response of the Council to the Commission's White Paper. See *Single European Act*, Luxembourg, 17 February 1986, The Hague, 28 February 1986, 1754 UNTS 3; 25 ILM 506; OJ L 169, 29.6.1987, p 1. Most importantly, the SEA provided for the completion of the "internal market" (Art 13). The SEA also provided for the cooperation of the European Parliament in the legislative process of the EC. See generally, H-J Glaesner, "The Single European Act" (1986) 6 *Yearbook of European Law* 283; Stefan A Riesenfeld, "The Single European Act" (1990) 13 *Hastings International and Comparative Law Review* 371.

[1.30] Maastricht Treaty

In 1993 a new European body (the European Union) was formed alongside the existing European Community. See *Treaty on European Union*, Maastricht, 7 February 1992, 1757 UNTS 3; 31 ILM 247; OJ C 191, 29.7.1992, p 1. The Treaty provided for the establishment of an Economic and Monetary Union (EMU). Economic Union involved the removal of exchange controls and the convergence of the economic policies of the Member States. The Monetary Union required the adoption of a single European currency (the Euro) by 1999.

The Treaty introduced a co-decision procedure for the enactment of legislation by the Parliament and Council. It provided for broader EU authority over the environment, health, research, culture and industrial and social policy. The Treaty also introduced the concept of subsidiarity according to which things which can be done better at local or regional level should be done at that level.

[1.35] Treaty of Amsterdam

In 1997 the Treaty of Amsterdam introduced many reforms of the founding Treaties. See *Treaty of Amsterdam*, Amsterdam, 2 October 1997, 37 ILM 56; OJ C 340, 10.11.1997, p 1. The Treaty provided authority for EU measures against discrimination based upon specific grounds such as race, sex, religion, disability, age and sexual orientation. Sustainable development was added to the objectives of the EU. This Treaty provided a framework for enhanced cooperation between some but not all EU Member States. The Treaty also expanded the range of areas subject to qualified majority voting and co-decision.

New provisions relating to police and judicial cooperation in criminal matters were inserted into the Treaty on European Union. Under the Treaty the European Union consisted of "three pillars": the European Community (EC), the Common Foreign and Security Policy (CFSP) and Police and Judicial Co-operation in Criminal Matters (PJCC). See Eileen Denza, *The Intergovernmental Pillars of the European Union* (Oxford: Oxford University Press, 2002).

See generally, Philippe Manin, "The Treaty of Amsterdam" (1998) 4 *Columbia Journal of European Law* 1; Jo Shaw, "The Treaty of Amsterdam: Challenges of Flexibility and Legitimacy" (1998) 4 *European Law Journal* 63; Michel Petite, "The Treaty of Amsterdam", *Jean Monnet Working Paper* No 2/98, http://www.jeanmonnetprogram.org; European Commission, *The Amsterdam Treaty: A Comprehensive Guide* (Luxembourg: Office for Official Publications of the European Communities, 1999).

[1.40] Charter of Fundamental Rights

In 2000 the EU adopted the *Charter of Fundamental Rights*, Nice, 7 December 2000, OJ C 364, 18.12.2000, p 1 (as originally adopted), as amended at Strasbourg, 12 December 2007, OJ C 303, 14.12.2007, p 1 (as amended). This Charter was based upon the case law of the European Court of Justice regarding the protection of fundamental rights as general principles of EU law.

As well as the usual civil and political rights, the Charter guarantees rights such as the freedom to conduct a business (Art 16), the right to strike and to bargain collectively (Art 28), information and consultation rights for employees (Art 27), protection against unjustified dismissal (Art 30), paid maternity leave and parental leave (Art 23(2)) and the protection of personal data (Art 8).

When the Charter was adopted it was a non-binding instrument. See *Pyres v Commission* (T-256/01) [2005] ECR-SC II-99 at [66]; *Re Validity of Directive 2003/86: Parliament v Council* (C-540/03) [2006] ECR I-5769 at [38]; [2006] 3 CMLR 28 (p 779). Since the entry into force of the Treaty of Lisbon the Charter has become legally binding upon the EU itself and the Member States when they implement EU law (Art 6(1) TEU; Art 51(1) Charter). The Charter possesses the "same legal value as the Treaties" (Art 6(1) TEU).

The Charter does not apply to the United Kingdom and Poland. See Protocol (No 30) on the Application of the Charter of Fundamental Rights of the European Union to Poland and to the United Kingdom. In October 2009 the European Council announced that the Treaty will be amended so that the Charter will not apply to the Czech Republic. See Brussels European Council 29/30 October 2009—Presidency Conclusions (15265/09) at [2], available at http://register.consilium.europa.eu. See generally, Steve Peers and Angela Ward, *The European Union Charter of Fundamental Rights* (Oxford: Hart, 2004).

[1.45] Treaty of Nice

Given the increasing number of Member States, the Treaty of Nice reduced the number of members of the Commission. See *Treaty of Nice*, Nice, 26 February 2001, OJ C 80, 10.3.2001, p 1; UKTS 2003 No 22 (Cm 5879). A new weighting of votes in the Council of Ministers was also introduced. The range of matters subject to qualified majority voting and co-decision were again expanded. A complicated system of voting in the Council was introduced, with three different majorities required for approval of a measure. See generally, Jean-Claude Piris, "The Treaty of Nice: An Imperfect Treaty but a Decisive Step towards Enlargement" (2000) 3 *Cambridge Yearbook of European Legal Studies* 15; Jo Shaw, "The Treaty of Nice: Legal and Constitutional Implications" (2001) 7 *European Public Law* 195; René Barents, "Some Observations on the Treaty of Nice" (2001) 8 *Maastricht Journal of European and Comparative Law* 121; Dimitris Melissas and Ingolf Pernice (eds), *Perspectives of the Nice Treaty and the Intergovernmental Conference in 2004* (Baden-Baden: Nomos, 2002), available at http://www.ecln.net

[1.50] European Constitution

In 2001 a European Convention began to draft a Constitutional Treaty for the EU. See http://european-convention.eu.int; Vaughne Miller, *The Convention on the Future of Europe: Institutional Reform* (House of Commons Library Research Paper 03/56), available at http://www.parliament.uk. After agreement was reached at an Intergovernmental Conference, the Constitution was signed by the Member States in October 2004. See *Treaty Establishing a Constitution for Europe*, Rome, 29 October 2004, OJ C 310,

16.12.2004, p 1; EC 2004 No 8 (Cm 6429). The proposed Constitution never entered into force. In June 2007 it was permanently shelved after the failure of several governments to ratify the treaty. See generally, Ingolf Pernice and Jirí Zemánek (eds), *A Constitution for Europe: The IGC, the Ratification Process and Beyond* (Baden-Baden: Nomos, 2005), available at http://www.ecln.net; Jean-Claude Piris, *The Constitution for Europe: A Legal Analysis* (Cambridge: Cambridge University Press, 2006).

[1.55] Treaty of Lisbon

After the Constitution was abandoned, a new amending treaty adopted many of its features. See *Treaty of Lisbon*, Lisbon, 13 December 2007, OJ C 306, 17.12.2007, p 1; EC 2007 No 13 (Cm 7294). The changes introduced by this Treaty are discussed in the relevant places throughout this book. A few points should be noted here. The Treaty establishing the European Community (EC) was renamed the Treaty on the Functioning of the European Union (TFEU). The three pillar system was superseded. That is, the European Community was fully merged within the European Union (Art 1 TEU). Police and Judicial Co-operation in Criminal Matters (PJCC) was replaced by an "Area of Freedom, Security and Justice" (Art 67 TFEU). However, the Common Foreign and Security Policy remained (Art 24(2) TEU). See Steve Peers, "Finally 'Fit for Purpose'? The Treaty of Lisbon and the End of the Third Pillar Legal Order" (2008) 27 *Yearbook of European Law* 47.

The EU has issued consolidated versions of the TEU and the TFEU as amended by the Treaty of Lisbon. See OJ C 83, 30.3.2010, p 1. The British Foreign Office has also issued an unofficial consolidated version. See Cm 7310.

The Treaty of Lisbon came into force on 1 December 2009. The ratification process faced significant obstacles in several Member States. In June 2008 Irish voters rejected the Treaty at a referendum. See John O'Brennan, "Ireland says No (again): The 12 June 2008 Referendum on the Lisbon Treaty" (2009) 62 *Parliamentary Affairs* 258; Gerard Hogan, "The Lisbon Treaty and the Irish Referendum" (2009) 15 *European Public Law* 163. On 2 October 2009 ratification was approved at a second referendum. See Vaughne Miller, *The Treaty of Lisbon after the Second Irish Referendum* (House of Commons Library Research Paper 09/75), available at http://www.parliament.uk. Ireland ratified the Treaty on 23 October 2009. In July 2008 the Polish President indicated that he would not ratify the Treaty until Ireland had ratified. On 10 October 2009 Poland ratified the Treaty following the second referendum.

The ratification of Germany was delayed while the national Constitutional Court deliberated upon constitutional challenges to the Treaty. On

30 June 2009 the Court rejected these challenges (2 BvE 2/08 & 5/08; 2 BvR 1010/08, 1022/08, 1259/08 & 182/09). However, as a consequence of the Court's decision statutory amendments strengthening legislative supervision of EU matters were enacted prior to ratification. Germany ratified the Treaty on 25 September 2009.

On 26 November 2008 the Czech Constitutional Court rejected a constitutional challenge to ratification (Pl US 19/08). In May 2009 the Treaty was approved by the Czech Parliament. In September 2009 Czech Senators brought another constitutional challenge to the Treaty. On 3 November 2009 the Court again held that the Treaty could be ratified (Pl US 29/09). On 13 November the Czech Republic ratified the Treaty.

The provisions of the EU treaties have been renumbered by several of the amending treaties, which can create confusion when reading older cases. However, comparative tables show the former and new numbers of every provision following each amendment. For the Treaty of Amsterdam, see OJ C 340, 10.11.1997, p 85. For the Treaty of Lisbon, see OJ C 115, 9.5.2008, p 361; Cm 7294, pp 235ff; Cm 7311. Comparative tables for both revisions appear in the Appendices to this book.

See generally, Grainne de Burca, "Reflections on the Path from the Constitutional Treaty to the Lisbon Treaty", *Jean Monnet Working Paper* No 03/08, http://www.jeanmonnetprogram.org; Stefan Griller and Jacques Ziller (eds), *The Lisbon Treaty: EU Constitutionalism without a Constitutional Treaty?* (Wien: Springer, 2008); Stephen C Sieberson, "The Treaty of Lisbon and its Impact on the European Union's Democratic Deficit" (2008) 14 *Columbia Journal of European Law* 445; Richard Crowe, "The Treaty of Lisbon: A Revised Legal Framework for the Organisation and Functioning of the European Union" (2008) 9 *ERA Forum* 163; Joakim Nergelius, *The EU Constitution in a Comparative and Historical Perspective: An Analysis of the Lisbon Treaty and its Importance* (Berlin: Springer, 2009); Ingolf Pernice, "The Treaty of Lisbon: Multilevel Constitutionalism in Action" (2009) 15 *Columbia Journal of European Law* 349.

[1.60] Relations Between the EU and the United States

The following sections discuss the relations between the European Union and various non-member nations, in particular those that have substantial English speaking populations. The discussion will focus upon trade relations.

The United States is the European Union's most important trading partner. In 2006 the EU was the largest exporter to the United States (18.5% of all imports). The EU was the second largest importer of US exports (20.6%). The EU was by far the largest source of foreign investment in the United States (62%). See *EU Insight* (Delegation of the European Commission to the USA), November 2006, p 1.

Some bilateral treaties between the EU and the United States regulate trade in specific products. See e.g. *Agreement on Trade in Wine*, London, 10 March 2006, OJ L 87, 24.3.2006, p 2; State Dept No 06-127. The United States does not have a free trade agreement with the EU.

The United States and the EU have also entered into an agreement for the mutual recognition of conformity assessment procedures. See *Agreement on Mutual Recognition*, London, 18 May 1998, OJ L 31, 4.2.1999, p 3; State Dept No 99-53. This mutual recognition applies only to specific categories of goods, including telecommunications, electrical safety, medical devices and pharmaceuticals (see Sectoral Annexes).

Several other treaties deal with cooperation regarding the competition laws of the EU and the United States and mutual notification of investigations. See *Agreement regarding the Application of Competition Laws*, Washington, 23 September 1991, OJ L 95, 27.4.1995, p 47; 30 ILM 1487; [1991] 4 CMLR 823; *Agreement on the Application of Positive Comity Principles in the Enforcement of their Competition Laws*, Brussels-Washington, 3–4 June 1998, OJ L 173, 18.6.1998, p 28; TIAS 12958; 37 ILM 1070. The texts of these treaties are available at http://ec.europa.eu/world/agreements/default.home.do.

Numerous trade disputes between the EU and the United States have been settled through the World Trade Organisation (WTO) dispute settlement process. Complaints brought by the United States and other nations against EU laws and practices are discussed in Chapter 13. The EU has brought complaints against many US laws and practices. For example, complaints have concerned the Anti-Dumping Act of 1916 (DS136), the imposition of trade sanctions under the Trade Act of 1974 (DS152) and the non-payment of royalties for the playing of music in public places (DS160).

Some of these complaints have resulted in the authorisation of countermeasures by the EU. In 2003 the Appellate Body held that the US "Byrd Amendment" violated the WTO Agreement. See *United States—Continued Dumping and Subsidy Offset Act of 2000*, Report of the Appellate Body, DS217, 16 January 2003, DSR 2003: I, 375; 42 ILM 427. The Byrd Amendment provided that the proceeds of anti-dumping fines paid by foreign companies would be paid to the US companies that complained about the dumping. See Simone Hartmann-Tröger, "Antidumping and Countervailing Duties—The Byrd Amendment" (2007) 11 *International Trade and Business Law Review* 269.

In 2003 the WTO Arbitrators authorised retaliatory action by the EU. See Decision by the Arbitrator under Art 22.6 of the DSU, DS217, 31 August 2004, DSR 2004: IX, 4591. In 2005 the Council of the European Union imposed a 15% additional duty upon specific products of US origin as a retaliatory measure. See Council Regulation 673/2005 of 25 April 2005 establishing additional customs duties on imports of certain products originating in the United States of America (OJ L 110, 30.4.2005, p 1).

The EU lodged a complaint regarding US tax treatment of foreign sales corporations. The Arbitrator determined that the EU should be authorised to take counter-measures against the US by suspending certain concessions. See *United States—Tax Treatment for "Foreign Sales Corporations"*, Recourse to Art 22.6 Arbitration Report, DS108, 30 August 2002, DSR 2002: VI, 2517; 41 ILM 1400. The DSB authorised such counter-measures. The EU's retaliatory actions entered into force on 1 March 2004.

Retaliatory action by the United States against EU trade is taken under s 301 of the Trade Act 1974 (19 USC 2411). For example, in 1999 the US Trade Representative imposed 100% ad valorem duties on several products from EU Member States for failure to implement the WTO Appellate Body ruling in the Banana dispute. See 64 Fed Reg 19,209 (19 April 1999); *European Communities—Regime for the Importation, Sale and Distribution of Bananas*, Report of the Appellate Body, DS27, 25 September 1997, DSR 1997: II, 589. In 2001 these sanctions were lifted after an agreement was reached between the parties. See 64 Fed Reg 35,689 (6 July 2001); Sally J Cummins and David P Stewart (eds), *Digest of United States Practice in International Law 2001* (Washington: International Law Institute, 2002), 650–651.

Indeed trade disputes between the EU and the US are often settled by agreement between the parties. For example, in 1996 the EU brought a WTO complaint (DS38) regarding the Helms-Burton Act (22 USC 6021), which restricted trade with Cuba. In 1998 the dispute was resolved by agreement between the parties and the complaint lapsed. See Sally J Cummins and David P Stewart (eds), *Digest of United States Practice in International Law 1991–1999* (Washington: International Law Institute, 2005), 1445–1446, 1976–1977; Stefaan Smis and Kim Van der Borght, "The EU-US Compromise on the Helms-Burton and D'Amato Acts" (1999) 93 *American Journal of International Law* 227.

The European Union maintains a Delegation in the United States. The Delegation's website is at http://www.eurunion.org. The website of the US Mission to the EU is at http://useu.usmission.gov.

[1.65] Relations Between the EU and Australia

The EU and Australia enjoy substantial trade and economic interactions. Australia represents one of the EU's most important and reliable sources of raw materials. Australia's largest trading partner is the European Union. Australia ranks at number 20 among the EU's trading partners. In 2006 the most important Australian exports to the EU were minerals, base metals, foodstuffs, machinery and chemical products. In that year the most important EU exports to Australia were machinery, chemical products, vehicles, medical and other instrumentation, and base metals. See *Statistics in Focus*, 4/2008, p 9, available at http://ec.europa.eu/eurostat.

The economic links between Australia and the EU have been summarised as follows: "The EU is Australia's largest partner in both two-way trade in goods (e.g. coal, medicaments, motor vehicles and alcohol) and two-way trade in services (e.g. travel and transportation) .... It is the largest investor in Australia and second largest destination for Australian investment overseas." See "EU-Australia Economic Relationship", *EU Insight* (Delegation of the European Commission to Australia and New Zealand), September 2009, available at http://www.delaus.ec.europa.eu. The Australian Department of Foreign Affairs and Trade publishes an annual publication entitled *Australia's Trade with the European Union*, the most recent issue of which is available at http://www.dfat.gov.au/publications/stats-pubs/trade_eu.html.

Australia and the EU have entered into several bilateral treaties which have significance for trade. One agreement concerns the wine trade. See *Agreement on Trade in Wine*, Brussels, 1 December 2008, [2008] ATNIF 20; OJ L 28, 30.1.2009, p 3. Another agreement relating to trade in certain meats expired on 30 June 1995. See [1999] ATS 38 Part I p 67; *Agreement concerning Trade in Mutton, Lamb and Goatmeat*, Brussels, 14 November 1980, 1641 UNTS 287; [1980] ATS No 32; OJ, L 275, 18.10.1980, p 20. Australia does not have a free trade agreement with the EU. A new Partnership agreement is currently under negotiation.

In 1998 Australia and the EU entered into a Mutual Recognition Agreement. See *Agreement on Mutual Recognition in relation to Conformity Assessment*, Canberra, 24 June 1998, 2076 UNTS 245; [1999] ATS No 2; OJ L 229, 17.8.1998, p 3. Many EU Member States have regulatory requirements concerning particular imported goods. Testing for compliance with these requirements is usually conducted in the country that imports the goods. Under this agreement testing according to European standards can be conducted in Australia (Art 2(1)). Similarly, testing according to Australian standards can be conducted in the EU (Art 2(2)). This treaty applies only to particular categories of goods, including pharmaceuticals, telecommunications terminal equipment, automotive products, machinery and low voltage electrical equipment (see Sectoral Annexes). This agreement is implemented by ss 25B and 26AA of the *Therapeutic Goods Act* 1989 (Cth).

The Agreement only applies to products that originate in Australia or the EU (Art 4(1)). The Australian Government considered that under EU rules of origin products that are assembled in Australia from imported components would be classified as being of Australian origin. See Joint Standing Committee on Treaties, *Report 20* (1999) at [2.40]–[2.42]. This Report is available at http://www.aph.gov.au/house/committee/jsct/index.htm. The texts of these treaties are available at http://www.austlii.edu.au/au/other/dfat

Relations between Australia and the EU have not been without disagreement. Successive Australian governments have lodged protests with the EU Commission about the Common Agricultural Policy (CAP). Australia brought a complaint under GATT concerning the Common Sugar Policy. See *European Communities—Refunds on Exports of Sugar*, GATT Panel Report, L/4833, adopted 6 November 1979, BISD 26S/290; 20 ILM 862.

The CAP has excluded many Australian agricultural products from European markets. Another detrimental effect of the CAP has been the invasion of markets previously supplied by Australia, assisted by the EU's extensive use of export subsidies. The Australian Department of Foreign Affairs and Trade has stated that the CAP "creates distortions and instability on world agricultural markets; causes internal EU prices to be higher than the international market level for many commodities and limits access to the EU agricultural market." See Nina Markovic, *Courted by Europe? Advancing Australia's Relations with the European Union in the New Security Environment*, Commonwealth Parliamentary Library Research Paper no 1, 2009–10, pp 43–44, available at http://www.aph.gov.au/library/pubs/index.htm.

Relatively few disputes between the EU and Australia have been brought before the WTO dispute settlement process. The European Communities brought a complaint relating to Australia's quarantine system, but it was settled by a mutually agreed solution (WT/DS287/8). Australia brought complaints concerning EU export subsidies on sugar (DS265) and trademarks and geographical indications (DS290).

The European Union maintains a Delegation in Australia (http://www.delaus.ec.europa.eu). The website of the Australian Mission to the European Communities is at http://www.belgium.embassy.gov.au/bsls/home. Organisations promoting business links between Australia and the EU include Australian Business In Europe (http://www.abie.com.au) and the European Australian Business Council (http://www.eabc.com.au). See generally, Matthew Harvey and Michael Longo, *European Union Law: An Australian View* (Sydney: Lexis Nexis, 2008), Ch 7.

[1.70] Relations Between the EU and Canada

The EU is Canada's second most important trading partner. The EU has entered into an agreement with Canada concerning the wine trade. See *Agreement on Trade in Wines and Spirit Drinks*, Niagara-on-the-Lake, 16 September 2003, OJ L 35, 6.2.2004, p 3. Canada and the EU have also concluded a Mutual Recognition Agreement. See *Agreement on Mutual Recognition*, London, 14 May 1998, OJ L 280, 16.10.1998, p 3; Can TS 1998 No 40. Each party shall accept the results of conformity assessments performed by the other party in particular sectors (Art II(2)–(3)). The Agreement applies to conformity assessment in sectors such as pharmaceuticals, medical devices, telecommunications terminal equipment, information technology and electrical safety (see Sectoral Annexes).

Another agreement relates to competition law. See *Agreement regarding the Application of Competition Laws*, Bonn, 17 June 1999, 2101 UNTS 23; OJ L 175, 10.7.1999, p 50; Can TS 1999 No 38. This Agreement is discussed in Chapter 6. In December 2008 the EU and Canada initialled an air services agreement. The texts of these treaties are available at http://ec.europa.eu/world/agreements/default.home.do.

Canada does not have a free trade agreement with the EU. In June 2009 EU and Canada began negotiations for a Comprehensive Economic and Trade Agreement. See Press Release, IP/09/896, 10 June 2009, available at http://europa.eu/rapid/searchAction.do. Canada has entered into a free trade agreement with the European Free Trade Area states, but it has not yet entered into force. See *Free Trade Agreement between Canada and the States of the European Free Trade Association*, Davos, Switzerland, 26 January 2008. The text of this agreement is available at http://www.efta.int. This treaty is implemented by the *Canada-EFTA Free Trade Agreement Implementation Act* (SC 2009 c 6).

Relatively few trade disputes between Canada and the EU have been resolved through the WTO panel system. The EU brought complaints against Canadian patent protection for pharmaceuticals (DS114) and import duty exemptions for automobiles (DS142). Canada has brought complaints concerning hormonal treatment of meat (DS48), asbestos (DS135) and biotech products (DS292).

The European Union maintains a Delegation in Canada (http://www.delcan.ec.europa.eu). The website of the Canadian Mission to the EU is at http://www.international.gc.ca/canada-europa/eu/menu-en.asp. The Canada Europe Roundtable for Business promotes business between Canada and the EU (http://www.canada-europe.org).

[1.75] Relations Between the EU and New Zealand

In 2007 16.9% of imports to New Zealand originated in the EU, while 15.4% of New Zealand's exports were destined for the EU. See *European Union—New Zealand Economic Relations*, p 1. For a discussion of EU-New Zealand economic relations, see Matthew Gibbons (ed), *New Zealand and the European Union* (Auckland: Pearson, 2008).

New Zealand does not have a free trade agreement with the EU. There is an Agreement concerning trade in several types of meat. See *Exchange of Notes comprising an Agreement on Trade in Mutton, Lamb and Goatmeat*, Brussels, 17 October 1980, 1324 UNTS 239; OJ L 275, 18.10.1980, p 28; NZTS 1980 No 13. This treaty has been amended on numerous occasions.

The EU-New Zealand Mutual Recognition Agreement applies to conformity assessment in relation to products such as medicines, medical devices, low voltage equipment, telecommunications terminal equipment, and machinery. See *Agreement on Mutual Recognition in relation to*

Conformity Assessment, Wellington, 25 June 1998, 2071 UNTS 429; OJ L 229, 17.8.1998, p 62; NZTS 1998 No 4. The texts of these treaties are available at http://www.nzlii.org/nz/other/mfat/NZTS.

Few disputes between the EU and New Zealand have been brought into the WTO dispute settlement process. The EC brought a complaint concerning New Zealand measures affecting butter. The complaint was settled by a mutually agreed solution (WT/DS72/7).

EU law has had an important effect upon the New Zealand dairy trade. The *Egenberger* decision of the European Court of Justice had a substantial impact upon that trade:

> "a German company claimed that New Zealand's import arrangements with the EU were discriminatory. This was because import licences for butter were awarded by the United Kingdom authorities only for New Zealand butter and those licences were issued only to subsidiaries of Fonterra. Fonterra ... enjoys an export monopoly on butter from New Zealand. The decision in favour of the German company which suspended New Zealand butter exports caused shockwaves in the dairy export community in New Zealand. The European Commission as a consequence of the decision proposed ... more restrictive arrangements for the import of New Zealand butter into the EU." See A H Angelo and Rebekah C Plachecki, "Towards a Celebration of 50 Years of European Union" (2007) 38 *Victoria University of Wellington Law Review* 5 at 6; *Franz Egenberger GmbH Molkerei und Trockenwerk v Bundesanstalt für Landwirtschaft und Ernährung* (C-313/04) [2006] ECR I-6331.

The European Union maintains a Delegation in New Zealand (http://www.delaus.ec.europa.eu). The website of the New Zealand Mission to the EU is at http://www.nzembassy.com/home.cfm?c=24. The New Zealand Europe Business Council maintains a website at http://www.eu.org.nz.

[1.80] Relations Between the EU and South Africa

The European Union has concluded a free trade agreement with South Africa. See *Agreement on Trade, Development and Cooperation*, Pretoria, 11 October 1999, OJ L 311, 4.12.1999, p 3. Under the agreement the EU and South Africa will establish a free trade area (Art 5(1)). Establishment of the free trade area will take place over a transitional period of up to 12 years (Art 5(2)). The free trade area will encompass freedom of movement of goods, services and capital (Art 5(3)).

Quantitative restrictions upon imports and exports and measures with an equivalent effect are to be abolished in relation to trade between South Africa and the EU (Art 19(1)). The parties will abolish charges that have an equivalent effect to customs duties (Art 9). The parties aim to fully liberalise movement of capital between the EU and South Africa (Art 33(2)). Other articles prohibit certain anti-competitive practices (Art 35) and various forms of public aid (Art 41). The agreement entered into force on 1 May 2004.

The EU and South Africa have also entered into treaties that specifically regulate the trade in wine and spirits. See *Agreement on Trade in Wine*, Paarl, 28 January 2002, OJ L 28, 30.1.2002, p 4; *Agreement on Trade in Spirits*, Paarl, 28 January 2002, OJ L 28, 30.1.2002, p 113. No trade disputes between South Africa and the EU have been brought through the WTO process. The European Union maintains a delegation to South Africa (http://www.eusa.org.za).

[1.81] Relations Between the EU and Other Common Law Jurisdictions

There are extensive trading links between the EU and India. For example, "[i]n 2003, actual EU foreign direct investment (FDI) in India amounted to EUR 535 million, as compared to EUR 337 million for the USA and EUR 76.5 million for Japan. The EU is also India's biggest trading partner, sourcing 16.7% of India's imports and taking 23.7% of exports in 2004." See *The European Union and India: A Strategic Partnership for the Twenty-First Century* (Directorate-General for External Relations, European Commission, 2006).

In October 2006 India and the European Union decided to begin negotiations towards a trade and investment treaty. See Written Answer to Starred Question 114, Lok Sabha Debates, 29 November 2006, available at http://loksabha.nic.in. The Agreement has not yet been signed or ratified. The EU has concluded a Customs Cooperation Agreement with India. See *Agreement on Customs Cooperation and Mutual Administrative Assistance in Customs Matters*, Brussels, 28 April 2004, OJ L 304, 30.9.2004, p 25. The EU and India have also entered into a scientific cooperation agreement. See *Agreement for Scientific and Technological Cooperation*, New Delhi, 23 November 2001, OJ L 213, 9.8.2002, p 30. The EU maintains a delegation to India (http://www.delind.ec.europa.eu).

Hong Kong is a separate customs territory. See Art 116, *Basic Law of Hong Kong SAR* (1990); Art 3(10) and Annex I(XI), *Agreement on the Future of Hong Kong (Joint Declaration between the United Kingdom and China)*, Peking, 19 December 1984, 1399 UNTS 33; 23 ILM 1366. The EU has entered into a Customs Cooperation Agreement with Hong Kong. See *Agreement on Cooperation and Mutual Administrative Assistance in Customs Matters*, Hong Kong, 13 May 1999, OJ L 151, 18.6.1999, p 21. The EU maintains an Office in Hong Kong and Macao (http://www.delhkg.ec.europa.eu), while the Hong Kong government has an Economic and Trade Office in Brussels (http://www.hongkong-eu.org).

There are no relevant bilateral trade agreements between the EU and Malaysia or Singapore. The websites of the EU delegations to Malaysia and Singapore are at http://www.delmys.ec.europa.eu (Malaysia) and http://www.delsgp.ec.europa.eu (Singapore).

[1.85] Political Institutions of the European Union

The EU has four main political institutions. They are:

The European Commission;
The Council;
The European Parliament; and
The European Council (Art 13(1) TEU).

[1.90] Commission

The European Commission consists of Commissioners appointed by the Governments of the Member States for a period of 5 years (Art 17(3) TEU). Until 2014 there will be one Commissioner from each Member State (Art 17(4) TEU). From 2014 the Commission will be reduced in size. The number of Commissioners will be two thirds of the total number of Member States, based upon a rotation of states (Art 17(5) TEU; Art 244 TFEU). The President of the Commission is elected by the European Parliament (Art 14(1) TEU).

Though the Commissioners have been proposed by their own national governments, they are completely independent in the performance of their duties. In the performance of their duties, the Commissioners "shall neither seek nor take instructions from any government or other institution" (Art 17(3) TEU). They are expected to develop policies which, while in the best interests of the EU, may be incompatible with the policies of their own national governments.

The Commission undertakes executive functions (Art 17(1) TEU). It ensures the application of the EU Treaties (Art 17(1) TEU). The Commission is thus the "guardian of the Treaty" because it ensures that the provisions of the Treaty are applied. See *Commission v Germany* (C-20/01) [2003] ECR I-3609 at [30]. The Commission has its own power to make secondary legislation.

The Commission operates according to a principle of collegiality under which decisions are adopted by "collective deliberation". All members of the Commission thus "bear collective responsibility on the political level for all decisions adopted". See *AKZO Chemie BV v Commission* (5/85) [1986] ECR 2585 at [30]; [1987] 3 CMLR 716; *Commission v BASF AG* (C-137/92 P) [1994] ECR I-2555 at [63]; *Commission v Germany* (C-191/95) [1998] ECR I-5449 at [39]; [1999] 2 CMLR 1265; *Re Ban on British Beef: Commission v France* (C-1/00) [2001] ECR I-9989 at [79]; [2002] 1 CMLR 22 (p 627).

The Commission can be removed en bloc by the European Parliament. If a motion of censure of the Commission is carried by a two-thirds majority of the votes cast, representing a majority of the component members of the Parliament, the entire Commission must resign (Art 234 TFEU). Thus far the Parliament has not availed itself of the opportunity to retire the Commission.

The mere threat of such action may be enough to persuade the Commission to resign. In March 1999 the entire Commission resigned following the presentation of the report of a Committee of Independent Experts regarding allegations of nepotism on the part of Commissioners. See Bulletin of the European Union 3-1999 at [1.10.11]–[2.3.1]; Angelina Topan, "The Resignation of the Santer-Commission: The Impact of 'Trust' and 'Reputation'" (2002) 6 no 14 *European Integration Online Papers*, http://eiop.or.at/eiop. No censure motion was brought: the Commission resigned to avoid being dismissed by such a motion. The Court of First Instance thus held that the Commissioners voluntarily resigned and were not dismissed through the censure mechanism. See *British Airways plc v Commission* (T-219/99) [2003] ECR II-5917 at [50]–[51]; [2004] 4 CMLR 19 (p 1008).

EU legislation often confers implementing powers upon the Commission. Various Committees monitor the implementation of legislation by the Commission pursuant to such powers. This Committee procedure is known as "comitology". The comitology procedure is governed by Council Decision 1999/468 laying down the Procedures for the Exercise of Implementing Powers Conferred on the Commission (OJ L 184, 17.7.1999, p 23). The Decision sets out criteria for the choice of the appropriate procedure for the adoption of implementation measures by the Commission (Art 2). These criteria are not legally binding, but if the Council does not comply with these criteria it must give reasons for its stance. See *Commission v Parliament* (C-378/00) [2003] ECR I-937 at [49]–[55]. The Commission is to provide regular information to the European Parliament about the proceedings of these Committees (Art 7(3)).

See generally, Koen Lenaerts and Amaryllis Verhoeven, "Towards a Legal Framework for Executive Rule-Making in the EU? The Contribution of the New Comitology Decision" (2000) 37 *Common Market Law Review* 645; Carl Fredrik Bergström, *Comitology: Delegation of Powers in the European Union and the Committee System* (Oxford: Oxford University Press, 2005); Gregor Schusterschitz and Sabine Kotz, "The Comitology Reform of 2006. Increasing the Powers of the European Parliament Without Changing the Treaties" (2007) 3 *European Constitutional Law Review* 68; Christine Neuhold, "Taming the 'Trojan Horse' of Comitology? Accountability issues of Comitology and the Role of the European Parliament" (2008) 12, 2 *European Integration Online Papers*, http://eiop.or.at/eiop.

The website of the Commission is at http://ec.europa.eu. See generally, Mike Cuthbert and Sarah Willis, "The European Commission: Should it be at the Heart of the Future European Union?" in Takis Tridimas and Paolisa Nebbia (eds), *European Union Law for the Twenty-First Century* (Oxford: Hart, 2004), I: 143; David Spence (ed), *The European Commission* (3rd ed, London: John Harper, 2006); Deirdre Curtin, *Executive Power in the European Union: Law, Practice, and Constitutionalism* (Oxford: Oxford University Press, 2009).

[1.95] Council

The Council undertakes a policy-making and coordinating role (Art 16(1) TEU). It exercises legislative and budgetary powers jointly with the Parliament (Art 16(1) TEU). The Council is composed of one national Minister from each Member State (Art 16(3) TEU). The members of the Council act on the instructions of their governments. In contrast to the Commission, the Council thus considers the interests of the Member States when making its decisions. The Presidency of the Council is rotated among the Member States (Art 16(9) TEU).

Except where otherwise provided by the Treaties, the Council acts by qualified majority. A qualified majority requires that a proposed law be supported by 55% of the Member States, which must constitute 65% of the total population of the EU. This system of double majority voting will begin to operate in 2014 (Art 16(4) TEU; but see derogations in Art 238 TFEU). Before that date the triple majority system applying under the Treaty of Nice will continue to apply. See generally, Stefaan van den Bogaert, "Qualified Majority Voting in the Council: First Reflections on the New Rules" (2008) 15 *Maastricht Journal of European and Comparative Law* 97. The Council's website is at http://www.consilium.europa.eu.

The Council is assisted by a Committee of Permanent Representatives, commonly known by its French acronym "Coreper". Coreper prepares the work of the Council (Art 16(7) TEU; Art 240(1) TFEU). The Committee is thus an "auxillary body of the Council" and is not an EU institution with powers of its own. See *Commission v Council* (C-25/94) [1996] ECR I-1469 at [26]. For a discussion of the Council, see Martin Westlake and David Galloway (eds), *The Council of the European Union* (3rd ed, London: John Harper, 2004).

[1.100] Parliament

The European Parliament is directly elected by universal suffrage for a 5 year term (Art 14(3) TEU). The Parliament represents the citizens of the EU (Arts 10(2), 14(2) TEU). The participation of the Parliament in the EU legislative process "reflects the fundamental democratic principle that the people should take part in the exercise of power through the intermediary of a representative assembly". See *Parliament v Council* (C-392/95) [1997] ECR I-3213 at [14]; [1997] 3 CMLR 896; see similarly, *Re Adoption of Decision 2006/1016: Parliament v Council* (C-155/07) [2009] 1 CMLR 23 (p 632) at [78].

The Parliament exercises political control over the executive institutions (Art 14(1) TEU). The Commission is obliged to answer questions asked of it by members of the Parliament (Art 230 TFEU). Members of the Commission may attend all meetings of the Parliament and shall, at their request, be heard on behalf of the Commission (Art 230 TFEU). The meetings of the Parliament shall be held in public (Art 15(2) TFEU).

The Parliament exercises legislative powers. The ordinary legislative procedure is as follows. The Commission submits a legislative proposal to the Parliament and Council. The Parliament adopts a position about the proposal and informs the Council. If the Council's approves the Parliament's position, the act is adopted. If the Council does not approve the Parliament's position, the Council informs the Parliament of its own position. If the Parliament approves the Council's position or does not make a decision, the act is treated as adopted. If the Parliament rejects the Council's position, the act is not adopted.

If the Parliament proposes amendments, those amendments are submitted to the Council and Commission. If the Council accepts those amendments, the act is approved. If the Council does not accept those amendments, a Conciliation Committee is formed. The Committee seeks to agree a joint text for the act. If the Committee does not agree upon a joint text, the legislative proposal is not adopted. If the Committee does agree upon a joint text, the Parliament and the Council have a period of 6 weeks in which to adopt that text. If the Parliament and the Council do not do so, the legislative proposal does not become law (Art 294 TFEU).

The Parliament also exercises budgetary powers. The Commission produces a draft annual budget which it submits to the Parliament and the Council. The Council adopts a position regarding the budget and informs the Parliament of that position. If the Parliament approves the Council's position or does not make a decision, the budget is treated as adopted. If the Parliament adopts amendments to the budget, a Conciliation Committee is formed. The Committee seeks to agree upon a joint text for the budget. If the Committee does agree upon a text, the Parliament and Council have 14 days in which to approve that text. If both the Parliament and the Council approve the text or both do not make a decision, the budget is treated as adopted.

The Commission shall submit a new draft budget in the following situations:

- if both the Parliament and Council reject the text, or one rejects it while the other does not make a decision, or
- if the Parliament rejects the text and the Council approves it, or
- if the Conciliation Committee cannot agree upon a joint text (Art 314 TFEU).

If a budget is not adopted before the start of the new financial year, the EU temporarily operates under the previous year's budget (Art 315 TFEU).

The Parliament also possesses important powers with regard to the admission of new Member States. A European state's application for EU membership is addressed to the Council, which acts unanimously after consulting the Commission and after receiving the assent of the Parliament (Art 49 TEU).

See generally, Richard Corbett, Francis Jacobs and Michael Shackleton, *The European Parliament* (7th ed, London: John Harper, 2007); Edward Best, "Legislative Procedures after Lisbon: Fewer, Simpler, Clearer?" (2008) 15 *Maastricht Journal of European and Comparative Law* 85; Julian Priestley, *Six Battles That Shaped Europe's Parliament* (London: John Harper, 2008); Sean Ó Neachtain, "The Growing Power of the European Parliament in Europe" (2008) 15 *Irish Journal of European Law* 19; Marianne van de Steeg, "Public Accountability in the European Union: Is the European Parliament able to hold the European Council Accountable?" (2009) 13 no 3 *European Integration Online Papers*, http://eiop.or.at/eiop. The Parliament's website is at http://www.europarl.europa.eu.

[1.105] European Council

The European Council sets the "general political directions and priorities" of the EU (Art 15(1) TEU). It does not exercise legislative power (Art 15(1) TEU). It is composed of the Heads of State or Government of each Member State (Arts 10(2), 15(2) TEU). Its decisions are generally made on a basis of consensus (Art 15(4) TEU).

Before the Treaty of Lisbon the office of President of the European Council was rotated among the Member States every 6 months. Since the Lisbon Treaty the President holds office for two and a half years and may be reappointed once only (Art 15(5) TEU). The President is chosen by a qualified majority vote of the European Council (Art 15(5) TEU). See generally, Jan Werts, *The European Council* (London: John Harper, 2008).

[1.110] EU Courts

There are several other EU institutions and bodies. These include courts, banks, committees and various officials.

The most important EU court is the European Court of Justice (ECJ). This chapter does not deal with the Court, which is considered in detail in Chapter 11. One point should be made at this stage. In this book the decisions of the Court are discussed as illustrations of how legal rules apply in practice rather than as precedents in the strict common law sense. EU law does not have a doctrine of *stare decisis*.

At this stage the form of citation for the Court's cases should be noted. The decisions of the Court are reported in an official series of law reports, the *European Court Reports* (Office for Official Publications of the European Communities, 1954-) (abbreviated ECR). Since 1990 the decisions of the Court of Justice and the Court of First Instance/General Court are reported in separate sections of these reports, each with different page numbering. The page references for the decisions of the Court of Justice are preceded by the Roman numeral I, while those for decisions of the Court of First Instance/General Court are preceded by the Roman numeral II. Since 2005 some minor decisions of both courts are not reported in full, but are merely noted with a brief summary of their subject matter. The page references for these decisions include an asterisk.

The Court's decisions are also published in unofficial reports such as the *Common Market Law Reports* (Sweet & Maxwell/Thomson, 1962-) (abbreviated CMLR). Since 2001 cases in the CMLR are no longer cited by the page number at which the case appears within the volume. Decisions are now cited by a case number based upon the order in which the cases are reported within the volume. For more convenient access to the printed volumes of these reports, in this book the page number is also given in brackets at the end of the citation. ECJ decisions are also reported in other less commonly available series. See *All England Law Reports: European Cases* (Butterworths, 1995-) (abbreviated All ER (EC)) and *European Community Cases* (CCH, 1989-) (abbreviated CEC). The Court's decisions are freely available on its website (http://curia.europa.eu).

Each judgment of the Court is divided into numbered paragraphs. These paragraphs are the same in each series of law reports and in the cases reproduced on the Internet. In this book specific points *within* decisions are cited by paragraph number rather than page numbers in the law reports. This form of citation will allow readers to find the same point in any of the major sources of the Court's judgments, including the Internet.

The Court of Auditors audits the finances of the EU (Art 285 TFEU). The Court examines whether revenue and expenditure have been properly handled (Art 287 TFEU). It consists of one national from every Member State (Art 285 TFEU). The members of the Court are appointed by the Council after consulting the Parliament. They serve for a term of 6 years (Art 282(2) TFEU). The Court's website is at http://eca.europa.eu.

[1.115] European Central Bank

The Treaties establish a European System of Central Banks (ESCB) and a European Central Bank (ECB) (Art 127(1) TFEU). The ESCB is composed of the ECB and the central banks of the Member States (Art 282(1) TFEU). The primary objective of the ESCB is to maintain price stability (Arts 127(1), 282(2) TFEU). The basic tasks of the ESCB are "to define and implement the monetary policy of the Union, to conduct foreign exchange operations..., to hold and manage the official foreign reserves of the Member States, [and] to promote the smooth operation of payment systems" (Art 127(3) TFEU).

The ECB has the exclusive right to authorise the issue of Euro banknotes within the Union, which may be issued by the ECB and the national central banks (Arts 128(1), 282(3) TFEU). To carry out its tasks the ECB is given legal personality (Art 282(3) TFEU). The ECB is independent of EU institutions and the governments of the Member States (Arts 130, 282(3) TFEU).

See generally, Chiara Zilioli and Martin Selmayr, "The European Central Bank: An Independent Specialized Organization of Community Law" (2000) 37 *Common Market Law Review* 591; José María Fernández Martin and Pedro Gustava Texeira, "The Imposition of Regulatory Sanctions by the European Central Bank" (2000) 25 *European Law Review* 391; Nikolaos Lavranos, "The Limited, Functional Independence of the ECB" (2004) 29 *European Law Review* 115; Chiara Zilioli and Martin Selmayr, "Recent Developments in the Law of the European Central Bank" (2006) 25 *Yearbook of European Law* 1; Chiara Zilioli and Martin Selmayr, "The Constitutional Status of the European Central Bank" (2007) 44 *Common Market Law Review* 355; Lorenzo Bini Smaghi, "Central Bank Independence in the EU: From Theory to Practice" (2008) 14 *European Law Journal* 446; Fabian Amtenbrink and Kees van Duin, "The European Central Bank before the European Parliament: Theory and Practice after 10 Years of Monetary Dialogue" (2009) 34 *European Law Review* 561. The ECB's website is at http://www.ecb.eu.

[1.120] EU Committees

There are also a number of EU Committees. The European Economic and Social Committee consists of representatives of various sectors of economic and social life, such as employers and employees (Art 300(2) TFEU). The Committee has advisory status (Art 13(4) TEU; Art 300(1) TFEU). It must be consulted by the Council or the Commission where the Treaty so provides (Art 304 TFEU). See generally, Stijn Smismans, "The European Economic and Social Committee: Towards Deliberative Democracy via a Functional Assembly" (2000) 4, 12 *European Integration Online Papers*, http://eiop.or.at/eiop; Martin Westlake, *The European Economic and Social Committee* (London: John Harper, 2009). The Committee's website is at http://eesc.europa.eu.

The Committee of the Regions is an advisory body representing the regional and local governments of the EU (Art 300(4) TFEU). The Commission and Council are required to consult the Committee regarding issues with a regional or local impact (Art 307 TFEU). The issues that require mandatory consultation include economic and social cohesion (Art 175 TFEU); trans-European networks in the fields of transport, energy and telecommunications (Art 172 TFEU); environment (Art 192(1) TFEU); public health (Art 168(4)–(5) TFEU); education and vocational training (Art 165(4) TFEU); culture (Art 167(5) TFEU); employment (Art 148(2) TFEU); energy (Art 194(2) TFEU); social policy and transport (Art 91 TFEU).

The Committee can challenge an EU legal measure before the ECJ as an infringement of its prerogatives (Art 263 TFEU). The Committee can also challenge an EU legislative act which has been adopted in breach of the requirement for mandatory consultation with the Committee (Art 8, Protocol (No 2) on the Application of the Principles of Subsidiarity and Proportionality). See generally, Jan Kottmann, "Europe and the Regions: Subnational Entity Representation at Community Level" (2001) 26 *European Law Review* 159; Tony Cole, "The Committee of the Regions and Subnational Representation to the European Union" (2005) 12 *Maastricht Journal of European and Comparative Law* 49. The Committee's website is at http://cor.europa.eu.

[1.125] Other Officials

The European Ombudsman investigates complaints of maladministration on the part of EU administrators. EU citizens, corporations and associations are able to bring such complaints (Art 228(1) TFEU). The Ombudsman provides a non-judicial alternative to litigation before the EU courts. However, a party must choose between pursuing a judicial or non-judicial remedy. They may not simultaneously avail themselves of both an action before the EU courts and a complaint before the Ombudsman. See *Lamberts v European Mediator* (T-209/00) [2002] ECR II-2203 at [65]–[66]; [2003] 1 CMLR 32 (p 942); *Internationaler Hilsfonds eV v Commission* (T-294/04) [2005] ECR II-2719 at [48].

The Ombudsman's website is at http://ombudsman.europa.eu. See generally, Alexandros Tsadiras, "The Position of the European Ombudsman in the Community System of Judicial Remedies" (2007) 35 *European Law Review* 607; Alexandros Tsadiras, "Navigating Through the Clashing Rocks: The Admissibility Conditions and the Grounds for Inquiry into Complaints by the European Ombudsman" (2007) 26 *Yearbook of European Law* 157.

Finally, the European Data Protection Supervisor monitors the observance by EU institutions of the privacy of personal information. See Hjelke Hijmans, "The European Data Protection Supervisor: The Institutions of the EC Controlled by an Independent Authority" (2006) 43 *Common Market Law Review* 1313. The Supervisor's website is at http://www.edps.europa.eu.

[1.130] Distribution of Powers Between the EU and the Member States

The EU may act only within the powers that are assigned to it by its founding Treaties (Art 5(2) TEU). The Member States retain competence over any matter to which jurisdiction has not been assigned to the EU by the Treaties (Arts 4(1), 5(2), TEU). The Member States must exercise their retained powers consistently with EU law. For example, the ECJ held that an exercise of a Member State's retained competence over foreign affairs had to be in accordance with an EU Regulation adopted under the common commercial policy. See *R v H M Treasury; Ex parte Centro-COM Srl* (C-124/95) [1997] ECR I-81 at [24]–[25]; [1997] 1 CMLR 555.

There are numerous similar examples regarding other retained competences:

- direct taxation: *Marks & Spencer plc v Halsey* (C-446/03) [2005] ECR I-10837 at [29]; [2006] 1 CMLR 18 (p 480); *Cadbury Schweppes plc v Commissioners of Inland Revenue* (C-196/04) [2006] ECR I-7995 at [40]; [2007] 1 CMLR 2 (p 43); *Rewe Zentralfinanz eG v Finanzamt Köln-Mitte* (C-347/04) [2007] ECR I-2647 at [21]; [2007] 2 CMLR 42 (p 1111); *Amurta v Belastingdienst* (C-379/05) [2007] ECR I-9569 at [16]; [2008] 1 CMLR 33 (p 851); *Skatteverket v A* (C-101/05) [2007] ECR I-11531 at [19]; [2009] 1 CMLR 35 (p 975); *Columbus Container Services BVBA & Co v Finanzamt Bielefeld-Innenstadt* (C-298/05) [2007] ECR I-10451 at [28]; [2009] 1 CMLR 8 (p 241);
- freedom of association: *International Transport Workers' Federation v Viking Line ABP* (C-438/05) [2007] ECR I-10779 at [39]–[40]; [2008] 1 CMLR 51 (p 1372) (retained competence over freedom of association);
- education: *Morgan v Bezirksregierung Köln* (C-11/06) [2007] ECR I-9161 at [24]; [2009] 1 CMLR 1 (p 1); and
- social security: *Richards v Secretary of State for Work and Pensions* (C-423/04) [2006] ECR I-3585 at [33]; [2006] 2 CMLR 49 (p 1242); *Government of the French Community v Flemish Government* (C-212/06) [2008] ECR I-1683 at [43]; [2008] 2 CMLR 31 (p 859); *Re Supply of Medicines by Pharmacies to Nearby Hospitals: Commission v Germany* (C-141/07) [2008] ECR I-6935 at [22]–[23]; [2008] 3 CMLR 48 (p 1479).

The EU has exclusive competence over a small number of subject matters. These are the customs union, competition rules for the internal market, monetary policy for the Eurozone, marine biological resource conservation and the common commercial policy (Art 3(1) TEU). In general the EU alone may adopt laws concerning these areas, though it may authorise the Member States to make laws regarding these matters (Art 2(1) TFEU).

The EU and the Member States share jurisdiction over a somewhat larger group of subject matters. These include the internal market, social policy, agriculture and fisheries, environment, consumer protection, transport, energy, and the area of freedom, security and justice (Art 4(2) TFEU). Where the EU and the Member States share jurisdiction over a matter, they will both have competence to make laws regarding that matter. However, the Member States exercise their competence to the extent that the EU has not exercised its jurisdiction over the matter. The Member States may also exercise jurisdiction if the EU has ceased to exercise its jurisdiction over the area (Art 2(2) TFEU).

The EU also has jurisdiction to "support, coordinate or supplement the actions of the Member States" concerning a number of other subject matters (Art 2(5) TFEU). These matters include human health, industry, culture, tourism, education and vocational training (Art 6 TFEU).

The TFEU also contains a "flexibility clause". Art 352(1) TFEU provides that "[i]f action by the Union should prove necessary, within the framework of the policies defined in the Treaties, to attain one of the objectives set out in the Treaties, and the Treaties have not provided the necessary powers" the Council may adopt "appropriate measures" upon a unanimous vote and with the consent of the Parliament. The requirement for unanimity in the Council constitutes a significant limitation upon this power. The exercise of this competence is also subject to the subsidiarity procedure discussed below (Art 352(2) TFEU). This power also does not provide a basis for the harmonisation of law where the Treaties exclude such harmonisation (Art 352(3) TFEU). See generally, Carl Lebeck, "Implied Powers Beyond Functional Integration? The Flexibility Clause in the Revised EU Treaties" (2008) 17 *Florida State University Journal of Transnational Law and Policy* 303.

For discussions of the distribution of powers between the EU and the Member States, see George A Bermann, "Competences of the Union" in Takis Tridimas and Paolisa Nebbia (eds), *European Union Law for the Twenty-First Century* (Oxford: Hart, 2004), I: 65; Anthony Dawes and Orla Lynskey, "The Ever-longer Arm of EC law: The Extension of Community Competence into the Field of Criminal Law" (2008) 45 *Common Market Law Review* 131; Gráinne de Búrca, *The Constitutional Limits of EU Action* (Oxford: Oxford University Press, 2008).

[1.135] Subsidiarity

The exercise of power by the EU must respect the principle of subsidiarity (Art 5(1) TEU). Subsidiarity is defined as follows: "in areas which do not fall within its exclusive competence, the Union shall act only if and insofar as the objectives of the proposed action cannot be sufficiently achieved by the Member States, either at central level or at regional and local level, but can rather, by reason of the scale or effects of the proposed action, be better achieved at Union level" (Art 5(3) TEU).

In *R v Secretary of State for Health; Ex parte British American Tobacco (Investments) Ltd* (C-491/01) [2002] ECR I-11453; [2003] 1 CMLR 14 (p 395) a Directive restricted the manufacturing and marketing of cigarettes. The Court considered whether the objective of the Directive could be better achieved at the EU level (at [180]). One objective of the Directive was to eliminate barriers to the operation of the internal market caused by differences between national laws regarding the manufacture, presentation and sale of cigarettes (at [181]). This objective could not be adequately achieved at the national level, given the great diversity of the previously applicable national laws (at [182]). The objective could thus be better achieved at the EU level (at [183]). The specific provisions adopted did not go beyond what was necessary to achieve this objective (at [184]).

Since the Treaty of Lisbon one third of all of the national legislatures are able to require the reconsideration of a proposed EU law that they believe does not respect the principle of subsidiarity. If the majority of national legislatures reject the proposed law, and the Council and Parliament demur to their objections, the proposed law will be blocked (Arts 6-7, Protocol (No 2) on the Application of the Principles of Subsidiarity and Proportionality). The ECJ has jurisdiction in actions alleging infringement of the principle of subsidiarity by an EU legal act (Art 8, Protocol).

See generally, Gabriël A Moens, "The Subsidiarity Principle and EC Directive 93/104" (Spring 1997) no 34 *Australia and World Affairs* 51; Gabriël A Moens, "The Subsidiarity Principle in European Union Law and the Irish Abortion Issue" in Guenther Doeker-Mach and Klaus A Ziegert (eds), *Law, Legal Culture and Politics in the Twenty First Century* (Stuttgart: Franz Steiner Verlag, 2004), 424; Christoph Ritzer, Marc Ruttloff and Karin Linhart, "How to Sharpen a Dull Sword—The Principle of Subsidiarity and its Control" (September 2006) 7, 9 *German Law Journal* 733, http://www.germanlawjournal.com; Gareth Davies, "Subsidiarity: The Wrong Idea, in the Wrong Place, at the Wrong Time" (2006) 43 *Common Market Law Review* 63; Florian Sander, "Subsidiarity Infringements before the European Court of Justice: Futile Interference with Politics or a Substantial Step towards EU Federalism?" (2006) 12 *Columbia Journal of European Law* 517; Philipp Kiiver, "The Treaty of Lisbon, the National Parliaments and the Principle of Subsidiarity" (2008) 15 *Maastricht Journal of European and Comparative Law* 77; Jean-Victor Louis, "National Parliaments and the Principle of Subsidiarity—Legal Options and Practical Limits" (2008) 4 *European Constitutional Law Review* 429.

[1.140] Proportionality

Proportionality is another limitation upon the powers of EU institutions. As expressed in the Treaty, under this principle the actions of the EU "shall not exceed what is necessary to achieve the objectives of the Treaties" (Art

5(4) TEU). According to the Court of Justice, this doctrine "requires that measures implemented through Community provisions be appropriate for attaining the objective pursued and must not go beyond what is necessary to achieve it". See *R (on the Application of ABNA Ltd) v Secretary of State for Health* (C-453/03) [2005] ECR I-10423 at [68]; [2006] 1 CMLR 48 (p 1290).

The decisions of the Court of Justice give an indication of how the concept of proportionality limits the exercise of power by EU institutions. In *United Kingdom v Council* (C-84/94) [1996] ECR I-5755; [1996] 2 CMLR 671 the Court noted that it did not review the expediency of EU legal measures, only their legality (at [23]). In reviewing the proportionality of EU measures concerning "political, economic and social policy choices", the Court is restricted to considering whether those measures are "vitiated by manifest error or misuse of powers, or whether the institution concerned has manifestly exceeded the limits of its discretion" (at [58]).

The Court has held that the EU legislature has to be accorded a "broad discretion" in areas that involve "political, economic and social choices". In such areas an EU measure will only be beyond power if it is "manifestly inappropriate having regard to the objective which the competent institutions are seeking to pursue". See *R v Secretary of State for Health; Ex parte British American Tobacco (Investments) Ltd* (C-491/01) [2002] ECR I-11453 at [123]; [2003] 1 CMLR 14 (p 395); *R (on the Application of International Air Transport Association) v Department for Transport* (C-344/04) [2006] ECR I-403 at [80]; [2006] 2 CMLR 20 (p 557); *Re Tobacco Advertising Directive 2003/33: Germany v Council* (C-380/03) [2006] ECR I-11573 at [145]; [2007] 2 CMLR 1 (p 1).

In *R v Secretary of State for Health; Ex parte British American Tobacco (Investments) Ltd* (C-491/01) [2002] ECR I-11453; [2003] 1 CMLR 14 (p 395) the challenged Directive regulated the manufacturing and marketing of cigarettes. The objectives of the Directive were to improve the functioning of the internal market and to safeguard public health (at [124]). One provision prohibited the circulation or marketing of cigarettes that contained more than a specified percentage of nicotine (at [15]). The Court held that this provision did not go beyond what was necessary to achieve the objective of safeguarding public health (at [126]).

The same provision also prohibited the manufacture of cigarettes that exceeded the maximum level of nicotine. This provision was designed to prevent the undermining of the internal market through the illegal trafficking of cigarettes. The Court held that this provision did not exceed the discretion to be afforded to the legislature (at [129]).

Another provision required manufacturers to print on the packaging both the nicotine level of the cigarette and a health warning (at [17]). These requirements were appropriate measures for the achievement of public health, as they would reduce tobacco consumption and guide consumers towards products with a lower toxicity (at [131]).

Another provision prohibited the use of certain words such as "light" or "mild" on the packaging (at [19]). The purpose of this prohibition was to protect consumers from being deceived into thinking that cigarettes bearing those descriptions were less harmful to health than other cigarettes (at [134], [138]). This prohibition was an appropriate measure for the protection of public health, since consumers would be given objective information about the hazardous nature of the product (at [135]–[136]). There was no less restrictive alternative means by which the objective of health protection could be as efficiently achieved (at [139]).

In *R (on the Application of ABNA Ltd) v Secretary of State for Health* (C-453/03) [2005] ECR I-10423 at [68]; [2006] 1 CMLR 48 (p 1290) the Directive at issue required that manufacturers of feedstuff for animals indicate the composition of the feed. This Directive was introduced in the wake of an outbreak of bovine spongiform encephalopathy (BSE), commonly known as "Mad Cow Disease". The Court held that an obligation to indicate the percentages of the ingredients in the feed was appropriate for enabling governments and farmers to respond to a potential food crisis. This requirement facilitated the rapid identification of potentially contaminated feedstuffs (at [76]). The provision was proportionate to the objective of protecting public health.

Another article provided that manufacturers must provide the exact composition by weight of the feed to any customer who requested that information (at [81]). This obligation jeopardised the commercial interests of manufacturers, potentially revealing their formulas to competitors (at [82]). The Court held that this provision was invalid (at [85]). It went beyond what was required to protect public health and was disproportionate to that objective. The other provision requiring the disclosure of the percentages of the ingredients was sufficient for the protection of public health (at [80]).

The Member States must also observe the principle of proportionality when they implement EU law. This obligation arises from the status of proportionality as a general principle of EU law. See *R (on the Application of Teleos Plc) v Commissioners of Customs and Excise* (C-409/04) [2007] ECR I-7797 at [45]; [2008] 1 CMLR 6 (p 98). See generally, Junko Ueda, "Is the Principle of Proportionality the European Approach? A Review and Analysis of Trade and Environment Cases before the European Court of Justice" (2003) 14 *European Business Law Review* 557.

[1.145] Cooperation Between and Secession of Member States

Member States are obliged to adopt any national legal acts that are necessary for the implementation of EU legal acts (Art 291(1) TFEU). The Treaties provide a framework for enhanced cooperation between some but not all EU Member States (Art 20 TEU; Art 326 TFEU). The legal acts that are created under this framework bind only the Member States that are participating in this cooperation (Art 20(4) TEU).

Amendments to the Treaties must be ratified by all Member States (Art 48(4), (6) TEU). The founding Treaties are "concluded for an unlimited period" (Art 53 TEU; Art 356 TFEU). However, a Member State may "secede" from the EU. Since the Treaty of Lisbon the Member States have the power to withdraw from the EU (Art 50 TEU).

[1.150] EU Legislation

The legal acts that may be adopted by EU institutions are listed in the TFEU:

> To exercise the Union's competences, the institutions shall adopt regulations, directives, decisions, recommendations and opinions.
>
> A regulation shall have general application. It shall be binding in its entirety and directly applicable in all Member States.
>
> A directive shall be binding, as to the result to be achieved, upon each Member State to which it is addressed, but shall leave to the national authorities the choice of form and methods.
>
> A decision shall be binding in its entirety. A decision which specifies those to whom it is addressed shall be binding only on them.
>
> Recommendations and opinions shall have no binding force. (Art 288 TFEU)

This Article thus recognises the following EU legal instruments:

(i) Regulations,
(ii) Directives,
(iii) Decisions,
(iv) Recommendations, and
(v) Opinions.

However, this provision does not provide an exhaustive list of EU legal acts. There are also legal acts *sui generis* (in a class of their own).

Regulations are directly applicable in the sense that they automatically become part of the domestic law of the Member States and need not be the subject of further legislative action by the national parliaments. Regulations have general application. The ECJ has stated that a regulation "is of general application..., for it is applicable to objectively determined situations and involves legal consequences for categories of persons viewed in a general and abstract manner". See *Zuckerfabrik Watenstedt GmbH v Council* (6/68) [1968] ECR 409 at 415; [1969] CMLR 26 at 37; *Sadam Zuccherifici v Council* (C-41/99) [2001] ECR I-4239 at [24]; *Yusuf v Council* (T-306/01) [2005] ECR II-3533 at [185]; [2005] 3 CMLR 49 (p 1335).

Directives stipulate a result which Member States are expected to achieve but leave the choice of means to the discretion of national authorities. The

Member States must "choose the most appropriate forms and methods to ensure the effectiveness of directives, in the light of their objective". See *Adeneler v Ellinikos Organismos Galaktos* [2006] ECR I-6057 at [93]; [2006] 3 CMLR 30 (p 867); *Boehringer Ingelheim KG v Swingward Ltd* (C-348/04) [2007] ECR I-3391 at [58]; [2007] 2 CMLR 52 (p 1445).

Achieving that result may not necessarily require the enactment of specific implementing legislation if national law is already sufficient for implementing the Directive. See *Commission v Netherlands* (C-144/99) [2001] ECR I-3541 at [17]; *Commission v Italy* (C-456/03) [2005] ECR I-5335 at [51]; *Commission v Luxembourg* (C-32/05) [2006] ECR I-11323 at [34]; *Kofoed v Skatteministeriet* (C-321/05) [2007] ECR I-5795 at [44]; [2007] 3 CMLR 33 (p 875).

An example is provided by Council Directive 2008/118 of 16 December 2008 concerning the general arrangements for excise duty (OJ L 9, 14.1.2009, p 12). It imposes upon Member States an obligation to "adopt and publish, not later than 1 January 2010, the laws, regulations and administrative provisions necessary to comply with this Directive" (Art 49(1)).

Decisions are exclusively directed at individual addressees and are the usual means by which EU institutions deal with individual cases. While Regulations have a general application, Decisions do not. See *Giuffrida v Council* (64/80) [1981] ECR 693 at [3], [6]; *Salerno v Commission* (87/77) [1985] ECR 2523 at [29].

Recommendations and opinions are not binding and give rise to no legal obligations on the part of the addressees. Recommendations are generally made on the initiative of EU institutions whereas opinions are delivered as a result of outside initiatives. An opinion may contain a general assessment of certain facts and may prepare the ground for subsequent legal proceedings.

EU legal acts begin with a preamble that sets out the general objective pursued by the measure. EU legislation must state the reasons upon which it is based (Art 296 TFEU). The purpose of the statement of reasons is to inform those affected by a legal act of the reasons for its adoption and to facilitate judicial review of the measure by the Court of Justice. See *Petrotub SA v Council* (C-76/00 P) [2003] ECR I-79 at [81]; *Re Tariff Preferences for Canned Tuna Imports: Spain v Council* (C-342/03) [2005] ECR I-1975 at [54]; [2006] 1 CMLR 8 (p 173); *Germany v Commission* (C-465/02) [2005] ECR I-9115 at [106]. The failure of a legal act to provide an adequate statement of reasons amounts to an infringement of an essential procedural requirement under Art 263 TFEU. See *Bertelsmann AG v Independent Music Publishers and Labels Association* (C-413/06 P) [2008] ECR I-4951 at [174]; [2008] 5 CMLR 17 (p 1073).

It is not necessary for the legislator to state "every relevant point of fact and law". See *Re Working Time Directive: United Kingdom v Council* (C-84/94) [1996] ECR I-5755 at [74]; [1996] 2 CMLR 671; *Re Tobacco Advertising Directive 2003/33: Germany v Council* (C-380/03) [2006] ECR I-11573 at [107]; [2007] 2 CMLR 1 (p 1). In the case of an act of general application, it is sufficient to state the "essential objective" of the act. It is not necessary to state the reason for every "technical choice" made by the legislator. See *R (on the Application of International Air Transport Association) v Department for Transport* (C-344/04) [2006] ECR I-403 at [67]; [2006] 2 CMLR 20 (p 557).

Council and Commission acts that impose pecuniary obligations are enforceable in the law of the Member States (Art 299 TFEU). For discussions of EU legal acts, see Sacha Prechal, *Directives in EC Law* (2nd ed, Oxford: Oxford University Press, 2005); Bartlomiej Kurcz and Adam Lazowski, "Two Sides of the Same Coin? Framework Decisions and Directives Compared" (2006) 25 *Yearbook of European Law* 177; Tadas Klimas and Jūratė Vaičiukaitė, "The Law of Recitals in European Community Legislation" (2008) 15 *ILSA Journal of International and Comparative Law* 61; Paul Craig, "The Legal Effect of Directives: Policy, Rules and Exceptions" (2009) 34 *European Law Review* 349.

Prior to the Treaty of Lisbon there was another category of legislation: framework decisions. This category was abolished along with the three pillar system to which it was linked. For discussions of this former type of legislation, see Carl Lebeck, "Sliding Towards Supranationalism? The Constitutional Status of EU Framework Decisions after *Pupino*" (May 2007) 8, 5 *German Law Journal* 502, http://www.germanlawjournal.com; Matthias Borgers, "Implementing Framework Decisions" (2007) 44 *Common Market Law Review* 1361; Eleanor Spaventa, "Opening Pandora's Box: Some Reflections on the Constitutional Effects of the Decision in *Pupino*" (2007) 3 *European Constitutional Law Review* 5; Alicia Hinarejos, "On the Legal Effects of Framework Decisions and Decisions: Directly Applicable, Directly Effective, Self-executing, Supreme?" (2008) 14 *European Law Journal* 620.

[1.155] Public Availability of EU Legal Acts

The legal principle of publicity requires the publication of certain EU legal acts in the *Official Journal of the European Union* (OJ). The TFEU provides that "Legislative acts shall be published in the Official Journal…. They shall enter into force on the date specified in them or, in the absence thereof, on the 20th day following that of their publication" (Art 297 TFEU).

An EU legal act cannot be enforced against individuals or corporations until it has been published in the Official Journal, giving those parties an opportunity to familiarise themselves with its requirements. See *Racke v Hauptzollamt Mainz* (98/78) [1979] ECR 69 at [15]. Thus an unpublished annex to a Regulation could not be enforced against individuals. See *Proceedings brought by Heinrich* (C-345/06) [2009] 3 CMLR 7 (p 219) at [42]–[43], [62].

EU legal acts must be published in all of the official languages of the Union. They may not be enforced against individuals or corporations in a Member State until they have been published in the official language of that State. See *Skoma-Lux sro v Celní ředitelství Olomouc* (C-161/06) [2007] ECR I-10841 at [38]; [2008] 1 CMLR 50 (p 1336).

EU legal acts are freely available on the Internet. An electronic version of the Official Journal is available at http://eur-lex.europa.eu/JOIndex.do. The Official Journal prints the texts of laws as they were originally adopted and does not consolidate amendments to the original legislation. Consolidated versions of EU legislation may be found at http://eur-lex.europa.eu. For preparatory materials for EU legislation, see http://ec.europa.eu/prelex/apcnet.cfm?CL=en. A frequently updated Directory of EU Legislation in Force is available at http://eur-lex.europa.eu/en/legis/index.htm. Summaries of numerous EU legal acts are available at http://europa.eu/legislation_summaries/index_en.htm.

Information about recent EU legislation may be found in the annual *General Report of the Activities of the European Union* (http://europa.eu/generalreport/en/welcome.htm) and the monthly *Bulletin of the European Union* (http://europa.eu/bulletin/en/welcome.htm). A directory of proposed legislation is available at http://eur-lex.europa.eu/en/prep/latest/index.htm. Numerous EU publications are freely available on the website of the EU Bookshop (http://bookshop.europa.eu).

There is also a "freedom of information" right of access to some internal documentation of EU institutions. EU citizens and businesses registered in an EU Member State have a right of access to EU documentation (Art 15(3) TFEU). See also Regulation 1049/2001 of the European Parliament and of the Council of 30 May 2001 regarding Public Access to European Parliament, Council and Commission documents (OJ L 145, 31.5.2001, p 43); Magdalena Elisabeth de Leeuw, "The Regulation on Public Access to European Parliament, Council and Commission Documents in the European Union: Are Citizens better off?" (2003) 28 *European Law Review* 324; Joni Heliskoski and Païvi Leino, "Darkness at the Break of Noon: The Case Law on Regulation No 1049/2001 on Access to Documents" (2006) 43 *Common Market Law Review* 735; Ian Harden, "The Revision of Regulation 1049/2001 on Public Access to Documents" (2009) 15 *European Public Law* 239.

[1.160] Conclusion

The EU constitutes an internal market with free movement of goods, persons, services and capital. It is a customs union without customs duties or quantitative restrictions on imports and exports between the Member States. The EU has a common currency, the Euro, which has been adopted by more than half of the Member States. Through a series of accession Treaties the EU has expanded to its present membership of 27 nations. There are extensive relations between the EU and many common law nations.

The European Commission undertakes executive functions and ensures the application of the founding Treaties. The Council and the directly elected European Parliament jointly exercise legislative and budgetary powers. The European Council is composed of the heads of state or government of the Member States. It sets the "general political directions and priorities" of the EU. The judicial power of the EU is exercised by courts such as the European Court of Justice and the Court of Auditors. There are many other EU institutions and bodies such as the European Central Bank, the Committee of the Regions and the European Ombudsman.

The EU may act only within the powers assigned to it by the founding Treaties. Competence over matters that are not assigned to the EU is retained by the Member States. The exercise of power by the EU must respect the principles of subsidiarity and proportionality. The most important EU legal instruments are Regulations, Directives and Decisions. Regulations are directly applicable. Directive must be implemented by the Member States. Decisions are directed to individual addresses. EU legislative acts must be published.

Further Reading

A. *Journals*

Cambridge Yearbook of European Legal Studies (Hart, 1998–).

Columbia Journal of European Law (Parker School of Foreign and Comparative Law, 1995–).

Common Market Law Review (Kluwer, 1963–).

ERA Forum (Springer, 2000–).

European Law Review (Sweet & Maxwell, 1975–).

European Law Journal (Blackwell, 1995–).

European Research Papers Archive (http://eiop.or.at/erpa).

Jean Monnet Working Papers (http://www.jeanmonnetprogram.org).

Yearbook of European Law (Oxford University Press, 1981–).

B. *General Works About EU Law*

Arnull, Anthony et al. *Wyatt and Dashwood's European Union Law* (5th ed, London: Sweet & Maxwell, 2006).

Barnard, Catherine. *The Substantive Law of the EU: The Four Freedoms* (2nd ed, Oxford: Oxford University Press, 2007).

Bermann, George A et al. *Cases and Materials on European Union Law* (2nd ed, St Paul, MN: West, 2002).

Berry, Elspeth and Sylvia Hargreaves. *European Union Law Textbook* (2nd ed, Oxford: Oxford University Press, 2007).

Bishop, Bernard. *European Union Law for International Business: An Introduction* (Port Melbourne, VIC: Cambridge University Press, 2009).

Chalmers, Damian; Christos Hadjiemmanuil, Giorgio Monti, and Adam Tomkins. *European Union Law: Text and Materials* (Cambridge: Cambridge University Press, 2006).

Craig, Paul and Grainne de Burca. *EU Law: Text, Cases and Materials* (4th ed, Oxford: Oxford University Press, 2007).

Davies, Karen. *Understanding European Union Law* (3rd ed, Abingdon, England: Routledge-Cavendish, 2007).

European Law Books (http://www.europeanlawbooks.org) (extensive collection of book reviews).

Fairhurst, John. *Law of the European Union* (7th ed, Harlow, Essex: Pearson, 2009).

Folsom, Ralph. *European Union Law in a Nutshell* (6th ed, St Paul, MN: Thomson/West, 2008).

Foster, Nigel G. *Foster on EU Law* (2nd ed, Oxford: Oxford University Press, 2009).

Foster, Nigel G. *Blackstone's EC Legislation 2006–2007* (17th ed, Oxford: Oxford University Press, 2006).

Gordon, Marcel. "Welcome to Europe – An Introduction to EU Law for Businesses" (2008) 5 *Macquarie Journal of Business Law* 171.

Hartley, T C. *The Foundations of European Community Law* (6th ed, Oxford: Oxford University Press, 2007).

Hartley, T C. *European Law in a Global Context: Text, Cases and Materials* (Cambridge: Cambridge University Press, 2004).

Horspool, Margot and Matthew Humphreys. *European Union Law* (5th ed, Oxford: Oxford University Press, 2008).

Kaczorowska, Alina. *European Union Law* (London: Routledge-Cavendish, 2008).

Kennedy, T P et al. *European Law* (4th ed, Oxford: Oxford University Press, 2008).

McDonnell, A M; Paul J G Kapteyn, Kamiel Mortelmans and Christian W A Timmermans. *The Law of the European Union and the European Communities* (4th rev ed, Alphen aan den Rijn: Kluwer, 2008).

Mathijsen, P S R F. *A Guide to European Union Law* (9th ed, London: Sweet & Maxwell, 2007).

Steiner, Jo; Lorna Woods and Christian Twigg-Flesner. *EU Law* (10th ed, Oxford: Oxford University Press, 2009).

Toth, A G (ed). *The Oxford Encyclopaedia of European Community Law* (Oxford: Clarendon Press, 1990–2005).

Weatherill, Stephen. *Cases and Materials on EU Law* (8th ed, Oxford: Oxford University Press, 2007).

C. Books About EU Institutions

Bogdandy, Armin von and Jürgen Bast (eds). *Principles of European Constitutional Law* (2nd ed, Oxford: Hart, 2009).

Chalmers, Damian and Adam Tomkins. *European Union Public Law: Text and Materials* (Cambridge: Cambridge University Press, 2007).

Curtin, Deirdre. *Executive Power in the European Union: Law, Practice and Constitutionalism* (Oxford: Oxford University Press, 2009).

Douglas-Scott, Sionaidh. *Constitutional Law of the European Union* (Harlow, Essex: Pearson, 2002).

Judge, David et al. *The European Parliament* (2nd ed, Basingstoke, Hampshire: Palgrave Macmillan, 2008).

Lasok, K P E. *Law and Institutions of the European Union* (7th ed, London: Butterworths, 2001).

Lenaerts, Koen; Piet van Nuffel and Robert Bray, *Constitutional Law of the European Union* (2nd ed, London: Sweet & Maxwell, 2005).

Peterson, John and Michael Shackleton (eds). *The Institutions of the European Union* (2nd ed, Oxford: Oxford University Press, 2006).

Tobler, Christa and Jacques Beglinge. *Essential EC Law in Charts* (Budapest: HVG-ORAC Publishing House, 2007). Companion website: http://www.eur-charts.eu.

D. Research Sources

Alford, Duncan E. "European Union Legal Materials: A Guide for Infrequent Users" (2005) 97 *Law Library Journal* 49.

Davies, Eric. *Eurojargon: A Dictionary of European Union Acronyms, Abbreviations and Terminology* (7th ed, Manchester: European Information Association, 2004).

Directory of EU Information Sources (18th ed, London: Routledge, 2009).

European Current Law Monthly Digest (Sweet and Maxwell, 1992–).

Eurovoc Theasaurus (Edition 4.2, Luxembourg: European Communities, 2007), available at http://eurovoc.europa.eu

Furlong, John. "How to find European Law: A Basic Introduction" (2009) 9 *Legal Information Management* 89.

Jones, Alistair. *A Glossary of the European Union* (Edinburgh: Edinburgh University Press, 2008).

Legal Bibliography of European Integration (Luxembourg: Court of Justice of the European Communities, 1981–), available at http://bookshop.europa.eu

Overy, Patrick. *European Information: A Guide to Official Sources* (Manchester: European Information Association, 2006).

Phinnemore, David and Lee McGowan. *A Dictionary of the European Union* (3rd ed, London: Routledge, 2006).

Chapter 2
Free Movement of Goods

[2.05] Introduction

Arts 28–32 and 34–36 TFEU deal with the free movement of goods, the customs union, the common customs tariff and the elimination of quantitative restrictions between Member States. These provisions are very important to non-EU companies that export goods to the European Union. Their importance stems from the fact that exporters need to know whether the EU has established a common external customs tariff with regard to their products and on whether their products gain free circulation throughout the Union once they have been landed in a Member State. This chapter deals with these issues.

[2.10] Customs Union

Art 28 TFEU provides for the establishment of an EU customs union. As part of this customs union the imposition by Member States of customs duties and charges having an equivalent effect are prohibited. Art 28(1) TFEU states that the "Union shall comprise a customs union which shall cover all trade in goods and which shall involve the prohibition between Member States of customs duties on imports and exports and of all charges having equivalent effect". As the goods themselves benefit from the prohibition of the imposition of customs duties, the nationality of the consignor, bailee or consignee is irrelevant.

The term "goods" in Art 28 has been given a broad meaning. In *Commission v Italy* (7/68) [1968] ECR 423; [1969] CMLR 1 it was held that goods are "products which can be valued in money and which are capable, as such, of forming the subject of commercial transactions" (at ECR 428; CMLR 8). In that case the Court held that articles of artistic or historic value fell within this definition (at ECR 428–429; CMLR 8). The Court has also held that recyclable and non-recyclable waste constitutes goods.

G. Moens, J. Trone, *Commercial Law of the European Union*,
Ius Gentium: Comparative Perspectives on Law and Justice 4,
DOI 10.1007/978-90-481-8774-4_2,

See *Commission v Belgium* (C-2/90) [1992] ECR I-4431 at [28]; [1993] 1 CMLR 365. Slot machines are also goods. See *Läärä v Kihlakunnansyyttäjä* (C-124/97) [1999] ECR I-6067 at [20], [24]; [2001] 2 CMLR 14 (p 257).

However, the definition of "goods" is not boundless. In *Jägerskiöld v Gustafsson* (C-97/98) [1999] ECR I-7319; [2000] 1 CMLR 235 the Court held that fishing rights were not goods. The fact that such rights may be traded does not make them goods (at [36]). The Court observed that intellectual property rights also did not fall within the concept of "goods" (at [38]). Similarly, lotteries are not "goods" but are considered to be "services". See *H M Customs and Excise v Schindler* (C-275/92) [1994] ECR I-1039 at [24]–[25]; [1995] 1 CMLR 4. Means of payment such as banknotes and coins are not goods. See *Criminal Proceedings Against Bordessa* (C-358/93) [1995] ECR I-361 at [12], [15]; [1996] 2 CMLR 13.

Art 30 TFEU stipulates that "Customs duties on imports and exports and charges having equivalent effect shall be prohibited between Member States. This prohibition shall also apply to customs duties of a fiscal nature." The customs union between the Member States thus requires not only the abolition of customs duties but also the abolition of charges having an effect equivalent to customs duties. In *Commission v Italy* (24/68) [1969] ECR 193; [1971] CMLR 611 the Court provided a classic description of the scope of Art 12 EC (now Art 30 TFEU):

> any pecuniary charge, however small and whatever its designation and mode of application, which is imposed unilaterally on domestic or foreign goods by reason of the fact that they cross a frontier, and which is not a customs duty in the strict sense, constitutes a charge having equivalent effect…, even if it is not imposed for the benefit of the State, is not discriminatory or protective in effect and if the product on which the charge is imposed is not in competition with any domestic product (at [9]).

See similarly, *Nygård v Svineafgiftsfonden* (C-234/99) [2002] ECR I-3657 at [19]; *Stadtgemeinde Frohnleiten v Bundesminister für Land- und Forstwirtschaft, Umwelt und Wasserwirtschaft* (C-221/06) [2007] ECR I-9643 at [27]; [2008] 1 CMLR 30 (p 779); *Brzeziński v Dyrektor Izby Celnej w Warszawie* (C-313/05) [2007] ECR I-513 at [22]; [2007] 4 CMLR 4 (p 121).

Arts 28 and 30 TFEU prohibit customs duties and charges having an equivalent effect. In *Commission v Italy* (C-173/05) [2007] ECR I-4917 an Italian regional government levied an "environmental tax" upon gas pipelines between Italy and Algeria, a non-Member State. The gas was distributed within Italy and exported to other Member States (at [41]). The chargeable event was the ownership of the pipelines (at [36]). The tax was assessed upon the volume of the gas in the pipelines (at [6]). The Court held that the tax was a charge with an effect equivalent to a customs duty (at [42]).

The Italian government argued that the tax was directed at the infrastructure (pipelines) rather than the goods (the gas). However, the Court pointed out that the tax was payable only if there was gas in the pipelines (at [37]). The tax was a fiscal charge levied upon goods imported from a non-Member State for distribution within a Member State or in transit to other Member States (at [39]). The tax infringed Arts 23 and 25 EC (now Arts 28 and 30 TFEU) (at [40]). The Italian government also argued that the tax was justifiable since its only purpose was environmental protection. The Court held that charges with an effect equivalent to a customs duty were prohibited whatever their purpose or the use to which the funds raised was put (at [42]).

The Court has exempted certain fees for services from the concept of charges with an equivalent effect. The Court has held that a charge will not have an equivalent effect "if it relates to a general system of internal dues applied systematically and in accordance with the same criteria to domestic products, and imported or exported products alike, if it represents payment for a specific service actually and individually rendered to the trader of a sum in proportion to that service or, in certain circumstances, if it is levied on account of inspections carried out for the purpose of fulfilling obligations imposed by Community law." See *Lamaire NV v Nationale Dienst voor Afzet van Land- en Tuinbouwprodukten* (C-130/93) [1994] ECR I-3215 at [14]; [1995] 3 CMLR 534.

The customs union implies free movement of goods within each Member State of the Union. Art 30 TFEU thus applies to charges levied upon goods that move from one region to another region of the same Member State, so customs duties and measures with an equivalent effect cannot be levied upon such goods. See *Jersey Produce Marketing Organisation Ltd v States of Jersey* (C-293/02) [2005] ECR I-9543 at [63]–[64]; [2006] 1 CMLR 29 (p 738).

In *Édouard Dubois et Fils SA v Garoner Exploration SA* (C-16/94) [1995] ECR I-2421; [1995] 2 CMLR 771 the Court held that Arts 9 and 12 EC (now Arts 28 and 30 TFEU) required the governments of the Member States to bear the costs of customs and other inspections associated with the movement of goods across national borders (at [14]). Thus a Member State may not require private parties to bear the costs of customs or veterinary inspections of goods crossing national frontiers (at [19]).

[2.15] Common Customs Tariff

Art 28(1) TFEU also provides for the adoption by EU Member States of a common customs tariff "in their relations with third countries". The Court has stated the common customs tariff is "intended to achieve an equalization of customs charges levied at the frontiers of the Community on products imported from third countries, in order to avoid any deflection of trade in relation with those countries and any distortion of free internal circulation or of competitive conditions". See *Sociaal Fonds voor de*

Diamantarbeiders v Indiamex NV (37/73) [1973] ECR 1609 at [9]; [1976] 2 CMLR 222; *Société Cadi Surgelés v Ministre des Finances* (C-126/94) [1996] ECR I-5647 at [14]; [1997] 1 CMLR 795; *Commission v Italy* (C-173/05) [2007] ECR I-4917 at [29].

The common customs tariff is defined in considerable detail in Art 33(2) of the Community Customs Code. See Regulation 450/2008 of the European Parliament and of the Council of 23 April 2008 laying down the Community Customs Code (OJ L 145, 4.6.2008, p 1). This Regulation provides that goods are subject to customs supervision upon their entry into the EU customs territory (Art 91(1)).

Goods are valued under the Community Customs Code. The transaction value is the price actually paid or payable when the goods were sold for export to the country of importation (Art 41(1)). If the circumstances are such that the invoice price cannot be relied upon, the Regulation provides for an alternative method of calculation (Art 42).

An EU Decision provides that the Commission and the Member States must establish electronic custom systems for the exchange of information set out in customs declarations and certificates. See Art 1, Decision 70/2008 of the European Parliament and of the Council of 15 January 2008 on a paperless environment for customs and trade (OJ L 23, 26.1.2008, p 21).

The EU is party to the *International Convention on the Harmonized Commodity Description and Coding System*, Brussels, 14 June 1983, 1503 UNTS 3; [1988] ATS 30; OJ L 198, 20.7.1987, p 3. The Convention was ratified by the EEC on 22 September 1987: 1503 UNTS 168. This treaty is the basis for Council Regulation 2658/87 on the tariff and statistical nomenclature and on the Common Customs Tariff (OJ L 256, 7.9.1987, p 1).

Once imported into the Union, goods exported by third countries are able to circulate freely within any part of the EU. Art 28(2) TFEU stipulates that the rules concerning the customs union and customs cooperation also "apply to products originating in Member States and to products coming from third countries which are in free circulation in Member States." In accordance with Art 29 TFEU such products are considered "to be in free circulation in a Member State if the import formalities have been complied with and any customs duties or charges having equivalent effect which are payable have been levied in that Member State, and if they have not benefited from a total or partial drawback of such duties or charges".

[2.20] Rules of Origin

For the purpose of the application of the common customs tariff, it is necessary to determine the origin of goods. Art 36(2) of the Community Customs Code provides: "Goods the production of which involved more than one country or territory shall be deemed to originate in the country or territory where they underwent their last substantial transformation."

A different definition appeared in the predecessors to this Regulation. See Art 5, Council Regulation 802/68 of 27 June 1968 on the common definition of the concept of the origin of goods (OJ L 148, 28.6.1968, p 1); Art 24, Council Regulation 2913/92 of 12 October 1992 establishing the Community Customs Code (OJ L 302, 19.10.1992, p 1). The 1968 definition provided: "A product in the production of which two or more countries were concerned shall be regarded as originating in the country in which the last substantial process or operation that is economically justified was performed..."

The former definitions included the additional requirement that the last substantial process was "economically justified". The case law relates to these repealed definitions. However, it may give some insight into the issues that may arise under the new definition.

In *Gesellschaft fur Überseehandel mbH v Handelskammer Hamburg* (49/76) [1977] ECR 41 the Court stated that "the determination of the origin of goods must be based on a real and objective distinction between raw material and processed product, depending fundamentally on the specific material qualities of each of those products" (at [5]). The last process "is only "substantial"... if the product resulting therefrom has its own properties and a composition of its own, which it did not possess before that process or operation" (at [6]). The Court decided that the cleaning, grinding and packaging of a product within the EU did not confer Union origin upon those goods.

However, a more complete manufacturing process would confer EU origin upon the goods. In *Yoshida Nederland BV v Kamer van Koophandel en Fabrieken voor Friesland* (34/78) [1979] ECR 115; [1979] 2 CMLR 747 the Court held that assembly operations which were economically justified, carried on in an appropriately equipped factory, and which resulted in a new product coming into existence, conferred a Community origin upon the goods. The companies concerned were manufacturers of zip fasteners. Plants in the Community wove, bound and dyed the tapes, pressed the metal scoops and fixed them to the tapes, fixed the end lugs, inserted a slider and cut the zippers to the appropriate length. The actual slider was imported from Japan. The Court held that the factories were manufacturing a new product which was quite distinct from the products from which it was made. The slider was only one item from which the whole was made and its price would not be decisive in the search for the origin of the goods. The slider would not be of great utility until integrated into the zip fastener, which was done in the Community. The zip fasteners were EU goods (at [11]).

[2.25] Added Value

The former Regulation did not refer to the amount of value added to the goods. This is an important element in the search for their origin, especially where the goods have not changed their intrinsic nature. In *Criminal*

Proceedings Against Cousin (162/82) [1983] ECR 1101; [1984] 2 CMLR 780 it was held that the gassing, dying, mercerising and spooling of cotton yarn, through which the value of the yarn had increased by 159%, could confer EU origin notwithstanding that the goods were still cotton yarn (at [9]–[10]).

In *Brother International GmbH v Hauptzollamt Giessen* (26/88) [1989] ECR 4253; [1990] 3 CMLR 658 the Court considered whether the assembly of previously manufactured parts originating in another country was sufficient to confer on the resulting product the origin of the country of assembly. The Court had to determine whether mere assembly constituted a "substantial process or operation".

The Court held that simple assembly operations which do not require specially equipped plants or a skilled workforce do not confer upon the resulting goods the origin of the country of assembly. An assembly operation confers origin only if "it represents from a technical point of view and having regard to the definition of the goods in question the decisive production stage during which the use to which the component parts are to be put becomes definite and the goods in question are given their specific qualities" (at [19]).

Where consideration on the basis of technical criteria is not decisive in the determination of the origin of goods, "it is necessary to take account of the value added by the assembly as an ancillary criterion" (at [20]). In particular, the Court decided that an added value of less than 10% was insufficient to confer on the resulting goods the origin of the country of assembly. The Court stated:

> the mere assembly of . . . goods in one country from previously manufactured parts originating in the other is not sufficient to confer on the resulting product the origin of the country of assembly if the value added there is appreciably less than the value imparted in the other country. . . . in such a situation value added of less than 10% . . . cannot in any event be regarded as sufficient to confer on the finished product the origin of the country of assembly (at [23]).

[2.30] Elimination of Quantitative Restrictions Between Member States

Art 34 TFEU (formerly Art 30 EC) stipulates that "Quantitative restrictions on imports and all measures having equivalent effect shall be prohibited between Member States". Art 35 TFEU contains a similar prohibition of quantitative restrictions upon exports.

In *Geddo v Ente Nazionale Risi* (2/73) [1973] ECR 865; [1974] 1 CMLR 13 the Court indicated that "measures which amount to a total or partial restraint of . . . imports, exports, or goods in transit" constitute quantitative restrictions (at [7]). If a measure adopted by a Member State restricts the quantity of goods which may be imported into that State, the measure would involve a quantitative restriction upon goods and would thus breach Art 34.

In *Rosengren v Riksåklagaren* (C-170/04) [2007] ECR I-4071; [2007] 3 CMLR 10 (p 239) the retail sale of alcohol was carried out by a state monopoly. Alcohol could only be imported by the state monopoly and authorized wholesalers. Swedish law prohibited the importation of alcohol by individuals, though small quantities could be brought back by travelers. An individual could only obtain alcohol from another country by placing an order with the state monopoly. The monopoly could refuse to fulfill an order from a customer (at [5], [16]).

The Court held that the importation system was a quantitative restriction upon imports since individuals were prohibited from importing alcohol and the monopoly did not have a counter-balancing obligation to import alcohol for customers in every case (at [33]). In any event, importation through the state monopoly had many inconveniences that would not have been faced by an individual who imported alcohol on their own (at [34]). The price charged by the state monopoly for imported alcohol also included a 17% surcharge that an individual would not have had to pay if they imported alcohol by themselves (at [35]).

[2.35] Measures with an Equivalent Effect

Most of the decided cases concern measures having an effect equivalent to a quantitative restriction. National restrictions upon goods that have been exported with the sole intention of reimportation so as to circumvent a national law do not constitute measures with an equivalent effect. See *Association des Centres distributeurs Édouard Leclerc v SARL "Au blé vert"* (229/83) [1985] ECR 1 at [27]; [1985] 2 CMLR 286; *R v Competition Commission; Ex parte Milk Marque Ltd* (C-137/00) [2003] ECR I-7975 at [115]; [2004] 4 CMLR 6 (p 293); *Deutscher Apothekerverband EV v 0800 Docmorris NV* (C-322/01) [2003] ECR I-14887 at [128]–[129]; [2005] 1 CMLR 46 (p 1205).

The Court has defined a measure with an equivalent effect as "all trading rules enacted by Member States which are capable of hindering, directly or indirectly, actually or potentially, intra-Community trade". See *Procureur du Roi v Dassonville* (8/74) [1974] ECR 837 at [5]; [1974] 2 CMLR 436; *Vereinigte Familiapress Zeitungsverlags- und Vertriebs GmbH v Heinrich Bauer Verlag* (C-368/95) [1997] ECR I-3689 at [7]; [1997] 3 CMLR 1329; *Rosengren v Riksåklagaren* (C-170/04) [2007] ECR I-4071 at [32]; [2007] 3 CMLR 10 (p 239); *Dynamic Medien Vertriebs GmbH v Avides Media AG* (C-244/06) [2008] ECR I-505 at [26]; [2008] 2 CMLR 23 (p 651).

A broad range of regulations fall within the concept of measures having an equivalent effect. Art 34 prohibits national measures that impact upon the sale of goods, such as advertising codes, purity codes, and "buy local products campaigns". Art 34 may be infringed by rules "relating to [the] designation, form, size, weight, composition, presentation, labeling, [and] packaging" of goods. See *Criminal Proceedings Against Keck* (C-267/91) [1993] ECR I-6097 at [15]; [1995] 1 CMLR 101; *Meyhui NV v Schott Zwiesel Glaswerke AG* (C-51/93) [1994] ECR I-3879 at [10]; *Colim NV v Bigg's Continent Noord NV* (C-33/97) [1999] ECR I-3175 at [38]; [2000] 2 CMLR 135; *Dynamic Medien Vertriebs GmbH v Avides Media AG* (C-244/06) [2008] ECR I-505 at [27]; [2008] 2 CMLR 23 (p 651).

The Court will look beyond the form to the substance of a measure to see if Art 34 has been breached. The cases concern a wide variety of national regulations. Only a selection of the challenged laws can be examined herein.

[2.40] Import Authorisation

In *Freistaat Bayern v Eurim-Pharm GmbH* (C-347/89) [1991] ECR I-1747; [1993] 1 CMLR 616 the Court held that a national requirement for authorisation to import certain products was a measure with an equivalent effect (at [24]).

[2.45] Production Quotas

In *Officier van Justitie v van Haaster* (190/73) [1974] ECR 1123; [1974] 2 CMLR 521 the ECJ held that national production quotas amounted to measures having an effect equivalent to quantitative restrictions (at [17]).

[2.50] Transport Restrictions

In *Re Ban on Night Lorry Traffic: Commission v Austria* (C-320/03) [2005] ECR I-9871; [2006] 2 CMLR 12 (p 337) an Austrian province prohibited trucks of greater than a certain tonnage from traveling along a section of one of the main highways between Germany and Italy (at [68]). The Court held that this prohibition hindered the free movement of goods. The prohibition was an obstacle to free movement despite the availability of alternative routes (at [67]). It constituted a measure having an equivalent effect (at [69]).

[2.55] Maximum Prices

Legislation fixing a maximum retail price for a product is also a measure having an effect equivalent to a quantitative restriction. In *Società SADAM v Comitato Interministeriale dei Prezzi* (88–90/75) [1976] ECR 323; [1977] 2 CMLR 183 the Court stated:

> A maximum price ... constitutes ... a measure having an effect equivalent to a quantitative restriction, especially when it is fixed at such a low level that, having regard to the general situation of imported products compared to that of domestic products, dealers wishing to import the product in question into the member-State concerned can do so only at a loss (at [15]).

[2.60] Packaging, Labeling and Product Description Rules

In *Walter Rau Lebensmittelwerke v de Smedt PVBA* (261/81) [1982] ECR 3961; [1983] 2 CMLR 496 a Belgian law required that margarine be sold in cube shaped packs (at [3]). The asserted purpose of this requirement was to allow a ready distinction to be made between butter and margarine (at [5]). However, the practical effect was to make margarine more expensive, thereby making it more difficult for margarine manufacturers to compete with butter producers. Specially packaging margarine for the small Belgian market was relatively uneconomic (at [3]). The ECJ held that the requirement for cube shaped tubs was a measure having an effect equivalent to a quantitative restriction (at [20]).

In *PIAGEME v BVBA Peeters* (C-369/89) [1991] ECR I-2971; [1993] 3 CMLR 725 a company located in the Flemish (Dutch) speaking region of Belgium sold mineral water in bottles labeled in French and German only (at [2]). Belgian legislation required that the labels of foodstuffs must be written in the language of the region in which the products are sold (at [3]). The Court held that this law violated Art 30 EC (now Art 34 TFEU) when another language could be easily understood by the purchasers (at [17]). See similarly, *Criminal Proceedings Against Geffroy* (C-366/98) [2000] ECR I-6579 at [24]–[28]; [2001] 2 CMLR 25 (p 525).

In *Re Marketing of Chocolate: Commission v Spain* (C 12/00) [2003] ECR I-459; [2005] 2 CMLR 33 (p 799) Spanish legislation prohibited the marketing as chocolate of products that contained fats other than cocoa butter. Such products could only be marketed as "chocolate substitute" (at [81]). In some other Member States these products could be legally marketed as chocolate (at [78]).

The Court observed that such a rule made the marketing of the product more difficult, inhibiting interstate trade (at [79]). The rule might force manufacturers to use different packaging for different national markets, leading to higher packaging costs and inhibiting interstate trade (at [80]). The product name "chocolate substitute" was likely to have a negative impact upon consumer views about the product (at [81]). The obligatory use of product names that are less well regarded by consumers impedes interstate trade (at [82]). See similarly, *De Groot en Slot Allium BV v Ministere de l'Economie, des Finances et de l'Industrie* (C-147/04) [2006] ECR I-245 at [74]; [2009] 1 CMLR 22 (p 603).

[2.65] Indications of Origin

In *Procureur du Roi v Dassonville* (8/74) [1974] ECR 837; [1974] 2 CMLR 436 a Belgian statute prohibited the importation and sale of spirits that carried an authorised designation of origin, unless the importer or seller possessed a certificate of origin. The product in question was Scotch whisky. The Belgian authorities only accepted as a valid certificate of origin a document issued by the British customs authorities. However, the defendant had made a parallel import of some bottles of Scotch whisky into Belgium from France.

The Court held that the law constituted a measure having an effect equivalent to quantitative restrictions. A parallel importer who imported whisky which was already in free circulation in France could only obtain the document with great difficulty, "unlike the importer who imports directly from the producer country" (at [4]). A parallel importer may find it cumbersome to obtain the relevant document from the British customs authorities after the product had already been exported to another Member State.

In *Re Origin Marking of Retail Goods: Commission v United Kingdom* (207/83) [1985] ECR 1201; [1985] 2 CMLR 259 it was held that the United Kingdom infringed Art 34 TFEU by prohibiting the retail sale of certain goods imported from other Member States unless they are marked with an indication of origin. The Court stated that "it has to be recognised that the purpose of indications of origin... is to enable consumers to distinguish between domestic and imported products and that this enables them to assert any prejudices which they may have against foreign products" (at [17]).

The Court added that "the origin-marking requirement... also has the effect of slowing down economic interpenetration in the Community by handicapping the sale of goods produced as the result of a division of labour between Member-States" (at [17]). The United Kingdom had argued unsuccessfully that the legislation was necessary to protect consumers (at [19]). The Court considered that the manufacturers, as opposed to the Member State, could affix an indication of origin onto the relevant products (at [21]).

[2.70] Advertising Restrictions

In *Buet v Ministere Public* (C-382/87) [1989] ECR 1235; [1993] 3 CMLR 659 the Court observed that forcing a trader to cease using an advertising or sales promotion scheme that it considers to be effective may constitute an obstacle to imports (at [7]). A right to cancel a doorstop sale was normally sufficient to protect against ill-considered purchases (at [12]). However, since doorstep sales of educational services exposed potential customers to a greater risk of long term harm from an ill-considered purchase, a complete ban upon such sales did not infringe Art 30 EC (now Art 34 TFEU) (at [14]–[15]).

In *GB-INNO-BM NV v Confédération du Commerce Luxembourgeois ASBL* (362/88) [1990] ECR I-667; [1991] 2 CMLR 801 the Court held that advertising lawfully distributed in another Member State could not be made subject to special national rules (at [18]). National legislation that prohibits or restricts advertising could restrict the volume of trade by affecting marketing opportunities (at [7]).

[2.75] Prohibition of Prize Competitions

In *Vereinigte Familiapress Zeitungsverlags- und Vertriebs GmbH v Heinrich Bauer Verlag* (C-368/95) [1997] ECR I-3689; [1997] 3 CMLR 1329 Austrian law prohibited magazine competitions offering prizes (at [2]). The Court held that since this law required interstate traders to change the contents of their magazines if they wished to sell them in Austria, it impeded the access of foreign magazines to the Austrian market and thus hindered the free movement of goods (at [12]).

[2.80] Censorship Classification

In *Dynamic Medien Vertriebs GmbH v Avides Media AG* (C-244/06) [2008] ECR I-505; [2008] 2 CMLR 23 (p 651) a German statute provided that DVDs for sale by mail order must have been classified by an official body and contain a sticker stating the age classification issued by that body (at [2]). The Court held that these requirements made the task of importing DVDs more difficult and costly, which might deter businesses in other Member States from selling such products in the German market (at [34]). The law could potentially constitute a measure with an equivalent effect.

[2.85] Sunday Closing Laws

In *Stoke-on-Trent City Council v B & Q plc* (C-169/91) [1992] ECR I-6635; [1993] 1 CMLR 426 the Court confirmed that while laws providing that shops must close on Sundays reduced the trade of those shops, the reduction affected both national and imported goods and did not advantage local goods over imports (at [10]). These laws were directed towards fulfilling a permissible aim under EU law: the protection of national cultural characteristics (at [11]). Such laws did not infringe Art 30 EC (now Art 34 TFEU) "where the restrictive effects on Community trade which might result from them did not exceed the effects intrinsic to such rules" (at [12]).

[2.90] Creation of Individual Rights

Art 34 TFEU can be relied upon by an individual in a national court to defeat the purported effect of incompatible national legislation. The ECJ confirmed the direct effect of Art 30 EC (now Art 34 TFEU) in *Iannelli & Volpi SpA v Ditta Paolo Meroni* (74/76) [1977] ECR 557; [1977] 2 CMLR 688. The Court stated:

> The prohibition of quantitative restrictions and measures having equivalent effect ... is mandatory and explicit and its implementation does not require any subsequent intervention of the Member States or Community institutions. The prohibition therefore has direct effect and creates individual rights which national courts must protect (at [13]).

See similarly, *Pigs Marketing Board (Northern Ireland) v Redmond* (83/78) [1978] ECR 2347 at [66]–[67]; [1979] 1 CMLR 177; *Brasserie du Pecheur SA v Germany* (C-46/93) [1996] ECR I-1029 at [54]; [1996] 1 CMLR 889.

[2.95] Arts 120 and 121 TFEU

Art 121(1) TFEU provides that "Member States shall regard their economic policies as a matter of common concern and shall coordinate them within the Council". In *Società SADAM v Comitato Interministeriale dei Prezzi* (88–90/75) [1976] ECR 323; [1977] 2 CMLR 183 the Court held that a Member State could not rely on Art 103 EC (now Art 121 TFEU) to avoid the implementation of Art 30 EC (now Art 34 TFEU) (at [13]). The Treaty further states that Member States should "conduct their economic policies with a view to contributing to the achievement of the objectives of the Union" and "act in accordance with the principle of an open market economy with free competition, favouring an efficient allocation of resources" (Art 120 TFEU).

[2.100] Treaty Exceptions to Art 34 TFEU

Art 36 TFEU provides an exception to Art 34. It stipulates that Art 34 "shall not preclude prohibitions or restrictions on imports ... justified on grounds of public morality, public policy or public security; the protection of health and life of humans, animals or plants; the protection of national treasures possessing artistic, historic or archaeological value; or the protection of industrial and commercial property". However, these "prohibitions or restrictions shall not ... constitute a means of arbitrary discrimination or a disguised restriction on trade between Member States".

There is an extensive jurisprudence concerning Art 36 TFEU. However, it suffices to give a few examples of the operation of this Article. Public morality is one of the permitted justifications. In *Conegate Ltd v Customs and Excise Commissioners* (121/85) [1986] ECR 1007; [1986] 1 CMLR 739 the British customs authorities had seized inflatable love dolls imported from Germany (at [2]). The English importer argued that his right to import these goods was protected by Art 30 EC (now Art 34 TFEU) (at [3]). In contrast, the United Kingdom relied upon the "public morality" exception of Art 36 EC (now Art 36 TFEU). The manufacture of such products was not prohibited in the United Kingdom (at [13]). The Court held that a Member State could not invoke the public morality exception where the manufacture and distribution of the product was not prohibited by its national law (at [16], [20]).

If the national legislation with regard to the transmission, distribution or display of these products is non-discriminatory and applies to all interstate and local products, the law would fall within the public morality exception in Art 36 TFEU. In *Quietlynn Ltd v Southend Borough Council* (C-23/89) [1990] ECR I-3059; [1990] 3 CMLR 55 a British law gave local authorities the power to decide that trade in sex articles could only be carried on with a licence (at [3]). The law effectively prohibited the sale of lawful sex articles by unlicensed establishments. The Court pointed out that "in similar cases concerning rules governing the marketing of certain products the Court has held Article 30 of the Treaty not to be applicable" (at [10]).

The protection of health is a permitted justification under Art 36 TFEU. The Court has upheld measures protecting against human exposure to dangerous substances. In *Kemikalieinspektionen v Toolex Alpha AB* (C-473/98) [2000] ECR I-5681 a national law prohibited the use of the hazardous chemical trichloroethylene for industrial purposes. An undertaking could obtain an exemption from the prohibition, which would be subject to compliance with safety conditions (at [34]). The Court held that in view of the difficulty of ascertaining the level of exposure at which exposure to this chemical was hazardous, this restriction was justifiable on the ground of protecting human health (at [45]). Similarly, in *Criminal Proceedings Against Nijman* (125/88) [1989] ECR 3533; [1991] 1 CMLR 92 the prohibition of unauthorized plant protection products was held to be justifiable on the ground of the protection of human health (at [13]–[15]).

The deterrence of the harmful effects of alcohol consumption falls within the protection of public health. See *Ahokainen v Virallinen syyttäjä* (C-434/04) [2006] ECR I-9171 at [28]; [2007] 1 CMLR 11 (p 345); *Rosengren v Riksåklagaren* (C-170/04) [2007] ECR I-4071 at [40]; [2007] 3 CMLR 10 (p 239).

In *Rosengren* Swedish law prohibited the importation of alcohol by individuals. An individual could only obtain alcohol from another country by placing an order with the state monopoly. The Court held that a national law would not fall within the Art 36 exception if health could be protected as effectively by a law that was less restrictive of interstate trade (at [43]).

The Swedish government argued that the law was justified by a need to limit alcohol consumption (at [44]). The Swedish law did not specify the grounds upon which the monopoly could decline to import alcohol for an individual. The facts before the Court did not show that in practice the monopoly refused to import alcohol for an individual due to their excessive consumption (at [46]). The prohibition had only a marginal effect upon the limitation of alcohol consumption (at [47]).

In *R v Medicines Control Agency; Ex parte Rhône-Poulenc Rorer Ltd* (C-94/98) [1999] ECR I-8789; [2000] 1 CMLR 409 a medicine had received marketing authorization in the country of export. The marketing authorization for that product had been withdrawn in the country of import because authorization had been given for a new product with the same active ingredients and therapeutic effects (at [15]–[16]). A company imported the earlier version of the medicine, which no longer had marketing authorization in the country of import.

The Court held that where the authorities of the country of import had granted a previous marketing authorization and already held all necessary information regarding the safety and effectiveness of the product, the protection of health did not require that the importer submit the same information once again for a practically identical product (at [26]). The authorities of the country of import must not hinder parallel importation by requiring the importer to fulfill the requirements applicable when a company applies for marketing authorization for a new medicine, provided that public health is not jeopardized (at [40]).

In *Konsumentombudsmannen (KO) v Gourmet International Products AB* (C-405/98) [2001] ECR I-1795; [2001] 2 CMLR 31 (p 672) a Swedish law prohibited advertisements for alcohol. The law was challenged as contrary to free movement of goods. The Court indicated that such an obstacle to free movement could be justified on public health grounds (at [26]). However, the challenged law must be proportionate to the objective of protecting public health. It must not be a form of arbitrary discrimination or a disguised restriction upon interstate trade (at [28]). A prohibition of alcohol advertising will not infringe Art 30 EC (now Art 34 TFEU) unless in the particular national circumstances public health may be protected by measures that have a lesser impact upon trade between Member States (at [34]).

In *Re Garlic Preparations in Capsule Form: Commission v Germany* (C-319/05) [2007] ECR I-9811; [2008] 1 CMLR 36 (p 943) the German government required that garlic capsules receive marketing authorization as a medicine (at [11]). The capsules contained only garlic, which was otherwise readily obtainable as a foodstuff. The Court emphasized that as an exception to free movement of goods the protection of health was to be construed strictly. A Member State relying upon the health exception must demonstrate that marketing of a product would constitute "a real risk for public health" (at [88]). The German rule was not necessary for the protection of public health. The risk to health from garlic consumption was not such as to justify the use of the onerous procedure of marketing authorization for medicines (at [94]). Warning labels about any health risks would have sufficed (at [95]).

In *Re Supply of Medicines by Pharmacies to Nearby Hospitals: Commission v Germany* (C-141/07) [2008] ECR I-6935; [2008] 3 CMLR 48 (p 1479) the Commission argued that cumulative conditions required by the German legislation on pharmacies made it "impossible in practice" for pharmacies in other Member States to supply German hospitals (at [1]). The effect of the cumulative conditions was that a pharmacy supplying a hospital needed to be quite close to the hospital (at [34]). The Court held that the challenged provisions were a measure with an equivalent effect (at [43]). The objective of the provisions was to ensure that the supply of medicines to hospitals was "reliable and of good quality", which clearly related to considerations of public health (at [47]).

The Court held that the provisions were appropriate for securing the objective pursued by the law (the protection of public health) (at [57]). By requiring that medicines be supplied by a pharmacy close to the hospital, the German law ensured that the supply of medicines was reliable and of good quality (at [49]).

The Court held that the provisions did not go beyond what was necessary to attain the objective pursued. Similar cumulative conditions applied to supplying pharmacies that were within the hospital itself (at [55]–[55]). Applying the same conditions to both internal and external pharmacies ensured the "unity and balance" of the system for the supply of medicines to German hospitals (at [56]). Allowing pharmacies that were not close to the hospital to supply medicines would undermine the unity and balance of the supply system and thereby undermine the level of protection of public health sought by the German government (at [58]). If pharmacies that were not close to hospital were allowed to supply medicines, hospitals could not employ a single pharmacy supplier and would thereby incur additional costs (at [59]). The provisions thus fell within the treaty exception for measures protecting public health (at [63]).

The protection of health is not restricted to human health. Art 36 TFEU expressly provides that the protection of animal and plant health is a justification for restricting the free movement. In *Criminal Proceedings Against Bluhme* (C-67/97) [1998] ECR I-8033; [1999] 1 CMLR 612 the Court upheld a national law that prohibited the introduction to an island of any species of bee other one specific indigenous subspecies (at [14]). The Court held that by safeguarding biodiversity through the protection of that subspecies, the law fell within the protection of animal health (at [33]–[34]).

The protection of industrial and commercial property is another permissible justification for restricting importation of goods. In *Pharmacia & Upjohn SA v Paranova A/S* (C-379/97) [1999] ECR I-6927; [2000] 1 CMLR 51 a pharmaceutical company marketed a drug under different trade marked names in different national markets (at [5]). It marketed the drug under different names in France and Denmark. Another company bought French versions of the drug and repackaged them for sale in Denmark under the Danish name (at [7]). The pharmaceutical company sought to prevent the sale as a violation of its trade mark.

Referring to Art 36 EC (now Art 36 TFEU), the Court held that a trade mark proprietor was entitled to oppose the repackaging of its goods with a replaced trade mark unless that opposition helped to create the "artificial partitioning of the markets between Member States" (at [31]). The Court explained the artificial portioning of markets as follows: "where the trade-mark rights in the importing Member State allow the proprietor of the trade mark to prevent it being reaffixed after repackaging of the product or being replaced, and where the repackaging with reaffixing or the replacement of the trade mark is necessary to enable the products to be marketed by the parallel importer in the importing Member State, there are obstacles to intracommunity trade giving rise to artificial partitioning of the markets between Member States..., whether or not the proprietor intended such partitioning" (at [39]).

The Art 36 TFEU exceptions are not a source of residual sovereignty for Member States and are permitted only in the absence of relevant European Union rules. When the EU adopts rules designed to protect public policy, public health or the other matters mentioned in Art 36, those rules are prima facie exhaustive. Unless such measures provide otherwise, there is no longer any room for national measures under Art 36. In *Denkavit Futtermittel GmbH v Minister für Ernährung* (251/78) [1979] ECR 3369; [1980] 3 CMLR 513 the Court stated that "when ... Community directives provide for the harmonisation of the measures necessary to guarantee the protection of ... health and when they establish procedures to check that they are observed, recourse to Article 36 is no longer justified" (at [14]). See also *Commission v Ireland* (C-235/91) [1992] ECR I-5917 at [5]; [1993] 1 CMLR 325; *Kemikalieinspektionen v Toolex Alpha AB* (C-473/98) [2000] ECR I-5681 at [25].

However, the exceptions in Art 36 TFEU remain available unless there has been full harmonisation. In *Belgium v Motte* (247/84) [1985] ECR 3887; [1987] 1 CMLR 663, the Court indicated that "it is only when Community directives make provision for the full harmonisation of all the measures needed to ensure the protection of health and institute Community procedures to monitor compliance therewith that recourse to Article 36 ceases to be justified" (at [16]). See similarly, *Criminal Proceedings Against Muller* (304/84) [1986] ECR 1511 at [14]; *Re Supply of Medicines by Pharmacies to Nearby Hospitals: Commission v Germany* (C-141/07) [2008] ECR I-6935 at [25]; [2008] 3 CMLR 48 (p 1479).

[2.105] Rule of Reason

There is also a judicial exception to Art 34 TFEU. This exception has become known as the "rule of reason". It was developed in a long line of cases by the Court. This judicial exception was first elaborated in *Procureur du Roi v Dassonville* (8/74) [1974] ECR 837; [1974] 2 CMLR 436. The Court stated:

> In the absence of a Community system guaranteeing for consumers the authenticity of a product's designation of origin, if a Member-State takes measures to prevent unfair practices in this connection it is subject to the condition that these measures should be reasonable and... they must not, in any case... constitute a means of arbitrary discrimination or a disguised restriction on trade between member-States (at [6]).

The effect of the rule of reason enunciated in *Dassonville* is that in the absence of relevant EU regulations the Member States may take measures to prevent unfair business practices. These measures are exempted from the prohibition in Art 34 TFEU if they do not constitute a means of arbitrary discrimination. Although even reasonable rules will not survive if they constitute a means of arbitrary discrimination, in *Dassonville* the Court failed to provide guidelines enabling the determination of when national measures are reasonable.

The rule of reason was further developed in the leading case of *Rewe-Zentral AG v Bundesmonopolverwalting für Branntwein* (120/78) [1979] ECR 649; [1979] 3 CMLR 494 (popularly referred to as the *Cassis de Dijon* case). The plaintiff proposed to import into West Germany a consignment of Cassis de Dijon (a French liquor) for the purpose of marketing it in that country. He was informed by the German Federal Monopoly Administration for Spirits that the liquor did not have the characteristics required for it to be marketed in West Germany. In particular, the product had insufficient alcoholic strength (at [2]).

In its judgment, the Court restated the rule of reason in the following language:

> In the absence of common rules relating to the production and marketing of alcohol... it is for the member-States to regulate all matters relating to the production and marketing of alcohol and alcoholic beverages on their own territory. Obstacles to movement within the Community resulting from disparities between the national laws relating to the marketing of the products in question must be accepted in so far as those provisions may be recognised as being necessary in order to satisfy mandatory requirements relating in particular to the effectiveness of fiscal supervision, the protection of public health, the fairness of commercial transactions and the defence of the consumer (at [8]).

This statement lists four mandatory aims which national measures are allowed to achieve. These aims are mandatory in the sense that they are indispensable for the welfare of a Member State. These aims are the fairness of commercial transactions, the effectiveness of fiscal supervision, the protection of public health and consumer protection. The Court stipulated that national laws restricting the free movement of goods must be necessary in order to satisfy these aims.

In this case the West German Government relied upon health and consumer protection concerns to justify its legislation. With regard to health, Germany argued that its rules relating to minimum alcohol content were justified since beverages with an alcohol content lower than that envisaged by the legislation would more readily create tolerance for alcohol than would higher strength beverages (at [10]). The ECJ rejected this argument since German consumers could buy a wide range of low alcohol products and many beverages with a high alcohol content were drunk in a diluted form (at [11]).

The German government also submitted that its rules were designed to protect the consumer against unfair practices on the part of producers of alcoholic beverages. It argued that a lowering of the alcohol content would secure an undue competitive advantage to low alcohol beverages since the high alcohol beverages are usually more expensive. The Court admitted that "the fixing of limits in relation to the alcohol content of beverages may lead to the standardisation of products placed on the market and of their designations" (at [13]). Nevertheless, the Court considered that the fixing of limits was unnecessary for guaranteeing the fairness of commercial transactions, because the protection of consumers could be ensured by affixing appropriate information on the packaging of products (at [13]).

In *Re Disposable Beer Cans: Commission v Denmark* (302/86) [1988] ECR 4607; [1989] 1 CMLR 619 Danish legislation required that all beer and soft drinks sold in Denmark be packaged in containers that were re-useable and which had been approved by the National Environmental Protection Agency. The Agency could refuse to approve a new type of container, especially if the container was not technically adapted to a system of return or did not ensure actual re-use of a sufficient proportion of containers, or if a container of general capacity which was both available and suited to its intended use had already been approved (at [2]). In order to avoid the possible adverse consequences of these national rules for interstate trade, the Danish government allowed the use of non-approved containers provided that a deposit and return system had been set up, "but excluding metal containers, within a limit of 3,000 hl per producer per year" (at [3]).

The Court reiterated its adherence to the rule of reason:

> in the absence of common rules relating to the marketing of the products in question, obstacles to free movement within the Community resulting from disparities between the national laws must be accepted in so far as such rules, applicable to domestic and imported products without distinction, may be recognized as being

necessary in order to satisfy mandatory requirements recognized by Community law. Such rules must also be proportionate to the aim in view. If a Member State has a choice between various measures for achieving the same aim, it should choose the means which least restricts the free movement of goods (at [6]).

This case clarified the rule of reason because the Court clearly indicated that a national rule would inevitably be incompatible with Art 34 TFEU if it discriminated between domestic and imported products. See generally, Richard Whish and Brenda Sufrin, "Article 85 and the Rule of Reason" (1987) 7 *Yearbook of European Law* 1; Annette Schrauwen (ed), *Rule of Reason: Rethinking Another Classic of European Legal Doctrine* (Groningen: Europe Law Publishing, 2005).

EU law distinguishes two categories of national rules: distinctly applicable and indistinctly applicable measures. Distinctly applicable measures "apply specifically to, or affect only, imported goods" and thus "explicitly *distinguish* between domestic and foreign goods". Indistinctly applicable measures "affect both home-produced and imported products, but . . . have a harsher impact on imported products" and thus do not explicitly distinguish between domestic and imported goods. See John Fairhurst, *Law of the European Union* (6th ed, Harlow, Essex: Pearson, 2007), 564, 565, 571.

[2.110] Permissible Grounds for Limitation of Free Movement of Goods

As has been discussed above, in the *Cassis de Dijon* case the Court identified four permissible justifications for the limitation of free movement of goods: "the effectiveness of fiscal supervision, the protection of public health, the fairness of commercial transactions and the defence of the consumer". See *Rewe-Zentral AG v Bundesmonopolverwaltung für Branntwein* (120/78) [1979] ECR 649 at [8]; [1979] 3 CMLR 494.

In *Re Disposable Beer Cans: Commission v Denmark* (302/86) [1988] ECR 4607; [1989] 1 CMLR 619 the Court extended the list of mandatory requirements to include the protection of the environment (at [9]). The Court held that the re-use of containers was necessary for the achievement of a mandatory requirement (environmental protection) and that a deposit-and-return system was an essential element of such a system (at [13]). Nevertheless, the Danish rules were incompatible with Art 30 EC (now Art 34 TFEU). The legislative requirement that only approved containers were to be used was not necessary to achieve the aim of environmental protection (at [14]–[17]). The concession for the limited marketing of beverages in unapproved containers was insufficient to remedy the defect (at [18]–[21]).

The protection of the environment is an EU rather than a purely national mandatory requirement. Indeed, the Court confirmed that the protection of the environment is "one of the Community's essential objectives" which may justify certain restrictions on the principle of the free movement of goods. See *Procureur de la République v Association de Défense des Brûleurs D'huiles Usagées* (240/83) [1985] ECR 531 at [13]; see similarly, *Re Ban on Night Lorry Traffic: Commission v Austria* (C-320/03) [2005] ECR I-9871 at [70], [72]; [2006] 2 CMLR 12 (p 337). The TFEU provides that EU action "shall be based on the precautionary principle and on the principles that preventive action should be taken, that environmental damage should as a priority be rectified at source and that the polluter should pay" (Art 191(2) TFEU). The TEU mandates that environmental protection policies are to form a part of all European Union policies (Art 11 TEU).

Consumer protection is another permissible justification. See *Fratelli Graffione SNC v Ditta Fransa* (C-313/94) [1996] ECR I-6039 at [17]; [1997] 1 CMLR 925; *Konsumentombudsmannen (KO) v De Agostini (Svenska) Förlag AB* (C-34/95) [1997] ECR I-3843 at [46]; [1998] 1 CMLR 32; *Cidrerie Ruwet SA v Cidre Stassen SA* (C-3/99) [2000] ECR I-8749 at [50]; [2000] 3 CMLR 1390; *Criminal Proceedings Against Guimont* (C-448/98) [2000] ECR I-10663 at [27]; [2003] 1 CMLR 3 (p 52); *De Groot en Slot Allium BV v Ministere de l'Economie, des Finances et de l'Industrie* (C-147/04) [2006] ECR I-245 at [75]; [2009] 1 CMLR 22 (p 603); *A-Punkt Schmuckhandels GmbH v Schmidt* (C-441/04) [2006] ECR I-2093 at [27]; [2006] 2 CMLR 33 (p 873).

In *Re Marketing of Chocolate: Commission v Spain* (C-12/00) [2003] ECR I-459; [2005] 2 CMLR 33 (p 799) Spanish legislation prohibited the marketing as chocolate of products that contained fats other than cocoa butter. In some other Member States such products could be legally marketed as chocolate (at [78]).

The Court held that overriding requirements of consumer protection could justify a restriction of free movement of goods (at [83]). It was permissible for a Member State to require that consumers be given proper information about products offered for sale (at [84]). Where the difference between national and foreign products is minor, the consumer may be provided with sufficient information through the product label (at [86]). The use of fats other than cocoa butter did not transform the product into a different product (at [92]). The need to supply consumers with adequate information would have been satisfied by noting on the label the use of fats other than cocoa butter (at [93]). The prohibition of marketing the product as chocolate was not necessary for the purpose of consumer protection (at [94]).

The protection of fundamental rights may constitute a justification for restricting the free movement of goods. In *Vereinigte Familiapress Zeitungsverlags- und Vertriebs GmbH v Heinrich Bauer Verlag* (C-368/95) [1997] ECR I-3689; [1997] 3 CMLR 1329 the Court held that the protection of press diversity was another permissible ground for limiting free movement of goods (at [18]). This was because press diversity helped protect freedom of expression, a fundamental right protected as a general principle of EU law (see Chapter 12). In *Dynamic Medien Vertriebs GmbH v Avides Media AG* (C-244/06) [2008] ECR I-505; [2008] 2 CMLR 23 (p 651) the Court held that the protection of children was another justification for limiting free movement of goods (at [42]). The Court cited numerous international instruments guaranteeing the rights of the child (at [39]–[41]).

The Court has held that protection of certain cultural interests may provide a valid justification. In *Fachverband der Buch- und Medienwirtschaft v LIBRO Handelsgesellschaft mbH* (C-531/07) [2009] 3 CMLR 26 (p 972) Austrian legislation prohibited importers of German language books from setting a price other than that recommended by the publisher in the state where the book was published (at [3]–[4]). The Austrian government sought to justify the law on cultural grounds (at [30]).

The Court accepted that the "protection of books as cultural objects" was a permissible justification for restricting free movement of goods (at [34]). In this case that interest could have been safeguarded by less restrictive measures: an importer could be permitted to set a price that takes account of the specific conditions of the Austrian market (at [35]).

Road safety is another permissible ground for limiting free movement of goods. See *Snellers Auto's BV v Algemeen Directeur van de Dienst Wegverkeer* (C-314/98) [2000] ECR I-8633 at [55]; [2000] 3 CMLR 1275; *Commission v Italy* (C-110/05) [2009] ECR I-519 at [60]; [2009] 2 CMLR 34 (p 876).

[2.115] Restriction of Selling Arrangements

The Court has held that certain restrictions upon selling arrangements fall outside the scope of Art 34 TFEU. In *Criminal Proceedings Against Keck* (C-267/91) [1993] ECR I-6097; [1995] 1 CMLR 101 French legislation prohibited the resale of goods at a loss (at [2]). The Court held that this legislation did not violate Art 30 EC (now Art 34 TFEU). The Court qualified its earlier case law, permitting some legislation that restricted selling arrangements for goods. The Court stated:

> contrary to what has previously been decided, the application to products from other Member States of national provisions restricting or prohibiting certain selling arrangements is not such to hinder directly or indirectly, actually or potentially, trade between Member States…, so long as those provisions apply to all relevant traders operating within the national territory and so long as they affect in the same manner, in law and in fact, the marketing of domestic producers and of those from other Member States (at [16]).

Such national laws do not infringe Art 30 EC (now Art 34 TFEU) (at [17]). The Court justified its reformulation on the ground that free movement of goods had become a means for traders to challenge any limitation of their commercial freedom even where the limitation was not directed at imports from other Member States (at [14]).

The Court held that a prohibition of television advertising in a specific business sector was a selling arrangement for products in that sector. See *Société d'Importation Edouard Leclerc-Siplec v TF1 Publicité SA* [1995] ECR I-179 at [27]; [1995] 3 CMLR 422; *Konsumentombudsmannen (KO) v De Agostini (Svenska) Förlag AB* (C-34/95) [1997] ECR I-3843 at [39]; [44]; [1998] 1 CMLR 32.

In *Commission v Greece* (C-391/92) [1995] ECR I-1621; [1996] 1 CMLR 359 Greek legislation provided that only pharmacies could sell processed milk for babies (at [2]). The Court held that the law regulated the selling arrangements for these goods (at [15]). The law applied irrespective of the origin of the goods. It applied to all traders within Greece. The effect of the law upon imports was no different from its effect upon domestic products (at [16]). It did not matter that Greece did not manufacture infant formula. The application of freedom of movement of goods does not depend upon such fortuitous circumstances. If the operation of this guarantee depended upon such circumstances, the same law would infringe free movement in some Member States but not others (at [17]). The Greek law did not infringe Art 30 EC (now Art 34 TFEU) (at [21]).

In *Konsumentombudsmannen (KO) v Gourmet International Products AB* (C-405/98) [2001] ECR I-1795; [2001] 2 CMLR 31 (p 672) a Swedish law prohibited advertisements for alcohol. The law was challenged as contrary to free movement of goods. The ECJ examined the law as a restriction upon selling arrangements. The Court held that because consumption of alcohol was linked to local customs, a prohibition of alcohol advertising was more likely to impede market access by imports than domestic goods, since consumers were likely to be already more aware of the domestic products (at [21]). The law affected the marketing of imports more than the marketing of domestic goods (at [25]).

In *Re Marketing of Chocolate: Commission v Spain* (C-12/00) [2003] ECR I-459; [2005] 2 CMLR 33 (p 799) Spanish legislation prohibited the marketing as chocolate of products that contained fats other than cocoa butter (at [81]). In some other Member States such products could be legally marketed as chocolate (at [78]). The Court held that the Spanish law was not a selling arrangement because it necessitated the alteration of the packaging of the imported goods (at [76]).

In *Dynamic Medien Vertriebs GmbH v Avides Media AG* (C-244/06) [2008] ECR I-505; [2008] 2 CMLR 23 (p 651) a German statute required that DVDs for sale by mail order must have been classified by an official body and contain a sticker indicating their age classification (at [2]). The purpose of the scheme was to protect children from unsuitable material. The ECJ held that the German law was not a selling arrangement (at [32]). The law did not prohibit mail order sales, but imposed a national classification procedure and labeling requirements (at [33]).

See generally, Laurence Gormley, "Reasoning Renounced? The Remarkable Judgment in *Keck and Mithouard*" (1994) 5 *European Business Law*

Review 63; Stephen Weatherill, "After *Keck*: Some Thoughts on how to Clarify the Clarification" (1996) 33 *Common Market Law Review* 885; Panos Koutrakos, "On Groceries, Alcohol and Olive Oil: More on Free Movement of Goods after *Keck*" (2001) 26 *European Law Review* 391; Stefan Enchelmaier, "The Awkward Selling of a Good Idea, or a Traditionalist Interpretation of *Keck*" (2003) 22 *Yearbook of European Law* 249; Tim Connor, "Accentuating the Positive: The 'Selling Arrangement', the First Decade, and Beyond" (2005) 54 *International and Comparative Law Quarterly* 127; Daniel Wilsher, "Does *Keck* Discrimination make any sense? An Assessment of the Non-discrimination Principle within the European Single Market" (2008) 33 *European Law Review* 3.

[2.120] Necessity Principle

The application of the necessity principle may result in the adoption of the least restrictive and thus the most basic level of product regulation in the EU, thereby potentially affecting the quality and safety of consumer products. Assume that Member State A enacts legislative measures prohibiting the use of flavouring additives in beer. State A deems these measures to be necessary to protect the health of its citizens. Assume that Member State B also wants to protect the health of its citizens but decides that, in addition to prohibiting the use of flavouring additives, a number of other purity requirements are also necessary to achieve this aim.

The totality of measures taken by State B are more likely than those taken by State A to inhibit interstate trade within the EU, as interstate products which do not satisfy the more stringent health requirements of State B cannot be marketed. The Court would be tempted to decide that the measures decided upon by State B are disproportionate, in the sense that they are not strictly necessary to attain the state's legitimate interest in protecting the health of its citizens. If the Court is faced with two sets of health regulations, the Court may well give preference to the set of regulations that least impedes interstate trade.

However, if the Court were to give absolute preference to national measures that least inhibit interstate trade, the necessity principle could easily become meaningless. Taken to its logical extreme, such an application of the necessity principle could lead to the conclusion that, in cases where a State does not consider it necessary at all to legislate for the protection of the health of its citizens, any relevant legislative measure taken by another State could be interpreted as violating Art 34 TFEU. On this interpretation of the necessity principle, any product that is legally produced and sold in one Member State can be legally marketed in another.

The above analysis is supported by the Court's judgment in *Re Purity Requirements for Beer: Commission v Germany* (178/84) [1987] ECR

1227; [1988] 1 CMLR 780. German food purity laws laid down stringent rules regarding the permitted ingredients for beer, prohibiting all additives. Beers from other Member States that contained other ingredients but had no additives could be imported into Germany but could not be marketed as beer. If beverages from other Member States contained additives they could not be marketed in Germany at all (at [7]). The German government conceded that the rule on designation was merely intended to protect consumers. It argued that German consumers associated "beer" with a beverage produced in conformity with German legislation. The government also pointed out that its purity rule could be complied with by foreign producers that wished to export their product to Germany (at [26]).

The Court held that the German rule prohibiting the designation of a beverage as beer if it contained non-approved ingredients was not necessary to protect consumers. The Court stated:

> It is admittedly legitimate to seek to enable consumers who attribute specific qualities to beers manufactured from particular raw materials to make their choice in the light of that consideration. However, ... that possibility may be ensured by means which do not prevent the importation of products which have been lawfully manufactured and marketed in other Member-States and, in particular, 'by the compulsory affixing of suitable labels giving the nature of the product sold'. By indicating the raw materials utilised in the manufacture of beer 'such a course would enable the consumer to make his choice in full knowledge of the facts and would guarantee transparency in trading and in offers to the public' (at [35]).

The Court also held that the absolute prohibition upon the marketing of beers containing additives could not be justified on human health grounds. The Court applied the necessity requirement to the exception in Art 36 EC (now Art 36 TFEU). The ECJ unequivocally indicated that it would prefer the set of State regulations which is least restrictive of interstate trade. The Court pointed out that other Member States also have strict rules on the utilisation of additives in foodstuffs "and do not authorise the use of any given additive until thorough tests have established that it is harmless" (at [38]).

The Court held that "in so far as the German rules on additives in beer entail a general ban on additives, their application to beers imported from other member-States is contrary to the requirements of Community law..., since that prohibition is contrary to the principle of proportionality" (at [53]). It also approvingly referred to the Commission's view that "there should be a presumption that beers manufactured in other Member-States which contain additives authorised there represent no danger to public health" and that if a Member State "wishes to oppose the importation of such beers then it bears the onus of proving that such beers are a danger to public health" (at [38]).

There are a number of problems with the application of the necessity principle to Art 34 TFEU. First, the principle does not usually involve a scientific examination of the extent to which a set of national measures are necessary to attain the State's aim. Secondly, the effect of the rigid application of the necessity principle is that the least restrictive national rules would usually be selected as a yardstick by which to determine the extent to which a measure is necessary. In preferring the least cumbersome national measures, the principle may undermine the achievement of the legitimate aims of Member States that introduce protective measures.

The Court has ameliorated the stringency of the necessity principle. The ECJ has held that the fact that one Member State imposes a lower level of protection of public health than is imposed by another Member State does not mean that the higher level of protection is disproportionate. See *Re "Loi Evin": Commission v France* (C-262/02) [2004] ECR I-6569 at [37]; [2004] 3 CMLR 1 (p 1); *Criminal Proceedings Against Schreiber* (C-443/02) [2004] ECR I-7275 at [48]; [2004] 3 CMLR 10 (p 211); *Re Supply of Medicines by Pharmacies to Nearby Hospitals: Commission v Germany* (C-141/07) [2008] ECR I-6935 at [51]; [2008] 3 CMLR 48 (p 1479). The Court has made the same point in relation to the protection of road safety. See *Commission v Italy* (C-110/05) [2009] ECR I-519 at [65]; [2009] 2 CMLR 34 (p 876).

[2.125] Proportionality

The necessity principle and the proportionality principle are closely related. This relatedness stems from the fact that disproportionate measures are unnecessary to enable the State to achieve its mandatory aims. However, while they overlap these two principles are different from one another. If one states that a particular measure or law is "necessary" that does not say anything about the *specific* measure that may legitimately be adopted. The proportionality principle discloses some information about the specific measure: it requires the measure to be proportionate to the problem that the State seeks to combat.

In *Officier van Justitie v De Peijper* (104/75) [1976] ECR 613; [1976] 2 CMLR 271 the Court held that Art 36 EC (now Art 36 TFEU) did not justify the adoption of restrictions that are disproportionate to the interest sought and which were motivated primarily by a concern to facilitate the task of the authorities (at [18]). In *Glocken GmbH v Unita Sanitaria Locale Centro-Sud* (407/85) [1988] ECR 4233 the Court decided that a complete prohibition on the importation and marketing of pasta products made from common wheat or a mixture of common wheat and durum wheat necessarily containing additives or colorants was contrary to the principle of proportionality and was not justified on the ground of the protection of public health (at [14]). See similarly, *Criminal Proceedings Against Zoni* (90/86) [1988] ECR 4285 at [14].

The rule of reason has been reduced to the simple proposition that once products have lawfully been produced and marketed in one Member State their importation and sale in another Member State cannot be prevented without contravening Art 34 TFEU. In *Schutzverband Gegen Unwesen in der Wirtschaft v Weinvertriebs GmbH* (59/82) [1983] ECR 1217; [1984] 1 CMLR 319 the Court held that goods not manufactured in accordance with the rules of the country of origin but in accordance with those of the country of destination are equally entitled to free movement throughout the European Union (at [7]–[9]).

In *Stoke on Trent City Council v B&Q Plc* (C-169/91) [1992] ECR I-6635; [1993] 1 CMLR 426 the Court indicated that the proportionality principle requires an appraisal of both the national objective and the EU's interest in the free movement of goods:

> Appraising the proportionality of national rules which pursue a legitimate aim under Community law involves weighing the national interest in attaining that aim against the Community interest in ensuring the free movement of goods. . . . in order to verify that the restrictive effects on intra-Community trade of the rules at issue do not exceed what is necessary to achieve the aim in view, it must be considered whether those effects are direct, indirect or purely speculative and whether those effects do not impede the marketing of imported products more than the marketing of national products (at [15]).

In *Rosengren v Riksåklagaren* (C-170/04) [2007] ECR I-4071 at [40]; [2007] 3 CMLR 10 (p 239) Swedish law prohibited the importation of alcohol by individuals. An individual could only obtain alcohol from another country by placing an order with the state monopoly. The Swedish government argued that the law protected youth from alcohol consumption since the state monopoly was obliged to ascertain the ages of those seeking imported alcohol (at [48]). The Court held that the prohibition was disproportionate. It went beyond what was necessary for achieving the objective since the prohibition applied to people of all ages (at [51]). There was a less restrictive alternative: a purchaser could be required to declare that they were above the legal age for alcohol consumption when placing an order. The making of false declarations could be punished by criminal penalty (at [56]).

In *Criminal Proceedings Against Gysbrechts* (C-205/07) [2008] ECR I-9947; [2009] 2 CMLR 2 (p 45) the Belgian consumer protection law provided that traders could not require that consumers make any deposit or payment before the end of the withdrawal period. If the consumer exercised the right of withdrawal from the contract, the trader was required to refund any amounts paid by the consumer (at [6]). The Belgian government interpreted this provision as prohibiting a trader from requiring a consumer to provide their credit card number in a distance sale (at [17]).

The Court held that this provision had the aim of protecting the consumer's right to withdraw from the contract (at [58]). This prohibition was "clearly necessary" for the level of consumer protection intended by the legislation (at [56]). It was appropriate and proportionate to attaining its objective (at [61]).

The prohibition upon requiring the giving of the customer's credit card number was also a measure with an equivalent effect (at [44]). This prohibition pursued the same aim as the prohibition upon requiring a deposit or payment (at [58]). The protective effect of this prohibition was only to remove any risk that the trader might collect payment before the end of the withdrawal period (at [60]). However, if the trader did that it would breach the prohibition upon requiring the making of a deposit or payment (at [61]). The prohibition went beyond what was necessary to attain its objective (at [62]).

[2.130] Private Action Threatening Interstate Trade

Art 34 TFEU prohibits discrimination by the Member States so while the ECJ has held that a "buy local campaign" by a Member State will breach this Article, such a campaign run by a private group such as a trade association would not infringe Art 34. However, the inaction of a Member State in relation to certain actions by private individuals threatening interstate trade may infringe Art 34 TFEU. In *Commission v France* (C-265/95) [1997] ECR I-6959 private individuals in France had obstructed the free movement of imported fruit and vegetables from other Member States (at [1]). These disruptions included destruction of consignments of food and the making of threats against truck drivers and businesses stocking imported farm produce (at [2]). The Commission argued that the French government had remained passive in the face of these actions.

The Court held that Art 30 EC (now Art 34 TFEU) required Member States to take measures against obstacles to free movement of goods that were not created by the State (at [30]). Inaction against such obstacles was as likely to hinder trade within the internal market as would a positive action by the State (at [31]). The French government had instituted only one prosecution despite the widespread nature of the disruption (at [51]). This response was "manifestly inadequate" for the protection of intra-Community trade in fruit and vegetables (at [52]).

In *Eugen Schmidberger, Internationale Transporte und Planzüge v Austria* (C-112/00) [2003] ECR I-5659; [2003] 2 CMLR 34 (p 1043) a demonstration caused the closure of a major international motorway for almost 30 hours (at [47], [63]). The national authorities permitted the demonstration on the grounds of freedom of expression and assembly (at [69]). The Court held that the freedoms of expression and assembly must be considered in determining whether a Member State is justified in refusing to prohibit a demonstration that will constitute an obstacle to the free movement of goods (at [77]–[78], [82]).

The factual situation was quite different from that in *Commission v France*. Here the demonstration had been authorized by the authorities, was limited to a particular geographical area and took place for a relatively short period of time, was not directed at trade in goods of a specific type or from a specific source, and did not create a "climate of insecurity" regarding free movement of goods (at [84]–[86], [88]). The authorities had taken precautions to minimize the disruptive effect upon traffic (at [87]). The national authorities were entitled to consider that respect for fundamental rights could not have been achieved by measures that were less restrictive of free movement of goods (at [89]–[93]).

The EU has adopted a Regulation that seeks to deter private obstacles to free movement of goods between the Member States. See Council Regulation 2679/98 of 7 December 1998 on the functioning of the internal market in relation to the free movement of goods among the Member States (OJ L 337, 12.12.1998, p 8). The Regulation defines an "obstacle" as an obstacle to the free movement of goods between the Member States that is attributable to a Member State by reason of its action or inaction. The obstacle must lead to a serious disruption of free movement of goods by preventing or delaying their import into or passage through a Member State. The obstacle must cause serious loss to individuals and must necessitate immediate action for its removal (Art 1(1)). When an obstacle occurs on its territory a Member State must take all necessary and proportionate measures to restore free movement of goods. The Member State must inform the Commission of these measures (Art 4(1)).

[2.135] Harmonisation

The European Union is engaged in the harmonisation of national rules concerning the free movement of goods. In harmonising national rules, the EU not only creates rules which are valid throughout the Union but it also obviates the need for the Court to apply the necessity principle, both in its judicial and Treaty versions. Indeed, the Court has often indicated that the judicial and Treaty exceptions to Art 34 TFEU only apply in the absence of exhaustive harmonized EU rules. See *Criminal Proceedings Against Guimont* (C-448/98) [2000] ECR I-10663 at [27]; [2003] 1 CMLR 3 (p 52); *Radiosistemi Srl v Prefetto di Genova* (C-388/00) [2002] ECR I-5845 at [41]; *Deutscher Apothekerverband EV v 0800 Docmorris NV* (C-322/01) [2003] ECR I-14887 at [64]; [2005] 1 CMLR 46 (p 1205).

The EU has enacted a considerable volume of harmonizing measures. Only a few examples will be given here. An EU Directive provides common standards for the labeling and advertising of food. See Directive 2000/13 of the European Parliament and of the Council on the approximation of the laws of the Member States relating to the labeling, presentation and advertising of foodstuffs (OJ L 109, 6.5.2000, p 29). The Directive states that differences between national standards regarding labeling inhibit the free movement of goods (Preamble Recital 2). The approximation of such standards would enhance the operation of the internal market (Preamble Recital 3). The Directive sets out certain information that must be provided on the labels of foodstuffs. These include ingredients, net quantity, use by date, storage conditions, the identity of the manufacturer or a seller located within the EU, and their place of origin (Art 3(1)). The Directive also contains other consumer protection measures. For example, the labeling of foodstuffs must not "be such as could mislead the purchaser to a material degree" (Art 2(1)).

The EU has introduced a legal framework for electronic signatures. See Directive 1999/93 of the European Parliament and of the Council of 13 December 1999 on a Community framework for electronic signatures (OJ L 13, 19.1.2000, p 12). The Directive states that the introduction of essential standards for electronic signature products will promote the free movement of goods within the Union (Preamble Recital 5). The Directive seeks to encourage the use of electronic signatures and their legal recognition (Art 1). Electronic signature products that are in accordance with this Directive must be permitted to circulate freely within the internal market (Art 4(2)).

Another Directive requires the payment of interest for late payment in certain commercial transactions. See Directive 2000/35 of the European Parliament and of the Council of 29 June 2000 on combating late payment in commercial transactions (OJ L 200, 8.8.2000, p 35). "Commercial transactions" are defined as transactions between undertakings (or between undertakings and public authorities) for the supply of goods or services (Art 2(1)). The Directive does not apply to transactions with consumers (Preamble Recital 13). Late payment occurs when the contractual or legislative time for payment has elapsed (Art 2(2)). Interest is to be payable from the date for payment provided by the contract (Art 3(1)(a)). Where the contract does not fix a date for payment, interest is payable 30 days from the date of the receipt of an invoice by the debtor (Art 3(1)(b)). If the contract contains a retention of title clause the seller will retain title in the goods until full payment is made (Art 4(1)). See generally, Reinhard Schulte-Braucks and Steven Ongena, "The Late Payment Directive – A Step Towards an Emerging European Private Law?" (2003) 11 *European Review of Private Law* 519; M del Pilar Perales Viscasillas, "Late Payment Directive 2000/35 and the CISG" (2007) 19 *Pace International Law Review* 125.

[2.140] Technical Standards

The adoption of EU-wide standards benefits both EU and non-Union companies because their goods can now be produced or manufactured in accordance with a single set of specifications. European subsidiaries of non-EU firms are able to sell their products or services anywhere within the EU knowing that there is only one set of norms, standards, testing or certification procedures that will have to be satisfied.

The EU has adopted safety, health, consumer and environmental protection requirements with which products must comply. Evidence of compliance is provided by attestation by an appropriate body. The European Committee for Standardization (http://www.cen.eu), the European Committee for Electrotechnical Standardization (http://www.cenelec.eu) and the European Telecommunications Institute (http://www.etsi.org) publish EU-wide standards. These European standards are based upon standards developed by international bodies such as the International Organisation for Standardization (http://www.iso.org) and the International Electrotechnical Association (http://www.iec.ch). European manufacturers usually conform to these EU standards. Alternatively, manufacturers may through independent testing and attestation establish that their product complies with the essential requirements of EU law.

The EU has set out a procedure for the provision of information concerning technical standards. See Directive 98/34 of the European Parliament and of the Council of 22 June 1998 laying down a procedure for the provision of information in the field of technical standards and regulations and of rules on Information Society services (OJ L 24, 21.7.1998, p 37).

[2.145] Mutual Acceptance of Goods

The enormous number of Directives needed to harmonise the existing national restrictions upon free movement of goods has precipitated the development of the principle of mutual acceptance of goods. This principle involves the recognition by Member States of the different national standards concerned, with the result that goods lawfully manufactured or marketed in one Member State are deemed to comply with the specifications of other Member States. The Member States are thus able to control the production and manufacturing of products on their own territory, but they may not prevent the importation or sale of interstate products which have legally been made in another Member State.

The implementation of this principle avoids the single most disadvantageous consequence of the application of the necessity principle, namely the potential erosion of national standards of excellence. The principle of mutual acceptance of goods also promotes competition because the Member States retain the privilege to implement their vision of product excellence, which will be compared by consumers with similar interstate products.

[2.150] European Economic Area (EEA) Agreement

The European Economic Area (EEA) consists of all EU Member States along with Iceland, Liechtenstein and Norway, which are members of the European Free Trade Association (EFTA). See Art 2, *Agreement on the European Economic Area*, Porto, 2 May 1992, 1801 UNTS 3; OJ L 1, 3.1.1994, p 3. The other member of EFTA (Switzerland) is not part of the EEA.

Under the EEA Agreement key elements of European Union law are applied by these three nations. As far as its provisions are substantially identical with provisions of the EU founding Treaties, the EEA Agreement is to be interpreted in conformity with the rulings of the ECJ (Art 6).

Acts mentioned in this Treaty and Decisions of the EEA Joint Committee are binding upon the parties (Art 7). Those EEA Acts that correspond to EU Regulations are part of the internal law of the parties. The parties have a choice regarding the method of application of EEA Acts that correspond to EU Directives. An important difference between EU law and EEA law is that EEA law does not have direct effect. See *Karlsson v Iceland* (E-4/01) [2002] EFTA Ct Rep 240 at [28]–[29]; *Criminal Proceedings Against A* (E-1/07) [2007] EFTA Ct Rep 246 at [40]; [2008] 1 CMLR 37 (p 982); *L'Oréal Norge AS v Per Aarskog AS* (E-9/07) [2008] EFTA Ct Rep 259 at [22]; [2008] ETMR 60 (p 943).

Under the EEA Agreement the internal market of the EU is extended to these three EFTA countries. See *Ospelt v Schlossle Weissenberg Familienstiftung* (C-452/01) [2003] ECR I-9743 at [29]; [2005] 3 CMLR 40 (p 1125). The Agreement provides for the extension to these states of the four fundamental freedoms and the rules on competition. There is freedom of movement of goods between the parties (Art 8(1)). This freedom applies only to goods that originate within the parties (Art 8(2)). The rules of origin are detailed in a Protocol to the Agreement (Art 9(2) and Protocol 4).

The Agreement prohibits customs duties and charges having an equivalent effect upon exports and imports between the parties (Art 10). The Agreement also prohibits quantitative restrictions on trade and measures having an equivalent effect (Arts 11–12). This prohibition is subject to restrictions on the grounds of public policy, national security, public health, the protection of national artistic treasures and the protection of intellectual property rights. However, these measures must not be used as a disguised restriction upon trade and may not be arbitrarily applied (Art 13).

The EEA Agreement also prohibits the imposition, whether directly or indirectly, of any internal tax in excess of that charged upon local products or the reimbursement of tax paid upon exported products at an amount higher than that actually paid (Arts 14–15).

The procurement policies of state monopolies operating on a commercial basis must be adjusted to preclude discrimination on the ground of nationality (Art 16). A notification procedure must be followed if a party intends to reduce duties applicable to third parties (Art 22). Where compliance with the prohibitions of customs duties upon imports or exports and quantitative restrictions upon exports (Arts 10 and 12) leads to re-export to a third party subject to quantitative restrictions or export duties, or where there is a threat of serious shortages of an essential product, a party may take safeguard measures (Art 25). The Agreement sets out procedures for taking such measures (Arts 112–114). Unless the Agreement otherwise specifies, anti-dumping duties and measures having an equivalent effect are not to be applied as between the parties (Art 26). See generally, Tor-Inge Harbo, "The European Economic Area Agreement: A Case of Legal Pluralism" (2009) 78 *Nordic Journal of International Law* 201.

The implementation of the EEA is supervised by the EFTA Court (http://www.eftacourt.lu). The Court's decisions are officially published in the annual *Report of the EFTA Court* (EFTA Court, 1994-), available at http://www.eftacourt.int/index.php/court/publication/reports. Many of the Court's decisions are also published in the *Common Market Law Reports*. See generally, Carl Baudenbacher, "The EFTA Court: An Actor in the European Judicial Dialogue" (2005) 28 *Fordham International Law Journal* 353.

The implementation of the EEA is monitored by an EFTA Surveillance Authority (http://www.eftasurv.int). See generally, Alexandra Antoniadis, "The EFTA Surveillance Authority's Practice in the Field of State Aid" [2002] *European State Aid Law Quarterly* 157. The EFTA website is at http://www.efta.int.

[2.155] Conclusion

The EU is a customs union with a common customs tariff in its relations with third countries. Member States may not impose customs duties or charges having an equivalent effect. The rules relating to the origin of goods determine whether products are EU products and thus exempt from the payment of customs duty. Goods the production of which involved more than one country shall be deemed to originate in the country where they underwent their last substantial transformation.

Quantitative restrictions on imports and measures having an equivalent effect are prohibited between Member States. This prohibition has direct effect. The Court has defined measures with an equivalent effect as all trading rules adopted by Member States that are capable of hindering intra-Community trade. Examples of measures that have been held to be measures with an equivalent effect include import authorization requirements, production quotas, maximum price laws and packaging and labeling laws.

There are several Treaty exceptions to the prohibition against quantitative restrictions and measures having an equivalent effect. These Treaty exceptions include prohibitions or restrictions justified on the grounds of public morality, public policy, public security, protection of human, animal or plant health and life and the protection of industrial or commercial property.

The rule of reason is a judicial exception to the prohibition upon quantitative restrictions and measures having an equivalent effect. The measures permitted under this exception include mandatory requirements relating to the effectiveness of fiscal supervision, the protection of public health, the fairness of commercial transactions, consumer protection and environmental protection.

National measures adopted under the Treaty and judicial exceptions must comply with the necessity and proportionality principles. These exceptions only apply in the absence of exhaustive harmonized EU rules. Certain restrictions upon selling arrangements fall outside the prohibition upon quantitative restrictions and measures having an equivalent effect.

Further Reading

Andenas, Mads and Jukka Snell. "Exploring the Outer Limits – Restrictions on the Free Movement of Goods and Services" (1999) 10 *European Business Law Review* 252.

Dawes, Anthony. "Importing and Exporting Poor Reasoning: Worrying Trends in relation to the Case Law on the Free Movement of Goods" (August 2007) 8, 8 *German Law Journal* 761, http://www.germanlawjournal.com

Dawes, Anthony. "A Freedom Reborn? The New yet Unclear Scope of Article 29 EC" (2009) 34 *European Law Review* 639.

Enchelmaier, Stefan. "The ECJ's Recent Case Law on the Free Movement of Goods: Movement in All Sorts of Directions" (2007) 26 *Yearbook of European Law* 115.

Enchelmaier, Stefan. "The Inexhaustible Question – Free Movement of Goods and Intellectual Property in the European Court of Justice's Case Law, 2002–2006" (2007) 38 *International Review of Intellectual Property and Competition Law* 453.

Commission of the European Communities. *Free Movement of Goods – Guide to the Application of Treaty Provisions Governing Free Movement of Goods (Articles 28–30 EC)* (SEC(2009) 673 final), available at http://ec.europa.eu/ enterprise/regulation/goods/docs/art2830/new_guide_en.pdf

Ginter, Carri. "Free Movement of Goods and Parallel Imports in the Internal Market of the EU" (2005) 7 *European Journal of Law Reform* 505.

Gormley, Laurence W. "Silver Threads Among the Gold ... 50 Years of the Free Movement of Goods" (2008) 31 *Fordham International Law Journal* 1637.

Gormley, Laurence W. *EU Law of Free Movement of Goods and Customs Union* (Oxford: Oxford University Press, 2008).

Jarvis, Malcolm A. *The Application of EC Law by National Courts: The Free Movement of Goods* (Oxford: Clarendon Press, 1998).

Koutrakos, Panos. "In Search of a Common Vocabulary in Free Movement of Goods: The Example of Repackaging Pharmaceuticals" (2003) 28 *European Law Review* 53.

Kraft, David. "Advertising Restrictions and the Free Movement of Goods – The Case Law of the ECJ" (2007) 18 *European Business Law Review* 517.

Leidenmühler, Franz. "The Free Movement of Goods within an EC-Wide Market: Still a Work in Progress" (2004) 12 *Cardozo Journal of International and Comparative Law* 163.

Moens, Gabriël A. "Freedom of Movement of Goods in the European Community" (1990) 17 *Melbourne University Law Review* 733.

Molyneux, Candido Garcia. "The Trade Barriers Regulation: The European Union as a Player in the Globalisation Game" (1999) 5 *European Law Journal* 375.

Oliver, Peter. *Free Movement of Goods in the European Union* (5th ed, London: Sweet & Maxwell, 2010).

Oliver, Peter and Stefan Enchelmaier. "Free Movement of Goods: Recent Developments in the Case Law" (2007) 44 *Common Market Law Review* 649.

Puig, Gonzalo Villalta. "Free Movement of Goods: The European Experience in the Australian Context" (2001) 75 *Australian Law Journal* 639.

Roth, Wulf-Henning. "Export of Goods and Services within the Single Market: Reflections on the Scope of Articles 29 and 49 EC" in Takis Tridimas and Paolisa Nebbia (eds), *European Union Law for the Twenty-First Century: Volume 2* (Oxford: Hart, 2004), 33.

Shuibhne, Niamh Nic. "The Free Movement of Goods and Article 28 EC: An Evolving Framework" (2002) 27 *European Law Review* 408.

Shuibhne, Niamh Nic. "Margins of Appreciation: National Values, Fundamental Rights and EC Free Movement Law" (2009) 34 *European Law Review* 230.

Snell, Jukka. "True Proportionality and Free Movement of Goods and Services" (2000) 11 *European Business Law Review* 50.

Torgersen, Ole-Andreas. "The Limitations of the Free Movements of Goods and the Freedom to Provide Services – in Search of a Common Approach" (1999) 10 *European Business Law Review* 371.

Weatherill, Stephen. "Recent Case Law Concerning the Free Movement of Goods: Mapping the Frontiers of Market Deregulation" (1999) 36 *Common Market Law Review* 51.

Weatherill, Stephen. "Recent Developments in the Law Governing the Free Movement of Goods in the EC's Internal Market" (2006) 2 *European Review of Contract Law* 90.

Woods, Lorna. *Free Movement of Goods and Services within the European Community* (Aldershot: Hampshire, 2004).

Chapter 3
Free Movement of Persons and Services

[3.05] Introduction

Title IV of Part Three of the TFEU has three relevant chapters concerning the free movement of persons and the provision of services: Chapter 1 (workers), Chapter 2 (right of establishment) and Chapter 3 (services). A consideration of the relevant law involves an examination of Arts 45, 49 and 56 TFEU. These Articles deal with the rights of "workers" (Art 45), self-employed persons (Art 49) and the providers of services (Art 56) respectively.

[3.10] Freedom of Movement for Workers

Art 45 TFEU concerns the free movement of workers. This Article reads as follows:

> 1. Freedom of movement for workers shall be secured within the Union.
> 2. Such freedom of movement shall entail the abolition of any discrimination based on nationality between workers of the Member States as regards employment, remuneration and other conditions of work and employment.
> 3. It shall entail the right, subject to limitations justified on grounds of public policy, public security or public health:
>
>   (a) to accept offers of employment actually made;
>   (b) to move freely within the territory of Member States for this purpose;
>   (c) to stay in a Member State for the purpose of employment in accordance with the provisions governing the employment of nationals of that State laid down by law, regulation or administrative action;
>   (d) to remain in the territory of a Member State after having been employed in that State, subject to conditions which shall be embodied in regulations to be drawn up by the Commission.
>
> 4. The provisions of this Article shall not apply to employment in the public service.

G. Moens, J. Trone, *Commercial Law of the European Union*,
Ius Gentium: Comparative Perspectives on Law and Justice 4,
DOI 10.1007/978-90-481-8774-4_3, © Springer Science+Business Media B.V. 2010

[3.15] Application of Art 45 TFEU

Art 45 TFEU has direct effect. See *Union Royale Belge des Sociétés de Football Association ASBL v Bosman* (C-415/93) [1995] ECR I-4921 at [93]; [1996] 1 CMLR 645. This provision has horizontal effect against individual private employers who discriminate on the basis of nationality. See *Angonese v Cassa di Risparmio di Bolzano SpA* (C-281/98) [2000] ECR I-4139 at [36]; [2000] 2 CMLR 1120; *Raccanelli v Max-Planck-Gesellschaft zur Förderung der Wissenschaften eV* (C-94/07) [2008] ECR I-5939 at [45]–[46]; [2008] 3 CMLR 25 (p 751). This Article protects both workers and the employers who wish to employ them. See *Clean Car Autoservice GmbH v Landeshauptmann von Wien* (C-350/96) [1998] ECR I-2521 at [19]–[20], [25]; [1998] 2 CMLR 637.

Situations that are "wholly internal to a Member State" are not covered by Art 45 TFEU. See *Moser v Land Baden-Württemberg* (180/83) [1984] ECR 2539 at [15]; [1984] 3 CMLR 720; *Union Royale Belge des Sociétés de Football Association ASBL v Bosman* (C-415/93) [1995] ECR I-4921 at [89]; [1996] 1 CMLR 645; *Land Nordrhein-Westfalen v Uecker* (C-64/96) [1997] ECR I-3171 at [16]; [1997] 3 CMLR 963; *My v Office National des Pensions* (C-293/03) [2004] ECR I-12013 at [40]; [2005] 1 CMLR 37 (p 937).

[3.20] Concept of "Worker" in Art 45 TFEU

Under the specific language of Art 45 TFEU, freedom of movement benefits only "workers". The term "worker" is not defined in the TFEU. The Court has held that a "worker" is any employed person. In *Raulin v Minister van Onderwijs en Wetenschappen* (C-357/89) [1992] ECR I-1027; [1994] 1 CMLR 227 the Court stated that the "essential characteristic of an employment relationship is that . . . a person performs services for and under the direction of another person in return for which he receives remuneration" (at [10]–[11]). See similarly, *Collins v Secretary of State for Work and Pensions* (C-138/02) [2004] ECR I-2703 at [26]; [2004] 2 CMLR 8 (p 147); *Trojani v Centre public d'aide sociale de Bruxelles* (C-456/02) [2004] ECR I-7573 at [15]; [2004] 3 CMLR 38 (p 820); *Alevizos v Ipourgos Ikonomikon* (C-392/05) [2007] ECR I-3505 at [67]; [2007] 2 CMLR 51 (p 1404).

For example, a professional sportsperson is regarded as a worker because professional sport is an economic activity. See *Walrave v Association Union Cycliste Internationale* (36/74) [1974] ECR 1405 at [4]; [1975] 1 CMLR 320; *Donà v Mantero* (13/76) [1976] ECR 1333 at [12]; [1976] 2 CMLR 578; *Union Royale Belge des Sociétés de Football Association ASBL v Bosman* (C-415/93) [1995] ECR I-4921 at [73]; [1996] 1 CMLR 645; *Meca-Medina v Commission* (C-519/04 P) [2006] ECR I-6991 at [22]–[23]; [2006] 5 CMLR 18 (p 1023).

The fact that employment is for a short fixed term does not prevent a person from being a "worker" under Art 45. See *Ninni-Orasche v Bundesminister für Wissenschaft, Verkehr und Kunst* (C-413/01) [2003] ECR I-13187 at [25], [32]; [2004] 1 CMLR 19 (p 638); *Vatsouras v Arbeitsgemeinschaft (ARGE) Nürnberg 900* (C-22/08) [2009] All ER (EC) 747 at [29].

[3.25] "Worker" Is Defined in EU Law Not National Law

In *Hoekstra v Bestuur der Bedrijfsvereniging voor Detailhandel en Ambachten* (75/63) [1964] ECR 177; [1964] CMLR 319 the Court emphasised that the concept of "worker" must be given an EU rather than a national meaning:

> Articles 48 to 51 of the Treaty [now Arts 45–48 TFEU], by the very fact of establishing freedom of movement for 'workers', have given Community scope to this term.
>
> If the definition of this term were a matter within the competence of national law, it would therefore be possible for each Member State to modify the meaning of the concept of 'migrant worker' and to eliminate at will the protection afforded by the Treaty to certain categories of persons.
>
> Moreover nothing in Articles 48 to 51 of the Treaty leads to the conclusion that these provisions have left the definition of the term 'worker' to national legislation. On the contrary, the fact that Article 48(2) [now Art 45(2) TFEU] mentions certain elements of the concept of 'workers', such as employment and remuneration, shows that the Treaty attributes a Community meaning to that concept. Articles 48 to 51 would therefore be deprived of all effect and the abovementioned objectives of the Treaty would be frustrated if the meaning of such a term could be unilaterally fixed and modified by national law.
>
> The concept of 'workers' in the said Articles does not therefore relate to national law, but to Community law (at ECR 184; CMLR 331).

As an EU concept the meaning of "worker" thus cannot vary from one Member State to another. The Court has continued to emphasise that the term "worker" has an EU meaning and must not be interpreted narrowly. See *Ninni-Orasche v Bundesminister für Wissenschaft, Verkehr und Kunst* (C-413/01) [2003] ECR I-13187 at [23]; [2004] 1 CMLR 19 (p 638); *Trojani v Centre public d'aide sociale de Bruxelles* (C-456/02) [2004] ECR I-7573 at [15]; [2004] 3 CMLR 38 (p 820); *Kranemann v Land Nordrhein-Westfalen* (C-109/04) [2005] ECR I-2421 at [12]; [2005] 2 CMLR 15 (p 341); *Petersen v Arbeitsmarktservice Niederösterreich* (C-228/07) [2008] ECR I-6989 at [45]; [2009] 1 CMLR 2 (p 43). The Court has also reiterated that the term "worker" is not to be interpreted in the light of national law. See *Levin v Secretary of State for Justice* (53/81) [1982] ECR 1035 at [10]–[11]; [1982] 2 CMLR 454; *Kempf v Staatssecretaris van Justitie* (139/85) [1986] ECR 1741 at [15]; [1987] 1 CMLR 764; *de Jaeck v Staatssecretaris van Financiën* (C-340/94) [1997] ECR I-461 at [25]; [1997] 2 CMLR 779.

[3.30] Workers with Low Incomes

The Court has indicated that the rights derived from Art 45 TFEU only cover the pursuit of "genuine and effective" economic activities, not "purely marginal and ancillary" economic activities. See *Levin v Secretary of State for Justice* (53/81) [1982] ECR 1035; [1982] 2 CMLR 454; *Bernini v Minister van Onderwijs en Wetenschappen* (C-3/90) [1992] ECR I-1071 at [14]; *Jany v Staatssecretaris van Justitie* (C-268/99) [2001] ECR I-8615 at [33]; [2003] 2 CMLR 1 (p 1); *Kurz v Land Baden-Württemberg* (C-188/00) [2002] ECR I-10691 at [32]; *Mattern v Ministre du Travail et de l'Emploi* (C-10/05) [2006] ECR I-3145 at [23]; [2006] 2 CMLR 42 (p 1080).

The requirement that the worker's economic activities be genuine and effective was somewhat eroded in *Steymann v Staatssecretaris van Justitie* (196/87) [1988] ECR 6159; [1989] 1 CMLR 449. The Court held that "activities performed by members of a community based on religion or another form of philosophy as part of the commercial activities of that community constitute economic activities in so far as the services which the community provides to its members may be regarded as the indirect quid pro quo for genuine and effective work" (at [14]). A person who worked for the Bhagwan community and was supported by that community was thus a worker within Art 48 EC (now Art 45 TFEU).

In *Trojani v Centre public d'aide sociale de Bruxelles* (C-456/02) [2004] ECR I-7573; [2004] 3 CMLR 38 (p 820) a French national worked for the Salvation Army in Belgium. He worked for around 30 hours each week in a reintegration programme. For that work he received benefits in kind and a small amount of pocket money (at [20]). The Court held that this could constitute a paid employment relationship, since it was one of paid remuneration in return for subordination to the employer (at [22]). The national court was required to determine whether the remunerated activity was "real and genuine", in particular whether the services rendered could be regarded as "part of the normal labour market" (at [23]–[24]).

A person may thus be classified as a "worker" notwithstanding that their income from employment is below subsistence level. See *Nolte v Landesversicherungsanstalt Hannover* (C-317/93) [1995] ECR I-4625 at [19]; *Megner v Innungskrankenkasse Vorderpfalz* (C-444/93) [1995] ECR I-4741 at [18]; *Vatsouras v Arbeitsgemeinschaft (ARGE) Nürnberg 900* (C-22/08) [2009] All ER (EC) 747 at [28].

[3.35] Right of Residence

In *Collins v Secretary of State for Work and Pensions* (C-138/02) [2004] ECR I-2703 at [36]; [2004] 2 CMLR 8 (p 147) the Court observed that Art 45 TFEU allows non-nationals to reside in other Member States for the purpose of seeking or undertaking paid employment (at [36]). In the absence of relevant EU provisions, the Member States may fix a reasonable time within which workers from other Member States must find work. At the end of that time, a worker cannot be compelled to leave the country if they can prove that they are seeking work and have a realistic prospect of being employed (at [37]).

[3.40] Discrimination Based on Nationality of Worker

Art 45(2) TFEU provides that "freedom of movement shall entail the abolition of any discrimination based on nationality between workers of the Member States as regards employment, remuneration and other conditions of work and employment."

This provision aims at abolishing discriminatory provisions which subject nationals of other Member States to more onerous treatment than nationals in the same circumstances. Art 45 prohibits both overt and covert discrimination. Overt (direct) discrimination is explicitly based on nationality. Covert (indirect) discrimination adopts other criteria, but in practice achieves the same discriminatory result. See *Merino García v Bundesanstalt für Arbeit* (C-266/95) [1997] ECR I-3279 at [33]; *Clean Car Autoservice GmbH v Landeshauptmann von Wien* (C-350/96) [1998] ECR I-2521 at [27]; [1998] 2 CMLR 637; *Graf v Filzmoser Maschinenbau GmbH* (C-190/98) [2000] ECR I-493 at [14]; [2000] 1 CMLR 741.

The Court has stated that national provisions are indirectly discriminatory where they apply without regard to nationality but "affect essentially migrant workers . . . or the great majority of those affected are migrant workers . . ., where they are indistinctly applicable but can more easily be satisfied by national workers than by migrant workers . . . or where there is a risk that they may operate to the particular detriment of migrant workers". See *O'Flynn v Adjudication Officer* (C-237/94) [1996] ECR I-2617 at [18]; [1996] 3 CMLR 103; see similarly, *Borawitz v Landesversicherungsanstalt Westfalen* (C-124/99) [2000] ECR I-7293 at [25]; *Celozzi v Innungskrankenkasse Baden-Württemberg* (C-332/05) [2007] ECR I-563 at [24]; *Klöppel v Tiroler Gebietskrankenkasse* (C-507/06) [2008] ECR I-943 at [18].

The Court has often pointed out that national rules that distinguish on the basis of residence are likely to work to the detriment of non-nationals, since non-residents are usually non-nationals. See *Clean Car Autoservice GmbH v Landeshauptmann von Wien* (C-350/96) [1998] ECR I-2521 at [29]; [1998] 2 CMLR 637 (free movement of workers); *Ciola v Land Vorarlberg* (C-224/97) [1999] ECR I-2517 at [14]; [1999] 2 CMLR 1220 (freedom to provide services). For example, in the *Clean Car* case the Court held that a Member State indirectly discriminated on the basis of nationality by providing that the owner of an undertaking could not appoint a non-resident manager (at [26], [30]).

In *Collins v Secretary of State for Work and Pensions* (C-138/02) [2004] ECR I-2703; [2004] 2 CMLR 8 (p 147) an Irish national seeking work in the United Kingdom was denied the jobseeker's allowance on the ground that he was not habitually resident in the country. The Court held that this requirement was more readily satisfied by UK nationals and placed work seekers from other Member States at a disadvantage (at [65]).

This requirement could be justified only if it was "based on objective considerations that are independent of the nationality of the persons concerned and proportionate to the legitimate aim of the national provisions" (at [66]). It was legitimate for a Member State to pay the allowance only after a genuine link between the jobseeker and the State's employment market had been shown (at [69]). A residence requirement was thus permissible, but it had to be proportionate to the State's legitimate objective. The application of the residence requirement must be based on clear rules known beforehand and judicial redress must be available. The period of residence must not be longer than necessary for demonstrating that the person is genuinely seeking work (at [72]).

In *Schöning-Kougebetopoulou v Freie und Hansestadt Hamburg* (C-15/96) [1998] ECR I-47; [1998] 1 CMLR 931 a collective agreement provided for promotion on the basis of 8 years seniority. However, periods of employment in the same capacity in the public service of another Member State were not included when calculating seniority. The Court held that this exclusion operated to the detriment of migrant workers and violated the prohibition against non-discrimination (at [23]).

[3.45] Obstacles to Freedom of Movement

Provisions that prevent or discourage an EU citizen from leaving their home State to work in another Member State constitute an obstacle to freedom of movement even if they apply to both nationals and non-nationals. See *Union Royale Belge des Sociétés de Football Association ASBL v Bosman* (C-415/93) [1995] ECR I-4921 at [96]; [1996] 1 CMLR 645; *Graf v Filzmoser Maschinenbau GmbH* (C-190/98) [2000] ECR I-493 at [23]; [2000] 1 CMLR 741; *Proceedings brought by Turpeinen* (C-520/04) [2006] ECR I-10685 at [15]; [2007] 1 CMLR 28 (p 783); *ITC Innovative Technology Center GmbH v Bundesagentur für Arbeit* (C-208/05) [2007] ECR I-181 at [33]; [2008] 1 CMLR 15 (p 343); *Commission v Germany* (C-318/05) [2007] ECR I-6957 at [115].

In *Union Royale Belge des Sociétés de Football Association ASBL v Bosman* (C-415/93) [1995] ECR I-4921; [1996] 1 CMLR 645 national football association rules for the transfer of players between clubs required the new club to pay a fee to the player's former club (at [100]). The Court held that this rule was an obstacle to free movement of workers even though it did not discriminate on the ground of nationality. The rule "directly affect[ed] player's access to the employment market in other Member States" and could impede free movement (at [103]). The Court held that the rule violated the freedom of movement for workers (at [114]).

[3.50] Exceptions to Free Movement of Workers

Two main exceptions will be examined here: the public policy exception and public service employment.

[3.55] Public Policy

The policy exception is provided for in Art 45(3) TFEU according to which the right of freedom of movement may be limited "on grounds of public policy, public security or public health". The Court has indicated that reliance on the concept of public policy presupposes the existence of a "genuine and sufficiently serious threat to the requirements of public policy affecting one of the fundamental interests of society". See *R v Bouchereau* (30/77) [1977] ECR 1999 at [35]; [1977] 2 CMLR 800; *Clean Car Autoservice GmbH v Landeshauptmann von Wien* (C-350/96) [1998] ECR I-2521 at [40]; [1998] 2 CMLR 637; *Ministre de l'Intérieur v Olazabal* (C-100/01) [2002] ECR I-10981 at [39]; [2005] 1 CMLR 49 (p 1297); *Commission v Germany* (C-441/02) [2006] ECR I-3449 at [35].

The Court has emphasised that as an exception to a fundamental freedom the concept of "public policy" should be interpreted strictly. See *Rutili v Minister for the Interior* (36/75) [1975] ECR 1219 at [27]; [1976] 1 CMLR 140; *Orfanopoulos v Land Baden-Württemberg* (C-482/01) [2004] ECR I-5257 at [64]–[65]; [2005] 1 CMLR 18 (p 433); *Commission v Spain* (C-503/03) [2006] ECR I-1097 at [45].

The public policy exception was considered in *Rutili v Minister for the Interior* (36/75) [1975] ECR 1219; [1976] 1 CMLR 140. An Italian resident in France received from the French immigration authorities a residence card that prohibited him from residing in four specific French départements (provinces) (at [4]). The reason for the imposition of this restriction was that Rutili had participated in political and union disturbances (at [6]). The decision to restrict his freedom of movement was based on the expectation that his presence in these départements could result in disturbances of the peace (at [6]).

The Court held that Member States cannot unilaterally decide upon the scope of the proviso but its interpretation is subject to control by the institutions of the EU (at [27]). In cases involving union rights activities, the public policy exception cannot be invoked for the purposes of limiting a person's freedom of movement (at [31]). The right to freedom of movement in Art 48 EC (now Art 45 TFEU) extends to the whole territory of a Member State (at [46]). Prohibitions upon residence thus may relate only to the entire national territory (at [48]).

In *Ministre de l'Interieur v Olazabal* (C-100/01) [2002] ECR I-10981; [2005] 1 CMLR 49 (p 1297) a French court had sentenced a Spanish national to imprisonment for conspiring to disturb public order by intimidation or terror (at [12]). He was associated with a terrorist group that sought Basque independence from Spain. After the Spanish national was released from jail, the French government prohibited him from residing in French départements near the Spanish border. He was later required to obtain permission before leaving the département in which he resided (at [15]).

The Court distinguished the *Rutili* case. In *Rutili* the residence of the foreign national had been restricted on the ground of his political and trade union activities (at [34]). In the present case the Spanish national had been sentenced to imprisonment for offences related to terrorism. He was a member of an armed group that was a threat to public order in France. Measures countering these activities fell within the ground of public security (at [35]).

The Court held that "where nationals of other Member States are liable to banishment or prohibition of residence, they are also capable of being subject to less severe measures consisting of partial restrictions on their right of residence, justified on grounds of public policy, without it being necessary that identical measures be capable of being applied by the Member State in question to its own nationals" (at [41]).

The public policy proviso was also considered in *van Duyn v Home Office* (41/74) [1974] ECR 1337; [1975] 1 CMLR 1. A Dutch woman was refused entry into the United Kingdom because she proposed to work for the Church of Scientology, which the British government regarded as socially harmful (at [2]–[3]). The Government justified its decision to refuse entry by reference to the public policy proviso.

The Court considered the interpretation of Art 3(1)) of Directive 64/221 (now Art 27(2) of Directive 2004/38). That provision stated that "Measures taken on grounds of public policy or of public security shall be based exclusively on the personal conduct of the individual concerned". Thus, EU law does not dictate to the Member States what constitutes public policy, but measures taken in pursuit of public policy must be based solely on the conduct of the individual concerned.

The Court indicated that the particular circumstances justifying recourse to the concept of public policy may vary between Member States and at different times. The Member States have a discretion in this area (at [18]). A Member State is allowed to rely on the public policy concept whenever it has clearly defined its viewpoint regarding the relevant behaviour and has taken administrative measures. Thus, it is not necessary, before a State can rely on the public policy concept, to make such activities unlawful (at [19]).

However, the validity of this conclusion is doubtful in the light of the Court's later decision in *Adoui v Belgium* (115/81) [1982] ECR 1665; [1982] 3 CMLR 631. In that case the Court indicated that a Member State may only expel from its territory a national of another Member State or deny him access to that territory if it has adopted "with respect to the same conduct on the part of its own nationals, repressive measures or other genuine and effective measures intended to combat such conduct" (at [8]). See similarly, *Ministre de l'Interieur v Olazabal* (C-100/01) [2002] ECR I-10981 at [42]; [2005] 1 CMLR 49 (p 1297).

[3.60] Public Service Employment

Art 45(4) TFEU provides that freedom of movement for workers does not apply to employment in the public service. As an exception to a fundamental freedom, this exclusion is to be strictly construed. See *Re Employees of the Consiglio Nazionale delle Ricerche (National Research Council): Commission v Italy* (225/85) [1987] ECR 2625 at [7]; [1988] 3 CMLR 635; *Colegio de Oficiales de la Marina Mercante Española v Administración del Estado* (C-405/01) [2003] ECR I-10391 at [41], [44]; [2005] 2 CMLR 13 (p 279); *Anker v Germany* (C-47/02) [2003] ECR I-10447 at [60], [63]; [2004] 2 CMLR 35 (p 845).

In *Re Public Employees (No 2): Commission v Belgium* (149/79) [1982] ECR 1845; [1982] 3 CMLR 539 the Court held that not all public service positions are exempted but that the scope of the exception must be limited to posts "entrusted with the exercise of powers conferred by public law and with responsibility for safeguarding the general interests of the State" (at [7]). See similarly, *Re French Nurses: Commission v France* (307/84) [1986] ECR 1725 at [12]; [1987] 3 CMLR 555; *Bleis v Ministère de l'Education Nationale* (C-4/91) [1991] ECR I-5627 at [6]; [1994] 1 CMLR 793; *Commission v Germany* (C-103/01) [2003] ECR I-5369 at [44]; *Alevizos v Ipourgos Ikonomikon* (C-392/05) [2007] ECR I-3505 at [69]; [2007] 2 CMLR 51 (p 1404).

The purpose of this exception is to allow Member States to restrict access to positions that "presume on the part of those occupying them the existence of a special relationship of allegiance to the State and reciprocity of rights and duties which form the foundation of the bond of nationality". See *Colegio de Oficiales de la Marina Mercante Española v Administración del Estado* (C-405/01) [2003] ECR I-10391 at [39]; [2005] 2 CMLR 13 (p 279); *Anker v Germany* (C-47/02) [2003] ECR I-10447 at [58]; [2004] 2 CMLR

35 (p 845); *Alevizos v Ipourgos Ikonomikon* (C-392/05) [2007] ECR I-3505 at [70]; [2007] 2 CMLR 51 (p 1404).

The Court has held that the following public sector positions do not constitute "employment in the public service":

- school teachers: *Bleis v Ministère de l'Education Nationale* (C-4/91) [1991] ECR I-5627 at [7]; [1994] 1 CMLR 793; *Re Public Service Employment: Commission v Luxembourg* (C-473/93) [1996] ECR I-3207 at [33]–[34]; [1996] 3 CMLR 981; *Österreichischer Gewerkschaftsbund v Austria* (C-195/98) [2000] ECR I-10497 at [36]; [2002] 1 CMLR 14 (p 375);
- specialist doctors: *Schöning-Kougebetopoulou v Freie und Hansestadt Hamburg* (C-15/96) [1998] ECR I-47 at [13], [25]; [1998] 1 CMLR 931;
- nurses in public hospitals: *Re French Nurses: Commission v France* (307/84) [1986] ECR 1725 at [13]; [1987] 3 CMLR 555;
- managers in hospitals: *Burbaud v Ministère de l'Emploi et de la Solidarité* (C-285/01) [2003] ECR I-8219 at [40]; [2003] 3 CMLR 21 (p 635);
- most water, gas and electricity distribution positions: *Commission v Belgium* (C-173/94) [1996] ECR I-3265 at [17], [20];
- researchers at a national research centre: *Re Employees of the Consiglio Nazionale delle Ricerche (National Research Council): Commission v Italy* (C-225/85) [1987] ECR 2625 at [9]; [1988] 3 CMLR 635;
- university researchers: *Petrie v Università degli Studi di Verona* (C-90/96) [1997] ECR I-6527 at [27]–[29]; [1998] 1 CMLR 711; and
- university foreign language assistants: *Allué v Università degli studi di Venezia* (33/88) [1989] ECR 1591 at [9]; [1991] 1 CMLR 283.

Obviously, employees in the private sector generally do not fall within the public service exception. See *Commission v Italy* (C-283/99) [2001] ECR I-4363 at [25]; *Kranemann v Land Nordrhein-Westfalen* (C-109/04) [2005] ECR I-2421 at [19]; [2005] 2 CMLR 15 (p 341). However, the public service exemption can include those in private employment who regularly exercise public functions as more than a minimal part of their activities. See *Colegio de Oficiales de la Marina Mercante Española v Administración del Estado* (C-405/01) [2003] ECR I-10391 at [43]–[44]; [2005] 2 CMLR 13 (p 279); *Anker v Germany* (C-47/02) [2003] ECR I-10447 at [62]; [2004] 2 CMLR 35 (p 845).

In *Sotgiu v Deutsche Bundespost* (152/73) [1974] ECR 153 the Court held that discriminatory measures cannot be justified once a person had been admitted to positions within the "public service" under Art 45(4) TFEU since that admission shows that the interests justifying the exemption were not applicable in this case (at [4]). See similarly, *Re Employees of the Consiglio Nazionale delle Ricerche (National Research Council): Commission v Italy* (225/85) [1987] ECR 2625 at [11]; [1988] 3 CMLR 635; *Echternach v Minister van Onderwijs en Wetenschappen* (389/87) [1989] ECR 723 at [14]; [1990] 2 CMLR 305; *Allué v Università degli studi di Venezia* (33/88) [1989] ECR 1591 at [8]; [1991] 1 CMLR 283; *Österreichischer Gewerkschaftsbund v Austria* (C-195/98) [2000] ECR I-10497 at [37]; [2002] 1 CMLR 14 (p 375); *Alevizos v Ipourgos Ikonomikon* (C-392/05) [2007] ECR I-3505 at [70]; [2007] 2 CMLR 51 (p 1404).

See generally, David O'Keeffe, "Judicial Interpretation of the Public Service Exception to the Free Movement of Workers" in Deirdre Curtin and David O'Keeffe (eds), *Constitutional Adjudication in European Community and National Law* (Dublin: Butterworths, 1992), 89; Jolanda E Beenen, *Citizenship, Nationality and Access to Public Service Employment: The Impact of European Community Law* (Groningen: Europa Law Publishing, 2001).

[3.65] Secondary Legislation Regarding Free Movement of Workers

The major secondary legislation regarding the freedom of movement of persons is Regulation 1612/68 of the Council of 15 October 1968 on freedom of movement for workers within the Community (OJ L 257, 19.10.1968, p 2).

Under the Regulation "[a] worker who is a national of a Member State may not, in the territory of another Member State, be treated differently from national workers by reason of his nationality in respect of any conditions of employment and work, in particular as regards remuneration, dismissal, and should he become unemployed, reinstatement or re-employment" (Art 7(1)). Such a worker is also entitled to equality of treatment with regard to membership of trade unions and the exercise of rights attaching to such membership (Art 8(1))

A worker who is a national of a Member State shall, in the territory of another Member State, "enjoy the same social and tax advantages as national workers" (Art 7(2)). This Article prohibits both overt and covert discrimination. See *Kaba v Secretary of State for the Home Department* (C-356/98) [2000] ECR I-2623 at [27]; [2003] 1 CMLR 39 (p 1150). This provision is not to be given a restrictive construction. See *Meints v Minister van Landbouw, Natuurbeheer en Visserij* (C-57/96) [1997] ECR I-6689 at [39]; [1998] 1 CMLR 1159. All social and tax advantages are included, whether or not attached to the contract of employment. See *Cristini v Sociéte Nationale des Chemins de fer Français* (32/75) [1975] ECR 1085 at [13]; [1976] 1 CMLR 573.

The concept of social advantage has been considered in many cases. In *Netherlands v Reed* (59/85) [1986] ECR 1283; [1987] 2 CMLR 448 Reed was a British national living with a British citizen who had residence status in the Netherlands. Ms Reed was ordered to leave the Netherlands because she was unemployed and was thereby effectively denied the right to live with her partner (at [4]). This is a right that would have been granted to her if her companion had Dutch nationality (at [6]).

The Court held that the "concept of social advantage ... must include all advantages which ... are generally granted to national workers primarily because of their objective status as workers or by virtue of the mere fact of their residence on the national territory and the extension of which to workers who are nationals of other member countries therefore seems suitable to facilitate their mobility within the Community" (at [26]). Therefore, the "possibility for a migrant worker of obtaining permission for his unmarried companion to reside with him ... must ... be regarded as falling within the concept of a social advantage" (at [28]). See similarly, *Martínez Sala v Freistaat Bayern* (C-85/96) [1998] ECR I-2691 at [25]; *Commission v Greece* (C-185/96) [1998] ECR I-6601 at [20]; [2001] 1 CMLR 28 (p 744).

The following benefits are among those that have been held to constitute social advantages under the Regulation:

- child-raising allowances: *Martínez Sala v Freistaat Bayern* (C-85/96) [1998] ECR I-2691 at [22], [24], [26];
- benefits for large families: *Cristini v Sociéte Nationale des Chemins de fer Français* (32/75) [1975] ECR 1085 at [13]; [1976] 1 CMLR 573; *Commission v Greece* (C-185/96) [1998] ECR I-6601 at [21]; [2001] 1 CMLR 28 (p 744);
- disability allowances: *Schmid v Belgium* (C-310/91) [1993] ECR I-3011 at [18]; [1995] 2 CMLR 803;
- payment of funeral costs: *O'Flynn v Adjudication Officer* (C-237/94) [1996] ECR I-2617 at [14]; [1996] 3 CMLR 103;
- tideover allowances: *Office national de l'emploi v Ioannidis* (C-258/04) [2005] ECR I-8275 at [34]; [2005] 3 CMLR 47 (p 1285); and
- study finance: *Meeusen v Hoofddirectie van de Informatie Beheer Groep* (C-337/97) [1999] ECR I-3289 at [19]; [2000] 2 CMLR 659; *Fahmi v Bestuur van de Sociale Verzekeringsbank* (C-33/99) [2001] ECR I-2415 at [45]; [2003] 1 CMLR 45 (p 1280).

The benefit must be generally granted to workers. The payment of pension contributions as part of a compensatory arrangement for those called up for military service was not a social advantage generally granted to workers. See *de Vos v Stadt Bielefeld* (C-315/94) [1996] ECR I-1417 at [21]–[23]. Similarly, compensation granted to former prisoners of war did not constitute a social advantage because it was not granted generally to workers. See *Baldinger v Pensionsversicherungsanstalt der Arbeiter* (C-386/02) [2004] ECR I-8411 at [19], [21]; [2005] 1 CMLR 20 (p 499).

There are fewer cases interpreting the concept of a tax advantage under the Regulation. The joint assessment to taxation of married couples was held to be a tax advantage. See *Zurstrassen v Administration des Contributions Directes* (C-87/99) [2000] ECR I-3337 at [26]; [2001] 3 CMLR 66 (p 1715).

The Court has held that Art 7(2) of the Regulation also prohibits discrimination regarding social and tax advantages that disadvantage the dependent children of a worker. See *Meeusen v Hoofddirectie van de Informatie Beheer Groep* (C-337/97) [1999] ECR I-3289 at [22]; [2000] 2 CMLR 659; *Office national de l'emploi v Ioannidis* (C-258/04) [2005] ECR I-8275 at [35]–[36]; [2005] 3 CMLR 47 (p 1285).

Other EU legal acts relating to free movement of workers include:

- Council Directive 98/49 of 29 June 1998 on safeguarding the supplementary pension rights of employed and self-employed persons moving within the Community (OJ L 209, 25.7.1998, p 46);
- Regulation 883/2004 of the European Parliament and of the Council of 29 April 2004 on the coordination of social security systems (OJ L 200, 7.6.2004, p 1); and
- Decision 2241/2004 of the European Parliament and of the Council of 15 December 2004 on a single Community framework for the transparency of qualifications and competences (Europass) (OJ L 390, 31.12.2004, p 6).

Under Art 48 TFEU the EU shall adopt such social security measures as are necessary for the free movement of European workers. These measures must include aggregation and the payment of benefits to EU migrant workers resident in a Member State.

[3.70] Freedom of Establishment

The purpose of freedom of establishment is to allow an EU national "to participate, on a stable and continuing basis, in the economic life of a Member State other than his State of origin and to profit therefrom". See *Cadbury Schweppes plc v Inland Revenue Commissioners* (C-196/04) [2006] ECR I-7995 at [53]; [2007] 1 CMLR 2 (p 43); see similarly, *Gebhard v Consiglio dell'Ordine degli Avvocati e Procuratori di Milano* (C-55/94) [1995] ECR I-4165 at [25]; [1996] 1 CMLR 603; *Centro di Musicologia Walter Stauffer v Finanzamt München für Körperschaften* (C-386/04) [2006] ECR I-8203 at [18]; [2009] 2 CMLR 31 (p 777).

Arts 49 and 54 TFEU deal with the freedom of establishment of individuals and companies respectively. Art 49 TFEU primarily aims at facilitating the establishment of professionals in a Member State other than the one of which they are a citizen. In its relevant part it reads as follows:

> [R]estrictions on the freedom of establishment of nationals of a Member State in the territory of another Member State shall be prohibited. Such prohibition shall also apply to restrictions on the setting-up of agencies, branches or subsidiaries by nationals of any Member State established in the territory of any Member State.
>
> Freedom of establishment shall include the right to take up and pursue activities as self-employed persons and to set up and manage undertakings... under

> the conditions laid down for its own nationals by the law of the country where such establishment is effected, subject to the provisions of the Chapter relating to capital.

Self-employed persons have a freedom of establishment. A self-employed person works "outside any relationship of subordination concerning the choice of that activity, working conditions and conditions of remuneration; ... under that person's own responsibility; and ... in return for remuneration paid to that person directly and in full". See *Jany v Staatssecretaris van Justitie* (C-268/99) [2001] ECR I-8615 at [70]; [2003] 2 CMLR 1 (p 1); see similarly, *Criminal Proceedings Against Nadin* (C-151/04) [2005] ECR I-11203 at [31]; [2006] 2 CMLR 15 (p 435).

Art 54 TFEU stipulates that "Companies or firms formed in accordance with the law of a Member State and having their registered office, central administration or principal place of business within the Union shall ... be treated in the same way as natural persons who are nationals of Member States."

[3.75] Establishment by Professionals

The right of establishment facilitates the establishment of professionals in a Member State other than the one of which they are a citizen. By way of example this section discusses briefly a number of judgments relating to the right of professionals to establish themselves in any Member State.

The second paragraph of Art 49 TFEU stipulates that EU citizens who wish to avail themselves of the right of establishment must satisfy the conditions which are laid down by the State of establishment for its own nationals. A Member State would be able to manipulate this Article for the purpose of preferring its own nationals by the expedient device of selecting conditions which cannot easily be met by non-nationals. The Court has endeavoured to limit the Member States' discretion in this area by requiring that these conditions are reasonable and non-discriminatory in their effect.

All EU practising lawyers have an enforceable right under the TFEU to establish themselves as practitioners in any Member State provided they are able to satisfy the stringent national legislative measures or professional rules which apply equally to nationals and non-nationals alike.

In *Thieffry v Paris Bar Council* (71/76) [1977] ECR 765; [1977] 2 CMLR 373 Thieffry's Belgian law degree had been recognised by a French university as equivalent to the French licentiate's degree in law. In accordance with French legislation he successfully sat for an examination and obtained a qualifying certificate for the profession of *avocat* (at [2]). Nevertheless, his application for admission to the French bar was rejected because he did not have the relevant French licentiate's degree (at [3]). The Court stated:

> when a national of one member-State desirous of exercising a professional activity such as the profession of advocate in another member-State has obtained a diploma in his country of origin which has been recognised as an equivalent qualification by the competent authority under the legislation of the country of establishment and which has thus enabled him to sit and pass the special qualifying examination for the profession in question, the act of demanding the national diploma prescribed by the legislation of the country of establishment constitutes... a restriction incompatible with the freedom of establishment (at [27]).

In *Ordre des Advocats au Barreau de Paris v Klopp* (107/83) [1984] ECR 2971; [1985] 1 CMLR 99 Klopp was established in Germany as a lawyer. He sought registration on the training list of the Paris Bar, while living in Düsseldorf and remaining a member of the Bar of that city (at [2]). His application was rejected on the ground that he did not meet the admission rule "that an advocate can maintain chambers in one place only, which is in the territorial jurisdiction of the Tribunal... with which he is registered" (at [3]). The Paris Bar argued that this rule was justified "by the need for the advocate actually to practice within the jurisdiction of a certain court so that both the court and his clients can have ready access to him" (at [16]).

The Court responded that modern transport and communications facilitated contact with the court and clients (at [21]). The Court concluded that the freedom of establishment prevents "the competent authorities of any member-State from refusing... a national of another member-State the right to join and to practice the profession of advocate merely because he at the same time maintains chambers in another member-State" (at [22]). In effect, the Court's judgment signifies that the national requirement constituted an unreasonable restriction that would have made the right of establishment meaningless.

In *Gullung v Conseil de L'ordre des Avocats* (292/86) [1988] ECR 111; [1988] 2 CMLR 57 a French legislative provision imposed upon legal practitioners an obligation to become members of a Bar if they proposed to establish themselves in France as *avocats* (at [24]). The Court emphasised that such a national rule pursued "an objective which merits protection" (at [29]). In particular, the objective was "to guarantee good character and observance of the rules of professional conduct" (at [29]). The Court decided that "Member-States whose legislation imposes an obligation to become a member of a Bar on those who wish to establish themselves in their territory as avocats... may impose the same requirement on avocats from other member-States who invoke the right of establishment" (at [30]).

In *Vlassopoulou v Ministerium für Justiz* (C-340/89) [1991] ECR I-2357; [1993] 2 CMLR 221 the Court provided guidance for national authorities when examining the adequacy of credentials from other Member States in considering applications by non-nationals for admission to the bar. The Court held that:

> Article 52 EEC [Art 49 TFEU] must be interpreted as requiring the national authorities of a member-State to which an application for admission to the profession of lawyer is made by a Community subject who is already admitted to practise as a lawyer in his country of origin . . . to examine to what extent the knowledge and qualifications attested by the diploma obtained by the person concerned in his country of origin correspond to those required by the rules of the host State; if those diplomas correspond only partially, the national authorities in question are entitled to require the person concerned to prove that he has acquired the knowledge and qualifications which are lacking (at [23]).

In *Commission v France* (96/85) [1986] ECR 1475; [1986] 3 CMLR 57 French law required doctors and dentists established in another Member State to give up their registration there in order to become a practitioner in France (at [1]). The French government justified its system on the ground that it was important for medical practitioners to be close to their patients (at [6]). The Court held that the French law unreasonably restricted the free movement of persons and services. In particular, restrictions on free movement are only "justified in view of the general obligations inherent in the proper practice of the professions in question and apply to nationals and foreigners alike" (at [11]).

[3.80] Establishment by Companies

Art 54 TFEU provides that entities must satisfy two requirements in order to be considered a "company". First, the entity must have been formed in accordance with the law of a Member State and have its registered office, central administration or principal place of business within the EU. The entity must have a legal personality in the sense that its assets must be separate from those of its owners. It must have the capacity to sue and to be sued. Secondly, Art 54 stipulates that a company is a profit-making entity.

A Member State may define the connecting factors required for a company to be incorporated under its law and for it to continue to retain that status. In *Proceedings re Cartesio Oktató és Szolgáltató bt* (C-210/06) [2008] ECR I-9641; [2009] 1 CMLR 50 (p 1394) the Court held that a Member State could withdraw recognition of the incorporation of a company under its law if the company transferred its seat to another Member State, thus severing the connecting factor required under its law for incorporation (at [110], [124]). See António Frada de Sousa, "Company's Cross-border Transfer of Seat in the EU after *Cartesio*", *Jean Monnet Working Paper* No 07/09, http://www.jeanmonnetprogram.org.

[3.85] Establishment of Subsidiaries

Companies established in a Member State may establish themselves in another Member State by means of a "subsidiary company". See

Commission v France (270/83) [1986] ECR 273 at [27]; [1987] 1 CMLR 401. However, in accordance with Arts 49 and 54 TFEU such establishment in another Member State will still be subject to non-discriminatory requirements laid down by the host country.

In *Imperial Chemical Industries plc v Colmer* (C-264/96) [1998] ECR I-4695; [1998] 3 CMLR 293 the Court held that while freedom of establishment was primarily directed at protecting companies operating in another Member State against discrimination by the host state, it also prohibited a Member State from obstructing its own companies' establishment of subsidiaries in other Member States (at [21]). See similarly, *Rewe Zentralfinanz eG v Finanzamt Köln-Mitte* (C-347/04) [2007] ECR I-2647 at [26]; [2007] 2 CMLR 42 (p 1111); *Columbus Container Services BVBA & Co v Finanzamt Bielefeld-Innenstadt* (C-298/05) [2007] ECR I-10451 at [33]; [2009] 1 CMLR 8 (p 241).

EU law makes a distinction between "branches" and "subsidiaries". A non-EU company with a branch in the Union would not be able to avail itself of the right to establishment because it does not meet the requirements of Art 54 TFEU. In particular, as a branch is merely an offshoot of a firm established in a third country, it does not have a statutory registered office or central administration or principal place of business within the EU. In contrast, subsidiaries are distinct from their parent companies, by which they have been set up, in that they have a statutory registered office or principal place of business within the European Union.

There are specific EU provisions relating to the establishment of branches by particular types of businesses. Insurance undertakings are one such example. See Directive 2009/138 of the European Parliament and of the Council of 25 November 2009 on the taking-up and pursuit of the business of Insurance and Reinsurance (Solvency II) (recast) (OJ L 335, 17.12.2009, p 1). An insurance undertaking that wishes to establish a branch in another Member State must notify the government of its home Member State (Art 145(1)). The home Member State of an undertaking is the Member State in which its head office is located (Art 13(8)). The undertaking must supply certain information to its home government (Art 145(2)).

The government of the home state communicates this information to the authorities of the other Member State. The home government can refuse to forward the application where, for example, it has reason to doubt the undertaking's financial situation or the good repute and qualification of its management (Art 146(1)). An undertaking has the right to appeal to the courts against a refusal to forward its information to the other Member State (Art 146(2)). The home government must attest that the undertaking satisfies the minimum solvency margins set by the Directive (Art 146(1)).

Within 2 months of receiving the information, the government of the other Member State may set conditions required in the "general good" for the operation of the branch (Art 146(3)). Two months after the receipt of the information by the other Member State the undertaking may establish the branch (Art 146(3)).

A similar process applies under Directive 2004/39 of the European Parliament and of the Council of 21 April 2004 on markets in financial instruments (OJ L 145, 30.4.2004, p 1). Investment services or activities may be provided in another Member State through the establishment of a branch (Art 32(1)). An investment firm wishing to establish a branch in another Member State must notify certain information to the authorities of its home Member State. This information includes the intended host Member State, a programme of intended business operations, and the names of those who will manage the branch (Art 32(2)).

The government of the home state communicates this information to the authorities of the other Member State. It can refuse to forward this information where, for example, it has reason to doubt the adequacy of the financial situation of the firm (Art 32(3)). The home state must also communicate the particulars of the accredited compensation scheme of which the firm is a member (Art 32(4)). Two months after receipt of the communication from the home state, the branch may be established and begin business (Art 32(6)).

EU Member States may not give more favourable treatment to EU branches of non-EU credit institutions rules than that given to EU credit institutions. See Art 38(1), Directive 2006/48 of the European Parliament and of the Council of 14 June 2006 relating to the taking up and pursuit of the business of credit institutions (OJ L 177, 30.6.2006, p 1).

[3.90] Removal of Discrimination

Paragraph 2 of Art 49 TFEU stipulates that the right of establishment includes "the right to take up and pursue activities as self-employed persons... under the conditions laid down for its own nationals by the law of the country where such establishment is effected". Such requirements may include the requirement that the applicant has been licensed in a technical school and has a satisfactory knowledge of the language of the state of establishment. However, it is obvious that some conditions could easily be manipulated by the state of establishment in order to accord a de facto preference to its own nationals. This stems from the fact that some conditions may more easily be satisfied by nationals than citizens of another EU Member State.

Art 49 provides that a Member State may not discriminate against the applicant on grounds of nationality. In *Scholz v Opera Universitaria di Cagliari* (C-419/92) [1994] ECR I-505; [1994] 1 CMLR 873 the ECJ explained that Art 48 EC (now Art 49 TFEU) "prohibits not only overt discrimination by reason of nationality but also all covert forms of discrimination which, by the application of other distinguishing criteria, lead in fact to the same result" (at [7]). See similarly, *R v Inland Revenue Commissioners; Ex parte Commerzbank AG* (C-330/91) [1993] ECR I-4017 at [14]; [1993] 3 CMLR 457; *Halliburton Services BV v Staatssecretaris van Financiën* (C-1/93) [1994] ECR I-1137 at [15]; [1994] 3 CMLR 377; *Geurts v Administratie van de BTW, registratie en domeinen* (C-464/05) [2007] ECR I-9325 at [20]; [2008] 1 CMLR 29 (p 755); *Finanzamt Dinslaken v Meindl* (C-329/05) [2007] ECR I-1107 at [21]; [2007] 2 CMLR 12 (p 255).

A combined reading of Arts 49 and 54 TFEU reveals that the freedom of establishment benefits businesses that are incorporated in a Member State even if they are a subsidiary of a foreign company. Provided that they are formed in accordance with the law of a Member State, these subsidiaries are treated as EU firms. They cannot be discriminated against on grounds of nationality because they are regarded as EU companies.

[3.95] When the Protection Applies

Art 49 TFEU protects EU nationals who propose to establish themselves in a Member State of which they are not nationals. This Article means that a self-employed person cannot be prevented from establishing themselves in a Member State of which they are not a national, simply because of their nationality. The Article also requires that they are not discriminated against with respect to any decisions which may affect a person's ability to function effectively as a self-employed person.

For example, in *Steinhauser v City of Biarritz* (197/84) [1985] ECR 1819; [1986] 1 CMLR 53 the Court was confronted with a decision of a French city to refuse an application by a German citizen to rent lock-ups for the purpose of exhibiting and selling works of art (at [3]). His application was denied on the ground of his nationality (at [4]). The Court pointed out that the freedom of establishment "includes the right not only to take up activities as a self-employed person but also to pursue them in the broad sense of the term" and that the "renting of premises for business purposes furthers the pursuit of an occupation" (at [16]). Thus Art 49 TFEU disallows a tendering procedure for the allocation of public property belonging to a city if it makes the acceptance of applications conditional upon nationality (at [17]).

Art 49 TFEU is not applicable to a situation that is purely internal to a Member State. See *Ministère Public v Gauchard* (20/87) [1987] ECR 4879 at [13]; [1989] 2 CMLR 489; *Steen v Deutsche Bundespost* (C-332/90) [1992] ECR I-341 at [12]; [1992] 2 CMLR 406; *Criminal Proceedings Against Van Buynder* (C-152/94) [1995] ECR I-3981 at [10]; *Criminal Proceedings Against Gervais* (C-17/94) [1995] ECR I-4353 at [24]; *Asscher v Staatssecretaris van Financiën* (C-107/94) [1996] ECR I-3089 at [32]; [1996] 3 CMLR 61.

[3.100] Limitations upon Freedom of Establishment

The right of establishment does not apply to activities connected with the exercise of official authority. There are also a number of permissible justifications for limiting freedom of establishment. These justifications include public policy, public health, consumer protection, the prevention of crime, the prevention of tax avoidance and collective industrial action. Only a few of the cases concerning these justifications will be examined here.

[3.105] Exercise of Official Authority

Art 51 TFEU stipulates that the right of establishment "shall not apply, so far as any given Member State is concerned, to activities which in that State are connected, even occasionally, with the exercise of official authority".

As an exception to fundamental freedoms Art 51 TFEU must be strictly interpreted. See *Re Private Teaching: Commission v Greece* (147/86) [1988] ECR 1637 at [7]; [1989] 2 CMLR 845; *Re Inspection of Organic Produce by Private Bodies: Commission v Germany* (C-404/05) [2007] ECR I-10239 at [37], [46]; [2008] 1 CMLR 43 (p 1148). It is limited to acts that are "directly and specifically connected" with the exercise of official authority. See *Thijssen v Controledienst voor de verzekeringen* (C-42/92) [1993] ECR I-4047 at [8]; *Re Inspection of Organic Produce by Private Bodies: Commission v Austria* (C-393/05) [2007] ECR I-10195 at [36]; [2008] 1 CMLR 42 (p 1121); *Jundt v Finanzamt Offenburg* (C-281/06) [2007] ECR I-12231 at [37].

In *Re Private Teaching: Commission v Greece* (147/86) [1988] ECR 1637; [1989] 2 CMLR 845 the Court held that the establishment of a private school or the giving of private lessons were not connected with the exercise of official authority. Therefore these activities were not exempt from the application of the freedom of establishment provisions (at [9]).

[3.110] Public Policy Exception

The public policy exception appears in Art 52(1) TFEU which stipulates that the right of establishment "shall not prejudice the applicability of provisions laid down by law, regulation or administrative action providing for special treatment for foreign nationals on grounds of public policy, public security or public health".

The public health exception was raised in *Apothekerkammer des Saarlandes v Saarland* (C-171/07) [2009] 3 CMLR 31 (p 1133). Under national legislation only pharmacists were permitted to own and operate a pharmacy (at [2]). The Court held that this restriction was justified on health protection grounds: ensuring the quality and reliability of medicines supplied to the public (at [28]). Medicines were distinguishable from most other goods because of the potential harm to health caused by incorrectly supplied medicines (at [32]–[32]). The viability of social security systems would also be undermined by the unnecessary consumption of medicines (at [33]). The professional independence of pharmacists provided a greater safeguard of these interests than would be given by the supply of medicines by non-pharmacists (at [35], [38]). It was not demonstrated that a less restrictive measure would provide as effective protection (at [55]).

[3.115] Consumer Protection

In *Criminal Proceedings Against Placanica* (C-338/04) [2007] ECR I-1891; [2007] 2 CMLR 25 (p 607) Italian legislation required that gambling operators be subject to licensing and authorization by the police. These requirements were enforced by criminal penalties. The Court observed that consumer protection was a reason of overriding general interest that would justify a limitation of freedom of establishment (at [45]–[46]). Member States may seek to protect their citizens from the harmful consequences of gambling, but the measures they take must satisfy the requirement of proportionality (at [48]).

The Italian government sought to justify the licensing requirement based upon the objective of reducing the opportunity of its citizens to gamble (at [52]). The Court held that this objective had to be based upon a determination to genuinely reduce those opportunities (at [53]). In this case the Italian government had actually sought to expand gambling in order to increase its tax revenue, so this justification was not persuasive (at [54]).

[3.120] Prevention of Crime

In *Criminal Proceedings Against Placanica* (C-338/04) [2007] ECR I-1891; [2007] 2 CMLR 25 (p 607) the Italian government also sought to justify the licensing requirement on the basis of preventing crime (at [52]). The Court acknowledged that a controlled expansion of the gambling sector could be consistent with an objective of encouraging gamblers away from illegal gaming (at [55]). A licensing requirement could be an efficient means of ensuring that gambling providers did not engage in illegal activity. However, the facts before the Court were insufficient to enable it to decide whether the limitation of the number of licences furthered the objective of preventing crime (at [57]). The national courts had to determine that issue (at [58]).

The requirement for police authorization was consistent with the objective of preventing crime (at [65]). The defendants in this case were prepared to undergo police authorization but were prevented from doing so because they were unable to be issued with a gambling licence (at [66]). Since the licensing requirement violated EU law, the Italian government could not validly exact a criminal penalty if the defendants provided gambling services without a licence or police authorization (at [69]–[70]).

The Italian law also required that the shareholders of gambling providers had to be immediately identifiable at all times. The major EU providers of gambling services did not satisfy this requirement (at [59]). The Court held that this requirement went further than was necessary for the prevention of crime. There were satisfactory alternatives that were less restrictive of freedom of establishment, such as gathering information about the major shareholders in gambling businesses (at [62]).

In *Liga Portuguesa de Futebol Profissional v Departamento de Jogos da Santa Casa da Misericórdia de Lisboa* (C-42/07) [2010] 1 CMLR 1 (p 1) Portuguese legislation provided that a non-profit organization had the exclusive right to offer Internet gambling. The law thus prohibited the offering of gambling services by providers from other Member States (at [50]). The Portuguese government justified the law on the ground of preventing crime, in particular the prevention of fraud by gambling providers (at [62]).

Gambling carries a high risk of fraud by operators (at [63]). Limiting the offer of Internet gambling to one provider subject to rigorous state control was appropriate for preventing fraud by gambling providers (at [67]). Given the absence of direct contact between gamblers and gambling providers, Internet gambling involves an even greater risk of fraud by gaming operators (at [70]). It cannot be ruled out that gambling providers could be able to influence the outcome of sporting events (at [71]). The prohibition was thus justified by the aim of crime prevention (at [72]).

[3.125] Prevention of Tax Avoidance

In *Marks & Spencer plc v Halsey* (C-446/03) [2005] ECR I-10837 at [29]; [2006] 1 CMLR 18 (p 480) British tax legislation did not permit a company to deduct from its profits the losses of a subsidiary that was resident in another Member State, whereas such a deduction was available where the subsidiary was resident in the United Kingdom. The Court held that denial of the deduction hindered freedom of establishment since it discouraged a company from establishing a subsidiary in another Member State (at [33]). This limitation of freedom of establishment would be permissible only if it served a legitimate objective and was justified by compelling reasons in the public interest. The limitation must also be appropriate for achieving the objective and must not go further than what was necessary to achieve that objective (at [35]).

While residence could constitute a valid justification for different treatment, it would not always justify different treatment since that would drain freedom of establishment of any significance (at [37]). The different treatment of non-resident companies must be justified on objective grounds (at [38]). The United Kingdom justified the discrimination on three grounds: profits and losses must be treated symmetrically in national taxation law, it was necessary to avoid double counting of the losses and it prevented tax avoidance (at [43]). The Court held that these were legitimate objectives, justified by compelling reasons in the public interest and the limitation was appropriate for achieving the objective (at [51]). However, the limitation at issue went beyond what was necessary for achieving those objectives (at [55]).

[3.130] Collective Action

In *International Transport Workers' Federation v Viking Line ABP* (C-438/05) [2007] ECR I-10779; [2008] 1 CMLR 51 (p 1372) a Finnish company operated a Finnish registered vessel with a Finnish crew. The ship travelled between Finland and Estonia (at [6]–[7]). The wages of Estonian crews were lower than those paid to Finnish crews. The company sought to register the vessel in Estonia and operate it with an Estonian crew (at [9]). An international federation of employees threatened to take industrial action against the company (at [2]).

The Court held that freedom of establishment could be violated by collective action taken by a trade union (at [32]–[33]). A company could invoke freedom of establishment against a trade union (at [61]). The registration of a vessel in another Member State was part of the company's freedom of establishment in that Member State (at [70]). The threatened industrial action restricted the company's freedom of establishment (at [72]–[73]).

The right to take collective action was a fundamental right under EU law (at [44]). The observance of fundamental rights was a legitimate interest that could justify a limitation of freedom of establishment (at [45], [77]). Freedom of establishment must be balanced against the social objectives of the EU Treaty (at [79]). The national court had to decide whether the objective of the industrial action was the protection of workers (at [80]). The national court also had to determine whether the industrial action went further than was necessary and whether less restrictive alternatives existed (at [87]).

[3.135] Abuse of Freedom of Establishment

Member States are permitted to adopt measures seeking to prevent improper circumvention of their national laws or the improper or fraudulent use of freedom of establishment. See *Criminal Proceedings Against Bouchoucha* (C-61/89) [1990] ECR I-3551 at [14]; [1992] 1 CMLR 1033; *Centros Ltd v Erhvervs- og Selskabsstyrelsen* (C-212/97) [1999] ECR I-1459 at [24]; [1999] 2 CMLR 551; *Cadbury Schweppes plc v Inland Revenue Commissioners* (C-196/04) [2006] ECR I-7995 at [35]; [2007] 1 CMLR 2 (p 43).

The Court has held that it is not in itself an abuse of freedom of establishment to set up a company in the Member State with the least restrictive company law. Abuse of the freedom of establishment is not proved by the fact that the company does not carry on any business in the Member State in which its registered office is located, while carrying on business only through a branch in another Member State with a less restrictive company law. See *Centros Ltd v Erhvervs- og Selskabsstyrelsen* (C-212/97) [1999] ECR I-1459 at [27], [29]; [1999] 2 CMLR 551; *Kamer Van Koophandel en Fabrieken Voor Amsterdam v Inspire Art Ltd* (C-167/01) [2003] ECR I-10155 at [96], [98], [138]–[139]; [2005] 3 CMLR 34 (p 937).

In *Cadbury Schweppes plc v Inland Revenue Commissioners* (C-196/04) [2006] ECR I-7995; [2007] 1 CMLR 2 (p 43) the Court held that it is not an abuse of freedom of establishment for a company to be established in a Member State to take advantage of a more favourable legislative regime (at [37]). The Court also held that a limitation of freedom of establishment may be justifiable where it is directed at entirely artificial arrangements that seek to circumvent the taxation legislation of the Member State (at [51], [55]). Freedom of establishment is predicated upon genuine economic activity (at [54]).

[3.140] Establishment of Service Providers

The EU has adopted a Directive that deals generally with freedom of establishment of service providers. See Directive 2006/123 of the European Parliament and of the Council of 12 December 2006 on services in the internal market (OJ L 376, 27.12.2006, p 36). The Directive applies to services supplied by service providers that are established in an EU Member State (Art 2(1)). A number of services are excluded from the operation of the Directive, including financial services, electronic communications services and networks, and transport services (Art 2(2)).

Member States may only make access to or exercise of a service activity subject to authorisation if the system does not discriminate against providers, is justified by overriding reasons relating to the public interest and the objective cannot be achieved by a less restrictive alternative (especially if an inspection after establishment would be too late to be effective) (Art 9(1)). "Overriding reasons relating to the public interest" are defined by reference to the case law of the ECJ (Art 4(8)).

Member States may not make access to, or exercise of, a service activity subject to requirements based directly or indirectly on nationality, prohibitions against maintaining an establishment in more than one Member State, an economic test of the effects of or need for the activity, or the involvement of competitors in the granting of authorisation (Art 14).

[3.145] EU Company Law

The EU has adopted numerous legal acts regulating company law. These acts concern:

- incorporation and operation of companies: Second Council Directive 77/91 of 13 December 1976 on coordination of safeguards which, for the protection of the interests of members and others, are required by Member States of companies, in respect of the formation of public limited liability companies and the maintenance and alteration of their capital, with a view to making such safeguards equivalent (OJ L 26, 31.1.1977, p 1); Directive 2009/101 of the European Parliament and of the Council of 16 September 2009 on coordination of safeguards which, for the protection of the interests of members and third parties, are required by Member States of companies within the meaning of the second paragraph of Article 48 of the Treaty, with a view to making such safeguards equivalent (OJ L 258, 1.10.2009, p 11);
- the structure of companies: Third Council Directive 78/855 of 9 October 1978 concerning mergers of public limited liability companies (OJ L 295, 20.10.1978, p 36); Sixth Council Directive 82/891 of 17 December 1982 concerning the division of public limited liability companies (OJ L 378, 31.12.1982, p 47); Directive 2005/56 of the European Parliament and of the Council of 26 October 2005 on cross-border mergers of limited liability companies (OJ L 310, 25.11.2005, p 1); Directive 2009/102 of the European Parliament and of the Council of 16 September 2009 in the area of company law on single-member private limited liability companies (OJ L 258, 1.10.2009, p 20);
- takeover bids: Directive 2004/25 of the European Parliament and of the Council of 21 April 2004 on takeover bids (OJ L 142, 30.4.2004, p 12); Blanaid Clarke, "The Takeover Directive: Is a Little Regulation Better than no Regulation?" (2009) 15 *European Law Journal* 174; Paul Van Hooghten, *The European Takeover Directive and its Implementation* (Oxford: Oxford University Press, 2009);
- cooperation between firms of different Member States and the harmonisation of information disclosure requirements: Eleventh Council

Directive 89/666 of 21 December 1989 concerning disclosure requirements in respect of branches opened in a Member State by certain types of company governed by the law of another State (OJ L 395, 30.12.1989, p 36); and

- accounting procedures: Fourth Council Directive 78/660 of 25 July 1978 on the annual accounts of certain types of companies (OJ L 222, 14.8.1978, p 11); Seventh Council Directive 83/349 of 13 June 1983 on consolidated accounts (OJ L 193, 18.7.1983, p 1); Directive 2006/43 of the European Parliament and of the Council of 17 May 2006 on statutory audits of annual accounts and consolidated accounts (OJ L 157, 9.6.2006, p 87); Regulation 1606/2002 of the European Parliament and of the Council of 19 July 2002 on the application of international accounting standards (OJ L 243, 11.9.2002, p 1).

The EU has created a special category of company, known as the European Company (SE—Societas Europaea). Such companies do not depend upon the national laws of the Member States. See Council Regulation 2157/2001 of 8 October 2001 on the Statute for a European company (SE) (OJ L 294, 10.11.2001, p 1).

See generally, Carla Tavares Da Costa and Alexandra de Meester Bilreiro, *The European Company Statute* (The Hague: Kluwer, 2003); Susanne Braun, "The European Private Company: A Supranational Company Form for Small and Medium-sized Enterprises?" (November 2004) 5, 11 *German Law Journal* 1393, http://www.germanlawjournal.com; Dirk Van Gerven and Paul Storm, *The European Company* (Cambridge: Cambridge University Press, 2006); Wolf-Georg Ringe, "The European Company Statute in the Context of Freedom of Establishment" (2007) 7 *Journal of Corporate Law Studies* 185; Christine Hodt Dickens, "Establishment of the SE Company: An Overview over the Provisions Governing the Formation of the European Company" (2007) 18 *European Business Law Review* 1423; Florian Drinhausen and Nicolas Nohlen, "The Limited Freedom of Establishment of an SE" (2009) 6 *European Company Law* 14.

Another Directive facilitates worker participation in the management of European Companies. See Council Directive 2001/86 of 8 October 2001 supplementing the Statute for a European company with regard to the involvement of employees (OJ L 294, 10.11.2001, p 22); Charlotte Villiers, "The Directive on Employee Involvement in the European Company: Its Role in European Corporate Governance and Industrial Relations" (2006) 22 *International Journal of Comparative Labour Law and Industrial Relations* 183.

The EU has also created a European Cooperative (SCE—Societas Cooperativa Europaea). See Council Regulation 1435/2003 of 22 July 2003 on the Statute for a European Cooperative Society (SCE) (OJ L 207, 18.8.2003, p 1).

The European Economic Interest Grouping (EEIG) is a legal form of business cooperation between companies, individuals and other legal bodies from different Member States which are able to coordinate certain non-profit making aspects of their operations without eroding their independence. See Council Regulation 2137/85 of 25 July 1985 on the European Economic Interest Grouping (EEIG) (OJ L 199, 31.7.1985, p 1). A grouping is not a means for companies to avoid the application of EU competition rules.

The EU has adopted a regulation concerning cross-border insolvency proceedings where the debtor is a company or an individual. See Council Regulation 1346/2000 of 29 May 2000 on insolvency proceedings (OJ L 160, 30.6.2000, p 1).

[3.150] Freedom to Provide Services

The right of EU nationals to provide services to people living in another Member State is encapsulated in Art 56 TFEU:

> restrictions on freedom to provide services within the Union shall be prohibited in respect of nationals of Member States who are established in a Member State other than that of the person for whom the services are intended.
>
> The European Parliament and the Council, acting in accordance with the ordinary legislative procedure, may extend the provisions of the Chapter to nationals of a third country who provide services and who are established within the Union.

This provision has direct effect. See *ITC Innovative Technology Center Gmbh v Bundesagentur für Arbeit* (C-208/05) [2007] ECR I-181 at [67]; [2008] 1 CMLR 15 (p 343); *Laval un Partneri Ltd v Svenska Byggnadsarbetareförbundet* (C-341/05) [2007] ECR I-11767 at [97]; [2008] 2 CMLR 9 (p 177).

This provision applies to barriers caused by the exercise of legal authority by bodies that are not governed by public law. See *Union Royale Belge des Sociétés de Football Association ASBL v Bosman* (C-415/93) [1995] ECR I-4921 at [98], [1996] 1 CMLR 645; *Laval un Partneri Ltd v Svenska Byggnadsarbetareförbundet* (C-341/05) [2007] ECR I-11767 at [98]; [2008] 2 CMLR 9 (p 177).

The freedom to provide services does not apply to situations that are "purely internal" to a Member State. See *Unità Socio-Sanitaria Locale n° 47 di Biella v Istituto nazionale per l'assicurazione contro gli infortuni sul lavoro* (C-134/95) [1997] ECR I-195 at [19].

The Court has stated that the chapter on freedom to provide services is "subordinate" to the chapter concerning freedom of establishment. See *Gebhard v Consiglio dell'Ordine degli Avvocati e Procuratori di Milano* (C-55/94) [1995] ECR I-4165 at [22]; [1996] 1 CMLR 603; *Broede v Sandker* (C-3/95) [1996] ECR I-6511 at [19]; [1997] 1 CMLR 224.

Where a challenged national law implicates both the freedom to provide services and the free movement of capital, the Court considers the extent to which those freedoms are affected by the law, and whether one of those freedoms should take precedence over the other freedom because it is secondary in the circumstances. See *Fidium Finanz AG v Bundesanstalt für Finanzdienstleistungsaufsicht* (C-452/04) [2006] ECR I-9521 at [34]; [2007] 1 CMLR 15 (p 489).

[3.155] Services Defined

Art 57 TFEU defines "services":

> Services shall be considered to be 'services' within the meaning of the Treaties where they are normally provided for remuneration, in so far as they are not governed by the provisions relating to freedom of movement for goods, capital and persons. 'Services' shall in particular include:
>
> (a) activities of an industrial character;
> (b) activities of a commercial character;
> (c) activities of craftsmen;
> (d) activities of the professions.
>
> Without prejudice to the provisions of the Chapter relating to the right of establishment, the person providing a service may, in order to do so, temporarily pursue his activity in the Member State where the service is provided, under the same conditions as are imposed by that State on its own nationals.

It would appear that only commercial activities are covered by Art 57 and therefore charitable and religious activities and state education are excluded from the scope of this Article.

[3.160] Broad Interpretation of "Services"

The concept of "services" has been broadly interpreted by the Court. The following examples illustrate some of the activities that have been held to constitute "services":

- tourism: *Oulane v Minister voor Vreemdelingenzaken en Integratie* (C-215/03) [2005] ECR I-1215 at [37]; *Criminal Proceedings Against Donatella Calfa* (C-348/96) [1999] ECR I-11 at [16]; [1999] 2 CMLR 1138;
- education financed by private fees: *Schwarz v Finanzamt Bergisch Gladbach* (C-76/05) [2007] ECR I-1721 at [40], [47]; [2007] 3 CMLR 47 (p 1283);
- television transmission: *De Coster v Collège des bourgmestre et échevins de Watermael-Boitsfort* (C-17/00) [2001] ECR I-9445 at [28]; [2002] 1

CMLR 12 (p 285); *United Pan-Europe Communications Belgium SA v Belgium* (C-250/06) [2007] ECR I-11135 at [28]; [2008] 2 CMLR 2 (p 45);
- medical treatment: *Müller-Fauré v Onderlinge Waarborgmaatschappij OZ Zorgverzekeringen UA* (C-385/99) [2003] ECR I-4509 at [38]; [2004] 2 CMLR 33 (p 777);
- abortion services: *Society for the Protection of Unborn Children v Grogan* (C-159/90) [1991] ECR I-4685 at [18]; [1991] 3 CMLR 849;
- sports betting: *Criminal Proceedings Against Gambelli* (C-243/01) [2003] ECR I-13031 at [52]; [2006] 1 CMLR 35 (p 913); and
- lotteries: *H M Customs and Excise v Schindler* (C-275/92) [1994] ECR I-1039 at [24]–[28]; [1995] 1 CMLR 4.

However, publicly funded courses of study provided by a technical institute as part of secondary schooling under the national education system are not services within the meaning of Art 57 TFEU because the State undertakes these activities to fulfil its duty to its people in the social, cultural and educational fields rather than to obtain remuneration. See *Belgium v Humbel* (263/86) [1988] ECR 5365 at [15]–[18]; [1989] 1 CMLR 393; see similarly, *Wirth v Landeshauptstadt Hannover* (C-109/92) [1993] ECR I-6447 at [15]–[16].

Sometimes the boundary between the free movement of goods and the free movement of services is at issue. For example, while the importation of slot machines falls within the freedom of movement of goods, the operation of such machines falls within the freedom of movement of services. See *Associação Nacional de Operadores de Máquinas Recreativas (Anomar) v Portugal* (C-6/01) [2003] ECR I-8621 at [55]–[56]; [2004] 1 CMLR 43 (p 1357).

[3.165] Scope of Protection

Art 56 TFEU protects the right of the recipient of services to travel to the Member State in which the provider of services resides. See *Luisi v Ministero del Tesoro* (286/82) [1984] ECR 377 at [16]; [1985] 3 CMLR 52; *Cowan v Tresor Public* (186/87) [1989] ECR 195 at [15]; [1990] 2 CMLR 613; *Ciola v Land Vorarlberg* (C-224/97) [1999] ECR I-2517 at [11]; [1999] 2 CMLR 1220; *FKP Scorpio Konzertproduktionen GmbH v Finanzamt Hamburg-Eimsbüttel* (C-290/04) [2006] ECR I-9461 at [64]; [2007] 1 CMLR 33 (p 937); *Schwarz v Finanzamt Bergisch Gladbach* (C-76/05) [2007] ECR I-1721 at [36]; [2007] 3 CMLR 47 (p 1283); *Presidente del Consiglio dei Ministri v Regione Sardegna* (C-169/08) [2009] ECR at [25].

However, this right does not allow a recipient of services to set up a principal residence so that they may be provided with the services for an indefinite period. See *Chen v Secretary of State for the Home Department* (C-200/02) [2004] ECR I-9925 at [22]; [2004] 3 CMLR 48 (p 1060).

A provider of services may rely upon Art 56 against its own state of establishment if the services are to be provided to a party in another Member State. See *Sodemare SA v Regione Lombardia* [1997] ECR I-3395 at [37]; [1997] 3 CMLR 591; *ITC Innovative Technology Center GmbH v Bundesagentur für Arbeit* (C-208/05) [2007] ECR I-181 at [56]; [2008] 1 CMLR 15 (p 343); *United Pan-Europe Communications Belgium SA v Belgium* (C-250/06) [2007] ECR I-11135 at [31]; [2008] 2 CMLR 2 (p 45).

In *Alpine Investments BV v Minister Van Financiën* (C-384/93) [1995] ECR I-1141; [1995] 2 CMLR 209 the Court held that the freedom to provide services applies to telephone offers of services to persons in another Member State even where the service provider will remain in their home Member State while providing the service (at [20]–[22]). The freedom to provide services operates as a limitation upon national restrictions laid down by either the state of origin or destination of services (at [30]). Art 56 TFEU similarly applies to services offered through the Internet to recipients in another Member State where the service provider does not move from their Member State. See *Criminal Proceedings Against Gambelli* (C-243/01) [2003] ECR I-13031 at [53]–[54]; [2006] 1 CMLR 35 (p 913).

The activities of employed people and self-employed people are excluded from the scope of Art 56 TFEU. Companies are also covered by Art 56 TFEU. Thus, the right of a British television company to travel to Spain to make a television serial would be covered by Art 56 TFEU but the employees of the company would be covered by Art 45 TFEU (freedom of movement for workers).

[3.170] Discrimination Based on Nationality of Service Provider

The Court has held that Art 56 TFEU prohibits discrimination based on the nationality of a service provider or the fact that it is established in another Member State. See *Commission v Germany* (C-490/04) [2007] ECR I-6095 at [83]; *Laval un Partneri Ltd v Svenska Byggnadsarbetareförbundet* (C-341/05) [2007] ECR I-11767 at [114]; [2008] 2 CMLR 9 (p 177).

In *Oulane v Minister voor Vreemdelingenzaken en Integratie* (C-215/03) [2005] ECR I-1215 the practical outcome of Dutch immigration rules was that nationals of other Member States were required to carry identification with them at all times, whereas no such requirement applied to Dutch nationals (at [31]). The Court held that EU law did not prohibit a requirement that identification be carried at all times, provided that the obligation applied both to nationals and citizens from other Member States (at [34]).

The Dutch rules violated free movement of services since they did not apply to nationals and non-nationals alike (at [35]).

In *Säger v Dennemeyer & Co Ltd* (C-76/90) [1991] ECR 4221; [1993] 3 CMLR 639 a British company provided a German patent renewal service for its British clients (at [3]). The company was sued in a German Court for violating a German statute that reserved such activity to licensed patent agents (at [5]–[6]). Therefore, the requirement that foreign renewers of a German patent be licensed amounted to a requirement for them to be established in Germany (at [13]).

[3.175] Obstacles to Provision of Services

Apart from prohibiting discrimination on the basis of nationality, the Court has held that Art 56 TFEU requires the "abolition of any restriction . . . which is liable to prohibit, impede or render less advantageous the activities of a provider of services established in another Member State where he lawfully provides similar services". See *Société Civile Immobilière Parodi v Banque H Albert de Bary et Cie* (C-222/95) [1997] ECR I-3899 at [18]; [1998] 1 CMLR 115; see similarly, *Säger v Dennemeyer & Co Ltd* (C-76/90) [1991] ECR 4221 at [12]; [1993] 3 CMLR 639; *Re Work Visa Regime: Commission v Germany* (C-244/04) [2006] ECR I-885 at [30]; [2006] 2 CMLR 23 (p 631); *Commission v Spain* (C-514/03) [2006] ECR I-963 at [24]; *Cipolla v Fazari* (C-94/04) [2006] ECR I-11421 at [56]; [2007] 4 CMLR 8 (p 286); *Commission v Germany* (C-490/04) [2007] ECR I-6095 at [63]; *Re Inspection of Organic Produce by Private Bodies: Commission v Austria* (C-393/05) [2007] ECR I-10195 at [31]; [2008] 1 CMLR 42 (p 1121); *United Pan-Europe Communications Belgium SA v Belgium* (C-250/06) [2007] ECR I-11135 at [29]; [2008] 2 CMLR 2 (p 45).

For example, in *Konsumentombudsmannen (KO) v Gourmet International Products AB* (C-405/98) [2001] ECR I-1795; [2001] 2 CMLR 31 (p 672) national legislation prohibited the advertising of alcohol in publications directed at the public (at [4]). The Court held that the legislation restricted the right of publications in the Member State to offer advertising to firms established in other Member States (at [38]). It thus constituted a restriction upon the freedom to provide services (at [39]). National legislation that prohibited the holding of lotteries constituted an obstacle to the free provision of services. See *H M Customs and Excise v Schindler* (C-275/92) [1994] ECR I-1039 at [43]–[45]; [1995] 1 CMLR 4.

The freedom to provide services prohibits "national rules which have the effect of making the provision of services between Member States more difficult than the provision of services purely within one Member State". See *Cipolla v Fazari* (C-94/04) [2006] ECR I-11421 at [57]; [2007] 4

CMLR 8 (p 286); see similarly, *Schwarz v Finanzamt Bergisch Gladbach* (C-76/05) [2007] ECR I-1721 at [67]; [2007] 3 CMLR 47 (p 1283); *Stamatelaki v NPDD Organismos Asfaliseos Eleftheron Epangelmation* (C-444/05) [2007] ECR I-3185 at [25]; [2007] 2 CMLR 44 (p 1185); *United Pan-Europe Communications Belgium SA v Belgium* (C-250/06) [2007] ECR I-11135 at [30]; [2008] 2 CMLR 2 (p 45).

[3.180] Limitations to Freedom to Provide Services

By the combined operation of Arts 51 and 62 TFEU, freedom to provide services does "not apply, so far as any given Member State is concerned, to activities which in that State are connected, even occasionally, with the exercise of official authority".

Under Arts 52(1) and 62 TFEU, freedom to provide services is subject to national measures "providing for special treatment for foreign nationals on grounds of public policy, public security or public health". This constitutes the sole justification for discriminatory rules.

To be compatible with the Treaty a limitation upon the freedom to provide services must pursue a legitimate objective, be justified by an overriding reason of public interest, be suitable for attaining the objective and not go further than what is necessary for attaining that objective. See *Cipolla v Fazari* (C-94/04) [2006] ECR I-11421 at [61]; [2007] 4 CMLR 8 (p 286); *Servizi Ausiliari Dottori Commercialisti v Calafiori* (C-451/03) [2006] ECR I-2941 at [37]; [2006] 2 CMLR 45 (p 1135); *Laval un Partneri Ltd v Svenska Byggnadsarbetareförbundet* (C-341/05) [2007] ECR I-11767 at [101]; [2008] 2 CMLR 9 (p 177).

The public health exception was raised in *Müller-Fauré v Onderlinge Waarborgmaatschappij OZ Zorgverzekeringen UA* (C-385/99) [2003] ECR I-4509; [2004] 2 CMLR 33 (p 777). Dutch social security law required that reimbursement for medical treatment abroad was subject to prior authorisation by the patient's sickness fund, other than in exceptional circumstances (at [18]). The Court held that the national objective of a universally available high quality public health system fell within the public health exception (at [67]). The risk of undermining the financial balance of the public health system was an overriding general interest reason that could justify such a restriction (at [73]).

The requirement that reimbursement for hospital treatment abroad receive prior authorisation was necessary and reasonable in view of the high cost of such treatment (at [80]–[81]). However, to prevent arbitrary action a scheme of prior authorisation must be based upon "objective non-discriminatory criteria which are known in advance". The system must deal with requests impartially within a reasonable time. Refusal of authorisation must be subject to challenge by at least quasi-judicial proceedings (at [85]).

[3.185] Consumer Protection

Apart from the express Treaty exceptions, there are judicially recognised exceptions known as overriding reasons in the public interest. Consumer protection is such a permissible justification for restricting free provision of services. See *Konsumentombudsmannen (KO) v De Agostini (Svenska) Förlag AB* (C-34/95) [1997] ECR I-3843 at [53]; [1998] 1 CMLR 32; *Cipolla v Fazari* (C-94/04) [2006] ECR I-11421 at [64]; [2007] 4 CMLR 8 (p 286); *Criminal Proceedings Against Placanica* (C-338/04) [2007] ECR I-1891 at [46]; [2007] 2 CMLR 25 (p 607); *Re Inspection of Organic Produce by Private Bodies: Commission v Germany* (C-404/05) [2007] ECR I-10239 at [50]; [2008] 1 CMLR 43 (p 1148).

In *H M Customs and Excise v Schindler* (C-275/92) [1994] ECR I-1039; [1995] 1 CMLR 4 the Court held that Member States were entitled to prohibit lotteries on consumer protection grounds (at [59]). The general approach of Member States was to restrict gambling. Lotteries have a substantial risk of crime or fraud. They also encourage spending which may have harmful consequences (at [60]). Where a Member State prohibits the advertising of lotteries, a prohibition of the importation of advertisements for lotteries conducted in other Member States was not an unjustified restriction of the freedom to provide services (at [62]).

In *Alpine Investments BV v Minister Van Financiën* (C-384/93) [1995] ECR I-1141; [1995] 2 CMLR 209 a national law prohibited the offering of financial services by cold calling (at [23]). The Court observed that the operation of financial markets depended upon investor confidence (at [42]). Preservation of the good reputation of the financial market in a Member State constituted an imperative reason of public interest (at [44]).

A consumer who received a cold call was not well placed to judge the risks inherent in the services offered or to make comparisons with the offerings of competitors. Given the complicated nature of the investment market, it was necessary to protect consumers against aggressive sales methods adopted by cold callers (at [46]). The prohibition was appropriate for achieving the aim of protecting the good reputation of financial markets (at [49]).

The Court considered that the prohibition of cold calling was necessary for the achievement of this objective. It was argued that a requirement to tape telephone calls was sufficient to protect consumers (at [50]). The Court responded that the fact that one Member State adopted less stringent requirements than another Member State did not mean that the stricter requirements were disproportionate (at [51]).

It was also argued that the prohibition was an unnecessary burden on firms that had not been the object of consumer complaints (at [52]). The Court held that restricting the prohibition to particular firms based on their prior conduct might not be adequate for achieving the aim of protecting investor confidence (at [53]).

[3.190] Protection of Fundamental Rights

The protection of fundamental rights is another permissible justification for restricting the freedom to provide services. See *Omega Spielhallen- und Automatenaufstellungs-GmbH v Oberbürgermeisterin der Bundesstadt Bonn* (C-36/02) [2004] ECR I-9609 at [35]; [2005] 1 CMLR 5 (p 91).

In *Laval un Partneri Ltd v Svenska Byggnadsarbetareförbundet* (C-341/05) [2007] ECR I-11767; [2008] 2 CMLR 9 (p 177) a union blockade sought to compel an employer established in another Member State to negotiate a collective agreement (at [30], [34]). The Court held that the right to take collective action for the protection of workers against social dumping could constitute an overriding reason of public interest (at [103]). However, the specific actions at issue were incompatible with freedom to provide services (at [111]).

A national cultural policy may constitute an overriding requirement of public interest. See *United Pan-Europe Communications Belgium SA v Belgium* (C-250/06) [2007] ECR I-11135 at [41]; [2008] 2 CMLR 2 (p 45).

[3.195] EU Secondary Legislation Regarding Provision of Services

The EU has adopted a large number of Directives and Regulations concerning the provision of services. This secondary legislation concerns (among others) services in the internal market, professional services, transport services, electronic commerce and communications, insurance services and cross-border mediation.

[3.200] Services in the Internal Market

The EU has adopted a Directive that deals generally with the free movement of services. See Directive 2006/123 of the European Parliament and of the Council of 12 December 2006 on services in the internal market (OJ L 376, 27.12.2006, p 36).

This Directive applies to services supplied by service providers that are established in an EU Member State (Art 2(1)). A number of services are excluded from the operation of the Directive, including financial services, electronic communications services and networks, and transport services (Art 2(2)). Where the Directive conflicts with a Directive concerning a particular services sector, the specific Directive prevails (Art 3(1)).

Member States must respect the right of service providers to provide services in Member States other than the State of establishment. The Member

State in which a service is provided must allow free access to and exercise of the service. That Member State may not make access to and exercise of a service subject to requirements that do not respect the principles of necessity, proportionality and non-discrimination on the ground of nationality (Art 16(1)).

Member States may not require that an inter-state service provider have an establishment on their territory or require that they receive an authorisation except where provided for by EU law (Art 16(2)). A Member State may not impose restrictive requirements upon recipients of services from an inter-state provider, such as a requirement to seek an official authorisation (Art 19).

[3.205] Professional Services

Under the second paragraph of Art 56 TFEU the Parliament and Council may extend the right to provide services to nationals of a third (non-EU) country who are already established in the Union.

An EU Directive governs the recognition of professional qualifications obtained in other Member States. See Directive 2005/36 of the European Parliament and of the Council of 7 September 2005 on the recognition of professional qualifications (OJ L 255, 30.9.2005, p 22). The Directive sets out rules for the recognition of qualifications and allows the holder of recognised qualifications to practice their profession in another Member State (Art 1). It applies to regulated professions (Art 2(1)), which are professions the pursuit of which is subject to the holding of specific professional qualifications (Art 3(1)(a)).

Recognition of a qualification allows its holder to practice their profession in the recognising Member State on the same conditions as nationals (Art 4(1)). There are numerous provisions relating to specific professions, including medical doctors (Art 24), nurses (Art 31), dentists (Art 34), veterinarians (Art 38), midwives (Art 40), pharmacists (Art 44) and architects (Art 46). See generally Miek Peeters, "Free Movement of Medical Doctors: The new Directive 2005/36/EC on the Recognition of Professional Qualifications" (2005) 12 *European Journal of Health Law* 373.

The EU has adopted a Directive regulating the provision of services in a Member State by a lawyer who is permanently established in another Member State. See Council Directive 77/249 of 22 March 1977 to facilitate the effective exercise by lawyers of freedom to provide services (OJ L 78, 26.3.1977, p 17). The Directive does not deal with a legal practitioner's right of establishment under Art 49 TFEU.

Under Art 4(1) of the Directive "[a]ctivities relating to the representation of a client in legal proceedings or before public authorities shall be pursued in each host Member State under the conditions laid down for lawyers established in that State, with the exception of any conditions requiring residence, or registration with a professional organization, in that State." For the pursuit of reserved activities relating to the representation of a client in legal proceedings, a Member State may require lawyers to be introduced "to the presiding judge and, where appropriate, to the President of the relevant Bar in the host Member State" and to work with a lawyer who practices before that court (Art 5).

Another Directive assists the permanent practice of lawyers in Member States other than the one in which they qualified. See Art 1(1), Directive 98/5 of the European Parliament and of the Council of 16 February 1998 to facilitate practice of the profession of lawyer on a permanent basis in a Member State other than that in which the qualification was obtained (OJ L 77, 14.3.1998, p 36).

Lawyers have the right to practice in any Member State under their home country professional title (Art 2). They must register with the competent authority in that Member State (Art 3(1)). That authority must register the lawyer upon presentation of proof of registration in their home Member State (Art 3(2)). This is the only condition for registration, so registration cannot be subject to a test for proficiency in a local language. See *Wilson v Ordre des avocats du barreau de Luxembourg* (C-506/04) [2006] ECR I-8613 at [65]–[70]; [2007] 1 CMLR 7 (p 217).

After registration lawyers may provide advice regarding the law of the host Member State, the law of their home Member State or EU law (Art 5(1)). The host State may require that a lawyer from another Member State work with a local lawyer when representing a client in court (Art 5(3)). Lawyers from another Member State are subject to local rules of professional conduct (Art 6(1)) and disciplinary procedures (Art 7) in relation to their activities in the host State.

[3.210] Transport Services

Freedom to provide transport services is regulated by specific provisions in the TFEU (Arts 58(1), 90–100 TFEU). Art 90 TFEU provides that the objectives of the founding Treaties shall, in matters of transport, "be pursued within the framework of a common transport policy".

Art 95(1) TFEU prohibits discriminatory rates and conditions for transportation within the EU. That Article provides: "In the case of transport within the Union, discrimination which takes the form of carriers charging different rates and imposing different conditions for the carriage of the same goods over the same transport links on grounds of the country of origin or of destination of the goods in question shall be prohibited."

[3.215] Rail Transport

The EU has adopted several Directives concerning rail transport:

- Council Directive 91/440 of 29 July 1991 on the development of the Community's railways (OJ L 237, 24.8.1991, p 25);
- Council Directive 96/48 of 23 July 1996 on the interoperability of the trans-European high-speed rail system (OJ L 235, 17.9.1996, p 6);
- Directive 2001/14 of the European Parliament and of the Council of 26 February 2001 on the allocation of railway infrastructure capacity and the levying of charges for the use of railway infrastructure and safety certification (OJ L 75, 15.3.2001, p 29); and
- Directive 2001/16 of the European Parliament and of the Council of 19 March 2001 on the interoperability of the conventional rail system (OJ L 110, 20.4.2001, p 1).

The European Railway Agency seeks to improve the interoperability of the railway systems of the Member States. See Art 1, Regulation 881/2004 of the European Parliament and of the Council of 29 April 2004 establishing a European Railway Agency (OJ L 220, 21.6.2004, p 3). The Agency's website is at http://www.era.europa.eu.

[3.220] Air Transport

In the area of air transport, the EU has adopted a number of Regulations and Directives that liberalise the industry:

- Council Regulation 3976/87 of 14 December 1987 on the application of Article 85(3) of the Treaty to certain categories of agreements and concerted practices in the air transport sector (OJ L 374, 31.12.1987, p 9);
- Council Directive 91/670 of 16 December 1991 on the mutual acceptance of licences for persons working in civil aviation (OJ L 373, 31.12. 1991, p 21);
- Council Regulation 3922/91 of 16 December 1991 on the harmonization of technical requirements and administrative procedures in the field of civil aviation (OJ L 373, 31.12.1991, p 4);
- Council Regulation 2407/92 of 23 July 1992 on licensing of air carriers (OJ L 240, 24.8.1992, p 1);
- Council Regulation 2408/92 of 23 July 1992 on access for Community air carriers to intra-Community air routes (OJ L 240, 24.8.1992, p 8);
- Council Regulation 95/93 on common rules for the allocation of slots at EU airports (OJ L 14, 21.2.1993, p 1); and

- Regulation 549/2004 of the European Parliament and of the Council of 10 March 2004 laying down the framework for the creation of the Single European Sky (OJ L 96, 31.3.2004, p 1).

The European Aviation Safety Agency provides technical assistance regarding the formulation and implementation of EU air safety standards. See Art 2(3), Regulation 1592/2002 of the European Parliament and of the Council of 15 July 2002 on common rules in the field of civil aviation and establishing a European Aviation Safety Agency (OJ L 240, 7.9.2002, p 1). The website of the Agency is at http://www.easa.europa.eu.

Under the EU-United States Open Skies Agreement any EU and US airline has the right to provide international flights between any point in the EU and any point in the US. While US airlines are permitted to offer flights between EU destinations, EU airlines are not permitted to offer US domestic flights. See Art 3(1)(c), *Air Transport Agreement between the European Community and the United States*, Washington, 30 April 2007, OJ L 134, 25.5.2007, p 4; 46 ILM 470.

[3.225] Inland Waterways and Maritime Transport

The aim of the common transport policy in the areas of inland waterways and maritime transport is to ensure freedom to provide these services but also to protect EU undertakings from unfair pricing by non-EU shipowners. The Regulations and Directives adopted by the European Union include the following measures:

- Council Regulation 4055/86 of 22 December 1986 applying the principle of freedom to provide services to maritime transport between Member States and between Member States and third countries (OJ L 378, 31.12.1986, p 1);
- Council Regulation 3921/91 of 16 December 1991 laying down the conditions under which non-resident carriers may transport goods or passengers by inland waterway within a Member State (OJ L 373, 31.12.1991, p 1);
- Council Regulation 3577/92 of 7 December 1992 applying the principle of freedom to provide services to maritime transport within Member States (maritime cabotage) (OJ L 364, 12.12.1992, p 7);
- Council Regulation 1356/96 of 8 July 1996 on common rules applicable to the transport of goods or passengers by inland waterway between Member States with a view to establishing freedom to provide such transport services (OJ L 175, 13.7.96, p 7);
- Directive 2002/6 of the European Parliament and of the Council of 18 February 2002 on reporting formalities for ships arriving in and/or

departing from ports of the Member States of the Community (OJ L 67, 9.3.2002, p 31); and
- Directive 2009/45 of the European Parliament and of the Council of 6 May 2009 on safety rules and standards for passenger ships (Recast) (OJ L 163, 25.6.2009, p 1).

The European Maritime Safety Agency provides technical assistance in the implementation of EU maritime safety legislation. See Art 1(2), Regulation 1406/2002 of the European Parliament and of the Council of 27 June 2002 establishing a European Maritime Safety Agency (OJ L 208, 5.8.2002, p 1). The Agency's website is at http://www.emsa.europa.eu.

[3.230] Road Transport

Several important Regulations concerning transportation of goods by road have been adopted:

- Council Regulation 3916/90 of 21 December 1990 on measures to be taken in the event of a crisis in the market in the carriage of goods by road (OJ L 375, 30.12.1990, p 10);
- Council Regulation 881/92 of 26 March 1992 on access to the market in the carriage of goods by road within the Community to or from the territory of a Member State or passing across the territory of one or more Member States (OJ L 95, 9.4.1992, p 1); and
- Council Regulation 3118/93 of 25 October 1993 laying down the conditions under which non-resident carriers may operate national road haulage services within a Member State (OJ L 279, 12.11.1993, p 1).

The EU has also adopted several Regulations concerning transportation of passengers by road:

- Council Regulation 684/92 of 16 March 1992 on common rules for the international carriage of passengers by coach and bus (OJ L 74, 20.3.1992, p 1); and
- Council Regulation 12/98 of 11 December 1997 laying down the conditions under which non-resident carriers may operate national road passenger transport services within a Member State (OJ L 4, 8.1.1998, p 10).

[3.235] Electronic Commerce and Communications

The EU has adopted a Directive promoting the operation of the internal market through the free movement of electronic commerce services. See Directive 2000/31 of the European Parliament and of the Council of 8 June

2000 on certain legal aspects of information society services, in particular electronic commerce, in the Internal Market (OJ L 178, 17.2.2000, p 1). This Directive seeks to facilitate the operation of the internal market by ensuring the free movement of information society services between the members of the Union (Preamble Recital 8; Art 1(1)). The Directive provides for the harmonisation of matters such as the establishment of service providers, commercial communications, electronic contracts, intermediary liability and codes of conduct (Art 1(2)).

Several provisions are specifically directed at the operation of the internal market. EU Members may not restrict the freedom to provide information society services from another Member State for reasons within the coordinated field (Art 3(2)). The coordinated field concerns requirements that service providers must fulfil in relation to the establishment of an information society service (e.g. qualifications or authorisation) and requirements for the operation of such a service (e.g. the behaviour of the providers, quality of service and provider liability) (Art 2(h)). Certain derogations from the freedom to provide information society services are permitted (Art 3(4)).

The authorisation of electronic communications networks is regulated by Directive 2002/20 of the European Parliament and of the Council of 7 March 2002 on the authorisation of electronic communications networks and services (Authorisation Directive) (OJ L 108, 24.4.2002, p 21). Member States must ensure the freedom to provide electronic communication networks and services (Art 3(1)). The provision of electronic communication networks and services is only subject to a general authorisation (Art 3(2)). After receiving a general authorisation an undertaking has the right to provide such networks and services (Art 4(1)).

Another Directive provides a harmonised framework for the regulation of electronic communications networks and services. See Art 1(1), Directive 2002/21 of the European Parliament and of the Council of 7 March 2002 on a common regulatory framework for electronic communications networks and services (Framework Directive) (OJ L 108, 24.4.2002, p 33).

Member States must guarantee the independence of their regulatory authorities (Art 3(1)). The authorities must exercise their powers in an impartial and transparent manner (Art 3(3)). Any user or provider of such networks or services has the right to appeal to an independent body against decisions that affect them (Art 4(1)). Providers must provide to the national authority all information necessary for verifying compliance with the EU Directives in this area (Art 5(1)). The national authorities shall assist in the development of the internal market by removing obstacles to the provision of networks and services at the European level and by encouraging the development of trans-European networks (Art 3(3)).

EU law provides for universal service obligations for operators of electronic communications networks. See Directive 2002/22 of the European Parliament and of the Council of 7 March 2002 on universal service and users' rights relating to electronic communications networks and services (Universal Service Directive) (OJ L 108, 24.4.2002, p 51). Various services must be available to all users at an affordable price, regardless of their geographical location (Art 3(1)). If the national authorities consider that the universal service obligation constitutes an unfair burden upon service providers, they may calculate the cost of providing the service (Art 12(1)). If the national authority finds that the cost is an unfair burden, it must compensate the providers or share the burden between the various providers (Art 13(1)).

[3.240] Postal Services

EU postal users have the "right to a universal service involving the permanent provision of a postal service of specified quality at all points in their territory at affordable process for all users". See Art 3(1), Directive 97/67 of the European Parliament and of the Council of 15 December 1997 on common rules for the development of the internal market of Community postal services and the improvement of quality of service (OJ L 15, 21.1.1998, p 14).

[3.245] Insurance and Investment Services

There are specific provisions relating to the free movement of services provided by insurance undertakings. See Directive 2009/138 of the European Parliament and of the Council of 25 November 2009 on the taking-up and pursuit of the business of Insurance and Reinsurance (Solvency II) (recast) (OJ L 335, 17.12.2009, p 1). An undertaking that relies upon the freedom to provide services in order to carry on business for the first time in another Member State must first notify the authorities of its home Member State of the commitments it intends to cover (Art 147).

The home Member State must provide the other Member State with a certificate that the undertaking has the minimum required solvency margin. The home State must also inform the other State of the classes of insurance which the undertaking has been authorised to offer and the commitments that the undertaking intends to cover (Art 148(1)). The undertaking may commence business in the other State once it has been informed that its home State has communicated this information to the other State (Art 148(4)).

A similar process also applies under Directive 2004/39 of the European Parliament and of the Council of 21 April 2004 on markets in financial instruments (OJ L 145, 30.4.2004, p 1). Member States shall ensure that an investment firm authorised under the Directive may freely perform investment services or activities in accordance with the authorisation. They may not impose additional requirements on investment firms in relation to matters regulated by the Directive (Art 31(1)).

An investment firm that wants to operate in another Member State must communicate certain information to the authorities of its home Member State. The following information must be provided: the Member State in which it wishes to operate and the investment services or activities it intends to offer in that State (Art 31(2)). Within 1 month of receiving this information the home State forwards the information to the state in which the investment is made (the host State). The firm may then commence operations in the host State (Art 31(3)). The host State may take certain precautionary measures in relation to investment firms from other States (Art 62).

[3.250] Payment Services

Another Directive concerns the operation of the single market in relation to payment services. See Directive 2007/64 of the European Parliament and of the Council of 13 November 2007 on payment services in the internal market (OJ L 319, 5.12.2007, p 1). See generally, Despina Mavromati, *The Law of Payment Services in the EU: The EC Directive on Payment Services in the Internal Market* (Alphen aan den Rijn: Kluwer, 2008).

[3.255] Cross-Border Mediation

The functioning of the internal market is assisted by the introduction of measures for judicial cooperation in civil matters. To this end the EU has adopted legislation promoting cross border mediation. See Preamble Recital 1 and Art 1(1), Directive 2008/52 of the European Parliament and of the Council of 21 May 2008 on certain aspects of mediation in civil and commercial matters (OJ L 136, 45.5.2008, p 3).

The Directive applies to cross-border disputes regarding civil and commercial matters (Art 1(2)). A cross-border dispute is one in which a party is domiciled or habitually resident in a Member State that is different from that of another party (Art 2(1)). If an action is brought in a court, the court may invite the parties to settle their dispute by mediation (Art 5(1)). A party may request that an agreement arising from the mediation be made legally enforceable (Art 6(1)). The agreement shall be enforceable unless its content is contrary to the law of the Member State or if such an agreement is not enforceable under the law of that State (Art 6(1)).

[3.256] International Commercial Arbitration

Commercial disputes between parties in different nations are often settled by arbitration. See generally, John Trone and Gabriël A Moens, "The International Arbitration Act 1974 (Cth) as a Foundation for International Commercial Arbitration in Australia" (2007) 4 *Macquarie Journal of Business Law* 293. The EU Regulation on jurisdiction in civil and commercial matters provides that it does not apply to arbitration. See Art 1(2)(d), Council Regulation 44/2001 of 22 December 2000 on jurisdiction and the recognition and enforcement of judgments in civil and commercial matters (OJ L 12, 16.1.2001, p 1). However, the Regulation does have a significant impact upon arbitration. The Regulation provides that a person domiciled in a Member State may be sued in a tort case in another Member State where the harmful event took place (Art 5(3)).

In *Allianz SpA v West Tankers Inc* (C-185/07) [2009] All ER (EC) 491; 48 ILM 485 a party sought from a United Kingdom court an anti-suit injunction prohibiting another party from continuing proceedings in the courts of another Member State in breach of an arbitration agreement (at [11]–[12]). The other party had brought a tort claim in an Italian court (at [11]). The ECJ held that such an anti-suit injunction would undermine the effectiveness of the Regulation because it would prevent the court of the other Member State from exercising jurisdiction that was conferred by the Regulation (at [24]).

Under the Regulation the Italian court had exclusive jurisdiction to determine the objection to jurisdiction based on the arbitration agreement (at [27]). Issuance of an anti-suit injunction to prevent a foreign court from deciding a tort dispute that was within its jurisdiction under the Regulation would strip that court of the power to determine its own jurisdiction under the Regulation (at [28]). In general the Regulation did not authorize a court of a Member State to review the jurisdiction of a court in another Member State (at [29]). Such a use of an anti-suit injunction was contrary to the trust that Member States place in the courts of other Member States (at [30]).

[3.260] Provision of Services by Non-EU Citizens

The freedom to provide services may be invoked only by EU nationals. See *Fidium Finanz AG v Bundesanstalt für Finanzdienstleistungsaufsicht* (C-452/04) [2006] ECR I-9521 at [25]; [2007] 1 CMLR 15 (p 489).

Some EU secondary acts make provision for the delivery of services by non-EU undertakings. For example, provision of insurance by undertakings that have a head office outside the EU is subject to official authorisation by the Member State concerned. See Art 162(1), Directive 2009/138 of the European Parliament and of the Council of 25 November 2009 on the taking-up and pursuit of the business of Insurance and Reinsurance (Solvency II) (recast) (OJ L 335, 17.12.2009, p 1). Authorisation may be granted if the undertaking satisfies the following conditions (inter alia): it is entitled to provide such services under its national law, it establishes an agency or branch in the Member State, it undertakes to keep its accounts and records for the agency or branch at the place of management of that agency or branch, it designates a general representative, it complies with minimum capital requirements, it undertakes to fulfil solvency capital requirements and it submits a scheme of operations (Art 162(2)).

[3.265] Freedom of Movement and Residence for EU Citizens Within the Union

As the internal market comprises "an area... without internal frontiers, in which the free movement of persons is ensured" (Art 3(2) TEU; Art 26(2) TFEU), it is mandatory to remove any remaining physical barriers that divide the Member States. On 1 January 1993 all border posts between EU countries disappeared, thereby enabling EU nationals to move freely within the Union.

Art 21(1) TFEU provides: "Every citizen of the Union shall have the right to move and reside freely within the territory of the Member States, subject to the limitations and conditions laid down in the Treaties and by the measures adopted to give them effect."

This Article has a broader operation than the other Treaty provisions regarding freedom of movement. This provision has direct effect. See *Trojani v Centre public d'aide sociale de Bruxelles* (C-456/02) [2004] ECR I-7573 at [30]–[31]; [2004] 3 CMLR 38 (p 820); *Re Expulsion of Foreign Nationals: Commission v Netherlands* (C-50/06) [2007] ECR I-4383 at [32]; [2007] 3 CMLR 8 (p 168). This Article does not apply to activities that have no connection to EU law and which take place solely within a single Member State. See *Metock v Minister for Justice, Equality and Law Reform* (C-127/08) [2008] ECR I-6241 at [77]; [2008] 3 CMLR 39 (p 1167).

[3.270] Secondary Legislation

An EU Directive regulates the freedom of movement and residence of EU citizens. See Directive 2004/38 of the European Parliament and of the Council of 29 April 2004 on the right of citizens of the Union and their family members to move and reside freely within the territory of the Member States (OJ L 229, 29.6.2004, p 35) (hereafter "Directive 2004/38"). The Commission has adopted guidelines for the implementation of the Directive. See Communication from the Commission to the European Parliament and the Council on guidance for better transposition and application of Directive 2004/38/EC on the right of citizens of the Union and their family members to move and reside freely within the territory of the Member States (COM(2009) 313 final).

This Directive applies to EU citizens who move to or reside in a Member State of which they are not a citizen and the family members who accompany them (Art 3(1)). "Family member" is defined to include the spouse or registered partner, direct descendants who are under 21 years of age or are dependents, and dependent parents (Art 2(2)). The host Member State must also facilitate the entry and residence of a partner with whom the citizen maintains a "durable relationship" (Art 3(2)(b)).

Member States must issue to their citizens an identity card or passport attesting to their nationality (Art 4(3)). All EU citizens with a valid identity card or passport have the right to leave a Member State to travel to another Member State. Their family members who are not EU citizens have the same right. These rights are subject to national provisions regarding travel documents applying to border controls (Art 4(1)). An exit visa is not required (Art 4(2)).

[3.275] Right of Entry

Under Directive 2004/38 Member States must grant entry to EU citizens with a valid identity card or passport. Their family members who are not EU citizens have the same right. This right is subject to national provisions regarding travel documents applicable to border controls. An entry visa is not required (Art 5(1)).

Member States may require entrants to report their presence to the authorities within a reasonable and non-discriminatory time (Art 5(5)). A breach of these immigration controls is not of itself sufficient to justify deportation. The sanctions available appear to be refusal of entry if the person has not entered the host country and does not possess the requisite documentation or a small fine if the person has entered the host Member State but the penalties must not be disproportionate to the gravity of the offence. See *Italy v Watson* (118/75) [1976] ECR 1185 at [20]–[21]; [1976] 2 CMLR 552. In *Oulane v Minister voor Vreemdelingenzaken en Integratie*

(C-215/03) [2005] ECR I-1215 the Court held that deportation for breach of national requirements for the carrying of identification is disproportionate to the gravity of the infringement (at [40]).

[3.280] Right of Residence

Under Directive 2004/38 EU citizens have the right of residence in another Member State for up to 3 months without any formality other than a passport or identity card (Art 6(1)). Their family members who are not EU citizens have the same right (Art 6(2)).

EU citizens have the right to reside for longer than 3 months if they are workers or are self-employed in the host State. EU citizens also have that right if they have sufficient resources and sickness insurance (Art 7(1)). Once again, their family members who are not EU citizens have the same right (Art 7(2)). In some circumstances the right of residence of non-EU citizen family members may be retained after divorce (Art 13(1)).

Member States may require an EU citizen to register with the authorities if they will reside for longer than 3 months. If EU citizens fail to register, they may be subject to proportionate and non-discriminatory penalties (Art 8(1)).

A person who ceases to be a worker or self-employed person retains that status where (among others) they are temporarily unable to work due to illness or accident, they are involuntarily unemployed after being employed for over a year, or they are undertaking vocational training (Art 7(4)).

EU citizens have a right of residence while they are not an unreasonable burden on the social security system of the host State (Art 14(1)). Expulsion may not be the automatic consequence of use of the social security system (Art 14(3)). Workers or self-employed persons may not be expelled except on the grounds of public policy, public security or public health (Art 14(4)(a)). The right of residence extends to the entire territory of the host State (Art 22).

EU citizens who have resided lawfully for a continuous period of 5 years have the right of permanent residence (Art 16(1)). Family members who are not EU citizens have the same right (Art 16(2)). Temporary absences do not affect continuity of residence (Art 16(3)). The right of permanent residence is lost only by absence for longer than two consecutive years (Art 16(4)). See generally Alina Tryfonidou, "Family Reunification Rights of (Migrant) Union Citizens: Towards a More Liberal Approach" (2009) 15 *European Law Journal* 634.

[3.285] Restrictions upon Free Movement of EU Citizens

Under Directive 2004/38 Member States may restrict the freedom of movement of EU citizens on the grounds of public order, public security or public health (Art 27(1)). Such measures must observe the principle of proportionality and must be based solely on the personal conduct of the individual. That conduct must constitute a "genuine, present and sufficiently serious threat affecting one of the fundamental interests of society". In particular, "[p]revious criminal convictions shall not in themselves constitute grounds for taking such measures" (Art 27(2)).

The predecessor of this provision (Art 3 of Directive 64/221) was applied in *Criminal Proceedings Against Donatella Calfa* (C-348/96) [1999] ECR I-11; [1999] 2 CMLR 1138. In that case a Greek court convicted an Italian national of drug possession for personal use. Upon conviction the Italian national was subject to an automatic penalty of expulsion from Greece for life (at [2], [9]).

The Court held that a previous criminal conviction may "only be taken into account in so far as the circumstances which gave rise to that conviction are evidence of personal conduct constituting a present threat to the requirements of public policy" (at [24]). An EU national could only be expelled if, apart from their conviction under narcotics laws, their "personal conduct created a genuine and sufficiently serious threat affecting one of the fundamental interests of society" (at [25]). The expulsion occurred automatically upon conviction, with no consideration given to the personal conduct of the foreign national (at [27]). The conditions set by the Directive were thus not satisfied (at [28]).

Art 27 of Directive 2004/38 was applied in *Ministerul Administraţiei şi Internelor—Direcţia Generală de Paşapoarte Bucureşti v Jipa* (C-33/07) [2008] ECR I-5157; [2008] 3 CMLR 23 (p 715). A Romanian citizen was repatriated after illegally residing in Belgium (at [9]). Under Romanian legislation a government Minister sought a national court order prohibiting the citizen from traveling to Belgium for a 3 year period (at [10]).

The ECJ observed that freedom of movement within the EU would be meaningless if Member States were able to prohibit their nationals from traveling to other Member States without needing to demonstrate a valid justification for the prohibition (at [18]). The freedom of movement is not unconditional (at [21]).

The Court applied Art 27 of Directive 2004/38. Measures restricting free movement on the grounds of public policy or public security must be based upon those interests in the Member State adopting the measure, rather than solely on reasons put forward by another Member State when removing the individual concerned (at [25]). The measure had been sought based upon the individual's actions in another Member State. No allegation had been made that he constituted a threat to the public policy or public security of Romania (at [27]).

Before expelling a person on the ground of public policy or public security, the host State must consider the person's length of residence, age, health, family and economic situation, integration into the host State and links with their home State (Art 28(1) of Directive 2004/38). A person with permanent residence status may not be expelled other than for serious grounds of public policy or public security (Art 28(2)). A person may not be expelled if they have resided in the host State for the last 10 years, except on imperative grounds of public security (Art 28(3)(a)). A minor may not be expelled, unless the expulsion is in the best interests of the child or is based upon imperative grounds of public security (Art 28(3)(b)).

Freedom of movement may be restricted to prevent the spread of epidemic diseases (Art 29(1)). The Member States may introduce proportionate measures to withdraw rights obtained by abusive or fraudulent practices, including fraudulent marriages (Art 35).

[3.290] Schengen Agreement

In 1985 France, Germany and the Benelux countries concluded the Schengen Agreement. See *Agreement between the States of the Benelux Economic Union, Germany and France on the Gradual Abolition of Checks at their Common Frontiers*, Schengen, Luxembourg, 14 June 1985, OJ L 239, 22.9.2000, p 13; 30 ILM 73. In 1990 a Convention elaborating upon the application of the Schengen Agreement was adopted. See *Convention Applying the Schengen Agreement*, Schengen, Luxembourg, 19 June 1990, OJ L 239, 22.9.2000, p 19; 30 ILM 84. The Schengen Acquis is set out in OJ L 239, 22.9.2000, p 1.

The Schengen Agreement provides for free internal border crossings by EU nationals and non-EU nationals. Free movement within the Schengen zone applies to non-EU nationals once they have crossed the frontier of any of the participating countries. The Agreement provides for identity checks on all travellers at the external frontiers of the Schengen area in order to determine the status of nationals of non-EU countries. The substance of the Agreement is incorporated into Art 77(1) TFEU, which provides that there shall be no border controls at the internal borders while thorough border checks will be carried out at the external frontiers.

The Schengen Borders Code regulates the system in much more detail. See Regulation 562/2006 of the European Parliament and of the Council of 15 March 2006 establishing a Community Code on the rules governing the movement of persons across borders (Schengen Borders Code) (OJ L 105, 13.4.2006, p 1). The external borders of the EU may be crossed only at border crossing points (Art 4(1)). External borders include airports and sea ports (Art 2(2)). There shall be borders checks at the external borders (Art 7(1)). All persons must be subject to identity checks at the external border (Art 7(2)).

Nationals of non-EU Member States are subject to more thorough checks at the external borders (Art 7(3)). For stays of less than 3 months per 6 months period, nationals of non-EU Member States require a valid travel document authorising them to cross the border and a valid visa if required for their country (Art 5).

There shall be no border checks for both EU and non-EU nationals at the internal borders of the Union. The internal borders may be crossed at any point (Art 20). The national police may carry out spot checks that are not equivalent to border checks (Art 21). Border controls may be temporarily reintroduced where there is a "serious threat to public policy or internal security" (Art 23). A Member State temporarily reintroducing border controls must inform the European Parliament of its action (Art 25).

All EU Member States are party to the Schengen Agreement. However, the United Kingdom and Ireland have opted out of full participation. Those two states participate only in certain aspects of the Agreement (police and judicial cooperation in criminal matters, combat of drug trafficking and the Schengen Information System). See Council Decision 2000/365 of 29 May 2000 concerning the request of the United Kingdom of Great Britain and Northern Ireland to take part in some of the provisions of the Schengen acquis (OJ L 131, 1.6.2000, p 43); Council Decision 2004/926 of 22 December 2004 on the putting into effect of parts of the Schengen acquis by the United Kingdom of Great Britain and Northern Ireland (OJ L 395, 31.12.2004, p 70); Council Decision 2002/192 of 28 February 2002 concerning Ireland's request to take part in some of the provisions of the Schengen acquis (OJ L 64, 7.3.2002, p 20); Maria Fletcher, "Schengen, the European Court of Justice and Flexibility under the Lisbon Treaty: Balancing the United Kingdom's 'Ins' and 'Outs'" (2009) 5 *European Constitutional Law Review* 71.

A Protocol to the TFEU provides that the Schengen Acquis applies to all EU Member States except the United Kingdom and Ireland. See Art 2, Protocol (No 19) on the Schengen Acquis Integrated into the Framework of the European Union. The Agreement is not yet implemented in Bulgaria, Cyprus, Liechtenstein and Romania. Four non-EU Member States are also party to the Agreement: Iceland, Liechtenstein, Norway and Switzerland. The following table sets out the parties to the Agreement.

Parties to the Schengen Agreement

Party	Date of signature
Austria	28 April 1995 (OJ L 239, 22.9.2000, p 90)
Belgium	14 June 1985 (OJ L 239, 22.9.2000, p 13)
Bulgaria	1 January 2007 (Art 4, Protocol on Conditions for Admission)
Cyprus	1 May 2004 (Art 3, Act of Accession; OJ L 323, 8.12.2007, p 34)
Czech Republic	1 May 2004 (Art 3, Act of Accession; OJ L 323, 8.12.2007, p 34)
Denmark	19 December 1996 (OJ L 239, 22.9.2000, p 97)
Estonia	1 May 2004 (Art 3, Act of Accession; OJ L 323, 8.12.2007, p 34)
Finland	19 December 1996 (OJ L 239, 22.9.2000, p 106)
France	14 June 1985 (OJ L 239, 22.9.2000, p 13)
Germany	14 June 1985 (OJ L 239, 22.9.2000, p 13)
Greece	6 November 1992 (OJ L 239, 22.9.2000, p 83)

(continued)

Party	Date of signature
Hungary	1 May 2004 (Art 3, Act of Accession; OJ L 323, 8.12.2007, p 34)
Iceland	19 December 1996 (OJ L 176, 10.7.1999, p 36)
Ireland	16 June 2000 (OJ L 15, 20.1.2000, p 2)
Italy	27 November 1990 (OJ L 239, 22.9.2000, p 63)
Latvia	1 May 2004 (Art 3, Act of Accession; OJ L 323, 8.12.2007, p 34)
Liechtenstein	28 February 2008 (OJ L 83, 26.3.2008, p 18)
Lithuania	1 May 2004 (Art 3, Act of Accession; OJ L 323, 8.12.2007, p 34)
Luxembourg	14 June 1985 (OJ L 239, 22.9.2000, p 13)
Malta	1 May 2004 (Art 3, Act of Accession; OJ L 323, 8.12.2007, p 34)
Netherlands	14 June 1985 (OJ L 239, 22.9.2000, p 13)
Norway	19 December 1996 (OJ L 176, 10.7.1999, p 36)
Poland	1 May 2004 (Art 3, 2003 Accession; OJ L 323, 8.12.2007, p 34)
Portugal	25 June 1992 (OJ L 239, 22.9.2000, p 76)
Romania	1 January 2007 (Art 4, Protocol on Conditions for Admission)
Slovakia	1 May 2004 (Art 3, Act of Accession; OJ L 323, 8.12.2007, p 34)
Slovenia	1 May 2004 (Art 3, Act of Accession; OJ L 323, 8.12.2007, p 34)
Spain	25 June 1992 (OJ L 239, 22.9.2000, p 69)
Sweden	19 December 1996 (OJ L 239, 22.9.2000, p 115)
Switzerland	26 October 2004 (OJ L 370, 17.12.2004, p 78; OJ L 53, 27.2.2008, p 52)
United Kingdom	20 May 1999 (OJ L 15, 20.1.2000, p 2)

The Schengen Protocol makes clear that the applicability of the Schengen Acquis within the EU is subject to its compatibility with EU law, in particular the founding Treaties. See Art 1, Protocol (No 19) on the Schengen Acquis Integrated into the Framework of the European Union; *Commission v Spain* (C-503/03) [2006] ECR I-1097 at [34].

See generally, Steve Peers, "Caveat Emptor? Integrating the Schengen Acquis into the European Union Legal Order" (1999) 2 *Cambridge Yearbook of European Legal Studies* 87; Lora Borissova, "The Adoption of the Schengen and the Justice and Home Affairs Acquis: Two Stumbling Blocks on the Way to Successful Enlargement?" (December 2002) 3 *German Law Journal*, http://www.germanlawjournal.com; Richard J Hunter Jr and Leo V Ryan, "The Schengen System: Protecting the Borders and Security of the European Union" (2004) 37 *Business Law Review* 29.

[3.295] Non-EU Citizens

Long term residence for non-EU nationals is governed by Council Directive 2003/109 of 25 November 2003 concerning the status of third-country nationals who are long-term residents (OJ L 16, 23.1.2004, p 44). This Directive does not apply to the United Kingdom and Ireland (Preamble

Recital 25). A third country national is anyone who is not an EU citizen (Art 2(a)).

Member States are required to grant long-term resident status to non-EU citizens who have legally and continuously resided in their territory for 5 years (Art 4(1)). Non-EU citizens must show that they have sufficient resources to maintain themselves and their dependents without reliance upon social security (Art 5(1)(a)). They must also have sickness insurance (Art 5(1)(b)).

The grant of long-term resident status may be refused on the grounds of public policy or public security. In making such a decision, the Member State must consider the severity of any offence or the hazard posed by the person, along with the length of residence and any links to the country (Art 6(1)). Refusal of status may not be based upon economic considerations (Art 6(2)).

Long-term residence status is permanent (Art 8(1)). The Member State shall issue a residence permit to those with long-term residence status. The permit is valid for 5 years and is automatically renewable (Art 8(2)). Expiry of a permit does not result in the loss of long-term residence status (Art 9(6)).

A long-term resident loses that status if the status has been fraudulently obtained, they are expelled, or they are absent from the EU for 12 consecutive months (Art 9(1)). However, a Member State may provide that absences of longer than 12 consecutive months will not result in loss of long-term residence status (Art 9(2)). Member States may also provide that long-term residence status will be lost where the individual is a threat to public policy, considering the seriousness of the offences committed. However, this is not a reason for expulsion (Art 9(3)).

A Member State may expel a long-term resident only where they constitute "an actual and sufficiently serious threat to public policy or public security" (Art 12(1)). A decision to expel may not be based upon economic considerations (Art 12(2)).

Long-term residents are to receive equal treatment with nationals in relation to access to employment, education, recognition of professional qualifications, social security, tax benefits, access to goods and services, freedom of association and access to the entire national territory (Art 11(1)).

A long-term resident has the right to reside for longer than 3 months in Member States other than the one that granted that status (Art 14(1)). The "second Member State" is a Member State other than the one that first granted long term resident status (Art 2(d)). An application for a residence permit must be made within 3 months of entry into the second Member State (Art 15(1)). The grounds for granting or refusing residence are similar to those applying to long-term residence status (Arts 15(2), 17). However, residence of a second Member State may also be refused on the ground that the individual is a threat to public health because they have an infectious disease (Art 18(1)–(2)).

Another Directive regulates family reunification by non-EU nationals. See Council Directive 2003/86 of 22 September 2003 on the right to family reunification (OJ L 251, 3.10.2003, p 12). This Directive does not apply to the United Kingdom and Ireland (Preamble Recital 17). The entry and residence of highly qualified employees is regulated by a specific Directive. See Council Directive 2009/50 of 25 May 2009 on the conditions of entry and residence of third-country nationals for the purposes of highly qualified employment (OJ L 155, 18.6.2009, p 17).

There are EU minimum standards for sanctions against those who employ third country workers who remain illegally in a Member State. See Directive 2009/52 of the European Parliament and of the Council of 18 June 2009 providing for minimum standards on sanctions and measures against employers of illegally staying third-country nationals (OJ L 168, 30.6.2009, p 24).

The external frontiers of the EU are subject to border controls operated by the Member States. Those border controls are coordinated by Frontex, which was established by EU Regulation. See Council Regulation 2007/2004 of 26 October 2004 establishing a European Agency for the Management of Operational Cooperation at the External Borders of the Member States of the European Union (OJ L 349, 25.11.2004, p 1). The Frontex website is at http://www.frontex.europa.eu.

[3.300] Non-discrimination on the Ground of Nationality

Art 18 TFEU provides: "Within the scope of application of the Treaties, and without prejudice to any special provisions contained therein, any discrimination on grounds of nationality shall be prohibited." The Court of Justice has held that this Article prohibits discrimination against EU citizens, not discrimination against third country nationals. See Chloé Hublet, "The Scope of Article 12 of the Treaty of the European Communities vis-à-vis Third-Country Nationals: Evolution at Last?" (2009) 15 *European Law Journal* 757. This prohibition of discrimination "requires that comparable situations must not be treated differently unless such treatment is objectively justified". See *Schempp v Finanzamt München V* (C-403/03) [2005] ECR I-6421 at [28]; [2005] 3 CMLR 37 (p 1051).

In *Wood v Fonds de Garantie des Victimes des Actes de Terrorisme et d'Autres Infractions* (C-164/07) [2008] ECR I-4143; [2008] 3 CMLR 11 (p 265) a British national had lived and worked in France for more than 20 years. His partner was a French national (at [7]). One of their children died in a traffic accident outside France (at [3]). The family sought compensation for her death. The French criminal procedure code required that claimants for compensation must have French nationality if the injury occurred outside French territory (at [1]). The British national was refused compensation on this basis, while his partner received compensation (at [5]).

The Court held that this national rule violated the prohibition against discrimination on the ground of nationality. The British national had exercised his freedom of movement for workers by living and working in France, so his situation was within the area of application of the Treaties (at [11]–[12]). The British national and his partner were in a comparable situation. The only difference in their entitlement to compensation was their nationality (at [14]). The different treatment was direct discrimination. The French government conceded that there was no justification for the discrimination (at [15]).

[3.305] Conclusion

EU workers have freedom of movement within the Union. The essential characteristic of an employment relationship is that a person performs services for and under the direction of another person in return for which remuneration is paid. The term "worker" has an EU meaning and is given a broad interpretation.

This freedom covers the pursuit of genuine and effective economic activities, not purely marginal and ancillary economic activities. Non-nationals may reside in other Member States for the purpose of seeking or undertaking paid employment. Free movement entails the abolition of any discrimination based on nationality between workers of the Member States as regards employment, remuneration and other conditions of work and employment.

Provisions that prevent or discourage an EU citizen from leaving their home State to work in another Member State constitute an obstacle to freedom of movement even if they apply to both nationals and non-nationals. This freedom may be limited on grounds of public policy, public security or public health. Free movement does not apply to employment in the public service, which is narrowly defined.

The TFEU prohibits restrictions on the freedom of establishment of nationals of a Member State in the territory of another Member State. Companies also enjoy freedom of establishment. The right of establishment includes the right to pursue activities as self-employed persons under the conditions laid down by the state of establishment for its own nationals.

The right of establishment does not apply to activities connected with the exercise of official authority. Permissible justifications for limiting freedom of establishment include public policy, public security, public health, consumer protection, the prevention of crime, the prevention of tax avoidance and collective industrial action.

Member States are permitted to adopt measures seeking to prevent improper circumvention of their national laws or the improper or fraudulent use of freedom of establishment. It is not in itself an abuse of freedom of establishment to set up a company in the Member State with the least restrictive company law. The EU has created a special category of company, known as the European Company. Such companies do not depend upon the national laws of the Member States.

Restrictions on freedom to provide services are prohibited in respect of nationals of Member States who are established in a Member State different from that of the recipient of the services. Services fall within the protection of the Treaty where they are normally provided for remuneration. The concept of "services" has been broadly interpreted by the Court.

The freedom to provide services prohibits discrimination based on the nationality of a service provider or the fact that it is established in another Member State. This provision also requires the abolition of any restriction which is likely to prohibit, impede or render less advantageous the activities of a service provider from another Member State.

This freedom does not apply to the exercise of official authority. The freedom is also subject to national measures providing for special treatment for foreign nationals on grounds of public policy, public security or public health. Apart from the express Treaty exceptions, there are judicially recognised exceptions known as overriding reasons in the public interest, including consumer protection and the protection of fundamental rights.

To be compatible with the Treaty a limitation to the freedom to provide services must pursue a legitimate objective, be justified by an overriding reason of public interest, be suitable for attaining the objective and not go further than what is necessary for attaining that objective. EU secondary legislation concerning the provision of services regulates services in the internal market, professional services, transport services, electronic commerce and communications, insurance services and cross-border mediation.

EU citizens have the right to move and reside freely within the territory of the Member States. The Member States must grant entry to EU citizens with a valid identity card or passport. EU citizens have the right of residence in another Member State for up to 3 months without any formality other than a passport or identity card. Member States may restrict freedom of movement of EU citizens on the grounds of public order or public security or public health. Such measures must be based solely on the personal conduct of the individual.

The Schengen Agreement provides for free internal border crossings by EU nationals and non-EU nationals. Free movement within the Schengen zone applies to non-EU nationals once they have crossed the frontier of any of the participating countries. There are no border controls at the internal EU borders while thorough border checks are carried out at the external frontiers.

Member States are required to grant long-term resident status to non-EU citizens who have legally and continuously resided in their territory for 5 years. Within the scope of application of the EU Treaties any discrimination on the ground of nationality is prohibited.

Further Reading

A. *Free Movement of Persons*

Broberg, Morten and Nina Holst-Christensen. *Free Movement in the European Union* (2nd ed, Copenhagen: DJØF, 2007).

Carlier, Jean-Yves and Elspeth Guild (eds). *The Future of Free Movement of Persons in the EU* (Bruxelles: Bruylant, 2006).

Costello, Cathryn. "*Metock*: Free Movement and 'Normal Family Life' in the Union" (2009) 46 *Common Market Law Review* 587.

Cousins, Mel. "Free Movement of Workers, EU Citizenship and Access to Social Advantages" (2007) 14 *Maastricht Journal of European and Comparative Law* 343.

Currie, Samantha. "Accelerated Justice or a Step Too Far? Residence Rights of Non-EU Family Members and the Court's Ruling in *Metock*" (2009) 34 *European Law Review* 310.

de Mestral, Armand and Jan Winter. "Mobility Rights in the European Union and Canada" (2001) 46 *McGill Law Journal* 979 at 995 ff.

Daniele, Luigi. "Non-discriminatory Restrictions on the Free Movement of Persons" (1997) 22 *European Law Review* 191.

Jeffery, Mark. "The Free Movement of Persons Within the European Union: Moving from Employment Rights to Fundamental Rights?" (2001) 23 *Comparative Labor Law and Policy Journal* 211.

Kranz, Amikam Omer. "The *Bosman* Case: The Relationship Between European Union Law and the Transfer System in European Football" (1999) 5 *Columbia Journal of European Law* 431.

McGlynn, Clare. "Family Reunion and the Free Movement of Persons in European Union Law" (2005) 7 *International Community Law Review* 159.

Moore, Matthew. "The Freedom of Movement and Migrant Workers' Social Security: An Overview of the Court's Jurisprudence 1992–1997" (1998) 35 *Common Market Law Review* 409.

Moore, Matthew. "Freedom of Movement and Migrant Workers' Social Security: An Overview of the Case Law of the Court of Justice, 1997–2001" (2002) 39 *Common Market Law Review* 807.

O'Leary, Síofra. "Developing an Ever Closer Union Between the Peoples of Europe? A Reappraisal of the Case Law of the Court of Justice on the Free Movement of Persons and EU Citizenship" (2008) 27 *Yearbook of European Law* 167.

Reich, Norbert. "Free Movement v Social Rights in an Enlarged Union – The *Laval* and *Viking* Cases before the ECJ" (February 2008) 9, 2 *German Law Journal* 125, http://www.germanlawjournal.com

Rogers, Nicola and Rick Scannell. *Free Movement of Persons in the Enlarged European Union* (London: Sweet & Maxwell, 2005).

Sánchez, Sara Iglesias. "Free Movement of Third Country Nationals in the European Union? Main Features, Deficiencies and Challenges of the New Mobility Rights in the Area of Freedom, Security and Justice" (2009) 15 *European Law Journal* 791.

Shine, D Bruce. "The European Union's Right of Free Movement of Workers" (2000) 30 *University of Memphis Law Review* 817.

Shuibhne, Niamh Nic. "Free Movement of Persons and the Wholly Internal Rule: Time to Move on?" (2002) 39 *Common Market Law Review* 731.

Shuibhne, Niamh Nic. "Derogating from the Free Movement of Persons: When Can EU Citizens Be Deported?" (2006) 8 *Cambridge Yearbook of European Legal Studies* 187.

Skordas, Achilles. "Immigration and the Market: The Long-Term Residents Directive" (2006) 13 *Columbia Journal of European Law* 201.

Spaventa, Eleanor. *Free Movement of Persons in the EU: Barriers to Movement in Their Constitutional Context* (Alphen aan den Rijn, The Netherlands: Kluwer, 2007).

Toner, Helen. *Partnership Rights, Free Movement, and EU Law* (Oxford: Hart, 2004).

Tryfonidou, Alina. "C-200/02, *Kunqian Catherine Zhu and Man Layette Chen v Secretary of State for the Home Department*: Further Cracks in the 'Great Wall' of the European Union?" (2005) 11 *European Public Law* 527.

Tryfonidou, Alina. "In Search of the Aim of the EC Free Movement of Persons Provisions: Has the Court of Justice Missed the Point?" (2009) 46 *Common Market Law Review* 1591.

van der Mei, Anne Pieter. *Free Movement of Persons Within the European Community: Cross-Border Access to Public Benefits* (Oxford: Hart, 2003).

Weiss, Freidl and Frank Wooldridge. *Free Movement of Persons Within the European Community* (2nd ed, Alphen aan den Rijn, The Netherlands: Kluwer, 2007).

Woodruff, Brian J. "The Qualified Right to Free Movement of Workers: How the Big Bang Accession Has Forever Changed a Fundamental EU Freedom" (2008) 10 *Duquesne Business Law Journal* 127.

B. Freedom of Establishment

Davies, A C L. "The Right to Strike Versus Freedom of Establishment in EC Law: The Battle Commences" (2006) 35 *Industrial Law Journal* 75.

Garcia-Riestra, Manuel. "The Transfer of Seat of the European Company v Free Establishment Case-Law" (2004) 15 *European Business Law Review* 1295.

Johnston, Andrew. "EC Freedom of Establishment, Employee Participation in Corporate Governance and the Limits of Regulatory Competition" (2006) 6 *Journal of Corporate Law Studies* 71.

Kaldellis, Evangelos I. "Freedom of Establishment Versus Freedom to Provide Services: An Evaluation of Case-Law Developments in the Areas of Indistinctly Applicable Rules" (2001) 28 *Legal Issues of Economic Integration* 23.

Kiekebeld, Ben J and Daniel S Smit. "Freedom of Establishment and Free Movement of Capital in Association and Partnership Agreements and Direct Taxation" (2007) 16 *EC Tax Review* 216.

Mucciarelli, Federico M. "Company 'Emigration' and EC Freedom of Establishment: *Daily Mail* Revisited" (2008) 9 *European Business Organization Law Review* 267.

Rammeloo, Stephan. "At Long Last: Freedom of Establishment for Legal Persons in Europe Accomplished. ECJ Case C-167/01 *Kamer van Koophandel en Fabrieken voor Amsterdam v Inspire Art Ltd*" (2004) 11 *Maastricht Journal of European and Comparative Law* 379.

Rothe, Nicole. "Freedom of Establishment of Legal Persons Within the European Union: An Analysis of the European Court of Justice Decision in the *Uberseering* Case" (2004) 53 *American University Law Review* 1103.

Vaccaro, Enrico. "Transfer of Seat and Freedom of Establishment in European Company Law" (2005) 16 *European Business Law Review* 1348.

Vossestein, Gert-Jan. "Exit Restrictions on Freedom of Establishment After *Marks & Spencer*" (2006) 7 *European Business Organization Law Review* 863.

Vossestein, Gert-Jan. "Cross-Border Transfer of Seat and Conversion of Companies Under the EC Treaty Provisions on Freedom of Establishment" (2009) 6 *European Company Law* 115.

White, Robin C A. *Workers, Establishment and Services in the European Union* (Oxford: Oxford University Press, 2004).

Wooldridge, Frank. "*Überseering*: Freedom of Establishment of Companies Affirmed" (2003) 14 *European Business Law Review* 227.

C. Free Movement of Services

Andenas, Mads and Jukka Snell. "Exploring the Outer Limits – Restrictions on the Free Movement of Goods and Services" (1999) 10 *European Business Law Review* 252.

Barnard, Catherine. "Unravelling the Services Directive" (2008) 45 *Common Market Law Review* 323.

Davies, Gareth. "The Services Directive: Extending the Country of Origin Principle and Reforming Public Administration" (2007) 32 *European Law Review* 232.

Fernandes, Jose Maria and Siofra O'Leary. "Judicial Exceptions to the Free Provision of Services" (1995) 1 *European Law Journal* 308.

Gkoutzinis, Apostolos. "Free Movement of Services in the EC Treaty and the Law of Contractual Obligations Relating to Banking and Financial Services" (2004) 41 *Common Market Law Review* 119.

Hansen, Jesper Lau. "Full Circle: Is There a Difference Between the Freedom of Establishment and the Freedom to Provide Services?" (2000) 11 *European Business Law Review* 83.

Hatzopoulos, Vassilis. "Recent Developments of Case Law of the ECJ in the Field of Free Provision of Services, 1994–1999" (2000) 37 *Common Market Law Review* 43.

Hatzopoulos, Vassilis. "Assessing the Services Directive (2006/123/EC)" (2008) 10 *Cambridge Yearbook of European Legal Studies* 215.

Hatzopoulos, Vassilis and Thien Uyen Do. "The Case Law of the ECJ Concerning the Free Provision of Services: 2000–2005" (2006) 43 *Common Market Law Review* 923.

O'Leary, Síofra. "Judicially-Created Exceptions to the Free Provision of Services" (2000) 11 *European Business Law Review* 347.

Sharpston, Eleanor and José Maria F Martin. "Some Reflections on Schengen Free Movement Rights and the Principle of *ne bis in idem*" (2008) 10 *Cambridge Yearbook of European Legal Studies* 413.

Torgersen, Ole-Andreas. "The Limitations of the Free Movements of Goods and the Freedom to Provide Services – in Search of a Common Approach" (1999) 10 *European Business Law Review* 371.

Chapter 4
Free Movement of Capital

[4.05] Introduction

The Treaty provisions concerning free movement of capital were replaced by the Maastricht (Union) Treaty. Under the amended Treaty all restrictions on the movement of capital between Member States, and between Member States and third countries, are prohibited (Art 63(1) TFEU). This provision has direct effect. See *Criminal Proceedings Against Sanz de Lera* (C-163/94) [1995] ECR I-4821 at [48]; [1996] 1 CMLR 361; *Skatteverket v A* (C-101/05) [2007] ECR I-11531 at [21], [25]–[26]; [2009] 1 CMLR 35 (p 975).

The free movement of capital is one of the fundamental freedoms of the European Union. See *Re Casati* (203/80) [1981] ECR 2595 at [8]; [1982] 1 CMLR 365. The four fundamental freedoms are part of the internal market, which is "an area without internal frontiers in which the free movement of goods, persons, services and capital is ensured" (Art 26(2) TFEU).

Free movement of capital also applies to capital movements between the EU and third states. A restrictive measure that would violate free movement of capital if applied to capital movements between Member States may be justifiable if applied to capital movements between the EU and non-member states. The legal integration between Member States is obviously much closer than that between the EU and non-member states. The considerations that determine the justifiability of the same measure in each situation are thus not identical. See *Test Claimants in the FII Group Litigation v Commissioners of Inland Revenue* (C-446/04) [2006] ECR I-11753 at [171]; [2007] 1 CMLR 35 (p 1021); *Skatteverket v A* (C-101/05) [2007] ECR I-11531 at [37]; [2009] 1 CMLR 35 (p 975). All restrictions upon payments between Member States and between Member States and third countries will be prohibited (Art 63(2) TFEU).

G. Moens, J. Trone, *Commercial Law of the European Union*,
Ius Gentium: Comparative Perspectives on Law and Justice 4,
DOI 10.1007/978-90-481-8774-4_4,

[4.10] Movement of Capital Defined

"The Movement of Capital" is not defined in the TFEU. In 1988 the EU adopted Council Directive 88/361 of 24 June 1988 for the implementation of Article 67 of the Treaty (OJ L 178, 8.7.1988, p 5). Art 67 EC was repealed by the Treaty of Amsterdam. Nonetheless, the Court has regard to the terminology used in Annex I to this Directive in determining the meaning of the "movement of capital". See *Proceedings brought by Trummer* (C-22/97) [1999] ECR I-1661 at [21]; [2000] 3 CMLR 1143; *Re Golden Shares: Commission v Portugal* (C-367/98) [2002] ECR I-4731 at [37]; [2002] 2 CMLR 1213; *Centro di Musicologia Walter Stauffer v Finanzamt München für Körperschaften* (C-386/04) [2006] ECR I-8203 at [22]; [2009] 2 CMLR 31 (p 777); *Fidium Finanz AG v Bundesanstalt für Finanzdienstleistungsaufsicht* (C-452/04) [2006] ECR I-9521 at [41]; [2007] 1 CMLR 15 (p 489).

However, the list in Annex I of the Directive is not exhaustive. See *Reisch v Bürgermeister der Landeshauptstadt Salzburg* (C-515/99) [2002] ECR I-2157 at [13]; [2004] 1 CMLR 44 (p 1394); *van Hilten-van der Heijden v Inspecteur van de Belastingdienst* (C-513/03) [2006] ECR I-1957 at [39]; *Jäger v Finanzamt Kusel-Landstuhl* (C-256/06) [2008] ECR I-123 at [29]; [2008] 2 CMLR 10 (p 268); *Eckelkamp v Belgium* (C-11/07) [2008] ECR I-6845 at [38]; [2008] 3 CMLR 44 (p 1137); *Arens-Sikken v Staatssecretaris van Financiën* (C-43/07) [2008] ECR I-6887 at [29]; [2008] 3 CMLR 43 (p 1303).

This very detailed list is divided into the following categories:

I – Direct Investments
II – Investments in Real Estate
III – Operations in Securities Normally Dealt in on the Capital Market
IV – Operations in Units of Collective Investment Undertakings
V – Operations in Securities and Other Instruments Normally Dealt in on the Money Market
VI – Operations in Current and Deposit Accounts with Financial Institutions
VII – Credits Related to Commercial Transactions or to the Provision of Services in which a Resident is Participating
VIII – Financial Loans and Credits
IX – Sureties, Other Guarantees and Rights of Pledge
X – Transfers in Performance of Insurance Contracts
XI – Personal Capital Movements
XII – Physical Import and Export of Financial Assets
XIII – Other Capital Movements.

Based upon this list, the European Court of Justice has held that the following activities may constitute movements of capital:

- direct investments, that is, "investments of any kind undertaken by natural or legal persons and which serve to establish or maintain lasting and direct links between the person providing the capital and the undertaking to which that capital is made available in order to carry on an economic activity": *Test Claimants in the FII Group Litigation v Commissioners of Inland Revenue* (C-446/04) [2006] ECR I-11753 at [181]; [2007] 1 CMLR 35 (p 1021); *Federconsumatori v Comune di Milano* (C-463/04) [2007] ECR I-10419 at [20]; [2008] 1 CMLR 46 (p 1187); *Re Law on Privatisation of Equity in Volkswagenwerk GmbH: Commission v Germany* (C-112/05) [2007] ECR I-8995 at [18]; [2008] 1 CMLR 25 (p 643);
- "operations relating to shares, bonds and other securities which . . . can be valued in money and may be the subject of market transactions": *Jägerskiöld v Gustafsson* (C-97/98) [1999] ECR I-7319 at [34]; [2000] 1 CMLR 235; in particular, shareholdings in an undertaking: *Re Golden Shares: Commission v Spain* (C-463/00) [2003] ECR I-4581 at [53]; [2003] 2 CMLR 18 (p 557); *Re Golden Shares: Commission v United Kingdom* (C-98/01) [2003] ECR I-4641 at [40]; [2003] 2 CMLR 19 (p 598);
- investments by non-residents in real estate located in another Member State (also known as real property or immovable property): *Proceedings brought by Trummer* (C-22/97) [1999] ECR I-1661 at [21]; [2000] 3 CMLR 1143; *Reisch v Bürgermeister der Landeshauptstadt Salzburg* (C-515/99) [2002] ECR I-2157 at [30]; [2004] 1 CMLR 44 (p 1394); *Heirs of Barbier v Inspecteur van de Belastingdienst Particulieren/Ondernemingen Buitenland te Heerlen* (C-364/01) [2003] ECR I-15013 at [58]; [2004] 1 CMLR 40 (p 1283); *D v Inspecteur van de Belastingdienst/Particulieren/Ondernemingen Buitenland te Heerlen* (C-376/03) [2005] ECR I-5821 at [24]; [2005] 3 CMLR 19 (p 515); *Blanckaert v Inspecteur van de Belastingdienst/Particulieren/Ondernemingen Buitenland te Heerlen* (C-512/03) [2005] ECR I-7685 at [35]; [2005] 3 CMLR 39 (p 1097); *Europeenne et Luxembourgeoise D'investissements SA (Elisa) v Directeur General des Impots* (C-451/05) [2007] ECR I-8251 at [59]; [2008] 1 CMLR 13 (p 276); *Hollmann v Fazenda Pública* (C-443/06) [2007] ECR I-8491 at [31]; [2008] 1 CMLR 10 (p 216).
- the provision of consumer credit: *Fidium Finanz AG v Bundesanstalt für Finanzdienstleistungsaufsicht* (C-452/04) [2006] ECR I-9521 at [42]–[43]; [2007] 1 CMLR 15 (p 489);
- an inheritance bequeathed to a person resident in another Member State: *Jäger v Finanzamt Kusel-Landstuhl* (C-256/06) [2008] ECR I-123 at [25]; [2008] 2 CMLR 10 (p 268); *Eckelkamp v Belgium* (C-11/07) [2008] ECR I-6845 at [39]; [2008] 3 CMLR 44 (p 1337); *Arens-Sikken v Staatssecretaris van Financiën* (C-43/07) [2008] ECR I-6887 at [30]; [2008] 3 CMLR 43 (p 1303); *Block v Finanzamt Kaufbeuren* (C-67/08) [2009] ECR I-883 at [20]; [2009] 2 CMLR 39 (p 1015); and

- donations to charities established in another Member State, which may comprise gifts of property or money: *Persche v Finanzamt Lüdenscheid* (C-318/07) [2009] ECR I-359 at [24], [26]–[27]; [2009] 2 CMLR 32 (p 819).

The freedom of movement of capital does not apply to a movement of capital that is "purely internal" to one Member State. See *Arens-Sikken v Staatssecretaris van Financiën* (C-43/07) [2008] ECR I-6887 at [30]–[31]; [2008] 3 CMLR 43 (p 1303); *Block v Finanzamt Kaufbeuren* (C-67/08) [2009] ECR I-883 at [20]–[21]; [2009] 2 CMLR 39 (p 1015).

[4.15] Restrictions upon the Movement of Capital

The Court has held that the following measures constitute restrictions upon the movement of capital:

- national restrictions that are liable to deter investments by non-residents or investments in other Member States by residents: *Proceedings brought by Manninen* (C-319/02) [2004] ECR I-7477 at [22]–[24]; [2004] 3 CMLR 40 (p 881); *Skatteverket v A* (C-101/05) [2007] ECR I-11531 at [40]; [2009] 1 CMLR 35 (p 975); *Test Claimants in the CFC and Dividend Group Litigation v Inland Revenue Commissioners* (C-201/05) [2008] ECR I-2875 at [53]; [2008] 2 CMLR 53 (p 1482);
- measures that are "liable to prevent or limit the acquisition of shares in the undertakings concerned or to deter investors of other Member States from investing in their capital": *Re Law on Privatisation of Equity in Volkswagenwerk GmbH: Commission v Germany* (C-112/05) [2007] ECR I-8995 at [19]; [2008] 1 CMLR 25 (p 643); *Federconsumatori v Comune di Milano* (C-463/04) [2007] ECR I-10419 at [21]; [2008] 1 CMLR 46 (p 1187);
- less favourable treatment of foreign source dividends than those from a domestic source: *Test Claimants in the FII Group Litigation v Commissioners of Inland Revenue* (C-446/04) [2006] ECR I-11753 at [184]–[185]; [2007] 1 CMLR 35 (p 1021);
- legislation providing that a bank must be established within a Member State for borrowers within its territory to qualify for an interest rate subsidy offered by the national government: *Svensson v Ministre du Logement et de l'Urbanisme* (C-484/93) [1995] ECR I-3955 at [10]; *Proceedings brought by Trummer* (C-22/97) [1999] ECR I-1661 at [26]; [2000] 3 CMLR 1143; *Sandoz v Finanzlandesdirektion für Wien, Niederösterreich und Burgenland* (C-439/97) [1999] ECR I-7041 at [19]; [2001] 3 CMLR 63 (p 1639);
- less favourable taxation treatment of foreign residents than domestic residents: *Blanckaert v Inspecteur van de Belastingdienst/Particulieren/*

Ondernemingen Buitenland te Heerlen (C-512/03) [2005] ECR I-7685 at [39]; [2005] 3 CMLR 39 (p 1097); *Hollmann v Fazenda Pública* (C-443/06) [2007] ECR I-8491 at [37]–[40]; [2008] 1 CMLR 10 (p 216);

- a less favourable rate of taxation for foreign source revenue compared to that for revenue from domestic sources: *Lenz v Finanzlandesdirektion für Tirol* (C-315/02) [2004] ECR I-7063 at [20]–[21]; [2004] 3 CMLR 13 (p 274);
- a tax credit that is available only for dividends paid by domestic companies: *Proceedings brought by Manninen* (C-319/02) [2004] ECR I-7477 at [20]–[23]; [2004] 3 CMLR 40 (p 881);
- measures that have the effect of reducing "the value of the inheritance of a resident of a State other than the Member State in which the assets concerned are situated and which taxes the inheritance of those assets": *Jäger v Finanzamt Kusel-Landstuhl* (C-256/06) [2008] ECR I-123 at [31]; [2008] 2 CMLR 10 (p 268); *Eckelkamp v Belgium* (C-11/07) [2008] ECR I-6845 at [44]; [2008] 3 CMLR 44 (p 1337); *Arens-Sikken v Staatssecretaris van Financiën* (C-43/07) [2008] ECR I-6887 at [37]; [2008] 3 CMLR 43 (p 1303);
- legislation requiring authorization for the export of currency: *Criminal Proceedings Against Sanz de Lera* (C-163/94) [1995] ECR I-4821 at [23]–[25]; [1996] 1 CMLR 361;
- legislation denying a tax deduction for donations to charities that are not established in the Member State where the deduction is claimed: *Persche v Finanzamt Lüdenscheid* (C-318/07) [2009] ECR I-359 at [38]–[39]; [2009] 2 CMLR 32 (p 819);
- legislation requiring prior authorization of foreign direct investment: *Église de Scientologie de Paris v Prime Minister* (C-54/99) [2000] ECR I-1335 at [14]; or the sale of agricultural land: *Ospelt v Schlossle Weissenberg Familienstiftung* (C-452/01) [2003] ECR I-9743 at [33]–[34]; [2005] 3 CMLR 40 (p 1125); or the acquisition of plots of building land: *Re Salzmann* (C 300/01) [2003] ECR I-4899 at [41]; [2004] 1 CMLR 29 (p 959); and
- legislation providing that the purchase of a particular type of land would be invalid unless a written declaration regarding the sale was submitted before a deadline: *Burtscher v Stauderer* (C-213/04) [2005] ECR I-10309 at [41]–[43]; [2006] 2 CMLR 13 (p 382).

A case example illustrates the way in which the Court determines whether a national measure constitutes a restriction upon the movement of capital. In *Re Law on Privatisation of Equity in Volkswagenwerk GmbH: Commission v Germany* (C-112/05) [2007] ECR I-8995; [2008] 1 CMLR 25 (p 643) a German law permitted the federal and state governments to each appoint two representatives to Volkswagen's supervisory board. The governments had this right provided that they held shares in the company, but it applied irrespective of the level of their investments (at [7]). These provisions departed from the general law that would otherwise apply in these circumstances (at [9], [63]).

The Court held that the right to appoint representatives to the board gave the federal and state governments the power to exercise influence over the company beyond the level of their investments. The influence of other shareholders could thereby be reduced below the level of their investments (at [64]). This provision was liable to deter investors from other Member States from investing in the company (at [66]). It was irrelevant that investors had nevertheless displayed strong interest in acquiring the company's shares (at [67]). The provision constituted a restriction upon the movement of capital (at [68]). See similarly, *Federconsumatori v Comune di Milano* (C-463/04) [2007] ECR I-10419 at [22]–[24]; [2008] 1 CMLR 46 (p 1187); Alessandro Spano, "Free Movement of Capital and Golden Shares: A New Perspective on Corporate Control?" (2010) 13 *International Trade and Business Law Review* 291.

A national measure may restrict the free movement of capital even if it does not discriminate between nationals and non-nationals. In *Re Golden Shares: Commission v Portugal* (C-367/98) [2002] ECR I-4731; [2002] 2 CMLR 1213 national legislation required prior governmental authorisation for the acquisition of holdings in particular national undertakings above a certain level (at [39]). The national government sought to justify the legislation on the ground that it applied to both national investors and those from other Member States (at [43]).

The Court rejected this argument, holding that Art 73b EC (now Art 63(1) TFEU) "lays down a general prohibition on restrictions on the movement of capital between Member States" which "goes beyond the mere elimination of unequal treatment, on grounds of nationality" (at [44]). The Court held that the legislation constituted a restriction upon the movement of capital (at [45]–[46]).

[4.20] Justifications for Restrictive Measures

The TFEU expressly permits certain restrictions upon the free movement of capital. The Treaty preserves tax laws that distinguish between taxpayers in accordance with residence or the place where capital is invested (Art 65(1)(a) TFEU). The Member States are also permitted to adopt measures for preventing the infringement of national laws such as taxation laws, the prudential supervision of financial institutions, mandatory declaration of capital movements for the purposes of administrative or statistical information, and measures justified by public policy or public security (Art 65(1)(b) TFEU). Such measures are not to constitute a means of arbitrary discrimination or a disguised restriction on the free movement of capital and payments (Art 65(3) TFEU).

The ECJ has held that as exceptions to a fundamental freedom, these justifications should be "interpreted strictly". See *Eckelkamp v Belgium* (C-11/07) [2008] ECR I-6845 at [57]; [2008] 3 CMLR 44 (p 1137); *Arens-Sikken v Staatssecretaris van Financiën* (C-43/07) [2008] ECR I-6887 at [51]; [2008] 3 CMLR 43 (p 1303). The Treaty distinguishes between unequal treatment authorised by Art 65(1) and the arbitrary discrimination that is prohibited by Art 65(3) TFEU. See *Proceedings brought by Manninen* (C-319/02) [2004] ECR I-7477 at [28]–[29]; [2004] 3 CMLR 40 (p 881).

The Court has held that a taxation law distinguishing between resident and non-resident persons or companies will not violate free movement of capital if the "difference in treatment... concern[s] situations which are not objectively comparable". See *Amurta SGPS v Inspecteur van de Belastingdienst* (C-379/05) [2007] ECR I-9569 at [32]; [2008] 1 CMLR 33 (p 851); *Eckelkamp v Belgium* (C-11/07) [2008] ECR I-6845 at [59]; [2008] 3 CMLR 44 (p 1137); *Persche v Finanzamt Lüdenscheid* (C-318/07) [2009] ECR I-359 at [41]; [2009] 2 CMLR 32 (p 819).

For example, it is not inherently discriminatory for a Member State to grant tax benefits to residents that it does not grant to non-residents because these two groups of taxpayers are not in a comparable situation. See *D v Inspecteur van de Belastingdienst/Particulieren/Ondernemingen Buitenland te Heerlen* (C-376/03) [2005] ECR I-5821 at [28], [38]; [2005] 3 CMLR 19 (p 515). In that case the Court held that free movement of capital was not violated by a national law under which non-resident taxpayers who held most of their wealth in their State of residence did not receive tax benefits that were granted to residents (at [43]).

The TFEU permits the maintenance of certain restrictions on capital movements to or from third countries under national or EU law that existed on 31 December 1993 (31 December 1999 for Bulgaria, Estonia and Hungary). These restrictions concern direct investment establishment, the provision of financial services or the admission of securities to capital markets (Art 64(1) TFEU). However, the Parliament and the Council may adopt measures in these areas (Art 64(2) TFEU). Measures which constitute a "step back" in EU law as regards the liberalisation of the movement of capital to or from third countries require unanimity in the Council (Art 64(3) TFEU).

[4.25] Overriding Requirements

Apart from the reasons listed in Art 65(1) TFEU, the Court has held that free movement of capital may be restricted for "overriding requirements of the general interest" by measures "which are applicable to all persons and undertakings pursuing an activity in the territory of the host Member

State". See *Re Golden Shares: Commission v Portugal* (C-367/98) [2002] ECR I-4731 at [49]; [2002] 2 CMLR 1213.

In the absence of EU harmonising measures protecting such overriding requirements, it is "for the Member States to decide on the degree of protection which they wish to afford to such legitimate interests and on the way in which that protection is to be achieved". See *Re Law on Privatisation of Equity in Volkswagenwerk GmbH: Commission v Germany* (C-112/05) [2007] ECR I-8995 at [73]; [2008] 1 CMLR 25 (p 643); *Federconsumatori v Comune di Milano* (C-463/04) [2007] ECR I-10419 at [40]; [2008] 1 CMLR 46 (p 1187).

The Court has indicated a number of justifications that may constitute overriding requirements of the general interest. Preserving the cohesion of the tax system is a permissible justification for restricting the free movement of capital. See *Proceedings brought by Manninen* (C-319/02) [2004] ECR I-7477 at [29], [42]; [2004] 3 CMLR 40 (p 881); *Meilicke v Finanzamt Bonn-Innenstadt* (C-292/04) [2007] ECR I-1835 at [25]–[28]; [2007] 2 CMLR 19 (p 469); *Amurta SGPS v Inspecteur van de Belastingdienst* (C-379/05) [2007] ECR I-9569 at [46]; [2008] 1 CMLR 33 (p 851).

The prevention of tax evasion is another permissible justification. See *Europeenne et Luxembourgeoise D'investissements SA (Elisa) v Directeur General des Impots* (C-451/05) [2007] ECR I-8251 at [81]; [2008] 1 CMLR 13 (p 276); *X v Staatssecretaris van Financiën* (C-155/08) [2009] All ER (EC) 888 at [45].

Ensuring the effectiveness of fiscal supervision is also a valid justification. See *Centro di Musicologia Walter Stauffer v Finanzamt München für Körperschaften* (C-386/04) [2006] ECR I-8203 at [47]; [2009] 2 CMLR 31 (p 777); *Skatteverket v A* (C-101/05) [2007] ECR I-11531 at [55]; [2009] 1 CMLR 35 (p 975); *Persche v Finanzamt Lüdenscheid* (C-318/07) [2009] ECR I-359 at [52]; [2009] 2 CMLR 32 (p 819).

The issue of fiscal supervision was raised in *Persche v Finanzamt Lüdenscheid* (C-318/07) [2009] ECR I-359; [2009] 2 CMLR 32 (p 819). A German resident sought a tax deduction for a donation to a charity that was established in another Member State (at [12]). The German government denied the exemption on the ground that German law required that the charity be established in Germany (at [15]).

The Court held that where a charity recognised by a Member State satisfies the conditions set by another Member State for recognition as a charity, the latter Member State cannot deny recognition on the ground that the charity is not established in its territory (at [49]). Tax deductions for donations to such charities cannot be denied on the ground that it is difficult to check whether they fulfil the legal requirements for recognition as a charity or to monitor the operation of the charity (at [51]).

The government could not invoke the need to protect fiscal supervision to justify a law that denied the taxpayer the opportunity to provide evidence that the charity met the national standards for recognition as a charity (at

[60]). A taxpayer may be able to provide sufficient evidence that will allow the government to verify the "nature and genuineness" of the donation (at [53]). The government is entitled to adopt verification measures, such as requiring the provision of annual accounts and activity reports (at [55]). Under EU law the government was entitled to request assistance from other Member States in ascertaining the taxpayer's tax liability (at [61]).

Different considerations apply in relation to third states. In *Skatteverket v A* (C-101/05) [2007] ECR I-11531; [2009] 1 CMLR 35 (p 975) the Swedish government refused to grant a Swedish resident a tax exemption for dividends distributed as shares in a subsidiary by a company formed in a third state (at [2]). The Swedish government sought to justify the restriction as necessary for the effectiveness of fiscal supervision (at [54]). The Court held that a Member State is justified in refusing an exemption if it is impossible to obtain the information from the third state because that state is not obliged to provide information necessary for verifying the taxpayer's entitlement to the exemption (at [63]).

Protection of minority shareholders is another permissible justification. See *Re Law on Privatisation of Equity in Volkswagenwerk GmbH: Commission v Germany* (C-112/05) [2007] ECR I-8995 at [77]; [2008] 1 CMLR 25 (p 643). The protection and promotion of national languages is another overriding interest. See *United Pan-Europe Communications Belgium SA v Belgium* (C-250/06) [2007] ECR I-11135 at [43]; [2008] 2 CMLR 2 (p 45); *Unión de Televisiones Comerciales Asociadas v Administración General del Estado* (C-222/07) [2009] 3 CMLR 2 (p 34) at [26]–[27].

The Court has identified certain interests that will not justify a restriction upon free movement of capital. Except as provided in relation to taxation by Art 65(1) TFEU, the financial interests of a Member State do not constitute a valid justification. See *Re Golden Shares: Commission v Portugal* (C-367/98) [2002] ECR I-4731 at [52]; [2002] 2 CMLR 1213. The avoidance of a reduction in taxation revenue is not a permissible justification. See *Centro di Musicologia Walter Stauffer v Finanzamt München für Körperschaften* (C-386/04) [2006] ECR I-8203 at [59]; [2009] 2 CMLR 31 (p 777); *Persche v Finanzamt Lüdenscheid* (C-318/07) [2009] ECR I-359 at [46]; [2009] 2 CMLR 32 (p 819).

An EU citizen does not lose the protection of the free movement of capital simply because they are "profiting from tax advantages which are legally provided for by the rules in force in a Member State other than [their] State of residence". See *Eckelkamp v Belgium* (C-11/07) [2008] ECR I-6845 at [66]; [2008] 3 CMLR 44 (p 1137).

A system of prior authorisation for acquisition of a shareholding in a company above a set level must "be based on objective, non-discriminatory criteria which are known in advance to the undertakings concerned, and all persons affected by a restrictive measure of that type must have a legal remedy available to them". See *Re Golden Shares: Commission v Portugal* (C-367/98) [2002] ECR I-4731 at [30], [50]; [2002] 2 CMLR 1213.

[4.30] Proportionality

Restrictions of free movement of capital must satisfy the proportionality test. They must be appropriate for attaining their objective and the means employed must not go beyond what is necessary for achieving that objective. See *Criminal Proceedings Against Sanz de Lera* (C-163/94) [1995] ECR I-4821 at [23]; [1996] 1 CMLR 361; *Église de Scientologie de Paris v Prime Minister* (C-54/99) [2000] ECR I-1335 at [18]; *Skatteverket v A* (C-101/05) [2007] ECR I-11531 at [56]; [2009] 1 CMLR 35 (p 975).

An example illustrates how the Court assesses whether a restriction passes the proportionality test. In *Re Law on Privatisation of Equity in Volkswagenwerk GmbH: Commission v Germany* (C-112/05) [2007] ECR I-8995; [2008] 1 CMLR 25 (p 643) a German law limited the voting rights of all shareholders in Volkswagen to 20% of the company's share capital (at [5]–[6]). The law required that resolutions of the general assembly of the company be passed by a majority of over 80%. The law also permitted the federal and state governments to each appoint two representatives to Volkswagen's supervisory board. The governments had this right provided that they held shares in the company, but it applied irrespective of the level of their investments (at [7]). These provisions departed from the general law relating to these matters (at [9], [63]).

The German government argued that the limitations upon the rights of shareholders were necessary for the protection of workers from a major shareholder. The Court held that the government had not explained why it was appropriate and necessary for the protection of workers that the federal and State governments "maintain a strengthened and irremovable position in the capital of the company" (at [74]). Furthermore, so far as representation on the supervisory board was concerned, under German law workers were already entitled to representation on the board (at [75]).

The government also argued that the limitations upon the rights of shareholders were necessary for the protection of minority shareholders (at [77]). The Court held that the government had not shown why enhancing the position of the government as a shareholder was necessary for the protection of minority shareholders (at [78]).

Nevertheless, the Court has acknowledged that "certain concerns may justify the retention by Member States of a degree of influence within undertakings that were initially public and subsequently privatised, where those undertakings are active in fields involving the provision of services in the public interest or strategic services". See *Federconsumatori v Comune di Milano* (C-463/04) [2007] ECR I-10419 at [41]; [2008] 1 CMLR 46 (p 1187).

[4.35] Protective Measures

Where in "exceptional circumstances" capital movement threaten to cause "serious difficulties" for the economic and monetary union the Council may adopt "strictly necessary" safeguard measures regarding third countries for up to 6 months (Art 66 TFEU). The Council may also adopt necessary measures for the interruption or reduction of economic relations with one or more third countries (Art 215(1) TFEU).

In order to combat terrorism, the EU may "define a framework for administrative measures with regard to capital movements and payments, such as the freezing of funds, financial assets or economic gains belonging to, or owned or held by, natural or legal persons, groups or non-State entities" (Art 75 TFEU). The EU has adopted legislation directed against terrorist financing. See Directive 2005/60 of the European Parliament and of the Council of 26 October 2005 on the prevention of the use of the financial system for the purpose of money laundering and terrorist financing (OJ L 309, 25.11.2005, p 15).

[4.40] Money Laundering

The EU has adopted legislation directed against money laundering. See Directive 2005/60 of the European Parliament and of the Council of 26 October 2005 on the prevention of the use of the financial system for the purpose of money laundering and terrorist financing (OJ L 309, 25.11.2005, p 15). The Directive observes that money launderers could seek to take advantage of the free movement of capital if preventive measures are not taken at the EU level (Preamble Recital 3).

Member States must prohibit money laundering (Art 1(1)). Money laundering includes the following activities:

- the conversion or transfer of property, knowing that it is derived from criminal activity, for the purpose of concealing its criminal origins;
- the concealment of the true nature, location or ownership of property, knowing that it is derived from criminal activity;
- the acquisition, possession or use of property, knowing that it was derived from criminal activity; or
- aiding or abetting any of these actions (Art 1(2)).

"Criminal activity" is defined as "any kind of criminal involvement in the commission of a serious crime" (Art 3(4)). "Serious crime" includes drug trafficking, the activities of criminal organisations, fraud, corruption, and all offences punishable by imprisonment for a year or more (Art 3(5)).

The Directive applies to a broad range of natural and legal persons, including credit and financial institutions, auditors, external accountants, tax advisers, independent legal professionals, notaries, real estate agents, goods traders where payment of €15,000 or more is made in cash and casinos (Art 2(1)).

Anonymous credit and financial institution accounts must be prohibited (Art 6). All natural and legal persons covered by the Directive must apply customer due diligence when a business relationship is established, when carrying out transactions that total at least €15,000, when money laundering is suspected, or when there are doubts about the accuracy of previously supplied customer identification information (Art 7). Customer identification must occur before a business relationship is established or the transaction is carried out (Art 9(1)).

Customer due diligence involves reliable identification of the customer or beneficial owner and scrutinising transactions to verify whether they are consistent with the person's knowledge of the customer and their business and risk profile (Art 8(1)). Enhanced measures of due diligence apply in situations where the risk of money laundering is higher (Art 13(1)).

The money laundering Directive is complemented by controls on movements of cash. See Preamble Recital 2, Regulation 1889/2005 of the European Parliament and of the Council of 26 October 2005 on controls of cash entering or leaving the Community (OJ L 309, 25.11.2005, p 9). Any person entering or leaving the EU who is carrying cash of €10,000 or more must declare that sum to the authorities of the Member State that they are entering or leaving (Art 3(1)). Cash includes currency, negotiable instruments the title to which passes upon delivery and incomplete instruments (Art 2(2)). The Regulation is without prejudice to national controls of cash movements that are consistent with free movement of capital (Art 1(2)).

[4.45] Banking

The general objective of the European Union in the area of financial services is the achievement of freedom of establishment and freedom to provide services in any Member State. Under Art 54 TFEU the subsidiaries of non-EU banks are treated as EU banks subject to EU law. The EU has adopted legislation to harmonise banking laws and to provide a level playing field. Only a few of these Directives can be examined here due to space constraints.

The EU eliminated some obstructions to the operation of credit institutions by adopting Directive 2006/48 of the European Parliament and of the Council of 14 June 2006 relating to the taking up and pursuit of the business of credit institutions (OJ L 177, 30.6.2006, p 1). The Directive provides that credit institutions will be granted a single licence recognised throughout the EU and prudential supervision will be undertaken by the home Member State of the institution (Preamble Recital 7).

The EU has regulated capital adequacy requirements. See Directive 2006/49 of the European Parliament and of the Council of 14 June 2006 on the capital adequacy of investment firms and credit institutions (recast) (OJ L 177, 30.6.2006, p 201). These requirements apply to both credit institutions and investment firms (Art 1(1)). A Member State may impose more demanding requirements (Art 1(2)). Capital means the "own funds" of the credit institution or investment firm (Art 3(1)(s)). The Directive sets out requirements for the initial capital of these institutions (Arts 4–9), provision against risks (Arts 18–21) and monitoring and control of large exposures (Arts 28–32).

Another Directive regulates cross-border credit transfers executed by credit institutions. See Directive 97/5 of 27 January 1997 of the European Parliament and of the Council on cross-border credit transfers (OJ L 43, 14.2.1997, p 25). A cross-border credit transfer is a transaction carried out on behalf of the originator through an institution in one Member State with a view to making available an amount of money to a beneficiary at an institution in another Member State (Art 2(f)).

The originator's institution must execute the transfer within the time limit agreed with the originator. If the transfer is not made within the agreed time limit, the originator's institution shall compensate the originator. If no time limit is agreed, the originator's institution shall compensate the originator if the transfer is not made within five business days after the day the transfer was ordered (Art 6(1)).

The beneficiary's institution shall make the funds available to the beneficiary within the time limit agreed with the beneficiary. If the transfer is not made within the agreed time limit, the beneficiary's institution shall compensate the beneficiary. If no time limit is agreed, the beneficiary's institution must compensate the beneficiary if it has not credited the funds to the beneficiary's account by the end of the business day after the day on which the beneficiary institution received the funds (Art 6(2)). The Directive applies to transfers of amounts up to €50,000 (Art 1).

Other Directives concerning financial institutions include:

- Council Directive 87/102 of 22 December 1986 for the approximation of the laws, regulations and administrative provisions of the Member States concerning consumer credit (OJ L 42, 12.2.1987, p 48);
- Directive 94/19 of the European Parliament and of the Council of 30 May 1994 on deposit-guarantee schemes (OJ L 135, 31.5.1994, p 5);
- Directive 2001/24 of the European Parliament and of the Council on the reorganisation and winding-up of credit institutions (OJ L 125, 5.5.2001, p 15);

- Directive 2002/47 of the European Parliament and of the Council of 6 June 2002 on financial collateral arrangements (OJ L 168, 27.6.2002, p 43);
- Directive 2002/87 of the European Parliament and of the Council of 16 December 2002 on the supplementary supervision of credit institutions, insurance undertakings and investment firms in a financial conglomerate (OJ L 35, 11.2.2003, p 1);
- Directive 2007/64 of the European Parliament and of the Council of 13 November 2007 on payment services in the internal market (OJ L 319, 5.12.2007, p 1); and
- Directive 2009/110 of the European Parliament and of the Council of 16 September 2009 on the taking up, pursuit and prudential supervision of the business of electronic money institutions (OJ L 267, 10.10.2009, p 7).

[4.50] Securities

Parallel to the banking field, a series of measures have been adopted to harmonise securities regulation in the Union. The EU has adopted measures directed against market abuse. See Directive 2003/6 of the European Parliament and of the Council of 28 January 2003 on insider dealing and market manipulation (market abuse) (OJ L 96, 12.4.2003, p 16). Market abuse means insider dealing or market manipulation (Preamble Recital 12).

Persons possessing inside information must not use that information by acquiring or disposing of financial instruments to which the information relates (Art 2(1)). "Inside information" is defined as precise information that is not publicly available and which would have a significant effect upon the prices of a financial instrument if it were made public (Art 1(1)).

Those possessing inside information through their involvement in management, holding of capital, or their employment or professional activity must not disclose that information except in the normal course of their work. They must not recommend that other persons acquire or dispose of financial instruments to which the information relates (Art 3).

Market manipulation must be prohibited by the Member States (Art 5). "Market manipulation" means transactions that give false or misleading signals regarding the supply, demand or price of a financial instrument, transactions employing fictitious devices or deception and dissemination of information which gives false or misleading signals regarding financial instruments (Art 1(2)(a)–(c)). A "financial instrument" includes transferable securities, units in collective investment undertakings, money-market instruments, financial-futures contracts and interest-rate, currency and equity swaps (Art 1(3)).

Persons acting in a managerial capacity within an issuer of financial instruments must notify the appropriate authority of their transactions in shares in the issuer or financial instruments linked to such shares (Art 9(4)). Professionals who arrange transactions in financial instruments must notify the appropriate authority if they reasonably suspect that a transaction involves insider dealing or market manipulation (Art 6(9)).

Investment advice is regulated by Directive 2004/39 of the European Parliament and of the Council of 21 April 2004 on markets in financial instruments (OJ L 145, 30.4.2004, p 1). The Directive applies to investment firms and regulated markets (Art 1(1)). "Investment firm" is defined as any legal person providing investment services to third parties or the performance of investment activities on a professional basis (Art 4(1)(1)). Investment services and activities are defined in Sections A and C of Annex 1 (Art 4(1)(2)). "Investment advice" is the provision of recommendations to a client regarding transactions relating to financial instruments (Art 4(1)(4)).

The performance of investment services or activities as a regular business must be subject to prior authorisation (Art 5(1)). The authorisation must specify the investment services or activities that the investment firm may provide (Art 6(1)). Persons who effectively direct the investment firm must be of good repute and sufficient experience to ensure that the firm is soundly and prudently managed (Art 9(1)). When providing investment services a firm must "act honestly, fairly and professionally in... the best interests of its clients" (Art 19(1)). Each Member State must have a competent authority to monitor the activities of investment firms to ensure that they follow these standards (Art 25(1)).

Other EU measures deal with the following matters:

- Council Directive 93/22 of 10 May 1993 on investment services in the securities field (OJ L 141, 11.6.1993, p 27);
- Directive 97/9 of the European Parliament and of the Council of 3 March 1997 on investor-compensation schemes (OJ L 84, 26.3.1997, p 22);
- Directive 2001/34 of the European Parliament and of the Council on the admission of securities to official stock exchange listings and on information to be published on those securities (OJ L 184, 6.7.2001, p 1);
- Directive 2003/71 of the European Parliament and of the Council of 4 November 2003 on the prospectus to be published when securities are offered to the public or admitted to trading (OJ L 345, 31.12.2003, p 64);
- Directive 2004/109 of the European Parliament and of the Council of 15 December 2004 on the harmonisation of transparency requirements in relation to information about issuers whose securities are admitted to trading on a regulated market (OJ L 390, 31.12.2004, p 38); and
- Directive 2009/65 of the European Parliament and of the Council of 13 July 2009 on the coordination of laws, regulations and administrative provisions relating to undertakings for collective investment in transferable securities (UCITS) (OJ L 302, 17.11.2009, p 32).

See generally, Niamh Moloney, *EC Securities Regulation* (2nd ed, Oxford: Oxford University Press, 2008).

[4.55] Insurance

An EU Directive regulates the establishment and pursuit of insurance businesses. See Directive 2009/138 of the European Parliament and of the Council of 25 November 2009 on the taking-up and pursuit of the business of Insurance and Reinsurance (Solvency II) (recast) (OJ L 335, 17.12.2009, p 1).

The taking up of the business of direct insurance is subject to prior authorisation from the home Member State (Art 14). The home Member State of an undertaking is the Member State in which its head office is located (Art 13(8)). That authorisation allows the undertaking to carry on business throughout the EU, relying upon the right of establishment and the freedom to provide services (Art 15(1)). Where there are close links between an insurance undertaking and another natural or legal person, the home Member State must not grant an authorisation if it cannot effectively exercise supervision over the undertaking (Art 19).

Life assurance and non-life insurance must be separately managed (Art 74(1)). The home Member State must require assurance undertakings to make sufficient technical provisions for all of their insurance obligations (Art 76(1)). The value of the technical provisions must "correspond to the current amount insurance and reinsurance undertakings would have to pay if they were to transfer their insurance and reinsurance obligations immediately to another insurance or reinsurance undertaking" (Art 76(2)).

Other provisions relate to reinsurance (Arts 172-175) and reorganisation and winding-up of insurance undertakings (Arts 267–296). A separate Directive regulates insurance mediation. See Directive 2002/92 of the European Parliament and of the Council of 9 December 2002 on insurance mediation (OJ L 9, 15.1.2003, p 3).

[4.60] Conclusion

The free movement of capital is one of the fundamental freedoms of the European Union. This freedom applies to capital movements between Member States and between the EU and third states. The term "movement of capital" is not defined in the TFEU. The ECJ has defined that term by reference to a detailed list contained in an EU Directive. The Court has held that a broad range of national measures constitute restrictions upon the free movement of capital. This freedom may be legitimately restricted under several Treaty provisions and for certain overriding requirements. Limitations must satisfy a proportionality test. To prevent abuse of the freedom of capital movement, the EU has adopted legislation directed against money laundering. This Chapter also outlined EU measures concerning the banking, securities and insurance industries.

Further Reading

Brohmer, Jurgen. "The Free Movement of Capital in the European Union and the Problem of "Golden Shares" and Similar Instruments" (2007) 25 *Law in Context* 144.

Cordewener, Axel. "Free Movement of Capital Between EU Member States and Third Countries: How Far Has the Door Been Closed?" (2009) 18 *EC Tax Review* 260.

Flynn, Leo. "Coming of Age: The Free Movement of Capital Case Law 1993–2002" (2002) 39 *Common Market Law Review* 773.

Katz, Sherman E. "The Second Banking Directive" (1992) 12 *Yearbook of European Law* 249.

Kronenberger, Vincent. "The Rise of the 'Golden' Age of Free Movement of Capital: A Comment on the Golden Shares Judgments of the Court of Justice of the European Communities" (2003) 4 *European Business Organization Law Review* 115.

Landsmeer, Arie. "Movement of Capital and Other Freedoms" (2001) 28 *Legal Issues of Economic Integration* 57.

Mohamed, Sideek. *European Community Law on the Free Movement of Capital and EMU* (The Hague: Kluwer, 1999).

O'Brien, Martha. "Taxation and the Third Country Dimension of Free Movement of Capital in EU Law: The ECJ's Rulings and Unresolved Issues" (2008) 6 *British Tax Review* 628.

Peers, Steve. "Free Movement of Capital: Learning Lessons or Slipping on Spilt Milk" in Catherine Barnard and Joanne Scott (eds), *Law of the Single European Market: Unpacking the Premises* (Oxford: Hart, 2002), 333.

Prechal, Sacha. "Free Movement and Procedural Requirements: Proportionality Reconsidered" (2008) 35 *Legal Issues of Economic Integration* 201.

Usher, John A. "Capital Movements and the Treaty on European Union" (1992) 12 *Yearbook of European Law* 35.

Usher, John A. "The Evolution of the Free Movement of Capital" (2008) 31 *Fordham International Law Journal* 1533.

Vossestein, Gert-Jan. "*Volkswagen*: The State of Affairs of Golden Shares, General Company Law and European Free Movement of Capital" (2008) 5 *European Company and Financial Law Review* 115.

Weber, Dennis. "*Fidium Finann AG v Bundesanstalt fur Finanzdienstleistungsaufsicht*: The ECJ Gives the Wrong Answer About the Applicability of the Free Movement of Capital Between the EC Member States and Non-member Countries" (2007) 6 *British Tax Review* 670.

Chapter 5
Commercial Law and Policy

[5.05] Introduction

The common external tariff is only one aspect of the EU's commercial policy. This Chapter discusses another plank of this policy, namely measures which may be taken by the EU to protect trade, in particular the imposition of anti-dumping and countervailing duties.

Provisions against the dumping of goods by non-Member States have been adopted as part of the common commercial policy. If the export price is below the normal price, the goods are considered to be dumped. If the dumped goods are causing or threatening to cause injury, an anti-dumping duty may be imposed.

If goods have been the subject of a direct or indirect subsidy in the country of manufacture, a countervailing duty may be imposed to offset the effect of the subsidy, where the subsidy causes injury in the EU. A subsidy is (1) a financial contribution by government in the country of origin or any form of income or price support (2) by which a benefit is conferred.

[5.06] Common Commercial Policy

Under the TFEU the EU pursues a common commercial policy. The Member States must conform to EU measures adopted under that policy when they exercise their retained competences, including those relating to foreign and security policy. See *R v H M Treasury; Ex parte Centro-COM Srl* (C-124/95) [1997] ECR I-81 at [24]–[27], [30]; [1997] 1 CMLR 555.

The common commercial policy of the European Union is based upon Arts 206 and 207 TFEU. Art 206 reads as follows:

> By establishing a customs union…, the Union shall contribute, in the common interest, to the harmonious development of world trade, the progressive abolition of restrictions on international trade and on foreign direct investment, and the lowering of customs and other barriers.

G. Moens, J. Trone, *Commercial Law of the European Union*,
Ius Gentium: Comparative Perspectives on Law and Justice 4,
DOI 10.1007/978-90-481-8774-4_5,

This Article seems to indicate that the commercial policy of the EU is essentially concerned with the import and export of goods. However, a reading of Art 207 TFEU suggests that the scope of the commercial policy is much wider.

Art 207(1) TFEU contains a non-exhaustive list of matters that come within the scope of the policy:

> The common commercial policy shall be based on uniform principles, particularly with regard to changes in tariff rates, the conclusion of tariff and trade agreements relating to trade in goods and services, and the commercial aspects of intellectual property, foreign direct investment, the achievement of uniformity in measures of liberalisation, export policy and measures to protect trade such as those to be taken in the event of dumping or subsidies. The common commercial policy shall be conducted in the context of the principles and objectives of the Union's external action.

[5.10] Broad Interpretation of Art 207

In *Re International Agreement on Natural Rubber* (Opinion 1/78) [1979] ECR 2871; [1979] 3 CMLR 639 it was held that that the international commodity agreement regarding rubber fell within the common commercial policy. The Court argued that Art 113 (now Art 207 TFEU) must be accorded a wide interpretation. The Court stated:

> Article 113 empowers the Community to formulate a commercial 'policy', based on 'uniform principles' thus showing that the question of external trade must be governed from a wide point of view and not only having regard to the administration of precise systems such as customs and quantitative restrictions. The same conclusion may be deduced from the fact that the enumeration in Article 113 of the subjects covered by commercial policy... is conceived as a non-exhaustive enumeration which must not, as such, close the door to the application in a Community context of any other process intended to regulate external trade. A restrictive interpretation of the concept of common commercial policy would risk causing disturbances in intra-Community trade by reason of the disparities which would then exist in certain sectors of economic relations with non-member countries (at [45]).

The EU may thus harmonize measures beyond the direct import and export of goods.

In *OTO SpA v Ministero delle Finanze* (C-130/92) [1994] ECR I-3281; [1995] 1 CMLR 84 the Court indicated that "although Article 113 [now Art 207 TFEU] confers upon the Community powers which enable it to take any appropriate measure concerning the common commercial policy, it nevertheless does not in itself contain any legal criterion which is sufficiently precise to enable assessment of the contested national rules to be made" (at [20]). See similarly, *Società Italiana per l'Oleodotto Transalpino v Ministero delle Finanze* (266/81) [1983] ECR 731 at [29]; [1984] 2 CMLR 231.

The EU also adopts common policies regarding capital and payments (Arts 63–66 TFEU) and the imposition of sanctions in the event of international crises (Art 215 TFEU).

[5.15] Treaty-Making by the European Union

Art 207(1) TFEU provides for the conclusion by the EU of tariff and trade agreements with third countries. By way of introduction, it is useful to briefly review the power of the EU to enter into international agreements with third countries.

Art 216(1) TFEU provides that the EU may conclude agreements between the Union and any one or more non-member States or any international organisation. Once an international agreement enters into force, it becomes an "integral part" of EU law. See *A Racke GmbH & Co v Hauptzollamt Mainz* (C-162/96) [1998] ECR I-3655 at [41]; [1998] 3 CMLR 219; *Re Dispute over Mox Plant: Commission v United Kingdom* (C-459/03) [2006] ECR I-4635 at [82]; [2006] 2 CMLR 59 (p 1429); *Merck Genéricos Produtos Farmacêuticos Lda v Merck & Co Inc* (C-431/05) [2007] ECR I-7001 at [31]; [2007] 3 CMLR 49 (p 1339); *R (on the Application of International Association of Independent Tanker Owners) v Secretary of State for Transport* (C-308/06) [2008] ECR I-4057 at [53]; [2008] 3 CMLR 9 (p 203).

A Member State and EU institutions may request that the ECJ give its opinion regarding the compatibility of a proposed international agreement with the founding Treaties (Art 218(11) TFEU). The Court may be called upon to give such an opinion at any time prior to ratification of the agreement. See *Re Uruguay Round Treaties* (Opinion 1/94) [1994] ECR I-5267 at [12]; [1995] 1 CMLR 205. Where the Court decides that the agreement is incompatible with the Treaties, the agreement may not be ratified unless the agreement or the founding Treaties are amended accordingly (Art 218(11) TFEU). This procedure may also be used to resolve doubts about the proper EU competence for concluding a proposed international agreement, since proceeding on an incorrect basis will invalidate the agreement. See *Re Cartagena Protocol on Biosafety* (Opinion 2/00) [2001] ECR I-9713 at [5]–[6]; [2002] 1 CMLR 28 (p 809).

The Court has often been asked to give its opinion regarding the compatibility of a proposed international agreement with the founding Treaties. See e.g. *Re Draft Treaty on the European Economic Area (No 1)* (Opinion 1/91) [1991] ECR I-6079; [1992] 1 CMLR 245; *(No 2)* (Opinion 1/92) [1992] ECR I-2821; [1992] 2 CMLR 217; *Re ILO Convention No 170 concerning Safety in the Use of Chemicals at Work* (Opinion 2/91) [1993] ECR I-1061; [1993] 3 CMLR 800; *Re Accession by the Community to the European Convention on Human Rights* (Opinion 2/94) [1996] ECR I-1759; [1996] 2 CMLR 265;

Re Cartagena Protocol on Biosafety (Opinion 2/00) [2001] ECR I-9713; [2002] 1 CMLR 28 (p 809); *Re Lugano Convention* (Opinion 1/03) [2006] ECR I-1145.

Art 207(3) TFEU provides that trade and tariff agreements are to be concluded in accordance with Art 218, subject to compliance with several specific requirements laid down in Art 207 itself. Art 218 TFEU sets out the general procedure through which the EU may enter into treaties. The Council authorises the commencement of negotiations and the conclusion of an agreement (Art 218(2)–(3), (6)). Before concluding some types of agreements, the Council must obtain the consent of the European Parliament (Art 218(6)). In other cases the Council is to consult the Parliament (Art 218(6)). In all cases the Parliament is to be kept informed during the treaty-making process (Art 218(10)). The Council acts by a qualified majority throughout the treaty-making procedure, apart from association and accession treaties (among others), which require unanimity (Art 218(8)). The Council does not need to approve non-binding agreements. See *France v Commission* (C-233/02) [2004] ECR I-2759 at [33]–[35]. The Member States, the Parliament, the Council and the Commission all have the right to request that the Court of Justice render an opinion concerning the compatibility of a proposed agreement with the founding Treaties. If the Court decides that the proposed agreement is incompatible with the Treaties, the proposed treaty may not be concluded unless it is amended or the Treaties are revised (Art 218(11)).

The general treaty-making procedure laid down in Art 218 TFEU is expressed to be without prejudice to the specific requirements for trade and tariff agreements set out in Art 207 (see Art 218(1)). Under Art 207 the Council shall authorise the Commission to begin negotiations. A special committee appointed by the Council assists the Commission in negotiating the agreement. The Commission informs the committee and the Parliament about the progress of the negotiations (Art 207(3)). The Council acts by a qualified majority when concluding the agreement. Some treaties concerning trade in services, the commercial aspects of intellectual property, foreign direct investment, trade in cultural and audiovisual services, and trade in social, education and health services may require the unanimous approval of the Council (Art 207(4)). Special provision is made for the negotiation of transport agreements (Arts 207(5), 90–100 TFEU).

[5.20] Scope of the EU's Treaty-Making Power

The European Union has (international) legal personality (Art 47 TEU). When adopting the Treaty of Lisbon, the Member States declared that "the fact that the European Union has a legal personality will not in any way authorise the Union to legislate or to act beyond the competences conferred upon it by . . . the Treaties." See Declaration (No 24) concerning the Legal Personality of the European Union. The Member States retain their own international personalities. See Enzo Cannizzaro, "Fragmented Sovereignty? The European Union and its Member States in the International Arena" (2003) 13 *Italian Yearbook of International Law* 35.

The TFEU provides that the EU may conclude agreements where its founding Treaties so authorise or "where the conclusion of an agreement is necessary in order to achieve, within the framework of the Union's policies, one of the objectives referred to in the Treaties, or is provided for in a legally binding Union act or is likely to affect common rules or alter their scope" (Art 216(1) TFEU).

There are a number of specific provisions in the founding Treaties that expressly grant to the EU the power to enter into particular types of international agreements with third countries. These agreements may concern:

- implementation of the common foreign and security policy (Art 37 TEU);
- readmission of third country nationals (Art 79(3) TFEU);
- environmental cooperation (Art 191(4) TFEU);
- the common commercial policy (Art 207(3) TFEU);
- development cooperation (Art 209(2) TFEU);
- the achievement of objectives such as the consolidation of democracy, rule of law, human rights and respect for international law; preservation of peace; eradication of poverty in developing countries; international economic integration and environmental protection (Art 21 TEU; Art 209(2) TFEU);
- economic, financial and technical cooperation with third countries (Art 212(3) TFEU);
- humanitarian aid (Art 214(4) TFEU); and
- establishment of "an association involving reciprocal rights and obligations, common action and special procedure" (Art 217 TFEU).

[5.25] Express or Implied Treaty-Making Powers?

The question arises whether the general provisions of Art 216(1) TFEU are to be read down or limited by express provisions provided elsewhere in the founding Treaties. Thus, it may be argued that the EU has no inherent powers to enter into agreements with third countries and possesses only those powers expressly conferred upon it by the provisions of the Treaties. According to this view, Art 216(1) is merely a general enabling provision but does not constitute a substantive treaty-making power.

The opposite view is that the EU's treaty-making power is not limited to the express provisions of the Treaty but extends to all matters which fall within the EU's internal jurisdiction. Such a view is usually justified by reference to the theory of implied powers. According to this theory, the existence of an express internal power implies also the existence of any other power which is reasonably necessary for the proper exercise of the express power. Therefore, the EU's treaty-making power should reflect its internal powers. It would be illogical for the Union to have powers in a particular field within its internal jurisdiction and yet be unable, in respect of the same field, to enter into an international agreement. Thus, on this view, if the EU has an express internal power, then it is also authorized to enter into international agreements with regard to the subject matter of that internal power.

[5.30] Implied Powers Recognised

The theory of implied powers was given recognition by the Court in *Re European Road Transport Agreement: Commission v Council* (22/70) [1971] ECR 263; [1971] CMLR 335. In that case the Court considered whether the EEC's authority to implement the common transport policy applied to the conclusion of transport agreements with non-EEC countries. The Court held that the treaty-making power of the EEC extended beyond those powers expressly granted by the EEC Treaty. The Court considered that when EEC legislation had removed matters from the jurisdiction of the Member States the Union then became competent to conclude treaties with third countries regarding those matters. The Court stated:

> each time the Community, with a view to implementing a common policy envisaged by the Treaty, adopts provisions laying down common rules, whatever form these may take, the Member States no longer have the right, acting individually or even collectively, to undertake obligations with third countries which affect those rules. As and when such common rules come into being, the Community alone is in a position to assume and carry out contractual obligations towards third countries affecting the whole sphere of application of the Community legal system. With regard to the implementation of the provisions of the Treaty the system of internal Community measures may not therefore be separated from that of external relations (at [17]–[19]).

This means that not only is the EU competent to conclude treaties on matters specifically assigned to it, it may also make treaties concerning other matters which have become the subject of Union law. The Court adopted a doctrine of parallelism. In this case the doctrine was enunciated in a weaker form, but the theory of implied powers was expanded in subsequent decisions.

In *Officier van Justitie v Kramer* (3/76) [1976] ECR 1279; [1976] 2 CMLR 440 the Court indicated that the mere existence of an internal power automatically implies the existence of a power to enter into an international agreement with regard to the subject matter of that power (at [19]–[20]). This approach was confirmed in *Draft Agreement establishing a European Laying-up Fund for Inland Waterway Vessels* (Opinion 1/76) [1977] ECR

741 at [3]–[4]; [1977] 2 CMLR 279 and *Re ILO Convention No 170 concerning Safety in the Use of Chemicals at Work* (Opinion 2/91) [1993] ECR I-1061 at [7]; [1993] 3 CMLR 800.

The Court clarified the extent of the EU's exclusive external competence in *Re Uruguay Round Treaties* (Opinion 1/94) [1994] ECR I-5267; [1995] 1 CMLR 205. An internal competence of the EU would only become an exclusive external power of the EU when the internal power had been exercised (at [89]). The Court held that "[w]henever the Community has included in its internal legislative acts provisions relating to the treatment of nationals of non-member countries or expressly conferred on its institutions powers to negotiate with non-member countries, it acquires exclusive external competence in the spheres covered by those acts" (at [95]).

The Court concluded that the Community and the Member States were jointly competent to conclude the Agreement on Trade Related Aspects of Intellectual Property Rights and the General Agreement on Trade in Services (at [98], [105]). The Community and the Member States were under an obligation to cooperate in relation to the negotiation, conclusion and fulfilment of international agreements that were within joint competence (at [109]–[110]). See also Meinhard Hilf, "The ECJ's Opinion 1/94 on the WTO—No Surprise, but Wise?" (1995) 6 *European Journal of International Law* 245; Andrea Appella, "Constitutional Aspects of Opinion 1/94 of the ECJ Concerning the WTO Agreement" (1996) 45 *International and Comparative Law Quarterly* 440.

In *Re Lugano Convention* (Opinion 1/03) [2006] ECR I-1145 the Court summarised its prior case law regarding the EU's exclusive competence to conclude international agreements. Where common or harmonised rules have been adopted by the EU, the Member States do not have the right to conclude treaties that would affect those rules. The EU has exclusive treaty-making competence in that situation (at [116], [118]).

The Court observed that it was not necessary for exclusive EU jurisdiction to exist that the proposed treaty and existing EU law completely overlap. It is enough that the area is already largely regulated by EU rules. The foreseeable future development of EU law in the area may also be taken into account (at [126]). The "uniform and consistent application" of EU law must be preserved (at [127]). The Court held that the proposed treaty would affect the "uniform and consistent application" of EU rules relating to the recognition and enforcement of judgments and the jurisdiction of courts. Conclusion of the treaty was within the exclusive jurisdiction of the EU (at [172]–[173]).

A treaty entered into by the EU may not infringe the "constitutional principles" of the founding Treaties, including the protection of fundamental rights. See *Kadi v Commission* (C-402/05 P) [2008] ECR I-6351 at [285]; [2008] 3 CMLR 41 (p 1207). In that case the Court held that it was empowered to review the validity of EU legal acts that had been adopted to fulfil international law obligations arising under a United Nations Security

Council resolution (at [326]). See also Sebastian Recker, "European Court of Justice Secures Fundamental Rights from UN Security Council Resolutions" (2009) 1 *Göttingen Journal of International Law* 159.

Finally, EU secondary law may affect the scope of the treaty-making competence of the Member States. In *Re Dutch Air Transport Agreement: Commission v Netherlands* (C-523/04) [2007] ECR I-3267; [2007] 2 CMLR 48 (p 1299) the Court held that the Member States may not enter into treaties that contain "provisions capable of affecting rules adopted by the Community or of altering their scope" (at [75]). In that case a bilateral treaty entered into by a Member State was inconsistent with an EU Regulation (at [76]).

EU legislation requires Member States to notify the Commission before negotiating bilateral air services treaties. See Art 1, Regulation 847/2004 of the European Parliament and of the Council of 29 April 2004 on the negotiation and implementation of air service agreements between Member States and third countries (OJ L 195, 2.6.2004, p 3).

There is an extensive literature regarding the foreign relations powers of the European Union. See David D Knoll, "From the Inside Looking Out: Comparing the External Capacities, Powers and Functions of the Commonwealth of Australia and the European Communities" (1985) 15 *Federal Law Review* 253; Moshe Kaniel, *The Exclusive Treaty-making Power of the European Community: up to the Period of the Single European Act* (The Hague: Kluwer Law International, 1996); Piet Eeckhout, *External Relations of the European Union* (Oxford: Oxford University Press, 2004); Panos Koutrakos, *EU International Relations Law* (Oxford: Hart, 2006); Bruno de Witte and Marise Cremona (eds), *EU Foreign Relations Law: Constitutional Fundamentals* (Oxford: Hart, 2008); Rass Holdgaard, *External Relations Law of the European Community* (Alphen aan den Rijn: Kluwer Law International, 2008); Gert De Baere, *Constitutional Principles of EU External Relations* (Oxford: Oxford University Press, 2008).

[5.31] Common Rules on Imports and Exports

With certain exceptions such as textiles, imports from third countries may be freely imported into the EU and may not be subject to quantitative restrictions. See Art 1, Council Regulation 260/2009 of 26 February 2009 on the common rules for imports (OJ L 84, 31.3.2009, p 1). However, Member States must inform the Commission if import trends show a need for surveillance or safeguard measures (Art 2). The Commission may impose surveillance measures if there is a threat of serious injury to EU producers and the interests of the EU require such measures (Art 11). Safeguard measures may be imposed if a product is imported in such increased quantities as to cause or threaten to cause serious injury to EU producers. Safeguard measures may make importation of the product subject to authorisation (Art 16(1)). Quotas may be established (Art 16(3)). Safeguard measures may not remain in force for longer than 4 years (Art 20(1)).

Export of products from the EU to third states may not be subject to any quantitative restriction. See Art 1, Council Regulation 1061/2009 of 19 October 2009 establishing common rules for exports (OJ L 291, 7.11.2009, p 1). The Commission may make the export of an essential product in short supply subject to authorisation (Art 6(1)).

[5.35] Anti-dumping and Subsidies

The EU will be naturally concerned about unfair trade practices of third countries or foreign producers of goods. Art 207(1) TFEU identifies dumping and subsidies as two examples of unfair trade practices and provides for the introduction of anti-dumping and countervailing duties. The EU has adopted a number of measures aimed at combating these practices.

[5.40] WTO Obligations

The *General Agreement on Tariffs and Trade 1994* (hereafter "GATT 1994") provides the international trade law basis for EU law regarding anti-dumping and countervailing duties. The content of GATT 1994 is defined in Annex 1A to the *Marrakesh Agreement establishing the World Trade Organization*, Marrakesh, 15 April 1994, 1867 UNTS 190; OJ L 336, 23.12.1994, p 20; [1995] ATS 8 p 14. The European Community, Australia, Canada, Hong Kong, India, Malaysia, New Zealand, Singapore, South Africa and the United States are all party to the WTO Agreement: 1867 UNTS 154–155.

Art VI of GATT 1994 provides:

> 1. The contracting parties recognize that dumping, by which products of one country are introduced into the commerce of another country at less than the normal value of the products, is to be condemned if it causes or threatens material injury to an established industry in the territory of a contracting party or materially retards the establishment of a domestic industry.... [A] product is to be considered as being introduced into the commerce of an importing country at less than its normal value, if the price of the product exported from one country to another
>
> (a) is less than the comparable price, in the ordinary course of trade, for the like product when destined for consumption in the exporting country....
>
> 3. No countervailing duty shall be levied on any product of the territory of any contracting party imported into the territory of another contracting party in excess of an amount equal to the estimated bounty or subsidy determined to have been granted, directly or indirectly, on the manufacture, production or export of such product in the country of origin or exportation, including any special subsidy to the transportation of a particular product.

Art VI of GATT 1994 indicates that dumping involves the unfair trade practice of selling products in an export market for less than the price charged for comparable goods in the producer's or manufacturer's home market. Dumping involves a foreign exporter selling goods imported into the EU market at a price lower than that prevailing in the exporter's home market. It is important to realise that selling products more cheaply than similar products in the importing state does not constitute dumping. The cheapness of goods is not of itself an indication of dumping.

The scope of Art VI is explained in detail in the *Agreement on Implementation of Art VI of GATT 1994*, 1868 UNTS 201; OJ L 336, 23.12.1994, p 103; [1995] ATS 8 p 143 (hereafter "Anti-dumping Agreement"). Materials produced by the WTO Committee on Anti-dumping Practices (Art 16) may be found at http://www.wto.org/English/Tratop_E/adp_e/adp_e.htm. See generally, Pierre Didier, "The WTO Anti-dumping Code and EC Practice, Issues for Review in Trade Negotiations" (2001) 35 *Journal of World Trade* 33; James P Durling and Matthew R Nicely, *Understanding the WTO Anti-dumping Agreement: Negotiating History and Subsequent Interpretation* (London: Cameron May, 2002); E C Schlemmer, "Anti-dumping in the WTO Framework" (2003) 28 *South African Yearbook of International Law* 306; Edwin Vermulst, *The WTO Anti-dumping Agreement: A Commentary* (Oxford: Oxford University Press, 2005); Douglas R Nelson and Hylke Vandenbussche (eds), *The WTO and Anti-dumping* (Northhampton, MA: Edward Elgar, 2005); Gabriël Moens and Peter Gillies (eds), *International Trade and Business: Law, Policy and Ethics* (2nd ed, Abingdon, Oxon: Routledge/Cavendish, 2006), Chapter 7; Henrik Andersen, *EU Dumping Determinations and WTO Law* (Alphen aan den Rijn: Kluwer Law International, 2009).

An agreement regarding subsidies was adopted as part of the WTO Agreement. See *Agreement on Subsidies and Countervailing Measures*, 1869 UNTS 14; OJ L 336, 23.12.1994, p 156; [1995] ATS 8 p 238 (hereafter "Subsidies Agreement"). The following are defined as prohibited subsidies under the Agreement: "(a) subsidies contingent . . . upon export performance [or] (b) subsidies contingent . . . upon the use of domestic over imported goods" (Art 3(1)). The Agreement provides for the imposition of countervailing duties (Art 19), which must be consistent with Art VI of GATT (Art 10).

Materials produced by the WTO Committee on Subsidies and Countervailing Measures (Art 24) are available at http://www.wto.org/english/tratop_e/scm_e/scm_e.htm. See generally, Marc Benitah, *The Law of Subsidies under the GATT/WTO System* (The Hague: Kluwer, 2001); M M Slotboom, "Subsidies in WTO Law and in EC Law: Broad and Narrow Definitions" (2002) 36 *Journal of World Trade* 517; Peggy A Clarke and Gary N Horlick, "The Agreement on Subsidies and Countervailing Measures" in Patrick F J Macrory et al. (eds), *The World Trade Organization: Legal, Economic and Political Analysis* (New York: Springer, 2005), II: 679; Anwarul Hoda and Rajeev Ahuja, "Agreement on Subsidies and Countervailing Measures:

Need for Clarification and Improvement" (2005) 39 *Journal of World Trade* 1009; Claus-Dieter Ehlermann and Martin Goyette, "The Interface between EU State Aid Control and the WTO Disciplines on Subsidies" [2006] *European State Aid Law Quarterly* 695; Luca Rubini, *The Definition of Subsidy and State Aid: WTO and EC Law in Comparative Perspective* (Oxford: Oxford University Press, 2008).

[5.45] Anti-dumping Legislation

In the following sections the concept of dumping will be examined, followed by a discussion of the concept of subsidies. Anti-dumping provisions have been adopted as part of the common commercial policy. See Council Regulation 1225/2009 of 30 November 2009 on protection against dumped imports from countries not members of the European Community (OJ L 343, 22.12.2009, p 51) (hereafter "Anti-dumping Regulation"). This Regulation deals with dumping from countries that are not members of the European Union. Dumping by a Member State into another Member State is dealt with under Arts 101 and 102 TFEU. The Regulation was adopted to implement the EU's obligations under the Anti-dumping Agreement. See *Petrotub SA v Council* (C-76/00 P) [2003] ECR I-79 at [55]; *Reliance Industries Ltd v Council* (T-45/06) [2008] ECR II-2399 at [1], [89]–[90].

The Commission is responsible for the investigation of complaints lodged under the anti-dumping law (Art 6(1)). The Regulation provides that an "anti-dumping duty may be applied to any dumped product whose release for free circulation within the [EU] causes injury" (Art 1(1)). The purpose of an anti-dumping duty is protective rather than punitive. In *Industrie des Poudres Sphériques v Council* (C-458/98) [2000] ECR I-8147 the Court stated that the duty "is not a penalty relating to earlier behaviour but is a protective and preventive measure against unfair competition resulting from dumping practices" (at [91]).

[5.50] Dumping

A determination of dumping involves a comparison of the export price with the domestic price of the goods (known as the "normal value"). The price at which the exporter exports to the EU is known as the "export price" (Art 2(8)). The normal value is the price at which the goods are sold in the producer's or manufacturer's home market (Art 2(1)). Any dumping investigation requires the ascertainment of both prices. The two prices are compared at the same level of trade (Art 2(10)). If the export price is below the normal price, the goods are considered to be dumped (Art 2(2)).

The dumping margin is the amount by which the normal value exceeds the export price (Art 2(12)). If the dumped goods are causing or threatening to cause injury, an anti-dumping duty may be imposed (Art 1(1)). The dumping margin will become smaller if, following an anti-dumping investigation, the normal price of the relevant product is decreased and the export price is increased.

The period covered by the Commission's investigation will usually include the 6 months immediately preceding the investigation (Art 6(1)). The 6 month period is for guidance only and is not mandatory. See *Industrie des Poudres Sphériques v Council* (C-458/98) [2000] ECR I-8147 at [88]. Art 3 of the Regulation confers upon the Commission a wide discretion regarding the period to be taken into account for the purposes of determining an injury to EU industry. In *Epichirisseon Metalleftikon Viomichanikon Kai Naftiliakon AE v Council* (C-121/86) [1989] ECR 3919 the Court held that the equivalent provision of the 1984 Regulation allowed a period of 4 years to be taken into account in the circumstances of that case (at [20]–[23]).

[5.55] Normal Value

The normal price or value of goods is usually "based on the prices . . . payable, in the ordinary course of trade, by independent customers in the exporting country" (Art 2(1)). This is the appropriate method where like products are on sale in the ordinary course of trade on the domestic market. A like product is one that is identical to the exported product or, when an identical product is not on sale, a product that has characteristics closely resembling those of the goods that were allegedly dumped (Art 1(4)).

Sales to related companies in the domestic market are not considered as being in the ordinary course of trade (Art 2(1)). Products that are sold at less than the cost of their production are not sold in the "ordinary course of trade". Such sales are thus excluded from ascertaining the normal value. See *Goldstar Co Ltd v Council* (C-105/90) [1992] ECR I-677 at [13]; [1992] 1 CMLR 996; *Thai Bicycle Industry & Co Ltd v Council* (T-118/96) [1998] ECR II-2991 at [47]; *Ajinomoto Co Inc v Council* (C-76/98 P) [2001] ECR I-3223 at [38]; [2001] 2 CMLR 40 (p 989).

[5.60] Constructing the Normal Value

Where there is no domestic market in the ordinary course of trade, the normal value will be the price of the goods as exported to a third market or a constructed price (Art 2(3)). A constructed price is calculated by adding to the cost of production "a reasonable amount for selling, general and administrative costs and for profits" (Art 2(3)). In constructing the normal value, the aim is to determine the price at which the product would sell if it were for sale on the domestic market.

In *NTN Toyo Bearing Co Ltd v Council* (240/84) [1987] ECR 1809; [1989] 2 CMLR 76 the applicant challenged the Regulation imposing the anti-dumping duty on the ground that in determining the dumping margin the normal value had been established on the basis of a weighted average of the prices paid on the domestic market while the export price had been calculated using the transaction-by-transaction method (at [11]–[12]). The Court rejected this argument. It held that Art 2(13)(b) of the 1984 Regulation (Art 2(1) of the current Regulation) was specifically intended to ensure that the most appropriate method was employed for the purpose of preventing damage to Community industry arising from dumping goods onto the EU Market (at [22]). Where dumping is disguised by charging different prices, some above and some below normal value, the transaction-by-transaction method is the only method that can effectively deal with the practice. If the weighted average method had been used to determine the export price, it would have concealed the dumping (at [23]).

This principle has been applied in many cases. See *Nachi Fujikoshi Corporation v Council* (255/84) [1987] ECR 1861 at [24]–[25]; [1989] 2 CMLR 76; *Nippon Seiko KK v Council* (258/84) [1987] ECR 1923 at [25]; [1989] 2 CMLR 76; *Minebea Co Ltd v Council* (260/84) [1987] ECR 1975 at [19]–[20]; [1989] 2 CMLR 76; *Ritek Corporation v Council* (T-274/02) [2006] ECR II-4305 at [55].

In calculating a constructed normal value, EU institutions may not use unreliable accounting data, since the method of calculation used must be applied so that the calculation is reasonable. See *Acme Industry & Co Ltd v Council* (T-48/96) [1999] ECR II-3089 at [37]; [1999] 3 CMLR 823. Where the European Union institutions have a discretion in the choice of means to protect EU industry from dumping, exporters may not rely upon the doctrine of legitimate expectations to prevent the EU institutions from altering the means originally chosen to curb the impugned behaviour. See *Koyo Seiko Co Ltd v Council* (256/84) [1987] ECR 1899 at [20]; [1989] 2 CMLR 76.

[5.65] Constructed Value Includes Sales Costs

In the construction of the normal value of a product, it may be appropriate to include the costs of a subsidiary of the manufacturer where the subsidiary executes the tasks normally handled by a sales department. In *Tokyo Electric Co Ltd v Council* (260/85) [1988] ECR 5855; [1989] 1 CMLR 169 Tokyo Electric had entrusted its domestic sales to a subsidiary. These tasks could have been handled by a sales department of the manufacturer. Even though the electronic typewriters at issue were not sold on the domestic market, the costs of the subsidiary were taken into account in constructing the normal value. By taking into account the subsidiary's costs, it was possible to ensure that costs that were undoubtedly part of the selling price of the product were included in the normal price of the goods (at [27]–[35]). See also *Sharp Corporation v Council* (301/85) [1988] ECR 5813 at [13]; [1989] 1 CMLR 381.

[5.70] Constructed Value Includes Profit

When the normal value is constructed, a reasonable amount is added for a profit margin (Art 2(3)). When they assess the profit margin the EU institutions are under no obligation to select the profit margin of the parent or the sales subsidiary but may add the two profit margins together. In determining the profit margin, the EU institutions may have to use confidential information belonging to competitors of the impugned enterprise. This may lead to a degree of unforeseeability as the enterprise will not know the profit margins of its competitors, but such references must be made when an actual price is not available.

These principles were applied in *Tokyo Electric Co Ltd v Council* (260/85) [1988] ECR 5855; [1989] 1 CMLR 169. The Court indicated that a profit margin had to be included in the normal price or there would be a risk of discrimination against competitors who sold like models on the domestic market when a definitive anti-dumping duty was imposed (at [16]). Where a profit margin attributed to a producer subject to a definitive anti-dumping duty is discriminatory because it is higher than that attributed to another company in similar circumstances that is not subject to the duty, the anti-dumping duty would not be annulled if it was adopted on the basis of findings properly made during the investigation in accordance with the appropriate EU legislation (at [17]–[18]).

In *Canon Inc v Council* (277/85) [1988] ECR 5731; [1989] 1 CMLR 915 it was argued that Art 2(3)(b) of Regulation 2176/84 (Art 2(3) of the current Regulation) required that the EU institutions should take the price of the product when exported to a third country as the normal value, when the domestic prices are not representative or do not permit a proper comparison. The ECJ rejected this argument. The Court pointed out that the Article "does not indicate that use of the price for exportation to a third country is to take precedence over construction of the normal value" (at [17]). The EU institutions have a discretion regarding the price to be used as the normal price and the onus is on the applicant to show that the discretion has been abused (at [17]).

[5.75] Constructed Value Where No Sale in the Ordinary Course of Trade

If the goods are not purchased in the ordinary course of trade the constructed price will be based upon the best available estimate as to the price that would have been paid in the ordinary course of trade. The calculations are based on available accounting data for the domestic market with costs appropriated in proportion to the turnover for the market under consideration. The Commission usually requires the submission of prices charged in third states but has shown a preference to calculate the normal value based upon a constructed price. It might be speculated that the reason for this preference lies in the fact that goods dumped in one market are likely to have been dumped in another.

In *Brother Industries Ltd v Commission* (250/85) [1988] ECR 5655; [1990] 1 CMLR 792 it was argued that the Council should follow the attitude of the major trading partners of the EU when determining its position regarding the protection of EU industry from dumping. The Court rejected this argument, stating that the attitude of a major trading partner such as the United States could not influence the application of EU law (at [13]). See similarly, *Canon Inc v Council* (277/85) [1988] ECR 5731 at [15]; [1989] 1 CMLR 915; *Nashua Corporation v Council* (C-133/87) [1990] ECR I-719 at [30]; [1990] 2 CMLR 6.

In *Brother Industries Ltd v Commission* (250/85) [1988] ECR 5655; [1990] 1 CMLR 792 the Court held that, as the Commission was given a discretion under the Anti-dumping Regulation, the Commission was not obliged to give the person being investigated a detailed explanation in advance as to how it intended to exercise its discretion. The absence of such an explanation did not render the decision void for lack of legal certainty (at [28]–[29]).

[5.80] Export Price

The export price is usually the price paid for the product by the EU importer (Art 2(8)). However, there are two circumstances where a constructed export price will be used in the calculation of the export price:

- where there is no export price (such as in situations of barter), or
- where there appears to be an association between the exporter and importer or some other party (e.g. an importer who is also a subsidiary of the exporter, though if prices charged by related parties are reasonable the Commission may accept them) (Art 2(9)).

The constructed export price is calculated by reference to the price of the goods when they are first sold to an independent reseller, along with an allowance for the costs incurred between importation and resale and a reasonable profit margin (Art 2(9)). If there is no sale to an independent reseller, or the goods are not sold in the same condition, then the constructed export price is calculated on a reasonable basis (Art 2(9)).

In *Silver Seiko Ltd v Council* (273/85) [1988] ECR 5927; [1989] 1 CMLR 249 the Court pointed out that under Art 2(8)(b) of Regulation 2176/84 (Art 2(9) of the current Regulation) the EU institutions could disregard a price paid by a EU subsidiary to the parent and rely upon the price paid by an independent importer (at [25]). In that case the profit margin of the EU subsidiary was therefore irrelevant to the construction of the export price.

[5.85] Comparison of the Export Price and Normal Value

There must be a "fair comparison" between the export price and the normal value. Adjustments shall be made "for differences in factors which are... demonstrated to affect prices and price comparability" (Art 2(10)). These differences include physical characteristics; import charges and indirect taxes; discounts, rebates and quantities; level of trade; transport and handling costs; credit; after-sales costs and currency conversions (Art 2(10)(a)–(e), (g), (h), (j)). For example, normal value shall be adjusted by "an amount corresponding to any import charges or indirect taxes borne by the like product and by materials physically incorporated therein, when intended for consumption in the exporting country and not collected or refunded in respect of the product exported to the Community" (Art 2(10)(b)).

In *Sharp Corporation v Council* (301/85) [1988] ECR 5813; [1989] 1 CMLR 381 the manufacturer did not have a sales department, but sold its products through an associated exclusive distributor. In those circumstances the prices charged by the manufacturer were not the product's normal value, and the prices charged by the distributor had to be considered instead. The Court decided that the EU institutions may calculate the dumping margin by comparing export prices at the "ex-factory level" with a constructed normal value at the "ex-exclusive distributor" level. It was irrelevant that the exclusive dealer does not sell the dumped product since the normal value must be constructed as if the product was sold on the domestic market (at [12]–[13]). See also *Brother Industries Ltd v Council* (250/85) [1988] ECR 5683 at [15]–[16]; [1990] 1 CMLR 792.

A comparison between the normal value and the export price for the purpose of determining the dumping margin will necessitate a consideration of exchange rates. The Regulation provides that "[f]luctuations in exchange rates shall be ignored and exporters shall be granted 60 days to reflect a sustained movement in exchange rates during the investigation period" (Art 2(10)(j)).

[5.90] Dumping Margin

In the simplest case, the dumping margin is simply the amount by which the normal value exceeds the export price (Art 2(12)). However, in most cases dumping margins vary greatly. In such cases, the Commission may establish a weighted average dumping margin (Art 2(12)). The ascertainment of the dumping margin aims to obviate the effects that exports of goods from non-member states at dumped prices will have upon the EU industry.

The WTO Agreement sets out three methods for calculating the dumping margin. See Art 2.4.2, Anti-dumping Agreement. There are two "symmetrical" methods and one "asymmetrical" method. The first symmetrical method is "a comparison of a weighted average normal value with a weighted average of prices of all export transactions to the Community". The second symmetrical method is "a comparison of individual normal values and individual export prices to the Community on a transaction-to-transaction basis". The asymmetrical method involves a comparison of "a normal value established on a weighted average basis . . . to prices of all individual export transactions to the Community". The Regulation gives effect to the Anti-dumping Agreement by using the same methods for calculating the dumping margin (Art 2(11)).

The Anti-dumping Agreement requires the giving of a specific explanation for the use of the asymmetrical method. The Regulation does not contain such an express requirement. In *Petrotub SA v Council* (C-76/00 P) [2003] ECR I-79 the ECJ interpreted the previous Regulation in the light of the Anti-dumping Agreement (at [56]). Against that background the Court held that the general obligation of EU institutions to give reasons for their legal acts (Art 296 TFEU) extended to giving the specific explanation required by the Anti-dumping Agreement (at [58], [60]).

[5.95] Subsidies Legislation

Thus far the concept of dumping has been examined. The concept of subsidies must now be explained. Goods could be made less costly in export markets through the public subsidization of producers and manufacturers. A subsidy does not always involve a monetary payment to the producer by the supporting state, but involves an advantage or favour granted directly or indirectly by a government to its producers in order to promote exports. Subsidised imports to the EU are regulated by Council Regulation 597/2009 of 11 June 2009 on protection against subsidised imports from countries not members of the European Community (OJ L 188, 18.7.2009, p 93) (hereafter "Subsidies Regulation"). This Regulation was adopted to implement the EU's obligations under the WTO Subsidies Agreement. See *Reliance Industries Ltd v Council* (T-45/06) [2008] ECR II-2399 at [2], [89]–[90].

[5.100] Subsidy

If goods have been the subject of a direct or indirect subsidy in the country of manufacture, a countervailing duty may be imposed to offset the effect of the subsidy, where the subsidy causes injury in the EU (Art 1(1) Subsidies

Regulation). A subsidy is defined as (1) a financial contribution by government in the country of origin or any form of income or price support (2) by which a benefit is conferred (Art 3 Subsidies Regulation). Annex I of the Regulation contains an illustrative list of export subsidies. The benefit of the subsidy is calculated in accordance with Arts 6 and 7 of the Regulation.

In many countries exports are exempted from commodity charges and other charges assessed upon domestically manufactured goods. Such an exemption does not constitute a subsidy. Art VI(4) of GATT 1994 states that "[n]o product of the territory of any contracting party imported into the territory of any other contracting party shall be subject to . . . countervailing duty by reason of the exemption of such product from duties or taxes borne by the like product when destined for consumption in the country of origin or exportation, or by reason of the refund of such duties or taxes". See also the Note to Art XVI of GATT 1994. This principle is incorporated in Art 3(1)(a)(ii) of the Subsidies Regulation.

[5.105] Countervailable Subsidies

Countervailable duties may only be applied to subsidies that are specific to an enterprise or industry (Art 4(1)–(2) Subsidies Regulation). The following subsidies are considered to be specific:

(a) where the granting authority expressly limits availability of the subsidy to certain enterprises (Art 4(2)(a));
(b) where the availability of the subsidy is limited to certain enterprises within a particular geographical region (Art 4(3));
(c) where the subsidy is contingent upon export performance (Art 4(4)(a)); or
(d) where the subsidy is contingent upon the use of domestic goods in preference to imports (Art 4(4)(b) Subsidies Regulation).

The following subsidy is not considered to be specific:

(a) where the granting authority has set objective criteria for eligibility for the subsidy, provided that the criteria are rigidly observed and eligibility is automatic upon satisfaction of those criteria (Art 4(2)(b) Subsidies Regulation).

Where some factors indicate that a subsidy is non-specific, but there are reasons to consider that the subsidy may actually be specific, other factors may be taken into account. Such other factors include the predominant use of the subsidy by certain enterprises and the granting of disproportionately large subsidies to certain enterprises (Art 4(2)(c) Subsidies Regulation).

The amount of the countervailable subsidy is the benefit conferred upon the recipient of the subsidy, as found during the investigation period (Art 5 Subsidies Regulation).

[5.110] Amount of the Subsidy

The amount of the subsidy is usually determined per unit of the goods exported to the EU (Art 7(1) Subsidies Regulation). Any application fee or other cost necessarily incurred to obtain the subsidy or any export taxes, duties or other charges levied on the export of the product to the EU specifically intended to offset the subsidy are deducted from the value of the subsidy if the interested party is able to show that the deduction is justified (Art 7(1)(a) and (b) Subsidies Regulation).

Where the subsidy is not granted on a per unit basis, the amount of the subsidy is determined by allocating the subsidy over an appropriate period, normally the accounting year of the recipient of the subsidy (Art 7(2) Subsidies Regulation). Where the subsidy is based on the acquisition of fixed assets, the value of the subsidy is determined by spreading the subsidy across a period which reflects the normal depreciation of such assets in the industry concerned. Where the assets are non-depreciating, the subsidy is valued as an interest-free loan (Art 7(3) Subsidies Regulation).

[5.115] Material Injury

Much of the law relating to dumping and subsidies is similar, so both Regulations will be discussed throughout the remainder of this Chapter. The effect of the dumped or subsidised imports is tested against EU production of like products (Art 3(8) Anti-dumping Regulation; Art 8(7) Subsidies Regulation). The dumped or subsidized imports must be causing or threatening to cause material injury to an established Community industry or materially retarding the establishment of such an industry (Art 3(1) Anti-dumping Regulation; Art 2(d) Subsidies Regulation).

If the difficulties faced by the Community industries are not caused by the dumped or subsidized imports, the Commission is not able to make an adverse determination to those goods. Such factors as an increase in volume of imports and decrease in price of imports which are not dumped or subsidized, or the decrease in demand for EU products, are thus not attributed to dumping or the subsidization of imports (Art 3(7) Anti-dumping Regulation; Art 8(6) Subsidies Regulation).

[5.120] Injury Calculated as a Whole

The injury caused by dumped imports to an established Community industry is calculated as a whole. It is not necessary to calculate the injury attributable to each of the persons responsible for the impugned behaviour. In an action disputing the quantum of the anti-dumping duty imposed upon its goods a company may not assert that, owing to its small market share, the injury caused by it is exceeded by the duty imposed. This is especially so where the duty imposed does not exceed the dumping margin. See *Nachi Fujikoshi Corporation v Council* (255/84) [1987] ECR 1861 at [45]–[48]; [1989] 2 CMLR 76; *Arne Mathisen AS v Council* (T-340/99) [2002] ECR II-2905 at [123]; *Shanghai Teraoka Electronic Co Ltd v Council* (T-35/01) [2004] ECR II-3663 at [163].

[5.125] Each Determination of Injury Is Independent

Each determination of injury depends upon its own facts. The Regulations list the factors to be considered by the EU authorities in an anti-dumping or subsidy investigation:

> The examination of the impact of the [subsidized or dumped products] on the Community industry concerned shall include an evaluation of all relevant economic factors... having a bearing on the state of the industry, including: the fact that an industry is still in the process of recovering from the effects of past subsidization or dumping, the magnitude of [the amount of countervailable subsidies or the actual margin of dumping], actual and potential decline in sales, profits, output, market share, productivity, return on investments, utilization of capacity; factors affecting Community prices; actual and potential negative effects on cash flow, inventories, employment, wages, growth, ability to raise capital or investments.... This list is not exhaustive, nor can any one or more of these factors necessarily give decisive guidance (Art 3(5) Anti-dumping Regulation; Art 8(4) Subsidies Regulation).

In *Silver Seiko Ltd v Council* (273/85) [1988] ECR 5927; [1989] 1 CMLR 249 the Court held that as this list is merely indicative, the Commission and Council are free to form an opinion as to which of the factors are the most important (at [40]). Non-consideration of one of the factors does not necessarily mean that a finding of injury is fatally flawed.

Similarly, where the dumped products come from many countries, all the exports may be aggregated to examine their effect upon the Community industry, even if the relevant exports of each country are small. See *Technointorg v Commission* (294/86) [1988] ECR 6077 at [41]; [1989] 1 CMLR 281; *Swedish Match Philippines Inc v Council* (T-171/97) [1999] ECR II-3241 at [66].

It is possible to establish injury during a period where the sales of the Community industry actually increased. In *Canon Inc v Council* (277/85) [1988] ECR 5731; [1989] 1 CMLR 915 the evidence showed that the Union producers did not maintain their share of an otherwise rapidly expanding market. In such circumstances, the Commission was able to find that due to the dumping their market share was not maintained (at [58]).

In fashioning an anti-dumping duty the EU institutions must consider only the injury that is attributable to the dumping, and must disregard any injury that is attributable to other factors such as the conduct of EU producers. See *Extramet Industrie SA v Council* (C-358/89) [1991] ECR I-2501 at [19]; [1993] 2 CMLR 619; *Mukand Ltd v Council* (T-58/99) [2001] ECR II-2521 at [39], [48]; [2002] 3 CMLR 13 (p 336). The Council thus made an error of law in considering the impact of a recession in an industry when determining the duty. See *Commission v NTN Corporation* (C-245/95 P) [1998] ECR I-401 at [43].

A finding of injury is not restricted to cases where dumping or subsidies are the sole or principal cause of the injury. In *Canon Inc v Council* (277/85) [1988] ECR 5731; [1989] 1 CMLR 915 the Court held a finding of injury by dumping may be made even if the injury is a small part of a more extensive injury primarily caused by other factors. The Court emphasised that if the injury was not all attributable to the dumping the anti-dumping duty could only be set at a level necessary to remove the injury caused by the dumping (at [62]).

[5.130] Finding of Injury Gives Rise to a Discretion

In *Brother Industries Ltd v Council* (250/85) [1988] ECR 5683; [1990] 1 CMLR 792 the Court indicated that, where the existence of dumping and injury had been established, the Council and the Commission in their discretion will decide whether intervention is necessary in the interests of the European Union (at [29]). The fact "that a Community producer is facing difficulties attributable in part to causes other than dumping is not a reason for depriving that producer of all protection against the injury caused by the dumping" (at [42]). See similarly, *Sinochem National Chemicals Import & Export Corporation v Council* (T-97/95) [1998] ECR II-85 at [100].

Where an exporter was under investigation for having dumped products in the EU, and EU manufacturers had imported some of the exporter's lower priced models, which they sold under their own brand name, but the number of those models imported was always small, there was no reason why the importing manufacturers should be excluded from being found to have been injured by the dumping. See *Tokyo Electric Co Ltd v Council* (260/85) [1988] ECR 5855 at [46]–[47]; [1989] 1 CMLR 169.

The imposition of an anti-dumping duty is justified where the continued existence of the Community industry might be in doubt if a duty is not imposed. This is especially so where the industry is needed to retain or develop technology required for the manufacture of the goods concerned and to protect employment within the EU. This need to protect an industry may override the short term interests of consumers. The EU interest may require the strengthening of the Community industry by the imposition of anti-dumping duties, particularly when the EU institutions have no reason to suspect that the strengthened position will be abused. See *Gestetner Holdings Plc v Council of Ministers* (C-156/87) [1990] ECR I-781 at [65]; [1990] 1 CMLR 820.

[5.135] Threat of Injury

Under the Regulations, "the totality of the factors considered must lead to the conclusion that further [dumped or subsidized imports] are imminent and that, unless protective action is taken, material injury will occur" (Art 3(9) Anti-dumping Regulation; Art 8(8) Subsidies Regulation). The Commission takes the following factors into account in determining whether a situation will cause material injury:

(1) (in a subsidy case) the nature of the subsidy and the likely effects of that subsidy upon trade in those goods;
(2) a significant rate of increase in the import of the dumped or subsidized goods into the EU, "indicating the likelihood of substantially increased imports";
(3) the export capacity of the exporter indicates the likelihood of substantially increased dumped or subsidised exports to the EU;
(4) whether imports are entering at prices that would, to a significant degree, depress prices or prevent price increases which otherwise would have occurred, and would probably increase demand for further imports; and
(5) inventories of the product (Art 3(9) Anti-dumping Regulation; Art 8(8) Subsidies Regulation).

In determining the nature of a threat of injury the Commission usually examines the subsidy in detail. If the subsidy is a purely domestic or internal subsidy, it will not pose the same problem for the EU as a subsidy payable only upon exports. Domestic subsidies are governmental measures, such as retraining programs, which have some reasonable purpose apart from promoting exports. However, a subsidy designed to stimulate local consumption might be considered as a threat of injury if current production meets the local demand. This stems from the fact that surplus production is likely to be exported.

[5.140] Community Industry

Community industry includes the producers of the Union who make like products or those producers whose collective output accounts for a major proportion of the production of those products within the EU (Art 4(1) Anti-dumping Regulation; Art 9(1) Subsidies Regulation). However, there are two exceptions to this definition.

Related Producers

Under the first exception to this definition, if a producer is related to the exporters or importers of dumped or subsidised goods, the Community industry encompasses the remainder of the industry without that producer (Art 4(1)(a) Anti-dumping Regulation; Art 9(1)(a) Subsidies Regulation). But the Council and the Commission do not automatically exclude from the relevant "Community industry" those producers who are related to exporters or importers or who are themselves importers of goods alleged to be dumped or subsidised. The exclusion of such persons from the relevant "Community industry" involves an exercise of discretion by the EU authorities, based upon the facts of the case under consideration. See *Gestetner Holdings Plc v Council of Ministers* (C-156/87) [1990] ECR I-781 at [41]–[43]; [1990] 1 CMLR 820.

Such a rule prevents a producer from frustrating the remainder of the industry when the others make a complaint to the Commission concerning the alleged misbehaviour. If the producer were a major producer of the goods and had to be taken into account during the Commission's investigation, the other producers could have difficulty showing that they had the necessary interest to complain. Such a rule precludes that producer from profiting from the impugned behaviour because it cannot prevent the Commission from making a finding of injury.

Division of Market Within the EU

Under the second exception to this definition, in exceptional circumstances the EU may be divided into two or more competitive (regional) markets (Art 4(1)(b) Anti-dumping Regulation; Art 9(1)(b) Subsidies Regulation). Such exceptional circumstances arise when the producers of a particular region sell all or almost all their production within that region and the regional demand for those goods is not met in any substantial way by producers located elsewhere within the Union. If these two conditions are met and the Commission finds that there is a concentration of dumped or subsidized products in that region which are causing injury to all or almost all the producers within the region, the Commission may make a finding of injury even though the major proportion of the "Community industry" is not injured.

[5.145] Community Interest

If the Commission has found that dumping has occurred or that subsidies have been paid and that material injury has resulted, the Commission will still have to consider the Community interest before it takes remedial measures (Art 9(4) Anti-dumping Regulation; Art 15(1) Subsidies Regulation). The Regulations elaborate upon the concept of Community interest (Art 21 Anti-dumping Regulation; Art 31 Subsidies Regulation). The Commission only takes remedial measures if they are in the overall interest of the Union. The interest most often opposed to the imposition of countervailing duties is the processing industry. This industry has an interest in obtaining its raw materials at the lowest possible price.

[5.150] Investigation of Complaints

The investigation is initiated by a complaint in writing lodged with the Commission on behalf of a Community industry (Art 5(1) Anti-dumping Regulation; Art 10(1) Subsidies Regulation). If it considers that it has sufficient evidence to justify an inquiry, the Commission must publish its intention to investigate in the *Official Journal of the European Union* (Art 5(9) Anti-dumping Regulation; Art 10(11) Subsidies Regulation). There must be sufficient evidence of dumping before an investigation may be begun. See *Rima Eletrometalurgia SA v Council* (C-216/91) [1993] ECR I-6303 at [16]; *Commission v NTN Corporation* (C-245/95 P) [1998] ECR I-401 at [38]. The Commission must advise the relevant exporters and importers and representative associations, the exporting country and the complainant that it has opened an investigation (Art 5(11) Anti-dumping Regulation; Art 10(13) Subsidies Regulation).

An investigation does not prevent the customs service clearing the goods for EU consumption (Art 5(12) Anti-dumping Regulation; Art 10(14) Subsidies Regulation). The provider of information for the purposes of the investigation must supply reasons why that information should remain confidential. The Commission may evaluate the claim for confidentiality and if it is not satisfied that the reasons are valid, the information may be disregarded unless the provider agrees to make that information public or to authorise its disclosure in generalised or summary form (Art 19(3) Anti-dumping Regulation; Art 29(3) Subsidies Regulation).

The exporter or importer is entitled to be given the facts and reasons upon which the Commission intends to recommend the imposition of an anti-dumping or countervailing duty. In *Timex Corporation v Council* (264/82) [1985] ECR 849; [1985] 3 CMLR 550 the Court had to balance the right of Timex Corporation to know the basis upon which the Commission was to make its decision, against the right of the suppliers of information to have that information remain confidential. The Court held that the Commission should make every effort that was compatible with the maintenance of business secrets, to provide to Timex information that was relevant to the defence of its interests. Mere disclosure of the items included within the calculation of the normal value, especially where the normal value is a constructed value, without the provision of the figures upon which that reconstruction was made, was deemed to be inadequate (at [30]).

The previous anti-dumping and subsidies Regulation did not confer upon the Commission the power to compel an exporter or producer to produce information or assist in the investigation. See *Acme Industry & Co Ltd v Council* (T-48/96) [1999] ECR II-3089 at [42]; [1999] 3 CMLR 823. The current Regulation also does not confer such powers. Where a party refuses access to required information or "significantly impedes" the investigation, the Commission may decide on the basis of the facts available (Art 18(1) Anti-dumping Regulation; Art 28(1) Subsidies Regulation). If a party fails to cooperate and does not supply relevant information, the result of the investigation may be less favourable to that party than if they had cooperated with the Commission (Art 18(6) Anti-dumping Regulation; Art 28(6) Subsidies Regulation).

The Commission may visit the interested parties in order to verify the information that they have supplied (Art 16 Anti-dumping Regulation; Art 26 Subsidies Regulation). Given the strict time limits for the investigation, where the number of parties, types of products and transactions are very large the Commission is permitted to investigate a reasonable sample only (Art 17 Anti-dumping Regulation; Art 27 Subsidies Regulation).

[5.155] Termination of the Investigation and the Proceeding

The conclusion of an investigation is usually marked by its termination or by a definitive action. The Regulations state that investigations must "in all cases" be concluded within 13 months of their initiation (in a subsidy investigation) or 15 months from their initiation (in a dumping investigation) (Art 6(9) Anti-dumping Regulation; Art 11(9) Subsidies Regulation). The conclusion of the investigation is not necessarily the end of the proceeding because anti-dumping or countervailing duties may be reviewed after a year (Art 11(3) Anti-dumping Regulation; Art 19(1) Subsidies Regulation).

If the Commission, after consultation with the Advisory Committee, is of opinion that protective measures are unnecessary, the proceeding will be terminated (Art 9(2) Anti-dumping Regulation; Art 14(2) Subsidies Regulation). If an objection is raised by the Advisory Committee, the Commission reports the matter to the Council. If the Council does not determine within 1 month that the proceeding is to continue, it is automatically terminated (Art 9(2) Anti-dumping Regulation; Art 14(2) Subsidies Regulation). Where an undertaking is accepted, the investigation will usually be terminated (Art 8(5) Anti-dumping Regulation; Art 13(5) Subsidies Regulation).

[5.160] Undertakings

The purpose of allowing a proceeding to be terminated on the acceptance of undertakings is to encourage producers or exporters to voluntarily cease the behaviour which is the cause of injury. The Commission may accept voluntary undertakings that:

1. (in the case of subsidies) the government of the exporting country eliminates or limits the subsidy; or
2. (in the cases of both subsidies and dumping) prices will be revised or exports cease to the extent that the Commission is satisfied that the injurious effect of the dumping or subsidy will be eliminated (Art 8(1) Anti-dumping Regulation; Art 13(1) Subsidies Regulation).

A normal incident of an undertaking is for the undertaker to periodically supply information to the Commission and to permit that information to be verified. Non-compliance with these conditions is a breach of the undertaking (Art 8(7) Anti-dumping Regulation; Art 13(7) Subsidies Regulation).

The Commission has a discretion as to whether it will accept an undertaking. See *Arne Mathisen AS v Council* (T-340/99) [2002] ECR II-2905 at [57]. The Commission may invite the investigated producer or exporter to offer undertakings. But the producer's non-acceptance of an invitation to give an undertaking does not prejudice consideration of the case under investigation. "However, it may be determined that a threat of injury is more likely to be realized" if the subsidised or dumped imports continue (Art 8(2) Anti-dumping Regulation; Art 13(2) Subsidies Regulation).

The Commission has adopted a practice of not accepting undertakings offered by importers. The Court held that this practice was justified. The Regulation provided for the imposition of an anti-dumping duty for breach of an undertaking by an exporter, not an importer. Undertakings might actually encourage the importer to continue to obtain supplies at dumped prices. If a large number of companies were involved monitoring compliance with the undertakings could be extremely difficult. See *Nashua Corporation v Council* (C-133/87) [1990] ECR I-719 at [45]–[46]; [1990] 2 CMLR 6; *Gestetner Holdings Plc v Council of 7 Ministers* (C-156/87) [1990] ECR I-781 at [70]–[71]; [1990] 1 CMLR 820.

The undertaking lapses if the Commission makes a finding that no injury has been caused, except where that finding is due to the existence of the undertaking. In such a case, the Commission may require the undertaking to be preserved for a reasonable period (Art 8(6) Anti-dumping Regulation; Art 13(6) Subsidies Regulation).

The Commission may withdraw its acceptance of an undertaking because it has been breached or circumvented. See *Miwon Co Ltd v Council* (T-51/96) [2000] ECR II-1841 at [52]; *Arne Mathisen AS v Council* (T-340/99) [2002] ECR II-2905 at [57]. Where an undertaking has been withdrawn or breached, the Commission may apply provisional anti-dumping or countervailing duties (Art 8(9) Anti-dumping Regulation; Art 13(9) Subsidies Regulation). When the circumstances so warrant undertakings are subject to review (Art 11(2)–(3) Anti-dumping Regulation; Arts 18–19 Subsidies Regulation). The principle of legal certainty does not prevent measures previously adopted from being reviewed. See *Nippon Seiko KK v Council* (258/84) [1987] ECR 1923 at [32]; [1989] 2 CMLR 76.

[5.165] Anti-dumping and Countervailing Duties

When a finding of injury has been made, an anti-dumping duty may be applied to dumped goods to counter the dumping margin (Art 1(1) Anti-dumping Regulation). A countervailing duty may be applied to offset the subsidy granted in the country of origin or export (Art 1(1) Subsidies Regulation).

Countervailing or anti-dumping duties, whether provisional or definitive, are imposed by Regulation (Art 14(1) Anti-dumping Regulation; Art 24(1) Subsidies Regulation). For example, a Council Regulation imposed a definitive anti-dumping duty upon biodiesel imported from the United States. See Council Regulation 599/2009 of 7 July 2009 imposing a definitive anti-dumping duty and collecting definitively the provisional duty imposed on imports of biodiesel originating in the United States of America (OJ L 179, 10.7.2009, p 26).

The regulation imposing the duty must state the product covered, the names of the exporters or countries involved, and the material questions of fact upon which the measure is based (Art 14(2) Anti-dumping Regulation; Art 24(2) Subsidies Regulation).

As the duty is to counter the dumping margin or the subsidy granted, the duty must not exceed this amount but should be less if that will be sufficient to remove the injury (Arts 7(2), 9(4) Anti-dumping Regulation; Arts 12(1), 15(1) Subsidies Regulation). The imposition of the duty is intended to remove the injury to the Community industry, not to ensure that all importers enjoy the same profit margin. See *Nashua Corporation v Council* (C-133/87) [1990] ECR I-719 at [41]; [1990] 2 CMLR 6.

The EU institutions may take into account the risk of circumvention of a duty when determining its scope. See *Climax Paper Converters Ltd v Council* (T-155/94) [1996] ECR II-873 at [96]; [1996] 3 CMLR 1031; *Shanghai Bicycle Corporation v Council* (T-170/94) [1997] ECR II-1383 at [108]; *International Potash Co v Council* (T-87/98) [2000] ECR II-3179 at [53]. The Regulations make specific provision in relation to circumvention of trade protection measures (Art 13 Anti-dumping Regulation; Art 23 Subsidies Regulation).

In *Silver Seiko Ltd v Council* (273/85) [1988] ECR 5927; [1989] 1 CMLR 249 the Court held that if it were established that the exclusion of a manufacturer from a group of companies subject to definitive anti-dumping duties amounted to a discrimination in favour of that manufacturer, that discrimination would not lead to an annulment of the Regulation imposing the duty where the duty was adopted on the basis of findings correctly made in the course of the investigation (at [55]).

[5.170] Provisional Duty

Where the preliminary investigation shows dumping or a subsidy and consequential injury to Community industry, if the interests of the Union require the injury to be abated during the proceeding, the Commission may impose a provisional anti-dumping or countervailing duty (Art 7(1) Anti-dumping Regulation; Art 12(1) Subsidies Regulation). In cases of extreme urgency the Commission may inform Member States and impose a duty, but consultations must take place within 10 days (Art 7(4) Anti-dumping Regulation; Art 12(3) Subsidies Regulation). When a Member State requests immediate intervention by the Commission, a decision regarding the imposition of a provisional duty must be taken within five working days (Art 7(5) Anti-dumping Regulation; Art 12(4) Subsidies Regulation).

The imposition of provisional duty does not entail the payment of the relevant sums. Instead, the release of the products for free circulation or consumption in the EU is conditional upon the provision of security for the duty levied (Art 7(3) Anti-dumping Regulation; Art 12(2) Subsidies Regulation). A provisional anti-dumping duty is valid for 6 months but may be extended for a further 3 months (Art 7(7) Anti-dumping Regulation). A provisional countervailing duty is valid for 4 months only (Art 12(6) Subsidies Regulation).

[5.175] Definitive Duty

Once dumping (or a subsidy) and injury have been established, if the interests of the EU call for intervention, the Council must apply a definitive duty (Art 9(4) Anti-dumping Regulation; Art 15(1) Subsidies Regulation). The duty is imposed by the Council acting on a proposal from the Commission after the Commission has consulted the Advisory Committee (Art 9(4) Anti-dumping Regulation; Art 15(1) Subsidies Regulation). In *Epichirisseon Metalleftikon Viomichanikon Kai Naftiliakon AE v Council* (C-121/86) [1989] ECR 3919 the Court held that it was clear that the Council was competent to rule on all of the conditions which must be satisfied for the imposition of an anti-dumping duty without being obliged to adopt every proposal made by the Commission (at [30]).

[5.180] Duty Applies Prospectively

Anti-dumping or Countervailing duties shall only be applied to products which enter free circulation after the time when the duty enters into force (Art 10(1) Anti-dumping Regulation; Art 16(1) Subsidies Regulation). However, some retroactivity is permissible in relation to such duties.

A definitive anti-dumping duty may be imposed on products which were entered for consumption up to 90 days prior to the application of provisional measures but not before the investigation began, provided that there is a history of dumping over an extended period; and there is a further substantial rise in imports which is likely to seriously undermine the remedial effect of the anti-dumping duty (Art 10(4) Anti-dumping Regulation).

A definitive countervailing duty may be imposed on products which were entered for consumption up to 90 days prior to the application of provisional measures but not before the initiation of the investigation, provided that (a) injury which is difficult to repair is caused by massive imports of a subsidised product in a relatively short period of time and (b) it is deemed necessary to prevent the recurrence of such injury by assessing countervailing duties retroactively on those imports (Art 16(4) Subsidies Regulation). Some retroactivity is similarly permitted in relation to duties applied for breaches or withdrawals of undertakings (Art 10(5) Anti-dumping Regulation; Art 16(5) Subsidies Regulation).

[5.185] Duty Applied Generally

Where the product is sourced from more than one country, the duty is applied in a non-discriminatory manner to all imports found to be dumped or subsidized and which are causing injury except where undertakings have been accepted (Art 9(5) Anti-dumping Regulation; Art 15(2) Subsidies Regulation). Where the Community industry has been interpreted as being producers in a region of the EU, the Commission must give the exporters an opportunity to offer undertakings, but if those undertakings are not promptly offered, the duty may be applied to the whole EU (Art 4(3) Anti-dumping Regulation; Art 9(3) Subsidies Regulation). The duty is collected by the Member States separately from customs duties, taxes and other charges imposed on imports (Art 14(1) Anti-dumping Regulation; Art 24(1) Subsidies Regulation).

[5.190] Refund of Duty

Where the importer can show that the duty applied exceeds the dumping margin or the amount of the subsidy, the excess must be refunded (Art

11(8) Anti-dumping Regulation; Art 21(1) Subsidies Regulation). The application for refund is made through the Member State on whose territory the goods were entered for EU consumption within 6 months of the determination of the amount of the duty or the decision definitively to collect the provisional duty (Art 11(8) Anti-dumping Regulation; Art 21(2) Subsidies Regulation).

[5.195] Review by the Council

The need for the continuation of the anti-dumping or countervailing duty may be reviewed on the initiative of the Commission or at the request of a Member State. After at least 1 year has passed since its imposition, the duty may also be reviewed upon a request by the exporter, importer, Community producers, or the country of origin or export (Art 11(3) Anti-dumping Regulation; Art 19(1) Subsidies Regulation).

The request for review must contain sufficient evidence that the continuation of the duty is no longer necessary to offset the dumping or subsidy and/or that the injury would be unlikely to continue or occur again if the duty was removed (Art 11(3) Anti-dumping Regulation; Art 19(2) Subsidies Regulation). When conducting a review the possibility that expiry of a duty may lead to renewed injury or threat of injury must be considered. See *Commission v NTN Corporation* (C-245/95 P) [1998] ECR I-401 at [41].

[5.200] Judicial Review of Findings

The EU courts do not subject anti-dumping decisions to an exacting standard of review, but recognise that the EU institutions have a "wide discretion" in this area. See *Shanghai Bicycle Corporation v Council* (T-170/94) [1997] ECR II-1383 at [63]; *Mukand Ltd v Council* (T-58/99) [2001] ECR II-2521 at [38]; [2002] 3 CMLR 13 (p 336). The breadth of this discretion is a consequence of the complicated economic, legal and political considerations that arise in the trade protection context. See *Miwon Co Ltd v Council* (T-51/96) [2000] ECR II-1841 at [94]; *Arne Mathisen AS v Council* (T-340/99) [2002] ECR II-2905 at [53].

In *Thai Bicycle Industry & Co Ltd v Council* (T-118/96) [1998] ECR II-2991 the Court stated that its review "must be limited to verifying whether the relevant procedural rules have been complied with, whether the facts on which the contested choice is based have been accurately stated and whether there has been a manifest error of assessment of the facts or a misuse of power" (at [33]). See similarly, *Rotexchemie v Hauptzollamt Hamburg-Waltershof* (C-26/96) [1997] ECR I-2817 at [11]; *Euroalliages v Commission* (T-132/01) [2003] ECR II-2359 at [49].

In such a review, the Court is required to exercise its normal powers of review over the exercise of a discretion by an EU institution, even though the Court has no power under the Regulation to intervene in the exercise of the discretion of the EU authorities. See *Timex Corporation v Council* (264/82) [1985] ECR 849 at [16]; [1985] 3 CMLR 550.

In *EEC Seed Crushers' and Oil Processors' Federation (FEDIOL) v Commission* (191/82) [1983] ECR 2913; [1984] 3 CMLR 244 the Court summarized its view regarding an applicant's right to challenge anti-dumping procedures:

> complainants . . . have a right to bring an action where it is alleged that the Community authorities have disregarded rights which have been recognized specifically in the regulation, namely the right to lodge a complaint, the right, which is inherent in the aforementioned right, to have that complaint considered by the Commission with proper care and according to the procedure provided for, the right to receive information within the limits set by the regulation and finally, if the Commission decides not to proceed with the complaint, the right to receive information comprising at the least the explanations guaranteed by . . . the regulation (at [28]).

In *Timex Corporation v Council* (264/82) [1985] ECR 849; [1985] 3 CMLR 550 the Court held that a manufacturer had standing to challenge a regulation imposing anti-dumping duties that was of direct and individual concern to it (at [15]–[16]). The rejection by the Commission of undertakings offered by an exporter does not constitute a measure having any binding legal effects affecting an applicant, because the Commission could decide to revoke its decision or the Council may decide not to impose an anti-dumping duty. Such a rejection is a step leading to the final decision and as such is not a reviewable act. See *Nashua Corporation v Council* (C-133/87) [1990] ECR I-719 at [9]; [1990] 2 CMLR 6; *Gestetner Holdings Plc v Council of Ministers* (C-156/87) [1990] ECR I-781 at [8]; [1990] 1 CMLR 820.

In *Allied Corporation v Commission* (239/82) [1984] ECR 1005; [1985] 3 CMLR 572 the Court held that measures imposing anti-dumping duties are liable to be of direct and individual concern to the producers and exporters identified in the measures or that were affected by the investigation (at [12]). See similarly, *Allied Corporation v Council of Ministers* (53/83) [1985] ECR 1621 at [4]; [1986] 3 CMLR 605; *Sinochem Heilongjiang v Council* (T-161/94) [1996] ECR II-695 at [46]; [1997] 3 CMLR 214; *Shanghai Bicycle Corporation v Council* (T-170/94) [1997] ECR II-1383 at [36]; *Euromin v Council* (T-597/97) [2000] ECR II-2419 at [45].

Similarly, measures imposing anti-dumping duties are liable to be of direct and individual concern to specific producers or exporters where the regulation does not lay down general rules that apply to a whole group of producers or exporters but imposes different anti-dumping duties upon each individual. But in such a case only the provisions that specifically affect the individual will be of direct and individual concern to that individual producer or exporter. See *NTN Toyo Bearing Co Ltd v Council* (240/84) [1987] ECR 1809 at [6]–[7]; [1989] 2 CMLR 76; *Gestetner Holdings Plc v Council of Ministers* (C-156/87) [1990] ECR I-781 at [12]; [1990] 1 CMLR 820; *Rendo NV v Commission* (T-16/91) [1992] ECR II-2417 at [73]; *Nachi Europe GmbH v Hauptzollamt Krefeld* (C-239/99) [2001] ECR I-1197 at [22].

It therefore follows that one of the persons so affected could not bring an action to annul the whole Regulation. Importers who are associated with an exporter may also have the required direct and individual concern, particularly where the export prices have been calculated by reference to the selling prices of the relevant goods within the EU. See *Allied Corporation v Commission* (239/82) [1984] ECR 1005 at [15]; [1985] 3 CMLR 572; *Canon Inc v Council* (277/85) [1988] ECR 5731 at [8]; [1989] 1 CMLR 915; *British Shoe Corporation Footwear Supplies Ltd v Council* (T-598/97) [2002] ECR II-1155 at [47]; [2002] 2 CMLR 7 (p 110). The reviewability of legal acts is discussed in more detail in Chapter 11.

[5.205] Conclusion

Under the TFEU the EU pursues a common commercial policy. Once an international agreement enters into force, it becomes an integral part of EU law. The EU may conclude agreements where its founding Treaties so authorise or where the conclusion of an agreement is necessary to achieve one of the objectives referred to in the Treaties, or is provided for in a legally binding Union act or is likely to affect common rules or alter their scope.

Provisions against the dumping of goods by Non-member States have been adopted as part of the common commercial policy. If the export price is below the normal price, the goods are considered to be dumped. If the dumped goods are causing or threatening to cause injury, an anti-dumping duty may be imposed.

The normal price or value of the goods is usually based on the prices payable in the ordinary course of trade by independent customers in the exporting country. Where there is no domestic market, the normal value will be the price of the goods as exported to a third market or the constructed price. The constructed price is calculated by adding to the cost of production a reasonable amount for selling, general and administrative costs and for profits. The export price is usually the price paid for the product by the EU importer, although in some circumstances a constructed export price will be used.

If goods have been the subject of a direct or indirect subsidy in the country of manufacture, a countervailing duty may be imposed to offset the effect of the subsidy, where the subsidy causes injury in the EU. A subsidy is (1) a financial contribution by government in the country of origin or any form of income or price support (2) by which a benefit is conferred. Countervailable duties may only be applied to subsidies that are specific to an enterprise or industry.

Many legal issues are common to both dumping and subsidies. The dumped or subsidised imports must be causing or threatening to cause material injury to an established Community industry or materially retarding the establishment of such an industry. "Community industry" includes the producers of the Union who make the products or those producers whose collective output accounts for a major proportion of the production of those goods within the EU. There are two exceptions to this definition: related producers and the division of the EU into regional markets.

A proceeding may be terminated on the acceptance of an undertaking by a producer or exporter. The Commission only takes remedial measures if they are in the overall interest of the Union. Countervailing or anti-dumping duties are applied by Regulation. The Commission may impose a provisional duty if the interests of the Union require the abatement of the injury during the proceeding. Once dumping (or a subsidy) and injury have been established, if the interests of the EU require intervention, the Council must apply a definitive duty. The EU courts do not subject anti-dumping decisions to an exacting standard of review, but recognise that the EU institutions have a wide discretion in this area.

Further Reading

Adamantopoulos, Kostantinos and Maria Pereyra-Friedrichsen. *EU Anti-subsidy Law & Practice* (2nd ed, London: Sweet & Maxwell, 2007).

Giannakopoulos, Themistoklis K. *A Concise Guide to the EU Anti-dumping/Anti-subsidies Procedures* (Alphen aan den Rijn: Kluwer, 2006).

Dominik, Lasok. *The Trade and Customs Law of the European Union* (3rd ed, London: Kluwer Law International, 1998), Chapter 14.

Ostoni, Lucia. "Anti-dumping Circumvention in the EU and the US: Is There a Future for Multilateral Provisions Under the WTO?" (2005) 10 *Fordham Journal of Corporate and Financial Law* 407.

Van Bael, Ivo and Jean-François Bellis. *Anti-dumping and Other Trade Protection Laws of the EC* (4th ed, The Hague: Kluwer, 2004).

Vermulst, Edwin. "The 10 Major Problems with the Anti-dumping Instrument in the European Community" (2005) 39 *Journal of World Trade* 105.

Wenig, Harald. "The European Community's Anti-dumping System: Salient Features" (2005) 39 *Journal of World Trade* 787.

Chapter 6
Competition Law

[6.05] Introduction

Private agreements or arrangements between undertakings may interfere with interstate trade by creating divisions in the European Union. For example, undertakings may agree to the allocation of interstate markets in order to avoid having to compete with one another in these markets. In such cases, the undertakings concerned may face legal action under EU competition rules.

The competition law of the EU is found in Arts 101–109 TFEU. Section 1 (Arts 101–106) deals with competition rules applicable to undertakings. Arts 101 and 102 contain the basic rules of competition. Arts 103–106 prescribe the implementation and administration of these rules. Section 2 (Arts 107–109) concerns aid granted to undertakings by EU Member States.

The competition rules in Arts 101 and 102 do not deal with governmental "measures" but are directed at private restrictive agreements or practices by undertakings. See *Criminal Proceedings Against Asjes* (209/84) [1986] ECR I-1425 at [71]; [1986] 3 CMLR 173; *Vereniging van Vlaamse Reis bureaus v Sociale Dienst van de Plaatselijke en Gewestelijke Overheids-diensten* (311/85) [1987] ECR 3801 at [10]; [1989] 4 CMLR 213. These rules apply only to voluntary conduct by undertakings, not to conduct that is compelled by national law. See *Commission v Ladbroke Racing Ltd* (C-359/95 P) [1997] ECR I-6265 at [33]; [1998] 4 CMLR 27; *Altair Chimica SpA v ENEL Distribuzione SpA* (C-207/01) [2003] ECR I-8875 at [30]; [2003] 5 CMLR 17 (p 867).

The competition law provisions do have an important consequence for national law. Member States may not take measures that could render ineffective the competition rules that apply to undertakings. See *Criminal Proceedings Against Corbeau* (C-320/91) [1993] ECR I-2533 at [11]; [1995] 4 CMLR 621; *Arduino v Compagnia Assicuratrice RAS SpA* (C-35/99) [2002] ECR I-1529 at [34]; [2002] 4 CMLR 25 (p 866); *Cipolla v Fazari* (C-94/04) [2006] ECR I-11421 at [46]; [2007] 4 CMLR 8 (p 286).

G. Moens, J. Trone, *Commercial Law of the European Union*,
Ius Gentium: Comparative Perspectives on Law and Justice 4,
DOI 10.1007/978-90-481-8774-4_6,

The EU has exclusive competence to establish "the competition rules necessary for the functioning of the internal market" (Art 3(1)(b) TEU). A Protocol to the TFEU commits the EU to ensuring undistorted competition: "the internal market... includes a system ensuring that competition is not distorted.... To this end, the Union shall, if necessary, take action under the provisions of the Treaties" (Protocol (No 27) on the Internal Market and Competition).

[6.10] Direct Effect of the Competition Rules

The ECJ has held that "[a]s the prohibitions of Arts 85(1) and 86 [now Art 101(1) and 102] tend by their very nature to produce direct effects in relations between individuals, these articles create direct rights in respect of the individuals concerned which the national courts must safeguard". See *Belgische Radio en Televisie v SV Sabam* (127/73) [1974] ECR 51 at [16]; [1974] 2 CMLR 238; see similarly, *Guérin Automobiles v Commission* (C-282/95 P) [1997] ECR I-1503 at [39]; [1997] 5 CMLR 447; *Courage Ltd v Crehan* (C-453/99) [2001] ECR I-6297 at [23]; [2001] 5 CMLR 28 (p 1058); *Masterfoods Ltd v HB Ice Cream Ltd* (C-344/98) [2000] ECR I-11369 at [47]; [2001] 4 CMLR 14 (p 449); *Manfredi v Lloyd Adriatico Assicurazioni SpA* (C-295/04) [2006] ECR I-6619 at [39]; [2006] 5 CMLR 17 (p 980).

[6.15] Art 101 TFEU

The aim of EU competition law is to prevent restrictive trade practices that are likely to interfere with trade between Member States or lead to a distortion of competition in the Union. To that end, Art 101(1) TFEU declares that certain restrictive trade practices are incompatible with the internal market, namely "all agreements between undertakings, decisions by associations of undertakings and concerted practices which may affect trade between Member States and which have as their object or effect the prevention, restriction or distortion of competition within the internal market".

The "agreements" referred to in Art 101 include horizontal and vertical agreements. Horizontal agreements are agreements between companies at the same level of commercial activity, namely competitors. Vertical agreements involve arrangements between manufacturers and the distributors of their goods. Art 101(1) applies to the supply of both goods and services.

[6.20] Voidness of Prohibited Agreements

Agreements prohibited by Art 101(1) TFEU are "automatically void" by virtue of Art 101(2). The void agreement has no effect between the parties and may not be set up against third parties. See *Beguelin Import Co v SA GL Import-Export* (22/71) [1971] ECR 949 at [29]; [1972] CMLR 81; *Société de Vente de Ciments et Betons de L'Est SA v Kerpen & Kerpen GmbH* (319/82) [1983] ECR 4173 at [11]; [1985] 1 CMLR 511; *Courage Ltd v Crehan* (C-453/99) [2001] ECR I-6297 at [22]; [2001] 5 CMLR 28 (p 1058); *Manfredi v Lloyd Adriatico Assicurazioni SpA* (C-295/04) [2006] ECR I-6619 at [57]; [2006] 5 CMLR 17 (p 980).

Only the provisions of the impugned agreement or practice that violate Art 101(1) are void. Where part of an agreement is void because it is incompatible with Art 101 TFEU, the validity of the remainder of the agreement falls to be considered under national law. See *Société de Vente de Ciments et Betons de L'Est SA v Kerpen & Kerpen GmbH* (319/82) [1983] ECR 4173 at [11]–[12]; [1985] 1 CMLR 511; *VAG France SA v Établissements Magne SA* (10/86) [1986] ECR 4071 at [14]–[15]; [1988] 4 CMLR 98. The whole agreement will be void if the void parts are unable to be severed from the remainder of the agreement. See *Delimitis v Henninger Brau AG* (C-234/89) [1991] ECR I-935 at [40]; [1992] 5 CMLR 210; *CEPSA Estaciones de Servicio SA v LV Tobar e Hijos SL* (C-279/06) [2008] ECR I-6681 at [78]; [2008] 5 CMLR 19 (p 1327). See generally, Mario Libertini and Maria Rosaria Maugeri, "Infringement of Competition Law and Invalidity of Contracts" (2005) 1 *European Review of Contract Law* 250.

A party to a restrictive agreement can rely on the breach of Art 101 TFEU by the agreement. Recognising such a right of action improves the enforcement of EU competition law since restrictive agreements are usually kept secret. See *Courage Ltd v Crehan* (C-453/99) [2001] ECR I-6297 at [24], [27]; [2001] 5 CMLR 28 (p 1058).

[6.25] Concept of an "Undertaking"

The TFEU does not define the concept of an "undertaking" for the purposes of the competition rules. The Court has held that the term "undertaking" "encompasses every entity engaged in an economic activity, regardless of the legal status of the entity and the way in which it is financed." See *Höfner v Macrotron GmbH* (C-41/90) [1991] ECR I-1979 at [21]; [1993] 4 CMLR 306; see similarly, *Federación Española de Empresas de Tecnología Sanitaria (FENIN) v Commission* (C-205/03 P) [2006] ECR I-6295 at [25]; [2006] 5 CMLR 7 (p 559); *Autorità Garante della Concorrenza e del Mercato v Ente Tabacchi Italiani—ETI SpA* (C-280/06) [2007] ECR I-10893 at [38]; [2008] 4 CMLR 11 (p 277). An organisation that does not engage in an economic activity is not an undertaking. See *Wouters v Algemene Raad van de Nederlandse Orde van Advocaten* (C-309/99) [2002] ECR I-1577 at [112]; [2002] 4 CMLR 27 (p 913).

An economic activity is "any activity consisting in offering goods and services on a given market". See *Re Customs Agents: Commission v Italy* (C-35/96) [1998] ECR I-3851 at [36]; [1998] 5 CMLR 889; *Federación Española de Empresas de Tecnología Sanitaria (FENIN) v Commission* (C-205/03 P) [2006] ECR I-6295 at [25]; [2006] 5 CMLR 7 (p 559); *Motosykletistiki Omospondia Ellados NPID (MOTOE) v Dimosio* (C-49/07) [2008] ECR I-4863 at [22]; [2008] 5 CMLR 11 (p 790).

The concept of economic activity has been widely construed. For example, it includes employment procurement. See *Höfner v Macrotron GmbH* (C-41/90) [1991] ECR I-1979 at [21]–[22]; [1993] 4 CMLR 306. It also includes the legal services of the national bar. See *Wouters v Algemene Raad van de Nederlandse Orde van Advocaten* (C-309/99) [2002] ECR I-1577 at [48]–[49]; [2002] 4 CMLR 27 (p 913).

By contrast, sickness funds that had "an exclusively social function" were not undertakings since they were wholly non-profit and benefits were determined by statute and not by contributions. See *Poucet v Assurances Générales de France* (C-159/91) [1993] ECR I-637 at [18]–[19]; *AOK Bundesverband v Ichthyol-Gesellschaft Cordes* (C-264/01) [2004] ECR I-2493 at [51]–[54]; [2004] 4 CMLR 22 (p 1261). A private body that was entrusted by the state with surveillance of environmental pollution offences was not an undertaking since such a responsibility was generally one of a public authority and was not of an economic character. See *Diego Calì & Figli Srl v Servizi Ecologici Porto di Genova (SEPG)* (C-343/95) [1997] ECR I-1547 at [23]; [1997] 5 CMLR 484.

A body that is vested with public powers may be an undertaking in relation to its economic activities. In *Motosykletistiki Omospondia Ellados Npid v Dimosio* (C-49/07) [2008] ECR I-4863; [2008] 5 CMLR 11 (p 790) Greek law provided that the holding of motorcycle competitions required authorization by ELPA, a non-profit national body representing the International Motorcycling Federation (at [3]). MOTOE was an association of motorcycling clubs (at [4]). MOTOE applied for authorization to hold a competition (at [5]). ELPA did not consent to the competition (at [10]).

The Court held that the exercise of public power is not an activity of an economic nature that would fall under the competition rules (at [24]). However, a body that is vested with public powers may fall under the competition rules in relation of any of its activities that are of an economic nature (at [25]). The role of ELPA in authorizing competitions must be distinguished from its economic activities in organizing motorcycling events. ELPA thus could be an undertaking in relation to its economic activities (at [26]). The fact that ELPA's economic activities had a non-profit intent did not preclude it from being an undertaking, because its economic activities were in competition with those of profit-making entities (at [27]). ELPA was thus an undertaking under Art 82 EC (Art 101 TFEU) (at [29]). The law of competition as it applies to governmental undertakings is discussed in Chapter 8.

[6.30] Single Economic Unit

Art 101 TFEU does not apply to companies that form a single economic unit in which the subsidiary has no independence to formulate its strategic course of action and any arrangements between these companies are concerned with the allocation of tactical tasks. See *Centrafarm BV v Sterling Drug Inc* (15/74) [1974] ECR 1147 at [41]; [1974] 2 CMLR 480; *Viho Europe BV v Commission* (C-73/95 P) [1996] ECR I-5457 at [16]–[17]; [1997] 4 CMLR 419; *Micro Leader Business v Commission* (T-198/98) [1999] ECR II-3989 at [38].

In *Viho Europe BV v Commission* (C-73/95 P) [1996] ECR I-5457; [1997] 4 CMLR 419 a manufacturer of pens (Parker) sold its products through subsidiaries and independent distributors (at [4]). An office equipment company argued that Parker prohibited its subsidiaries and distributors from exporting its products from their national territories, which divided the EU into a series of national markets (at [5], [7]). The subsidiaries were fully owned by Parker. Sales and marketing by the subsidiaries were directed by a team appointed by Parker (at [15]). The Court held that Parker and its subsidiaries constituted a single economic unit (at [16]). Parker's policy of dividing the national markets thus did not infringe Art 101 TFEU, though it could potentially infringe Art 102 TFEU if the conditions set out in that provision were satisfied (at [17]). (Art 102 TFEU deals with abuse of a dominant position. It is discussed at para [6.105] of this chapter).

An undertaking that is resident in a non-member state but has a subsidiary in a Member State that must act according to its instruction is regarded as being resident in the European Union. Such an undertaking is subject to EU competition law because it and its subsidiary are treated as one economic entity. Agreements between the subsidiary and its parent company do not come within the ambit of Art 101(1) TFEU because they are part of the same economic entity.

[6.35] Associations of Undertakings

Where the rules, decisions and behaviour of an association of undertakings, typically an association of traders, impinge upon the trading behaviour of the members, Art 101 TFEU will be applicable. See *NV IAZ International Belgium SA v Commission* (96/82) [1983] ECR 3369 at [20]; [1984] 3 CMLR 276; *Fédération nationale de la coopération bétail and viande*

(FNCBV) v Commission (T-217/03) [2006] ECR II-4987 at [49]; [2005] 5 CMLR 12 (p 465), appeal dismissed sub nom *Coop de France bétail et viande v Commission* (C-101/07 P) [2008] ECR I-10193; [2009] 4 CMLR 15 (p 743). It is irrelevant that the association of undertakings does not trade as it is a non-profit undertaking. Art 101 is similarly applicable to an association which is itself an association of associations. See *Piau v Commission* (T-193/02) [2005] ECR II-209 at [69]; appeal dismissed (C-171/05 P) [2006] ECR I-37*.

[6.40] Undertakings Situated Outside the EU

Undertakings that are situated outside the Union may be subject to EU competition rules. For example, if the behaviour is that of a subsidiary located within the Union, the parent company will be subject to EU law even though the parent company is located outside the Union. See *Imperial Chemical Industries Ltd v Commission* (48/69) [1972] ECR 619 at [131]–[132], [137], [140]–[141]; [1972] CMLR 557.

In *Beguelin Import Co v SA GL Import-Export* (22/71) [1971] ECR 949; [1972] CMLR 81 the Court held that Art 85 EC (Art 101 TFEU) does not apply to a parent-subsidiary relationship because the subsidiary, "although having separate legal personality, enjoys no economic independence" (at [8]). See similarly, *Bodson v SA Pompes funèbres des régions libérées* (30/87) [1988] ECR 2479 at [19]–[20]; [1989] 4 CMLR 984; *Compagnie Maritime Belge Transports SA v Commission* (C-395/96 P) [2000] ECR I-1365 at [35]; [2000] 4 CMLR 1076. The Court has thus applied the "economic entity" approach.

Actual Control Test

The test applied by the Court is whether the parent company is actually controlling the subsidiary and that control has been the cause of the impugned behaviour. See *Europemballage Corporation v Commission* (6/72) [1973] ECR 215 at [15]; [1973] CMLR 199; *Metsä-Serla Oyj v Commission* (C-294/98 P) [2000] ECR I-10065 at [27]; *Stora Kopparbergs Bergslags AB v Commission* (C-286/98 P) [2000] ECR I-9925 at [26]; [2001] 4 CMLR 12 (p 370); *Siderúrgica Aristrain Madrid SL v Commission* (C-96/99 P) [2003] ECR I-11005 at [96]; *Dansk Rørindustri v Commission* (C-13/02 P) [2005] ECR I-5425 at [117]; [2005] 5 CMLR 17 (p 796).

Effects Theory

The "effects theory" holds that EU competition rules may be invoked where the behaviour of an undertaking situated outside the EU would have a direct, immediate, reasonably foreseeable and substantial effect upon competition within the Union. The ECJ adopted this theory in *Re Wood Pulp Cartel: A Ahlström Osakeyhtiö v Commission* (89/85) [1988] ECR 5193; [1988] 4 CMLR 901.

In that case the Commission had assumed jurisdiction under the rules of competition over thirty-six undertakings, located outside the Community. The ECJ held that the decisive factor in applying the competition rules to agreements, decisions or concerted practices was the place of their implementation as opposed to the place of formation. The Court stated that where "wood pulp producers established in those countries sell directly to purchasers established in the Community and engage in price competition in order to win orders from those customers, that constitutes competition within the common market" (at [12]).

The Court concluded: "where those producers concert on the prices to be charged to their customers in the Community and put that concertation into effect by selling at prices which are actually co-ordinated, they are taking part in concertation which has the object and effect of restricting competition within the common market within the meaning of" Art 85 EC (Art 101 TFEU) (at [13]). The Court added that "[i]f the applicability of prohibitions laid down under competition law were made to depend on the place where the agreement, decision or concerted practice was formed, the result would obviously be to give undertakings an easy means of evading those prohibitions. The decisive factor is therefore the place where it is implemented" (at [16]). See similarly, *Atlantic Container Line AB v Commission* (T-395/94) [2002] ECR II-875 at [72].

It would therefore appear that either the economic entity approach or the effects theory will be adequate to ground jurisdiction for the purposes of EU competition law.

[6.45] Concept of "Agreement"

The ECJ has held that an agreement "arises from an expression, by the participating undertakings, of their joint intention to conduct themselves on the market in a specific way". See *Commission v Anic Partecipazioni SpA* (C-49/92 P) [1999] ECR I-4125 at [130]; [2001] 4 CMLR 17 (p 602); see similarly, *Bayerische Hypo- und Vereinsbank AG v Commission* (T-56/02) [2004] ECR II-3495 at [59]; [2004] 5 CMLR 29 (p 1592); *Brasserie Nationale SA v Commission* (T-49/02) [2005] ECR II-3033 at [118]; *BPB plc v Commission* (T-53/03) [2008] ECR II-1333 at [79].

Private arrangements that have been held to constitute an "agreement" for the purposes of Art 101 TFEU include:

- a non-binding agreement which amounts to a faithful expression of the intention of the parties: *Tréfileurope Sales SARL v Commission*

(T-141/89) [1995] ECR II-791 at [96]; *HFB Holding für Fernwärmetechnik Beteiligungsgesellschaft mbH & Co KG v Commission* (T-9/99) [2002] ECR II-1487 at [200]; appeal dismissed (C-189/02 P) [2005] ECR I-5425; [2005] 5 CMLR 17 (p 796);
- an oral agreement: *Tepea BV v Commission* (28/77) [1978] ECR 1391 at [41]; [1978] 3 CMLR 392; *Dunlop Slazenger International Ltd v Commission* (T-43/92) [1994] ECR II-441 at [54];
- an agreement between two trading associations made on behalf of their members: *Vereniging ter Bevordering van het Vlaamse Boekwezen (VBVB) v Commission* (43/82) [1984] ECR 19 at [45]; [1985] 1 CMLR 27;
- common intentions between undertakings in relation to price initiatives and sales volume: *BASF AG v Commission* (T-4/89) [1991] ECR II-1523 at [238]; *SA Hercules Chemicals NV v Commission* (T-7/89) [1991] ECR II-1711 at [256]; appeal dismissed (C-51/92 P) [1999] ECR I-4235; [1999] 5 CMLR 976;
- assent by a member undertaking to the decision of an association of undertakings: *Heintz van Landewijck Sarl v Commission* (209/78) [1980] ECR 3125 at [85]–[86]; [1981] 3 CMLR 134; and
- a compromise reached as the result of litigation: *BAT Cigaretten-Fabriken GmbH v Commission* (35/83) [1985] ECR 363 at [33]; [1985] 2 CMLR 470.

A party that participates in meetings at which an anti-competitive agreement was reached takes part in the agreement unless it expresses its opposition to the anti-competitive agreement. That tacit approval amounts to passive participation in the agreement. See *Aalborg Portland A/S v Commission* (C-204/00 P) [2004] ECR I-123 at [81]; [2005] 4 CMLR 4 (p 251); *Dansk Rørindustri v Commission* (C-13/02 P) [2005] ECR I-5425 at [142]–[143]; [2005] 5 CMLR 17 (p 796); *Archer Daniels Midland Co v Commission* (C-510/06 P) [2009] 4 CMLR 20 (p 889) at [119].

[6.50] Unilateral Acts

A unilateral act or policy does not constitute an "agreement", which requires the assent of more than one party. In *Bayer AG v Commission* (C-2/01 P) [2004] ECR I-23; [2004] 4 CMLR 13 (p 653) Bayer manufactured the pharmaceutical drug Adalat. Bayer operated through national subsidiaries in EU Member States. The price of Adalat was fixed by the government in most Member States. The price of the drug was considerably lower in Spain and France than in the United Kingdom. Spanish and French wholesalers exported the drug to the United Kingdom. Sales of the drug by the United Kingdom subsidiary fell drastically. Bayer then stopped supplying the large orders of the Spanish and French wholesalers (at [2]). Bayer reduced the orders supplied to wholesalers if they exported the drug (at [5]).

The issue for the Court was whether a unilateral measure applied by one party in a continuing commercial relationship was able to constitute an "agreement" (at [98]). The Court held that a policy that was unilaterally adopted by one party and which did not require the assistance of others could not constitute an "agreement" (at [101]). An agreement could be reached by tacit acceptance where both parties agreed to jointly achieve an anti-competitive goal (at [102]).

The co-existence of an agreement that is neutral to competition and a unilateral anti-competitive policy does not constitute an "agreement". The mere fact that the manufacturer's unilateral measure occurred in the context of a continuing commercial relationship with the wholesalers did not justify the conclusion that an "agreement" had been reached (at [141]).

In *Commission v Volkswagen AG* (C-74/04 P) [2006] ECR I-6585; [2008] 4 CMLR 16 (p 1297) Volkswagen cars were sold by authorised dealers (at [3]). The dealership agreements provided that dealers would obey instructions issued by Volkswagen. Recommendations concerning prices were non-binding (at [4]). The Commission alleged that Volkswagen had agreed with its German dealers to enforce price discipline for one of the manufacturer's models (at [6]).

The Court held that a call by a car manufacturer to its dealers could amount to an "agreement" if there is a "concurrence of wills" between the manufacturer and the individual dealers (at [36]). An apparently unilateral act would constitute an "agreement" if it gave rise to a concurrence of wills between more than one party (at [37]). The will of the parties could result from the "tacit acquiescence" of the dealers to a call by the manufacturer (at [39]). The Commission bears the onus of proving that there was such a concurrence of wills (at [36], [38]). It was possible that a call by the manufacturer that violated competition law could be authorised by apparently neutral provisions in the dealership agreement (at [44], [53]). However, the calls in this case did not constitute an "agreement" (at [54]).

[6.55] Types of Prohibited Agreements

Art 101(1) TFEU offers examples of agreements that are likely to distort competition in the European Union. They include price fixing between competitors, market manipulation or restriction, discrimination in trading terms, agreements on market shares or production quotas, and tie-in clauses that oblige a buyer of one product or service to buy another product or service which is not connected to the first by nature of its commercial usage. As will be seen in the following section, exclusive purchasing agreements have the potential to infringe Art 101(1) TFEU.

[6.60] Exclusive Purchasing Agreements

In *Neste Markkinointi Oy v Yötuuli Ky* (C-214/99) [2000] ECR I-11121; [2001] 4 CMLR 27 (p 993) Yötuuli was a member of Neste's distribution chain pursuant to a contract. Under the agreement Yötuuli exclusively purchased and sold Neste's petrol in its service stations (at [3], [5]). The contract had a 10 year term. After that time a party could terminate the agreement with 12 months notice (at [4]). Yötuuli terminated the contract without the 12 months notice (at [6]–[7]). Neste brought an action seeking compensation for losses resulting from Yötuuli's termination without the required notice (at [7]). Yötuuli argued that the action should be dismissed since the agreement contained an exclusive purchasing clause that violated Art 85(1) EC (Art 101(1) TFEU) (at [8]).

The Court held that the effects of the clause must be assessed in the economic and legal context of the contract, including any interaction with other restrictive agreements. The Court must examine the effect of the clause upon the prospects of competitors to enter the market or expand their market share (at [25]). Agreements that individually make a minor contribution to closing off the market do not fall under Art 101(1) TFEU. Where the duration of the contract is "manifestly excessive" in comparison to the average length of contracts on the market in question, the contract falls under Art 101(1) TFEU (at [27]).

An exclusive purchasing agreement for petrol is different from those for other products because only one brand of petrol is sold in a petrol station (at [31]). The most important consideration is thus the duration of the agreement rather than the exclusive purchasing obligation itself (at [32]). Long fixed term contracts are more likely to limit market access than would short term contracts (at [33]). A notice period of 12 months provides reasonable protection for the interests of the parties and reduces the anti-competitive effects of the agreement (at [35]). Contracts that may be terminated with 12 months notice were a small proportion of all the exclusive purchasing agreements concluded by Neste and did not make a significant contribution to closing off the market (at [36]).

[6.65] Object of the Agreement

Art 101(1) TFEU applies to agreements "which have as their object or effect the prevention, restriction or distortion of competition within the internal market". The effect of the agreement upon competition must be assessed in both its economic and legal context. See *Unilever Bestfoods (Ireland) Ltd v Commission* (C-552/03 P) [2006] ECR I-9091 at [53]–[54]; [2006] 5 CMLR 27 (p 1494). The agreement is examined in its economic context in order to determine whether its object or effect is to restrict competition.

"Competition" in the context of Art 101(1) means the competition which would occur if the agreement did not exist. See *Société Technique Miniére v Maschinenbau Ulm GmbH* (56/65) [1966] ECR 235 at 250; [1966] CMLR 357 at 375; *John Deere Ltd v Commission* (C-7/95 P) [1998] ECR I-3111 at [76]; [1998] 5 CMLR 311; *New Holland Ford Ltd v Commission* (C-8/95 P) [1998] ECR I-3175 at [90]; *General Motors BV v Commission* (C-551/03 P) [2006] ECR I-3173 at [72]; [2006] 5 CMLR 1 (p 1).

For the purpose of testing the existence of competition, it is not necessary to consider the actual effect of the agreement. In *Établissements Consten SàRL v Commission* (56/64) [1966] ECR 299; [1966] CMLR 418 the Court held that "there is no need to take account of the concrete effects of an agreement once it appears that it has as its object the prevention, restriction or distortion of competition" (at ECR 342; CMLR 473). See similarly, *Commission v Anic Partecipazioni SpA* (C-49/92 P) [1999] ECR I-4125 at [99]; [2001] 4 CMLR 17 (p 602); *Hüls AG v Commission* (C-199/92 P) [1999] ECR I-4287 at [178]; [1999] 5 CMLR 1016; *Montecatini SpA v Commission* (C-235/92 P) [1999] ECR I-4539 at [122]; [2001] 4 CMLR 18 (p 691); *Limburgse Vinyl Maatschappij v Commission* (C-238/99 P) [2002] ECR I-8375 at [491]; [2003] 4 CMLR 10 (p 397).

The agreement may therefore be held to be incompatible with Art 101(1) TFEU even before the agreement comes into effect or if the attempt to restrict competition fails. If the intended effect of the agreement does not reveal an attempt to restrict competition then the operation of the agreement is examined to test its actual effect upon competition.

[6.70] Prevention, Restriction or Distortion

The terms "prevention, restriction or distortion" in Art 101(1) TFEU overlap. It is not necessary to inquire which term most accurately describes the impugned agreement or practice. The agreement need not necessarily prevent, restrict or distort competition between the parties to be incompatible with Art 101(1). If an agreement affects a third party then it may also be incompatible with that Article.

Any clause in a contract of sale which restricts the freedom of the purchaser in using the goods in the purchaser's unfettered economic interest is a restriction of competition. See *Société de Vente de Ciments et Betons de L'Est SA v Kerpen & Kerpen GmbH* (319/82) [1983] ECR 4173 at [6]; [1985] 1 CMLR 511.

[6.75] Effect upon Trade Between Member States

The agreement or practice must affect trade between Member States in order to fall within Art 101(1) TFEU. "Trade" has a very wide meaning in EU competition law. The Commission has stated that trade includes "all forms of economic activity including establishment". See *Decision COMP/A.37.507/F3 AstraZeneca*, 15 June 2005 at [864], available at http://ec.europa.eu/competition/antitrust/cases/index.html.

For example, trade has been held to include:

- banking: *Züchner v Bayerische Vereinsbank AG* (172/80) [1981] ECR 2021 at [18]; [1982] 1 CMLR 313;
- insurance: *Decision 85/75 Re Fire Insurance* OJ L 35, 7.2.1985, p 20 at [22]; [1985] 3 CMLR 246; and
- telecommunications: *Italy v Commission* (41/83) [1985] ECR 873 at [18]; [1985] 2 CMLR 368.

The requirement that the agreement affects trade between Member States is a limiting factor and as such sets the boundary between EU and national competition law. Conduct which affects the trade only within a single Member State is covered by the law of that Member State. See *Hugin Kassaregister AB v Commission* (22/78) [1979] ECR 1869 at [17]; [1979] 3 CMLR 345.

There must be a perceptible effect, actual or potential, on trade between Member States. See *Criminal Proceedings Against Morais* (C-60/91) [1992] ECR I-2085 at [12]; [1992] 2 CMLR 533. The effect on trade must have the potential to impair the operation of the internal market. It is not necessary that an agreement must have actually affected trade in order to violate Art 101(1) TFEU. It is only necessary that the agreement have that potential. See *Ferriere Nord SpA v Commission* (C-219/95 P) [1997] ECR I-4411 at [19]; [1997] 5 CMLR 575; *Bagnasco v Banca Popolare di Novara soc coop arl (BNP)* (C-215/96) [1999] ECR I-135 at [48]; [1999] 4 CMLR 624. Arrangements that operate in one State are still subject to EU competition law if they impede the importation of goods from other Member States.

What is particularly important "is whether the agreement is capable of constituting a threat, either direct or indirect, actual or potential, to freedom of trade between Member States in a manner which might harm the attainment of the objectives of a single market between States". See *Établissements Consten SàRL v Commission* (56/64) [1966] ECR 299 at 341; [1966] CMLR 418 at 472; see similarly, *Ambulanz Glöckner v Landkreis Südwestpfalz* (C-475/99) [2001] ECR I-8089 at [47]; [2002] 4 CMLR 21 (p 726).

If an agreement is capable of having such an effect it will be incompatible with Art 101(1) TFEU. For example, in *Miller International Schallplatten Gmbh v Commission* (19/77) [1978] ECR 131; [1978] 2 CMLR 334 a contractual clause prevented the export of recordings in the German language (at [4]). The Court rejected the argument that the recordings were made for the German home market and were of only marginal interest to speakers of other languages and none of the purchasers were interested in exporting the recordings (at [11]–[14]). This clause violated Art 85(1) EC (Art 101(1) TFEU) by its mere inclusion in the agreement (at [15]).

In *Coöperatieve Stremsel-en Kleurselfabriek v Commission* (61/80) [1981] ECR 851; [1982] 1 CMLR 240 Dutch cheese producers bound themselves to purchase rennet exclusively from a Netherlands cooperative (at [3]). The agreement precluded the purchase of rennet from other Member States. The Court held that Art 85(1) EC (now Art 101(1) TFEU) was infringed even though the evidence was that the producers would continue to purchase the rennet from the Dutch cooperative (at [13]).

The effect upon trade usually results from a combination of several factors that taken individually may not be decisive. See *Oude Luttikhuis v Verenigde Coöperatieve Melkindustrie Coberco BA* (C-399/93) [1995] ECR I-4515 at [17]; *Bagnasco v Banca Popolare di Novara soc coop arl (BNP)* (C-215/96) [1999] ECR I-135 at [47]; [1999] 4 CMLR 624; *British Sugar plc v Commission* (C-359/01 P) [2004] ECR I-4933 at [27]; [2004] 5 CMLR 8 (p 329); *Manfredi v Lloyd Adriatico Assicurazioni SpA* (C-295/04) [2006] ECR I-6619 at [43]; [2006] 5 CMLR 17 (p 980); *Asnef-Equifax, Servicios de Información sobre Solvencia y Crédito, SL v Asociación de Usuarios de Servicios Bancarios (Ausbanc)* (C-238/05) [2006] ECR I-11125 at [35]; [2007] 4 CMLR 6 (p 224). See generally Commission Notice: Guidelines on the effect on trade concept contained in Articles 81 and 82 of the Treaty (OJ C 101, 27.4.2004, p 81).

[6.80] De Minimis Effect

Art 101(1) TFEU is not infringed unless competition is appreciably affected by being prevented, distorted or restricted. In *Völk v Etablissements J Vervaecke SPRL* (5/69) [1969] ECR 295; [1969] CMLR 273 the Court held that "an agreement falls outside the prohibition in Article 85 [Art 101 TFEU] when it has only an insignificant effect on the markets, taking into account the weak position which the persons concerned have on the market of the product in question" (at [7]). See similarly, *John Deere Ltd v Commission* (C-7/95 P) [1998] ECR I-3111 at [77]; [1998] 5 CMLR 311; *New Holland Ford Ltd v Commission* (C-8/95 P) [1998] ECR I-3175 at [91]; *Asnef-Equifax, Servicios de Información sobre Solvencia y Crédito, SL v Asociación de Usuarios de Servicios Bancarios (Ausbanc)* (C-238/05) [2006] ECR I-11125 at [50]; [2007] 4 CMLR 6 (p 224).

The *Völk* case involved an exclusive dealing agreement that provided for absolute territorial protection by prohibiting parallel imports. The Court found that the agreement escaped the prohibition in Art 85(1) EC (Art 101(1) TFEU) because it did not appreciably hinder the attainment of the objectives of the Community. However, where the market was divided amongst many brands so that each manufacturer held only a small percentage share of that market the Court refused to apply the de minimus principle to the holder of one of the largest market shares. See *Musique Diffusion Française SA v Commission* (100/80) [1983] ECR 1825 at [85]–[86]; [1983] 3 CMLR 221; *European Night Services Ltd v Commission* (T-374/94) [1998] ECR II-3141 at [103].

The Commission has published a Notice regarding agreements of minor importance. See Commission Notice on agreements of minor importance which do not appreciably restrict competition under Article 81(1) of the Treaty establishing the European Community (de minimis) (OJ C 368, 22.12.2001, p 13). The principles stated in the Notice do not constitute a conclusive interpretation of Art 101(1). The Commission recognises this by stating that the Notice is given without prejudice to the decisions of the Court (at [6]).

The Notice states that an agreement does not appreciably restrict competition in the following cases:

> (a) if the aggregate market share held by the parties to the agreement does not exceed 10 % on any of the relevant markets affected by the agreement, where the agreement is made between undertakings which are actual or potential competitors on any of these markets (agreements between competitors); or
> (b) if the market share held by each of the parties to the agreement does not exceed 15 % on any of the relevant markets affected by the agreement, where the agreement is made between undertakings which are not actual or potential competitors on any of these markets (agreements between non-competitors) (at [7]).

Art 101(1) TFEU is not infringed where there is no possibility of competition, for example, where extensive government regulation severely restricts the possibility of competition. See *Cöoperatieve Vereniging 'Suiker Unie' UA v Commission* (40/73) [1975] ECR 1663 at [67]–[72]; [1976] 1 CMLR 295.

[6.85] Justification for Limitations

A restriction upon competition may be justified by a legitimate objective. For example, in *Meca-Medina v Commission* (C-519/04 P) [2006] ECR I-6991; [2006] 5 CMLR 18 (p 1023) the Court held that the anti-doping rules for Olympic sports were inherent in the proper conduct of sport (at [45]). However, the limitations adopted must not go beyond what is necessary for the proper conduct of sporting competitions (at [47]).

Social policy objectives may constitute legitimate objectives justifying limitations upon competition. For example, agreements entered into during collective negotiations regarding labour do not fall within Art 101(1) TFEU. See *Brentjens' Handelsonderneming BV v Stichting Bedrijfspensioenfonds voor de Handel in Bouwmaterialen* (C-115/97) [1999] ECR I-6025 at [56]–[57]; [2000] 4 CMLR 566; *Albany International BV v Stichting Bedrijfspensioenfonds Textielindustrie* (C-67/96) [1999] ECR I-5751 at [59]–[60]; [2000] 4 CMLR 446.

[6.90] Declaration of Inapplicability

An agreement falling within Art 101(1) TFEU may be subject to a declaration of inapplicability under Art 101(3). Provision is made in Art 101(3) for exemptions to be granted to agreements that are economically beneficial.

Art 101(3) provides that an exemption will only be granted to an agreement, decision or concerted practice "which contributes to improving the production or distribution of goods or to promoting technical or economic progress, while allowing consumers a fair share of the resulting benefit, and which does not: (a) impose on the undertakings concerned restrictions which are not indispensable to the attainment of these objectives; (b) afford such undertakings the possibility of eliminating competition in respect of a substantial part of the products in question". Thus, the harmful effects of the agreement must be counterbalanced by a number of beneficial elements if the agreement is to benefit from an exemption.

A restrictive agreement can only be declared void by a national court under Art 101(2) TFEU if it could not possibly benefit from an exemption under Art 101(3). See *Delimitis v Henninger Brau AG* (C-234/89) [1991] ECR I-935 at [55]; [1992] 5 CMLR 210. See generally, Commission Notice: Guidelines on the application of Article 81(3) of the Treaty (OJ C 101, 27.4.2004, p 97); Paul Lugard and Leigh Hancher, "Honey I Shrunk the Article! A Critical Assessment of the Commission's Notice on Article 81(3) of the EC Treaty" (2004) 25 *European Competition Law Review* 410.

[6.95] Block Exemptions

Due to the voluminous number of agreements reached in the EU between undertakings, the Commission has adopted a number of block exemptions. Block exemptions have been granted for:

- specialisation agreements: Commission Regulation 2658/2000 of 29 November 2000 on the application of Article 81(3) of the Treaty to categories of specialisation agreements (OJ L 304, 5.12.2000, p 3);
- supply and distribution agreements: Commission Regulation 2790/1999 of 22 December 1999 on the application of Article 81(3) of the Treaty to categories of vertical agreements and concerted practices (OJ L 336, 29.12.1999, p 21); Christoffer Gniechwitz, "Commission Regulation (EC) No 2790/1999—The European Commission's Block Exemption for Vertical Agreements" (2004) 1 *Macquarie Journal of Business Law* 73;
- research and development agreements: Commission Regulation 2659/2000 of 29 November 2000 on the application of Article 81(3) of the Treaty to categories of research and development agreements (OJ L 304, 5.12.2000, p 7);

- technology transfer agreements: Commission Regulation 772/2004 of 27 April 2004 on the application of Article 81(3) of the Treaty to categories of technology transfer agreements (OJ L 123, 27.4.2004, p 11); see also Commission Notice: Guidelines on the application of Article 81 of the EC Treaty to technology transfer agreements (OJ C 101, 27.4.2004, p 2);
- certain types of insurance agreements: Commission Regulation 358/2003 of 27 February 2003 on the application of Article 81(3) of the Treaty to certain categories of agreements, decisions and concerted practices in the insurance sector (OJ L 53, 28.2.2003, p 8); and
- motor vehicle distribution and servicing agreements: Commission Regulation 1400/2002 of 31 July 2002 on the application of Article 81(3) of the Treaty to categories of vertical agreements and concerted practices in the motor vehicle sector (OJ L 203, 1.8.2002, p 30).

In *Delimitis v Henninger Brau AG* (C-234/89) [1991] ECR I-935; [1992] 5 CMLR 210 the Court held that a national court could not extend the scope of a block exemption regulation in order to cover agreements that do not come within the terms of the regulation (at [46]). If one provision of the agreement did not fall within the block exemption, the whole agreement was deemed to be outside the exemption. That did not mean that the whole agreement would be void under Art 85(2) EC (Art 101(2) TFEU) (at [40]).

[6.100] Concerted Practices

Art 101(1) TFEU also prohibits "concerted practices which may affect trade between Member States and which have as their object or effect the prevention, restriction or distortion of competition within the internal market". In *Züchner v Bayerische Vereinsbank AG* (172/80) [1981] ECR 2021; [1982] 1 CMLR 313 the Court defined "concerted practices" as follows:

> a form of coordination between undertakings which, without having reached the stage where an agreement properly so called has been concluded, knowingly substitutes practical cooperation between them for the risks of competition .... [T]he criteria of coordination and cooperation necessary for the existence of a concerted practice in no way require the working out of an actual 'plan' but must be understood in the light of the concept inherent in the provisions of the Treaty relating to competition, according to which each trader must determine independently the policy which he intends to adopt on the common market and the conditions which he intends to offer his customers. Although it is correct to say that this requirement of independence does not deprive traders of the right to adapt themselves intelligently to the existing or anticipated conduct of their competitors, it does however strictly preclude any direct or indirect contract between such traders, the object or effect of which is to create conditions of competition which do not correspond to the normal conditions of the market in question, regard being had to the nature of the products or services offered, the size and number of the undertakings and the volume of the said market (at [12]–[14]).

See similarly, *John Deere Ltd v Commission* (C-7/95 P) [1998] ECR I-3111 at [86]–[87]; [1998] 5 CMLR 311; *Thyssen Stahl AG v Commission* (C-194/99 P) [2003] ECR I-10821 at [82]–[83]; *T-Mobile Netherlands BV v Raad van bestuur van de Nederlandse Mededingingsautoriteit* (C-8/08) [2009] 5 CMLR 11 (p 1701) at [26].

Thus similar or even identical behaviour is not per se a concerted practice which is incompatible with the TFEU. Indeed, such behaviour may be the result of independent judgment and assessment of the market. However if the undertakings do not operate independently but their representatives meet with the object or effect of influencing the behaviour of the other undertaking or of disclosing their proposed behaviour, that is sufficient to constitute a concerted action regardless of whether the undertakings have calculated a plan.

If a practice is adopted by an undertaking on the mutual understanding that the practice will also be adopted by another undertaking that will amount to concerted behaviour. For example, in *Tepea BV v Commission* (28/77) [1978] ECR 1391; [1978] 3 CMLR 392 where manufacturers and their distributors cooperated to identify parallel importers, that constituted a concerted practice (at [40]–[45]). See also *Hasselblad (GB) Ltd v Commission* (86/82) [1984] ECR 883 at [24]–[29]; [1984] 1 CMLR 559. It is possible for a concerted practice to arise from a single meeting between competitors. See *T-Mobile Netherlands BV v Raad van bestuur van de Nederlandse Mededingingsautoriteit* (C-8/08) [2009] 5 CMLR 11 (p 1701) at [59]–[60].

A concerted practice is prohibited by Art 101(1) TFEU even where it has no anti-competitive effect upon the market since an anti-competitive object is sufficient to fall within the prohibition. See *Hüls AG v Commission* (C-199/92 P) [1999] ECR I-4287 at [163]–[164]; [1999] 5 CMLR 1016; *Montecatini SpA v Commission* (C-235/92 P) [1999] ECR I-4539 at [123]–[124]; [2001] 4 CMLR 18 (p 691); *Commission v Anic Partecipazioni SpA* (C-49/92 P) [1999] ECR I 4125 at [122]–[123]; [2001] 4 CMLR 17 (p 602).

[6.105] Abuse of a Dominant Position

Art 102 TFEU prohibits the abuse of a dominant position in the European Union. A dominant position is not in itself illegal because such a position may be the result of the company's efficiency. Art 102 is violated if three requirements are met: (1) there must be a dominant position, (2) an abuse of that position and (3) the abuse is prejudicial to trade between the Member States.

It is possible for a practice to violate both Arts 101 and 102 TFEU. However, the aims of those provisions are different. Art 101 applies without regard to the position of the undertakings on the market, while Art 102 applies to abuse of a dominant position on the market. See *Flugreisen v*

Zentrale zur Bekämpfung unlauteren Wettbewerbs eV (66/86) [1989] ECR 803 at [37]; [1990] 4 CMLR 102; *Compagnie Maritime Belge Transports SA v Commission* (C-395/96 P) [2000] ECR I-1365 at [33]–[34], [130]; [2000] 4 CMLR 1076.

[6.110] Dominant Position

The Court has defined "dominant position" as "a position of economic strength held by an undertaking, which enables it to prevent effective competition from being maintained on the relevant market by giving it the power to behave to an appreciable extent independently of its competitors, its customers and, ultimately, consumers". See *Autotrasporti Librandi Snc di Librandi F & C v Cuttica Spedizioni e Servizi Internazionali Srl* (C-38/97) [1998] ECR I-5955 at [27]; [1998] 5 CMLR 966; *Compagnie Maritime Belge Transports SA v Commission* (C-395/96 P) [2000] ECR I-1365 at [34]; [2000] 4 CMLR 1076; *Motosykletistiki Omospondia Ellados NPID (MOTOE) v Dimosio* (C-49/07) [2008] ECR I-4863 at [37]; [2008] 5 CMLR 11 (p 790); *France Télécom SA v Commission* (C-202/07 P) [2009] 4 CMLR 25 (p 1149) at [103].

A dominant position usually results from a combination of several factors that taken individually may not be decisive. See *Gøttrup-Klim ea Grovvareforeninger v Dansk Landbrugs Grovvareselskab AmbA* (C-250/92) [1994] ECR I-5641 at [47]; [1996] 4 CMLR 191. It is possible for legally independent entities to occupy a collective dominant position if they act as a collective entity in an economic sense. See *Compagnie Maritime Belge Transports SA v Commission* (C-395/96 P) [2000] ECR I-1365 at [36]; [2000] 4 CMLR 1076.

[6.115] Concept of Abuse

Art 102 TFEU expressly sets out several examples of abuse of a dominant position:

(a) directly or indirectly imposing unfair purchase or selling prices or other unfair trading conditions;
(b) limiting production, markets or technical development to the prejudice of consumers;
(c) applying dissimilar conditions to equivalent transactions with other trading parties, thereby placing them at a competitive disadvantage;
(d) making the conclusion of contracts subject to acceptance by the other parties of supplementary obligations which, by their nature or according to commercial usage, have no connection with the subject of such contracts.

These examples are not exhaustive. See *Tetra Pak International SA v Commission* (C-333/94 P) [1996] ECR I-5951 at [37]; [1997] 4 CMLR 662; *Compagnie Maritime Belge Transports SA v Commission* (C-395/96 P) [2000] ECR I-1365 at [112]; [2000] 4 CMLR 1076; *British Airways plc v Commission* (C-95/04 P) [2007] ECR I-2331 at [57]; [2007] 4 CMLR 22 (p 982).

An abuse may occur if an undertaking in a dominant position strengthens its position so that the level of dominance substantially fetters competition. In *Europemballage Corporation v Commission* (6/72) [1973] ECR 215; [1973] CMLR 199 the Court held that an abuse may exist when an undertaking of considerable strength in the market attempts to further increase its share in a particular market by taking over a rival enterprise. The Court remarked that an abuse may occur "if an undertaking in a dominant position strengthens such position in such a way that the degree of dominance reached substantially fetters competition, i.e. that only undertakings remain in the market whose behaviour depends on the dominant one" (at [26]). See similarly, *Compagnie Maritime Belge Transports SA v Commission* (C-395/96 P) [2000] ECR I-1365 at [113]; [2000] 4 CMLR 1076.

In *AKZO Chemie BV v Commission* (C-62/86) [1991] ECR I-3359; [1993] 5 CMLR 215 the Court held that competition by means of predatory pricing was illegitimate (at [70]). The Court defined one form of predatory pricing as follows: "Prices below average variable costs (that is to say, those which vary depending on the quantities produced) by means of which a dominant undertaking seeks to eliminate a competitor must be regarded as abusive" (at [71]). The Court also described another form of predatory pricing: "prices below average total costs, that is to say, fixed costs plus variable costs, but above average variable costs, must be regarded as abusive if they are determined as part of a plan for eliminating a competitor" (at [72]). See similarly, *Tetra Pak v Commission* (C-333/94 P) [1996] ECR I-5951 at [41]; [1997] 4 CMLR 662, *France Télécom SA v Commission* (C-202/07 P) [2009] 4 CMLR 25 (p 1149) at [109].

The issue of the indispensability of a dominant undertaking's services for other undertakings arose in *Oscar Bronner GmbH & Co KG v Mediaprint Zeitungs- und Zeitschriftenverlag GmbH & Co KG* (C-7/97) [1998] ECR I-7791; [1999] 4 CMLR 112. Bronner published a small daily newspaper in Austria (at [4]). Mediaprint published two newspapers that occupied a very large share of the Austrian newspaper market (at [5]–[6]). Mediaprint ran a national home delivery service for its newspapers (at [7]). Mediaprint refused to distribute Bronner's newspaper through its delivery service. Bronner argued that this refusal constituted an abuse of Mediaprint's dominant position. Bronner submitted that it would be unprofitable to establish its own delivery service given its small distribution. It also argued that postal distribution was not equivalent to home delivery since the newspapers would be delivered too late in the morning (at [8]).

The Court held that Mediaprint had not abused a dominant position (at [47]). Mediaprint's refusal would constitute an abuse if it was likely to eliminate all competition in the newspaper market by Bronner and the refusal was not objectively justifiable. Furthermore, the delivery service would need to be indispensable to Bronner's business, in that there was no alternative means of distribution (at [41]). In this case distribution by post and sale in stores were alternative means (at [43]).

There were also no "technical, legal or even economic obstacles" preventing newspaper publishers from setting up their own home delivery service, either alone or conjunction with others (at [44]). Indispensability could not be proved merely by showing that it was unprofitable for a newspaper to establish its own distribution scheme because of its small circulation (at [45]). Inclusion in the distribution service could be indispensable only if it was proved "at the very least . . . that that it is not economically viable to create a second home-delivery scheme for the distribution of daily newspapers with a circulation comparable to that of the daily newspapers distributed by the existing scheme" (at [46]).

The establishment of abuse does not require a finding of fault. There is also no requirement to establish a causal connection between the dominance of the undertaking and the behaviour constituting the abuse. Conduct that is incompatible with Art 102 TFEU is an abuse regardless of the means of procuring the behaviour.

[6.120] Special Responsibility of Dominant Undertakings

An undertaking in a dominant position has a "special responsibility not to allow its conduct to impair genuine undistorted competition on the common market". See *Atlantic Container Line AB v Commission* (T-191/98) [2003] ECR II-3275 at [1109]; [2005] 4 CMLR 20 (p 1283); *Compagnie Maritime Belge Transports SA v Commission* (C-395/96 P) [2000] ECR I-1365 at [37], [85]; [2000] 4 CMLR 1076; *France Télécom SA v Commission* (C-202/07 P) [2009] 4 CMLR 25 (p 1149) at [105].

An undertaking in a dominant position is entitled to take reasonable measures for the protection of its commercial interests, but it may not take measures designed to strengthen its dominant position and thus abuse that position. See *Irish Sugar plc v Commission* (T-228/97) [1999] ECR II-2969 at [112]; [1999] 5 CMLR 1300; *Sot Lelos kai Sia EE v GlaxoSmithKline AEVE Farmakeftikon Proionton* (C-468/06) [2008] ECR I-7139 at [50]; [2008] 5 CMLR 20 (p 1382); *Kanal 5 Ltd v Föreningen Svenska Tonsättares Internationella Musikbyrå (STIM) upa* (C-52/07) [2008] ECR I-9275 at [26]; [2009] 5 CMLR 18 (p 2175).

[6.125] Substantial Part of the Internal Market

To infringe Art 102 TFEU the abuse must be carried out "within the internal market or in a substantial part of it". A single Member State or a part thereof can constitute a substantial part of the internal market. See *Scandinavian Airlines System AB v Commission* (T-241/01) [2005] ECR II-2917 at [89]; [2005] 5 CMLR 18 (p 922). Areas which have been held to be a "substantial part" of the EU include Belgium and Luxembourg, Belgium, the southern part of Germany and the Netherlands.

The area in which the economic power of the undertaking is to be considered is the internal market. However, a determination of the power of an undertaking within the Union may also require an examination of its activities outside the Union including supply, transportation, research, technical knowledge and marketing. The fact that an undertaking may belong to a multinational group may also be relevant.

[6.130] Relevant Market

The concept of the relevant market for the product or service is also important. The Court has defined the relevant market as "all the products or services which in view of their characteristics are particularly suited to satisfy constant needs and are only to a limited extent interchangeable with other products or services". See *AKZO Chemie BV v Commission* (C-62/86) [1991] ECR I-3359 at [51]; [1993] 5 CMLR 215; *Oscar Bronner GmbH & Co KG v Mediaprint Zeitungs- und Zeitschriftenverlag GmbH & Co KG* (C-7/97) [1998] ECR I-7791 at [33]; [1999] 4 CMLR 112.

If there is competition between two products and that competition brings an advantage to the consumer, the relevant market contains both those products although they may not be exactly the same. For example, in *Kali und Salz AG v Commission* (19/74) [1975] ECR 499; [1975] 2 CMLR 154 potash fertiliser and compound potash fertiliser were in the one relevant product market (at [6]). A relevant market requires effective competition between products in that market and presupposes a sufficient degree of interchangeability between the goods in that market so far as a specific use of the goods is concerned.

The characteristics of the production of the goods which make them suitable for their use may be taken into account in defining the relevant market. If small price rises would lead to a large substitution of other goods for the goods under consideration, the substituted goods are part of the relevant product market. Where large price rises would lead to only a small amount of substitution the substituted goods are not part of the relevant product market.

The geographic market in which the existence or absence of a dominant position is considered "is an area where the objective conditions of competition applying to the product in question must be the same for all traders". See *United Brands Co v Commission* (27/76) [1978] ECR 207 at [44]; [1978] 1 CMLR 429; *Ambulanz Glöckner v Landkreis Südwestpfalz* (C-475/99) [2001] ECR I-8089 at [34]; [2002] 4 CMLR 21 (p 726).

Thus the geographic market only includes areas where the product is marketed under similar marketing conditions. In determining the geographic market it is relevant to compare the sales of the undertaking to the total sales of those products within the relevant area. To establish whether the area is of sufficient size to constitute a substantial part of the EU, the volume of production and consumption of the goods are considered. Other factors, such as the freight costs in comparison with the value of the goods must also be considered.

In *Tetra Pak v Commission* (C-333/94 P) [1996] ECR I-5951; [1997] 4 CMLR 662 the Court held that it is possible for Art 102 TFEU to apply to an act by an undertaking on another market that is different to the market that is dominated by the undertaking (at [25]). However, such an application of Art 102 TFEU is justified only in "special circumstances" (at [27]). Such special circumstances exist where the dominant position of the undertaking on one market enabled it to act independently of other undertakings on a related market that it did not dominate (at [29]). In that case the near monopoly of Tetra Pak in the aseptic packaging market enabled it to act as if it was in a dominant position in the non-aseptic packaging market, which it did not dominate (at [31]).

[6.135] Exercise of Industrial Property Rights

When industrial and commercial property rights are exercised in conformity with Art 36 TFEU, Art 102 is not necessarily infringed on the ground that the undertaking is in a dominant position. See *Hoffman-La Roche & Co AG v Centrafarm Vertriebsgesellschaft Pharmazeutischer Erzeugnisse mbH* (102/77) [1978] ECR 1139 at [15]–[16]; [1978] 3 CMLR 217. The refusal of an undertaking in a dominant position to grant a licence thus does not in itself constitute abuse of that position. Nevertheless, in "exceptional circumstances" refusal of a licence may constitute an abuse. See *Radio Telefis Eireann v Commission* (C-241/91) [1995] ECR I-743 at [49]–[50]; [1995] 4 CMLR 718; *Oscar Bronner GmbH & Co KG v Mediaprint Zeitungs- und Zeitschriftenverlag GmbH & Co KG* (C-7/97) [1998] ECR I-7791 at [39]; [1999] 4 CMLR 112; *IMS Health GmbH & Co OHG v NDC Health GmbH & Co KG* (C-418/01) [2004] ECR I-5039 at [34]–[35]; [2004] 4 CMLR 28 (p 1543).

In *Microsoft Corporation v Commission* (T-201/04) [2007] ECR II-3601; [2007] 5 CMLR 11 (p 846) the Court of First Instance summarised what constitutes "exceptional circumstances". Refusal of a licence may constitute an abuse where "the refusal relates to a product or service indispensable to the exercise of a particular activity on a neighbouring market; . . . the refusal is of such a kind as to exclude any effective competition on that neighbouring market; . . . [and] the refusal prevents the appearance of a new product for which there is potential consumer demand" (at [332]). This decision was not appealed.

In *Radio Telefis Eireann v Commission* (C-241/91) [1995] ECR I-743; [1995] 4 CMLR 718 each of the three broadcasters received in Ireland produced a television guide for its own programmes. There was no weekly guide that listed the programmes shown by all three broadcasters. Each network claimed copyright protection for its programme listings so as to prevent their use by other parties (at [7]). They made available their listings each day for reproduction in that day's listings in the newspapers (at [9]). Magill wished to produce a weekly guide for all three networks, but was prohibited from doing so by an injunction obtained by two of the broadcasters (at [10]).

The Court held that the broadcasters were in a dominant position since they had a "de facto monopoly" on the provision of programme information (at [47]). The Court affirmed that in exceptional circumstances refusal to grant a licence could constitute abuse of a dominant position (at [49]). The broadcaster's refusal to supply its programme information prevented the emergence of a new product (a weekly television guide), which constituted an abuse of their dominant positions (at [54]). The refusal was not justified by the activity of broadcasting or magazine publishing (at [55]). The broadcasters excluded competition in the market for weekly television guides by refusing to divulge the information necessary for such publications (at [56]).

The use of intellectual property rights by a dominant undertaking to prevent the importation of infringing copies is compatible with Art 102 TFEU (see Chapter 9). The fact that an undertaking charges a higher price for an article protected by a patent than is charged for an article not so protected is not necessarily evidence of an abuse of a dominant position. However, if the price cannot be justified by objective criteria such a high price may be a determining factor. See generally, Valentine Korah, *Intellectual Property Rights and the EC Competition Rules* (Oxford: Hart, 2006).

[6.140] Effect upon Trade

Art 102 TFEU requires that the abuse of a dominant position should affect trade between EU Member States. Trade is affected for the purposes of Art 102 if trade between Member States is diverted from normal commercial channels by the abuse or if the competitive pattern of the trade is distorted. The abuse need not have substantially affected trade; it need only have the potential to have that effect. See *Radio Telefis Eireann v Commission* (C-241/91) [1995] ECR I-743 at [69]; [1995] 4 CMLR 718.

[6.145] No Exemptions for Abuses

No exemption may be granted for an abuse of a dominant position. See *Flugreisen v Zentrale zur Bekämpfung Unlauteren Wettbewerbs eV* (66/86) [1989] ECR 803 at [32]; [1990] 4 CMLR 102; *Compagnie Maritime Belge Transports SA v Commission* (C-395/96 P) [2000] ECR I-1365 at [135]; [2000] 4 CMLR 1076.

[6.150] Merger Control Under the TFEU

The TFEU does not have a specific provision designed to regulate mergers or the acquisition of a shareholding in another enterprise. However, in *Europemballage Corporation v Commission* (6/72) [1973] ECR 215; [1973] CMLR 199 the Court applied Art 86 EC (Art 102 TFEU) in the context of a proposed merger. The Court held that a dominant position is abused when an undertaking of considerable strength in the market attempts to further increase its share by acquiring a rival company (at [28]–[30]). Thus, Art 102 TFEU does not allow mergers that eliminate competition.

In *British American Tobacco Co Ltd v Commission* (142/84) [1987] ECR 4487; [1988] 4 CMLR 24 the Court acknowledged that Art 85 EC (Art 101 TFEU) could be violated by the acquisition of a minority shareholding in a competing company. The Court stated:

> Although the acquisition by one company of an equity interest in a competitor does not in itself constitute conduct restricting competition, such an acquisition may nevertheless serve as an instrument for influencing the commercial conduct of the companies in question so as to restrict or distort competition on the market on which they carry on business.
>
> That will be true in particular where, by the acquisition of a shareholding or through subsidiary clauses in the agreement, the investing company obtains legal or de facto control of the commercial conduct of the other company or where the agreement provides for commercial co-operation between the companies or creates a structure likely to be used for such co-operation.
>
> That may also be the case where the agreement gives the investing company the possibility of reinforcing its position at a later stage and taking effective control of the other company. Account must be taken not only of the immediate effects of the agreement but also of its potential effects and of the possibility that the agreement may be part of a long-term plan . . . every agreement must be assessed in its economic context and in particular in the light of the situation on the relevant market (at [37]–[39]).

[6.155] Merger Control Under the EU Regulation

The EU has adopted a Regulation dealing with mergers. See Council Regulation 139/2004 of 20 January 2004 on the control of concentrations between undertakings (OJ L 24, 29.1.2004, p 1). The Regulation covers firms where their combined aggregate worldwide turnover is more than EUR 5,000 million, and the aggregate Community-wide turnover of each of at least two of the undertakings concerned is more than EUR 250 million (Art 1(2)). Lower thresholds apply in certain cases (Art 1(3)). The Regulation sets out the method for calculating turnover (Art 5).

A concentration with a Community dimension must be notified to the Commission "prior to... implementation and following the conclusion of the agreement, the announcement of the public bid, or the acquisition of a controlling interest" (Art 4(1)). A concentration is notified jointly by the parties to the merger or by those who acquire joint control (Art 4(2)). Following the notification of a concentration, the Commission publishes the fact of the notification, indicating the names of the parties and the nature of the concentration and the economic sectors involved (Art 4(3)).

In order to enable the Commission to examine the compatibility of the proposed concentration with the Regulation, the concentration is "suspended" until it has been declared to be compatible with the common market (Art 7(1)). The Commission may grant a derogation from the suspension after considering "the effects of the suspension on one or more undertakings concerned by the concentration or on a third party and the threat to competition posed by the concentration" (Art 7(3)).

A concentration is incompatible with the common market if it "would significantly impede effective competition, in the common market or in a substantial part of it, in particular as a result of the creation or strengthening of a dominant position" (Art 2(3)). In making its appraisal, the Commission must take into account the need to maintain effective competition in the EU. The Commission must also take into account "the market position of the undertakings concerned and their economic and financial power, the alternatives available to suppliers and users, their access to supplies or markets, any legal or other barriers to entry, supply and demand trends for the relevant goods and services, the interests of the intermediate and ultimate consumers, and the development of technical and economic progress provided that it is to consumers' advantage and does not form an obstacle to competition" (Art 2(1)).

The Commission may refer a concentration to the competition authorities of the Member States (Art 9(1)). If the Commission finds that the concentration was incompatible with the common market, it may order dissolution of the merger or the disposal of all shares or assets or any other action that may be appropriate in order to restore the conditions of effective competition (Art 8(4)).

The Commission may undertake investigations into undertakings in order to establish any infringement of the Regulation, including requesting all necessary information and undertaking necessary inspections of undertakings (Arts 11 and 13). Heavy fines may be imposed upon offending firms (Art 14). The ECJ has unlimited jurisdiction within the meaning of Art 261 TFEU to review the imposition and amounts of fines and may reduce, cancel or increase any such payments (Art 16).

The EU evaluates the competition law regimes of non-Member States, in order to examine the treatment accorded to EU undertakings with regard to concentrations in those countries. Whenever the Commission concludes that a non-Member State "does not grant undertakings having their seat or their principal fields of activity in the Community, treatment comparable to that granted by the Community to undertakings from that country, the Commission may submit proposals to the Council for an appropriate mandate for negotiation with a view to obtaining comparable treatment for undertakings having their seat or their principal fields of activity in the Community" (Art 24(3)).

The Commission has issued several guidelines for the application of the Regulation. See Guidelines on the assessment of horizontal mergers under the Council Regulation on the control of concentrations between undertakings (OJ C 31, 5.2.2004, p 5); Guidelines on the assessment of non-horizontal mergers under the Council Regulation on the control of concentrations between undertakings (OJ C 265, 18.10.2008, p 6).

[6.160] State Aid

Art 107(1) TFEU provides: "Save as otherwise provided in the Treaties, any aid granted by a Member State or through State resources in any form whatsoever which distorts or threatens to distort competition by favouring certain undertakings or the production of certain goods shall, in so far as it affects trade between Member States, be incompatible with the internal market."

In *Altmark Trans GmbH v Nahverkehrsgesellschaft Altmark GmbH* (C-280/00) [2003] ECR I-7747; [2003] 3 CMLR 12 (p 339) the Court summarised the conditions for classification as state aid: "First, there must be an intervention by the State or through State resources. Second, the intervention must be liable to affect trade between Member States. Third, it must confer an advantage on the recipient. Fourth, it must distort or threaten to distort competition" (at [75]). The Court also stated that "[m]easures which, whatever their form, are likely directly or indirectly to favour certain undertakings... or are to be regarded as an economic advantage which the recipient undertaking would not have obtained under normal market conditions . . . are regarded as aid" (at [84]). See similarly, *Syndicat français de l'Express international (SFEI) v La Poste* (C-39/94) [1996] ECR I-3547 at [60]; [1996] 3 CMLR 369; *Chronopost SA v Union française de l'express (Ufex)* (C-83/01 P) [2003] ECR I-6993 at [69]; [2003] 3 CMLR 11 (p 303); *Altmark Trans GmbH v Nahverkehrsgesellschaft Altmark GmbH* (C-280/00) [2003] ECR I-7747 at [84]; [2003] 3 CMLR 12 (p 339); *Essent Netwerk Noord BV v Aluminium Delfzijl BV* (C-206/06) [2008] ECR I-5497 at [79]; [2008] 3 CMLR 32 (p 895).

There are a number of block exemptions for aid. A Regulation exempts certain categories of aid from the duty of notification to the Commission, including regional aid, small and medium enterprise investment and employment aid, aid for the creation of small enterprises by women, aid for environmental protection, risk capital aid, research and development aid, training aid and aid for disadvantaged or disabled workers. See Art 1(1), Commission Regulation 800/2008 of 6 August 2008 declaring certain categories of aid compatible with the common market in application of Articles 87 and 88 of the Treaty (OJ L 214, 9.8.2008, p 3).

Another EU Regulation provides that if aid granted to an enterprise does not exceed EUR 200,000 over any 3 year period, the aid does not fall within Art 107(1) TFEU (formerly Art 87(1) EC). See Art 2(2), Commission Regulation 1998/2006 of 15 December 2006 on the application of Articles 87 and 88 of the Treaty to de minimis aid (OJ L 379, 28.12.2006, p 5). The Regulation does not apply to aid in the agriculture, fisheries, aquaculture and coal sectors (Art 1(1)). See generally Michael Berghofer, "The New De Minimis Regulation: Enlarging the Sword of Damocles?" [2007] *European State Aid Law Quarterly* 11.

Art 107(2) TFEU provides that several forms of aid are compatible with the internal market, including "aid having a social character, granted to individual consumers, provided that such aid is granted without discrimination related to the origin of the products concerned" and "aid to make good the damage caused by natural disasters or exceptional occurrences".

Art 107(3) TFEU provides that several forms of aid may be considered to be compatible with the internal market, including:

(a) aid to promote the economic development of areas where the standard of living is abnormally low or where there is serious underemployment. . .;
(b) aid to promote the execution of an important project of common European interest or to remedy a serious disturbance in the economy of a Member State;
(c) aid to facilitate the development of certain economic activities or of certain economic areas, where such aid does not adversely affect trading conditions to an extent contrary to the common interest;
(d) aid to promote culture and heritage conservation where such aid does not affect trading conditions and competition in the Union to an extent that is contrary to the common interest.

Under category (b) aid "to remedy a serious disturbance in the economy of a Member State" may be considered to be compatible with the internal market. For example, in March 2009 the Commission gave its approval for an emergency recapitalisation of the Bank of Ireland (N149/2009; IP/09/483). See generally, Raymond Luja, "State Aid and the Financial Crisis: Overview of the Crisis Framework" [2009] *European State Aid Law Quarterly* 145; Abel M Mateus, "The Current Financial Crisis and State Aid in the EU" (2009) 5 *European Competition Journal* 1.

The Commission constantly monitors all systems of aid in the Member States (Art 108(1) TFEU). Member States are under a duty to provide the Commission with prior notification of their intention to grant or alter aid and to temporarily suspend that aid to enable the Commission to examine the proposal. See Art 108(3) TFEU; *France v Commission* (C-332/98) [2000] ECR I-4833 at [32]; Arts 2(1), 3, Council Regulation 659/1999 of 22 March 1999 laying down detailed rules for the application of Article 93 of the EC Treaty (OJ L 83, 27.3.1999, p 1).

If the Commission finds that aid is incompatible with the internal market, it shall order that the State "abolish or alter" the aid (Art 108(2) TFEU). The purpose of this provision is to restore the position to that existing prior to the granting of the aid. See *Land Rheinland-Pfalz v Alcan Deutschland GmbH* [1997] ECR I-1591 at [23]; [1997] 2 CMLR 1034; *Re Aid to Seleco: Italy v Commission* (C-328/99) [2003] ECR I-4035 at [66]; [2005] 2 CMLR 48 (p 1169). State aid that has been granted in violation of EU law must be recovered. See *Italy v Commission* (C-298/00 P) [2004] ECR I-4087 at [75]. In the absence of relevant EU provisions, recovery is undertaken in accordance with national procedural law. See *Belgium v Commission* (C-142/87) [1990] ECR I-959 at [61]; [1991] 3 CMLR 213.

[6.165] Application of the Competition Rules

With certain exceptions, EU competition rules apply to the whole of the economic life of the European Union. Special provision is made in relation to the following cases: (a) agriculture, (b) transport, (c) undertakings granted special or exclusive rights and (d) services of general economic interest.

[6.170] Agriculture

The competition rules apply to the production and trade of agricultural products to the extent determined by the European Parliament and the Council (Art 42 TFEU). To this end, the EU adopted Council Regulation 1184/2006 of 24 July 2006 applying certain rules of competition to the production of and trade in certain agricultural products (OJ L 214, 4.8.2006, p 7). The Regulation provides that the competition rules of the TFEU apply to undertakings engaged in the production and trade of the agricultural products listed in Annex I of the Treaty (Arts 1 and 1a).

Art 101(1) TFEU does not apply to agreements that form an integral part of a national market organisation. Art 101(1) also does not apply to agreements which are necessary to achieve the objectives of Art 39 TFEU (Art 2(1)). The objectives of Art 39 are: (a) increasing agricultural productivity, (b) ensuring a fair standard of living for the agricultural community, (c) stabilising markets, (d) ensuring the availability of supplies and (e) ensuring that supplies reach consumers at reasonable prices (Art 39(1) TFEU).

In particular, the Regulation exempts from the application of the EU competition rules "agreements, decisions and practices of farmers, farmers' associations, or associations of such associations belonging to a single Member State which concern the production or sale of agricultural products or the use of joint facilities for the storage, treatment or processing of agricultural products, and under which there is no obligation to charge identical prices, unless the Commission finds that competition is thereby excluded or that the objectives of [Art 39 TFEU] are jeopardised" (Art 2(1)).

[6.175] Transport

EU competition rules apply to road, rail and inland waterway transportation. See Council Regulation 169/2009 of 26 February 2009 applying rules of competition to transport by rail, road and inland waterway (OJ L 61, 5.3.2009, p 1). This Regulation includes exemptions for technical agreements (Art 2) and groups of small and medium-sized undertakings (Art 3).

An EU Regulation allows the Commission to adopt block exemptions for several categories of agreements, decisions and concerted practices in air transportation. See Art 2(2), Council Regulation 3976/87 of 14 December 1987 on the application of Article 85(3) of the Treaty to certain categories of agreements and concerted practices in the air transport sector (OJ L 374, 31.12.1987, p 9).

Agreements, decisions and concerted practices concerning joint planning and coordination of the capacity of air transport and consultations regarding tariffs and airport slot allocation have been exempted from the operation of Art 101(1) TFEU. See Art 1, Commission Regulation 1617/93 of 25 June 1993 on the application of Article 85(3) of the Treaty to certain categories of agreements and concerted practices concerning joint planning and coordination of schedules, joint operations, consultations on passenger and cargo tariffs on scheduled air services and slot allocation at airports (OJ L 155, 26.6, 1993, p 18).

[6.180] Undertakings with Exclusive Rights

Art 106(1) TFEU provides: "In the case of public undertakings and undertakings to which Member States grant special or exclusive rights, Member States shall neither enact nor maintain in force any measure contrary to the [competition] rules contained in the Treaties".

The creation of a dominant position through the grant of special or exclusive rights does not necessarily violate Art 102(1) TFEU. That Article will only be infringed if the undertaking abuses its dominant position or will be led inevitably to abuse its position. See *Corsica Ferries France SA v Gruppo Antichi Ormeggiatori del Porto di Genova Coop arl* (C-266/96) [1998] ECR I-3949 at [40]; [1998] 5 CMLR 402; *Albany International BV v Stichting Bedrijfspensioenfonds Textielindustrie* (C-67/96) [1999] ECR I-5751 at [93]; [2000] 4 CMLR 446; *Entreprenørforeningens Affalds/Miljøsektion (FFAD) v Københavns Kommune* (C-209/98) [2000] ECR I-3743 at [66]–[67]; [2001] 2 CMLR 39 (p 936); *Motosykletistiki Omospondia Ellados NPID (MOTOE) v Dimosio* (C-49/07) [2008] ECR I-4863 at [48]–[49]; [2008] 5 CMLR 11 (p 790).

[6.185] Services of General Economic Interest

Art 106(2) TFEU provides: "Undertakings entrusted with the operation of services of general economic interest or having the character of a revenue-producing monopoly shall be subject to... the rules on competition, in so far as the application of such rules does not obstruct the performance, in law or in fact, of the particular tasks assigned to them."

For example, in *Criminal Proceedings Against Corbeau* (C-320/91) [1993] ECR I-2533; [1995] 4 CMLR 621 Belgian legislation provided that the post office had the exclusive right to carry mail (at [3]). Corbeau operated a local postal service in one city, picking up letters and delivering them by noon the next day within the town (at [4]). He was prosecuted for violating the exclusive right of the post office (at [2]).

The Court held that the Belgian post office had been entrusted with a service of general economic interest (delivery of mail at uniform costs throughout the national territory) (at [15]). Such a task required that the less profitable segments of the market be offset against the more profitable segments. This justified a limitation of competition in the more profitable segments of the market (at [17]). Permitting competition with the exclusive right holder in the more profitable sectors would allow the competitor to concentrate on those sectors without being hampered by the less profitable segments. In those circumstances the competitor would be able to offer lower prices than could be offered by the exclusive right holder (at [18]). The exclusion of competition would not be justified where the competitor offered additional services that went beyond those offered by the exclusive right holder, such as pickup from the sender and greater speed. However, those additional services must "not compromise the economic equilibrium of the service of general economic interest" (at [19]). See generally, Mustafa T Karayigit, "The Notion of Services of General Economic Interest Revisited" (2009) 15 *European Public Law* 575.

[6.190] Enforcement of the Competition Rules

Art 105(1) TFEU empowers the Commission, either of its own initiative or on application from a Member State, to investigate alleged infringements of Arts 101 or 102 and to make proposals to bring the behaviour to an end. Following the publication of a reasoned decision by the Commission, the Member States are authorised "to take the measures... needed to remedy the situation" (Art 105(2) TFEU).

[6.195] Regulation 1/2003

Art 103(1) TFEU confers upon the Council the power to adopt Regulations and Directives to give effect to the principles of Arts 101 and 102. In reliance upon this power, the Council adopted a Regulation providing for the enforcement of the competition rules. See Council Regulation 1/2003 of 16 December 2002 on the implementation of the rules on competition laid down in Articles 81 and 82 of the Treaty (OJ L 1, 4.1.2003, p 1).

Agreements that violate Art 101(1) TFEU and are not saved by Art 101(3) are prohibited without any need for a previous decision prohibiting them (Art 1(1)). Agreements that violate Art 101(1) but are saved by Art 101(3) are not prohibited and there is similarly no need for a previous decision to that effect (Art 1(2)). The abuse of a dominant position under Art 102 TFEU is prohibited without the need for any prior decision to that effect (Art 1(3)). The burden of proving a violation of Arts 101 or 102 TFEU lies with the party or authority that alleges the violation (Art 2).

The Commission may require the cessation of a violation of Arts 101 or 102 TFEU. It may impose behavioural or structural remedies to end the violation. These remedies must be proportionate to the violation and necessary to end the infringement. Structural remedies may be imposed only if there is no equally effective behavioural remedy that would be less burdensome than the structural remedy (Art 7(1)). The Commission has the power to order interim measures against a violation (Art 8(1)). The Commission may accept binding commitments by undertakings to end a violation (Art 9(1)).

[6.200] Investigation by the Commission

Under Regulation 1/2003 the Commission has various powers of investigation. It may require undertakings to provide necessary information (Art 18(1)), interview persons with their consent (Art 19(1)), and carry out inspections of undertakings (Art 20) and other premises (Art 21).

Another Regulation further elaborates upon the conduct of investigations by the Commission. See Commission Regulation 773/2004 of 7 April 2004 relating to the conduct of proceedings by the Commission pursuant to Articles 81 and 82 of the EC Treaty (OJ L 123, 27.4.2004, p 18). The Commission may record interviews (Art 3(2)–(3)) and explanations given during inspections (Art 4(1)–(2)). Natural and legal persons must demonstrate a legitimate interest for lodging a complaint about a violation of EU competition law (Art 5(1)). The Commission may reject a complaint if there are insufficient grounds for acting upon it (Art 7(1)). The parties have a right of access to the Commission's file in the case, though business secrets and other confidential information may not be revealed (Art 15). The Commission shall hold an oral hearing if that is requested by the parties (Art 12).

[6.205] Imposition of Fines

Under Regulation 1/2003 the Commission may impose fines to penalise violations of Arts 101 and 102 TFEU or breaches of a commitment (Art 23(2)). Fines may also be imposed for various forms of non-cooperation during the investigation such as the supply of incorrect or misleading information (Art 23(1)).

The amount of the fine is determined according to the gravity and duration of the violation (Art 23(3)). The fact that an undertaking played a minor part in an anti-competitive agreement may be taken into account when setting the fine since it goes to the gravity of the violation. See *Commission v Anic Partecipazioni* (C-49/92) [1999] ECR I-4125 at [90]; [2001] 4 CMLR 17 (p 602); *Aalborg Portland A/S v Commission* (C-204/00 P) [2004] ECR I-123 at [86]; [2005] 4 CMLR 4 (p 251); *Dansk Rørindustri A/S v Commission* (C-189/02) [2005] ECR I-5425 at [145]; [2005] 5 CMLR 17 (p 796). The Commission has issued a notice detailing its approach to giving immunity or reducing fines where an undertaking has cooperated in its investigation. See Commission Notice on Immunity from fines and reduction of fines in cartel cases (OJ C 298, 8.12.2006, p 17).

The Commission has often imposed very substantial fines. For example, in May 2009 the Commission fined Intel € 1.96 billion for abuse of its dominant position in the CPU market (IP/09/745, 13 May 2009). In *Britannia Alloys & Chemicals Ltd v Commission* (C-76/06 P) [2007] ECR I-4405; [2007] 5 CMLR 3 (p 251) the Court held the Commission's past practice regarding fines does not constitute a framework for the level of fines (at [60]). In particular, undertakings do not have a legitimate expectation that the Commission will not impose higher fines than those that have been previously imposed (at [61]).

Under Regulation 1/2003 the Commission may also impose periodic penalty payments (Art 24). The ECJ has unlimited jurisdiction to review decisions imposing a penalty (Art 31). Undertakings have a right of access to the Commission file in the case (Art 27(2)).

[6.210] Limitation Periods

Penalties may only be imposed within the specified limitation periods (Art 25(1), Regulation 1/2003). An EU Regulation places time limits upon the power of the Commission to impose fines. See Regulation 2988/74 of the Council of 26 November 1974 concerning limitation periods in proceedings and the enforcement of sanctions under the rules of the European Economic Community relating to transport and competition (OJ L 319, 29.11.1974, p 1). The limitation period for infringement of the provisions concerning applications or notifications of undertakings, requests for information or the carrying out of investigations is 3 years (Art 1(1)(a)). The limitation period for all other infringements is 5 years (Art 1(1)(b)).

Time begins to run from the date of the infringement except where there is a pattern of repeated or continuing infringements where time runs from the date when the infringement ceases (Art 1(2)). The limitation period is interrupted when the Commission, or a Member State at the request of the Commission, takes action amounting to a preliminary investigation or proceedings in the matter of the infringement (Art 2(1)). Time ceases to run on the day on which one of the participating undertakings is notified of the Commission's action.

Actions that interrupt the running of the limitation period include the following:

(a) written requests for information by the Commission, or by the competent authority of a Member State acting at the request of the Commission; or a Commission decision requiring the requested information;
(b) written authorisations to carry out investigations issued by the Commission or by the competent authority of any Member State at the request of the Commission; or a Commission decision ordering an investigation;
(c) the commencement of proceedings by the Commission;
(d) notification of the Commission's statement of objections (Art 2(1)).

Each interruption "shall start time running afresh" (Art 2(3)). However, the limitation period will expire at the latest on a day equal to a period twice as long as the original limitation period if the Commission has not imposed a fine or a periodic penalty payment (Art 2(3)). Time also does not run while a matter is before the Court (Art 3).

[6.215] Judicial Review of Commission Assessments

The Commission's margin of discretion in relation to economic matters does not preclude judicial review of its economic assessments in competition cases. See *Commission v Tetra Laval BV* (C-12/03) [2005] ECR I-987 at [39]; [2005] 4 CMLR 8 (p 573); *Spain v Lenzing AG* (C-525/04 P) [2007] ECR I-9947 at [56]; [2008] 1 CMLR 40 (p 1068); *Bertelsmann AG v Independent Music Publishers and Labels Association (Impala)* (C-413/06) [2008] ECR I-4951 at [145]; [2008] 5 CMLR 17 (p 1073).

However, the Court's review of economic assessments is marked by judicial restraint. In *Aalborg Portland A/S v Commission* (C-204/00 P) [2004] ECR I-123; [2005] 4 CMLR 4 (p 251) the Court stated that "[e]xamination by the Community judicature of the complex economic assessments made by the Commission must necessarily be confined to verifying whether the rules on procedure and on the statement of reasons have been complied with, whether the facts have been accurately stated and whether there has been any manifest error of appraisal or misuse of powers" (at [279]).

[6.220] Researching Commission Documents

The Commission produces many publications relating to its application of EU competition law. For example, the Commission issues an *Annual Report on Competition Policy*. All reports since 1971 are available at http://ec.europa.eu/competition/publications/annual_report/index.html. The Commission also publishes a *Competition Policy Newsletter* which summarises recent developments in competition law. All issues since 1994 are available on the Internet (http://ec.europa.eu/comm/competition/ publications/cpn).

Electronic versions of all Commission decisions in competition cases since 1964 are available at http://ec.europa.eu/competition/antitrust/cases/ index.html. Older decisions were reported in the *Official Journal of the European Union*. The Commission has also issued a series of compilations of decisions given in particular years. See Commission of the European Communities, *Reports of Commission Decisions Relating to Competition* (Office for Official Publications of the European Communities, 1993–). Commission decisions are also reported in the *Common Market Law Reports Antitrust Reports* (Sweet & Maxwell/Thomson, 1991–), which are volumes 4 and 5 of each year's reports. Prior to 1991 Commission decisions were reported in a separately paginated section of the *Common Market Law Reports*. The page numbers in the citations for such Commission decisions were preceded by the letter "D".

[6.225] Enforcement by National Competition Authorities

The Commission shares with the national authorities the power to rule upon the admissibility of agreements, decisions and concerted practices and abuses of a dominant position (Arts 104–105 TFEU). Under Regulation 1/2003 the competition authorities of the Member States are empowered to apply Arts 101 and 102 TFEU. To this end they may order that the violation cease, order interim measures, accept commitments and impose penalties (Art 5). The courts of the Member States are also empowered to apply Arts 101 and 102 TFEU (Art 6).

The Commission and the national competition authorities apply EU competition law in "close cooperation" (Art 11(1)). The national authorities must inform the Commission when they commence an investigation (Art 11(3)). The national authorities must also inform the Commission 30 days before ordering that a violation cease or accepting a commitment (Art 11(4)). If the Commission initiates proceedings the competence of the national authorities ends (Art 11(6)). The national courts or competition authorities may not adopt a decision on an agreement or practice that is contrary to a prior decision of the Commission on that agreement or practice (Art 16). See generally, Commission Notice on the co-operation between the Commission and the courts of the EU Member States in the application of Articles 81 and 82 EC (OJ C 101, 27.4.2004, p 54).

[6.230] Interaction of EU and National Competition Law

The Court has held that EU and national competition laws "apply in parallel, since they consider restrictive practices from different points of view." See *R v Competition Commission; Ex parte Milk Marque Ltd* (C-137/00) [2003] ECR I-7975 at [61]; [2004] 4 CMLR 6 (p 293); *Manfredi v Lloyd Adriatico Assicurazioni SpA* (C-295/04) [2006] ECR I-6619 at [38]; [2006] 5 CMLR 17 (p 980).

For example, in *Wilhelm v Bundeskartellamt* (14/68) [1969] ECR 1; [1969] CMLR 100 proceedings had been brought against the applicants under German competition law. The Commission also commenced proceedings under EC competition law, based upon the same facts. The Court held that a restrictive agreement could give rise to liability under both national and Community law. The Court observed that "in principle the national authorities in competition matters may take proceedings ... with regard to situations liable to be the object of a decision by the Commission". However, if the general aim of the Treaty is to be respected, "such parallel application of the national system should only be allowed in so far as it does not impinge upon the uniform application throughout the common market, of the Community rules on restrictive business agreements and of the full effect of the acts decreed in application of those rules" (at [4]). Conflicts between EU and national competition laws must be resolved in favour of EU law (at [6]).

In determining the amount of a fine for breach of EU competition law, natural justice requires that the Commission take account of any fine that has already been imposed by the competition authority of a Member State with respect of the same facts. See *Wilhelm v Bundeskartellamt* (14/68) [1969] ECR 1 at [11]; [1969] CMLR 100; *Boehringer Mannheim GmbH v Commission* (7/72) [1972] ECR 1281 at [3]; [1973] CMLR 864; *Tréfileurope Sales SARL v Commission* (T-141/89) [1995] ECR II-791 at [191]; *Sotralentz SA v Commission* (T-149/89) [1995] ECR II-1127 at [29]; *Kyowa Hakko Kogyo Co Ltd v Commission* (T-223/00) [2003] ECR II-2553 at [98].

Regulation 1/2003 provides that where Member States apply their national competition laws to agreements, decisions or concerted practices that may affect trade between Member States, they must also apply Art 101 TFEU (Art 3(1)). Where the Member States apply their national competition laws to the abuse of a dominant position, they must also apply Art 102 TFEU (Art 3(1)). Agreements, decisions or concerted practices may not be prohibited under national competition law if they do not restrict competition under Art 101(1) TFEU or are declared inapplicable under Art 101(3) TFEU (Art 3(2)).

The Member States are not "precluded from adopting and applying on their territory stricter national laws which prohibit or sanction unilateral conduct engaged in by undertakings" (Art 3(2)). These restrictions upon the application of national competition laws do not apply to national merger control laws. These limitations also do not "preclude the application of provisions of national law that predominantly pursue an objective different from that pursued by" Arts 101 and 102 TFEU (Art 3(3)).

[6.235] Cooperation with Non-member States

The EU and the United States have concluded a competition law cooperation agreement. See *Agreement regarding the Application of Competition Laws*, Washington, 23 September 1991, OJ L 95, 27.4.1995, p 47; [1991] 4 CMLR 823; 30 ILM 1487. This Agreement aims to promote cooperation and to lessen the impact of differences between the EU and the United States concerning the application of their competition laws.

The Agreement provides that "[e]ach Party shall notify the other whenever its competition authorities become aware that their enforcement activities may affect important interests of the other Party" (Art II(1)). If one of the parties considers that its important interests are adversely affected by anti-competitive activities occurring on the territory of the other party, it may request that the other party take enforcement action (Art V(2)). However, the other party is not obliged to take such action (Art V(4)). Each party is to consider the important interests of the other party in carrying out its enforcement activities (Art VI).

Another treaty between the EU and the United States adopts a positive comity approach to competition law investigations. See *Agreement on the Application of Positive Comity Principles in the Enforcement of their Competition Laws*, Brussels-Washington, 3–4 June 1998, OJ L 173, 18.6.1998, p 28; TIAS 12958; 37 ILM 1070. The US Department of Justice summarised the Agreement as follows: "the requesting government or party relies on its counterpart to take action under its own laws, consulting frequently in the process. A positive comity referral will lead to efficient enforcement as each side deals with conduct occurring primarily in its own territory". See Sally J Cummins and David P Stewart (eds), *Digest of United States Practice in International Law 1991–1999* (Washington: International Law Institute, 2005), 1544.

Under United States federal law a US District Court may order a resident of its District "to give his testimony or statement or to produce a document or other thing for use in a proceeding in a foreign or international tribunal" (28 USC 1782(a)). In *Intel Corporation v Advanced Micro Devices Inc* 542 US 241 (2004) the United States Supreme Court held that the European Commission is a "tribunal" when it makes a competition decision at first instance. The Court of Justice and the General Court are "tribunal[s]" but do not "use" evidence since they are limited to the record compiled by the Commission. A party could only "use" evidence by submitting it to the Commission during its investigation (at 257).

Canada and the EU have also entered into a treaty regarding competition law. See *Agreement regarding the Application of Competition Laws*, Bonn, 17 June 1999, 2101 UNTS 23; OJ L 175, 10.7.1999, p 50; Can TS 1999 No 38. The agreement provides for cooperation regarding anti-competitive activities that affect both parties (Art 4), coordination of enforcement (Art 4) and mutual notification of investigations (Art 2).

When assessing penalties for a cartel which operated both within and outside the EU, the Commission is *not* required to take account of penalties imposed by the competition authorities of non-Member States. See *Showa Denko KK v Commission* (C-289/04 P) [2006] ECR I-5859 at [56]–[57]; [2006] 5 CMLR 14 (p 840); *SGL Carbon AG v Commission* (C-308/04) [2006] ECR I-5977 at [33]; [2006] 5 CMLR 16 (p 922).

[6.240] Conclusion

Art 101(1) TFEU declares that certain restrictive trade practices are incompatible with the internal market, namely "all agreements between undertakings, decisions by associations of undertakings and concerted practices which may affect trade between Member States and which have as their object or effect the prevention, restriction or distortion of competition within the internal market". The agreements prohibited by this provision are "automatically void". Art 101(1) applies not only to horizontal agreements (agreements between competitors) but also to vertical agreements (such as between suppliers and acquirers of goods and services).

The term "undertaking" includes every entity engaged in an economic activity. An organisation that does not engage in an economic activity is not an undertaking. Art 101 also does not apply to companies that form a single economic unit in which the subsidiary has no independence to formulate its strategic course of action. Undertakings that are situated outside the Union may be subject to EU competition rules.

An agreement "arises from an expression, by the participating undertakings, of their joint intention to conduct themselves on the market in a specific way". A unilateral act or policy does not constitute an "agreement", which requires the assent of more than one party. The agreement or practice must affect trade between Member States. Agreements that have only an insignificant effect on the market do not fall under this Article. Art 101(1) also prohibits "concerted practices which may affect trade between Member States and which have as their object or effect the prevention, restriction or distortion of competition within the internal market".

Art 102 prohibits any abuse of a dominant position which affects trade between the Member States. The Court has defined a "dominant position" as "a position of economic strength held by an undertaking, which enables it to prevent effective competition from being maintained on the relevant market by giving it the power to behave to an appreciable extent independently of its competitors, its customers and, ultimately, consumers".

Art 102 expressly sets out several examples of abuse of a dominant position. These examples are not exhaustive. An abuse may also occur if an undertaking in a dominant position strengthens its position so that the level of dominance substantially fetters competition. Competition by means of predatory pricing is also illegitimate. In exceptional circumstances the refusal of an undertaking in a dominant position to grant a licence to use its industrial or commercial property may constitute an abuse of its dominant position. Art 102 requires that the abuse of a dominant position should affect trade between EU Member States. No exemption may be granted for an abuse of a dominant position.

The EU has adopted a Regulation dealing with mergers. A merger is incompatible with the common market if it "would significantly impede effective competition, in the common market or in a substantial part of it, in particular as a result of the creation or strengthening of a dominant position".

Art 107(1) provides that "any aid granted by a Member State or through State resources in any form whatsoever which distorts or threatens to distort competition by favouring certain undertakings or the production of certain goods shall, in so far as it affects trade between Member States, be incompatible with the internal market." If the Commission finds that aid is incompatible with the internal market, it shall order that the State "abolish or alter" the aid.

With certain exceptions, EU competition rules apply to the whole of the economic life of the European Union. Special provision is made in relation to (a) agriculture, (b) transport, (c) undertakings granted special or exclusive rights and (d) services of general economic interest.

The Commission is empowered to investigate alleged infringements of Arts 101 or 102. It may impose fines to penalise violations of those Articles. Agreements that violate Art 101(1) and are not saved by Art 101(3) are prohibited without any need for a previous decision prohibiting them. Agreements that violate Art 101(1) but are saved by Art 101(3) are not prohibited and there is similarly no need for a previous decision to that effect. The abuse of a dominant position under Art 102 is prohibited without the need for any prior decision to that effect. The competition authorities and courts of the Member States are also empowered to apply Arts 101 and 102. If the Commission initiates proceedings the competence of the national authorities ends.

Further Reading

A. *General Works About Competition Law*

Amato, Guiliano and Claus-Dieter Ehlermann (eds). *EC Competition Law: A Critical Assessment* (Oxford: Hart, 2007).

Andreangeli, Arianna. *EU Competition Enforcement and Human Rights* (Cheltenham, UK: Edward Elgar, 2008).

Barents, René. *Directory on EC Case Law on Competition* (Alphen aan den Rijn: Kluwer Law International, 2007).

Bechtold, Rainer; Ingo Brinker; Wolfgang Bosch and Simon Hirsbrunner. *European Competition Law: A Commentary* (3rd ed, Oxford: Hart, 2011).

European Competition Law Annual (Oxford: Hart, 1996–).

Faull, Jonathan and Ali Nikpay (eds). *The EC Law of Competition* (2nd ed, Oxford: Oxford University Press, 2007).

Furse, Mark. *Competition Law of the EC and UK* (6th ed, Oxford: Oxford University Press, 2008).

González-Orús, Jerónimo Maillo. "Beyond the Scope of Article 90 of the EU Treaty: Activities Excluded from the EC Competition Rules" (1999) 5 *European Public Law* 387.

Goyder, Joanna and Albertina Albors-Llorens. *EC Competition Law* (5th ed, Oxford: Oxford University Press, 2009).

Jones, Alison and Brenda Sufrin. *EC Competition Law* (3rd ed, Oxford: Oxford University Press, 2007).

Jones, Christopher and Marc van der Woude. *EC Competition Law Handbook, 2009/2010 Edition* (London: Sweet & Maxwell, 2009).

Kanninen, Heikki; Nina Korjus and Allan Rosas (eds). *EU Competition Law in Context: Essays in Honour of Virpi Tiili* (Oxford: Hart, 2009).

Kerse, Christopher and Nicholas Khan. *EC Antitrust Procedure* (5th ed, London: Sweet & Maxwell, 2005).

Kokkoris, Ioannis. *Competition Cases from the European Union* (London: Sweet & Maxwell, 2007).

Korah, Valentine. *Cases and Materials on EC Competition Law* (3rd ed, Oxford: Hart, 2006).

Korah, Valentine. *An Introductory Guide to EC Competition Law and Practice* (9th ed, Oxford: Hart, 2007).

Macnab, Andrew (ed). *Bellamy & Child: Materials on European Community Law of Competition* (Oxford: Oxford University Press, 2009).

Pace, Lorenzo Federico. *European Antitrust Law: Prohibitions, Merger Control and Procedures* (Cheltenham, UK: Edward Elgar, 2007).

Prosser, Tony. "Competition Law and Public Services: From Single Market to Citizenship Rights?" (2005) 11 *European Public Law* 543.

Ritter, Lennart and W David Brown. *European Competition Law: A Practitioner's Guide* (The Hague: Kluwer, 2004).

Rodger, Barry J and Angus MacCulloch. *Competition Law and Policy in the EC and UK* (4th ed, London: Routledge-Cavendish, 2009).

Roth, Peter and Vivien Rose. *Bellamy and Child: European Community Law of Competition* (6th ed, London: Sweet & Maxwell, 2008).

Tobler, Christa and Jacques Beglinge. *Essential EC Law in Charts* (Budapest: HVG-ORAC Publishing House, 2007). Companion website: http://www.eur-charts.eu

Van Bael, Ivo and Jean-Francois Bellis. *EC Competition Law Reporter* (Sweet & Maxwell, 1996–) (looseleaf).

Vogelaar, F O W. *The European Competition Rules: Landmark Cases of the European Courts and the Commission* (2nd ed, Groningen: Europa Law Publishing, 2007).

Wils, Wouter P J. "The Undertaking as Subject of EC Competition Law and the Imputation of Infringements to Natural or Legal Persons" (2000) 25 *European Law Review* 99.

B. *Agreements Between Undertakings*

Alese, Femi. "Unmasking the Masquerade of Vertical Price Fixing" (2007) 28 *European Competition Law Review* 514.

Black, Oliver. "Agreement: Concurrence of Wills, or Offer and Acceptance?" (2008) 4 *European Competition Journal* 103.

Davies, Gareth. "Article 86 EC, the EC's Economic Approach to Competition Law, and the General Interest" (2009) 5 *European Competition Journal* 549.

Ferro, Miguel Sousa. "Reassessing Borders Between Agreements and Unilateral Practices After Case C-74/04, *Volkswagen* II" (2007) 27 *European Competition Law Review* 205.

Joshua, Julian. "Single Continuous Infringement of Article 81 EC: Has the Commission Stretched the Concept Beyond the Limit of its Logic?" (2009) 5 *European Competition Journal* 451.

Krajewski, Markus and Martin Farley. "Non-economic Activities in Upstream and Downstream Markets and the Scope of Competition Law after *FENIN*" (2007) 32 *European Law Review* 111.

Odudu, Okeoghene. "The Meaning of Undertaking Within 81 EC" (2005) 7 *Cambridge Yearbook of European Legal Studies* 211.

Odudu, Okeoghene. *The Boundaries of EC Competition Law: The Scope of Article 81* (Oxford: Oxford University Press, 2006).

Singla, Tony. "The Remedies (Not) Available for Breaches of Article 81 EC" (2008) 29 *European Competition Law Review* 201.

Townley, Christopher. *Article 81 EC and Public Policy* (Oxford: Hart, 2009).

Wickihalder, Urs. "The Distinction Between an 'Agreement' Within the Meaning of Article 81(1) of the EC Treaty and Unilateral Conduct" (2006) 2 *European Competition Journal* 87.

C. *Abuse of a Dominant Position*

Albors-Llorens, Albertina. "The Role of Objective Justification and Efficiencies in the Application of Article 82 EC" (2007) 44 *Common Market Law Review* 1727.

Cahill, Dermot. "Competition and Protected Services in the EU: Abuse of Dominance by Public Sector Undertakings and the Onward March of Article 86" in Takis Tridimas and Paolisa Nebbia (eds), *European Union Law for the Twenty-First Century* (Oxford: Hart, 2004), II: 239.

Ezrachi, Ariel (ed). *Article 82 EC: Reflections on Its Recent Evolution* (Oxford: Hart Publishing, 2009).

Furse, Mark. "Excessive Prices, Unfair Prices and Economic Value: The Law of Excessive Pricing Under Article 82 EC and the Chapter II Prohibition" (2008) 4 *European Competition Journal* 59.

Kokkoris, Ioannis. *A Gap in the Enforcement of Article 82* (London: British Institute of International and Comparative Law, 2009).
Lang, John Temple. "Reprisals and Overreaction by Dominant Companies as an Anti-competitive Abuse Under Article 82(b)" (2008) 29 *European Competition Law Review* 11.
Maier-Rigaud, Frank P. "Article 82 Rebates: Four Common Fallacies" (2005) 2 *European Competition Journal* Special Supplement 85.
Monti, Giorgio. "The Concept of Collective Dominance Under Article 82" (2001) 38 *Common Market Law Review* 131.
Monti, Giorgio. "The Concept of Dominance in Article 82" (2005) 2 *European Competition Journal* Special Supplement 31.
O'Donoghue, Robert and Atilano Jorge Padilla. *The Law and Economics of Article 82 EC* (Oxford: Hart, 2006).
Oliver, Peter. "The Concept of 'Abuse' of a Dominant Position Under Article 82 EC: Recent Developments in Relation to Pricing" (2005) 1 *European Competition Journal* 315.
Ridyard, Derek. "Exclusive Contracts and Article 82 Enforcement: An Effects-Based Perspective" (2008) 4 *European Competition Journal* 579.
Stothers, Christopher. "Refusal to Supply as Abuse of a Dominant Position: Essential Facilities in the European Union" (2001) 22 *European Competition Law Review* 256.
Subiotto, Romano and Robert O'Donoghue. "Defining the Scope of the Duty of Dominant Firms to Deal with Existing Customers Under Article 82 EC" (2003) 24 *European Competition Law Review* 683.

D. Mergers

Bailey, David. "Standard of Proof in EC Merger Proceedings: A Common Law Perspective" (2003) 40 *Common Market Law Review* 845.
Bailey, David. "Damages Actions Under the EC Merger Regulation" (2007) 44 *Common Market Law Review* 101.
Blanke, Gordon. "The Use of Arbitration in EC Merger Control: Latest Developments" (2007) 28 *European Competition Law Review* 673.
Broberg, Morten P. *The European Commission's Jurisdiction to Scrutinise Mergers* (3rd ed, The Hague: Kluwer Law International, 2006).
Cook, John and Christopher Kerse. *EC Merger Control* (5th ed, London: Sweet and Maxwell, 2009).
Drauz, Götz and Christopher Jones. *EU Competition Law. Volume II: Mergers and Acquisitions* (Leuven, Belgium: Claeys & Casteels, 2006).
Fountoukakos, Kyriakos. "Judicial Review and EC Merger Control: Reflections on the Effectiveness of the System with Regard to the Standard of Review and Speed" (2008) 10 *Cambridge Yearbook of European Legal Studies* 133.

Harvey, Neil. *A Practitioner's Guide to Takeovers and Mergers in the European Union* (5th ed, Old Woking, Surrey: City & Financial Publishing, 2008).

Heimler, Alberto. "Was the Change of the Test for Merger Control in Europe Justified? An Assessment (Four Years after the Introduction of SIEC)" (2008) 4 *European Competition Journal* 85.

Kekelekis, Mihalis. *The EC Merger Control Regulation: Rights of Defence* (Alphen aan den Rijn: Kluwer, 2006).

Kent, Penelope; Vicky Allsopp and Penny English. "The Future of Merger Control in the EC" in Takis Tridimas and Paolisa Nebbia (eds), *European Union Law for the Twenty-First Century* (Oxford: Hart, 2004), II: 195.

Killick, James. "The *GE/Honeywell Judgment*: In Reality Another Merger Defeat for the Commission" (2007) 28 *European Competition Law Review* 52.

Lindsay, Alistair. *The EC Merger Regulation: Substantive Issues* (3rd ed, London: Sweet & Maxwell, 2009).

Monti, Giorgio. "The New Substantive Test in EC Merger Regulation—Bridging the Gap Between Economics and Law?" (2008) 10 *Cambridge Yearbook of European Legal Studies* 263.

Siems, Mathias M. "The European Directive on Cross-Border Mergers: An International Model?" (2005) 11 *Columbia Journal of European Law* 167.

Szilagyi, Pal. "The ECJ Has Spoken: Where Do We Stand with Standard of Proof in Merger Control?" (2008) 29 *European Competition Law Review* 726.

Temple Lang, John. "Two Important Merger Regulation Judgments: The Implications of *Schneider-Legrand* and *Tetra Laval-Sidel*" (2003) 28 *European Law Review* 259.

Vesterdorf, Bo. "Standard of Proof in Merger Cases. Reflections in the Light of Recent Case Law of the Community Courts" (2005) 1 *European Com petition Journal* 3.

Werden, Gregory J. "Unilateral Competitive Effects and the Test for Merger Control" (2008) 4 *European Competition Journal* 95.

E. State Aid

Arhold, Christoph. "The Case-Law of the European Court of Justice and the Court of First Instance on State Aids in 2003/2004" [2004] *European State Aid Law Quarterly* 167.

Arhold, Christoph. "The Case Law of the European Court of Justice and the Court of First Instance on State Aids in 2004/2005" [2005] *European State Aid Law Quarterly* 175.

Arhold, Christoph. "The Case Law of the European Court of Justice and the Court of First Instance on State Aids in 2005/2006" [2006] *European State Aid Law Quarterly* 215, 465.

Arhold, Christoph. "The Case Law of the European Court of Justice and the Court of First Instance on State Aids in 2006/2007" [2007] *European State Aid Law Quarterly* 151, 435.

Arhold, Christoph. "The 2007/2008 Case Law of the European Court of Justice and the Court of First Instance on State Aid" [2008] *European State Aid Law Quarterly* 441.

Bacon, Kelyn. *European Community Law of State Aid* (Oxford: Oxford University Press, 2009).

Biondi, Andrea et al. *The Law of State Aid in the European Union* (Oxford: Oxford University Press, 2004).

Bovis, Christopher H. "State Aid and European Union Transport: A Reflection on Law, Policy and Practice" (2005) 39 *Journal of World Trade* 587.

Braun, Jens-Daniel and Jürgen Kühling. "Article 87 EC and the Community Courts: From Revolution to Evolution" (2008) 45 *Common Market Law Review* 465.

Commission Notice on the Enforcement of State Aid Law by National Courts (OJ C 85, 9.4.2009, p 1).

D'Sa, Rose M. "When is Aid not State Aid? The Implications of the English Partnerships Decision for European Competition Law and Policy" (2000) 25 *European Law Review* 139.

de Cecco, Francesco. "The Many Meanings of 'Competition' in EC State Aid Law" (2007) 9 *Cambridge Yearbook of European Legal Studies* 111.

Gromnicka, Ewa. "Services of General Economic Interest in the State Aids Regime: Proceduralisation of Political Choices?" (2005) 11 *European Public Law* 429.

Hakenberg, Waltraud and Friedrich Erlbacher. "State Aid Law in the European Courts in 2001 and 2002" (2003) 24 *European Competition Law Review* 431.

Hancher, Leigh. "Towards a New Definition of a State Aid Under European Law: Is there a New Concept of State Aid Emerging?" [2003] *European State Aid Law Quarterly* 365.

Hancher, Leigh; Tom Ottervanger and Piet Jan Slot. *EC State Aids* (3rd ed, London: Sweet & Maxwell, 2006).

Hatton, Catriona and Jean-Michel Coumes. "European Commission Adopts Guidance on State Aids to the Financial Sector" (2008) 30 *European Competition Law Review* 51.

Heidenhain, Martin (ed). *European State Aid Law: A Handbook* (Oxford: Hart, 2009).

Heuninckx, Baudouin. "Defence Procurement: The Most Effective Way to Grant Illegal State Aid and Get Away with it...or is it?" (2009) 46 *Common Market Law Review* 191.

Hillger, Jens. "The Award of a Public Contract as State Aid Within the Meaning of Article 87(1) EC" (2003) 12 *Public Procurement Law Review* 109.

Honoré, Michael. "The Standing of Third Parties in State Aid Cases" [2006] *European State Aid Law Quarterly* 269.

Kroes, Neelie; Mario Monti and Karel van Miert (eds). *EC State Aid Law: Liber Amicorum in Honour Francisco Santaolalla* (Alphen aan den Rijn: Kluwer Law International, 2008).

Kurcz, Bartlomiej and Dimitri Vallindas. "Can General Measures Be... Selective? Some Thoughts on the Interpretation of a State Aid Definition" (2008) 45 *Common Market Law Review* 159.

Lindner, Nikolaus. "The Impact of the Decision of the European Court of Justice in *Ferring* on European State Aid Law" (2003) 9 *European Public Law* 359.

Mederer, Wolfgang; Nicola Pesaresi and Marc van Hoof (eds). *EU Competition Law. Volume IV: State Aid* (Leuven, Belgium: Claeys & Casteels, 2008).

Quigley, Conor. *European State Aid Law* (2nd ed, Oxford: Hart, 2008).

Rubini, Luca. *The Definition of Subsidy and State Aid: WTO and EC Law in Comparative Perspective* (Oxford: Oxford University Press, 2008).

Schohe, Gerrit and Christoph Arhold. "The Case-Law of the European Court of Justice and the Court of First Instance on State Aids in 2002/2003" [2003] *European State Aid Law Quarterly* 145.

Sinnaeve, Adinda. "State Financing of Public Services: The Court's Dilemma in the *Altmark* Case" [2003] *European State Aid Law Quarterly* 351.

Soltész, Ulrich and Holger Bielesz. "Judicial Review of State Aid Decisions—Recent Developments" (2004) 25 *European Competition Law Review* 133.

Vesterdorf, Peter and Mogens Uhd Nielsen. *State Aid Law of the European Union* (London: Sweet & Maxwell, 2008).

Völcker, Sven B. "Never the Twain Shall Meet: State Aid Considerations in EC Merger Control" [2003] *European State Aid Law Quarterly* 531.

Winter, Jan A. "Re(de)fining the Notion of State Aid in Article 87(1) of the EC Treaty" (2004) 41 *Common Market Law Review* 475.

Zuleger, Volker. "State Aid and Risk Capital" (2006) 27 *European Competition Law Review* 166.

F. Administration of Competition Law

Billiet, Philippe. "How Lenient Is the EC Leniency Policy? A Matter of Certainty and Predictability" (2009) 30 *European Competition Law Review* 14.

Brammer, Silke. *Co-operation Between National Competition Agencies in the Enforcement of EC Competition Law* (Oxford: Hart, 2009).

Grasso, Roberto. "The EU Leniency Program and US Civil Discovery Rules: A Fraternal Fight?" (2008) 29 *Michigan Journal of International Law* 565.

Komninos, Assimakis. "New Prospects for Private Enforcement of EC Competition Law: *Courage v Crehan* and the Community Right to Damages" (2002) 39 *Common Market Law Review* 447.

Komninos, Assimakis. *EC Private Antitrust Enforcement, Decentralised Application of EC Competition Law by National Courts* (Oxford: Hart, 2008).

Lucey, Mary Catherine. "Unforeseen Consequences of Article 3 of EU Regulation 1/2003" (2006) 27 *European Competition Law Review* 558.

Monti, Giorgio. "Anticompetitive Agreements: The Innocent Party's Right to Damages" (2002) 27 *European Law Review* 282.

Müller, Felix. "The New Council Regulation (EC) No 1/2003 on the Implementation of the Rules on Competition" (June 2004) 5, 6 *German Law Journal* 721, http://www.germanlawjournal.com

Nordsjo, Andreas. "Regulation 1/2003: Power of the Commission to Adopt Interim Measures" (2006) 27 *European Competition Law Review* 299.

O'Keeffe, Siún. "First Among Equals: The Commission and the National Courts as Enforcers of EC Competition Law" (2001) 26 *European Law Review* 301.

Rodger, Barry J. *Article 234 and Competition Law: An Analysis* (Alphen aan den Rijn: Kluwer Law International, 2008).

van den Bergh, Roger and Sonja Keske. "Private Enforcement of European Competition Law: Quo Vadis?" (2007) 3 *European Review of Contract Law* 468.

Venit, James. "Brave New World: The Modernization and Decentralization of Enforcement Under Articles 81 and 82 of the EC Treaty" (2003) 40 *Common Market Law Review* 545.

Walsh, Declan J. "Carrots and Sticks—Leniency and Fines in EC Cartel Cases" (2009) 30 *European Competition Law Review* 30.

Werden, Gregory J. "Sanctioning Cartel Activity: Let the Punishment Fit the Crime" (2009) 5 *European Competition Journal* 19.

Useful Websites

Commission decisions in competition cases http://ec.europa.eu/competition/anti-trust/cases/index.html

Annual Report on Competition Policy http://ec.europa.eu/comm/competition/annual_reports

Competition Policy Newsletter http://ec.europa.eu/comm/competition/publications/cpn

Chapter 7
Removal of Taxation Barriers to Trade

[7.05] Introduction

Art 26 TFEU affirms the EU's commitment to the operation of the internal market, namely an area without internal frontiers in which the free movement of goods, persons, services and capital is ensured. From its initiation the EU envisaged the abolition of internal customs duties and charges of equivalent effect. While necessary limits upon the power to impose internal taxation were also accepted, Member States were left with a considerable discretion in fiscal matters. The scope of that discretion is being gradually reduced through the harmonization of indirect taxes and certain direct business taxes.

The achievement of the internal market necessarily involved the abolition of tariffs, quotas, subsidies and other customs barriers to internal trade. However, the abolition of these tariff and non-tariff barriers could be subverted through the manipulation of any one Member State's taxation regime, which could thus be a barrier to the free movement of goods and services and the implementation of free competition. For example, such subversion may occur if a Member State imposes internal taxation on imported products after their importation. While Member States may still levy taxes, their taxation powers are limited by Art 110 TFEU. This chapter discusses this Article in detail.

[7.10] Customs Duties

Art 28 TFEU (formerly Art 9 EC) affirms that the EU is based upon a Customs Union which covers all trade in goods. That Article prohibits customs duties on internal trade (imports and exports of goods between Member States). The Customs Union is supplemented by a common customs tariff in relations with third countries.

The concept of a single market with a common external face to the world would be effectively eroded if internal customs duties could be disguised as,

G. Moens, J. Trone, *Commercial Law of the European Union*,
Ius Gentium: Comparative Perspectives on Law and Justice 4,
DOI 10.1007/978-90-481-8774-4_7,

for example, health regulations. Art 25 TFEU (formerly Art 12 EC) prohibits charges that have an effect equivalent to that of customs duties. This reaffirms the intent of Art 28 TFEU to examine the effect of charges, whatever their alleged purpose.

[7.15] Internal Taxation

The TFEU maintains a distinction between proscribed internal customs duties (including charges having an equivalent effect) and permitted, but regulated, internal taxation. The authority of Member States to impose internal taxes derives from Arts 110 and 111 TFEU. Art 110 TFEU provides as follows:

> No Member State shall impose, directly or indirectly, on the products of other Member States any internal taxation of any kind in excess of that imposed directly or indirectly on similar domestic products.
>
> Furthermore, no Member State shall impose on the products of other Member States any internal taxation of such a nature as to afford indirect protection to other products.

Art 110 thus provides that Member States are prevented from imposing upon the products of other Member States any internal tax in excess of that imposed upon "similar domestic products". Internal taxes may be direct or indirect. The key requirement is that internal taxes upon imports from other Member States must be no higher than those upon similar domestic products.

The Court of Justice has identified the purpose of Art 110 as ensuring the free movement of goods by preventing protection of domestic products through the adoption of discriminatory internal taxation. See *Nádasdi v Vám- és Pénzügyőrség Észak-Alföldi Regionális Parancsnoksága* (C-290/05) [2006] ECR I-10115 at [45]; [2007] 1 CMLR 21 (p 627); *Brzezińksi v Dyrektor Izby Celnej w Warszawie* (C-313/05) [2007] ECR I-513 at [27]; [2007] 4 CMLR 4 (p 121). Art 110 ensures that internal taxation is completely neutral in relation to competition between domestic products and imports. See *Commission v Denmark* (171/78) [1980] ECR 447 at [4]; [1981] 2 CMLR 688; *De Danske Bilimportører v Skatteministeriet, Told- og Skattestyrelsen* (C-383/01) [2003] ECR I-6065 at [37]; [2003] 2 CMLR 41 (p 1265); *Weigel v Finanzlandesdirektion für Vorarlberg* (C-387/01) [2004] ECR I-4981 at [66]; [2004] 3 CMLR 42 (p 931).

The TFEU provides that customs duties and charges that have an equivalent effect are prohibited between Member States (Art 30 TFEU). Art 110 supplements this prohibition by proscribing discriminatory or protectionist internal taxation. See *Air Liquide Industries Belgium SA v Ville de Seraing* (C-393/04) [2006] ECR I-5293 at [55]; [2006] 3 CMLR 23 (p 667); *Nádasdi v Vám- és Pénzügyőrség Észak-Alföldi Regionális*

Parancsnoksága (C-290/05) [2006] ECR I-10115 at [45]; [2007] 1 CMLR 21 (p 627); *Brzeziński v Dyrektor Izby Celnej w Warszawie* (C-313/05) [2007] ECR I-513 at [27]; [2007] 4 CMLR 4 (p 121).

However, a charge cannot infringe both Arts 30 and 110 TFEU, that is, it cannot constitute both discriminatory internal taxation and a customs duty or equivalent charge. See *Nygård v Svineafgiftsfonden* (C-234/99) [2002] ECR I-3657 at [17]; *De Danske Bilimportører v Skatteministeriet, Told- og Skattestyrelsen* (C-383/01) [2003] ECR I-6065 at [33]; [2003] 2 CMLR 41 (p 1265); *Stadtgemeinde Frohnleiten v Bundesminister für Land- und Forstwirtschaft, Umwelt und Wasserwirtschaft* (C-221/06) [2007] ECR I-9643 at [26]; [2008] 1 CMLR 30 (p 779).

Art 111 TFEU provides: "Where products are exported to the territory of any Member State, any repayment of internal taxation shall not exceed the internal taxation imposed on them whether directly or indirectly." Under this provision, where products are exported to another part of the EU any refund of internal taxation must not exceed the internal taxation imposed. Disguised subsidies for exports to other Member States are thus prohibited.

A tax must meet several conditions to be within the power of a Member State under Arts 110 and 111 TFEU. First, the charge must relate to a general system of taxation. Secondly, the tax must be imposed upon objective criteria regardless of the origin of the product. See *Commission v France* (90/79) [1981] ECR 283 at [14]; [1981] 3 CMLR 1; *Chemial Farmaceutici v DAF SpA* (140/79) [1981] ECR 1 at [12], [14]; [1981] 3 CMLR 350; *Commission v Italy* (319/81) [1983] ECR 601 at [8]; [1983] 2 CMLR 517. Thirdly, the tax or levy must be upon both imported and domestic similar products. See *Commission v Luxembourg* (2/62) [1962] ECR 425 at 434; [1963] CMLR 199 at 217–218.

[7.20] Customs Duty or an Internal Tax?

It is important to emphasize that the scheme in Arts 110 and 111 TFEU applies only to *internal* taxation, not to customs duties or to charges having an effect equivalent to a customs duty. Art 28 TFEU prohibits the imposition of internal customs duties or charges having equivalent effect. Art 110 permits internal taxes, provided there is no discrimination against EU imports. Internal taxes imposed upon imports must be the same as those imposed upon local products.

The distinction between customs duties and internal taxation thus necessitates a classification of the disputed legislation as internal taxation or a customs duty. See *United Foods NV v Belgium* (132/80) [1981] ECR 995 at [32]; [1982] 1 CMLR 273. The case law of the ECJ offers many examples of the Court's attempts to distinguish between a proscribed custom duty and a permitted internal tax.

The importance of the distinction is illustrated by *Commission v France* (90/79) [1981] ECR 283; [1981] 3 CMLR 1. The French government applied a levy upon photocopying machines and the publication of books (at [2]–[3]). It claimed that the purpose of the levy was to purchase French and foreign books for libraries (at [4]). The government claimed that another purpose was to reimburse authors for the loss of royalties from the use of reproductions made with photocopying machines (at [5]–[6]). The Commission pointed out that as the French made very few photocopying machines the levy fell almost exclusively upon foreign goods. The Commission argued that the levy therefore contravened Art 12 (now Art 25 TFEU) where the levy applied to photocopying machines made in other Member States (at [7]). The French government argued that the levy was not a customs duty or a charge with an equivalent effect (at [8]).

The ECJ dismissed the Commission's claim. The Court held that internal taxation may be imposed upon imported products even where there are no similar or competing domestic products, provided that the tax applies to similar or competing goods irrespective of their origin. The Court observed:

> the prohibition . . . in regard to charges having equivalent effect covers any charge exacted at the time of or on account of importation which, being borne specifically by an imported product to the exclusion of the similar domestic product, has the result of altering the cost price of the imported product thereby producing the same restrictive effect on the free movement of goods as a customs duty. The essential feature of a charge having an effect equivalent to a customs duty which distinguishes it from an internal tax therefore resides in the fact that the former is borne solely by an imported product as such whilst the latter is borne both by imported and domestic products (at [12]–[13]).

In *Ditta Fratelli Cucchi v Avez SpA* (77/76) [1977] ECR 987 Italian surcharges upon sugar involved a reimbursement to domestic producers (at [3]). The charges were levied indiscriminately upon domestically produced and imported sugar (at [13]). The Italian government argued that the levies constituted a permitted internal tax under Art 95 (now Art 110 TFEU) rather than an impermissible customs duty under Art 9 (now Art 28 TFEU). The Court held that as part of the proceeds of the levies were used for the purpose of wholly or partially reimbursing the domestic producers of sugar for the levies paid, they amounted to charges equivalent to customs duties (at [15]–[17]). However, the Court's ruling suggested that the levy would have to be wholly reimbursed to the domestic producer before the levy would constitute a charge having an equivalent effect to a customs duty.

The Italian surcharge was also at issue in *Commission v Italy* (73/79) [1980] ECR 1533. The surcharge imposed upon local and imported products was principally used for the purpose of financing adaptation aid for the sugar industry (at [2]). The Court stressed that, even if an equal charge is imposed upon domestic and imported products, it is still necessary to consider the purpose for which the revenue is used. The internal taxation was held to be incompatible with Art 95 (now Art 110 TFEU) because the revenue was used for the special benefit of the taxed domestic product (at [15]).

In *Denkavit Loire Sarl v France* (132/78) [1979] ECR 1923; [1979] 3 CMLR 605, the Court considered whether a levy should be regarded as an internal tax or was equivalent to a duty of customs. The Court stated:

> in order to relate to a general system of internal dues, the charge to which an imported product is subject must impose the same duty on national products and identical imported products at the same marketing stage and that the chargeable event giving rise to the duty must also be identical in the case of both products. It is therefore not sufficient that the objective of the charge imposed on imported products is to compensate for a charge imposed on similar domestic products – or which has been imposed on those products or a product from which they are derived – at a production or marketing stage prior to that at which the imported products are taxed (at [8]).

[7.25] Indirect Taxation

Once it has been determined that there is no customs duty or charge of equivalent effect it may be necessary to consider whether there is an indirect tax. Art 110 TFEU prohibits Member States from "directly or indirectly" imposing internal taxation of any kind in excess of that imposed directly or indirectly upon similar domestic products. This is reinforced by the requirement in Art 110 that taxation of imports from another Member State shall not be "of such a nature as to afford indirect protection to other products."

The Court thus has a mandate to look beyond the formal description of the tax in question, and to examine the total scheme established by the Member State. The Court has stated that "taxation might be indirectly discriminatory as a result of its effects". See *Nádasdi v Vám- és Pénzügyőrség Észak-Alföldi Regionális Parancsnoksága* (C-290/05) [2006] ECR I-10115 at [47]; [2007] 1 CMLR 21 (p 627).

In *Commission v Ireland* (55/79) [1980] ECR 481; [1980] 1 CMLR 734 the Court considered the Irish government's practice of permitting the payment of excise upon locally produced products to be deferred, but requiring the immediate payment of tax upon products imported from other Member States (at [2]). This discrimination was held to be incompatible with Art 95 (now Art 110 TFEU) (at [9]–[10]).

One question for the Court to determine is whether the tax is so remote from the final product that it does not amount to indirect internal taxation of the product. In *Molkerei-Zentrale Westfalen Lippe GmbH v Hauptzollamt Paderborn* (28/67) [1968] ECR 143; [1968] CMLR 187 the Court said that "[t]he first paragraph of Article 95 [now Art 110 TFEU] refers to all taxation which is actually and specifically imposed on the domestic product at all earlier stages of its manufacture and marketing or which corresponds to the stage at which the product is imported from other Member States" (at ECR 155; CMLR 220).

The same question could arise under the second paragraph of Art 110 TFEU. This paragraph prohibits a Member State from taxing the product of another Member State if the taxation is such as to afford indirect protection to other products produced in the taxing state. The effect would be to make the taxed product uncompetitive with the equivalent local product, so that the local product would be substituted for the taxed product. For example, this paragraph would presumably apply if a State producing goose meat taxed imports of duck meat so that cheap local goose meat was substituted for more expensive imported duck meat.

In *Firma August Stier v Hauptzollamt Hamburg-Ericus* (31/67) [1968] ECR 235 Germany taxed lemons that had been imported from Italy. As Germany produced no similar fruit and there could be no substitution of a German product for the imported product, the tax was upheld as a valid internal tax (at 241). The test seems to be whether there is in fact a locally produced product that may be substituted for the taxed article. See *Firma Fink-Frucht GmbH v Hauptzollamt München-Landsbergerstrasse* (27/67) [1968] ECR 223 at 231.

[7.30] Similar Domestic Products

Art 110 TFEU restricts only internal taxation of imports where there is a similar or competing domestic product. It does not offer protection against excessive taxation that has no protectionist effect. See *De Danske Bilimportører v Skatteministeriet, Told- og Skattestyrelsen* (C-383/01) [2003] ECR I-6065 at [38]; [2003] 2 CMLR 41 (p 1265). In that case Art 110 TFEU did not apply to Danish internal taxation of cars as there was no similar or competing domestic product since no cars were produced in Denmark (at [39]).

The word "products" has been widely interpreted. For example, transactions in relation to the disposal of waste have been held to fall within the scope of Art 110. See *Commission v Belgium* (C-2/90) [1992] ECR I-4431 at [25]–[26]; [1993] 1 CMLR 365; *Stadtgemeinde Frohnleiten v Bundesminister für Land- und Forstwirtschaft, Umwelt und Wasserwirtschaft* (C-221/06) [2007] ECR I-9643 at [36]–[38]; [2008] 1 CMLR 30 (p 779).

The question of what are "similar domestic products" under Art 110 TFEU is not always easily answered. In *H Hansen Jun v Hauptzollamt Flensburg* (148/77) [1978] ECR 1787; [1979] 1 CMLR 604 the Court conceded that "[d]ifficult problems regarding similar treatment can arise . . . in view of the elements to which the legislation of the different member-States has linked the granting of the tax advantages concerned" (at [18]). The

Court also pointed out that the application of Art 110 TFEU "is based not on a strict requirement that the products should be identical but on their 'similarity'" (at [18]).

This question of "similarity" has arisen in a number of cases. In *Commission v France* (168/78) [1980] ECR 347; [1981] 2 CMLR 631 the Commission sought to prevent France maintaining its policy of taxing spirits distilled from cereals (mainly imported) at higher rates than spirits distilled from wine and fruit (mainly produced in France) (at [17]). The Court did not provide a general answer to the question of what are "similar domestic products". It held that the French system was so obviously designed to protect the local distillers that the problem did not require an answer (at [39]). Such protection was incompatible with the second paragraph of Art 95 (now Art 110 TFEU).

A similar finding was made in *Commission v Denmark* (171/78) [1980] ECR 447; [1981] 2 CMLR 688. In that case the taxation upon aquavit was lower than that upon other spirits (at [22]). The Court stressed that the expression "similar products" should be interpreted flexibly. The criteria for describing products as "similar" did not involve an examination of the nature of the products themselves but whether they had a comparable use (at [5]).

In *Re Natural Sweet Wines: Commission v France* (196/85) [1987] ECR 1597; [1988] 2 CMLR 851 France had established a preferential system for the taxation of natural sweet wines (at [2]). The ECJ held that the French scheme did not violate the EEC Treaty. The Court stated:

> Community law does not restrict the freedom of Member States to lay down tax arrangements which differentiate between certain products, even products which are similar within the meaning of Article 95(1) [Art 110 TFEU], on the basis of objective criteria, such as the nature of the raw materials used or the production processes used. Such differentiation is compatible with Community law if it pursues objectives of economic policy which are themselves compatible with the requirements of the Treaty and its secondary law, and if the detailed rules are such as to avoid any form of discrimination, direct or indirect, in regard to imports from other member states or any form of protection of competing domestic products. . . .
>
> Article 95 EEC does not prohibit Member States, in the pursuit of economic or social aims from granting tax advantages, in the form of exemptions from or reduction of taxes, to certain types of spirits or to certain classes of producers, provided that such preferential systems are extended without discrimination to imported products conforming to the same conditions as preferred domestic products (at [6]–[7]).

The substitutability of wine and beer was considered in *Commission v United Kingdom* (170/78) [1980] ECR 417 and [1983] ECR 2265. British legislation taxed wine at £3.25 per gallon and beer at £0.61 per gallon. The Commission argued that Art 95 (Art 110 TFEU) had been violated because wine and beer stand in a competitive relationship to each other and the tax on wine was much heavier than that upon beer ([1980] ECR 417 at [2]). In determining the substitutability of beer and wine, the Court considered the whole EC market and not simply the United Kingdom market (at [14]). The Court held that two competing products should be taxed in the same manner if they possess the same characteristics from a fiscal point of view. The British tax system had the effect of imposing a higher tax burden upon imported wines than upon local beer, thereby protecting the local beer industry ([1983] ECR 2265 at [27]). In *Re VAT Rates on Wine: Commission v Belgium* (356/85) [1987] ECR 3299; [1988] 3 CMLR 277 the Court held that cheap wines were in competition with beer (at [11]).

In *F G Roders BV v Inspecteur der Invoerrechten en Accijnzen* (C-367/93) [1995] ECR I-2229 the ECJ stated that in determining whether there are similar domestic products the court must "consider whether they have similar characteristics and meet the same needs from the point of view of consumers, the test being not whether they are strictly identical but whether their use is similar and comparable" (at [27]). See similarly, *Commission v France* (C-302/00) [2002] ECR I-2055 at [23].

The cases reveal that the Court first examines whether the competing products are substitutable. If they are substitutable, the Court considers the tax burden. Art 110 TFEU will be infringed if the taxation imposed upon domestic and imported products is taxed in a different manner and according to different criteria that will in at least some cases lead to higher taxation of the imported products. See *Weigel v Finanzlandesdirektion für Vorarlberg* (C-387/01) [2004] ECR I-4981 at [67]; [2004] 3 CMLR 42 (p 931); *Brzezinski v Dyrektor Izby Celnej w Warszawie* (C-313/05) [2007] ECR I-513 at [29]; [2007] 4 CMLR 4 (p 121). A national law that limits the availability of a tax exemption to domestic products will infringe Art 110 because it is likely to lead to higher taxation of imports. See *Chevassus-Marche v Conseil régional de la Réunion* (C-212/96) [1998] ECR I-743 at [26]; [1998] 2 CMLR 330.

To be consistent with Art 110 a system of taxation must entirely preclude the possibility that imported products may be subject to higher taxation. See *Brzeziński v Dyrektor Izby Celnej w Warszawie* (C-313/05) [2007] ECR I-513 at [40]; [2007] 2 CMLR 4 (p 121); *Stadtgemeinde Frohnleiten v Bundesminister für Land- und Forstwirtschaft, Umwelt und Wasserwirtschaft* (C-221/06) [2007] ECR I-9643 at [50]; [2008] 1 CMLR 30 (p 779); *Krawczynski v Dyrektor Izby Celnej w Bialymstoku* (C-426/07) [2008] ECR I-6021 at [32].

[7.35] Harmonization of Indirect Taxation

Art 113 TFEU provides that "[t]he Council shall . . . adopt provisions for the harmonisation of legislation concerning turnover taxes, excise duties and other forms of indirect taxation to the extent that such harmonisation is necessary to ensure the establishment and the functioning of the internal market and to avoid distortion of competition."

[7.40] Value Added Tax (VAT)

Value Added Tax was introduced in 1967 as the method of collection of a Community-wide indirect tax. It is levied upon the production and distribution of goods and the provision of services performed within the territory of a Member State by a taxable person in their business activity and upon the imports of goods into that territory.

Art 110 TFEU applies to the value added tax. In *Gaston Schul BV v Inspecteur der Invoerrechten en Accijnzen* (15/81) [1982] ECR 1409; [1982] 3 CMLR 229 the Court held that the submission of goods to VAT in the importing State violated Art 95 (Art 110 TFEU) if the goods have already been charged VAT in the exporting Member State (at [40]). This violation stems from the fact that submission of imported goods to VAT in the importing State would result in imports carrying a heavier taxation burden than national products.

Harmonization of indirect taxes is being achieved through the adoption of a number of Directives. In 1967 a Directive provided that existing turnover taxes were to be replaced by a Value Added Tax levied on a common basis. See First Council Directive 67/227 on the harmonisation of legislation of Member States concerning turnover taxes (OJ L 71, 14.4.1967, p 1301).

In 1970 the Council decided that the Community should be financed through its own resources. See Council Decision 70/243 of 21 April 1970 on the replacement of financial contributions from Member States by the Communities' own resources (OJ L 94, 28.4.1970, p 19). Art 311 TFEU now stipulates that "[w]ithout prejudice to other revenue, the budget shall be financed wholly from own resources" and that the Council shall "adopt a decision laying down the provisions relating to the system of own resources of the Union". The EU's own resources include a proportion of VAT levied in each Member State. See Art 2(1)(b), Council Decision 2007/436 of 7 June 2007 on the system of the European Communities' own resources (OJ L 163, 23.6.2007, p 17).

A Council Directive sets out the framework for the value added tax. See Council Directive 2006/112 of 28 November 2006 on the common system of value added tax (OJ L 347, 11.12.2006, p 1). The common system "entails the application to goods and services of a general tax on consumption exactly proportional to the price of the goods and services, however many transactions take place in the production and distribution process before the stage at which the tax is charged. On each transaction, VAT . . . shall be chargeable after deduction of the amount of VAT borne directly by the various cost components. The common system . . . shall be applied up to and including the retail trade stage" (Art 1(2)). The taxable person is authorized to deduct from the tax they are liable to pay on goods and services supplied any tax paid on the acquisition of those goods and services (Art 168). The consumer does not benefit from any deduction.

The following transactions are subject to VAT: (1) the supply of goods and services within the territory of a Member State by a taxable person for consideration, (2) the intra-Community acquisition of goods within the territory of a Member State by (among others) a taxable person for consideration and (3) the importation of goods (Art 2(1)). The Directive harmonizes the legislation of Member States defining the concepts of taxable persons (Art 9); taxable transactions such as the supply of goods (Art 14) or services (Art 24) and the importation of goods (Art 30); chargeable events (Art 62); taxable amounts (Arts 73–87) and numerous exemptions (Arts 131 and following).

This Directive is a codification of the former Sixth Council Directive 77/388 of 17 May 1977 on the harmonization of the laws of the Member States relating to turnover taxes—Common system of value added tax: uniform basis of assessment (OJ L 145, 13.6.1977, p 1). In *Halifax plc v Customs and Excise Commissioners* (C-255/02) [2006] ECR I-1609; [2006] 2 CMLR 36 (p 943) the Court held that a transaction would constitute a supply of goods or services or an economic activity under the Sixth Council Directive if it fulfilled the objective criteria for those concepts, even though the transaction was made with the sole purpose of securing a tax advantage (at [58], [60]). Tax evasion by dishonest means would not fulfil those objective criteria (at [59]).

However, the Court also held that EU law could not be invoked for abusive or fraudulent purposes (at [68]). Transactions that were entered into with the sole intention of wrongfully obtaining an advantage under EU law and without any normal commercial purpose would constitute an abusive practice (at [69]). This principle applied to value added tax (at [70]). The Court acknowledged that it is permissible for businesses to structure their operations in a manner that reduces their liability to taxation (at [73]). A transaction would constitute an abusive practice only if it met two conditions. The first condition was that the transaction secured a tax advantage contrary to the purpose of the Directive and national implementing legislation while satisfying in form the conditions laid down in that legislation. The second condition was that objective factors showed that the essential purpose of the transaction was to secure a tax advantage (at [74]). See generally, Ad van Doesum et al., "The New Rules on the Place of Supply of Services in European VAT" (2008) 17 *EC Tax Review* 78; Ben Terra and Julie Kajus, *A Guide to the European VAT Directives 2009* (Amsterdam: IBFD Publications BV, 2009).

[7.45] Capital Taxation

A Directive regulates the levying of indirect taxes on contributions of capital to capital companies, their restructuring operations and the issue of some securities and debentures. See Art 1, Council Directive 2008/7 of 12

February 2008 concerning indirect taxes on the raising of capital (OJ L 46, 21.2.2008, p 11). Capital companies include "any company, firm, association or legal person the shares in whose capital or assets can be dealt in on a stock exchange" (Art 2(1)(b)).

The Directive provides that Member States shall not levy upon capital companies any indirect tax in relation to contributions of capital, formalities prior to commencing business, amendment of the company constitution or restructuring operations (among others) (Art 5(1)). Member States may not levy any indirect tax in relation to issues or dealings in shares or stocks or in respect of loans raised by the issue of negotiable securities (again among others) (Art 5(2)). However, Member States are permitted to levy duties on the transfer of securities, duties on the transfer of businesses, mortgage duties and value added tax (Art 6(1)).

Despite the prohibition upon indirect taxation of contributions of capital, the Directive permits those Member States that charged capital duty as at 1 January 2006 to continue to do so (Art 7(1)). The duty must be charged at a single rate (Art 8(1)), which must not exceed 1% (Art 8(3)). Capital duty is defined as "a duty on contributions of capital to capital companies" (Art 7(1)).

[7.50] Excise Duties

Excise duties are duties levied at a single stage on the production or distribution process. The rate of the excise may be either "ad valorem" (a percentage of the value) or specific (a fixed amount per volume or quantity of the product).

The EU has adopted general guidelines for excise duties. See Council Directive 2008/118 of 16 December 2008 concerning the general arrangements for excise duty (OJ L 9, 14.1.2009, p 12). The Directive applies to excise duty levied on the consumption of energy products, electricity, alcohol and tobacco (the "excise goods") (Art 1(1)). The Member States may levy taxes on other products but those taxes must not "give rise to formalities connected with the crossing of frontiers" (Art 1(3)).

Excise goods are subject to excise duty at the time of their production within the EU and their importation into the EU (Art 2). Excise duty is chargeable at the time and place of release for consumption (Art 7(1)). Excise duty on excise goods acquired by a private individual for his or her own use may be charged only in the Member State in which the goods were acquired (Art 32(1)). The Member States may lay down guide quantities as evidence of whether tobacco and alcohol are acquired for personal use (Art 32(3)).

The Council has adopted measures for the harmonization of excise upon manufactured tobacco and alcohol. See Council Directive 95/59 of 27 November 1995 on taxes other than turnover taxes which affect the consumption of manufactured tobacco (OJ L 291, 6.12.1995, p 40); Council Directive 92/83 of 19 October 1992 on the harmonisation of the structures of excise duties on alcohol and alcoholic beverages (OJ L 316, 31.10.1992, p 21).

The EU has also set minimum rates of excise duty applicable to tobacco and alcohol. See Council Directive 92/79 of 19 October 1992 on the approximation of taxes on cigarettes (OJ L 316, 31.10.1992, p 8); Council Directive 92/80 of 19 October 1992 on the approximation of taxes on manufactured tobacco other than cigarettes (OJ L 316, 31.10.1992, p 10); Council Directive 92/84 of 19 October 1992 on approximation of the rates of excise duty on alcohol and alcoholic beverages (OJ L 316, 31.10.1992, p 29).

Another Directive makes provision for minimum rates of taxation for mineral oils, coal, natural gas and electricity used for fuel or power. See Council Directive 2003/96 of 27 October 2003 restructuring the Community framework for the taxation of energy products and electricity (OJ L 283, 31.10.2003, p 51).

[7.55] Harmonization of Direct Taxes

Arts 110–113 TFEU are directed only to the harmonization of indirect taxes. Arts 115 and 116 TFEU provide for the approximation of legislation of the Member States which affects the establishment or functioning of the internal market or which creates distortions in the conditions of competition. The Council has adopted several measures in the field of direct company taxation. These measures concern company mergers, parent and subsidiary companies, arbitration in relation to double taxation and interest and royalties.

[7.60] Mergers Directive

The Mergers Directive applies to five types of transactions in which companies from two or more Member States are involved, namely mergers, divisions, partial divisions, transfers of assets, and exchanges of shares. See Art 1(a), Council Directive 90/434 of 23 July 1990 on the common system of taxation applicable to mergers, divisions, partial divisions, transfers of assets and exchanges of shares concerning companies of different Member States and to the transfer of the registered office, of an SE or SCE, between Member States (OJ L 225, 20.8.1990, p 1).

The Directive covers all companies set up under the law of a Member State and subject to corporation tax in a Member State (Art 3(b)). A "merger" is defined as an operation whereby:

- one or more companies, on being dissolved without going into liquidation, transfer all their assets and liabilities to another existing company in exchange for the issue to their shareholders of securities representing the capital of that other company, and, if applicable, a cash payment not exceeding 10% of the nominal value, or, in the absence of a nominal value, of the accounting par value of those securities,
- two or more companies, on being dissolved without going into liquidation, transfer all their assets and liabilities to a company that they form, in exchange for the issue to their shareholders of securities representing the capital of that new company, and, if applicable, a cash payment not exceeding 10% of the nominal value, or in the absence of a nominal value, of the accounting par value of those securities,
- a company, on being dissolved without going into liquidation, transfers all its assets and liabilities to the company holding all the securities representing its capital (Art 2(a)).

"Division" is defined as an operation whereby "a company, on being dissolved without going into liquidation, transfers all its assets and liabilities to two or more existing or new companies, in exchange for the pro rata issue to its shareholders of securities representing the capital of the companies receiving the assets and liabilities" (Art 2(b)). Thus, in both mergers and divisions, all the assets and liabilities are transferred and the existing company is dissolved without going into liquidation. The legislation provides that shares in the receiving company are allotted to the previous shareholders in the dissolved company. The Directive also applies to partial divisions (Art 2(b)(a)).

Mergers and divisions are fundamentally different from a transfer of assets. The Directive states that a transfer of assets is an operation whereby "a company transfers without being dissolved all or one or more branches of its activity to another company in exchange for the transfer of securities representing the capital of the company receiving the transfer" (Art 2(c)). Where a company transfers all of its activity to another, it continues to exist as a legal entity. The transferring company takes the new shares in the receiving company. Once it has transferred all of its activity, the transferring company becomes a holding company, whose assets consist entirely of a stake in the receiving company.

The provisions on "exchange of shares" deal with the case where "a company acquires a holding in the capital of another company such that it obtains a majority of the voting rights in that company" (Art 2(d)). In exchange, the acquiring company allocates shares to these existing shareholders in the acquiring company.

The central principle of the Mergers Directive is that after the merger or transfer a permanent establishment belonging to the receiving company in the State of the transferring company remains available for taxation in that State. The Directive allows the State of the acquired company or transferring company, which has now become the State of a permanent establishment only, to tax the transferred assets and liabilities at a later stage. In such circumstances, double taxation agreements will come into operation. See generally, Eva van den Brande, "The Merger Directive Amended: The Final Version" (2005) 14 *EC Tax Review* 119; G K Fibbe, "The Different Translations of the term 'Company' in the Merger Directive and the Parent Subsidiary Directive: A Babylonian Confusion of Tongues?" (2006) 15 *EC Tax Review* 95.

[7.65] Parent/Subsidiary Directive

Another Directive relates to parent and subsidiary companies. See Council Directive 90/435 of 23 July 1990 on the common system of taxation applicable in the case of parent companies and subsidiaries of different Member States (OJ L 225, 20.8.1990, p 6).

This Directive applies to:

- "distributions of profits received by companies ... which come from their subsidiaries of other Member States",
- "distributions of profits by companies ... to companies of other Member States of which they are subsidiaries",
- "distributions of profits received by permanent establishments ... of companies of other Member States which come from their subsidiaries of a Member State other than that where the permanent establishment is situated", and
- "distributions of profits by companies ... to permanent establishments situated in another Member State of companies of the same Member State of which they are subsidiaries" (Art 1(1)).

A "company of a Member State" takes one of the forms listed in the Annex to the Directive (Art 2(1)(a)). They are all joint stock companies. A "permanent establishment" is defined as "a fixed place of business situated in a Member State through which the business of a company of another Member State is wholly or partly carried on in so far as the profits of that place of business are subject to tax in the Member State in which it is situated" (Art 2(2)).

The status of parent company is attributed at least to any company of a Member State which has a minimum holding of 10% in the capital of a company of another Member State (the subsidiary) (Art 3(1)(a)). The use of the words "at least" and "minimum" indicates that Member States are free to provide for a privileged parent/subsidiary relationship even below this minimum holding. Member States have the option of "replacing, by means of bilateral agreement, the criterion of a holding in the capital by that of a holding of voting rights" (Art 3(2)).

This Directive has two legal consequences for distributions of profits by a subsidiary to a parent company resident for tax purposes in another Member State. The first consequence is that double taxation is abolished. Where a parent company or permanent establishment, by virtue of its association with its subsidiary, receives distributed profits, the State of the parent company is under an obligation either (a) to refrain from taxing such profits, or (b) "tax such profits while authorising the parent company and the permanent establishment to deduct from the amount of tax due that fraction of the corporation tax related to those profits and paid by the subsidiary…, up to the limit of the amount of the corresponding tax due" (Art 4(1)). Expressed more simply, the Member State in which the parent company is established shall exempt the dividends or, alternatively, tax them while at the same time imputing the tax charged in the Member State in which the subsidiary is established against it own tax.

The second legal consequence for such distributions of profits is that withholding tax is abolished. "Profits which a subsidiary distributes to its parent company shall be exempt from withholding tax" (Art 5). See generally, Cécile Brokelind, "Ten Years of Application of the Parent-Subsidiary Directive" (2003) 12 *EC Tax Review* 158; Guglielmo Maisto, "The 2003 Amendments to the EC Parent-Subsidiary Directive: What's Next?" (2004) 13 *EC Tax Review* 164.

[7.70] Arbitration Convention

The Arbitration Convention provides for the introduction of an arbitration procedure designed to avoid double taxation that occurs in connection with the adjustment of the profits of associated enterprises when an upward adjustment in an enterprise's profits in one Member State is not accompanied by a corresponding adjustment in the results of the other enterprise in another Member State. See Art 7, *Convention on the Elimination of Double Taxation in connection with the Adjustment of Profits of Associated Enterprises*, Brussels, 23 July 1990, 1847 UNTS 3; OJ L 225, 20.8.1990, p 10.

The Convention applies "where, for the purposes of taxation, profits which are included in the profits of an enterprise of a Contracting State are also included or are also likely to be included in the profits of an enterprise of another Contracting State" (Art 1(1)). In order to include adjustments of prices charged between an enterprise and its permanent establishments, a permanent establishment situated in another contracting State is deemed to be an enterprise of the State in which it is situated (Art 1(2)).

The Convention applies to the taxes that were levied on profits in the individual Member States at the time it was concluded (Art 2(2)). It is expressly stated that it will also apply to any identical or similar taxes imposed later (Art 2(3)). The Convention provides that the prices agreed between associated enterprises can be adjusted for tax purposes if they differ from those that would be charged under the same conditions between independent enterprises (the "arm's length" principle) (Art 4(1)). The same holds for adjustments relating to a permanent establishment (Art 4(2)).

The main purpose of the Convention is to resolve cases of double taxation as rapidly as possible. Tax authorities are accordingly required to inform the enterprise beforehand where they intend to make an adjustment of the kind covered by the Convention (Art 5). This will allow the intended adjustment to be discussed with the associated enterprise and the contracting State in which it is situated, and if all parties are in agreement the matter is resolved. The date on which the tax authority announces its intention of making an adjustment is also important for some of the time-limits governing later steps.

[7.75] Interest and Royalties Directive

This Directive ensures equality as between domestic and cross-border transactions in relation to the taxation of interest and royalty payments made between associated companies of different Member States. See Preamble Recital 4, Council Directive 2003/49 of 3 June 2003 on a common system of taxation applicable to interest and royalty payments made between associated companies of different Member States (OJ L 157, 26.6.2003, p 49).

The Directive seeks to ensure that such payments are subject to taxation once only by eliminating taxation in the Member State where they arise (Preamble Recitals 3 and 4). To this end the Directive provides that interest and royalty payments arising in a Member State are exempt from taxation in that State, provided that their beneficial owner is a company of another Member State or a Member State company's permanent establishment in another Member State (Art 1(1)).

Interest is widely defined as "income from debt-claims of every kind" and numerous specific examples are given (Art 2(a)). Royalties are defined as payments received as a consideration for the use of or the right to use various intellectual property rights (Art 2(b)). Certain payments such as distributions of profits, repayments of capital and a right to participate in the debtor's profits are excluded from the protection of the Directive (Art 41)). Where there is a special relationship between the payer and the beneficial owner of the interest or royalties, if the interest or royalties paid is greater than that which would have been agreed if there was no special relationship, the Directive protects only that lower amount from taxation (Art 4(2)).

[7.80] Taxation of Individuals

The Council has adopted a Directive concerning one aspect of the taxation of individuals. See Council Directive 2003/48 of 3 June 2003 on taxation of savings income in the form of interest payments (OJ L 157, 26.6.2003, p 38). The purpose of this Directive is to ensure that savings income from interest payments made in a Member State to an individual who is resident for tax purposes in another Member State is subject to taxation in that State of residence (Art 1(2)). The Directive was enacted because many recipients of such interest had not been taxed upon that income (Preamble Recital 5).

[7.85] Conclusion

EU Member States may not directly or indirectly impose upon products from other Member States any internal taxation exceeding that imposed upon similar domestic products. No Member State may impose on the products of other Member States any internal taxation that would afford indirect protection to other products. Discriminatory or protectionist internal taxation is thus prohibited. Where products are exported to the territory of any Member State, any repayment of internal taxation must not exceed the internal taxation imposed upon them.

These prohibitions apply only to internal taxation, not to customs duties or charges. The ECJ must thus classify a measure as internal taxation or a customs duty. Internal taxation is only restricted where there is a similar or competing domestic product.

The Council may adopt provisions for the harmonisation of turnover taxes, excise duties and other forms of indirect taxation. The EU has adopted a common system of value added tax. The EU's own resources include a proportion of VAT levied in each Member State. Subject to transitional arrangements, Member States may not levy upon capital companies any indirect taxation in relation to contributions of capital and their restructuring operations. The EU has regulated excise duties levied on the consumption of energy products, electricity, alcohol and tobacco. The EU has also adopted measures in the field of direct company taxation.

Under the Mergers Directive after the merger or transfer a permanent establishment belonging to the receiving company in the State of the transferring company remains available for taxation in that State. The State of the acquired or transferring company is permitted to tax the transferred assets or liabilities at a later stage. In such circumstances double taxation agreements will come into operation.

The Parent/Subsidiary Directive abolishes double taxation for distributions of profits by a subsidiary to a parent company resident for tax purposes in another Member State. Profits distributed by a subsidiary are exempt from withholding tax.

The Arbitration Convention provides for an arbitration procedure designed to avoid double taxation in connection with the adjustment of the profits of associated enterprises. The Interest and Royalties Directive seeks to ensure that interest and royalty payments made between associated companies of different Member States are subject to taxation once only by eliminating taxation in the Member State where they arise. Savings income from interest payments made in a Member State to an individual who is resident for tax purposes in another Member State will be subject to taxation in the State of residence.

Further Reading

Barents, René. *Directory of EC Case Law on Direct Taxation* (Alphen aan den Rijn: Kluwer Law International, 2009).

Gormley, Laurence W. *EU Taxation Law* (Richmond, UK: Richmond Law and Tax, 2005).

Henkow, Oskar. "Neutrality of VAT for Taxable Persons: A New Approach in European VAT" (2008) 17 *EC Tax Review* 233.

Slotboom, Marco M. "Do Different Treaty Purposes Matter for Treaty Interpretation?: The Elimination of Discriminatory Internal Taxes in EC and WTO Law" (2001) 4 *Journal of International Economic Law* 557.

Snell, Jukka. "Non-Discriminatory Tax Obstacles in Community Law" (2007) 56 *International and Comparative Law Quarterly* 339.

Terra, Ben J M and Peter J Wattel. *European Tax Law* (4th ed, The Hague: Kluwer, 2005).

Weber, Dennis. *European Direct Taxation: Case Law and Regulations* (Alphen aan den Rijn: Kluwer Law International, 2009).

Chapter 8
Public Procurement

[8.05] Introduction

Public procurement represents a significant proportion of the EU's gross domestic product. Government contracts have traditionally been awarded to national suppliers. One of the implicit aims of the EU is to remove discrimination in contracts for governmental procurement.

There are three types of government contracts:

(a) public supply contracts, namely those for the purchase of products, for example the supply of equipment to government schools and hospitals;
(b) public works contracts, relating to the execution of works, for example, the building of government schools and hospitals; and
(c) public service contracts, namely contracts between a service provider and a contracting authority but which are not public supply or public works contracts.

Public procurement is governed by two specific EU Directives, the more general principles of the TFEU and the WTO Agreement on Government Procurement.

The European Court of Justice has stated that "the principal objective of the Community rules in the field of public procurement is the free movement of services and the opening-up to undistorted competition in all the Member States". See *Stadt Halle, RPL Recyclingpark Lochau GmbH v Arbeitsgemeinschaft Thermische Restabfall- und Energieverwertungsanlage TREA Leuna* (C-26/03) [2005] ECR I-1 at [44]; [2006] 1 CMLR 39 (p 1027); *Carbotermo SpA v Comune di Busto Arsizio* (C-340/04) [2006] ECR I-4137 at [58]; [2006] 3 CMLR 7 (p 195).

G. Moens, J. Trone, *Commercial Law of the European Union*,
Ius Gentium: Comparative Perspectives on Law and Justice 4,
DOI 10.1007/978-90-481-8774-4_8, © Springer Science+Business Media B.V. 2010

[8.10] Public Works, Supplies and Services Directive

In 2004 the Council and Parliament adopted Directive 2004/18 on the coordination of procedures for the award of public works contracts, public supply contracts and public service contracts (OJ L 134, 30.4.2004, p 114).

[8.15] Exclusions from the Directive

The Directive does not apply to contracts awarded under international agreements (Art 15). Some services are excluded from the Directive, including employment contracts, contracts for the sale or rental of land or buildings, research and development services and financial services relating to securities (Art 16). It also does not apply to service concessions, where the consideration for the service consists wholly or partially in a concession to exploit the service (Arts 1(4), 17). The Directive does not apply to secret contracts (Art 14). Contracts in the water, energy, transport and postal services sectors are excluded from this Directive (Art 12). They are regulated by a separate Directive.

[8.20] Contracting Authorities Regulated by the Directive

The contracting authorities covered by the Directive include not only national, regional and local authorities in the Member States, but also "bodies governed by public law" and "associations formed by one or several of such authorities" (Art 1(9)). These include undertakings which are mainly financed by or are subject to administrative or managerial control by public authorities.

[8.25] Threshold Amounts

The Directive applies to contracts that have a value of at least a specified threshold amount. Subject to certain exceptions, the following threshold amounts apply:

(a) EUR 125,000 for public supply and service contracts awarded by the central governmental authorities listed in Annex IV of the Directive,
(b) EUR 193,000 for public supply and service contracts awarded by author ities not listed in Annex IV, and
(c) EUR 4,845,000 for public works contracts (Art 7).

These amounts exclude value added tax. The Commission revises these thresholds every 2 years (Art 78(1)).

[8.30] Definitions of Public Contracts

"Public contracts" are of three types: public works contracts, public supply contracts and public service contracts. "Public works contracts" are public contracts for the construction of, among other things, buildings, highways, airfields and water projects (Art 1(2)(b); Annex I). The Directive provides that "insofar as... works are incidental to the principal subject-matter of the contract,... the fact that such works are included in the contract does not justify the qualification of the contract as a public works contract" (Preamble Recital 10).

A "public supply contract" is a public contract for the purchase, lease, rental or hire purchase of products, unless it constitutes a public works contract (Art 1(2)(c)).

A "public service contract" is a public contract for the provision of various services, unless it constitutes a public works contract or a public supply contract (Art 1(2)(d)). The services that may constitute the subject of a public service contract are listed in Annex II. This Annex lists services under two categories (A and B). For the moment only the first category will be considered here, since it is subject to more detailed regulation.

[8.35] Requirements Applicable to Annex II A Services

Annex II A includes services such as maintenance and repair, land and air transportation, mail transport, telecommunications, banking, insurance, accounting, management and architectural services, research and development, market research and advertising, sanitation and computer services. The services listed in Annex II A are governed by Arts 23–55 of the Directive (Art 20). These provisions are summarised below.

[8.40] Non-discrimination Obligations of Contracting Authorities

Contracting authorities are required to treat service providers without discrimination and must act in a transparent way (Art 2). Equal treatment is a fundamental principle of the EU law relating to public procurement. See *Concordia Bus Finland Oy AB v Helsingin Kaupunki* (C-513/99) [2002] ECR I-7213 at [81]; [2003] 3 CMLR 20 (p 589); *Kauppatalo Hansel Oy v*

Imatran Kaupunki (C-244/02) [2003] ECR I-12139 at [36]; [2004] 3 CMLR 17 (p 366).

[8.45] Requirements as to Technical Specifications

Technical specifications must not create unjustifiable obstacles to the opening of government contracts to competition (Art 23(2)). Specifications are to be formulated by reference to European standards or national standards where European standards do not exist (Art 23(3)(a)). These requirements are without prejudice to mandatory national technical rules that are compatible with EU law (Art 23(3)). Performance or functional requirements may take account of environmental considerations (Art 23(3)(b)).

Technical specifications must not "refer to a specific make or source, or a particular process, or to trade marks, patents, types or a specific origin or production with the effect of favouring or eliminating certain undertakings or certain products." Such reference may be made where it is required by the subject-matter of the contract. Exceptionally, specifications may make such reference where necessary for precision or comprehensibility, but they must also state that an equivalent will be acceptable (Art 23(8)).

[8.50] Procedures for the Award of Public Contracts

Public contracts are awarded by four different procedures. These are open procedures, restricted procedures, competitive dialogue and negotiated procedures (Art 28). Under open procedures any provider may submit a tender (Art 1(11)). Under restricted procedures any provider may ask to tender but only those that are invited may actually tender (Art 1(11)).

Under competitive dialogue any provider may ask to participate and the contracting authority enters into discussions with selected candidates in order to find an acceptable alternative before inviting tenders from the candidates (Arts 1(11), 29(3)). The contract must be awarded on the basis of criteria for selecting the most economically advantageous tender (Arts 29(1), 53).

Under negotiated procedures the contracting authorities consult their chosen providers and negotiate the contract with one or more of them (Art 1(11)). A contract notice must generally be published beforehand (Art 30(1)). However, there are exceptions to this requirement of prior publication (Art 31). Negotiated procedures are available in several circumstances. For example, this procedure may be used where tenders have been irregular or unacceptable under national provisions. The procedure may also be used where the nature of the works, supplies or services prevents the adoption of a prior total price (Art 30(1)).

The Directive also makes provision for design contests (Arts 66–74). These procedures enable contracting authorities to obtain a design selected from competition entries (Art 1(11)).

[8.55] Publicity of Contracting Opportunities

Contracting authorities that intend to award a public contract by open, restricted or negotiated procedures or by competitive dialogue, must publicise that intention by a contract notice sent to the Commission (Art 35(2)). The Commission publishes these notices at EU expense (Art 36(4)). Each notice is published in one of the EU's official languages, along with a summary in the other languages (Art 36(4)). Notices may be published at the national level only after they have been published by the EU (Art 36(5)). Tendering notices are available online at http://ted.europa.eu.

The Directive sets minimum time limits for the receipt of tenders (Art 38). This facilitates the making of tenders by providers from other Member States.

[8.60] Award of Public Contracts

Contracting authorities shall award public contracts on the basis of (a) criteria related to the subject-matter of the contract where the contract will be awarded to the most economically advantageous tender or (b) the lowest price (Art 53(1)). Under a repealed public procurement Directive the Court held that in determining the most economically advantageous tender the contracting authority can take into account environmental considerations. However, those environmental considerations must relate to the subject-matter of the contract, must not give the authority an unlimited choice of contractor, must be set out in the tender notice and must not infringe the principle of non-discrimination. See *Concordia Bus Finland Oy Ab v Helsingin Kaupunki* (C-513/99) [2002] ECR I-7213 at [57], [59], [61]–[63]; [2003] 3 CMLR 20 (p 589). Contracting authorities are required to notify the Commission of the results of the award procedure (Art 35(4)).

[8.65] Requirements Applicable to Annex II B Services

The services that may constitute the subject of a public service contract are listed in Annex II. Thus far the more detailed requirements applicable to the services listed in Annex II A have been considered. Now the much less detailed requirements that apply to the services listed in Annex II B will be considered.

Annex II B includes services such as hotels and restaurants, water and rail transportation, legal services, personnel placement, security, education, recreation, and health and social services. The services listed in Annex II B are governed by Arts 23 and 35(4) of the Directive (Art 20). The provisions regarding technical specifications discussed above also apply to these services (Art 23). Contracting authorities are required to notify the Commission of the results of the award procedure (Art 35(4)).

[8.70] Qualification and Disqualification of Bidders

The Directive specifies qualitative criteria for the disqualification of bidders (Art 45). It also deals with the evidence contractors can produce to demonstrate their technical, financial and economic capacity (Arts 47–48), including evidence of their listing on a national official list of approved contractors (Art 46).

[8.75] Excluded Sectors

The public works, supplies and services Directive does not cover public procurement in the water, energy, transport and postal services sectors. These are the "excluded sectors" which are covered by Directive 2004/17 coordinating the procurement procedures of entities operating in the water, energy, transport and postal services sectors (OJ L 134, 30.4.2004, p 1). The Directive applies to governmental authorities, bodies governed by public law and public undertakings (Art 2). It does not apply to contracts awarded under international agreements (Art 22). The threshold values of contracts are EUR 3,87,000 for supply and service contracts and EUR 4,845,000 for public works contracts (Art 16). The threshold amounts are revised every 2 years (Art 69). See generally, Jan Hebly, *European Public Procurement: Legislative History of the Utilities Directive 2004/17/EC* (Alphen aan den Rijn: Kluwer Law International, 2008).

Some types of defence and security contracts are governed by a separate Directive. See Directive 2009/81 of the European Parliament and of the Council of 13 July 2009 on the coordination of procedures for the award of certain works contracts, supply contracts and service contracts by contracting authorities or entities in the fields of defence and security (OJ L 216, 20.8.2009, p 76). The contracts regulated by this Directive include those for the supply of military or sensitive equipment and works and services for specifically military purposes (Art 2).

[8.80] Enforcement of the Procurement Rules

In 1989 the Council adopted Directive 89/665 on the coordination of the laws, regulations and administrative provisions relating to the application of review procedures to the award of public supply and public works contracts (OJ 1989 L 395, 30.12.1989, p 33). The Directive aims to ensure that appropriate national remedies are available for breaches of the public procurement rules. The review procedures can result in the suspension of any decision taken by a contracting authority or discriminatory technical specifications may be declared inoperable. It also increases the powers of the Commission to ensure that national tendering authorities respect EU procurement rules.

Under the Directive all Member States are required to establish effective and rapid administrative and judicial remedies against any infringement of EU rules concerning public procurement. Art 1 of this Directive provides:

> (1) ... Member States shall take the measures necessary to ensure that, as regards contracts falling within the scope of Directive 2004/18/EC, decisions taken by the contracting authorities may be reviewed effectively and, in particular, as rapidly as possible ... on the grounds that such decisions have infringed [EU] law in the field of public procurement or national rules transposing that law ... .
>
> (3) Member States shall ensure that the review procedures are available, under detailed rules which the Member States may establish, at least to any person having or having had an interest in obtaining a particular contract and who has been or risks being harmed by an alleged infringement.
>
> (4) Member States may require that the person wishing to use a review procedure has notified the contracting authority of the alleged infringement and of his intention to seek review.

The bodies implementing the review procedures must have the power to suspend the award of contracts, to award damages, and to set aside any decisions taken unlawfully (Art 2(1)). Member States may set time limits for review applications (Art 2f). Where the Commission considers that there has been a "serious infringement" of the rules in a contract award procedure, it may intervene prior to the conclusion of a contract, requesting the correction of the infringement by the Member State concerned (Art 3).

There is an equivalent Directive concerning enforcement relating to public procurement in the excluded sectors. See Council Directive 92/13 coordinating the laws, regulations and administrative provisions relating to the application of Community rules on the procurement procedures of entities operating in the water, energy, transport and telecommunications sectors (OJ L 76, 23.3.1992, p 14).

[8.85] General Provisions of the TFEU

Public procurement contracts that are not regulated by either Directive are still subject to EU rules. The internal market provisions of the TFEU are applicable to contracts that are excluded from the Directives. See Commission Interpretative Communication (OJ C 179, 1.8.2006, p 2). For example, the prohibition upon discrimination upon the ground of nationality applies to contracts that do not fall under either Directive. See *Associazione Nazionale Autotrasporto Viaggiatori (ANAV) v Comune di Bari* (C-410/04) [2006] ECR I-3303 at [18]; [2006] 2 CMLR 63 (p 1544); *SECAP SpA v Comune di Torino* (C-147/06) [2008] ECR I-3565 at [20]; [2008] 2 CMLR 56 (p 1558).

As a consequence of the prohibition of indirect discrimination on the ground of nationality and the principle of equal treatment, public authorities are under an obligation of transparency in awarding public procurement contracts. See *Consorzio Aziende Metano v Comune di Cingia de' Botti* (C-231/03) [2005] ECR I-7287 at [16]–[19]; [2006] 1 CMLR 2 (p 17); *Coditel Brabant SA v Commune d'Uccle* (C-324/07) [2009] 1 CMLR 29 (p 789) at [25]. Public procurement contracts are also subject to the competition rules of the TFEU.

[8.90] Quantitative Restrictions

Art 34 TFEU prohibits quantitative restrictions on imports or exports and measures having an equivalent effect. This provision has direct effect, that is, it creates rights that are enforceable by individuals (see Chapter 12). Thus any requirement in public tendering documents which specifies that the products to be supplied or to be used in public works should be of domestic origin is inoperative. If public authorities of a Member State discriminate against goods imported from another Member State in the award of supply contracts, then that conduct constitutes a measure having an effect equivalent to a quantitative restriction prohibited by Art 34 TFEU. The same principle applies to public works contracts.

The Commission closely scrutinizes tenders which prefer or benefit domestic producers. Where necessary, the Commission initiates legal action under Art 258 TFEU for discontinuation of the impugned practice. For example, in *Re Dundalk Water Supply Scheme: Commission v Ireland* (45/87) [1988] ECR 4929; [1989] 1 CMLR 225 the Irish government invited the submission of tenders for the construction of an asbestos cement water main (at [2]). The Court held that the call for tenders was incompatible with Art 34 TFEU [then Art 30] insofar as the contractor had to certify that the asbestos cement pressure pipe used complied with the relevant Irish standards (at [27]). The Court stated:

> Article 30 [now Art 23 TFEU] envisages the elimination of all measures of the member-States which impede imports in intra-Community trade, whether the measures bear directly on the movement of imported goods or have the effect of indirectly impeding the marketing of goods from other member-States. . . . the fact that a public works contract relates to the provision of services cannot remove a clause in an invitation to tender restricting the materials that may be used from the scope of the prohibitions set out in Article 30 (at [16]–[17]).

[8.95] Competition Law Rules

Art 102 TFEU deals with the abuse by an undertaking of a dominant position within the internal market. This Article applies to:

- public bodies: *Italy v Sacchi* (155/73) [1974] ECR 409 at [14]; [1974] 2 CMLR 177; *Decision 82/861 Telespeed Services Ltd v United Kingdom Post Office* OJ L 360, 21.12.1982, p 36; [1983] 1 CMLR 457;
- statutory authorities: *Belgische Radio en Televisie v SV Sabam* (127/73) [1974] ECR 313 at [19]–[22]; [1974] 2 CMLR 238; *Centre Belge D'études de Marche Tele-Marketing SA v Compagnie Luxembourgeoise de Télédiffusion SA* (311/84) [1985] ECR 3261 at [16]; [1986] 2 CMLR 558;
- authorities given statutory powers: *Gesellschaft zur Verwertung von Leistungsschutzrechten mbH (GVL) v Commission* (7/82) [1983] ECR 483 at [29]–[32]; [1983] 3 CMLR 645; and
- non-profit organisations.

Where several undertakings hold a dominant position and the behaviour of those undertakings is characterised as concerted action that group of undertakings is regarded as an economic unit and the members of that unit are jointly and severally liable for damage caused. See *Istituto Chemioterapico Italiano SpA v Commission* (6/73) [1974] ECR 223 at [41]; [1974] 1 CMLR 309; *Siderúrgica Aristrain Madrid SL v Commission* (C-196/99 P) [2003] ECR I-11005 at [99]; *Dansk Rørindustri A/S v Commission* (C-189/02) [2005] ECR I-5425 at [118]; [2005] 5 CMLR 17 (p 796).

Art 106(1) TFEU provides that where public undertakings are concerned, the Member States may not enact or maintain in force any measure contrary to Art 102. If an undertaking abuses its dominant position that conduct is not excused by the fact that it was permitted or encouraged by national measures. The fact that the dominant position was created by national measures does not give the undertaking a defence against the application of Art 102 TFEU. Art 102 does not apply where the distortion of competition was caused by legislation of Member States. See *Cullet v Centre Leclerc à Toulouse* (231/81) [1985] ECR 305 at [16]; [1985] 2 CMLR 524. That Article also does not apply to national price freeze rules. See *Procureur Général v Buys* (5/79) [1979] ECR 3203 at [29]–[31]; [1980] 2 CMLR 493.

[8.100] WTO Agreement on Public Procurement

Directive 2004/18 (OJ L 134, 30.4.2004, p 114) provides that in awarding public contracts, "Member States shall apply in their relations conditions as favourable as those which they grant to economic operators of third countries" under the WTO Agreement on Government Procurement (Art 5). See *Agreement on Government Procurement*, Marrakesh, 15 April 1994, 1915 UNTS 103; OJ L 336, 23.12.1994, p 273; OJ C 256, 3.9.1996, p 1.

The European Community, United States, Canada, Hong Kong and Singapore are party to this treaty. See 1915 UNTS 103; 2065 UNTS 150, 152. As at 28 February 2010 Australia, India, Malaysia, New Zealand and South Africa were not party to the Agreement. As the European Union is a party to the Agreement, a considerable proportion of the EU's government contracts are open to direct competitive bidding from suppliers established in non-EU countries.

The Agreement applies to procurements valued above a minimum amount (Art I(4); Appendix I). Each Party shall provide to the products, services and suppliers of other Parties treatment no less favourable than that accorded to those from domestic sources (Art III(1)). Technical specifications shall not be applied with the effect of creating unnecessary obstacles to international trade (Art VI(1)). Each Party shall ensure that its tendering procedures are applied in a non-discriminatory manner (Art VII(1)). All procurements shall be preceded by a published invitation to participate (Art IX(1)). However, there are exceptions for limited tendering (Art XV). Time limits for tendering must be sufficient to allow suppliers from other Parties to prepare tenders before the closing date (Art XI(1)). See generally, Sue Arrowsmith, *Government Procurement in the WTO* (The Hague: Kluwer, 2003).

[8.105] Conclusion

This chapter deals with one of the largest customers within the EU, namely the national governments. There are three types of government contracts: public supply contracts for the purchase of products, public works contracts for the execution of works and public service contracts for the provision of services.

Contracting authorities must treat service providers without discrimination and must act in a transparent way. Technical specifications must not create unjustifiable obstacles to the opening of government contracts to competition. Public contracts are awarded by open procedures, restricted procedures, competitive dialogue and negotiated procedures. Contracting authorities that intend to award a public contract must publicise that intention by notice sent to the Commission.

EU Member States are required to establish effective and rapid administrative and judicial remedies against any infringement of EU rules concerning public procurement. The internal market and competition provisions of the TFEU are applicable to contracts that are excluded from the public procurement Directives. In awarding public contracts EU Member States must apply in their relations conditions as favourable as those that they grant to economic operators of non-EU Member States under the WTO Agreement on Government Procurement.

Further Reading

Arrowsmith, Sue. "The Entity Coverage of the EC Procurement Directives and UK Regu-lations: A Review" (2004) 13 *Public Procurement Law Review* 59.

Arrowsmith, Sue and Peter Kunzlik. *Social and Environmental Policies in EC Procurement Law: New Directives and New Directions* (Cambridge: Cambridge University Press, 2009).

Bartosch, Andreas. "The Relationship Between Public Procurement and State Aid Surveillance – The Toughest Standard Applies" (2002) 39 *Common Market Law Review* 551.

Bovis, Christopher H. "The New Public Procurement Regime of the European Union: A Critical Analysis of Policy, Law and Jurisprudence" (2005) 30 *European Law Review* 607.

Bovis, Christopher H. "The New Public Procurement Regime: A Different Perspective on the Integration of Public Markets of the European Union" (2006) 12 *European Public Law* 73.

Bovis, Christopher. "Public Procurement in the European Union: A Critical Analysis of the New Regime" (2006) 33 *Legal Issues of Economic Integration* 29.

Bovis, Christopher. "Public Procurement in the European Union: Lessons from the Past and Insights to the Future" (2006) 12 *Columbia Journal of European Law* 53.

Bovis, Christopher H. *EU Public Procurement Law* (Cheltenham, UK: Edward Elgar, 2007).

De Koninck, Constant and Peter Flamey. *European Public Procurement Law Part II – Remedies* (Alphen aan den Rijn: Kluwer Law International, 2009).

Doern, Alik. "The Interaction Between EC Rules on Public Procurement and State Aid" (2004) 13 *Public Procurement Law Review* 97.

Drijber, Berend Jan and Hélène Stergiou. "Public Procurement Law and Internal Market Law" (2009) 46 *Common Market Law Review* 805.

Golding, Jane and Paul Henty. "The New Remedies Directive of the EC: Standstill and Ineffectiveness" (2008) 17 *Public Procurement Law Review* 146.

Hebly, Jan M (ed). *European Public Procurement – Legislative History of the Classic Directive 2004/18/EC* (Alphen aan den Rijn: Kluwer Law International, 2007).

Leffler, Henrik. "Damages Liability for Breach of EC Procurement Law: Governing Principles and Practical Solutions" (2003) 12 *Public Procurement Law Review* 151.

Manunza, Elisabetta R. "Privatised Services and the Concept of 'Bodies Governed by Public Law' in EC Directives on Public Procurement" (2003) 28 *European Law Review* 273.

Mueller, Wolfgang, Nicholas Khan and Tibor Scharf. *EC and WTO Anti-dumping Law: A Handbook* (Oxford: Oxford University Press, 2009).

Nijholt, H. "Environmental Provisions in Public Procurement Directive 2004/18/EC" (2004) 21 *International Construction Law Review* 268.

Nijholt, H. "The Concept of a 'Body Governed by Public Law' in European Procurement Law" (2005) 22 *International Construction Law Review* 422.

Szydło, Marek. "Contracts Beyond the Scope of the EC Procurement Directives – Who is Bound by the Requirement for Transparency?" (2009) 34 *European Law Review* 720.

Taccogna, Gerolamo. "The Evolution of European Community Law on Public Procurement Between 2006 and 2008" (2008) 4 *European Review of Contract Law* 193.

Trepte, Peter. *Public Procurement in the EU: A Practitioner's Guide* (2nd ed, Oxford: Oxford University Press, 2007).

Treumer, Steen. "The Field of Application of Competitive Dialogue" (2006) 15 *Public Procurement Law Review* 307.

Treumer, Steen. "Damages for Breach of the EC Public Procurement Rules – Changes in European Regulation and Practice" (2006) 15 *Public Procurement Law Review* 159.

Williams, Rhodri. "The New Procurement Directives of the European Union" (2004) 13 *Public Procurement Law Review* 153.

Williams, Rhodri. "Contracts Awarded Outside the Scope of the Public Procurement Directives" (2007) 16 *Public Procurement Law Review* NA1.

Williams, Rhodri. "A New Remedies Directive for the European Community" (2008) 17 *Public Procurement Law Review* 19.

Williams, Sope. "The Mandatory Exclusions for Corruption in the New EC Procurement Directives" (2006) 31 *European Law Review* 711.

Useful Websites

European Commission: Public Procurement http://ec.europa.eu/internal_market/publicprocurement/index_en.htm

Chapter 9
Industrial and Commercial Property Rights

[9.05] Introduction

Industrial and commercial property rights are determined by the laws of the Member States of the Union. However, the exercise of those rights is subject to the TFEU, especially Arts 34, 36, 101 and 102 thereof. These rights are also protected by Art 345 TFEU which provides that the Treaty "shall in no way prejudice the rules in Member States governing the system of property ownership".

The European Parliament and the Council have power to adopt "measures for the creation of European intellectual property rights to provide uniform protection of intellectual property rights throughout the Union" (Art 118 TFEU). The process of harmonization of this area of law is impeded by the existence of an intractable difficulty. This problem arises from a fundamental disparity inherent in the applicable law.

On the one hand, Art 34 TFEU prohibits all quantitative restrictions or measures having equivalent effect in order to bring about free movement of goods. On the other hand, the territoriality principle of industrial and commercial property rights results in the creation of national markets, which hampers the free movement of goods within the European Union.

The first part of this chapter examines this potential conflict between the principle of free movement of goods and the territorial protection of industrial and commercial property rights. The second part of the chapter concerns the relationship between industrial and commercial property rights and EU competition law. The third part discusses the substantive law of the EU regarding the protection of industrial and commercial property, in particular the various harmonising Directives and Regulations.

[9.10] Compatibility of National Law with EU Law

In the absence of EU harmonising measures industrial and commercial property rights are determined by national law. See *Keurkoop BV v Nancy Kean Gifts BV* (144/81) [1982] ECR 2853 at [18]; [1983] 2 CMLR 47;

G. Moens, J. Trone, *Commercial Law of the European Union*,
Ius Gentium: Comparative Perspectives on Law and Justice 4,
DOI 10.1007/978-90-481-8774-4_9, © Springer Science+Business Media B.V. 2010

Thetford Corporation v Fiamma SpA (35/87) [1988] ECR 3585 at [12]; [1988] 3 CMLR 549; *Consorzio italiano della componentistica di ricambio per autoveicoli and Maxicar v Régie nationale des usines Renault* (53/87) [1988] ECR 6039 at [10]; [1990] 4 CMLR 265; *Radio Telefis Eireann v Commission* (C-241/91 P) [1995] ECR I-743 at [49]; [1995] 4 CMLR 718.

This national legislation must be consistent with EU law. For example, in *Collins v Imtrat Handelsgesellschaft mbH* (C-92/92) [1993] ECR I-5145; [1993] 3 CMLR 773 the German Copyright Act discriminated against non-nationals in that only German nationals were permitted to invoke the legislation (at [4]–[5]). The Court held that the German law violated the EC Treaty's prohibition of discrimination on the ground of nationality (at [33]).

The two primary characteristics of national industrial and commercial property rights are exclusivity and territoriality. In other words, national law gives to the owner the exclusive right to control the use of that property within the territory of the granting state. There is potential for this right to be used in such a way as to prevent goods, lawfully sold in one Member State, from being imported into another Member State. That would constitute a barrier to the free movement of goods.

Furthermore, the owner could seek to license others to exploit the right on a territorial basis with the possibility that the agreement would frustrate competition in the Union. If so, the exploitation of the property right may be incompatible with the competition rules of the TFEU. In ruling on the compatibility of national laws with the Treaty, the Court will therefore decide whether those national laws infringe the EU rules on competition and free movement of goods.

Arts 34 and 35 TFEU have the effect of prohibiting quantitative restrictions upon the import or export of goods to, from and within Member States. Art 36 TFEU sets out exceptions to these provisions. One of these exceptions relates to measures "for the protection of industrial and commercial property." Art 36 is subject to a proviso that "[s]uch prohibitions or restrictions shall not... constitute a means of arbitrary discrimination or a disguised restriction on trade between Member States." The purpose of this restriction "is to reconcile the requirements of the free movement of goods and the right of industrial and commercial property, by avoiding the maintenance or establishment of artificial barriers within the common market." See *Commission v France* (C-23/99) [2000] ECR I-7653 at [37]; *Administration des douanes et droits indirects v Rioglass SA* (C-115/02) [2003] ECR I-12705 at [23]; [2006] 1 CMLR 12 (p 273).

[9.15] Industrial and Commercial Property

The most important forms of industrial and commercial property are patents, designs, trade marks and copyright. Within the EU some Member States do not regard copyright as "industrial and commercial property" but rather as "intellectual or artistic property". In *Musik-Vertrieb Membran GmbH v Gema* (55/80) [1981] ECR 147; [1981] 2 CMLR 44 the Court held that the expression "industrial and commercial property" in Art 36 EC (Art 36 TFEU) includes copyright, "especially when exploited commercially in the form of licences capable of affecting distribution in the various Member States of goods incorporating the protected literary or artistic work" (at [9]). See similarly, *EMI Electrola GmbH v Patricia Im- und Export* (341/87) [1989] ECR 79 at [7]; [1989] 2 CMLR 413; *Parfums Christian Dior SA v Evora BV* (C-337/95) [1997] ECR I-6013 at [55]; [1998] 1 CMLR 737.

The Court has held that other types of intellectual property constitute "industrial and commercial property" under Art 36 TFEU:

- patents: *Generics (UK) Ltd v Smith Kline & French Laboratories Ltd* (C-191/90) [1992] ECR I-5335 at [23]; [1993] 1 CMLR 89;
- designs: *Keurkoop BV v Nancy Kean Gifts BV* (144/81) [1982] ECR 2853 at [14]; [1983] 2 CMLR 47; and
- designations of origin: *Belgium v Spain* (C-388/95) [2000] ECR I-3123 at [54]; *Ravil SARL v Bellon import SARL* (C-469/00) [2003] ECR I-5053 at [49]; *Consorzio del Prosciutto di Parma v Asda Stores Ltd* (C-108/01) [2003] ECR I-5121 at [64]; [2003] 2 CMLR 21 (p 639).

[9.20] Protection of Packaging

The protection of traditional type packaging indicative of an origin is not justified under Art 36 TFEU. In *Criminal Proceedings Against Prantl* (16/83) [1984] ECR 1299; [1985] 2 CMLR 238 the Court held that Germany could not prevent the importation of wine bottles from Italy in order to discourage unfair imitation of the similarly shaped "Bocksbeutel" wine bottle which has been used for many centuries in the German regions of Franconia and Baden.

The Court first considered whether the German legislation constituted a measure having an effect equivalent to a quantitative restriction in violation of Art 30 EC (now Art 34 TFEU). The government argued that consumers could be confused if wines from other regions were sold in this type of bottle (at [29]). The Court responded that "the provisions of Community law on the labelling of wines . . . are particularly comprehensive and enable the feared confusion to be avoided" (at [29]).

The German Government also argued that the packaging was "an indirect indication of geographical origin and therefore constitutes an industrial or commercial property right which belongs to the wine producers in the specific region and which the rules at issue may legitimately protect" (at [34]). The Court rejected this argument in unequivocal language:

measures having an effect equivalent to quantitative restrictions on imports arising from the fact that national legislation permits a specific shape of wine-bottle to be used only by certain national producers or dealers cannot be justified ... by the protection of industrial and commercial property on the ground that such a bottle is traditionally used by national producers if identical or similar bottles are used in another Member State in accordance with a fair and traditional practice for marketing wines produced in that State (at [38]).

[9.25] Art 36 TFEU Derogates from Free Movement of Goods

As Art 36 TFEU is an exception to the free movement of goods expressed in Arts 34 and 35, there is a potential for conflict between free movement and intellectual property rights. The holders of these property rights may attempt to use them to prevent the importation or marketing of goods by means of an infringement action, thereby subverting the principle of free movement of goods and partitioning the Union into national markets. However, the exercise of industrial and commercial property rights under Art 36 TFEU is restricted by the doctrine of the exhaustion of rights.

[9.30] Exhaustion of Rights: Copyright

The Court enunciated the "exhaustion of rights principle" in *Deutsche Grammophon Gesellschaft GmbH v Metro SB Großmärkte GmbH & Co KG* (78/70) [1971] ECR 487; [1971] CMLR 631. Deutsche Grammophon manufactured sound recordings in Germany which it exported to its subsidiary Polydor in France. Some of the recordings became the property of the supermarket chain Metro, which shipped them back to Germany for sale. Deutsche Grammophon then sought an injunction to prevent a breach of its German copyright.

The Court developed the "exhaustion of rights principle" as follows:

> Although it permits prohibitions or restrictions on the free movement of products, which are justified for the purpose of protecting industrial and commercial property, Article 36 [now Art 36 TFEU] only admits derogations from that freedom to the extent to which they are justified for the purpose of safeguarding rights which constitute the specific subject-matter of such property.
>
> If a right related to copyright is relied upon to prevent the marketing in a Member State of products distributed by the holder of the right or with his consent on the territory of another Member State on the sole ground that such distribution did not take place on the national territory, such a prohibition, which would legitimize the isolation of national markets, would be repugnant to the essential purpose of the Treaty, which is to unite national markets into a single market (at [11]–[12]).

The Court has continued to hold that the exclusive right of the copyright owner "is exhausted when a product has been lawfully distributed on the market in another Member State by the actual proprietor of the right or with his consent". See *Dansk Supermarked A/S v A/S Imerco* (58/80) [1981] ECR 181 at [11]; [1981] 3 CMLR 590; *Metronome Musik GmbH v Music Point Hokamp GmbH* (C-200/96) [1998] ECR I-1953 at [14]; [1998] 3 CMLR 919.

In *Foreningen AF Danske Videogramdistributorer v Laserdisken* (C-61/97) [1998] ECR I-5171; [1999] 1 CMLR 1297 the Court held that Arts 30 and 36 EC (now Arts 34 and 36 TFEU) were not violated where the holder of an exclusive rental right prohibited the rental of films in a Member State even though rental of those films was authorized in another Member State (at [23]). The Court pointed out that the right to authorize rental "would be rendered meaningless if it were held to be exhausted as soon as the object was first offered for rental" (at [18]).

Exhaustion of rights in computer programs is governed by Art 4(2), Directive 2009/24 of the European Parliament and of the Council of 23 April 2009 on the legal protection of computer programs (OJ L 111, 5.5.2009, p 16).

[9.35] Exhaustion of Rights: Patents

The "exhaustion of rights principle" was extended to patents in *Centrafarm BV v Sterling Drug Inc* (15/74) [1974] ECR 1147; [1974] 2 CMLR 480. The Court held that with regard to patents "the specific subject matter of the industrial property is the guarantee that the patentee... has the exclusive right to use an invention with a view to manufacturing industrial products and putting them into circulation for the first time, either directly or by the grant of licences to third parties, as well as the right to oppose infringements" (at [9]).

The Court continued that "a derogation from the principle of the free movement of goods is not... justified where the product has been put onto the market in a legal manner, by the patentee himself or with his consent, in the Member State from which it has been imported, in particular in the case of a proprietor of parallel patents" (at [11]). The Court emphasised that, once a product is lawfully marketed within the Community, the patentee has exhausted its rights with respect to that product. Thus, the Court made a distinction between the patentee's exclusive right to market the relevant product for the first time, on the one hand, and peripheral rights, on the other. The patentee cannot rely upon Art 36 TFEU to derogate from the principle of the free movement of goods once the product has been lawfully marketed.

The Court pointed out that "if a patentee could prevent the import of protected products marketed by him or with his consent in another Member State, he would be able to partition off national markets and thereby restrict trade where no such restriction was necessary to guarantee the essence of the exclusive rights flowing from the parallel patents" (at [12]).

[9.40] Exhaustion of Patent Rights: Compulsory Licences

In *Pharmon BV v Hoechst AG* (19/84) [1985] ECR 2281; [1985] 3 CMLR 775 the Court applied the exhaustion of rights principle in the context of a compulsory licence. Such a licence enables the licensee to manufacture the relevant product without the approval or consent of the holder of the patent, even though a royalty may be payable to the holder. The grant of a compulsory licence could be characterized as a penalty for the "non-use" of the patent by the holder in the granting Member State.

The Court considered the exhaustion of rights principle in the circumstance of the grant of a compulsory licence:

> where . . . the competent authorities . . . grant a third party a compulsory license which allows him to carry out manufacturing and marketing operations which the patentee would normally have the right to prevent, the patentee cannot be deemed to have consented to the operation of that third party. Such a measure deprives the patent proprietor of his right to determine freely the conditions under which he markets his products.
>
> . . . the substance of a patent right lies essentially in according the inventor an exclusive right of first placing the product on the market . . .. It is therefore necessary to allow the patent proprietor to prevent the importation and marketing of products manufactured under a compulsory licence in order to protect the substance of his exclusive rights under his patent (at [25]–[26]).

As the substance of a patent is the exclusive right of the patent holder to first place the invention on the market, and a compulsory licence abrogated that right, the Court held that national measures could be used to prevent importation and sale of the goods manufactured under a compulsory licence in another Member State. Thus the Court's judgment allowed the substance of the patent to be given effect.

A national compulsory licensing law must not discriminate against imports from Member States. The Court has held that a discriminatory compulsory licensing provision is incompatible with Art 36 TFEU. In *Re Compulsory Patent Licences: Commission v United Kingdom* (C-30/90) [1992] ECR I-829; [1992] 2 CMLR 709 a British statute provided that compulsory licenses could be granted if the United Kingdom demand for a patented invention was being met by imports rather than by domestically manufactured products (at [2]).

The Court held that to the extent to which a compulsory licence discriminated against imports from other Member States, it impeded interstate trade, and that it was not necessary to protect the specific subject matter of the patent, namely "the exclusive right for the patent proprietor to use an invention with a view to manufacturing industrial products and putting them into circulation for the first time, either directly or by the grant of licences to third parties, as well as the right to oppose infringements" (at [21]). The Court reiterated that Art 36 EC (Art 36 TFEU) only permits limitations to free movement that safeguard the right that is the specific subject matter of the property (at [20]). The national provision could not be justified by reference to Art 36 EC (Art 36 TFEU) and it therefore constituted an infringement of Art 30 EC (Art 34 TFEU).

[9.45] Exhaustion of Rights: Trade Marks

The exhaustion of rights principle has also been given effect in trade marks law. In *Centrafarm BV v Winthrop BV* (16/74) [1974] ECR 1183; [1974] 2 CMLR 480 the Court observed that the holder of a trade mark "has the exclusive right to use that trade mark for the purpose of putting products protected by the trade mark into circulation for the first time, and is therefore intended to protect him against competitors wishing to take advantage of the status and reputation of the trade mark by selling products illegally bearing that trade mark" (at [8]). But once the products have been marketed in another Member State by or with the consent of the holder of the trade mark, the holder would not be able to prevent the reimportation of those goods into the country of origin.

This rule was refined in *Hoffman-La Roche & Co AG v Centrafarm Vertriebsgesellschaft Pharmazeutischer Erzeugnisse mbH* (102/77) [1978] ECR 1139; [1978] 3 CMLR 217. A re-importer altered the packaging of the product before reapplying the original trade mark (at [1]). The Court was confronted with the question of whether the trade mark holder was entitled to claim that re-import may be prevented by virtue of the removal of the original trade mark in the course of repackaging, although it is replaced later.

The Court's judgment is truly Solomonic:

(a) The proprietor of a trade-mark right which is protected in two Member States at the same time is justified pursuant to... Article 36 [EC] [Art 36 TFEU] in preventing a product to which the trade-mark has lawfully been applied in one of those States from being marketed in the other Member State after it has been repacked in new packaging to which the trade-mark has been affixed by a third party.

(b) However, such prevention of marketing constitutes a disguised restriction on trade between Member States within... Article 36 where:

- ... the use of the trade-mark right by the proprietor, having regard to the marketing system which he has adopted, will contribute to the artificial partitioning of the markets between Member States;
- ... the repackaging cannot adversely affect the original condition of the product;

- The proprietor of the mark receives prior notice of the marketing of the repackaged product; and
- It is stated on the new packaging by whom the product has been repackaged (at [14]).

In *Boehringer Ingelheim KG v Swingward Ltd* (C-143/00) [2002] ECR I-3759; [2002] 3 CMLR 26 (p 623) Swingward imported Boehringer pharmaceuticals into the United Kingdom from another EU Member State. Swingward modified the packaging and information leaflets of those pharmaceuticals (at [6]). The Court reiterated that "where repackaging is necessary to allow the product imported in parallel to be marketed in the importing State" opposition to repackaging constitutes an artificial portioning of markets (at [15], see also [35]). An importer must give notice to the proprietor before putting a repackaged product on sale. The importer must also supply a sample where requested to do so by the proprietor (at [61]).

Producers will often use different trade marks in different countries for the same product. Importers often repack the product to affix the trade mark used in the country of importation. This situation arose in *Pfizer Inc v Eurim-Pharm GmbH* (1/81) [1981] ECR 2913; [1982] 1 CMLR 406. A broad spectrum antibiotic (vibramycin) was manufactured and marketed in the United Kingdom in packages of 10 and 50 capsules. In Germany the same antibiotic was sold in packages of 8, 16 or 40 capsules. The antibiotic was sold in the United Kingdom at a lower price than in Germany (at [3]).

Eurim-Pharm imported a quantity of the United Kingdom product. It repackaged the antibiotic in order to take account of the German usage. It removed the original blister packages from the original packs. It repacked the blister packs in packets which had windows that allowed the consumer to see the label bearing the trade mark "vibramycin" and the name of the manufacturer ("Pfizer") (at [4]).

The Court held that under Art 36 EC (now Art 36 TFEU) "the proprietor of a trade-mark ... may not rely on that right in order to prevent an importer from marketing a pharmaceutical ... manufactured in another Member State by the subsidiary of the proprietor and bearing the ... trade mark with his consent, where the importer ... confined himself to replacing the external wrapping without touching the internal packaging and made the trade mark affixed by the manufacturer to the internal packaging visible through the new external wrapping, [while] ... clearly indicating on the ... wrapping that the product is manufactured by the subsidiary ... and re-packaged by the importer" (at [13]).

The exhaustion of trade mark rights is now regulated by Art 7 of Directive 2008/95, which is discussed later in this chapter. See Directive 2008/95 of the European Parliament and of the Council of 22 October 2008 to approximate the laws of the Member States relating to trade marks (OJ L 299, 8.11.2008, p 25). National rules must now be assessed in the light of Art 7 of the Directive. See *Bristol-Myers Squibb v Paranova A/S* (C-427/93) [1996]

ECR I-3457 at [26]; [1997] 1 CMLR 1151. However, the Court has held that Art 30 EC (now Art 34 TFEU) and Art 7 of the Directive seek the same end and must receive the same interpretation. The case law under Art 30 EC thus provides the basis for the interpretation of Art 7 of the Directive. See *Boehringer Ingelheim KG v Swingward Ltd* (C-143/00) [2002] ECR I-3759 at [18]; [2002] 3 CMLR 26 (p 623). Another Regulation provides for the exhaustion of Community trade mark rights. See Art 13, Council Regulation 207/2009 of 26 February 2009 on the Community trade mark (OJ L 78, 24.3.2009, p 1).

[9.50] Exhaustion of Other Rights

EU legislation now provides for the exhaustion of other types of rights, such as designs and plant variety rights. See Art 16, Council Regulation 2100/94 of 27 July 1994 on Community plant variety rights (OJ L 227, 1.9.1994, p 1); Art 15, Directive 98/71 of the European Parliament and of the Council of 13 October 1998 on the legal protection of designs (OJ L 289, 28.10.1998, p 28); Art 21, Council Regulation 6/2002 of 12 December 2001 on Community designs (OJ L 3, 5.1.2002, p 1).

[9.55] Prevention of Deception of Consumers

Can the proprietor of industrial and commercial property use that property to prevent deception of consumers? This question was considered by the Court in *Terrapin (Overseas) Ltd v Terranova Industrie CA Kapferer & Co* (119/75) [1976] ECR 1039; [1976] 2 CMLR 482. Terranova was the owner of certain trade marks, one of which it used as its name. These marks were registered in Germany for use on building materials. Terrapin was a manufacturer of prefabricated buildings. It sought to register its name as a German trade mark for buildings. Terranova objected on the ground that the name sought to be registered was deceptively similar to its own name (at [2]).

The Court held that "it is compatible with . . . the free movement of goods for an undertaking . . ., by virtue of a right to a trade-mark . . ., to prevent the importation of products of an undertaking established in another Member State and bearing . . . a name giving rise to confusion with the trade-mark . . . of the first undertaking, provided that there are no agreements restricting competition and no legal or economic ties between the undertakings and that their respective rights have arisen independently of one another" (at [8]).

Thus, if the industrial or commercial property could be used as a means of deceiving consumers, the provisions of Arts 34 and 35 TFEU will not apply to allow the freedom of movement of those goods, but the national rights will prevail.

[9.60] Relationship with Competition Law

Art 101(1) TFEU prohibits agreements and concerted practices "which may affect trade between Member States and which have as their object or effect the prevention, restriction or distortion of competition within the internal market." Such agreements are automatically void (Art 101(2) TFEU).

The exemption in Art 36 for industrial and commercial property presents a difficulty whenever the owner of that property licenses a manufacturer to manufacture the relevant product. The agreement between the owner of that industrial and commercial property and the manufacturer appears to be incompatible with Art 101(1). A review of the case law reveals that, basically, the conflict may be resolved by reference to either one of three alternative theories regarding the relationship between Arts 36 and 101.

(1) Under the first theory, agreements restricting the use of industrial and commercial property rights are permissible and do not come within the ambit of Art 101.
(2) The second theory holds that the exceptions to Art 101 cannot be made to depend upon the protection granted by national law. As national laws vary as to the extent of protection given, reliance upon national law would prevent the development of a uniform EU law. The Court must consider whether a restraint of trade is incompatible with Art 101(1).
(3) The third theory assumes that all restraints of trade come within Art 101(1) but, if they are to be allowed to operate, Art 101(1) must be declared inapplicable under Art 101(3).

A review of the case law suggests that the Court has firmly adopted the second theory.

[9.65] Relationship Between Arts 36 and 101 TFEU

In *Établissements Consten SàRL v Commission* (56/64) [1966] ECR 299; [1966] CMLR 418 the Court decided that copyright has an essential core: the right to initially put the work onto the market. This right was protected by Art 36 EC (Art 36 TFEU). Once this right had been exercised, the rights under the copyright were exhausted. An agreement which sought by use of the copyright to prevent the reimportation of the sound recordings into the country of origin was held to be incompatible with Art 85 EC (now Art 101 TFEU).

In *EMI Records v CBS Schallplatten GmbH* (96/75) [1976] ECR 913; [1976] 2 CMLR 235 the trade mark "Columbia" had been originally owned by a United States corporation. The plaintiff acquired the rights to the trade mark in the European Community (at [2]). The defendants were locally incorporated subsidiaries of the CBS Inc, an American corporation which had become the owner of the trade mark in the United States. The plaintiff was totally independent of the defendants and their parent company. The CBS group had imported into several Member States sound recordings bearing the trade mark "Columbia", which had been lawfully affixed within the United States (at [3]). EMI sued for infringement of its trade mark.

The Court held that a trade mark does not come within the wording of Art 85 EC (Art 101 TFEU). However, the exercise of rights given by the trade mark could nevertheless be affected by Art 85(1) (Art 101(1) TFEU), especially if those rights were used to restrict competition (at [14]). If the trader within the EU had an agreement with a trader from a non-member State, the effect of which was to restrict trade within the EU, Art 85 EC (Art 101 TFEU) would render that agreement void. It did not matter if the agreement had ceased to have effect, as long as the undesirable effect of lessening of trade continued, the agreement was rendered void by Art 85 EC (Art 101 TFEU) (at [15]).

But in the circumstances of this case, the Court held that "the provisions on the free movement of goods and on competition do not prohibit the proprietor of the same mark in all the Member States... from exercising his trade-mark rights,... in order to prevent the sale by a third party in the Community of products bearing the same mark, which is owned in a third country, provided that the exercise of the[se]... rights does not manifest itself as the result of an agreement or of concerted practices which have as their object or effect the isolation or partitioning of the common market" (at [21]).

Terrapin (Overseas) Ltd v Terranova Industrie CA Kapferer & Co (119/75) [1976] ECR 1039; [1976] 2 CMLR 482 both resembles and differs from the *EMI Records* case. There are obvious similarities between the cases. In both cases the Court found that it was compatible with the provisions relating to free movement of goods to rely on trade marks to prevent the importation of goods. In each case the Court relied on the central core of the industrial and commercial property right.

The cases also differ from one another in important respects. In *Terrapin* the central core was the right of the proprietor to the exclusive use of the trade mark without another passing his goods off as the goods of the trade mark owner. In contrast, the central core in *EMI Records* consisted of the right to put goods on the market where the trade mark was registered under the appropriate national law. In neither case was there an agreement that would have divided the EU market between the parties. Hence no infringement of Art 85 EC (Art 101 TFEU) had occurred.

The relationship between Arts 34 and 101 TFEU may be summarized as follows. The existence of industrial and commercial property rights is not affected by EU law, but the exercise of those rights could be affected by EU competition rules. Art 101 will affect the exercise of those rights once the core rights are exhausted. Although Art 36 TFEU safeguards property rights in industrial and commercial property, Art 36 is subject to the competition rules of the TFEU. Any agreement which aims to use the industrial or industrial property right to prevent the reimportation of goods lawfully placed on the market by the owner of the property right (or their agent) is incompatible with the Treaty.

[9.70] Exemptions

The Commission may exempt from the operation of Art 101(3) TFEU certain agreements relating to industrial property rights. See Council Regulation 19/65 of 2 March 1965 on the application of Article 81(3) (formerly Article 85(3)) of the Treaty to certain categories of agreements and concerted practices (OJ P 36, 6.3.1965, p 533). The Commission may exempt categories of agreements between two undertakings which impose restrictions "in relation to the acquisition or use of industrial property rights, in particular of patents, utility models, designs or trade marks, or to the rights arising out of contracts for assignment of, or the right to use, a method of manufacture or knowledge relating to the use or to the application of industrial processes" (Art 1(1)(b)).

The Commission has exempted from the operation of Art 101(3) TFEU "technology transfer agreements entered into between two undertakings permitting the production of contract products". See Art 2, Commission Regulation 772/2004 of 27 April 2004 on the application of Article 81(3) of the Treaty to categories of technology transfer agreements (OJ L 123, 27.4.2004, p 11). This exemption is subject to market share thresholds (Arts 3, 8). Where the parties are competitors, the exemption does not apply to agreements that restrict a party's ability to set prices for sales to third parties, limit output or allocate markets or customers (Art 4(1)). The exemption is also subject to restrictions where the parties are not competitors (Art 4(2)). Certain contractual obligations fall outside the exemption (Art 5).

The Commission has also exempted some research and development agreements from the operation of Art 101(3) TFEU. See Commission Regulation 2659/2000 of 29 November 2000 on the application of Article 81(3) of the Treaty to categories of research and development agreements (OJ L 304, 5.12.2000, p 7).

[9.75] Systems of Property Ownership

Art 345 TFEU stipulates that the Treaty "shall in no way prejudice the rules in Member States governing the system of property ownership." The meaning of this Article was settled in *Parke, Davis & Co v Probel* (24/67) [1968] ECR 55; [1968] CMLR 47. Pharmaceuticals were imported into the Netherlands from Italy where drugs did not then enjoy patent protection (at ECR 70). Parke, Davis had registered a patent under Dutch law for the process of the manufacture of the pharmaceutical "choramphenicol". Parke, Davis attempted to use its patent to prevent the importation of the drugs from Italy into the Netherlands. The Court held that a patent was not, by its very existence, incompatible with the competition requirements of the Treaty, and in particular with the implied prohibition against partitioning the Community market into national segments (at ECR 71).

This decision was reinforced by the Court's judgment in *Pharmon BV v Hoechst AG* (19/84) [1985] ECR 2281; [1985] 3 CMLR 775. The Court held that a patent owner could use a patent to prevent the importation of goods made under a compulsory licence granted in another Member State as the patent owner had not exercised his right of voluntarily putting the goods on the market (at [25]–[26]). But if the exercise of the property right has the effect of lessening competition, or impedes the free movement of goods, then the compatibility of the right with Arts 30 and 85 will be examined by the Court.

The Court has held that Art 345 TFEU "cannot be interpreted as reserving to the national legislature, in relation to industrial and commercial property, the power to adopt measures which would adversely affect the principle of free movement of goods within the common market". See *Commission v Italy* (C-235/89) [1992] ECR I-777 at [14]; *Re Compulsory Patent Licences: Commission v United Kingdom* (C-30/90) [1992] ECR I-829 at [18]; [1992] 2 CMLR 709; *Re Medicinal Product Certificate: Spain v Council* (C-350/92) [1995] ECR I-1985 at [18]; [1996] 1 CMLR 415.

[9.80] Harmonisation of Copyright

The EU has adopted several Directives regulating various aspects of copyright law. The term of copyright protection is harmonised by Directive 2006/116 of the European Parliament and of the Council of 12 December 2006 on the term of protection of copyright and certain related rights (OJ L 372, 27.12.2006, p 12). Copyright protection of a literary or artistic work ends 70 years after the author's death (Art 1(1)). Protection of cinematographic or audiovisual work ends 70 years after the death of the last survivor among the director, screenplay writer or music composer (Art 2(2)). There are various terms of protection for related rights such as those of performers (Art 3(1)). Where a work originates in a third state and the author is not an EU national, copyright protection ends with the expiry of the protection granted in the country of origin. However, this is subject to an upper limit of 70 years after the author's death (Art 7(1)).

The EU has regulated rental and lending rights. See Directive 2006/115 of the European Parliament and of the Council of 12 December 2006 on rental right and lending right and on certain rights related to copyright in the field of intellectual property (OJ L 376, 27.12.2006, p 28). Member States must provide a right to authorise or prohibit the rental or lending of a copyright work (Art 1(1)). This right belongs to the author, performer, phonogram producer or film producer (Art 2(1)).

Authors and performers have an unwaivable right to equitable remuneration for rental of their work (Art 5(1)–(2)). Member States may provide for public lending provided that authors receive payment for that lending (Art 6(1)). Performers have the exclusive right to authorise or prohibit the broadcasting and communication to the public of their performances (Art 8(1)). Performers, phonogram producers and film producers have the exclusive right to make their works available to the public (Art 9(1)).

The author of an artwork receives a percentage of the price for any resale of their work. See Art 1(1), Directive 2001/84 of the European Parliament and of the Council of 27 September 2001 on the resale right for the benefit of the author of an original work of art (OJ L 272, 13.10.2001, p 32). This royalty is paid by the seller of the artwork (Art 1(4)).

[9.85] Copyright in the Information Society

Another Directive regulates copyright as it has been affected by the "information society". See Art 1(1), Directive 2001/29 of the European Parliament and of the Council of 22 May 2001 on the harmonisation of certain aspects of copyright and related rights in the information society (OJ L 167, 22.6.2001, p 10). The Directive provides for exclusive rights of reproduction, communication to the public, making available to the public and distribution.

Authors, performers, phonogram producers, film producers and broadcasters have the exclusive right to authorise reproduction of their copyright works (Art 2). Authors have the exclusive right to authorise communication to the public of their work (Art 3(1)). For example, cable transmission of a television signal by a hotel to sets in its guest rooms constitutes a communication to the public. See *Sociedad General de Autores y Editores de España (SGAE) v Rafael Hoteles SA* (C-306/05) [2006] ECR I-11519 at [23], [46]–[47]. Performers, phonogram producers, film producers and broadcasters have the exclusive right to authorise the making available to the public of their copyright works (Art 3(2)). Authors have the exclusive right to authorise distribution of their work to the public (Art 4(1)). The Directive sets out several exceptions to these exclusive rights (Art 5).

Member States must provide legal protection against the sale or rental of devices for the circumvention of technological measures for the protection of copyright (Art 6(1)). They must also provide legal protection against the removal of electronic rights-management information (Art 7(1)), which is information identifying the work and rightholder (Art 7(2)). Member States must provide sanctions and remedies for infringement of rights conferred by this Directive (Art 8(1)).

[9.90] Copyright in Computer Programs

An EU Directive affords protection against unauthorised reproduction of computer software. See Directive 2009/24 of the European Parliament and of the Council of 23 April 2009 on the legal protection of computer programs (OJ L 111, 5.5.2009, p 16). Computer programs are to be protected as literary works by exclusive rights under copyright law (Art 1(1)). Protection does not extend to the ideas and principles underlying the program (Art 1(2)).

As a general rule, the author of a program is its creator (Art 2(1)). In the case of computer programs created by a group of natural persons, the exclusive rights are exercised jointly (Art 2(2)). When a computer program is created in the course of employment, the employer is exclusively entitled to exercise all economic rights in respect of the program, unless otherwise provided by contract (Art 2(3)). The Directive also regulates decompilation, which involves the process of reproduction in order to obtain the information required to interconnect with other independently developed programs (Art 6(1)).

[9.95] Copyright in Databases

Database protection is governed by Directive 96/9 of the European Parliament and of the Council of 11 March 1996 on the legal protection of databases (OJ L 77, 27.3.1996, p 20). The Directive provides for the copyright protection of databases that are the author's intellectual creation by reason of the selection or arrangement of their contents (Art 3(1)). This copyright protection relates to the database itself rather than the contents of the database (Art 3(2)).

"Database" is defined as "a collection of independent works, data or other materials arranged in a systematic or methodical way and individually accessible by electronic or other means" (Art 1(2)). The author of a database is the person who created it (Art 4(1)). The author has several exclusive rights such as reproduction in whole or part, translation, alteration and distribution or communication to the public (Art 5). There are limited exceptions to these exclusive rights (Art 6(2)).

The Member States must create a sui generis right for the database maker where "there has been qualitatively and/or quantitatively a substantial investment in either the obtaining, verification or presentation of the contents to prevent extraction and/or re-utilization of the whole or of a substantial part, evaluated qualitatively and/or quantitatively, of the contents of that database" (Art 7(1)). The Court has held that the concept of "extraction" under Art 7(1) includes "the transfer of material from a protected database to another database following an on-screen consultation of the first database and an individual assessment of the material contained in that first database". See *Directmedia Publishing GmbH v Albert-Ludwigs-Universität Freiburg* (C-304/07) [2008] ECR I-7565 at [60]; [2009] 1 CMLR 7 (p 213).

A separate Directive regulates copyright in relation to satellite broadcasting and cable retransmission. See Council Directive 93/83 of 27 September 1993 on the coordination of certain rules concerning copyright and rights related to copyright applicable to satellite broadcasting and cable retransmission (OJ L 248, 6.10.1993, p 15).

[9.100] International Treaties Relating to Copyright

The EC is a party to the *Agreement on Trade-Related Aspects of Intellectual Property Rights, (TRIPS)*, Marrakesh, 15 April 1994, 1869 UNTS 299; OJ L 336, 23.12.1994, p 214; [1995] ATS 8 p 341. The TRIPS Agreement is discussed in Chapter 13.

The EC ratified the WIPO Copyright Treaty and the WIPO Performances and Phonograms Treaty on 14 December 2009. See *WIPO Copyright Treaty*, Geneva, 20 December 1996, 2186 UNTS 121; 36 ILM 65; OJ L 89, 11.4.2000, p 8; *WIPO Performances and Phonograms Treaty*, Geneva, 20 December 1996, 2186 UNTS 203; 36 ILM 76; OJ L 89, 11.4.2000, p 15.

Those WIPO treaties fall within the competence of both the EU and the Member States, and the EU ratified when the Member States became party to the Treaties. See Preamble Recitals 4–7, Council Decision 2000/278 of 16 March 2000 on the approval, on behalf of the European Community, of the WIPO Copyright Treaty and the WIPO Performances and Phonograms Treaty (OJ L 89, 11.4.2000, p 6).

[9.105] Patents

The EU has not yet adopted a system of Community Patents. An EC Patents Agreement was opened for signature in 1989 but did notenter into force

(OJ EPO 2009, 286). See *Agreement Relating to Community Patents*, Luxembourg, 15 December 1989, OJ L 401, 30.12.1989, p 1; EC 1991 No 22 (Cm 1452).

All EU Member States are party to the European Patent Convention (OJ EPO 2009, 283). See *Convention on the Grant of European Patents*, Munich, 5 October 1973, 1065 UNTS 199; 13 ILM 268. Under the Convention a single application may be made to the European Patent Office (EPO). The EPO is not formally associated with the European Union.

A patent application to the EPO must pass through four steps before being granted. These involve:

1. filing requirements,
2. determining that there is an element of novelty,
3. publicly announcing the patent request, and
4. being examined by three patent experts.

EPO decisions are reported in the *Official Journal of the European Patent Office* (Munich: European Patent Office, 1977–) and the *European Patent Office Reports* (London: Sweet & Maxwell, 1986–). The Official Journal is available on the EPO's website (http://www.epo.org). The proposed European Patent Litigation Agreement is a draft Protocol to the European Patent Convention. See Stefan Luginbuehl, "A Stone's Throw Away from a European Patent Court: The European Patent Litigation Agreement" (2003) 25 *European Intellectual Property Review* 256.

See generally, Ian Muir et al., *European Patent Law: Law and Procedure Under the EPC and PCT* (3rd ed, Oxford: Oxford University Press, 2002); Romuald Singer, *European Patent Convention: A Commentary* (3rd ed, London: Sweet & Maxwell, 2003); Richard Hacon and Jochen Pagenberg (eds), *Concise European Patent Law* (Alphen aan den Rijn, The Netherlands: Kluwer Law International, 2007); Derk Visser, *The Annotated European Patent Convention 2000* (17th ed, Veldhoven, Netherlands: H Tel, 2009); Tobias Bremi, *The European Patent Convention and Proceedings Before the European Patent Office* (Köln: Carl Heymanns, 2008); Adam Jolly and Jeremy Philpott, *The Handbook of European Intellectual Property Management: Protecting, Developing and Exploiting Your IP Assets* (2nd ed, London: Kogan Page, 2009).

The grant of a patent under national law provides legal protection only in that jurisdiction. Some temporary protection is granted by the Paris Convention. See *Paris Convention for the Protection of Industrial Property*, Paris, 20 March 1883, as revised at Stockholm, 14 July 1967, 828 UNTS 305; 24 UST 2140; TIAS 6923; [1972] ATS 12. The Convention gives priority to a patent application filed in a state that is party to the Convention (Art 4(A)(1)). Any subsequent filing in another state party is not defeated by another filing or exploitation of the invention, which will not give rise to third party rights (Art 4(B)). This priority lasts for 12 months from the date that the first application was filed (Art 4(C)(1)–(2)). All EU Member

States are party to the Convention. Australia, Canada, India, Malaysia, New Zealand, Singapore, South Africa and the United States are also parties (OJ EPO 2009, 266).

The Patent Cooperation Treaty provides for an international process for the filing of patent applications in the States that are party to the Treaty. See *Patent Cooperation Treaty*, Washington, 19 June 1970, 1160 UNTS 231; 28 UST 7645; TIAS 8733; [1980] ATS 6. An international application under the Treaty is filed with a Receiving Office (Arts 3, 10). The actual grant of a patent is performed by national authorities. All EU Member States are party to this treaty. Australia, Canada, India, Malaysia, New Zealand, Singapore, South Africa and the United States are also parties (OJ EPO 2009, 270).

The following are among the national statutes that implement the Patent Cooperation Treaty:

Australia: ss 88–96, *Patents Act* 1990;
Canada: ss 50–66, *Patent Rules* (SOR/96-423);
India: *Patents Act* 1970;
Ireland: ss 2(1), 127, *Patents Act* 1977;
Malaysia: *Patents Act* 1983 (Act 291);
New Zealand: ss 26A–26H, *Patents Act* 1958;
Singapore: *Patents Act* (Chapter 221);
South Africa: ss 43A–43F, *Patents Act* 1978;
United Kingdom: ss 89–89B, *Patents Act* 1977; and
United States: 35 USC 351–376.

EU Member States must provide patent protection for biotechnological inventions. See Art 1(1), Directive 98/44 of the European Parliament and of the Council of 6 July 1998 on the legal protection of biotechnological inventions (OJ L 213, 30.7.98, p 13). An invention may be patented even though it consists of biological material. To be patentable the invention must still be new, involve an inventive step and be capable of industrial application (Art 3(1)).

Plant and animal varieties may not be patented (Art 4(1)(a)). The human body including its gene sequences is not patentable (Art 5(1)). An invention is not patentable where its commercial exploitation would be against public order or morality (Art 6(1)). For example, a process for cloning human beings may not be patented (Art 6(2)(a)).

[9.110] Trade Marks

The ECJ has frequently emphasised that "the essential function of a trade mark is to guarantee the identity of origin of the marked goods or services to the consumer... by enabling him, without any possibility of confusion, to distinguish the goods or services from others which have another origin..... [A trade mark] offer[s] a guarantee that all the goods or services bearing it have been manufactured or supplied under the control of a single undertaking which is responsible for their quality". See *Koninklijke Philips Electronics NV v Remington Consumer Products Ltd* (C-299/99) [2002] ECR I-5475 at [30]; [2002] 2 CMLR 52 (p 1329); *Arsenal Football Club plc v Reed* (C-206/01) [2002] ECR I-10273 at [48]; [2003] 1 CMLR 12 (p 345); *Sieckmann v Deutsches Patent-und Markenamt* (C-273/00) [2002] ECR I-11737 at [35]; [2005] 1 CMLR 40 (p 1021); *Gillette Co v LA-Laboratories Ltd Oy* (C-228/03) [2005] ECR I-2337 at [26]; [2005] 2 CMLR 62 (p 1539); *Copad SA v Christian Dior couture SA* (C-59/08) [2009] ETMR 40 (p 683) at [22].

[9.115] Harmonisation of Trade Marks

The EU has adopted several pieces of secondary legislation regarding trade marks. One Directive regulates national legislation regarding trade marks. See Directive 2008/95 of the European Parliament and of the Council of 22 October 2008 to approximate the laws of the Member States relating to trade marks (OJ L 299, 8.11.2008, p 25). This Directive applies to every trade mark relating to goods or services which is registered or under application for registration in a Member State or as an international registration which has effect in a Member State (Art 1).

[9.120] Graphical Representation

The Directive provides that a trade mark "may consist of any signs capable of being represented graphically, particularly words, including personal names, designs, letters, numerals, the shape of goods or of their packaging, provided that such signs are capable of distinguishing the goods or services of one undertaking from those of other undertakings" (Art 2). A shape does not need to be embellished with a non-functional addition in order to distinguish the goods or services. See *Koninklijke Philips Electronics NV v Remington Consumer Products Ltd* (C-299/99) [2002] ECR I-5475 at [49]–[50]; [2002] 2 CMLR 52 (p 1329).

Under Art 2 a trade mark consists of a sign that is "capable of being represented graphically". Applying this provision, the Court held that an odour was incapable of registration as a trade mark. In *Sieckmann v Deutsches Patent-und Markenamt* (C-273/00) [2002] ECR I-11737; [2005] 1 CMLR 40 (p 1021) Sieckmann sought to register an odour by tendering its chemical formula, a sample in a container and a written description (at [11], [13]).

The Court held that a trade mark could be registered for a sign that could not be perceived visually, so long as it could be represented graphically (at [45]). The graphical representation must enable the sign to be "precisely identified" (at [46]). That precise identification was necessary if the trade mark office was to fulfil its role of examining trade mark applications. It was also necessary so that competitors would be able to ascertain what marks are already protected (at [50]–[51]). In the case at hand the chemical formula identified a substance but not its odour and thus did not precisely identify the sign (at [69]). The written description of an odour was also insufficiently precise (at [70]). A sample of an odour was not a graphical representation and was not durable (at [71]).

In *Libertel Groep BV v Benelux-Merkenbureau* (C-104/01) [2003] ECR I-3793; [2005] 2 CMLR 45 (p 1097) Libertel sought to register a colour in relation to telecommunications goods and services (at [14]). The Court held that a colour was capable of registration (at [27]). However, a sample of a colour was not sufficient for registration since it may change over time (at [32]). However, a written description of a colour was a sufficient graphical representation (at [34]). The use of an international identification code for a colour was also a sufficient graphical representation (at [37]). A combination of a sample and a written description was sufficient for registration (at [38]). The registration of colours may be limited for reasons of public interest (at [51]). In particular, the more extensive the goods and services for which an application is sought, the more likely it is that trade mark protection would distort competition (at [54], [56]).

In *Shield Mark BV v Kist* (C-283/01) [2003] ECR I-14313; [2005] 1 CMLR 41 (p 1046) the Court held that a sound could be registered as a trade mark, provided that it could be represented graphically (at [37]). Musical notes alone were not a sufficient graphical representation (at [61]). However, sheet music showing the pitch and duration of the sounds is sufficient graphical representation of a melody (at [62]).

[9.125] Distinctive Character

The following marks or signs (among others) may not be registered as trade marks: a mark that is "devoid of any distinctive character"; a mark that consists only of indications that show the kind, quality, quantity, purpose or origin of the goods; a sign that is merely the shape resulting from the nature of the goods; and marks that may deceive the public (Art 3(1)).

The concept of "distinctive character" has been examined in many cases. In *Koninklijke Philips Electronics NV v Remington Consumer Products Ltd* (C-299/99) [2002] ECR I-5475; [2002] 2 CMLR 52 (p 1329) Philips registered a trade mark for the shape and configuration of a three-headed rotary shaver (at [11]). Remington later sold a shaver with a similarly shaped head (at [12]). Philips commenced proceedings against Remington for infringement of its trade mark (at [13]). The Court held that "where a trader has been the only supplier of particular goods to the market, extensive use of a sign which consists of the shape of those goods may be sufficient to give the sign a distinctive character... where, as a result of that use, a substantial proportion of [consumers]... associate[] that shape with that trader and no other undertaking or believe[] that goods of that shape come from that trader" (at [65]).

In *Procter & Gamble Co v Office for Harmonisation in the Internal Market* (C-383/99 P) [2001] ECR I-6297; [2001] 5 CMLR 28 (p 1058) Proctor & Gamble sought to register BABY-DRY as a trade mark for disposable nappies (at [4]). The Court held that if a combination of words was purely descriptive it would be unable to be registered (at [41]). Here the "syntactically unusual juxtaposition" formed by these words was not a familiar expression (at [43]). This combination of words was not simply descriptive and gave a distinctive character to the mark. These words were thus eligible for registration (at [44]).

A trade mark may not be registered if it is identical to a prior trade mark and both marks concern similar goods or services. A trade mark may also not be registered if its similarity to a prior trade mark relating to similar goods or services may create confusion among the public (Art 4(1)).

[9.130] Prohibited Uses of Marks

The trade mark proprietor may prevent third parties from using in trade an identical sign in relation to goods or services that are identical to those for which the mark has been registered (Art 5(1)(a)). In *Arsenal Football Club plc v Reed* (C-206/01) [2002] ECR I-10273; [2003] 1 CMLR 12 (p 345) Arsenal Football Club had registered its name and emblems as trade marks for clothing and shoes (at [13]). Reed sold unofficial Arsenal merchandise outside the football stadium. The merchandise referred to the club name (at [15]). A sign at his stall stated that the merchandise was not official (at [17]).

The Court held that the use of the club name was not purely descriptive (at [55]). The use of the name created an impression of a commercial link between the goods and the trade mark proprietor (at [56]). The sign at the stall was not sufficient to dispel confusion about the origin of the goods (at [57]). The use of the club name on the goods placed at risk the guarantee of origin and quality that underlies a trade mark (at [58], [60]).

A trade mark may be used in a competitor's comparative advertising, unless there is (inter alia) a likelihood of confusion or the goods are presented as imitations of trade marked goods. See *O2 Holdings Ltd v Hutchison 3G UK Ltd* (C-533/06) [2008] ECR I-4231 at [45], [48]; [2008] 3 CMLR

14 (p 397) (confusion); *L'Oréal SA v Bellure NV* (C-487/07) [2009] ETMR 55 (p 987) at [80] (imitation). The trade mark proprietor may also prevent third parties from using in trade a similar sign in relation to similar goods or services where there is a likelihood of confusion among the public (Art 5(1)(b)).

Member States may provide that the proprietor has the right to prevent third parties from using in trade any identical or similar sign where such use "takes unfair advantage of, or is detrimental to, the distinctive character or the repute of the trade mark" (Art 5(2)). In *L'Oréal SA v Bellure NV* (C-487/07) [2009] ETMR 55 (p 987) the Court held that the taking of unfair advantage consists of attempting "to ride on the coat-tails of the mark with a reputation in order to benefit from the power of attraction, the reputation and the prestige of that mark and to exploit, without paying any financial compensation, the marketing effort expended by the proprietor of the mark" (at [50]). It is not necessary that "there be a likelihood of confusion or a likelihood of detriment to the distinctive character or the repute of the mark" (at [50]).

[9.135] Exhaustion of Trade Marks Rights

The Directive regulates exhaustion of rights. A trade mark proprietor is "not entitle[d] . . . to prohibit its use in relation to goods which have been put on the market in the Community under that trade mark by the proprietor or with his consent" (Art 7(1)). Putting of the goods on the market was considered in *Peak Holding AB v Axolin-Elinor AB* (C-16/03) [2004] ECR I-11313; [2005] 1 CMLR 45 (p 1182). Peak contended that a Swedish company sold trade marked goods that were subject to a contractual restriction upon resale in most European nations (at [12]). The Court stated that goods are not "put on the market" in the EU where the proprietor imports them with the intention of selling them within the EU. In such a case there is no transfer to a third party of the right to sell the goods (at [41]–[42]). The Court observed that exhaustion occurs where the proprietor puts the goods onto the EU market (at [53]). A contractual restriction upon resale cannot forestall the exhaustion of the proprietor's rights pursuant to the Directive (at [54]–[55]).

The requirements for consent by the proprietor under Art 7(1) were considered in *Zino Davidoff SA v Tesco Stores Ltd* (C-414/99) [2001] ECR I-8691; [2002] 1 CMLR 1 (p 1). The Court held that consent must be unequivocally shown (at [45]). The proprietor's consent will normally be through an express statement. However, consent may be implied from the circumstances (at [46]). Mere silence does not constitute implied consent (at [55]). The failure of a proprietor to communicate their opposition to trading also does not constitute implied consent (at [56]). A proprietor need not demonstrate their lack of consent. It is for a trader to demonstrate that consent was given (at [54]).

A trade mark proprietor will have the right to prohibit use of the mark in relation to goods "where there exist legitimate reasons for the proprietor to oppose further commercialisation of the goods, especially where the condition of the goods is changed or impaired after they have been put on the market" (Art 7(2)). The concept of legitimate reasons was considered in *Bayerische Motorenwerke AG v Deenik* (C-63/97) [1999] ECR I-905; [1999] 1 CMLR 1099. Deenik operated a garage that specialized in selling second hand BMWs. He was not an official BMW dealer (at [8]). He advertised that he was a BMW specialist (at [25]). This advertising constituted use of the mark (at [42]).

The Court held that there would be a "legitimate reason" under Art 7(2) if the advertisements for the sale of BMWs created the impression that there was a commercial link between the reseller and the proprietor of the mark, especially if the impression was created that the reseller was part of the official BMW network (at [51]). However, there would be no legitimate reason if the advertising did not create a risk that the public would believe that there was a commercial link between the reseller and the mark proprietor (at [53]). A reseller who was a specialist in BMWs would be unable to inform consumers of that fact without using the BMW mark. Such a use of the mark was necessary for exercising the right of resale (at [54]).

In *Boehringer Ingelheim KG v Swingward Ltd* (C-348/04) [2007] ECR I-3391; [2007] 2 CMLR 52 (p 1445) the ECJ held that repackaging or relabelling creates a risk for the guarantee of origin. The proprietor may thus prohibit repackaging or relabelling unless the changes are necessary for the marketing of parallel imports and the legitimate interests of the proprietor are respected (at [30]). Repackaging is "necessary" where the rules or practices of the importing country do not allow the pharmaceutical to be marketed in the same packaging (at [36]). However, repackaging was not "necessary" if it was done to obtain a commercial advantage (at [37]). The repackaging must not damage the reputation of the mark through its poor quality, defects or untidiness (at [43]–[44]).

[9.140] Violation of a Licensing Agreement

The proprietor may invoke its trade mark rights against a licensee who violates the licensing contract in relation to "(a) its duration; (b) the form covered by the registration in which the trade mark may be used; (c) the scope of the goods or services for which the licence is granted; (d) the territory in which the trade mark may be affixed; or (e) the quality of the goods manufactured or of the services provided by the licensee" (Art 8(2)).

In *Copad SA v Christian Dior couture SA* (C-59/08) [2009] ETMR 40 (p 683) Christian Dior entered into a licence agreement with Copad (at [7]). The agreement provided that in order to maintain the prestige of the brand Copad would not sell Dior products to stores that were not part of the selective distribution network (at [8]). In violation of this clause, Copad sold Dior products to a chain of discount stores (at [10]).

The Court held that the quality of luxury goods was in part the result of the prestigious image that gave them an "aura of luxury" (at [24]). Impairment of that aura of luxury affects the quality of the product (at [26]). The selective distribution network helped to maintain the aura of luxury surrounding the goods (at [29]). Selling luxury goods outside the selective network may affect the quality of the product so the contractual restriction fell under Art 8(2) of the Directive (at [30]). Thus the proprietor could invoke its trade mark rights against a licensee who sold to discount stores in violation of a contractual undertaking, if that violation damaged the prestigious image of the mark (at [37]).

[9.145] Revocation of a Trade Mark

A trade mark may be revoked if during a continuous period of 5 years it has not been put to genuine use in relation to the goods or services for which it was registered (Art 12(1)). Use of the mark on promotional items that were given to consumers without charge does not constitute a "genuine use" of the mark. See *Silberquelle GmbH v Maselli-Strickmode GmbH* (C-495/07) [2009] ECR I-137 at [18]–[20].

[9.150] Community Trade Marks

Registration of a Community trade mark confers protection in all EU Member States. See Council Regulation 207/2009 of 26 February 2009 on the Community trade mark (OJ L 78, 24.3.2009, p 1). A Community trade mark is a trade mark registered in accordance with this Regulation (Art 1). The mark is obtained by registration (Art 6). It has a "unitary character" and has equal effect throughout the EU (Art 1(2)). The criteria for registration (Arts 4, 7–8) are similar to those applying under Directive 2008/95. Provision is made for the exhaustion of rights (Art 13).

The Office of Harmonization for the Internal Market (OHIM) registers Community trade marks. OHIM decisions are reported in the *European Trade Mark Reports* (London: Sweet & Maxwell, 1996–). The decisions of the Office are also available on its website (http://oami.europa.eu). Previous OHIM decisions may be taken into account in determining whether a sign is entitled to registration as a Community trade mark, though they do not have decisive effect. See *Paul Reber GmbH & Co KG v Office for Harmonisation in the Internal Market* (T-304/06) [2008] ECR II-1927 at [53]; *Ferrero SpA v Office for Harmonisation in the Internal Market* (T-140/08) [2009] ECR at [35]. Notice of marks is provided in the *Community Trade Marks Bulletin* (Art 89(a)). The Bulletin is available at http://oami.europa.eu/ows/rw/pages/CTM/CTMBulletinList.em.do.

[9.155] International Registration of Trade Marks

On 1 July 2004 the EC acceded to the Madrid Protocol. See *Protocol Relating to the Madrid Agreement Concerning the International Registration of Marks*, Madrid, 27 June 1989, OJ L 296, 14.11.2003, p 22; [2001] ATS 7; Treaty Doc 106-41. The United States, Australia and Singapore are also parties to the Protocol (*Treaties in Force 2009* p 376).

The Protocol provides that where an application for registration of a mark is made in the trade marks office of a party to the Protocol, the applicant may obtain protection in all state parties by registering that mark in the register of the International Bureau of the World Intellectual Property Organization. A person who has obtained the registration of a mark in the trade marks office of a party has the same right (Art 2(1)). Upon registration with the International Bureau, the mark shall be protected in each state party as if it had been deposited in its national office (Art 4(1)(a)). Applications for international registration of a Community trade mark are governed by Arts 145–161, Council Regulation 207/2009 of 26 February 2009 on the Community trade mark (OJ L 78, 24.3.2009, p 1).

[9.160] Designs

An EU Directive has harmonised the legislation of the Member States regarding designs. See Directive 98/71 of the European Parliament and of the Council of 13 October 1998 on the legal protection of designs (OJ L 289, 28.10.1998, p 28). "Design" is defined as "the appearance of the whole or a part of a product resulting from the features of, in particular, the lines, contours, colours, shape, texture and/or materials of the product itself and/or its ornamentation" (Art 1(a)). Product is defined as "any industrial or handicraft item", including packaging and graphic symbols, but not a computer program (Art 1(b)).

The Member States must protect registered designs (Art 3(1)). A design is protected "to the extent that it is new and has individual character" (Art 3(2)). A design is new if no identical design was available to the public before the application for registration was filed. A design is considered to be identical if it differs "only in immaterial details" (Art 4).

A design has individual character if the "overall impression it produces on the informed observer" differs from that of any design made available to the public before the application for registration was filed (Art 5(1)). A design has been made available to the public if it has been published, exhibited, employed in trade or commerce or disclosed in another way (Art 6(1)).

The holder of a registered design has the exclusive right to use the design, including the sale of any product in which the design is incorporated (Art 12(1)). There are limited exceptions to these exclusive rights (Art 13). A design is protected for 5 years from the date of the application for registration, renewable up to 20 years from the date of filing (Art 10).

An EU Regulation provides for Community designs. See Council Regulation 6/2002 of 12 December 2001 on Community designs (OJ L 3, 5.1.2002, p 1). The provisions of this Regulation are "aligned" with those of Directive 98/71 (Preamble Recital 9). Many of the provisions of the Regulation are thus similar to those of the Directive, and the discussion here will focus upon the differences between the two instruments. A Community design is a design that fulfils the conditions laid down in the Regulation (Art 1(1)). The Community design has a "unitary character" and has "equal effect throughout" the Union (Art 1(3)).

A Community design may be registered or unregistered. An unregistered Community design is a design that is made available to the public in accordance with the Regulation (Arts 1(2), 7). A registered Community design has been registered in accordance with the Regulation (Art 1(2)). The holder of a registered Community design has the exclusive right to use the design, including putting on the market, exporting and importing (Art 19(1)). The holder of an unregistered design has the right to prevent these acts only if the use is the result of copying the unregistered design (Art 19(2)).

Applications for a registered Community design may be filed at the Office for Harmonisation in the Internal Market or a Member State's central industrial property office (Arts 2, 35(1)). The central industrial property office of a Member State must forward the application to the Office for Harmonisation (Art 35(2)). If the requirements for a registered Community design are satisfied the Office for Harmonisation will register the design in the Community design register (Arts 48, 72). Notice of registered Community designs is given in the *Community Designs Bulletin* (Arts 49, 73(1)). The Bulletin is available at http://www.oami.europa.eu/bulletin/rcd/rcd_bulletin_en.htm.

The European Community and Singapore are parties to the Geneva Act regarding international registration of designs. See *Geneva Act of the Hague Agreement Concerning the International Registration of Industrial Designs*, Geneva, 2 July 1999, 2279 UNTS 3; OJ L 386, 29.12.2006, p 30; Council Decision 2006/954 of 18 December 2006 approving the accession of the European Community to the Geneva Act of the Hague Agreement concerning the international registration of industrial designs (OJ L 386, 29.12.2006, p 28). Australia, Canada, India, Malaysia, New Zealand and South Africa are not party to this agreement.

[9.165] Plant Variety Rights

The EU has introduced a system for the protection of plant variety rights. See Council Regulation 2100/94 of 27 July 1994 on Community plant variety rights (OJ L 227, 1.9.1994, p 1). This system is the "exclusive form of Community industrial property rights for plant varieties" (Art 1). These rights have uniform effect throughout the EU (Art 2). A plant variety is eligible for protection if it is distinct, uniform, stable and new (novel) (Art 6). These concepts are elaborated upon in Arts 7–10.

Plant variety rights may be granted to the person who bred or discovered and developed the plant variety (Art 11(1)). The right holder has exclusive rights such as production, conditioning for propagation, sale, export and import (Art 13(2)). Farmers are permitted to use for propagation the product of their harvest of a variety protected by a plant variety right, other than hybrids or synthetic varieties (Art 14(1)). This propagation right is limited to specific varieties such as various fodder plants, oats, barley, rice, rye, wheat, spelt and potatoes (Art 14(2)).

Plant variety rights last for 25 years following the year in which they were granted, and 30 years following the year of grant in the case of vine and tree species (Art 19(1)). A civil action is available to enjoin infringement or obtain compensation or both (Art 94(1)). Time limits apply to these actions (Art 96). EU Member States retain the right to provide for national plant variety rights (Art 3). However, any variety protected by a Community plant variety right may not be the subject of a national plant variety right or patent (Art 92(1)). See generally, Margaret Llewelyn and Mike Adcock, *European Plant Intellectual Property* (Oxford: Hart, 2006).

The European Community is party to the UPOV Convention providing for the protection of plant varieties. See *International Convention for the Protection of New Varieties of Plants of 2 December 1961*, as Revised at Geneva on 10 November 1972, 23 October 1978 and 19 March 1991, OJ L 192, 22.7.2005, p 64; [2000] ATS 5; Treaty Doc 104-17. Australia, Canada, New Zealand, Singapore, South Africa and the United States are also party to the Convention, either as amended in 1978 or in 1991 (*Treaties in Force* 2009 p 424). The website of the International Union for the Protection of New Varieties of Plants (UPOV) is at http://www.upov.int.

[9.170] Semi-conductors

Another Directive governs the protection of legal rights in semi-conductor products. See Council Directive 87/54 of 16 December 1986 on the legal protection of topographies of semiconductor products (OJ L 24, 27.1.1987, p 36). Member States are required to protect the topographies of semiconductor products by using legislative provisions conferring exclusive rights (Art 2(1)). "Topography" is defined as "a series of related images… representing the three-dimensional pattern of the layers of which a semiconductor product is composed;…in which…each image has the pattern…of a surface of the semiconductor product" (Art 1(b)).

An application for registration in due form must be filed at the public authority within 2 years of its first commercial exploitation (Art 4(1)). In addition, Member States may require that material identifying or exemplifying the topography be deposited with the public authorities as well as a statement regarding the first commercial exploitation when a person applies for registration (Art 4(1)). The exclusive rights given under the Directive apply to reproduction and to commercial exploitation (Art 5(1)). These exclusive rights come to an end 10 years from the current year in which the topography is first commercially exploited or when re-registration is effected (Art 7(3)).

The right to protection can be extended by Council decisions to persons who do not benefit from protection under the provisions of the Directive (Art 3(7)). This has been done in favour of natural persons from most countries outside of the European Union, including all members of the World Trade Organisation. See Council Decision 93/16 of 21 December 1992 on the extension of the legal protection of topographies of semiconductor products to persons from the United States of America and certain territories (OJ L 11, 19.1.1993, p 20); Council Decision 94/700 of 24 October 1994 on the extension of the legal protection of topographies of semiconductor products to persons from Canada (OJ L 284, 1.11.1994, p 61); Council Decision 94/824 of 22 December 1994 on the extension of the legal protection of topographies of semiconductor products to persons from a Member of the World Trade Organization (OJ L 349, 31.12.1994, p 201).

[9.175] Geographical Indications

EU law provides for the protection of agricultural product or foodstuff names as geographical indications and designations of origin for agricultural products. See Council Regulation 510/2006 of 20 March 2006 on the protection of geographical indications and designations of origin for agricultural products and foodstuffs (OJ L 93, 31.3.2006, p 12).

Only names relating to certain agricultural products and foodstuffs may be protected under the Regulation (Art 1(1)). These agricultural products include hay, essential oils, flowers, wool, meat, fish, dairy, vegetables, fruit, nuts, coffee, tea, spices, cereals and sugar (Annex II of the Regulation;

Annex I TFEU). These foodstuffs include beer, bread, pastry, cake, confectionary, mustard and pasta (Annex I of the Regulation).

A geographical indication is defined as the name of a region or place used to describe an agricultural product originating from and produced in that region or place. The product or foodstuff must possess a particular quality or reputation attributable to this geographical origin (Art 2(1)(b)).

A designation of origin is defined as the name of a region or place used to describe an agricultural product or foodstuff originating from and produced in that region or place. The quality or characteristics of the product or foodstuff must be essentially due to the specific local environment (Art 2(1)(a)). A name that has become generic cannot be registered as a geographical indication or designation of origin (Art 3(1)). However, a name protected under the Regulation cannot become generic (Art 13(2)).

An association of producers or processors of the product or foodstuff may register a name as a protected geographical indication or designation of origin (Art 5(1)–(2)). A product specification indicating various qualities of the product or foodstuff must accompany the application (Art 4). If the Commission receives no objection to registration, it registers the name and publishes a notice of registration in the EU Official Journal (Art 7(4)). A registered name may be used by operators marketing products or foodstuffs that meet the product specification (Art 8(1)). These products or foodstuffs must be labelled "protected geographical indication" or "protected designation of origin" (Art 8(2)–(3)).

A registered name is protected against use in relation to products not covered by the registration where use of the registered name exploits the reputation of that name (Art 13(a)). The name is also protected against any imitation of the name, including where the true origin is disclosed or where words such as "style" or "imitation" are used (Art 13(b)). The name is protected against false or misleading indications regarding the origin or qualities of the product and any other practices that are likely to mislead consumers as to the origin of the product (Art 13(c)–(d)). See generally, Lilian V Faulhaber, "Cured Meat and Idaho Potatoes: A Comparative Analysis of European and American Protection and Enforcement of Geographic Indications of Foodstuffs" (2005) 11 *Columbia Journal of European Law* 623.

The EU's bilateral agreements regarding the wine trade also contain provisions regarding geographical indications. For example, under the wine agreement with Australia the parties agree that their wine producers will not use specific geographical indications customarily used by the other party. See Arts 12(1)(a)(I), 13 and Annex II, *Agreement on Trade in Wine*, Brussels, 1 December 2008, [2008] ATNIF 20; OJ L 28, 30.1.2009, p 3. As a result Australian wine producers will not use EU geographical indications such as champagne and sherry.

The other bilateral treaties concerning the wine trade also provide for the protection of geographical indications:

- *Canada*: Arts 10–11 and Annex III(a) and (b), *Agreement on Trade in Wines and Spirit Drinks*, Niagara-on-the-Lake, 16 September 2003, OJ L 35, 6.2.2004, p 3;
- *South Africa*: Arts 7–8 and Annex II, *Agreement on Trade in Wine*, Paarl, 28 January 2002, OJ L 28, 30.1.2002, p 4; and
- *United States*: Art 7(1) and Annex IV, Part A, *Agreement on Trade in Wine*, London, 10 March 2006, OJ L 87, 24.3.2006, p 2; State Dept No 06-127.

A bilateral agreement with South Africa makes provision for the protection of geographical indications for spirits. See Arts 5–6 and Annex, *Agreement on Trade in Spirits*, Paarl, 28 January 2002, OJ L 28, 30.1.2002, p 113.

[9.180] Enforcement Measures

The EU has adopted legislation applying to any violation of intellectual property rights as provided by EU law or the law of the Member State concerned. See Art 2(1), Directive 2004/48 of the European Parliament and of the Council of 29 April 2004 on the enforcement of intellectual property rights (OJ L 157, 30.4.2004, p 45). The Directive does not affect EU provisions concerning the substantive law of intellectual property (Art 2(3)(a)).

Where an aggrieved party presents evidence sufficient to support its claims, the courts may order the opposing party to present evidence in its control (Art 6(1)). The courts may also order the opposing party to produce banking, financial or commercial documents in their control (Art 6(2)). The courts may also make provisional orders for the preservation of evidence (Art 7(1)). In each case these powers are subject to the protection of confidential information. The courts may also order that the infringer provide information regarding the origin and distribution networks of infringing goods or services. Such an order may also be made against a person who possesses or uses infringing goods on a commercial scale (Art 8(1)).

The Directive sets out various provisional measures that may be issued against infringers. The courts may issue an interlocutory injunction to prevent the occurrence or continuation of an infringement (Art 9(1)(a)). The seizure or delivery up of infringing goods may also be ordered (Art 9(1)(b)). If the injured party shows that the recovery of damages may be frustrated, the courts may order the seizure of the real and personal property of the infringer (Art 9(2)). These orders may be made without hearing the alleged infringer (Art 9(4)). If the defendant has not infringed copyright, the applicant may be ordered to compensate the defendant for injury resulting from the making of these orders (Art 9(7)).

Other orders may be made after a decision on the merits has been given. If the court decides that the defendant infringed the applicant's intellectual property rights, the court may order that infringing goods be removed from commerce and destroyed (Art 10(1)). The court may also issue an injunction against continuation of the infringement (Art 11). If an infringer "acted unintentionally and without negligence", the court may order the infringer to pay compensation instead of making such orders, if those orders would cause the infringer disproportionate harm and compensation would be a satisfactory remedy (Art 12).

The courts may order an infringer with actual or constructive knowledge to pay damages for the infringement. These damages may take account of lost profits, unfair profits and moral prejudice to the applicant (Art 13(1)). Where the infringer did not have actual or constructive knowledge, the Member States may provide that their courts are empowered to order the recovery of profits or the payment of damages (Art 13(2)). See generally, Enrico Bonadio, "Remedies and Sanctions for the Infringement of Intellectual Property Rights Under EC Law" (2008) 30 *European Intellectual Property Review* 320.

[9.185] Counterfeit Goods

An EU Regulation provides that customs authorities may take action against counterfeit goods. See Council Regulation 1383/2003 of 22 July 2003 concerning customs action against goods suspected of infringing certain intellectual property rights and the measures to be taken against goods found to have infringed such rights (OJ L 196, 2.8.2003, p 7). The Regulation lays down "the conditions for action by the customs authorities when goods are suspected of infringing an intellectual property right... when they are entered for release for free circulation, export or re-export... [or] when they are found during checks on goods entering or leaving the Community customs territory" (Art 1(1)).

The free circulation of goods infringing intellectual property rights is prohibited (Art 16). Goods infringing intellectual property rights include counterfeit goods, pirated goods, and goods infringing a patent, plant variety right or designations of origin (Art 2(1)(c)). Counterfeit goods are any goods "bearing without authorisation a trademark identical to the trademark validly registered in respect of the same type of goods, or which cannot be distinguished in its essential aspects from such a trademark, and which thereby infringes the trademark-holder's rights under Community law,... or the law of the Member State in which the application for action by the customs authorities is made" (Art 2(1)(a)).

Pirated goods are defined as "goods which are... copies made without the consent of the holder of a copyright or related right or design right, regardless of whether it is registered in national law, or of a person authorised by the right-holder in the country of production in cases where the making of those copies would constitute an infringement of that right under [EU designs law]...or the law of the Member State in which the application for customs action is made" (Art 2(1)(b)).

An intellectual property owner may lodge an application for action by the customs authorities (Art 5(1)). The applicant may not be asked to pay a fee to cover the administrative costs incurred in processing the application (Art 5(7)). Once a decision has been made, the customs authorities shall inform the applicant of the result of the application (Art 5(7)).

Member States are to adopt measures necessary to allow the destruction of "goods found to infringe an intellectual property right or dispose of them outside commercial channels in such a way as to preclude injury to the right-holder, without compensation of any sort" (Art 17(1)(a)). They are also authorized to take any other measures having the effect of effectively depriving those responsible for importation of the economic benefits of the transaction (Art 17(1)(b)). Mere removal of the trademarks does not effectively deprive the importer of the economic benefits of the transaction (Art 17(1)(b)). See generally, Karel Daele, "Regulation 1383/2003: A New Step in the Fight Against Counterfeit and Pirated Goods at the Borders of the European Union" (2004) 26 *European Intellectual Property Review* 214.

[9.190] Conclusion

Art 34 TFEU prohibits all quantitative restrictions or measures having equivalent effect in order to bring about free movement of goods. However, the territoriality principle of industrial and commercial property rights results in the creation of national markets which hampers the free movement of goods within the European Union. There is thus a tension between the principle of free movement of goods and the territorial protection of industrial and commercial property rights.

Under Art 36 TFEU measures for the protection of industrial and commercial property constitute a permissible exception to free movement of goods. However, these restrictions may not "constitute a means of arbitrary discrimination or a disguised restriction on trade between Member States." The holders of intellectual property rights may attempt to use them to prevent the importation or marketing of goods by means of an infringement action, thereby subverting the principle of free movement of goods and partitioning the Union into national markets.

However, the exercise of industrial and commercial property rights under Art 36 TFEU is restricted by the doctrine of the exhaustion of rights. The Court has held that the exclusive right of the copyright owner "is exhausted when a product has been lawfully distributed on the market in another Member State by the actual proprietor of the right or with his consent".

Art 101(1) TFEU prohibits agreements and concerted practices "which may affect trade between Member States and which have as their object or effect the prevention, restriction or distortion of competition within the internal market." By Art 101(2), such agreements are automatically void. The existence of industrial and commercial property rights is not affected by EU law, but the exercise of those rights may be affected by EU competition rules. Art 101 will affect the exercise of those rights once the core rights are exhausted.

The EU has adopted several Directives regulating various aspects of copyright law, including the term of copyright protection, rental and lending rights and resale rights for artists. Other Directives concern copyright protection in particular contexts, such as the information society, computer programs and databases.

The EU has not yet adopted a system of Community Patents. Under the European Patent Convention a single application may be made to the European Patent Office. The Patent Cooperation Treaty provides for an international process for the filing of patent applications in the States that are party to the Treaty. A Directive provides that EU Member States must provide patent protection for biotechnological inventions.

An EU Directive approximates national trade marks laws. A trade mark may consist of any sign capable of being represented graphically. A mark may not be registered if it is devoid of any distinctive character. The trade mark proprietor may prevent third parties from using in trade an identical sign in relation to goods or services that are identical to those for which the mark has been registered.

The Directive provides for the exhaustion of trade mark rights. A proprietor is not entitled to prohibit its use in relation to goods which have been put on the market in the EU under that trade mark by the proprietor or with its consent. A proprietor has the right to prohibit use of the mark in relation to goods where there are legitimate reasons to oppose further commercialization of the goods.

Registration of a Community trade mark confers protection in all EU Member States. The Madrid Protocol facilitates the international registration of marks. The EU has also adopted legislation for the protection of designs, plant variety rights, semi-conductors and geographical indications. Other EU legislation provides for judicial enforcement measures against violation of intellectual property rights and customs measures against counterfeit goods.

Further Reading

A. General

Harris, Bryan. *Intellectual Property Law in the European Union* (Buffalo, NY: William S Hein, 2005).

Hays, Thomas. *Parallel Importation Under European Union Law* (London: Sweet & Maxwell, 2004).

Seville, Catherine. *EU Intellectual Property Law and Policy* (Cheltenham, UK: Edward Elgar, 2009).

Tritton, Guy. *Intellectual Property in Europe* (3rd ed, London: Sweet & Maxwell, 2008).

B. Free Movement of Goods

Enchelmaier, Stefan. "The Inexhaustible Question – Free Movement of Goods and Intellectual Property in the European Court of Justice's Case Law, 2002–2006" (2007) 38 *International Review of Intellectual Property and Competition Law* 453.

Ginter, Carri. "Free Movement of Goods and Parallel Imports in the Internal Market of the EU" (2005) 7 *European Journal of Law Reform* 505.

Keeling, David T. *Intellectual Property Rights in EU Law. Vol 1: Free Movement and Competition Law* (Oxford: Oxford University Press, 2003).

Subiotto, Romano and Claudia Annacker. "Free Movement of Goods and the Protection of Trademarks: Current Issues Concerning Repackaging, Relabelling and Rebranding in EC Law" (2002) 5 *Journal of World Intellectual Property* 933.

C. Copyright

Dreier, Thomas and P Bernt Hugenholtz (eds). *Concise European Copyright Law* (Alphen aan den Rijn, The Netherlands: Kluwer, 2006).

Horton, Kenneth L. "The Software Copyright Directive and the Internet: Collision on the Information Superhighway?" *Jean Monnet Working Paper* No 8/96, http://www.jeanmonnetprogram.org

Leistner, Matthias. "Copyright Law in the EC: Status Quo, Recent Case Law and Policy Perspectives" (2009) 46 *Common Market Law Review* 847.

Travers, Noel. "Rental Rights and the Specific Subject-Matter of Copyright in Community Law" (1999) 24 *European Law Review* 171.

van Eechoud, Mireille et al. *Harmonizing European Copyright Law: The Challenge of Better Lawmaking* (Alphen aan den Rijn: Kluwer Law International, 2009).

D. Patents

Hacon, Richard and Jochen Pagenberg (eds). *Concise European Patent Law* (2nd ed, Alphen aan den Rijn, The Netherlands: Kluwer Law International, 2007).

Volkheimer, Tim. "Patents and the Free Movement of Goods: A Shift Towards European Arbitrariness?" (2009) 15 *Columbia Journal of European Law* 495.

E. Trade Marks

Bertoli, Giuseppe. "Advances and Halts in the Recent Case-Law of the Court of First Instance Concerning the Community Trade Mark" (2009) 9 *ERA Forum* 609.

Clark, Julia. "Adorning Shavers with Clover Leaves: *Koninklijke Philips Electronics NV v Remington Consumer Products Ltd*" (2006) 28 *European Intellectual Property Review* 352.

Evrard, Sebastien J. "Trademark Law in the European Union: An Overview of the Court of Justice and the Court of First Instance (1997–2001)" (2002) 9 *Columbia Journal of European Law* 175.

Feaster, Trudy, James I Walsh, and Pat Treacy. "The Exhaustion and Unauthorised Exploitation of Trade Mark Rights in the European Union" (1999) 24 *European Law Review* 259.

Grassie, Gill. "Parallel Imports and Trade Marks: Where Are We? (Part 1)" (2006) 28 *European Intellectual Property Review* 474.

Grassie, Gill. "Parallel Imports and Trade Marks: The Repackaging Cases (Part 2)" (2006) 28 *European Intellectual Property Review* 513

Leistner, Matthias. "Harmonization of Intellectual Property Law in Europe: The European Court of Justice's Trade Mark Case Law 2004–2007" (2008) 45 *Common Market Law Review* 69.

Pehrson, Lars. "Interpretation of the Trade Mark Directive" (2007) 2 *Swedish Studies in European Law* 157.

Turner-Kerr, Peter M. "Trade Mark Tangles: Recent Twists and Turns in EC Trade Mark Law" (2004) 29 *European Law Review* 345.

Walmsley, Mike. "Too Transparent? ECJ Rules Dyson Cannot Register Transparent Collection Chamber as a Trade Mark" (2007) 29 *European Intellectual Property Review* 298.

Chapter 10
Social Dimension of the European Union

[10.05] Introduction

The social dimension of the European Union is of direct relevance to business people, especially those who propose to establish a subsidiary in the Union. European subsidiaries of non-EU parent companies must organize their business in accordance with the anti-discrimination and consumer protection laws of the Union. The completion of the internal market has been accompanied by vigorous attempts to harmonize the social policies of the Member States. The first part of this chapter discusses EU provisions relating to sex discrimination, the second part examines EU legislation regarding other forms of discrimination and the final part briefly deals with other social provisions such as vocational training, data protection and consumer protection.

[10.10] Equal Pay for Equal Work

Art 157 TFEU (formerly Art 119 EC) contains the "equal pay for equal work" principle. Art 157 reads as follows:

> 1. Each Member State shall ensure that the principle of equal pay for male and female workers for equal work or work of equal value is applied.
> 2. For the purpose of this article, 'pay' means the ordinary basic or minimum wage or salary and any other consideration, whether in cash or in kind, which the worker receives directly or indirectly, in respect of his employment, from his employer.
>
> Equal pay without discrimination based on sex means:
>
> (a) that pay for the same work at piece rates shall be calculated on the basis of the same unit of measurement;
> (b) that pay for work at time rates shall be the same for the same job.

In *Specialarbejderforbundet i Danmark v Dansk Industri* (C-400/93) [1995] ECR I-1275; [1996] 1 CMLR 515 most members of two groups of

G. Moens, J. Trone, *Commercial Law of the European Union*,
Ius Gentium: Comparative Perspectives on Law and Justice 4,
DOI 10.1007/978-90-481-8774-4_10, © Springer Science+Business Media B.V. 2010

factory employees were paid on a piece work basis, under which their salary was dependent upon their individual output (at [5]). The Court held that the principle of equal pay applied to piece work pay arrangements (at [12]–[13]). Art 157 TFEU expressly requires that payment for piece work "shall be calculated on the basis of the same unit of measurement".

[10.15] Equal Pay and the Elimination of Sex Discrimination

The social aim of the principle of equal pay for equal work is the elimination of discrimination based on sex. The right of a person to be free from discrimination on grounds of sex is a fundamental right protected as a general principle of EU law. See *Defrenne v SABENA (No 3)* (149/77) [1978] ECR 1365 at [26]–[27]; [1978] 3 CMLR 312; *P v S* (C-13/94) [1996] ECR I-2143 at [19]; [1996] 2 CMLR 247; *Deutsche Telekom AG v Schröder* (C-50/96) [2000] ECR I-743 at [56]; [2002] 2 CMLR 25 (p 583); *Rinke v Ärztekammer Hamburg* (C-25/02) [2003] ECR I-8349 at [25]; *Richards v Secretary of State for Work and Pensions* (C-423/04) [2006] ECR I-3585 at [23]; [2006] 2 CMLR 49 (p 1242). The TFEU provides that in all of its activities the EU "shall aim to eliminate inequalities, and to promote equality, between men and women" (Art 8 TFEU).

The ECJ has defined discrimination as "the application of different rules to comparable situations or the application of the same rule to different situations". See *Gillespie v Northern Health and Social Services Board* (C-342/93) [1996] ECR I-475 at [16]; [1996] 2 CMLR 969; *Hill v Revenue Commissioners* (C-243/95) [1998] ECR I-3739 at [22]; [1998] 3 CMLR 81; *Lewen v Denda* (C-333/97) [1999] ECR I-7243 at [36]; [2000] 2 CMLR 38; *Alabaster v Woolwich plc* (C-147/02) [2004] ECR I-3101 at [45]; [2004] 2 CMLR 9 (p 186).

[10.20] Defrenne (No 2) Litigation

The Court of Justice authoritatively examined the equal pay principle in *Defrenne v SABENA (No 2)* (43/75) [1976] ECR 455; [1976] 2 CMLR 98. Ms Defrenne was employed by Sabena as a flight attendant. Her employment was confirmed by a new contract of employment which provided that her employment would terminate upon reaching the age of 40 years. This provision was in accordance with Belgian law which required that female flight attendants retire at the age of 40. There was no such legal requirement in respect of male flight attendants.

Ms Defrenne initiated legal proceedings for compensation for the loss she had suffered in salary and allowances as a result of the fact that female and male members of the air crew performing identical duties did not receive equal pay. The Court had to determine whether Art 119 EC (now Art 157

TFEU) was directly effective in the sense that it could be relied upon by individuals in national courts even if Member States have not taken steps to implement it.

The ECJ held that Art 119 EC (now Art 157 TFEU) was directly effective and, therefore could be relied upon in national courts at least in cases of direct (as opposed to indirect) discrimination. The Court's decision was stated succinctly:

> a distinction must be drawn within the whole area of application of Article 119 between, first, direct and overt discrimination which may be identified solely with the aid of the criteria based on equal work and equal pay referred to by the article in question and, secondly, indirect and disguised discrimination which can only be identified by reference to more explicit implementing provisions of a Community or national character..... the principle of equal pay contained in Art 119 may be relied upon before the national courts and... these courts have a duty to ensure the protection of the rights which this provision vests in individuals, in particular as regards those types of discrimination arising directly from legislative provisions or collective labour agreements, as well as in cases in which men and women receive unequal pay for equal work which is carried out in the same establishment or service, whether private or public (at [18], [40]).

In adopting the distinction between direct and indirect discrimination, the Court effectively defeated the argument that Art 119 (now Art 157 TFEU) does not clearly define the concept of "equal work".

The Court also held that Art 119 is mandatory in nature and therefore the prohibition upon discrimination "applies not only to the action of public authorities, but also extends to all agreements which are intended to regulate paid labour collectively, as well as to contracts between individuals" (at [39]). See similarly, *Specialarbejderforbundet i Danmark v Dansk Industri* (C-400/93) [1995] ECR I-1275 at [45]; [1996] 1 CMLR 515; *Lawrence v Regent Office Care Ltd* (C-320/00) [2002] ECR I-7325 at [13]; [2002] 3 CMLR 27 (p 761); *Land Brandenburg v Sass* (C-284/02) [2004] ECR I-11143 at [25]; [2005] 1 CMLR 27 (p 681); *Hlozek v Roche Austria Gesellschaft mbH* (C-19/02) [2004] ECR I-11491 at [43]; [2005] 1 CMLR 28 (p 702). Thus, Art 157 TFEU (formerly Art 119 EC) is both vertically and horizontally directly effective. A vertical direct effect imposes obligations upon Member States, while a horizontal direct effect imposes obligations upon individuals.

[10.25] Equal Work Carried Out in the Same Establishment

In *Defrenne (No 2)* the Court fixed as the basis of comparison the work carried out in the same establishment or service, thereby making the principle of "equal pay for equal work" inapplicable to whole industries. The scope of this implied limitation was clarified in *Macarthys Ltd v Smith* (129/79) [1980] ECR 1275; [1980] 2 CMLR 205. In that case the applicant sought to establish a right to equal pay by means of a comparison with a former male employee who 4 months previously had held the same position and had been paid at a higher level of remuneration (at [2]).

The Court ruled on the admissibility of a comparison with a former employee of the opposite sex. The Court held that the scope of the principle of "equal pay for equal work" is not restricted to situations of contemporaneous employment of men and women (at [11]). The Court was eager to avoid the possibility of an employer evading the requirements of Art 119 EC (now Art 157 TFEU) by replacing a former male employee with a female employee doing the same work and paying her less than her male predecessor because of her sex. However, the Court also decided that a difference in pay between two workers who occupy the same post at a different period may be due to the operation of factors unrelated to sex discrimination (for example, inflationary trends). That is a question of fact to be decided by the national courts (at [12]).

The Court was also requested to decide whether Art 119 EC (now Art 157 TFEU) applied in a situation of alleged unequal pay where the work in question had not previously been performed by a man, given the fact that contemporaneity is not a necessary element of "equal work" (at [14]). In effect the Court was asked to rule on the continuing legality of segregated professions where, by definition, a male comparator cannot be found. However, the Court was unwilling to apply the principle of "equal pay for equal work" to segregated professions. The Court stated that occupational segregation involves "indirect and disguised discrimination, the identification of which . . . implies comparative studies of entire branches of industry and therefore requires, as a prerequisite, the elaboration by the Community and national legislative bodies of criteria of assessment" (at [15]). It concluded that for the purposes of a claim based on Art 119 EC (Art 157 TFEU) "comparisons are confined to parallels which may be drawn on the basis of concrete appraisals of the work actually performed by employees of different sex within the same establishment or service" (at [15]).

[10.30] Application of Art 157 TFEU to Indirect Discrimination

The distinction between direct and indirect discrimination introduced by the Court in *Defrenne (No 2)* was soon discarded. Art 157 TFEU prohibits indirect discrimination by "the application of provisions which maintain different treatment between men and women at work as a result of the application of criteria not based on sex where those differences of treatment are not attributable to objective factors unrelated to sex discrimination". See *R v Secretary of State for Employment; Ex parte Seymour-Smith* (C-167/97) [1999] ECR I-623 at [52]; [1999] 2 CMLR 273; *Elsner-Lakeberg v Land Nordrhein-Westfalen* (C-285/02) [2004] ECR I-5861 at [12]; [2004]

2 CMLR 36 (p 874); *Voss v Land Berlin* (C-300/06) [2007] ECR I-10573 at [25]; [2008] 1 CMLR 49 (p 1313).

In *Jenkins v Kingsgate (Clothing Productions) Ltd* (96/80) [1981] ECR 911; [1981] 2 CMLR 24 the Court considered whether Art 119 EC (Art 157 TFEU) applies to a situation involving different hourly wage rates for part-time and full-time employees where the majority of the part-time workers are women (at [6]–[7]). The Court held that the fact that part-time work is paid at an hourly rate lower than pay for full-time work does not amount per se to discrimination provided that the hourly rates are applied to workers belonging to either category without distinction based on sex (at [10]).

A violation of Art 119 (Art 157 TFEU) occurs when "the pay policy of the undertaking in question cannot be explained by factors other than discrimination based on sex" (at [13]). If the pay policy can be explained by factors other than discrimination based on sex, a violation of Art 119 would not arise "unless it is in reality merely an indirect way of reducing the level of pay of part-time workers on the ground that that group of workers is composed exclusively or predominantly of women" (at [15]). A difference in remuneration between part-time work and full-time work is contrary to Art 119 if the category of part-time employees is predominantly or exclusively composed of females and there are no objectively justifiable factors for the differences in pay.

In *Bilka-Kaufhaus GmbH v Von Hartz* (170/84) [1986] ECR 1607; [1986] 2 CMLR 701 the Court again held that statistical disparities may prove the existence of indirect discrimination. A department store (Bilka) had implemented a supplementary pension scheme for its employees (at [3]). Part-time employees were eligible for a supplementary pension only if they had been in full-time employment for 15 years out of a total of 20 (at [4]).

The applicant (Mrs Weber) argued that Bilka had violated the principle of equal pay for equal work. She contended that the requirement of a minimum period of full-time employment adversely affected female workers who "were more likely than their male colleagues to take part-time work so as to be able to care for their family and children" (at [6]). Bilka argued that its scheme was not discriminatory because the requirement of a minimum period of full-time employment was based on objectively justified economic grounds. Bilka emphasised that "the employment of full-time workers entails lower ancillary costs and permits the use of staff throughout opening hours" (at [7]).

The Court held that Art 119 EC (Art 157 TFEU) "is infringed by a department store company which excludes part-time employees from its occupational pension scheme, where that exclusion affects a far greater number of women than men, unless the undertaking shows that the exclusion is based on objectively justified factors unrelated to any discrimination on grounds of sex" (at [31]). If the factors chosen by the company "correspond to a real need on the part of the undertaking", are appropriate to achieving the objectives pursued and are necessary to that end, the fact that more women are affected is not sufficient to constitute an infringement of Art 119 EC (Art 157 TFEU) (at [36]). The words "appropriate" and "necessary" indicate the existence of a requirement of proportionality. The employer must show that the same result could not have been achieved by a less discriminatory method and that the means employed are necessary to achieve the desired purpose.

[10.35] Further Indirect Discrimination Rulings

In *Specialarbejderforbundet i Danmark v Dansk Industri* (C-400/93) [1995] ECR I-1275; [1996] 1 CMLR 515 one group of piece workers (machine operators) was entirely men, while the other group (product painters) was almost entirely women (at [6]). The average hourly pay of the primarily female group was less than that of the primarily male group (at [8]).

The Court held that the mere fact that the average pay of the two groups was different did not of itself establish discrimination (at [22]). The difference may be attributable to individual differences in output (at [25]). A difference in pay between groups doing work of equal value will not constitute discrimination if it is explainable by "objectively justified factors" that do not involve sex discrimination (at [41]).

In *R v Secretary of State for Employment; Ex parte Seymour-Smith* (C-167/97) [1999] ECR I-623; [1999] 2 CMLR 273 British legislation provided that an unfair dismissal claim could only be brought by an employee who had been continuously employed for at least 2 years (at [6]). The Court stated that the national court had to determine whether statistical evidence showed that a much smaller proportion of women than men were able to meet the requirement of 2 years employment. If the statistics did show that disparity it would be evidence of apparent discrimination unless the national legislation was justified by objective factors that were not related to sex discrimination (at [60]). A smaller but persistent and fairly constant disparity over a long time would also be evidence of apparent discrimination (at [61]).

The Court pointed out that if a Member State demonstrated that its legislation was based on a "necessary aim of its social policy" and that the measures taken were "suitable and necessary" for attaining that goal, the fact that legislation that affected far more women than men would not necessarily breach Art 119 EC (Art 157 TFEU) (at [69]). The national court must determine whether the aim of the legislation is unrelated to sex discrimination and whether the measures adopted were able to further its social policy aim (at [72]). The Member State must also show that "it could reasonably consider that the means chosen were suitable for achieving that aim" (at [77]).

In *Voss v Land Berlin* (C-300/06) [2007] ECR I-10573; [2008] 1 CMLR 49 (p 1313) part time teachers were paid less than full time teachers for the same number of hours worked (at [12]–[14]). The Court considered whether the legislation treated full time and part time workers differently, whether the different treatment affected many more women than men and whether there were objective factors entirely unrelated to sex discrimination that would justify the different treatment (at [27]–[28]). The Court held that full time and part time workers were treated differently (at [37]). The national court had to determine whether the different treatment affected many more men than women (at [40]). If it did affect a much greater number of women than men, that was evidence of apparent sex discrimination, and the legislation would need to be justified by objective factors unrelated to discrimination (at [42]).

[10.40] Concept of "Pay"

Art 157 TFEU defines the concept of "pay" as "the ordinary basic or minimum wage or salary and any other consideration, whether in cash or in kind, which the worker receives directly or indirectly, in respect of his employment, from his employer". The Court has indicated that this consideration may be received immediately or in the future. See *R v Secretary of State for Employment; Ex parte Seymour-Smith* (C-167/97) [1999] ECR I-623 at [23]; [1999] 2 CMLR 273.

The Court has adopted an expansive interpretation of the concept of "pay". The following are examples of "pay" under Art 157 TFEU:

- redundancy payments: *Barber v Guardian Royal Exchange Assurance Group* (C-262/88) [1990] ECR I-1889 at [20]; [1990] 2 CMLR 513;
- an employer's contribution to a company pension scheme: *Worringham v Lloyds Bank Ltd* (69/80) [1981] ECR 767 at [17]; [1981] 2 CMLR 1;
- survivors benefit paid under an occupational pension scheme: *Maruko v Versorgungsanstalt der Deutschen Bühnen* (C-267/06) [2008] ECR I-1757 at [45]; [2008] 2 CMLR 32 (p 914);
- pay during maternity leave: *Gillespie v Northern Health and Social Services Board* (C-342/93) [1996] ECR I-475; [1996] 2 CMLR 969; *Alabaster v Woolwich plc* (C-147/02) [2004] ECR I-3101 at [44]; [2004] 2 CMLR 9 (p 186);
- lump sum payment to workers on maternity leave: *Abdoulaye v Regie nationale des usines Renault SA* (C-218/98) [1999] ECR I-5723 at [14]; [2001] 2 CMLR 372;
- payment of wages during sickness: *North Western Health Board v McKenna* (C-191/03) [2005] ECR I-7631 at [29]; [2006] 1 CMLR 6 (p 121); and

- a Christmas bonus: *Lewen v Denda* (C-33/97) [1999] ECR I-7243 at [21]; [2000] 2 CMLR 38.

The cases provide many other examples of "pay" under Art 157 TFEU. In *Defrenne v Belgium (No 1)* (8/70) [1971] ECR 445; [1974] 1 CMLR 494 the Court ruled that an emolument arising out of employment did not come within Art 119 (Art 157 TFEU). The term "consideration" in Art 119 did not cover a retirement pension established within the framework of a national social security system governed directly by legislation. Such a pension was the result of the implementation of national social policy rather than a concomitant of the relationship between employer and employee (at [7]).

In *Garland v British Rail Engineering Ltd* (12/81) [1982] ECR 359; [1982] 1 CMLR 696 the Court decided that the concept of "pay" included special concessionary travel facilities granted by an employer to former male (but not female) employees after their retirement (at [6]–[9]). The Court also pointed out that the fact that the employer was not contractually obliged to grant the concessions was irrelevant for the purposes of Art 119 (Art 157 TFEU) (at [10]). In *Grant v South-west Trains Ltd* (C-249/96) [1998] ECR I-621; [1998] 1 CMLR 993 the ECJ held that travel concessions provided by an employer under an employment contract to the spouse or same sex partner of an employee constituted "pay" (at [14]).

In *R v Secretary of State for Employment; Ex parte Seymour-Smith* (C-167/97) [1999] ECR I-623; [1999] 2 CMLR 273 the Court held that compensation paid to an employee in relation to their unfair dismissal was paid by reason of their employment and was intended to provide the employee with what they would have earned if they had not been unfairly dismissed (at [26], [28]). Such compensation thus constituted "pay".

The payment of a benefit after the end of the employment may constitute "pay" under Art 157 TFEU. See *Bestuur van het Algemeen Burgerlijk Pensioenfonds v Beune* (C-7/93) [1994] ECR I-4471 at [21]; [1995] 3 CMLR 30; *Maruko v Versorgungsanstalt der deutschen Bühnen* (C-267/06) [2008] ECR I-1757 at [44]; [2008] 2 CMLR 32 (p 914).

[10.45] Equal Pay Under EU Directives

The most important EU legislation relating to equal opportunities and equal treatment is the Equal Opportunities Directive. See Directive 2006/54 of the European Parliament and of the Council of 5 July 2006 on the implementation of the principle of equal opportunities and equal treatment of men and women in matters of employment and occupation (recast) (OJ L 204, 26.7.2006, p 23).

Art 4 of this Directive stipulates that "[f]or the same work or for work to which equal value is attributed, direct and indirect discrimination on grounds of sex with regard to all aspects and conditions of remuneration shall be eliminated.

In particular, where a job classification system is used for determining pay, it shall be based on the same criteria for both men and women and so drawn up as to exclude any discrimination on grounds of sex".

"Pay" is defined as including any "consideration, whether in cash or kind, which the worker receives directly or indirectly, in respect of his/her employment" (Art 2(1)(e)).

[10.50] Job Classification Schemes

The "principle of equal pay for equal work" and the "principle of equal pay for work of equal value" are distinct. The "principle of equal pay for equal work" refers to performance of the same work. The principle of "equal pay for work of equal value" requires that employees be paid an equal salary for work that is considered to be of equal value to their employer. It aims to establish wage parity among certain dissimilar types of employment on the claim that the jobs are of equal value to the employer. This issue is important for employers because they may have to pay equal salaries for different jobs.

The ECJ has given some guidance regarding the factors that may be used to determine the comparability of the value of work. In *Rummler v Dato-Druck GmbH* (237/85) [1986] ECR 2101; [1987] 3 CMLR 127 the different wage groups were divided according to the muscular effort, fatigue and physical hardship associated with the job (at [3]). The complainant sought to challenge these factors on the ground that they were discriminatory.

The Court decided that the scheme, based on the strength required to carry out such work or the degree of physical hardship which the work entailed, was not in violation of the former Equal Pay Directive provided that these factors were objectively justified (at [15]). Objective factors are those which are appropriate to the tasks to be carried out, and correspond to a genuine need of the undertaking. Factors "based on values appropriate only to workers of one sex" contain "a risk of discrimination" (at [23]).

In *Handels-Og Kontorfunktionaerernes Forbund v Dansk Arbejdsgiverforening* (109/88) [1989] ECR 3199; [1991] 1 CMLR 8 the Court decided that where the pay system is not transparent, if a female worker establishes, by comparison with a relatively large number of employees, that the average pay of female workers is lower than that of male workers, the onus is on the employer to prove that the factors used are justified (at [16]).

[10.55] Concept of "Sex" Discrimination

Several cases have examined the concept of "sex" discrimination. The Court has held that discrimination on the ground of gender reassignment constitutes discrimination on the basis of sex. See *P v S* (C-13/94) [1996] ECR I-2143 at [20]–[21]; [1996] 2 CMLR 247; *Richards v Secretary of State for Work and Pensions* (C-423/04) [2006] ECR I-3585 at [24]; [2006] 2 CMLR 49 (p 1242).

By contrast, the Court held that the prohibition of sex discrimination in relation to pay contained in Art 119 EC (now Art 157 TFEU) did not prohibit discrimination on the basis of sexual orientation. See *Grant v Southwest Trains Ltd* (C-249/96) [1998] ECR I-621 at [47]; [1998] 1 CMLR 993; Catherine Barnard, "Some are More Equal than Others: The Decision of the Court of Justice in *Grant v Southwest Trains*" (1998) 1 *Cambridge Yearbook of European Legal Studies* 147. Since that decision, the TFEU has been amended to authorise the EU to take action against discrimination on the ground of sexual orientation (Arts 10, 19(1) TFEU). However, Art 157 TFEU itself has not been amended.

[10.60] Equal Opportunities Directive

The Equal Opportunities Directive 2006/54 applies in the following contexts: access to employment, working conditions and occupational social security schemes (Art 1). Sexual harassment and other harassment on the basis of gender constitute sex discrimination (Art 2(2)(a)). Sexual harassment is defined as "any form of unwanted verbal, non-verbal or physical conduct of a sexual nature… with the purpose or effect of violating the dignity of a person, in particular when creating an intimidating, hostile, degrading, humiliating or offensive environment" (Art 2(1)(d)).

Direct discrimination is defined as "where one person is treated less favourably on grounds of sex than another is, has been or would be treated in a comparable situation" (Art 2(1)(a)). Indirect discrimination is defined as "where an apparently neutral provision, criterion or practice would put persons of one sex at a particular disadvantage compared with persons of the other sex, unless that provision, criterion or practice is objectively justified by a legitimate aim, and the means of achieving that aim are appropriate and necessary" (Art 2(1)(b)).

There may be no direct or indirect sex discrimination in relation to access to (among others) employment, vocational training, and employment and working conditions (including dismissals and pay) (Art 14(1)). This prohibition applies to both the public and private sectors. There must be no discrimination in occupational social security schemes (Art 5).

If a complainant establishes facts from which discrimination may be presumed, the respondent must prove that there was no prohibited discrimination (Art 19(1)). This burden of proof does not apply in criminal cases (Art 19(5)). Member States must adopt measures to prevent the victimisation of complainants (Art 24).

The Directive provides that "Member States shall ensure that ... judicial procedures for the enforcement of obligations under this Directive are available to all persons who consider themselves wronged by failure to apply the principle of equal treatment to them" (Art 17(1)). Member States are required to provide for compensation or reparation for the loss or damage caused by sex discrimination (Art 18).

[10.65] Genuine and Determining Occupational Requirements

The Equal Opportunities Directive permits an exception to the requirement that men and women be treated equally with regard to access to employment or vocational training. It states that the "Member States may provide ... that a difference of treatment which is based on a characteristic related to sex shall not constitute discrimination where, by reason of the nature of the particular occupational activities concerned or of the context in which they are carried out, such a characteristic constitutes a genuine and determining occupational requirement, provided that its objective is legitimate and the requirement is proportionate" (Art 14(2)).

The cases relating to the predecessor of this provision provide examples of the operation of such an exception. For example, the Court accepted sex as a determining factor in the case of the occupation of midwife. See *Commission v United Kingdom* (165/82) [1983] ECR 3431 at [20]; [1984] 1 CMLR 44. The Court also held that prison warders could be recruited on the basis of sex. See *Commission v France* (318/86) [1988] ECR 3559 at [12], [18]; [1989] 3 CMLR 663. The ECJ upheld the exclusion of women from the British Royal Marines. See *Sirdar v Secretary of State for Defence* (C-273/97) [1999] ECR I-7403 at [31]; [1999] 3 CMLR 559.

[10.70] Discrimination in the Supply of Goods and Services

The EU has also adopted legislation setting out a framework for national laws prohibiting sex discrimination in relation to the supply of goods and services. See Council Directive 2004/113 implementing the principle of equal treatment between men and women in the access to and supply of goods and services (OJ L 373, 21.12.2004, p 37). The Directive applies to all persons who supply goods and services to the public (Art 3(1)). It does not limit an individual's right to choose a contractual partner on any basis other than sex (Art 3(2)). Differential treatment is permissible where it is justified by a legitimate aim and achieved by appropriate and necessary means (Art 4(5)). See generally Christopher Krois, "Directive 2004/113/EC on Sexual Equality in Access to Goods and Services: Progress or Impasse in European Sex Discrimination Law?" (2006) 12 *Columbia Journal of European Law* 323.

[10.75] Discrimination Against Pregnant Workers

Under the former Equal Treatment Directive (Council Directive 76/207) the Court held that dismissal on the basis of pregnancy constituted direct discrimination on the basis of sex. See *Habermann-Beltermann v Arbeiterwohlfahrt Bezirksverband* (C-421/92) [1994] ECR I-1657 at [15]; [1994] 2 CMLR 681; *Webb v EMO Air Cargo (UK) Ltd* (C-32/93) [1994] ECR I-3567 at [19]; [1994] 2 CMLR 729; *Tele Danmark A/S v Handels-og Kontorfunktionoerernes Forbund I Danmark (HK)* (C-109/00) [2001] ECR I-6993 at [25]; [2002] 1 CMLR 5 (p 105). The Equal Opportunities Directive now provides that any less favourable treatment of a woman related to pregnancy or maternity leave constitutes sex discrimination (Art 2(2)(c)).

The Pregnant Workers Directive provides that Member States must prohibit the dismissal of workers "from the beginning of their pregnancy to the end of the maternity leave". See Art 10(1)), Council Directive 92/85 of 19 October 1992 concerning the implementation of measures to encourage improvements in the safety and health of pregnant workers, workers who have recently given birth and women who are breastfeeding (OJ L 348, 28.11.1992, p 1) (hereafter "Pregnant Workers Directive").

In *Mayr v Bäckerei und Konditorei Gerhard Flöckner OHG* (C-506/06) [2008] ECR I-1017; [2008] 2 CMLR 27 (p 759) an employee was dismissed because she was undergoing IVF treatment. On the date of dismissal the ova had been fertilized but had not been implanted in her womb (at [20], [29]). The Court held that this protection against dismissal operated only from the time the pregnancy commenced (at [37]). This protection would only begin when the fertilized ova were transferred into the womb since there could be many years between fertilization and transfer into the uterus (at [42]). However, the Court also held that dismissal of an employee because they were undergoing IVF treatment constituted direct discrimination on the ground of sex and was unlawful on that basis (at [50], [52]).

In *Dekker v Stichting Vormingscentrum voor Jonge Volwassenen Plus* (C-177/88) [1990] ECR I-3941 Mrs Dekker had applied for a job with a Dutch training centre. Her application was rejected by the management on the ground that she was 3 months pregnant. Mrs Dekker claimed that she had been denied equal access to a job because of her sex. The employer argued that it could not afford to hire Mrs Dekker because under applicable Dutch law it would be obliged to pay sickness benefits to her at a later stage and that its insurer would not reimburse that amount because she was already pregnant when she applied (at [3]).

The Court held that the financial consequences to the employer were no defence to a breach of the former Equal Treatment Directive (at [12]). Lack of any intention to discriminate was irrelevant under the Directive (at [22], [24]). The Court's decision was based on the rationale that acceptance of the employer's argument would have undermined the general impact and effectiveness of the Directive.

[10.80] Maternity Leave

The Equal Opportunities Directive provides that it "shall be without prejudice to provisions concerning the protection of women, particularly as regards pregnancy and maternity" (Art 28(1))). The predecessor of this article in the former Directive was interpreted as permitting the granting of maternity leave to a mother where paternity leave was denied to a father. See *Hofmann v Barmer Ersatzkasse* (184/83) [1984] ECR 3047 at [26]; [1986] 1 CMLR 242. The Equal Opportunities Directive allows Member States to provide for paternity leave (Art 16).

In *Gillespie v Northern Health and Social Services Board* (C-342/93) [1996] ECR I-475; [1996] 2 CMLR 969 the Court held that Art 119 EC (Art 157 TFEU) did not require that women receive full pay during maternity leave (at [20]). The Court stated that employees on maternity leave were "in a special position which requires them to be afforded special protection, but which is not comparable either with that of a man or . . . a woman actually at work" (at [17]). However, the level of pay during maternity leave must not be so low that the purpose of protecting women before and after birth was undermined (at [20]). See similarly, *North Western Health Board v McKenna* (C-191/03) [2005] ECR I-7631 at [50]; [2006] 1 CMLR 6 (p 121). The Pregnant Workers Directive provides that pay during maternity leave must not be lower than sick pay (Art 11(2)–(3)).

In *Abdoulaye v Regie nationale des usines Renault SA* (C-218/98) [1999] ECR I-5723 at [14]; [2001] 2 CMLR 372 a lump sum payment was made to employees going on maternity leave. The Court pointed out that workers going on maternity leave faced occupational disadvantages. For example, their period of service was reduced by the leave, they were not eligible for performance based pay increases, they miss out on training and rapid technological changes in some fields may make their reintegration into the workplace more difficult (at [19]). The Court thus held that the lump sum payment did not violate Art 119 (Art 157 TFEU) since it offset these disadvantages (at [20]).

In *Caisse Nationale d'Assurance Vieillesse des Travailleurs Salaries (Cnavts) v Thibault* (C-136/95) [1998] ECR I-2011; [1998] 2 CMLR 516 an employer declined to undertake a performance review for Mrs Thibault because she did not fulfill the condition of 6 months presence at work (at [13]). If she had not taken maternity leave she would have fulfilled that condition (at [14]). The failure to hold a performance review denied her a possibility for promotion (at [17]).

The Court held that the right to a performance review and thus to qualify for promotion was part of the conditions of work (at [27]). It would discriminatory for a female employee to be denied a performance review and the prospect of promotion because she had taken maternity leave and thus did not meet the condition of 6 months presence at work (at [29]). She had been discriminated against on the ground of pregnancy (at [32]).

Under the Equal Opportunities Directive a woman who has been on maternity leave is entitled to "return to her job or to an equivalent post on terms and conditions which are no less favourable to her and to benefit from any improvement in working conditions to which she would have been entitled during her absence" (Art 15).

[10.85] Prohibited Forms of Affirmative Action

The leading cases concerning affirmative action were decided under the now repealed Equal Treatment Directive. These decisions offer several examples of affirmative action that went beyond the bounds permitted under EU law. In *Kalanke v Freie Handestadt Bremen* (C-450/93) [1995] ECR I-3051; [1996] 1 CMLR 175 a Bremen law provided that where women comprised less than 50 percent of the employees in an individual pay bracket within the relevant personnel group within a department, priority was to be given to a female candidate over a male candidate where the candidates had the "same qualifications" (at [3]). That women comprised less than 50 percent of employees in any such pay bracket was deemed to be "under-representation", even if women did not comprise 50 percent of the relevant labour force.

The Court held that the Bremen law was inconsistent with the former Equal Treatment Directive. Art 2(1) of the Directive laid down an unqualified prohibition of direct and indirect sex discrimination. Art 2(4) allowed Member States to adopt "measures to promote equal opportunity for men and women, in particular by removing existing inequalities which affect women's opportunities".

The Court held that a law which gave automatic preference to women over equally qualified men in employment sectors in which women were "under-represented" constituted a discrimination based on sex (at [16]). The law would fall foul of the general prohibition of sex discrimination unless it could be justified as falling within the exception for measures promoting equal opportunity.

The ECJ held that the law was not saved by the exception for equal opportunity measures. The Court stated that "such a system substitutes for equality of opportunity as envisaged in [the Directive] the result which is only to be arrived at by providing such equality of opportunity" (at [23]). The Court thus drew a distinction between equality of opportunity, which was required by the Directive, and equality of result, which was compatible with the Directive only when it was the outcome of fair competition.

The Court ruled that laws "which guarantee women absolute and unconditional priority for appointment or promotion go beyond promoting equal opportunities" and thus violate the Directive as they could not be saved by Art 2(4) (at [22]). The Court did not explain what constituted an "absolute and unconditional priority", nor did it indicate why the Bremen law was "absolute and unconditional".

The Court made some general statements about what affirmative action measures were permitted by the derogation in Art 2(4). The Court stated that the exception would "allow measures which, although discriminatory in appearance, are in fact intended to eliminate or reduce actual instances of inequality which may exist in the reality of social life" (at [18]). It thus "permits national measures relating to access to employment, including promotion, which give a specific advantage to women with a view to improving their ability to compete on the labour market and to pursue a career on an equal footing with men" (at [19]).

In *Abrahamsson v Fogelqvist* (C-407/98) [2000] ECR I-5539 the Court examined a regulation which provided that a member of an under-represented sex who was qualified for the position could be selected in preference to the candidate who would otherwise have been selected, provided that the difference in their qualifications was not so significant that giving preference would be contrary to the principle of objectivity in the appointment process (at [9]).

The Court pointed out that the regulation allowed the appointment of a candidate who did not possess equal qualifications (at [45]). The preference thus did not operate as a tie-breaker. Under the Swedish regulation the assessment of qualifications was not based upon "clear and unambiguous criteria" that would address career disadvantages of members of the under-represented sex (at [50]). The regulation created an automatic preference (at [51]). The appointment was ultimately made on the basis of the sex of the applicant, even if they possessed lesser qualifications than another applicant. The appointment process did not involve an objective assessment of the particular candidates. The regulation was not justified by Art 2(4) of the Directive (at [53]).

[10.90] Permissible Forms of Affirmative Action

In *Marschall v Land Nordrhein Westfalen* (C-409/95) [1997] ECR I-6363; [1998] 1 CMLR 547 a German civil service law provided that where there were less women than men in higher posts, women who were of equal suitability and competence were to be given priority, unless there were reasons specific to a particular male applicant that tilted the balance in favour of his appointment (at [3]). The law examined in *Kalanke* did not contain such a "savings clause" allowing the appointment of a male candidate where there were specific reasons tilting the balance in his favour (at [24]).

The Court noted that female candidates were often overlooked for promotion based on cultural stereotypes (at [29]). The fact that a female candidate and a male candidate were equally qualified thus did not mean that they had equal chances of promotion (at [30]). A savings clause would mean that the preference for women was justified under Art 2(4) of the Equal Treatment Directive if all candidates were objectively assessed and individual characteristics taken into account so that the preference could be overcome if reasons specific to a male applicant tilted the balance in his favour (at [33]).

In *Proceedings for a Review of Legality by Badeck* (C-158/97) [2000] ECR I-1875; [2001] 2 CMLR 6 (p 79) another German civil service law gave priority to equally qualified female candidates in civil service areas where women were under-represented. The priority would operate where necessary for meeting binding affirmative action targets, provided that "no reasons of greater legal weight are opposed" (at [26], [33]). There were five reasons of greater legal weight overcoming the priority given to women candidates: former civil servants who left for family work, those who worked part time for family reasons and who now wished to return to full time work, former soldiers, disabled persons and the long term unemployed (at [35]). The Court held that the priority was not absolute and unconditional (at [36]).

The law also provided that binding affirmative action targets for temporary academic appointments must set a minimum representation for women of at least the percentage of graduates in each discipline who were female. The Court held that the law did not set an "absolute ceiling" (at [42]). This provision did not violate the Equal Treatment Directive (at [44]).

The German law also provided that in public service occupations in which women were under-represented and in which the state did not have a training monopoly, half of the training positions must be allocated to women (at (45]). The Court pointed out that the law did not reserve employment positions, but only training places (at [52]). This provision also did not infringe the Directive (at [55]).

The law also provided that in sectors where women were under-represented, where male and female candidates are equally qualified, female candidates must be interviewed (at [56]). Only qualified candidates need be interviewed (at [61]). The Court held that this measure promoted equal opportunity and was justified under Art 2(4) of the Directive (at [62]).

[10.95] Affirmative Action Under the Current Directive

The leading cases regarding affirmative action were decided under the now repealed Equal Treatment Directive. The Equal Opportunities Directive now provides that the Member States may adopt measures within the meaning of the Treaty "with a view to ensuring full equality in practice between men and women in working life" (Art 3). Art 157(4) TFEU provides: "With a view to ensuring full equality in practice between men and women in working life, the principle of equal treatment shall not prevent any Member

State from maintaining or adopting measures providing for specific advantages in order to make it easier for the underrepresented sex to pursue a vocational activity or to prevent or compensate for disadvantages in professional careers."

The EU Charter of Fundamental Rights recognises the permissibility of affirmative action measures: "The principle of equality shall not prevent the maintenance or adoption of measures providing for specific advantages in favour of the under-represented sex". See Art 23, Charter of Fundamental Rights, Nice, 7 December 2000, as amended at Strasbourg, 12 December 2007, OJ C 303, 14.12.2007, p 1.

There is an extensive literature regarding affirmative action under EU law. See generally, Gabriël A Moens, "Equal Opportunities Not Equal Results: 'Equal Opportunity' in European Law" (1997) 23 *Journal of Legislation* 43; Sandra Fredman, "After *Kalanke* and *Marschall*: Affirming Affirmative Action" (1998) 1 *Cambridge Yearbook of European Legal Studies* 199; Dagmar Schiek, "Sex Equality Law After *Kalanke* and *Marschall*" (1998) 4 *European Law Journal* 148; Albertine Veldman, "The Lawfulness of Women's Priority Rules in the EC Labour Market: Case C-409/95 *Hellmut Marschall v Land Nordrhein-Westfalen*" (1998) 5 *Maastricht Journal of European and Comparative Law* 403; Manfred Zuleeg, "Gender Equality and Affirmative Action Under the Law of the European Union" (1999) 5 *Columbia Journal of European Law* 319; Alina Tryfonidou, *Reverse Discrimination in EC Law* (The Hague: Kluwer Law International, 2009).

[10.100] Other Forms of Discrimination

EU anti-discrimination legislation is not restricted to combating sex discrimination. The TFEU authorises the EU to "take appropriate action to combat discrimination based on sex, racial or ethnic origin, religion or belief, disability, age or sexual orientation" (Art 19(1) TFEU).

A Directive has expanded the bases of discrimination regulated by EU law beyond sex discrimination. See Council Directive 2000/78 of 27 November 2000 establishing a general framework for equal treatment in employment and occupation (OJ L 303, 2.12.2000, p 16) (hereafter the "present Equal Treatment Directive"). In *Mangold v Helm* (C-144/04) [2005] ECR I-9981; [2006] 1 CMLR 43 (p 1132) the ECJ observed that this Directive "does not itself lay down the principle of equal treatment in the field of employment and occupation" (at [74]). It sets out a framework for national anti-discrimination laws. The principle that discrimination must be prohibited derives from international human rights law and the constitutional traditions of the Member States (at [74]).

This Directive applies to national anti-discrimination laws concerning discrimination on several grounds: religion, disability, age and sexual orientation (Art 1). It does not apply to racial and sexual discrimination, which are regulated by other Directives. It defines discrimination as including both direct and indirect discrimination (Art 2(1)). Harassment also constitutes discrimination (Art 2(3)).

The Directive applies to actions by all persons in relation to (among others) access to employment, vocational training and employment conditions (Art 3(1)). There is an exception permitting affirmative action (Art 7(1)). Member States may provide that differential treatment based upon a prohibited ground will not infringe the anti-discrimination principle if the prohibited ground is a genuine and determining occupational requirement (Art 4(1)). Religious belief may constitute a "genuine, legitimate and justified" occupational requirement for employment in churches and religious organisations (Art 4(2)).

If a complainant establishes facts from which discrimination may be presumed, the respondent must prove that there was no prohibited discrimination (Art 10(1)). This burden of proof does not apply in criminal cases (Art 10(3)). Member States must adopt measures to prevent the victimisation of complainants (Art 11).

[10.105] Racial Discrimination

The EU has adopted a specific Directive concerning racial discrimination. See Council Directive 2000/43 of 29 June 2000 implementing the principle of equal treatment between persons irrespective of racial or ethnic origin (OJ L 180, 19.7.2000, p 22) (hereafter "Racial Discrimination Directive"). The Directive applies to both direct and indirect discrimination (Art 2(1)). Harassment constitutes discrimination (Art 2(3)). The Directive applies to actions by all persons in relation to access to employment and vocational training, employment conditions including dismissal and pay, social security, and access to goods and services (Art 3(1)).

Discrimination on the ground of nationality is not regulated by the Directive (Art 3(2)). There is an exception for genuine and determining occupational requirements (Art 4). Member States may adopt affirmative action "measures to prevent or compensate for disadvantages linked to racial or ethnic origin" (Art 5). If facts are proved from which discrimination may be presumed the burden of proof falls to the respondent (Art 8(1)). Member States must adopt measures to prevent victimisation of complainants (Art 9). They must also establish a body for the promotion of equal treatment on the ground of race, such as an equal opportunity commission (Art 13(1)).

In *Centrum voor gelijkheid van kansen en voor racismbestrijding v Firma Feryn NV* (C-54/07) [2008] ECR I-5187; [2008] 3 CMLR 22 (p 695) an employer had made public statements indicating that it would not employ "immigrants" (at [15]–[16]). No complainant alleged that they had been denied employment (at [21]). The Court held that the absence of an identifiable complainant did not prevent the employer's selection policy from constituting direct discrimination on the ground of race (at [23]). Such public statements would be likely to deter would be applicants and constituted direct discrimination under the Racial Discrimination Directive (at [25]). See generally, Mark Bell, *Racism and Equality in the European Union* (Oxford: Oxford University Press, 2009); Erica Howard, *The EU Race Directive: Developing the Protection Against Racial Discrimination Within the EU* (London: Taylor and Francis, 2009); Kristin Henrard, "The First Substantive ECJ Judgment on the Racial Equality Directive: A Strong Message in a Conceptually Flawed and Responsively Weak Bottle", *Jean Monnet Working Paper* No 09/09, http://www.jeanmonnetprogram.org.

[10.110] Age Discrimination

The present Equal Treatment Directive allows Member States to set special conditions for access to employment on the basis of age to promote aims such as "legitimate employment policy, labour market and vocational training objectives". The means adopted must be appropriate and necessary. Permissible measures may include special conditions for access to employment for young and older workers for the promotion of their vocational integration. Member States may adopt minimum ages for employment and a maximum age for recruitment (Art 6(1)). Member States may exempt the armed forces from the prohibition of discrimination on the ground of age (Art 3(4)).

In *Mangold v Helm* (C-144/04) [2005] ECR I-9981; [2006] 1 CMLR 43 (p 1132) German law allowed employers to conclude a succession of fixed term contracts with employees over the age of 52 (at [57]). The purpose of the German law was to promote the vocational integration of older workers (at [59]). The Court pointed out that the measures adopted to achieve this aim must be "appropriate and necessary" (at [62]). The German legislation applied to all workers over the age of 52, irrespective of whether they were unemployed before the contract and the length of any period of unemployment. The legislation thus allowed a large number of workers to be excluded from the advantages of stable employment, based only on their age (at [64]). It had not been demonstrated that adopting this age criterion was objectively necessary for achieving the aim. The legislation went beyond what was appropriate and necessary to achieve the aim, and it was not justified by Art 6(1) of the Directive (at [65]).

In *Palacios de la Villa v Cortefiel Servicios SA* (C-411/05) [2007] ECR I-8531; [2008] 1 CMLR 16 (p 385) the Court considered a Spanish law that allowed employers to provide for compulsory retirement at the age of 65. The aim of the law was to promote "better access to employment, by means of a better distribution of work between the generations" (at [53]). The Court indicated that this aim was legitimate since it fell within Art 6(1) of the Directive (at [64]). Under that provision the measures adopted must be "appropriate and necessary" (at [66]). The Member States have a broad discretion in this area (at [68]). The law was appropriate and necessary for achieving its aim (at [72]). Workers were entitled to a pension upon reaching the retirement age and the level of that pension was reasonable (at [73]).

See generally, Clare McGlynn, "EC Legislation Prohibiting Age Discrimination—'Towards a Europe for All Ages'?" (2000) 3 *Cambridge Yearbook of European Legal Studies* 279; Marlene Schmidt, "The Principle of Non-discrimination in Respect of Age: Dimensions of the ECJ's *Mangold* Judgment" (May 2005) 7, 5 *German Law Journal* 505, http://www.germanlawjournal.com.

[10.115] Disability Discrimination

The present Equal Treatment Directive does not define "disability". In *Chacón Navas v Eurest Colectividades SA* (C-13/05) [2006] ECR I-6467; [2006] 3 CMLR 40 (p 1123) the Court defined "disability" as a "limitation which results in particular from physical, mental or psychological impairments and which hinders the participation of the person in professional life" (at [43]). Sickness did not fall within the concept of disability (at [44], [47]). A condition must be likely to persist for a "long time" to constitute a disability (at [45]).

In *Coleman v Attridge Law* (C-303/06) [2008] ECR I-5603; [2008] 3 CMLR 27 (p 777) the Court held that the protection of equal treatment under the Directive was not restricted to disabled persons alone, but also extended to their carers where they were subject to direct discrimination on the basis of the disabled person's disability (at [38], [56]).

Employers must make reasonable accommodation for disabled workers. However, employers need not adopt measures that would impose a disproportionate burden upon them (Art 5). Member States may exempt the armed forces from the anti-discrimination principle in relation to disability (Art 3(4)).

[10.120] Sexual Orientation Discrimination

In *Maruko v Versorgungsanstalt der deutschen Bühnen* (C-267/06) [2008] ECR I-1757; [2008] 2 CMLR 32 (p 914) surviving registered life partners of the same sex were not entitled to receive benefits under a compulsory pension scheme, while surviving spouses were entitled to such benefits (at [62]). The Court held that Arts 1 and 2 of the Directive precluded the legislation at issue if national law placed a life partner in a position comparable to that of a spouse (at [73]). The national court had to determine the comparability of the two legal relationships (at [72]).

[10.125] Other Social Provisions: Arts 151 and 153 TFEU

Art 151 TFEU sets out a broad aim in general terms. It states that Member States "shall have as their objectives the promotion of employment, improved living and working conditions, so as to make possible their harmonisation while the improvement is being maintained, proper social protection, dialogue between management and labour, the development of human resources with a view to lasting high employment and the combating of exclusion". Art 153(1) TFEU provides that the EU may "support and complement" the activities of the Member States in the following areas: occupational health and safety, social security, termination of employment, consultation of employees, co-determination, and "equality between men and women with regard to labour market opportunities and treatment at work". In these areas the EU may adopt Directives setting out "minimum requirements for gradual implementation" (Art 153(2)(b) TFEU).

The EU has regulated the protection of workers' rights where a business undertaking is transferred. See Council Directive 2001/23 of 12 March 2001 on the approximation of the laws of the Member States relating to the safeguarding of employees' rights in the event of transfers of undertakings, businesses or parts of undertakings or businesses (OJ L 82, 22.3.2001, p 16). The Directive applies to the transfer of an undertaking to another employer as a result of a legal transfer or merger (Art 1(1)(a)).

The Directive stipulates that the "transferor's rights and obligations arising from a contract of employment or from an employment relationship existing on the date of a transfer shall, by reason of such transfer, be transferred to the transferee" (Art 3(1)). The transfer is not in itself a sufficient justification for dismissal of employees (Art 4 (1)). Both the transferor and the transferee are required to inform employees affected by a transfer of the reasons for the transfer, the legal, economic and social implications of the transfer for the employees, and measures envisaged in relation to the employees (Art 7(1)).

[10.130] Charter of Fundamental Rights

The Charter of Fundamental Rights contains numerous provisions relating to the workplace. See Charter of Fundamental Rights, Nice, 7 December 2000, as amended at Strasbourg, 12 December 2007, OJ C 303, 14.12.2007, p 1. Since the Treaty of Lisbon the Charter has become legally binding upon the EU itself and the Member States when they implement EU law (Art 6(1) TEU; Art 51(1) Charter). The Charter possesses the "same legal value as the Treaties" (Art 6(1) TEU).

Everyone has the right to form and join trade unions (Art 12(1)). Workers, employers, unions and employee organisations have the right to bargain collectively and to take collective action such as a strike (Art 28).

Other provisions guarantee limitation of working hours, paid annual leave (Art 31(2)) and protection against unjust dismissal (Art 30).

Everyone has the right to freedom of occupation (Art 15) and free employment placement (Art 29). Employees have the right to be informed and consulted within the undertaking as provided for by EU and national law (Art 27). Child labour is prohibited (Art 32).

[10.135] Vocational Training

Art 166(1) TFEU provides that the EU shall adopt a policy regarding vocational training: "[t]he Union shall implement a vocational training policy which shall support and supplement the action of the Member States, while fully respecting the responsibility of the Member States for the content and organisation of vocational training." The Charter of Fundamental Rights provides that everyone has the right to have access to vocational training (Art 14(1)).

The ECJ has handed down a number of decisions dealing with access to vocational training. In *Gravier v City of Liège* (293/83) [1985] ECR 593; [1985] 3 CMLR 1 Ms Gravier, a French national, enrolled in a course of instruction at a Belgian academy. She sought an injunction to prevent the school from demanding payment of an enrolment fee (minerval) which was not imposed upon Belgian students (at [2]). She based her claim on Art 7 EC which stipulated that "[w]ithin the scope of application of this Treaty . . . any discrimination on grounds of nationality shall be prohibited" (now in Art 18 TFEU).

The Court held that since the costs of higher education were "not borne by students of Belgian nationality, whereas foreign students must bear part of that cost", the inequality of treatment on the basis of nationality had to be considered to be a form of discrimination prohibited by Art 7 EC (Art 18 TFEU) if it occurred in an area to which the Treaty applied (at [14]–[15]). The Court held that vocational training was covered by EU law (at [19]). In particular, access to vocational training in a Member State in which a student wants to practice was "likely to promote free movement of persons throughout the Community" (at [24]). The imposition of the minerval thus infringed Art 7 EC (Art 18 TFEU). See similarly, *Re University Fees: Commission v Belgium* (C-47/93) [1994] ECR I-1593 at [19]; [1994] 3 CMLR 723.

[10.140] Data Protection: Personal Information

The Charter of Fundamental Rights includes a right to the protection of personal data (Art 8). The EU has adopted several Directives that create obligations relating to data protection. The most important is Directive

95/46 of the European Parliament and of the Council of 24 October 1995 on the protection of individuals with regard to the processing of personal data and on the free movement of such data (OJ L 281, 23.11.1995, p 31). The Directive's harmonization of national laws regarding personal data protection is "generally complete". See *Criminal Proceedings Against Lindqvist* (C-101/01) [2003] ECR I-12971 at [96]; [2004] 1 CMLR 20 (p 673); *Huber v Germany* (C-524/06) [2008] ECR I-9705 at [51]; [2009] 1 CMLR 49 (p 1360).

"Personal data" is defined as "any information relating to an identified or identifiable person" (Art 3(1)). "Processing of personal data" is defined as "any operation ... which is performed upon personal data, whether or not by automatic means" such as collection, recording, storage, retrieval, disclosure, erasure or destruction (Art 3(1)). Processing of personal data includes placing the information on an Internet page. See *Criminal Proceedings Against Lindqvist* (C-101/01) [2003] ECR I-12971 at [25]–[26]; [2004] 1 CMLR 20 (p 673). The Directive applies to "the processing of personal data wholly or partly by automatic means, and to the processing otherwise than by automatic means of personal data which form part of a filing system" (Art 3(1)).

Certain types of personal data processing are excluded from the operation of the Directive. These include processing concerning public security, defence, State security and the criminal law (Art 3(2)). The Court held that access to airline passenger name records by customs authorities for the purpose of combating terrorism fell within this exclusion. The granting of this access constituted processing operations relating to public security and the activities of the State concerning criminal law. See *Re Validity of Decisions 2004/496 and 2004/535: Parliament v Council* (C-317/04) [2006] ECR I-4721 at [54]–[56]; [2006] 3 CMLR 9 (p 251).

The Directive also does not apply to personal data processing by an individual "in the course of a purely personal or household activity" (Art 3(2)). Making information publicly available on the Internet is not part of a purely personal or household activity, which is an activity "carried out in the course of [the] private or family life of individuals". See *Criminal Proceedings against Lindqvist* (C-101/01) [2003] ECR I-12971 at [46]–[48]; [2004] 1 CMLR 20 (p 673).

Personal data must be collected for specified and legitimate purposes (Art 6(1)(b)). The data must be relevant and not excessive for the purposes for which it is collected (Art 6(1)(c)). The information must be accurate and up to date. Inaccurate or out of date information must be modified (Art 6(1)(d)). Data may be kept in a personally identifiable form only for as long as is necessary for the purposes for which it was collected (Art 6(1)(e)).

Personal data may be processed only if (a) the subject of the data has consented, or (b) the processing is necessary for the performance of a contract to which the subject has consented, or (c) the processing is legally required, or (d) the processing is necessary for the protection of the vital interests of the subject, or (e) the processing is necessary for carrying out a task undertaken in the public interest or in the exercise of official authority, or (f) the processing is "necessary for the purposes of the legitimate interests pursued by the controller" of the data processing (Art 7).

In *Huber v Germany* (C-524/06) [2009] 1 CMLR 49 (p 1360) the Court held that access to data kept by national authorities for determining the right of residence of nationals of other Member States may only be granted to officials that have authority in that area (at [61]). The maintenance of a centralized register for these purposes may be "necessary" under Art 7(e) (at [62]). The keeping of data regarding population movements for statistical purposes will only be "necessary" where the data is anonymous (at [63]–[65]).

The Member States must prohibit processing of personal data revealing racial or ethnic origin, political opinions, religious or philosophical beliefs, and membership of trade unions. They shall also prohibit the processing of data regarding health or sex life (Art 8(1)). "Health" includes both physical and mental health. See *Criminal Proceedings against Lindqvist* (C-101/01) [2003] ECR I-12971 at [50]; [2004] 1 CMLR 20 (p 673). However, there are exceptions to these prohibitions. For example, these types of personal data may be processed with the express consent of the individuals concerned (Art 8(2)(a)).

The subject of personal data must be provided with certain information such as the controller of the data processing and the purposes of the data processing (Arts 10–11). Individuals have the right to know whether data concerning them is being processed and who has access to the data (Art 12(a)). This right relates to both present and past recipients of the data. See *College van burgemeester en wethouders van Rotterdam v Rijkeboer* (C-553/07) [2009] 3 CMLR 28 (p 1041) at [53]–[54], [70].

Individuals have the right to the correction of incomplete or inaccurate data (Art 12(b)). The Member States may restrict many of the obligations and rights under the Directive on grounds such as national security, defence, public security, and the investigation and prosecution of crime (Art 13(1)). The ECJ has held that several provisions of the Directive have direct effect (Arts 6(1)(c), 7(c), 7(e)). See *Rechnungshof v Österreichischer Rundfunk* (C-465/00) [2003] ECR I-4989 at [99]–[101]; [2003] 3 CMLR 10 (p 265).

[10.145] Transfer of Personal Data to Non-member States

Transfer of personal data to non-member States may only occur if the State ensures an "adequate level of protection" for personal data (Art 25(1)). The Commission may decide that a non-member State ensures an adequate level of protection in the light of its national law or treaty obligations (Art 25(6)). The Commission has decided that the national data protection regimes of Argentina, Canada and Switzerland provide adequate protection. See Commission Decision 2000/518 of 26 July 2000 on the adequate protection of personal data provided in Switzerland (OJ L 215, 25.8.2000, p 1); Commission Decision 2002/2 of 20 December 2001 on the adequate protection of personal data provided by the Canadian Personal Information Protection and Electronic Documents Act (OJ L 2, 4.1.2002, p 13); Commission Decision 2003/490 of 30 June 2003 on the adequate protection of personal data in Argentina (OJ L 168, 5.7.2003, p 19).

The Commission determined that the Safe Harbor Privacy Principles issued by the US Department of Commerce provides adequate protection for the purposes of the Directive. See Art 1, Commission Decision 2000/520 of 26 July 2000 on the adequacy of the protection provided by the safe harbour privacy principles and related frequently asked questions issued by the US Department of Commerce (OJ L 215, 25.8.2000, p 7). Extensive materials relating to the Principles are available at http://www.export.gov/safeharbor/eu/index.asp.

The effect of the Principles is to "grant US companies who are subject to the jurisdiction of the FTC or the Department of Transportation a presumption of 'adequacy' of protecting personal data for purposes of the Directive, thereby allowing data transfers from the EU to continue to that company." See *The EU Data Protection Directive: Implications for the US Privacy Debate. Hearing before the Subcommittee on Commerce, Trade and Consumer Protection of the Committee on Energy and Commerce, House of Representatives* 107th Cong (2001), 57.

See generally Barbara Crutchfield George, Patricia Lynch and Susan J Marsnik, "US Multinational Employers: Navigating Through the 'Safe Harbor' Principles to Comply with the EU Data Privacy Directive" (2001) 38 *American Business Law Journal* 735; Alexander Zinser, "The Safe Harbor Solution: Is it an Effective Mechanism for International Data Transfers Between the United States and the European Union?" (2004) 1 *Oklahoma Journal of Law and Technology* 11, available at http://www.okjolt.org; Daniel R Leathers, "Giving Bite to the EU-US Data Privacy Safe Harbor: Model Solutions for Effective Enforcement" (2009) 41 *Case Western Reserve Journal of International Law* 193.

Transfer of air passenger name data between EU and the United States is regulated by a bilateral treaty. See *Agreement between the European Union and the United States on the Processing and Transfer of Passenger Name Record (PNR) Data by Air Carriers to the United States Department of Homeland Security*, Brussels, 23 July 2007-Washington, 26 July 2007, OJ L 204, 4.8.2007, p 18.

[10.150] Data Protection: Electronic Communications

Another Directive "particularizes and complements" Directive 95/46 in the electronic communications context. See Art 1(2), Directive 2002/58 of the

European Parliament and of the Council of 12 July 2002 concerning the processing of personal data and the protection of privacy in the electronic communications sector (OJ L 201, 31.7.2002, p 37).

The tension between protection of copyright on the Internet and the confidentiality of Internet users was raised in *Productores de Música de España (Promusicae) v Telefónica de España SAU* (C-275/06) [2008] ECR I-271; [2008] 2 CMLR 17 (p 465). An association of music producers and publishers sought a judicial order that an Internet service provider disclose the identities of users of a file sharing programme (at [30]). The association sought this information so that it would be able to sue these Internet users for infringement of copyright (at [31]).

The Court pointed out that Directive 2002/58 required Internet service providers to ensure the confidentiality of Internet users (at [47]). However, confidentiality could be limited for the protection of the rights and freedoms of others, which included protection of the right to property and the right to judicial protection (at [53]). Directive 2002/58 thus permitted Member States to limit confidentiality in order to safeguard property rights through civil proceedings (at [54]). However, the Directive does not obligate Member States to require disclosure of personal data in those circumstances (at [55]).

The situation thus involved a potential conflict between the fundamental rights to property and judicial protection and the right to protection of personal data (the right to privacy) (at [62]–[63]). There was a need to reconcile the requirements of these rights (at [65]). The machinery for balancing these rights was provided by Directive 2002/58 itself (at [66]). When implementing the EU Directives concerning data protection and copyright enforcement the Member States must strike a "fair balance" between these fundamental rights (at [68]). See Christopher Kuner, "Data Protection and Rights Protection on the Internet: The *Promusicae* Judgment of the European Court of Justice" (2008) 30 *European Intellectual Property Review* 199.

The EU has also adopted a Directive that harmonises national provisions requiring the retention of certain data regarding usage of publicly available electronic communication services and communication networks. See Art 1(1), Directive 2006/24 of the European Parliament and of the Council of 15 March 2006 on the retention of data generated or processed in connection with the provision of publicly available electronic communications services or of public communications networks (OJ L 105, 13.4.2006, p 54).

The purpose of retaining data from these sources is the investigation of serious crime (Art 1(1)). The Directive applies to traffic and location data but not the content of communications (Arts 1(2), 5(2)). The data to be retained includes the source, destination, time and duration of telephone calls, and similar details relating to Internet and email usage (Art 5(1)). Data concerning unsuccessful call attempts is also to be retained (Art 3(2)). The data is to be retained for at least 6 months but no longer than 2 years from the date of the communication (Art 6).

[10.155] Consumer Protection

The TFEU provides that the EU must take consumer protection into account in determining and carrying out all of its activities (Art 12 TFEU). The Treaty also provides that the EU "shall contribute to protecting the health, safety and economic interests of consumers, as well as to promoting their right to information, education and to organise themselves in order to safeguard their interests" (Art 169(1) TFEU). To this end the EU has adopted a considerable body of consumer protection law. The Directives generally define a "consumer" as a natural person who makes the contract for purposes that do not relate to their trade, business or profession.

Some of what follows will be affected if a proposed Directive is adopted. In October 2008 the European Commission issued a proposal for a new Directive on Consumer Rights (COM(2008) 614 final). The proposal would consolidate four existing Directives: Sale of Consumer Goods (99/44), Unfair Contract Terms (93/13), Distance Selling (97/7) and Doorstep Selling (85/577). As at 28 February 2010 the proposal had not been approved by the European Parliament. See generally, Rohan Massey, "Sales for the Next Century: Europe's Draft Directive on Consumer Rights" (2009) 15 *Computer and Telecommunications Law Review* 23; Christian Twigg-Flesner and Daniel Metcalfe, "The Proposed Consumer Rights Directive – Less Haste, More Thought?" (2009) 5 *European Review of Contract Law* 368.

[10.160] Unfair Commercial Practices

An EU Directive prohibits unfair business-to-consumer commercial practices before, during and after a transaction concerning a product. See Art 3(1), Directive 2005/29 of the European Parliament and of the Council of 11 May 2005 concerning unfair business-to-consumer commercial practices in the internal market (OJ L 149, 11.6.2005, p 22). "Business-to-consumer commercial practices" are defined as a trader's acts or omissions that are directly connected to the promotion, sale or supply of a product to consumers (Art 2(d)).

Unfair commercial practices are prohibited (Art 5(1)). A practice is unfair if it is against the professional diligence required of traders and it materially distorts the economic behaviour of the average consumer in relation to the market (Art 5(2)). "Professional diligence" is defined as the "standard of special skill and care which a trader may reasonably be expected to exercise towards consumers, commensurate with honest market practice and/or the general principle of good faith in the trader's field of activity" (Art 2(h)). A commercial practice that is likely to distort the economic behaviour of only a class of consumers that is vulnerable because of mental or physical infirmity is to be considered from the standpoint of the average member of that class (Art 5(3)).

Misleading or aggressive commercial practices are unfair (Art 5(4)). A practice is misleading if it is untruthful or is likely to deceive the average consumer regarding a number of matters and is likely to cause the consumer to make a different purchasing decision. These matters include the main characteristics of the product, the trader's commitments and the price (Art 6(1)). A practice may also be misleading if it omits material information (Art 7(1)). A practice is aggressive if it involves harassment, coercion or undue influence that "is likely to significantly impair the average consumer's freedom of choice" regarding the product and is likely to cause the consumer to make a different purchasing decision (Art 8).

Annex I contains a list of commercial practices that are considered to be unfair in all circumstances (Art 5(5)). The misleading practices in this list include falsely claiming to be a signatory to a code of conduct, bait and switch techniques, falsely claiming that a product will only be available for a very short time, falsely claiming that a product will cure illness and falsely describing a product as "free" (Items 1, 6, 7, 17, 20). The aggressive practices in this list include giving the impression that a consumer will not be allowed to leave the premises until a contract is made, ignoring a consumer's request not to visit their home again and making persistent contact by telephone or other forms of electronic communication (Items 24, 25, 26).

See generally, Hugh Collins, "The Unfair Commercial Practices Directive" (2005) 1 *European Review of Contract Law* 417; Christian Handig, "The Unfair Commercial Practices Directive – A Milestone in the European Unfair Competition Law?" (2005) 16 *European Business Law Review* 1117; Geraint Howells et al., *European Fair Trading Law: The Unfair Commercial Practices Directive* (Aldershot, Hampshire: Ashgate, 2006); Giuseppe B Abbamonte, "The Unfair Commercial Practices Directive: An Example of the New European Consumer Protection Approach" (2006) 12 *Columbia Journal of European Law* 695; Julien Stuyck, Evelyne Terryn and Tom van Dyck, "Confidence Through Fairness? The New Directive on Unfair Business-to-Consumer Commercial Practices in the Internal Market" (2006) 43 *Common Market Law Review* 107; Stephen Weatherill and Ulf Bernitz (eds), *The Regulation of Unfair Commercial Practices Under EC Directive 2005/29: New Rules and New Techniques* (Oxford: Hart, 2007); Peter Shears, "Overviewing the EU Unfair Commercial Practices Directive: Concentric Circles" (2007) 18 *European Business Law Review* 781.

[10.165] Sale of Consumer Goods

An EU Directive approximates some aspects of the sale of consumer goods. See Art 1, Directive 1999/44 of the European Parliament and of the

Council of 25 May 1999 on certain aspects of the sale of consumer goods and associated guarantees (OJ L 171, 7.7.1999, p 12). The proposed Consumer Rights Directive (COM(2008) 614 final) would replace this Directive.

The seller must provide to the consumer goods that conform to the sale contract (Art 2(1)). Goods conform to the contract if they comply with the seller's description, have the same qualities as a sample, are fit for a purpose communicated to the seller, are fit for purposes for which such goods are ordinarily used, and have the quality and performance which is normal for such goods and which may be reasonably expected by the consumer (Art 2(2)). Goods are deemed to conform to the contract if at the time the contract was entered into the consumer was aware of the nonconformity (Art 2(3)).

The seller is liable to the consumer for a lack of conformity at the time of delivery (Art 3(1)). The seller must bring the goods into conformity "free of charge" by repair, replacement, reduction in the price or rescission of the contract (Art 3(2)). "Free of charge" means free of the "necessary costs incurred to bring the goods into conformity, particularly the cost of postage, labour and materials" (Art 3(4)).

The meaning of "free of charge" was considered in *Quelle AG v Bundesverband der Verbraucherzentralen und Verbraucherverbände* (C-404/06) [2008] ECR I-2685; [2008] 2 CMLR 49 (p 1347). A company delivered a stove-set to a consumer. The consumer returned the set for lack of conformity. Relying on German law, the company required the consumer to pay for the benefit of using the non-conforming appliance before its return (at [12]).

The Court held that the requirement that return must be free of charge seeks to protect consumers from financial costs that might deter them from exercising their rights under the Directive. The seller may not make any charge for remedying the lack of conformity of the goods (at [34]). A consumer is not unjustly enriched when they are provided with a replacement for goods that are not in conformity with the contract (at [41]). The Directive precludes a national law requiring the consumer to compensate the seller for the use of defective goods before their replacement (at [43]).

The seller is under a duty to bring the goods into conformity where the lack of conformity becomes known within a period of 2 years from the delivery of the goods (Art 5(1)). The Member States may require the consumer to inform the seller of the lack of conformity within 2 months of discovering the nonconformity (Art 5(2)).

Guarantees legally bind those who give them under the conditions set out in the guarantee document and advertising (Art 6(1)). A guarantee is an undertaking by a producer or seller to a consumer to refund the price or to repair consumer goods if they fail to meet the advertised standards (Art 1(2)(e)). Subject to certain exceptions, rights under the Directive may not be waived (Art 7(1)).

[10.170] Advertising Restrictions

The EU has prohibited misleading advertising and regulated comparative advertising. See Directive 2006/114 of the European Parliament and of the Council of 12 December 2006 concerning misleading and comparative advertising (codified version) (OJ L 376, 27.12.2006, p 21). Misleading advertising is likely to deceive consumers and injures competitors by affecting the purchasing decisions of consumers (Art 2(b)). The Member States must adopt adequate and effective measures to prevent misleading advertising, including permitting those with a legitimate interest to take legal action against such advertising (Art 5(1)).

Comparative advertising expressly or impliedly identifies a competitor or its goods or services (Art 2(b)). An advertisement may thus constitute comparative advertising if it refers by implication to the products of competitors. See *Toshiba Europe GmbH v Katun Germany GmbH* (C-112/99) [2001] ECR I-7945 at [31]; [2002] 3 CMLR 7 (p 164); *Pippig Augenoptik GmbH & Co KG v Hartlauer Handelsgesellschaft mbH* (C-44/01) [2003] ECR I-3095 at [35]; [2004] 1 CMLR 39 (p 1244); *De Landtsheer Emmanuel SA v Comité Interprofessionnel du Vin de Champagne* (C-381/05) [2007] ECR I-3115 at [16]; [2007] 2 CMLR 43 (p 1146); *O2 Holdings Ltd v Hutchison 3G UK Ltd* (C-533/06) [2008] ECR I-4231 at [42]; [2008] 3 CMLR 14 (p 397).

Comparative advertising is permitted if (inter alia) it is not misleading, compares goods and services that meet the same needs, objectively compares relevant features, does not disparage or take unfair advantage of the competitor's trade mark, and does not cause confusion between traders (Art 4). The Court has emphasised that comparative advertising can be beneficial for consumers: "comparative advertising helps to demonstrate objectively the merits of the various comparable products". See *Lidl Belgium GmbH & Co KG v Etablissementen Franz Colruyt* NV (C-356/04) [2006] ECR I-8501 at [22]; [2007] 1 CMLR 9 (p 269); *De Landtsheer Emmanuel SA v Comité Interprofessionnel du Vin de Champagne* (C-381/05) [2007] ECR I-3115 at [62]; [2007] 2 CMLR 43 (p 1146).

Subliminal advertising in audiovisual media is prohibited. See Art 3e(1)(b), Directive 89/552 of 3 October 1989 of the European Parliament and of the Council on the coordination of certain provisions laid down by law, regulation or administrative action in Member States concerning the provision of audiovisual media services (OJ L 298, 17.10.1989, p 23). Audiovisual media includes both television and on-demand services (Art 1(a)).

Tobacco advertising is prohibited in the printed media, information society services and on radio. See Arts 3–4, Directive 2003/33 of the European Parliament and of the Council of 26 May 2003 on the approximation of the laws, regulations and administrative provisions of the Member States relating to the advertising and sponsorship of tobacco products (OJ L 152, 20.6.2003, p 16). Sponsorship of events by tobacco companies is also prohibited (Art 5(1)).

[10.175] Unfair Terms

The EU has legislated to prohibit various unfair terms in contracts between sellers and consumers. See Art 1(1), Council Directive 93/13 of 5 April 1993 on unfair terms in consumer contracts (OJ L 95, 21.4.1993, p 29). The key provision of the Directive states that a "contractual term which was not individually negotiated shall be regarded as unfair if, contrary to the requirement of good faith, it causes a significant imbalance in the parties' rights and obligations arising under the contract, to the detriment of the consumer" (Art 3(1)). The Annex to the Directive gives examples of potentially unfair terms (Art 3(3)).

Unfair terms are not binding on the consumer. The contract will remain enforceable if the remainder can be validly severed from the unfair terms (Art 6(1)). Contractual terms are to be written in "plain, intelligible language". Where the meaning of a term is unclear, it shall be given the interpretation that is "most favourable to the consumer" (Art 5). The proposed Consumer Rights Directive (COM(2008) 614 final) would replace this Directive.

See generally, Hugh Collins, "Implementation and Interpretation of the EU Directive on Unfair Terms in Consumer Contracts in Member States" (2007) 8 *Contemporary Issues in Law* 99; Paolisa Nebbia, *Unfair Contract Terms in European Law* (Oxford: Hart, 2007); Florian Bruder, "Burden of Proof and the Unfair Terms in Consumer Contracts Directive" (2007) 15 *European Review of Private Law* 205.

[10.180] Unit Pricing

EU legislation requires traders to provide unit prices to facilitate price comparison by consumers. See Art 1, Directive 98/6 of the European Parliament and of the Council of 16 February 1998 on consumer protection in the indication of the prices of products offered to consumers (OJ L 80, 18.3.1998, p 27). Unit price is defined as the final price per kilogram, litre or metre of a product (Art 2(b)). The unit price is to be given in addition to the selling price for the individual item (Art 3(1)). Advertisements must mention both the selling price and the unit price (Art 3(4)).

[10.185] Product Labelling

There are many Directives regulating the labelling of various products, including:

- Council Directive 76/211 of 20 January 1976 on the approximation of the laws of the Member States relating to the making-up by weight or by volume of certain prepackaged products (OJ L 46, 21.2.1976, p 1);

- Council Directive 92/75 of 22 September 1992 on the indication by labelling and standard product information of the consumption of energy and other resources by household appliances (OJ L 297, 13.10.1992, p 16);
- Directive 94/11 of the European Parliament and of the Council of 23 March 1994 on the approximation of the laws, regulations and administrative provisions of the Member States relating to labelling of the materials used in the main components of footwear for sale to the consumer (OJ L 100, 19.4.1994, p 37);
- Directive 1999/94 of the European Parliament and of the Council of 13 December 1999 relating to the availability of consumer information on fuel economy and CO2 emissions in respect of the marketing of new passenger cars (OJ L 12, 18.1.2000, p 16); and
- Directive 2000/13 of the European Parliament and of the Council of 20 March 2000 on the approximation of the laws of the Member States relating to the labelling, presentation and advertising of foodstuffs (OJ L 109, 6.5.2000, p 29).

The provision of nutritional information is optional unless the label makes a nutritional claim. See Art 2, Council Directive 90/496 of 24 September 1990 on nutrition labelling for foodstuffs (OJ L 276, 6.10.1990, p 40). False or misleading nutritional or health claims are prohibited. See Art 3, Regulation 1924/2006 of the European Parliament and of the Council of 20 December 2006 on nutrition and health claims made on foods (OJ L 404, 30.12.2006, p 9).

[10.190] Distance Contracts

A separate Directive regulates distance contracts between consumers and suppliers. See Art 1, Directive 97/7 of the European Parliament and of the Council of 20 May 1997 on the protection of consumers in respect of distance contracts (OJ L 144, 4.6.1997, p 19). The proposed Consumer Rights Directive (COM(2008) 614 final) would replace this Directive.

A distance contract is a contract relating to goods and services entered into between a consumer and a supplier. The contract must have been entered into under a supplier scheme making exclusive use of means of distance communication (Art 2(1)). Annex I contains a non-exhaustive list of means of distance communication, including printed matter, letters, telephone, email, radio and television.

Once again, the consumer may not waive rights arising under the Directive (Art 12(1)). Consumers are to be provided with specified information prior to entering into the contract (Art 4(1)). The consumer has a right to withdraw from the contract within 7 working days of receipt of a written form with the specified information. If the consumer withdraws, the only cost that may be imposed upon the consumer is the direct cost of returning the goods (Art 6(1)).

In *Messner v Firma Stefan Krüger* (C-489/07) [2009] ECR German legislation provided that a consumer who withdrew from a distance contract must compensate the seller for the value of the use of the goods prior to their return (at [17]). The Court held that consumers would be deterred from exercising their right to withdraw if by doing so they would incur adverse costs (at [19]). The right to withdraw is intended to allow the consumer to inspect and test the goods (at [20]). The obligation to compensate the seller for use of the goods was incompatible with these objectives (at [22]). However, a Member State may require a consumer to compensate the seller where the goods have been used in a manner inconsistent with the principles of good faith or unjust enrichment (at [26]).

Another Directive regulates distance contracts concerning consumer financial services. See Directive 2002/65 of the European Parliament and of the Council of 23 September 2002 concerning the distance marketing of consumer financial services (OJ L 271, 9.10.2002, p 16). The Directive provides that consumers must be provided with certain information prior to entering the contract (Art 3) and have a right to withdraw from the contract (Art 6). The consumer's rights under the Directive may not be waived (Art 12(1)).

[10.195] Doorstep Selling

Another Directive regulates contracts concluded at the customer's home or workplace, unless that location was used at the request of the customer. See Art 1(1), Council Directive 85/577 of 20 December 1985 to protect the consumer in respect of contracts negotiated away from business premises (OJ L 372, 31.12.1985, p 31). The Directive seeks to protect consumers "from the element of surprise inherent in doorstep selling". See *Crailsheimer Volksbank eG v Conrads* (C-229/04) [2005] ECR I-9273 at [43]; [2006] 1 CMLR 21 (p 563). It is not necessary to prove that the trader intended to manipulate the customer by concluding the contract away from its business premises. See *Travel-Vac SL v Sanchís* (C-423/97) [1999] ECR I-2195 at [43]; [1999] 2 CMLR 1111.

The trader must give the consumer written notice of the right to withdraw from the contract (Art 4). The right to withdraw ends 7 days after receipt of written notice of the right to withdraw (Art 5(1)). This right protects consumers by allowing them to withdraw from a contract entered into at the initiative of the trader where the consumer may not have been able to appreciate all of the implications of the agreement. See *Bayerische Hypotheken- und Wechselbank AG v Dietzinger* (C-45/96) [1998] ECR I-1199; [1998] 2 CMLR 499. The right to withdraw may not be waived by the consumer (Art 6).

If the consumer withdraws from the contract they are released from any obligations under the contract (Art 5(2)). In *Travel-Vac SL v Sanchís* (C-423/97) [1999] ECR I-2195; [1999] 2 CMLR 1111 a contract provided that the purchaser could cancel the contract subject to payment of one quarter of the price as damages (at [12]). The Court held that cancellation of the contract extinguished the right to pay damages (at [58]). The Directive prohibits a contractual term providing for the payment of damages where the consumer exercises the right to withdraw (at [60]). The proposed Consumer Rights Directive (COM(2008) 614 final) would replace this Directive.

[10.200] Consumer Credit

Some aspects of consumer credit are regulated by an EU Directive. See Directive 2008/48 of the European Parliament and of the Council of 23 April 2008 on credit agreements for consumers (OJ L 133, 22.5.2008, p 66). With some exceptions, the Directive applies to credit agreements (Art 2(1)). The exceptions include credit agreements secured by a mortgage, those for the acquisition of property in land, and those for less than EUR 200 or more than EUR 75,000 (Art 2(2)). "Credit agreement" is defined as an agreement under which a creditor grants credit to a consumer in the form of a loan, deferred payment or other financial accommodation. It does not include agreements for the continuing provision of goods or services where the consumer pays by instalments (Art 3(c)).

The Directive sets out standard information that must be provided in advertisements for credit (Art 4(2)). Before a credit agreement is concluded the consumer must also be provided with standard information. This information includes the conditions governing the borrowing rate, the annual percentage rate, the total amount payable, the interest rate applying to late payment, the right of withdrawal and the right of early repayment (Art 5(1)). Similar information is to be given in the credit agreement (Art 10(2)).

Before granting credit the creditor must assess the credit worthiness of the consumer, based on the responses of the consumer and consultation of relevant databases (Art 8(1)). The consumer is to be provided with a copy of the credit agreement (Art 10(1)). Consumers are to be informed of changes to the borrowing rate before the change takes effect (Art 11(1)). Consumers have a right to withdraw from the credit agreement within 14 calendar days of concluding the agreement (Art 14(1)). The consumer is entitled to make early repayment at any time and to have the cost of credit reduced accordingly (Art 16(1)), though the creditor is entitled to fair compensation for costs associated with early repayment (Art 16(2)).

[10.205] Timeshare Contracts

The EU has regulated contracts for the use of real property on a timeshare basis. The Directive also regulates long-term holiday product, resale and exchange contracts. See Directive 2008/122 of the European Parliament and of the Council of 14 January 2009 on the protection of consumers in respect of certain aspects of timeshare, long-term holiday product, resale and exchange contracts (OJ L 33, 3.2.2009, p 10). The Annexes set out certain information that traders are required to provide to consumers before entering into these contracts (Art 4(1)). The purchaser has the right to withdraw from the contract within 14 calendar days of signature (Art 6(1)). Advance payments before the end of the period for withdrawal are prohibited (Art 9(1)). These rights may not be waived (Art 12(1)).

[10.210] Air and Rail Passengers

The EU has adopted several Regulations for the protection of air and rail passengers:

- Council Regulation 2299/89 of 24 July 1989 on a code of conduct for computerized reservation systems (OJ L 220, 29.7.1989, p 1);
- Regulation 261/2004 of the European Parliament and of the Council of 11 February 2004 establishing common rules on compensation and assistance to passengers in the event of denied boarding and of cancellation or long delay of flights (OJ L 46, 17.2.2004, p 1);
- Regulation 2111/2005 of the European Parliament and of the Council of 14 December 2005 on the establishment of a Community list of air carriers subject to an operating ban within the Community and on informing air transport passengers of the identity of the operating air carrier (OJ L 344, 27.12.2005, p 15);
- Regulation 1107/2006 of the Parliament and of the Council of 5 July 2006 concerning the rights of disabled persons and persons with reduced mobility when travelling by air (OJ L 204, 26.7.2006, p 1); and
- Regulation 1371/2007 of the European Parliament and of the Council of 23 October 2007 on rail passengers' rights and obligations (OJ L 315, 3.12.2007, p 14).

[10.215] Product Liability

The EU has adopted legislation concerning product liability. See Council Directive 85/374 of 25 July 1985 on the approximation of the laws, regulations and administrative provisions of the Member States concerning liability for defective products (OJ L 210, 7.8.1985, p 29). A producer is liable for damage caused by a defect in their product (Art 1). A product is defective if "it does not provide the safety which a person is entitled to expect", considering the product's presentation, its reasonably expected use and the time when it was circulated (Art 6(1)). A product is not defective simply because a better product was later circulated (Art 6(2)). "Damage" includes death, personal injury and property damage (Art 9).

"Producer" is defined as the manufacturer of the product or the producer of a raw material. The term also includes any person who presents themselves as producer by putting their name or trade mark on the product (Art 3(1)). An importer of the product into the EU is also deemed to be a producer (Art 3(2)). If the producer cannot be ascertained, the suppliers of the product are treated as its producer unless they identify the producer or their supplier (Art 3(3)). The liability of a producer may not be limited or excluded by contract (Art 12).

The producer will not be liable if they prove that they "did not put the product into circulation" (Art 7(a)). In *O'Byrne v Sanofi Pasteur MSD Ltd* (C-127/04) [2006] ECR I-1313; [2006] 2 CMLR 24 (p 656) a vaccine manufacturer sent its product to a subsidiary that distributed the product in another national market (at [11]–[12]). The subsidiary sold the product to a hospital which supplied it to a surgery (at [13]). The Court held that a product has been put into circulation "when it leaves the production process operated by the producer and enters a marketing process in the form in which it is offered to the public in order to be used or consumed" (at [27]).

[10.220] Product Safety

The EU has adopted a Directive imposing a general obligation of product safety. See Directive 2001/95 of the European Parliament and of the Council of 3 December 2001 on general product safety (OJ L 11, 15.1.2002, p 4). "Product" is defined as any product intended for consumers or likely to be used by consumers although not intended for them (Art 2(a)). Producers may place only safe products on the market (Art 3(1)). "Safe product" is defined as "any product which, under normal or reasonably foreseeable conditions of use... does not present any risk or only the minimum risks compatible with the product's use, considered to be acceptable and consistent with a high level of protection for the safety and health of persons" (Art 2(b)).

In the absence of EU legislation relating to the specific product, a product is deemed safe if it complies with the specific laws of the Member State in which it is marketed. A product is also deemed safe if it complies with voluntary national standards implementing European standards (Art 3(2)). Producers are also obliged to provide consumers with all necessary information regarding possible risks involved in the use of their products (Art 5(1)). Producers and distributors are required to inform the governments of the Member States of any risks associated with the product that come to their attention (Art 5(3)).

Other legislation concerns the safety of specific products. See, for example, Directive 2007/23 of the European Parliament and of the Council of 23 May 2007 on the placing on the market of pyrotechnic articles (OJ L 154, 14.6.2007, p 1); Directive 2009/48 of the European Parliament and of the Council of 18 June 2009 on the safety of toys (OJ L 170, 30.6.2009, p 1).

Some legislation is directed to health protection in relation to foodstuffs, including:

- Regulation 852/2004 of the European Parliament and of the Council on the hygiene of foodstuffs (OJ L 139, 30.4.2004, p 1);
- Regulation 1331/2008 of the European Parliament and of the Council of 16 December 2008 establishing a common authorisation procedure for food additives, food enzymes and food flavourings (OJ L 354, 31.12.2008, p 1);
- Regulation 1332/2008 of the European Parliament and of the Council of 16 December 2008 on food enzymes (OJ L 354, 31.12.2008, p 7);
- Regulation 1333/2008 of the European Parliament and of the Council of 16 December 2008 on food additives (OJ L 354, 31.12.2008, p 16);
- Regulation 1334/2008 of the European Parliament and of the Council of 16 December 2008 on flavourings and certain food ingredients with flavouring properties for use in and on foods (OJ L 354, 31.12.2008, p 34);
- Commission Directive 2008/84 of 27 August 2008 laying down specific purity criteria on food additives other than colours and sweeteners (OJ L 253, 20.9.2008, p 1); and
- Commission Regulation 41/2009 of 20 January 2009 concerning the composition and labelling of foodstuffs suitable for people intolerant to gluten (OJ L 16, 21.1.2009, p 3).

[10.225] Implementation by Member States

Consumer organisations and national consumer protection authorities may seek an injunction for the protection of the collective interests of consumers against intra-community infringements of certain EU Directives concerning consumer protection. See Arts 2–4, Directive 98/27 of the European Parliament and of the Council of 19 May 1998 on injunctions for the protection of consumers' interests (OJ L 166, 11.6.1998, p 51). The authorities of the Member States cooperate in relation to intra-community infringements of EU consumer protection law. See Regulation 2006/2004 of the European Parliament and of the Council of 27 October 2004 on cooperation between national authorities responsible for the enforcement of consumer protection laws (OJ L 364, 9.12.2004, p 1).

National legislation implementing the most important EU consumer protection legislation is available in the EU Consumer Law Acquis Database (http://www.eu-consumer-law.org). The Database also includes national judicial decisions applying these Directives. See also Hans Schulte-Nölke, Christian Twigg-Flesner and Martin Ebers (eds), *EC Consumer Law Compendium: The Consumer Acquis and its Transposition in the Member States* (Munich: Sellier 2007).

[10.230] Conclusion

EU Member States must ensure that the principle of equal pay for male and female workers for equal work or work of equal value is applied. The equal pay principle has direct effect. Both direct and indirect discrimination are prohibited. The Court has adopted an expansive interpretation of "pay". The principle of equal pay for equal work refers to performance of the same work. The principle of equal pay for work of equal value requires that employees be paid an equal salary for work that is considered to be of equal value to their employer.

Under the Equal Opportunities Directive there may be no direct or indirect sex discrimination in relation to access to employment, vocational training and employment and working conditions. If a complainant establishes facts from which discrimination may be presumed, the respondent must prove that there was no prohibited discrimination. Sexual harassment must be prohibited. Any less favourable treatment of a woman related to pregnancy or maternity leave constitutes sex discrimination. The Member States may adopt measures with a view to ensuring full equality between men and women in working life.

Another Directive sets out a framework for national laws prohibiting sex discrimination in relation to the supply of goods and services. The Equal Treatment Directive applies to national anti-discrimination laws concerning discrimination on the grounds of religion, disability, age and sexual orientation. There is a specific Directive concerning racial discrimination.

The EU has adopted a number of measures relating to labour law, including workers' rights in the transfer of undertakings and vocational training. The Data Protection Directive applies to the processing of personal data by automatic means and non-automatic processing of data that forms part of a filing system. Other Directives concern the processing of personal data in the electronic communications context and the retention of data regarding use of electronic communications services.

The EU has adopted a considerable body of consumer protection law. Unfair commercial practices are prohibited. In particular, misleading or aggressive commercial practices are unfair. The seller must provide to the consumer goods that conform to the sale contract. The seller must bring nonconforming goods into conformity "free of charge" by repair, replacement, reduction in the price or rescission of the contract.

EU Member States must adopt adequate and effective measures to prevent misleading advertising. Comparative advertising is permitted if (inter alia) it is not misleading, compares goods and services that meet the same needs, objectively compares relevant features, does not disparage or take unfair advantage of the competitor's trade mark, and does not cause confusion between traders.

Unfair contractual terms are not binding on the consumer. A term that was not individually negotiated will be regarded as unfair "if, contrary to the requirement of good faith, it causes a significant imbalance in the parties' rights and obligations . . . to the detriment of the consumer".

Before a consumer credit agreement is concluded the consumer must also be provided with standard information. Before granting credit the creditor must assess the credit worthiness of the consumer. Consumers have a right to withdraw from the credit agreement within 14 calendar days of concluding the agreement.

A producer is liable for damage caused by a defect in their product. A product is defective if "it does not provide the safety which a person is entitled to expect", considering the product's presentation, its reasonably expected use and the time when it was circulated.

Further Reading

A. *Anti-discrimination Law*

Ahtela, Karoliina. "The Revised Provisions on Sex Discrimination in European Law: A Critical Assessment" (2005) 11 *European Law Journal* 57.

Besson, Samantha. "Gender Discrimination Under EU and ECHR Law. Never Shall the Twain Meet?" (2008) 8 *Human Rights Law Review* 647.

Costello, Cathryn and Gareth Davies. "The Case Law of the Court of Justice in the Field of Sex Equality Since 2000" (2006) 43 *Common Market Law Review* 1567.

Ellis, Evelyn. "Recent Developments in European Community Sex Equality Law" (1994) 31 *Common Market Law Review* 43.

Ellis, Evelyn. "Recent Developments in European Community Sex Equality Law" (1998) 35 *Common Market Law Review* 379.

Ellis, Evelyn. "The Recent Jurisprudence of the Court of Justice in the Field of Sex Equality" (2000) 37 *Common Market Law Review* 1403.

Ellis, Evelyn. *EU Anti-discrimination Law* (Oxford: Oxford University Press, 2005).

Goldschmidt, Jenny E. "Reasonable Accommodation in EU Equality Law in a Broader Perspective" (2007) 8 *ERA Forum* 39.

Hervey, Tamara K. "Thirty Years of EU Sex Equality Law: Looking Backwards, Looking Forwards" (2005) 12 *Maastricht Journal of European and Comparative Law* 307.

Koukoulis-Spiliotopoulos, Sophia. "The Amended Equal Treatment Directive (2002/73): An Expression of Constitutional Principles/Fundamental Rights" (2005) 12 *Maastricht Journal of European and Comparative Law* 327.

Masselot, Annick. "The State of Gender Equality Law in the European Union" (2007) 13 *European Law Journal* 152.

Meenan, Helen. "Age Equality After the Employment Directive" (2003) 10 *Maastricht Journal of European and Comparative Law* 9.

Paparrigopoulou, Patrina. "Age Discrimination in European Union Law" (2009) 59 *Revue Hellenique de Droit International* 781.

Schiek, Dagmar. "A New Framework on Equal Treatment of Persons in EC Law?" (2002) 8 *European Law Journal* 290.

Schiek, Dagmar and Victoria Chege (eds). *European Union Non-discrimination Law* (London: Routledge-Cavendish, 2008).

Szyszczak, Erika. "Antidiscrimination Law in the European Community" (2009) 32 *Fordham International Law Journal* 624.

B. Vocational Training

Ertl, Hubert. "The European Union and Education and Training: An Overview of Policies and Initiatives" in David Phillips and Hubert Ertl (eds), *Implementing European Union Education and Training Policy. A Comparative Study of Issues in Four Member States* (The Hague: Kluwer, 2003), 13.

Ertl, Hubert. "European Union Policies in Education and Training: The Lisbon Agenda as a Turning Point?" (2006) 42 *Comparative Education* 5.

Flynn, James. "Vocational Training in Community Law and Practice" (1988) 8 *Yearbook of European Law* 59.

Freedland, Mark. "Vocational Training in EC Law and Policy – Education, Employment or Welfare?" (1996) 25 *Industrial Law Journal* 110.

C. Data Protection

Bignami, Francesca. "Privacy and Law Enforcement in the European Union: The Data Retention Directive" (2007) 8 *Chicago Journal of International Law* 233.

Bygrave, Lee A. "Automated Profiling: Minding the Machine: Article 15 of the EC Data Protection Directive and Automated Profiling" (2001) 17 *Computer Law and Security Review* 17.

Johnson, Elizabeth H. "Data Protection Law in the European Union" (2007) 54 *Federal Lawyer* 44.

Koritnik, Boştjan. "Discretion of the EU Member State when Implementing the Data Protection Directive 95/46/EC" (July 2005) 12, 1–2 *eLaw Journal: Murdoch University Electronic Journal of Law*, Available at https://elaw.murdoch.edu.au.

Oxman, Stephen A. "Exemptions to the European Union Personal Data Privacy Directive: Will they Swallow the Directive?" (2000) 24 *Boston College International and Comparative Law Review* 191.

Vilasau, Monica. "Traffic Data Retention v Data Protection: the New European Framework" (2007) 13 *Computer and Telecommunications Law Review* 52.

Wong, Rebecca and Joseph Savirimuthu. "All or Nothing: This is the Question? The Application of Article 3(2) Data Protection Directive 95/46/EC to the Internet" (2008) 25 *John Marshall Journal of Computer & Information Law* 241.

D. Consumer Protection

Betlem, Gerrit. "Public and Private Transnational Enforcement of EU Consumer Law" (2007) 18 *European Business Law Review* 683.

Gormley, Laurence W. "The Consumer Acquis and the Internal Market" (2009) 20 *European Business Law Review* 409.

Howells, Geraint. "The Scope of European Consumer Law" (2005) 1 *European Review of Contract Law* 360.

Nebbia, Paolisa and Tony Askham. *EU Consumer Law* (Richmond, UK: Richmond Law and Tax, 2004).

Palmigiano, Alessandro and Angela Bongiorno. "Overview of EU Legislation on Product Liability and Consumer Safety" (2005) 6 *Business Law International* 396.

Schurr, Francesco A. "The Relevance of the European Consumer Protection Law for the Development of the European Contract Law" (2007) 38 *Victoria University of Wellington Law Review* 131.

Weatherill, Stephen. *EU Consumer Law and Policy* (Cheltenham, UK: Edward Elgar, 2005).

Chapter 11
Judicial Review and the European Court of Justice

[11.05] Introduction

Although the EU legal system is regarded by many common lawyers as a derivative of the civil law system, it is moulded by the voluminous case law of the Court of Justice. As Hjalte Rasmussen put it, EU law "is as much a case law system as that of, say, the United States of America; or perhaps even as that of England." See Hjalte Rasmussen, *European Community Case Law: Summaries of Leading EC Court Cases* (Copenhagen: Handelshøjskolens Forlag, 1993), 8. Indeed, any meaningful consideration of EU law necessitates a study of the case law of the Court. This chapter sets out the function of the Court of Justice in the continuing development of the EU legal system. In particular, this chapter explains how legal proceedings may be initiated in the ECJ and by whom. It also explains the Court's methods of interpretation of EU laws.

[11.10] Composition of the Court

The Court of Justice exercises the jurisdiction conferred upon it under the EU founding Treaties. The ECJ consists of one judge from each Member State (Art 19(2) TEU). These judges sit as a Grand Chamber and in certain situations as a full Court (Art 251 TFEU; Art 16, Protocol (No 3) on the Statute of the Court of Justice (hereafter "Statute")). However, they may form Chambers (Art 251 TFEU), each consisting of three or five judges (Art 16, Statute).

Judges are "chosen from persons whose independence is beyond doubt and who possess the qualifications for appointment to the highest judicial offices in their respective countries or who are jurisconsults of recognized competence" (Art 253 TFEU). The Judges of the ECJ are appointed for staggered terms of 6 years (Art 19(2) TEU; Art 253 TFEU; Art 9, Statute).

G. Moens, J. Trone, *Commercial Law of the European Union*,
Ius Gentium: Comparative Perspectives on Law and Justice 4,
DOI 10.1007/978-90-481-8774-4_11,

[11.15] Independence of the Judges

The Judges cannot be dismissed by Member States but may be deprived of their office or of their right to a pension or other benefits if, in the unanimous opinion of the Judges, they no longer meet the obligations of the office (Art 6, Statute). The Judges are immune from legal proceedings. After they leave office the Judges continue to have immunity for acts done in their official capacity (Art 3, Statute).

Before taking up duties at the Court, a Judge must take an oath to carry out their duties "impartially and conscientiously" (Art 2, Statute). Judges may not hold political or administrative office (Art 4, Statute). They may not engage in any other occupation, unless granted permission by the Council (Art 4, Statute).

The judicial oath also requires a Judge "to preserve the secrecy of the deliberations of the Court" (Art 2, Statute; see also Art 35, Statute). The secrecy of deliberations shields the judges against retaliatory action by Member States. As the judgment is the judgment of the Court, it is impossible for outsiders to know what side a judge took during the deliberations regarding a case.

[11.20] Judgments of the Court

The Court delivers a collective judgment. The author of each judgment is not disclosed. Dissenting judgments are not published. Judgments state only the names of the Judges who participated in the decision (Art 36, Statute). As a consequence, judges are not able to make a name for themselves by their association with powerful dissenting or majority judgments. See generally, Julia Laffranque, "Dissenting Opinion in the European Court of Justice—Estonia's Possible Contribution to the Democratisation of the European Union Judicial System" 2004-I *Juridica International* 14, available at http://www.juridicainternational.eu. Judgments normally consist of four parts. The first part is a statement of the facts, the second part gives the reasons of the Court, the third part contains the Court's formal decision, while the fourth part deals with costs.

It is fair to say that until the mid-1970s the judgments of the Court sometimes lacked logical rigour and were often written in a somewhat cryptic manner. This may have to do with the fact that in continental legal systems judgments are not usually written in the form of a reasoned essay. This contrasts sharply with the elaborate reasoning usually offered by common law judges. The cryptic nature of much of the case law may also be due to the necessity to compromise in order to arrive at a collective judgment.

The EU legal system does not know the concept of stare decisis, the doctrine that requires a common law court to follow precedents. However, the ECJ routinely cites previous cases in its judgments and generally follows its prior decisions. Nevertheless, the Court occasionally declines to follow one of its decisions. See e.g. *SA CNL-SUCAL NV v HAG GF AG* (C-10/89) [1990] ECR I-3711 at [10]; [1990] 3 CMLR 571; *Criminal Proceedings Against Keck* (C-267/91) [1993] ECR I-6097 at [16]; [1995] 1 CMLR 101; *Collins v Secretary of State for Work and Pensions* (C-138/02) [2004] ECR I-2703 at [63]–[64]; [2004] 2 CMLR 8 (p 147); *Metock v Minister for Justice, Equality and Law Reform* (C-127/08) [2008] ECR I-6241 at [58]; [2008] 3 CMLR 39 (p 1167). See generally, Anthony Arnull, "Owning up to Fallibility: Precedent and the Court of Justice" (1993) 30 *Common Market Law Review* 247; John J Barcelo, "Precedent in European Community Law" in D Neil MacCormick and Robert S Summers (eds), *Interpreting Precedents: A Comparative Study* (Aldershot: Ashgate/Dartmouth, 1997), 407.

[11.25] Advocates-General

The Court is assisted by eight Advocates-General. The Advocates-General are independent and impartial advisors who make reasoned submissions on cases in order to assist the Court (Art 252 TFEU). In other words, they advise the Court as to how the case should be decided. Advocates-General have the same status as Judges but, for obvious reasons, they do not play any further part in deciding the case. They speak for the public interest.

In *Emesa Sugar (Free Zone) NV v Aruba* (C-17/98) [2000] ECR I-665 the Court stated that the opinion of the Advocate-General is "the individual reasoned opinion, expressed in open court, of a Member of the Court of Justice itself" (at [14]). By giving a reasoned opinion the Advocate-General participates in the decision-making process of the Court (at [15]). The Advocates-General are not subject to any authority and do not represent any "particular interest" in carrying out their functions (at [12]).

[11.30] Advice of the Advocates-General

In their opinions, Advocates-General need not limit themselves to a discussion of the arguments advanced by the parties to the dispute. Instead, they may advise the court to decide the case on grounds which have not been considered by the parties. A good example of the Advocates-General's wide freedom of argument is found in *Transocean Marine Paint Association v Commission* (17/74) [1974] ECR 1063; [1974] 2 CMLR 459.

Transocean Marine Paint Association was made up of medium-sized manufacturers of marine paint, some established in the EEC and some located outside the Community. It was a feature of the market in marine paints that manufacturers must be able to offer a world-wide service because shipowners do not purchase a brand of paint unless they know that a supply can be obtained in any part of the world where the ship happens to be. The Association enabled the participating companies to provide this service by cooperating with each other. The members of the Association marketed a brand known as Transocean, manufactured by them all over the world to an identical formula.

Art 85 of the EEC Treaty (now Art 101 TFEU) prohibited agreements that distorted competition. Following the adoption by the Commission of a Decision in 1967, the Association's agreement enjoyed an exemption under Art 85(3) EEC (Art 101(3) TFEU) for a period of 5 years. In 1972, the Association sought a renewal of the exemption. The Commission renewed the exemption but subjected the agreement to a number of new conditions. The Association claimed that the Commission failed to inform the Association of its intention to impose one of these conditions.

The parties to the agreement argued that the Commission had violated a number of EC secondary laws providing that the Commission should accord parties the right to be heard in particular contexts (at [4]). The Advocate-General advised the Court that the case should be decided on the basis of a general principle of law which did not yet exist under EC law, namely *audi alteram partem* or the right to be heard. The important point is that the Advocate-General did not limit himself to interpretation of that secondary legislation but recommended that the Court decide the case on grounds that had not been advanced by the parties.

The ECJ adopted the approach urged by the Advocate-General. The Court held that the secondary legislation did not create a right to be heard that would apply in this case (at [9]). However, the Court held that there was a general principle of EC law "that a person whose interests are perceptibly affected by a decision taken by a public authority must be given the opportunity to make his point of view known" (at [15]). The Court concluded that the right to be heard exists especially in the "case of conditions which ... impose considerable obligations having far-reaching effects" (at [15]). Thus an administrative authority before wielding a statutory power to the detriment of a particular person, must in general hear what that person has to say about the matter, even if the statute does not expressly require it.

[11.35] Role of the Advocate-General

It could be said that the Advocate-General fulfills, in the EU legal system, the role which is usually played by a court of first instance. Indeed, the Advocate-General's function is to provide the Court with a coherently and persuasively argued opinion. This opinion is in turn subject to rigorous scrutiny by the Court. The Court is free to depart from or reject altogether the advice given by the Advocate-General. For example, the Court did not follow the Advocate-General's advice in *Faccini Dori v Recreb Srl* (C-91/92) [1994] ECR I-3325; [1994] 1 CMLR 665 (see the Opinion at [73] and the Judgment at [23]–[24]). Nevertheless, the Advocate-General's opinion usually carries great weight.

See generally, Takis Tridimas, "The Role of the Advocate General in the Development of Community Law: Some Reflections" (1997) 34 *Common Market Law Review* 1349; Cyril Ritter, "A New Look at the Role and Impact of Advocates-General: Collectively and Individually" (2006) 12 *Columbia Journal of European Law* 751; Noreen Burrows and Rosa Greaves, *The Advocate General and EC Law* (Oxford: Oxford University Press, 2007).

[11.40] General Court

The TFEU provides for a General Court (formerly the Court of First Instance). The General Court has jurisdiction to hear first instance actions concerning the legality of EU acts, the failure of EU institutions to act, compensation for damage, staff disputes and actions under contractual arbitration clauses. Such judgments of the General Court can be appealed to the ECJ on matters of law only (Art 256(1) TFEU; Art 58, Statute).

The General Court also has jurisdiction to determine proceedings brought against decisions of the specialised courts of the EU (Art 256(2) TFEU). The Union is empowered to establish specialised courts to hear cases regarding "specific areas" of EU law (Art 257 TFEU). The decisions of these courts may exceptionally be appealed to the Court of Justice, where there is a serious risk that the unity or consistency of EU law will be affected (Art 256(2) TFEU).

After the Statute of the Court is amended, the General Court will have jurisdiction to determine a request for a preliminary ruling. The General Court may refer the request to the ECJ where it believes that the case requires it to make a ruling of legal principle that may affect the unity or consistency of EU law. The ECJ may also review a decision of the General Court on a preliminary ruling where there is a serious risk that the unity or consistency of EU law will be affected (Art 256(3) TFEU).

[11.45] Methods of Interpretation

The general task of the ECJ is to "ensure that in the interpretation and application of the Treaties the law is observed" (Art 19(1) TEU). The Court has a preference for methods of interpretation which take account of the "purposes" and the "objectives" of the EU Treaties. There are essentially four methods of interpretation that it has employed. The Court has referred to these approaches as the literal, historical, contextual and teleological methods of interpretation. See *Sumitomo Chemical Co Ltd v Commission* (T-23/02) [2005] ECR II-4065 at [102]; *Germany v Commission* (T-374/04) [2007] ECR II-4431 at [92], [149]; *Germany v Commission* (T-349/06) [2008] ECR II-2181 at [66].

It should be stressed that these methods of interpretation are not in any way rigid principles of interpretation. Rather, they represent the main discernible approaches adopted at different times by the Court when interpreting EU law. Furthermore, the Court may apply any one or a combination of these methods of interpretation in order to assist it in its task of interpretation. See generally, Joxerramon Bengoetxea, *The Legal Reasoning of the European Court of Justice: Towards a European Jurisprudence* (Oxford: Clarendon Press, 1993); Giulio Itzcovich, "The Interpretation of Community Law by the European Court of Justice" (May 2009) 10, 5 *German Law Journal* 537, http://www.germanlawjournal.com.

The ECJ also applies other interpretative rules. For example, wherever possible EU legislation is interpreted so as to be consistent with international law. See *Bettati v Safety Hi-Tech Srl* (C-341/95) [1998] ECR I-4355 at [20]; *Petrotub SA v Council* (C-76/00 P) [2003] ECR I-79 at [57]; *Sociedad General de Autores y Editores de España (SGAE) v Rafael Hoteles SA* (C-306/05) [2006] ECR I-11519 at [35].

[11.50] Literal Interpretation

Where legal provisions are clear, the Court will usually not depart from their literal (or plain) meaning. The Court has described the plain meaning as the "normal meaning of the words used". See *Denmark v Commission* (C-233/96) [1998] ECR I-5759 at [38]; *Germany v Commission* (C-245/97) [2000] ECR I-11261 at [72]. However, the ECJ has stated that a literal interpretation of legal provisions is not sufficient. See *Humblet v Belgium* (6/60) [1960] ECR 559 at 575.

If the literal meaning does not accord with the overall scheme of the Treaties or other legal instruments under consideration, the Court will disregard the plain wording in order to achieve an interpretation that promotes the main objectives of the Treaties or other legal instruments. For example, the Court rejected a literal interpretation of a Directive on the ground that it would result in inconsistency with another Directive. See *Toshiba Europe GmbH v Katun Germany GmbH* (C-112/99) [2001] ECR I-7945 at [35]; [2002] 3 CMLR 7 (p 164).

[11.55] Historical Interpretation

In most European civil law countries the judge seeks the subjective intention of the legislature by examining the *travaux préparatoires* of a law.

The Court cannot examine the *travaux préparatoires* of the original 1957 EEC Treaty because these are secret. However, preparatory materials are available for most of the amending Treaties.

The Court has made use of the preparatory documents for secondary legislation such as Directives. See *Stauder v City of Ulm* (29/69) [1969] ECR 419 at [5]; [1970] CMLR 112; *Deutsche Bakels GmbH v Oberfinanzdirektion Münich* (14/70) [1970] ECR 1001 at [6]–[10]; [1971] CMLR 188; *Kuwait Petroleum (GB) Ltd v Customs and Excise Commissioners* (C-48/97) [1999] ECR I-2323 at [23]; [1999] 2 CMLR 651; *Bowden v Tuffnell Parcels Express Ltd* (C-133/00) [2001] ECR I-7031 at [35], [42]; [2001] 3 CMLR 52 (p 1342); *Wilson v Ordre des avocats du barreau de Luxembourg* (C-506/04) [2006] ECR I-8613 at [68]; [2007] 1 CMLR 7 (p 217). These preparatory materials include debates in the European Parliament, Management Committee papers and explanatory notes to conventions. It thus considers the intention of the EU legislature when interpreting EU legal instruments. See *Gebrüder Knauf Westdeutsche Gipswerke v Hauptzollamt Hamburg-Jonas* (118/79) [1980] ECR 1183 at [5].

In *Commission v Greece* (C-306/89) [1991] ECR I-5863; [1994] 1 CMLR 803 a Member State argued for an interpretation of a Directive based upon a declaration by several national delegations at the Council meeting at which the Directive was adopted (at [6]). The Court responded that "the objective scope of rules of Community law can be derived only from those rules themselves, having regard to their context", not from such declarations (at [8]). See also *Libertel Groep BV v Benelux-Merkenbureau* (C-104/01) [2003] ECR I-3793 at [24]–[25]; [2005] 2 CMLR 45 (p 1097).

[11.60] Contextual Interpretation

This method of interpretation is also referred to as the systematic method. In interpreting EU law, the Court places reliance upon the system of the Treaties or the secondary legislation under consideration. It frequently has regard to the context of the provisions at issue. See *Vereniging voor Energie, Milieu en Water v Directeur van de Dienst uitvoering en toezicht Energie* (C-17/03) [2005] ECR I-4983 at [41]; [2005] 5 CMLR 8 (p 361); *Britannia Alloys & Chemicals Ltd v Commission* (C-76/06 P) [2007] ECR I-4405 at [21]; [2007] 5 CMLR 3 (p 251). In other words, the Court considers their place in relation to other provisions of EU law. Thus, in interpreting a particular paragraph of an Article of the Treaties, the Court would look at the position of that paragraph in relation to the other paragraphs of that Article and the position of that Article in the general scheme of the Treaties.

In *CILFIT Srl v Ministro della Sanita* (283/81) [1982] ECR 3415; [1983] 1 CMLR 472 the Court stated that "every provision of Community law must be placed in its context and interpreted in the light of the provisions of

Community law as a whole, regard being had to the objectives thereof and to its state of evolution at the date on which the provision in question is to be applied" (at [20]). The Court has stated that it would strictly interpret provisions of the Treaties which constitute an exception to the fundamental rules of the Union. See *Commission v Italy* (7/68) [1968] ECR 423 at 430; [1969] CMLR 1 at 10.

Where there is more than one possible literal interpretation of an expression, the Court considers the context in which the words are used, including the aim and scheme of the EU legislation concerned. See *Velvet & Steel Immobilien und Handels GmbH v Finanzamt Hamburg-Eimsbüttel* (C-455/05) [2007] ECR I-3225 at [20]; *R (on the Application of Teleos Plc) v Commissioners of Customs and Excise* (C-409/04) [2007] ECR I-7797 at [35]; [2008] 1 CMLR 6 (p 98).

[11.65] Teleological Interpretation

The expression "teleological" refers to an interpretation of the Treaties based upon the intention and purposes of the provisions under consideration. See *Criminal Proceedings Against Roudolff* (803/79) [1980] ECR 2015 at [6]. It goes beyond all three previously discussed methods of interpretation because it is not restricted by the wording, background or context of the provisions at issue. Rather, it is dynamic and purposeful in its application, seeking to give effect to the spirit or the overall scheme and objectives of the specific provisions under consideration, and those of the Treaty or any other legislation of which they form part.

The importance of the teleological method of interpretation in relation to EU law was recognized by Lord Denning in *Bulmer (H P) Ltd v J Bollinger SA* [1974] Ch 401 at 425–426; [1974] 2 CMLR 91 at 119–120:

> The Treaty is quite unlike any of the enactments to which we have become accustomed. The draftsmen of our statutes have striven to express themselves with the utmost exactness. They have tried to foresee all possible circumstances that may arise and to provide for them. They have sacrificed style and simplicity. They have forgone brevity. They have become long and involved. In consequence, the judges have followed suit. They interpret a statute as applying only to the circumstances covered by the very words. They give them a literal interpretation. If the words of the statute do not cover a new situation – which was not foreseen – the judges hold that they have no power to fill the gap. To do so would be a "naked usurpation of the legislative function"....
>
> How different is this Treaty! It lays down general principles. It expresses its aims and purposes. All in sentences of moderate length and commendable style. But it lacks precision. It uses words and phrases without defining what they mean. An English lawyer would look for an interpretation clause, but he would look in vain. There is none. All the way through the Treaty there are gaps and lacunae. These have to be filled in by the judges, or by Regulations or Directives. It is the European way.... Seeing these differences, what are the English courts to do when they are faced with a problem of interpretation? They must follow the

> European pattern. No longer must they examine the words in meticulous detail. No longer must they argue about the precise grammatical sense. They must look to the purpose or intent.... They must divine the spirit of the Treaty and gain inspiration from it. If they find a gap, they must fill it as best they can. They must do what the framers of the instrument would have done if they had thought about it.

See generally, Nial Fennelly, "Legal Interpretation at the European Court of Justice" (1997) 20 *Fordham International Law Journal* 656.

[11.70] All Language Versions Considered

When interpreting EU legislation the Court considers *all* of the different language versions so as to ensure the uniform interpretation and application of EU law. See *CILFIT Srl v Ministro della Sanita* (283/81) [1982] ECR 3415 at [18]; [1983] 1 CMLR 472; *Ferriere Nord SpA v Commission* (C-219/95 P) [1997] ECR I-4411 at [15]; [1997] 5 CMLR 575; *Skatteministeriet v Codan* (C-236/97) [1998] ECR I-8679 at [25]; [2001] 1 CMLR 36 (p 941); *Velvet & Steel Immobilien und Handels GmbH v Finanzamt Hamburg-Eimsbüttel* (C-455/05) [2007] ECR I-3225 at [16]; *García v Delegado del Gobierno en la Región de Murcia* (C-261/08) [2009] ECR at [55].

In *Stauder v City of Ulm* (29/69) [1969] ECR 419; [1970] CMLR 112 the Court explained the rationale for this rule as follows:

> when a single decision is addressed to all the Member States the necessity for uniform application and accordingly for uniform interpretation makes it impossible to consider one version of the text in isolation but requires that it be interpreted on the basis of both the real intention of its author and the aim he seeks to achieve, in the light in particular of the versions in all four languages (at [3]).

In principle all language versions carry the same weight. See *R v Commissioners of Customs and Excise; Ex parte EMU Tabac Sarl* (C-296/95) [1998] ECR I-1604 at [36]; [1998] 2 CMLR 1205; *Givane v Secretary of State for the Home Department* (C-257/00) [2003] ECR I-345 at [36]; [2003] 1 CMLR 17 (p 587); *Kyocera Electronics Europe GmbH v Hauptzollamt Krefeld* (C-152/01) [2003] ECR I-13821 at [32].

Of course, there may be significant differences between the different language versions of an EU legal measure. The Court adopts a uniform interpretation of the different language versions, and "in the case of divergence between the versions the provision in question must be interpreted by reference to the purpose and general scheme of the rules of which it forms a part." See *R v Bouchereau* (30/77) [1977] ECR 1999 at [14]; [1977] 2 CMLR 800; *Milk Marketing Board of England and Wales v Cricket St Thomas Estate* (C-372/88) [1990] ECR I-1345 at [19]; [1990] 2 CMLR 800; *Aannemersbedrijf P K Kraaijeveld BV ea v Gedeputeerde Staten van*

Zuid-Holland (C-72/95) [1996] ECR I-5403 at [28]; [1997] 3 CMLR 1; *Givane v Secretary of State for the Home Department* (C-257/00) [2003] ECR I-345 at [37]; [2003] 1 CMLR 17 (p 587). See generally, Geert van Calster, "The EU's Tower of Babel—The Interpretation by the European Court of Justice of Equally Authentic Texts Drafted in more than one Official Language" (1997) 17 *Yearbook of European Law* 363; Lawrence M Solan, "The Interpretation of Multilingual Statutes by the European Court of Justice" (2009) 34 *Brooklyn Journal of International Law* 277.

[11.75] Jurisdiction of the Court

As the ECJ is the supreme judicial body of a supranational organization, it may be tempting to compare it to a national constitutional court. In fact, the ECJ's nature and functions go well beyond those of a constitutional court. It also acts as an administrative court when it judicially reviews acts or omissions of other EU institutions. It also functions as an economic court when dealing with restrictive trade practices. It even acts as a general court when it adjudicates on claims for damages against an EU institution.

Broadly, the Court's jurisdiction is of four kinds: to give opinions on the compatibility of international agreements with the Treaties (Art 218(11) TFEU); to review the legality of the acts of EU institutions (Art 263 TFEU); to give preliminary rulings regarding the interpretation of the Treaties or the validity or interpretation of secondary law in respect of matters referred to it by national courts (Art 267 TFEU); and to hear appeals from the General Court on questions of law (Art 256(1) TFEU). Thus, it performs a number of functions which in the legal systems of the Member States are usually divided among the various branches of the judiciary. The ECJ only possesses the express powers that are enumerated in the Treaties.

[11.80] Causes of Actions

Any discussion of the functions of the Court must distinguish between causes of actions and grounds of review. These causes of actions include:

(i) actions for annulment (Art 263 TFEU);
(ii) actions for failure to act (Art 265 TFEU);
(iii) actions for non-fulfilment of obligations under Treaties (Arts 258–260 TFEU);
(iv) preliminary rulings (Art 267 TFEU); and
(v) indirect actions (Art 277 TFEU).

[11.85] Action for Annulment

Art 263 TFEU reads as follows:

> The Court of Justice of the European Union shall review the legality of legislative acts, of acts of the Council, of the Commission and of the European Central Bank, other than recommendations and opinions, and of acts of the European Parliament and of the European Council intended to produce legal effects vis-à-vis third parties. It shall also review the legality of acts of bodies, offices or agencies of the Union intended to produce legal effects vis-à-vis third parties.
>
> It shall for this purpose have jurisdiction in actions brought by a Member State, the European Parliament, the Council or the Commission on grounds of lack of competence, infringement of an essential procedural requirement, infringement of the Treaties or of any rule of law relating to their application, or misuse of powers....
>
> Any natural or legal person may, under the conditions laid down in the first and second paragraphs, institute proceedings against an act addressed to that person or which is of direct and individual concern to them, and against a regulatory act which is of direct concern to them and does not entail implementing measures....
>
> The proceedings provided for in this Article shall be instituted within two months of the publication of the measure, or of its notification to the plaintiff, or, in the absence thereof, of the day on which it came to the knowledge of the latter, as the case may be.

The action for annulment may be brought by, inter alia, the Council, the Commission or the Member States. A local or regional government is not regarded as a Member State under this provision, but is treated as a legal person. See *Région Wallonne v Commission* (C-95/97) [1997] ECR I-1787 at [6]; *Regione Siciliana v Commission* (C-417/04 P) [2006] ECR I-3881 at [21]; [2006] 2 CMLR 64 (p 1557).

As amended by the Treaty of Lisbon, this provision distinguishes between two types of proceedings brought by natural or legal persons (such as individuals or companies). A natural or legal person may bring an action against an act that is addressed to them "or which is of direct and individual concern to them". By contrast, such persons may bring an action against a regulatory act provided that it "is of direct concern to them and does not entail implementing measures".

An EU measure may be challenged by an action for annulment only if its "legal effects ... are binding on, and capable of affecting the interests of, the applicant by bringing about a distinct change in his legal position". See *Bossi v Commission* (346/87) [1989] ECR 303 at [23]; *Portugal v Commission* (C-249/02) [2004] ECR I-10717 at [35]; *R J Reynolds Tobacco Holdings Inc v Commission* (C-131/03 P) [2006] ECR I-7795 at [54]; [2007] 1 CMLR 1 (p 1); *Commission v Ferriere Nord SpA* (C-516/06 P) [2007] ECR I-10685 at [27]; [2008] 4 CMLR 10 (p 267). See generally, Carmen Martínez Capdevila, "The Action for Annulment, the Preliminary Reference on Validity and the Plea of Illegality: Complementary or Alternative Means?" (2006) 25 *Yearbook of European Law* 451.

Art 263 TFEU provides that an action for annulment must be brought "within 2 months of the publication of the measure, or of its notification to the plaintiff, or, in the absence thereof, of the day on which it came to the knowledge of the latter". If an action is not brought within this time, a decision becomes definitive against its addressee. See *TWD Textilwerke Deggendorf GmbH v Germany* (C-188/92) [1994] ECR I-833 at [13]; [1995] 2 CMLR 145; *Wiljo NV v Belgium* (C-178/95) [1997] ECR I-585 at [19]; [1997] 1 CMLR 627; *Commission v AssiDomän Kraft Products AB* (C-310/97 P) [1999] ECR I-5363 at [57]; [1999] 5 CMLR 1253.

The action for annulment aims at a declaration of invalidity of the relevant "acts". An EU act may be partially annulled if it is possible to sever the invalid part from the remainder of the act. See *Germany v Commission* (C-239/01) [2003] ECR I-10333 at [33]; *Re Cosmetic Products Directive: France v Parliament* (C-244/03) [2005] ECR I-4021 at [12]; [2005] 3 CMLR 6 (p 118).

If the act is annulled, then the Court usually declares it void with retrospective effect. See *Roquette Frères SA v Hauptzollamt Geldern* (C-228/92) [1994] ECR I-1445 at [17]. However, the Court may "state which of the effects of the act which it has declared void shall be considered as definitive" (Art 264 TFEU). The Court has interpreted this provision as giving it the power to "limit the temporal effect" of a ruling of invalidity. See *Roquette Frères SA v Hauptzollamt Geldern* (C-228/92) [1994] ECR I-1445 at [19]–[20]. This power will be exercised sparingly, and will only be used in exceptional cases. See *Ampafrance SA v Directeur des Services Fiscaux de Maine-et-Loire* (C-177/99) [2000] ECR I-7013 at [66]; *Stradasfalti Srl v Agenzia delle Entrate Ufficio di Trento* (C-228/05) [2006] ECR I-8391 at [72].

The Court has the power to order interim measures (Art 279 TFEU). The purpose of an order of interim measures is to enable a final judgment to have full effect. See *Martinez v Parliament* (T-222/99 R) [1999] ECR II-3397 at [79]; [2002] 1 CMLR 31 (p 893). The Court does not consider the admissibility of the main application when it hears an application for interim measures, except where it is argued that the main application is manifestly inadmissible. See *Martinez v Parliament* (T-222/99 R) [1999] ECR II-3397 at [60]; [2002] 1 CMLR 31 (p 893); *Rothley v Parliament* (T-17/00 R) [2000] ECR II-2085 at [45]; [2002] 2 CMLR 29 (p 737). The Court also has the power to order that the application of a challenged act be suspended while it considers the case (Art 278 TFEU).

See generally, Edurne Navarro Varona and Ilenar Gonzalez Durantez, "Interim Measures in Competition Cases before the European Commission and Courts" (2002) 23 *European Competition Law Review* 512; Dimitrios Sinaniotis, *Interim Protection of Individuals Before the European and National Courts* (Alphen aan den Rijn: Kluwer, 2006); F Castillo de la Torre, "Interim Measures in Community Courts: Recent Trends" (2007) 44 *Common Market Law Review* 273.

[11.90] Characteristic of a Reviewable Act

The ECJ reviews the legality of acts of the Council and the Commission intended to produce legal effects vis-à-vis third parties. It follows that the characteristic of a reviewable act in the EU is the binding nature of these acts. Only acts which have legal effect such as Regulations, Directives and Decisions are reviewable acts under Art 263 TFEU. Recommendations or opinions are excluded from the Court's review jurisdiction. Those instruments are not binding (Art 288 TFEU).

[11.95] Substance Not Form

In determining the reviewability of an act, the Court is concerned with the substance and not merely the form of the act. Thus, a decision expressed in the form of an opinion may in substance be a decision. Such will be the case where an act is expressed as a mere opinion if it has the effect of altering the legal position of the person to whom it is addressed.

This is illustrated by the case of *Re Noordwijks Cement Accoord* (8/66) [1967] ECR 75; [1967] CMLR 77. Several undertakings applied to the Court for the annulment of a "decision" constituted by a letter from the Commission. The Commission argued that the proceedings were inadmissible on the ground that its letter was a mere "opinion" which was not reviewable (at ECR 90, CMLR 102). The Court rejected the Commission's argument:

> The effect of the [letter] was that the undertakings ceased to be protected by [a provision] which exempted them from fines, and came under the contrary rules of [another provision] which thenceforth exposed them to the risk of fines. This measure deprived them of the advantages of a legal situation . . . and exposed them to a grave financial risk. Thus the said measure affected the interests of the undertakings by bringing about a distinct change in their legal position. It is unequivocally a measure which produces legal effects touching the interests of the undertakings concerned and which is binding on them. It thus constitutes not a mere opinion but a decision (at ECR 91, CMLR 102).

[11.100] Review Is Not Limited to Regulations, Decisions or Directives

In *Re European Road Transport Agreement: Commission v Council* (22/70) [1971] ECR 263; [1971] CMLR 335 the Council argued that an "act" was only reviewable if it was drafted in the form of a Regulation, Decision or Directive. The Council argued that its *discussion* regarding the negotiation and conclusion of the European Road Transport Agreement was "nothing more than a coordination of policies amongst Member States within the framework of the Council, and as such created no rights, imposed no obligations and did not modify any legal position" (at [36]). The ECJ rejected the Council's argument:

> Since the only matters excluded from the scope of the action for annulment open to the Member States and the institutions are 'recommendations or opinions' – which . . . are declared to have no binding force – Article 173 [now Art 263 TFEU] treats as acts open to review by the court all measures adopted by the institutions which are intended to have legal force. The objective of this review is to ensure . . . observance of the law in the interpretation and application of the Treaty. It would be inconsistent with this objective to interpret the conditions under which the action is admissible so restrictively as to limit the availability of this procedure merely to the categories of measures referred to by Article 189 [now Art 288 TFEU]. An action for annulment must therefore be available in the case of all measures adopted by the institutions, whatever their nature or form, which are intended to have legal effects (at [39]–[42]).

The Court continues to follow this interpretation. See *Commission v France* (C-366/88) [1990] ECR I-3571 at [8]; [1992] 1 CMLR 205; *Parliament v Council* (C-181/91) [1993] ECR I-3685 at [13]; [1994] 3 CMLR 317; *Commission v Council* (C-27/04) [2004] ECR I-6649 at [44]; *Italy v Commission* (C-301/03) [2005] ECR I-10217 at [19].

As a result, the number of reviewable acts is not limited or exhausted by the list provided in Art 288 TFEU. The fact that an act may not take the form of a Regulation, Directive or Decision should not, of itself, preclude its reviewability if in substance it is a legal act that has a legal effect upon the person, institution or Member State to whom or to which it is addressed. Art 263 TFEU thus refers to acts intended to produce legal effects vis-à-vis third parties. Acts that do not have "legal effects which are binding on and capable of affecting the interests of the individual" are excluded from review under Art 263. See *R J Reynolds Tobacco Holdings Inc v Commission* (C-131/03 P) [2006] ECR I-7795 at [55]; [2007] 1 CMLR 1 (p 1).

[11.105] Reviewability of "Acts" of the Institutions and Other Bodies

Art 263 TFEU expressly authorises the Court to review the validity of "acts" of the Council, Commission, European Central Bank, European Parliament and the European Council. Art 263 provides that the Member States, European Parliament, the Council and the Commission may bring actions concerning the legality of EU acts. The Court of Auditors, European Central Bank and the Committee of the Regions may bring actions for the purpose of protecting their prerogatives. An action for annulment may only be brought against the institution that adopted the challenged act, not against other EU institutions. See *Austria v Council* (C-445/00) [2003] ECR I-8549 at [32].

[11.106] Grounds of Review

The grounds of review are described in the second paragraph of Art 263 TFEU. One of the grounds of review is lack of competence, known in common law countries as ultra vires. It means that there is no power to adopt an act unless authorized to do so by a Treaty provision. The preamble of EU secondary legislation usually refers to the Treaty Article upon which the law is based. However, if an Article is nominated, it is necessary that the requirements stipulated in it are satisfied. See *Re Generalised Tariff Preferences: Commission v Council* (45/86) [1987] ECR 1493 at [13]; [1988] 2 CMLR 131.

The second ground of review is the infringement of an essential procedural requirement. Such a requirement could be laid down in a treaty provision or secondary legislation or a general principle of law. An example is the requirement to give reasons under Art 296 TFEU. The third ground of review is an infringement of the Treaties or of any rule of law relating to their application.

The fourth ground of review is misuse of power, which is the exercise of a power for a purpose other than that for which it was granted (improper purpose) or to "evad[e] a procedure specifically prescribed by the Treaty for dealing with the circumstances of the case". See *Netherlands v Commission* (C-452/00) [2005] ECR I-6645 at [114]; *Re New Cotton Support Scheme: Spain v Council* (C-310/04) [2006] ECR I-7285 at [69]; [2006] 3 CMLR 47 (p 1277); *Dalmine SpA v Commission* (C-407/04 P) [2007] ECR I-829 at [99].

This plea is rarely made out. However, misuse of power was established in *Giuffrida v Council* (105–75) [1976] ECR 1395. An internal promotions process was undertaken with the sole intention of appointing a particular candidate (at [10]). The Court held that this was a misuse of power since it was contrary to the purpose of any recruitment or promotion procedure (at [11]). See also *Schwierung v Court of Auditors* (142/85) [1986] ECR 3177 at [15].

[11.110] Action for Failure to Act

Under Art 265 TFEU claimants are able to proceed against the unlawful omission of an EU institution or other body. This article reads as follows:

> Should the European Parliament, the European Council, the Council, the Commission or the European Central Bank, in infringement of the Treaties, fail to act, the Member States and the other institutions of the Union may bring an action before the Court of Justice... to have the infringement established. This Article shall apply, under the same conditions, to bodies, offices and agencies of the Union which fail to act.

> The action shall be admissible only if the institution, body, office or agency concerned has first been called upon to act. If, within two months of being so called upon, the institution, body, office or agency concerned has not defined its position, the action may be brought within a further period of two months.
>
> Any natural or legal person may, under the conditions laid down in the preceding paragraphs, complain to the Court that an institution, body, office or agency of the Union has failed to address to that person any act other than a recommendation or an opinion.

Actions for failure to act may be brought by the Member States and the "other institutions" of the Union. The phrase "other institutions" includes the Parliament. In *Parliament v Council* (13/83) [1985] ECR 1513; [1986] 1 CMLR 138 the Court held that Art 175 (now Art 265 TFEU) gives the same right of action to all the Community institutions, including the Parliament (at [17]).

Art 265 is an application for a finding that various institutions or bodies have failed to take an action. The judgment of the Court only establishes the illegality of the specific failure to act. The Court does not order the taking of the necessary measures. However, in accordance with Art 266 TFEU "[t]he institution whose act has been declared void or whose failure to act has been declared contrary to the Treaties shall be required to take the necessary measures to comply with the judgment of the Court of Justice".

[11.115] Action for Failure to Fulfil a Treaty Obligation

An action for failure to fulfil a Treaty obligation is based on Art 258 TFEU:

> If the Commission considers that a Member State has failed to fulfil an obligation under the Treaties, it shall deliver a reasoned opinion on the matter after giving the State concerned the opportunity to submit its observations.
>
> If the State concerned does not comply with the opinion within the period laid down by the Commission, the latter may bring the matter before the Court of Justice of the European Union.

The importance of this Article lies in the fact that it is used often by the Commission to compel Member States to fulfil their obligations under the Treaties. For example, Art 258 TFEU (formerly Art 169 EU) has been relied upon by the Commission to compel Member States to cease violations of the Treaty's prohibition of quantitative restrictions on imports and measures having equivalent effect. See *Commission v Italy* (7/61) [1961] ECR 317; [1962] CMLR 39; *Re 'Buy Irish' Campaign: Commission v Ireland* (249/81) [1982] ECR 4005; [1983] 2 CMLR 104. The Commission may bring an action under Art 258 regarding an erroroneous interpretation of EU law by a national court. See *Commission v Spain* (C-154/08) [2009] ECR.

In *Commission v Germany* (C-20/01) [2003] ECR I-3609 the Court held that when the Commission brings an action for failure to fulfill an obligation under the Treaties, the Commission does not need to demonstrate a specific interest in so doing (at [29]). In bringing such an action the

Commission does not act in its own interest but in its role as "guardian of the Treaty" (at [29]–[30]). The Commission alone decides whether it is appropriate to bring such an action (at [30]). See similarly, *Commission v Greece* (C-394/02) [2005] ECR I-4713 at [14]–[16].

A Member State may also bring an action against another Member State alleging failure to fulfil an obligation under the Treaties (Art 259 TFEU). For rare examples of such actions, see *Belgium v Spain* (C-388/95) [2000] ECR I-3123; *Re Gibraltar European Elections: Spain v United Kingdom* (C-145/04) [2006] ECR I-7917; [2007] 1 CMLR 3 (p 87).

If the Court holds that a Member State has not fulfilled an obligation under the founding Treaties, the State must comply with the Court's judgment (Art 260(1) TFEU). The Member State must immediately begin the process for complying with the judgment and compliance must be achieved as soon as possible. See *Commission v Spain* (C-278/01) [2003] ECR I-14141 at [27].

The Court may impose a lump sum or penalty against a State that does not comply with its judgment (Art 260(2) TFEU). The Court has explained that a lump sum will be suitable where the Member State has persisted in its breach for a long period after the Court passed judgment. By comparison, a penalty seeks to persuade a Member State to cease its breach as soon as possible. See *Commission v Greece* (C-387/97) [2000] ECR I-5047 at [90]; *Commission v France* (C-304/02) [2005] ECR I-6263 at [81]; [2005] 3 CMLR 13 (p 275); *Commission v Greece* (C-568/07) [2009] ECR at [45].

Until 2005 it was the practice of the Commission to seek penalties in respect of non-compliance with EU law *after* the ECJ had delivered a judgment to that effect. The Commission did not seek penalties for non-compliance with Treaty obligations during the period *before* the ECJ rendered judgment. This practice meant that there was an incentive to delay compliance. Since 2005 where the Member State complies with its Treaty obligations after the case is brought but before judgment is delivered, the Commission will seek a lump sum for the entire period of the infringement. See *Communication from the Commission: Application of Article 228 of the EC Treaty* (SEC(2005) 1658) at [10.1], [11].

See generally, Maria A Theodossiou, "An Analysis of the Recent Response of the Community to Non-compliance with Court of Justice Judgments: Article 228(2) EC" (2007) 27 *European Law Review* 25; Stine Andersen, "Procedural Overview and Substantive Comments on Articles 226 and 228 EC" (2008) 27 *Yearbook of European Law* 121.

[11.120] Indirect Actions

Indirect actions are based on Art 277 TFEU. It states that notwithstanding the expiry of the 2 months period stipulated in Art 263, "any party may, in proceedings in which an act of general application adopted by an institution, body, office or agency of the Union is at issue, plead the grounds specified in Article 263, second paragraph, in order to invoke before the Court of Justice ... the inapplicability of that act."

Assume that the Council adopted a regulation which was not the subject of an annulment procedure under Art 263. Assume further that the regulation is the basis of a subsequent implementing measure which is addressed to an individual. The affected individual may, at that time, raise the illegality of the regulation in order to make it inapplicable to the applicant and consequently to annul the implementing measure based on it. In such circumstances, although the applicant cannot initiate annulment proceedings under Art 263, it is possible to challenge the regulation indirectly by arguing by way of defence that the regulation should be inapplicable to the applicant.

[11.125] Preliminary Rulings

Art 267 TFEU (formerly Art 177 EU) is one of the most important Articles of the Treaties. It deals with preliminary rulings. It aims to ensure the uniform application of EU law. In *CILFIT Srl v Ministro della Sanita* (283/81) [1982] ECR 3415; [1983] 1 CMLR 472 the Court stressed that the preliminary reference procedure "seeks to prevent the occurrence within the Community of divergences in judicial decisions on questions of Community law" (at [7]). The preliminary reference procedure "has the object of ensuring that in all circumstances this law is the same in all [Member] States". See *Rheinmühlen-Düsseldorf v Einfuhr- und Vorratsstelle für Getreide und Futtermittel* (166/73) [1974] ECR 33 at [2]; [1974] 1 CMLR 523.

For the purpose of facilitating a discussion of the relevant jurisprudence, it is desirable to set out most of the text of Art 267:

> The Court of Justice ... shall have jurisdiction to give preliminary rulings concerning:
>
> (a) the interpretation of the Treaties;
> (b) the validity and interpretation of acts of the institutions, bodies, offices or agencies of the Union;
>
> Where such a question is raised before any court or tribunal of a Member State, that court or tribunal may, if it considers that a decision on the question is necessary to enable it to give judgment, request the Court to give a ruling thereon.
>
> Where any such question is raised in a case pending before a court or tribunal of a Member State against whose decisions there is no judicial remedy under national law, that court or tribunal shall bring the matter before the Court.

Under Art 267 TFEU a national court or tribunal, in the course of proceedings, may refer questions involving the interpretation of the Treaty or the interpretation or validity of any EU legal act to the ECJ for a preliminary ruling. A ruling concerning validity is binding only on the national courts which have to reach a decision and therefore does not constitute a precedent.

A preliminary ruling must concern a question of EU law: the ECJ does not have jurisdiction over national legislation that is outside the scope of EU law. See *Criminal Proceedings Against Maurin* (C-144/95) [1996] ECR I-2909 at [12]; *Kremzow v Austria* (C-299/95) [1997] ECR I-2629 at [15]; [1997] 3 CMLR 1289; *Criminal Proceedings Against Vajnai* (C-328/04) [2005] ECR I-8577 at [12]–[13]; *Columbus Container Services BVBA & Co v Finanzamt Bielefeld-Innenstadt* (C-298/05) [2007] ECR I-10451 at [47]; [2009] 1 CMLR 8 (p 241). The interpretation of national law is the task of the national courts not the European Court. See *Wilson v Ordre des avocats du barreau de Luxembourg* (C-506/04) [2006] ECR I-8613 at [34]; [2007] 1 CMLR 7 (p 217); *Productores de Musica de España (Promusicae) v Telefonica de España SAU* (C-275/06) [2008] ECR I-271 at [38]; [2008] 2 CMLR 17 (p 465).

The Court has described the preliminary ruling system as involving a dialogue between courts. See *Willy Kempter AG v Hauptzollamt Hamburg-Jonas* (C-2/06) [2008] ECR I-411 at [42]; [2008] 2 CMLR 21 (p 586); *Eckelkamp v Belgium* (C-11/07) [2008] ECR I-6845 at [34]; [2008] 3 CMLR 44 (p 1137). The system is one of cooperation between the ECJ and the national courts. See *Union Royale Belge des Sociétés de Football Association ASBL v Bosman* (C-415/93) [1995] ECR I-4921 at [59]–[60]; [1996] 1 CMLR 645; *Kamer van Koophandel en Fabrieken voor Amsterdam v Inspire Art Ltd* (C-167/01) [2003] ECR I-10155 at [42], [45]; [2005] 3 CMLR 34 (p 937).

Following the Court's interpretation of the relevant Treaty provision or legal act, the matter is referred back to the national court for the application of the law in question in accordance with the preliminary ruling. See *Alabaster v Woolwich plc* (C-147/02) [2004] ECR I-3101 at [52]; [2004] 2 CMLR 9 (p 186); *Centrum voor gelijkheid van kansen en voor racismbestrijding v Firma Feryn NV* (C-54/07) [2008] ECR I-5187 at [19]; [2008] 3 CMLR 22 (p 695).

Under the preliminary ruling procedure the ECJ does not rule upon the compatibility of the law of the Member States with EU law. The national courts make that determination. However, the ECJ gives the national court all guidance necessary for the national court to determine the compatibility of a national law with EU law. See *Productores de Musica de España (Promusicae) v Telefonica de España SAU* (C-275/06) [2008] ECR I-271 at [38]; [2008] 2 CMLR 17 (p 465).

This interaction between the ECJ and national courts ensures that the jurisdiction of the national courts in respect of the application of EU law in any litigation remains exclusive. The Court of Justice does not act in a supervisory capacity or as an appellate court. Rather, it acts as an integral part of the national judicial system with the specific role of interpreting EU law and thereby facilitating the task of the national court in its application of EU law.

A preliminary ruling may relate to the validity of an EU legal measure. In *Woodspring District Council v Bakers of Nailsea Ltd* (C-27/95) [1997] ECR I-1847; [1997] 2 CMLR 266 the Court observed that the national courts do not need to seek a preliminary ruling if they consider an EU act to be valid (at [19]).

In contrast, a national court must seek a preliminary ruling if it considers that an EU legal measure is invalid. See *R (on the Application of International Air Transport Association) v Department for Transport* (C-344/04) [2006] ECR I-403 at [30]; [2006] 2 CMLR 20 (p 557). Only the ECJ may rule that an EU legal act is invalid. See *Krüger GmbH & Co KG v Hauptzollamt Hamburg-Jonas* [1997] ECR I-4517 at [51]; [1998] 1 CMLR 520; *Association Greenpeace France v Ministère de l'Agriculture et de la Pêche* (C-6/99) [2000] ECR I-1651 at [54]; [2001] 2 CMLR 45 (p 1129).

National courts thus do not have power to hold EU legal measures invalid. See *Foto-Frost v Hauptzollamt Lubeck-Ost* (314/85) [1987] ECR 4199 at [20]; [1988] 3 CMLR 571; *Gaston Schul Douane-expediteur BV v Minister van Landbouw, Natuur en Voedselkwaliteit* (C-461/03) [2005] ECR I-10513 at [17]. If they exercised such a power the unity of EU law and legal certainty would be imperilled. See *Woodspring District Council v Bakers of Nailsea Ltd* (C-27/95) [1997] ECR I-1847 at [20]; [1997] 2 CMLR 266. Decisions of national courts applying EU law are available on the free database Dec.Nat: National Decisions (http://www.juradmin.eu/en/jurisprudence/jurisprudence_en.lasso) and the subscription database Caselex (http://caselex.com). The decisions of British and Irish courts regarding issues of EU law are reported in the *European Law Reports* (Hart, 1997–).

The ECJ presumes that EU legal acts are valid. EU acts thus have legal effect until they are annulled or repealed. An EU act would only have no legal effect at all in an extreme case. See *Hüls AG v Commission* (C-199/92 P) [1999] ECR I-4287 at [84]–[86]; [1999] 5 CMLR 1016; *Montecatini SpA v Commission* (C-235/92 P) [1999] ECR I-4539 at [96]–[98]; [2001] 4 CMLR 18 (p 691).

EU decisions are not acts of general application. After the expiry of the 2 month period in Art 263 TFEU, they may not be challenged by the indirect means of the preliminary ruling procedure (Art 267 TFEU). See *TWD Textilwerke Deggendorf GmbH v Germany* (C-188/92) [1994] ECR I-833 at [17]–[18]; [1995] 2 CMLR 145; *Wiljo NV v Belgium* (C-178/95) [1997] ECR I-585 at [21]; [1997] 1 CMLR 627; *Nachi Europe GmbH v Hauptzollamt Krefeld* (C-239/99) [2001] ECR I-1197 at [29]–[30]. There is an urgent preliminary ruling procedure in relation to the area of freedom, security and justice. See Art 23a, Protocol (No 3) on the Statute of the Court of Justice.

See generally, Michael O'Neill, "Article 177 and the Limits to the Right to Refer: An End to the Confusion" (1996) 2 *European Public Law* 375; Anthony Arnull, "The Past and Future of the Preliminary Rulings Procedure"

(2002) 13 *European Business Law Review* 183; Caitríona McCarthy, "Europe's Iron Fist in a Judicial Velvet Glove? The Power of Article 234 and the Question of Reform" (2003) 4 *Hibernian Law Journal* 223; Information Note on References from National Courts for a Preliminary Ruling (OJ C 297, 5.12.2009, p 1); Jan Komárek, "In the Court(s) We Trust? On the Need for Hierarchy and Differentiation in the Preliminary Ruling Procedure" (2007) 32 *European Law Review* 467; Michal Bobek, "Learning to Talk: Preliminary Rulings, the Courts of the new Member States and the Court of Justice" (2008) 45 *Common Market Law Review* 1611; Alicia Farrell Miller, "The Preliminary Reference Procedure of the Court of Justice of the European Communities: A Model for the ICJ?" (2009) 32 *Hastings International and Comparative Law Review* 669; René Barents, *Directory of EU Case Law on the Preliminary Ruling Procedure* (Alphen aan den Rijn: Kluwer Law International, 2009).

[11.130] Concept of "Court or Tribunal" in Art 267 TFEU

In determining whether a body is a "court or tribunal" under Art 267 TFEU, the ECJ considers "whether the body is established by law, whether it is permanent, whether its jurisdiction is compulsory, whether procedure before it is inter partes, whether it applies rules of law, and whether it is independent". See *Jokela and Pitkäranta* (C-9/97) [1998] ECR I-6267 at [18]; *Abrahamsson v Fogelqvist* (C-407/98) [2000] ECR I-5539 at [29]; *Österreichischer Gewerkschaftsbund, Gewerkschaft öffentlicher Dienst v Austria* (C-195/98) [2000] ECR I-10497 at [24]; [2002] 1 CMLR 14 (p 375); *Proceedings brought by Standesamt Stadt Niebüll* (C-96/04) [2006] ECR I-3561 at [12]; [2006] 2 CMLR 58 (p 1414).

The requirement of independence means that the members of a court or tribunal have external independence (such as protection against dismissal from office) and internal independence (neutrality). See *Wilson v Ordre des avocats du barreau de Luxembourg* (C-506/04) [2006] ECR I-8613 at [51]–[53]; [2007] 1 CMLR 7 (p 217).

The requirement of an inter partes procedure is not an "absolute" one. See *Dorsch Consult Ingenieurgesellschaft mbH v Bundesbaugesellschaft Berlin mbH* (C-54/96) [1997] ECR I-4961 at [31]; [1998] 2 CMLR 237; *Gabalfrisa SL v Agencia Estatal de Administración Tributaria* (C-110/98) [2000] ECR I-1577 at [37]; [2002] 1 CMLR 13 (p 343); *De Coster v Collège des bourgmestre et échevins de Watermael-Boitsfort* (C-17/00) [2001] ECR I-9445 at [14]; [2002] 1 CMLR 12 (p 285).

The concept of "court or tribunal" in Art 267 has been very widely interpreted by the Court. For example, in *Broekmeulen v Huisarts Registratie Commissie* (246/80) [1981] ECR 2311; [1982] 1 CMLR 91, a professional registration body acting under a degree of governmental supervision was deemed to constitute a court or tribunal if that body created appeals procedures which could affect the rights or the exercise of the rights granted by EU law (at [17]).

Other bodies that have been held to be a court or tribunal include:

- the Austrian Supreme Court when giving a declaratory decision: *Österreichischer Gewerkschaftsbund, Gewerkschaft öffentlicher Dienst v Austria* (C-195/98) [2000] ECR I-10497 at [27]–[32]; [2002] 1 CMLR 14 (p 375);
- a national court that was required by an arbitration agreement to give a decision that was fair and reasonable: *Municipality of Almelo v NV Energiebedrijf Ijsselmij* (C-393/92) [1994] ECR I-1477 at [22]–[24];
- the Italian Council of State when giving its opinion on an extraordinary petition: *Garofalo v Ministero della Sanita* (C-69/96) [1997] ECR I-5603 at [5]–[14]; [1998] 1 CMLR 1087;
- the Finnish Rural Business Appeals Board: *Jokela and Pitkäranta* (C-9/97) [1998] ECR I-6267 at [20]–[24];
- a German Federal Board supervising the award of contracts: *Dorsch Consult Ingenieurgesellschaft mbH v Bundesbaugesellschaft Berlin mbH* (C-54/96) [1997] ECR I-4961 at [24]–[38]; [1998] 2 CMLR 237;
- an appeals board hearing appeals against university appointment decisions: *Abrahamsson v Fogelqvist* (C-407/98) [2000] ECR I-5539 at [30]–[38]; and
- a British Immigration Adjudicator: *El-Yassini v Secretary of State for the Home Department* (C-416/96) [1999] ECR I-1209 at [18]–[22]; [1999] 2 CMLR 32.

While broad, the concept of court or tribunal is not without boundaries. In *Nordsee Deutsche Hochseefischerei GmbH v Reederei Mond Hochseefischerei Nordstern AG & Co Ltd* (102/81) [1982] ECR 1095 the Court refused to recognise an arbitration tribunal as a court or tribunal within this Article. The parties were not legally or factually required to settle their disputes through arbitration (at [11]). The government of the Member State was not involved in the decision to choose arbitration and was not obliged to participate in the arbitration proceedings (at [12]). The link between the arbitration tribunal and the national judicial process was thus "not sufficiently close" for the arbitrator to constitute a court or tribunal under Art 267 (at [13]). See similarly, *Denuit v Transorient-Mosaïque Voyages and Culture SA* (C-125/04) [2005] ECR I-923 at [13]; [2005] 1 CMLR 48 (p 1291).

In *Synetairismos Farmakopoion Aitolias & Akarnanias (Syfait) v GlaxoSmithKline plc* (C-53/03) [2005] ECR I-4609; [2005] 5 CMLR 1 (p 1) the Court held that the Greek Competition Commission was not a "court or tribunal". The Commission was subject to ministerial supervision of its decisions (at [30]). There were insufficient safeguards for its members against dismissal (at [31]). The Commission was not separated from its fact finding secretariat, which had a role similar to that of a party in a competition case (at [33]). The ECJ also held that the Italian Office of the Public Prosecutor was not a court or tribunal. See *Criminal Proceedings Against X* (C-74/95) [1996] ECR I-6609 at [19]–[20].

The same national court may act as a "court or tribunal" when it carries out judicial functions, but will not act in that capacity when it carries out administrative functions. See *Azienda Nazionale Autonoma delle Strade* (C-192/98) [1999] ECR I-8583 at [22]. See generally, Morten Broberg, "Preliminary References by Public Administrative Bodies: When Are Public Administrative Bodies Competent to Make Preliminary References to the European Court of Justice?" (2009) 15 *European Public Law* 207.

[11.135] Scope of Art 267 TFEU

The scope of subparagraph 267(a) is clear and does not require any discussion: the provisions in any of the constitutive Treaties may be referred to the Court of Justice. The EU institutions referred to in subparagraph 267(b) are listed in Art 13(1) TEU: the European Parliament, European Council, Council, Commission, European Central Bank and the Court of Auditors. The provision also gives jurisdiction with respect to the validity and interpretation of acts of EU "bodies, offices or agencies."

The matters referred to the ECJ and the method of referral are left to the discretion of the national judges. As early as 1962 the Court admitted that its jurisdiction depends "solely on the existence of a request for a preliminary ruling" from the national court. See *Robert Bosch GmbH v Kleding Verkoopbedrijf de Geus en Uitdenbogerd* (13/61) [1962] ECR 45 at 50; [1962] CMLR 1 at 26.

The national court's discretion under Art 267 TFEU (formerly Art 177 EU) was considered by the ECJ in *Irish Creamery Milk Suppliers Association v Ireland* (36/80) [1981] ECR 735; [1981] 2 CMLR 455. The Court stated that "it is for the national court to decide at what stage in the proceedings it is appropriate for that court to refer a question to the court of justice for a preliminary ruling" (at [5]).

A national court requesting a preliminary ruling must set out the reasons why such a ruling is required. See *R (on the Application of International Air Transport Association) v Department for Transport* (C-344/04) [2006] ECR I-403 at [31]; [2006] 2 CMLR 20 (p 557). The referring Court must describe the factual and legislative context in which the question is raised. See *Telemarsicabruzzo SpA v Circostel* (C-320/90) [1993] ECR I-393 at [6]; *Re Laguillaumie* (C-116/00) [2000] ECR I-4979 at [15]; *Deutsche Lufthansa AG v ANA Aeroportos de Portugal SA* (C-181/06) [2007] ECR I-5903 at [33]. The Court gives a preliminary ruling only on the basis of the facts provided by the referring court. See *Assedic Pas-de-Calais*

AGS v Dumon (C-235/95) [1998] ECR I-4531 at [25]; [1999] 2 CMLR 113; *Eckelkamp v Belgium* (C-11/07) [2008] ECR I-6845 at [52]; [2008] 3 CMLR 44 (p 1137).

The jurisdiction of the European Court under Art 267 is limited to questions of EU law. See *Leur-Bloem v Inspecteur der Belastingdienst* (C-28/95) [1997] ECR I-4161 at [33]; [1998] 1 CMLR 157. In general where the questions referred by the national court relate to the interpretation of EU law, the ECJ is bound to give a preliminary ruling. See *PreussenElektra AG v Schleswag AG* (C-379/98) [2001] ECR I-2099 at [38]; [2001] 2 CMLR 36 (p 833); *Keller v Instituto Nacional de la Seguridad Social* (C-145/03) [2005] ECR I-2529 at [33]; *Mangold v Helm* (C-144/04) [2005] ECR I-9981 at [35]; [2006] 1 CMLR 43 (p 1132); *Chacón Navas v Eurest Colectividades SA* (C-13/05) [2006] ECR I-6467 at [32]; [2006] 3 CMLR 40 (p 1123); *Ministero dell'Industria, del Commercio e dell'Artigianato v Lucchini SpA* (C-119/05) [2007] ECR I-6199 at [43]; [2009] 1 CMLR 18 (p 501).

A presumption of relevance applies to the questions submitted by the referring court. See *Criminal Proceedings Against Pupino* (C-105/03) [2005] ECR I-5285 at [30]; [2005] 2 CMLR 63 (p 1569); *Cipolla v Fazari* (C-94/04) [2006] ECR I-11421 at [25]; [2007] 4 CMLR 8 (p 286); *Amurta v Belastingdienst* (C-379/05) [2007] ECR I-9569 at [64]; [2008] 1 CMLR 33 (p 851). The Court may decline to give a preliminary ruling only where the interpretation of EU law is not related to the main action, or the issue is hypothetical or the Court does not have the factual or legal material essential for giving a useful response to the questions asked. See *Kachelmann v Bankhaus Hermann Lampe KG* (C-322/98) [2000] ECR I-7505 at [17]; [2002] 1 CMLR 7 (p 155); *Vereniging voor Energie, Milieu en Water v Directeur van de Dienst uitvoering en toezicht Energie* (C-17/03) [2005] ECR I-4983 at [34]; [2005] 5 CMLR 8 (p 361); *Amurta v Belastingdienst* (C-379/05) [2007] ECR I-9569 at [64]; [2008] 1 CMLR 33 (p 851); *Eckelkamp v Belgium* (C-11/07) [2008] ECR I-6845 at [29]; [2008] 3 CMLR 44 (p 1137).

The Court does not render advisory opinions pursuant to the preliminary ruling procedure. See *Dias v Director da Alfândega do Porto* (C-343/90) [1992] ECR I-4673 at [17]; *Meilicke v ADV/ORGA F A Meyer AG* (C-83/91) [1992] ECR I-4871 at [25]; *Erasun v Instituto Nacional de Empleo* (C-422/93) [1995] ECR I-1567 at [29]; [1996] 1 CMLR 861. It will not give a preliminary ruling upon a hypothetical question. See *Meilicke v ADV/ORGA* (C-83/91) [1992] ECR I-4871 at [25]; *Kamer van Koophandel en Fabrieken voor Amsterdam v Inspire Art Ltd* (C-167/01) [2003] ECR I-10155 at [45]; [2005] 3 CMLR 34 (p 937); *Shield Mark BV v Kist* (C-283/01) [2003] ECR I-14313 at [52]–[53]; [2005] 1 CMLR 41 (p 1046); *EVN AG v Austria* (C-448/01) [2003] ECR I-14527 at [75], [83]; [2004] 1 CMLR 22 (p 739).

The Court may decline to give a ruling where the "interpretation of Community law or the examination of [its] validity . . . sought . . . bears no relationship to the true facts or the subject matter of the main proceedings." See *Imperial Chemical Industries plc v Colmer* (C-264/96) [1998] ECR I-4695 at [15]; [1998] 3 CMLR 293; *Arduino v Compagnia Assicuratrice RAS SpA* (C-35/99) [2002] ECR I-1529 at [25]; [2002] 4 CMLR 25 (p 866).

The Court has refused to reply to questions of interpretation which are merely procedural devices to obtain the view of the Court regarding an issue but which is not required for resolution of a dispute. See *Foglia v Novello (No 1)* (104/79) [1980] ECR 745 at [11]; [1981] 1 CMLR 45; *Foglia v Novello (No 2)* (244/80) [1981] ECR 3045 at [18]; [1981] 1 CMLR 585.

Where the submitted question has been improperly expressed, the Court has the power to extract the relevant issues of EU law from the grounds provided in the referral from the national court. See *Pigs Marketing Board v Redmond* (83/78) [1978] ECR 2347 at [26]; [1979] 1 CMLR 177; *Teckal Srl v Comune di Viano* (C-107/98) [1999] ECR I-8121 at [34]; *Oliehandel Koeweit BV v Minister van Volkshuisvesting* (C-307/00) [2003] ECR I-1821 at [105]; [2003] 2 CMLR 9 (p 273); *Chateignier v Office national de l'emploi* (C-346/05) [2006] ECR I-10951 at [19]; [2007] 1 CMLR 20 (p 618).

Where it finds it necessary to do so, the Court may consider provisions of EU law that were not referred to by the national court in its request for a preliminary ruling. See *Alevizos v Ipourgos Ikonomikon* (C-392/05) [2007] ECR I-3505 at [64]; [2007] 2 CMLR 51 (p 1404); *Mayr v Bäckerei und Konditorei Gerhard Flöckner OHG* (C-506/06) [2008] ECR I-1017 at [43]; [2008] 2 CMLR 27 (p 759).

[11.140] Obligatory References

The second paragraph of Art 267 gives a court or tribunal of a Member State the discretion to request the Court of Justice to give a preliminary ruling. However, where the national court considers that the arguments for invalidity are well founded, it must request a preliminary ruling. See *R (on the Application of International Air Transport Association) v Department for Transport* (C-344/04) [2006] ECR I-403 at [30]; [2006] 2 CMLR 20 (p 557).

Art 267 provides that a national court or tribunal against whose decisions there is no judicial remedy has an obligation to bring any such question before the Court of Justice. The principles governing the obligatory reference under Art 267 (formerly Art 177 EU) were considered in *CILFIT Srl v Ministro della Sanita* (283/81) [1982] ECR 3415; [1983] 1 CMLR 472. The Court held that Art 267 is not "a means of redress" for parties to a case in a national court (at [9]). The "mere fact" that a party raises a question within the meaning of Art 267 does not obligate a national court to refer the matter to the Court of Justice (at [9]). The national court against whose decisions there is no judicial remedy has the same discretion as any other national court to determine whether a decision on a question of EU law is necessary to enable it to give judgment (at [10]).

It would not be necessary for a question to be referred to the ECJ if it is "materially identical with a question which has already been the subject of a preliminary ruling in a similar case" (at [13]). Finally, where the correct application of EU law is "so obvious as to leave no scope for any reasonable doubt as to the manner in which the question raised is to be resolved", such a question need not be referred to the Court (at [16]). However, this obviousness must be equally apparent to the courts of other Member States and to the ECJ itself (at [16]).

In summary, the Court has held that a national court against whose decisions there is no judicial remedy is required to request a preliminary ruling unless the question at issue is irrelevant to the case, the ECJ has already interpreted the EU provision or the correct application of the EU provision is obvious. See *Gaston Schul Douane-expediteur BV v Minister van Landbouw, Natuur en Voedselkwaliteit* (C-461/03) [2005] ECR I-10513 at [16].

[11.145] Acts of the Institutions

The judicial law-making of the Court with regard to Art 267 mainly relates to its jurisdiction to give preliminary rulings concerning "the validity and interpretation of acts of institutions, bodies, offices or agencies of the Union". In *R & V Haegeman Sprl v Belgium* (181/73) [1974] ECR 449; [1975] 1 CMLR 515 the ECJ considered the Association Agreement between the EEC and Greece. The Agreement had been "concluded" by the Council. The Court held that the Agreement was an act of an institution of the Community (at [3]–[4]). The Court thus had jurisdiction to render preliminary rulings interpreting the Association Agreement (at [6]). See similarly, *Demirel v City of Schwäbisch* (12/86) [1987] ECR 3719 at [7]; [1989] 1 CMLR 421; *Sevince v Staatssecretaris van Justitie* (C-192/89) [1990] ECR I-3461 at [10]; [1992] 2 CMLR 57; *Andersson v Sweden* (C-321/97) [1999] ECR I-3551 at [26]; [2000] 2 CMLR 191.

T C Hartley accepted that the Court correctly held that it had jurisdiction to give a preliminary ruling in respect of the act of the Council providing for the conclusion of the Agreement. However, he argued that the Court should not have held that it had jurisdiction to give preliminary rulings in respect of the interpretation of the Agreement itself. Hartley argued that, as the party to the Agreement was the Community itself and not the Council, the Agreement could not constitute an act of an *institution* of the Community. See T C Hartley, *The Foundations of European Community Law* (6th ed, Oxford: Oxford University Press, 2007), 269. However, leaving the interpretation of treaties concluded by the EU to national courts would defeat the object of Art 267, namely ensuring the uniform interpretation of EU law.

[11.150] Judicial Policy-Making and Retroactivity

The Court's decisions have often been criticised on the ground that they involve judicial policy-making going beyond the function of a court. In particular, the Court's preference for methods of interpretation that take account of the "purposes" and "objectives" of the Treaties is often proffered by commentators as evidence of judicial policy-making.

The Court's judgment in *Defrenne v SABENA (No 2)* (43/75) [1976] ECR 455; [1976] 2 CMLR 98 provides an example of the Court's policy-making role. The Court held that the principle of "equal pay for equal work" in Art 119 (now Art 157 TFEU) could only be relied upon by workers who had already initiated legal proceedings before the date of the Court's judgment. The Court referred to the concerns expressed by the governments of several Member States regarding the adverse economic consequences of attributing direct effect to the Treaty provision at issue (at [69]).

The Court formulated a solution that removed the potential economic harm that might have resulted from the application of the doctrine of direct effect. The Court held that, exceptionally, the direct applicability of Art 119 would apply only to proceedings in national courts which were already pending or to those which were brought after the date of the judgment and related to events subsequent to the judgment. The Court decided that the principle of "equal pay for equal work" could not be used to support claims concerning pay periods prior to the date of its judgment, except as regards those workers who had already initiated legal proceedings (at [74]–[75]).

T C Hartley argues that the Court's reasoning was policy-based:

> the Court felt it expedient to sweeten the pill by ruling that only those workers who had instituted legal proceedings (or made equivalent claims) before the date of the judgment could rely on the direct effect of Article 141 [119] in order to claim back-pay for periods prior to that date. Thus Ms Defrenne won her case but the Member States were shielded from an avalanche of similar claims.
>
> This ruling neatly reconciled the Court's policy with the interests of the Member States. But it did so at the expense of legal principle: there was no possible ground in law for limiting the effect of the judgment in this way... if the Community is to fulfil the expectations of its founders, it must be firmly based on the rule of law: this could be jeopardized if policy is allowed to override clear provisions of law. See T C Hartley, *The Foundations of European Community Law* (6th ed, Oxford: Oxford University Press, 2007), 77–78.

The Court's judgment in *Defrenne (No 2)* created much controversy. The controversy arose because of the well-established rule of EU law that "the interpretation which... the Court gives to a rule of Community law clarifies and defines where necessary the meaning and scope of that rule as it must be or ought to have been understood and applied from the time of its coming into force". See *Blaizot v University of Liège* (24/86) [1988] ECR 379 at [27]; [1989] 1 CMLR 57. Limiting the temporal effect of a judgment constitutes an exception to that general rule.

[11.155] Blaizot Case

Another example of the policy-making role of the Court is provided by *Blaizot v University of Liège* (24/86) [1988] ECR 379; [1989] 1 CMLR 57. In a challenge to a supplementary university enrolment fee paid by foreign nationals, the national court sought a preliminary ruling whether the teaching of veterinary science was to be treated as vocational training (at [7]). If the Court interpreted the term "vocational training" as including university teaching, the national court sought a clarification regarding the temporal effect of that interpretation (at [9]).

The Court resorted to a policy argument in support of the proposition that university teaching constituted vocational training. It stated that the exclusion of university teaching from the concept of vocational training would "result in unequal application of the Treaty in different member-States" (at [18]). In some Member States veterinary sciences were taught in universities, in others it was taught in different institutions. The exclusion of university teaching from the concept of "vocational training" would result in the teaching of veterinary sciences being characterised as vocational in one State but not in another State.

The Court once again declined to give its decision full retroactive effect, with the result that it was not necessary to refund the supplementary fee paid by most of the students. The Court stated that "pressing considerations of legal certainty preclude any re-opening of the question of past legal relationships" which were established in good faith "where that would retroactively throw the financing of university education into confusion and might have unforeseeable consequences for the proper functioning of universities" (at [34]). It could be argued that the result in *Blaizot* conflicts with the right to equality, which requires that all those who are similarly situated should be treated equally.

The Court's doctrine regarding the retroactive effect of its decisions may be summarised as follows. In general the Court interprets a provision of EU law as it should have been applied from the time it entered into force. See *R (on the Application of Bidar) v London Borough of Ealing* (C-209/03) [2005] ECR I-2119 at [69]; [2005] 2 CMLR 3 (p 56). However, the Court has the power to limit the temporal effect of a decision interpreting a rule of EU law. The financial consequences for a Member State of a decision are not in themselves a reason for limiting the ruling's temporal effect. See *R v Secretary of State for Health; Ex parte Richardson* (C-137/94) [1995]

ECR I-3407 at [37]; [1995] 3 CMLR 376; *R (on the Application of Bidar) v London Borough of Ealing* (C-209/03) [2005] ECR I-2119 at [68]; [2005] 2 CMLR 3 (p 56).

Limitation of temporal effect will be justified only where there is a "risk of serious economic consequences" because of the number of transactions entered into on the basis that the challenged act was valid. See *Richards v Secretary of State for Work and Pensions* (C-423/04) [2006] ECR I-3585 at [42]; [2006] 2 CMLR 49 (p 1242); *Brzezinski v Dyrektor Izby Celnej W Warszawie* (C-313/05) [2007] ECR I-513 at [57]–[58]; [2007] 4 CMLR 4 (p 121). See generally, Christian Waldhoff, "Recent Developments relating to the Retroactive Effect of Decisions of the ECJ" (2009) 46 *Common Market Law Review* 173.

[11.160] Conclusion

The Advocates-General are independent and impartial advisers who make reasoned submissions on cases in order to assist the Court of Justice. The Court has applied four methods of interpreting legal texts: literal, historical, contextual and teleological. The Court considers all language versions when interpreting an EU legal text.

In an action for annulment the Court reviews the legality of EU legal acts. Such an action may be brought by an individual or a company if the challenged legal act directly and individually concerns them. An action for annulment must be brought within 2 months of the publication of the measure or of its notification to the plaintiff or, in the absence thereof, of the day on which it came to the knowledge of the plaintiff.

The Court has power to limit the temporal effect of a ruling of invalidity. The Court reviews acts intended to produce legal effects vis-à-vis third parties. The grounds of review are lack of competence, infringement of an essential procedural requirement, infringement of the Treaties and misuse of power.

Claimants are also able to proceed against the unlawful omission of an EU institution (action for failure to act). The Commission may bring an action against a Member State for failure to fulfil a Treaty obligation. Notwithstanding the expiry of the 2 month period for an action for annulment, any party may, in proceedings in which an act of general application is at issue, plead the grounds of invalidity in order to invoke the inapplicability of that act.

A national court or tribunal in the course of proceedings may refer questions involving the interpretation of the Treaty or the interpretation or validity of any EU legal act to the ECJ for a preliminary ruling. A national court must seek a preliminary ruling if it considers that an EU legal measure is invalid. The concept of "court or tribunal" has been widely interpreted by the Court.

Further Reading

Anderson, David W K and Marie Demetriou. *References to the European Court* (2nd ed, London: Sweet & Maxwell, 2002).

Arnull, Anthony. *The European Union and its Court of Justice* (2nd ed, Oxford: Oxford University Press, 2006).

Bernitz, Ulf. "The Duty of Supreme Courts to Refer Cases to the ECJ: The Commission's Action Against Sweden" (2006) 2 *Swedish Studies in European Law* 37.

Brown, Lionel Neville and Tom Kennedy. *The Court of Justice of the European Communities* (5th ed, London: Sweet & Maxwell, 2000).

Cruz, Julio Baquero. "The Changing Constitutional Role of the European Court of Justice" (2006) 34 *International Journal of Legal Information* 223.

De Búrca, Gráinne and J H H Weiler. *The European Court of Justice* (Oxford: Oxford University Press, 2001).

de La Serre and E Barbier. "Accelerated and Expedited Procedures before the EC Courts: A Review of the Practice" (2006) 43 *Common Market Law Review* 783.

Groussot, Xavier and Timo Minssen. "Res Judicata in the Court of Justice Case-Law" (2007) 3 *European Constitutional Law Review* 385.

Johnson, Herbert A. "Judicial Institutions in Emerging Federal Systems: The Marshall Court and the European Court of Justice" (2000) 33 *John Marshall Law Review* 1063.

Lasok, Paul. *Lasok's European Court Practice and Procedure* (3rd ed, Haywards Heath, West Sussex: Tottel, 2010).

Lasser, Mitchel. "Anticipating Three Models of Judicial Control, Debate and Legitimacy: The European Court of Justice, the Cour de cassation and the United States Supreme Court", *Jean Monnet Working Paper* No 1/03, http://www.jeanmonnetprogram.org.

Lavranos, Nikolaos. "The Scope of the Exclusive Jurisdiction of the Court of Justice" (2007) 32 *European Law Review* 83.

Lenaerts, Koenraad; Dirk Arts and Ignace Maselis. *Procedural Law of the European Union* (2nd ed, London: Sweet & Maxwell, 2006).

Levin, Ronald M (et al.). *Administrative Law of the European Union/Judicial Review* (Chicago, IL: ABA Section of Administrative Law and Regulatory Practice, 2008).

Moens, Gabriël and Ted Tzovaras. "Judicial Law-making in the European Court of Justice" (1992) 17 *University of Queensland Law Journal* 76.

Plender, Richard (ed). *European Courts Procedure* (London: Sweet & Maxwell, 2000).

Stein, Eric. "Lawyers, Judges, and the Making of a Transnational Constitution" (1981) 75 *American Journal of International Law* 1.

Türk, Alexander H. *Judicial Review in EU Law* (Cheltenham, UK: Edward Elgar, 2009).

Chapter 12
The Effect of EU Law upon National Law

[12.05] Introduction

This chapter discusses two of the essential pillars of EU law: the doctrines of direct effect and supremacy. The direct effect of EU law ensures that individuals can invoke some EU treaty provisions and legislation in legal proceedings in the courts of Member States. The doctrine of supremacy ensures that EU law prevails over any inconsistent law of a Member State, whether it be legislation or the national constitution.

In 1977 Lord Mackenzie Stuart wrote that the "unique feature of Community law is that commonly referred to as 'direct effect', that is to say the concept that Community law can in appropriate circumstances create rights in favour of individuals which national courts must protect". See Lord Mackenzie Stuart, *The European Communities and the Rule of Law* (London: Stevens, 1977), 18.

The importance of this "unique feature" lies in the fact that it is futile for business people to seek to invoke a legal act of an EU institution which could not be relied upon in a national court. Indeed, before legal proceedings are initiated, it is necessary to ascertain first whether a provision is directly effective in the sense that it can be relied upon by the potential litigant in a national court.

[12.10] van Gend en Loos Case

The earliest pronouncement of the ECJ regarding the doctrine of direct effect is found in *NV Algemene Transport- en Expeditie Onderneming van Gend en Loos v Nederlandse Administratie der Belastingen* (26/62) [1963] ECR 1; [1963] CMLR 105. A Dutch company sought to invoke Community law in proceedings brought against the Dutch customs authorities in a Dutch tribunal. The Dutch company had imported a product from Germany for use in the manufacture of glue. When the EEC Treaty came into force, the product's classification under Dutch law attracted an import

G. Moens, J. Trone, *Commercial Law of the European Union*, Ius Gentium: Comparative Perspectives on Law and Justice 4, DOI 10.1007/978-90-481-8774-4_12, © Springer Science+Business Media B.V. 2010

duty of 3%. However, on the date of importation the product was subject to another classification which attracted a higher import duty (8%). This re-classification was made on the basis of newer findings about the product's composition.

The Dutch company argued that the imposition of higher customs duties was contrary to Art 12 of the EEC Treaty. At that time Art 12 provided that "Member States shall refrain from introducing between themselves any new customs duties on imports or exports or any charges having equivalent effect, and from increasing those which they already apply in their trade with each other." The Dutch tribunal requested a preliminary ruling on the question of "whether Art 12 of the Treaty has direct application in national law in the sense that nationals of Member States may on the basis of this Article lay claim to rights which the national court must protect" (at ECR 11; CMLR 129).

The Dutch government disputed the jurisdiction of the ECJ on the ground that the request related not to the interpretation of the Treaty but to its application under Dutch constitutional law. The government argued that in cases involving alleged incompatibility between national provisions and EEC Treaty provisions recourse should be had to the provisions of the Treaty that authorised the Commission and the Member States to initiate proceedings before the Court challenging those national laws.

The Court held that Art 12 produced a direct effect and created individual rights which the national courts must protect. The Court's observations will be quoted extensively because of their importance for the development of EU law:

> To ascertain whether the provisions of an international treaty extend so far in their effects it is necessary to consider the spirit, the general scheme and the wording of those provisions.
>
> The objective of the EEC Treaty, which is to establish a Common Market, the functioning of which is of direct concern to interested parties in the Community, implies that this Treaty is more than an agreement which merely creates mutual obligations between the contracting states. This view is confirmed by the preamble to the Treaty which refers not only to governments but to peoples..... The fact that... the Treaty enable the Commission and the Member States to bring before the Court a State which has not fulfilled its obligations does not mean that individuals cannot plead these obligations, should the occasion arise, before a national court, any more than the fact that the Treaty places at the disposal of the Commission ways of ensuring that obligations imposed upon those subject to the Treaty are observed, precludes the possibility, in actions between individuals before a national court, of pleading infringements of these obligations.
>
> A restriction of the guarantees against an infringement of Article 12 by Member States to the procedures [by the Commission and the Member States]... would remove all direct legal protection of the individual rights of their nationals..... The vigilance of individuals concerned to protect their rights amounts to an effective supervision in addition to the supervision entrusted... to the diligence of the Commission and of the Member States (at ECR 12–13; CMLR 129–130).

The Court also pointed out that the procedure for preliminary rulings is predicated on the existence of directly effective Treaty provisions. If the provisions of the Treaty could not be directly effective the preliminary ruling procedure would be meaningless. The preliminary ruling procedure confirms that the Member States recognise that Community law "can be invoked by their nationals" before their courts (at ECR 12; CMLR 129).

In summary, the Court held that where a legal provision imposes an obligation upon Member States that affects private interests, that provision is capable of conferring a corresponding right upon the individual citizens of the Member States. In other words, that legal provision may be directly effective in that it grants individuals rights which are enforceable in national courts.

[12.15] Test for Direct Effect

In *van Gend en Loos* (26/62) [1963] ECR 1; [1963] CMLR 105 the Court formulated a test for determining whether a provision of the Treaty was directly effective:

> The wording of Article 12 contains a clear and unconditional prohibition which is not a positive but a negative obligation. This obligation, moreover, is not qualified by any reservation on the part of states which would make its implementation conditional upon a positive legislative measure enacted under national law. The very nature of this prohibition makes it ideally adapted to produce direct effects in the legal relationship between Member States and their subjects. The implementation of Article 12 does not require any legislative intervention on the part of the states (at ECR 13; CMLR 130).

This quotation reveals that a provision of the Treaty will be directly effective where (i) its text is clear and unambiguous; (ii) it imposes an unconditional prohibition in the sense that the rights it protects are not subject to the discretion of an EU institution or a Member State; and (iii) its implementation does not depend upon any further legislative action by the Member States. However, a limited state discretion is no bar to the direct effect of a Treaty provision. See *van Duyn v Home Office* (41/74) [1974] ECR 1337; [1975] 1 CMLR 1.

In *Alfons Lütticke GmbH v Hauptzollamt Saarlouis* (57/65) [1966] ECR 205; [1971] CMLR 674 the Court abandoned the suggestion in *van Gend en Loos* that only a negative prohibition could be directly effective. Art 95(3) EC imposed upon Member States an obligation to repeal or amend any provisions which conflicted with Art 95(1). Art 95(1) prohibited the imposition upon products from other Member States of internal taxation that was greater than that imposed upon similar domestic products (now Art 110 TFEU). The Court held that the obligation to amend or repeal inconsistent legislation could become directly effective (at ECR 210; CMLR 684).

[12.20] When Are Treaty Provisions Directly Effective?

Treaty provisions may become directly effective upon the expiration of any transitional period for which they provide, even if these provisions have not been implemented by the Member States. A good example of the Court's view on this issue is *Reyners v Belgium* (2/74) [1974] ECR 631; [1974] 2 CMLR 305. The Court stated that "[a]fter the expiry of the transitional period the Directives provided for by the chapter on the right of establishment have become superfluous with regard to implementing the rule on nationality, since this is henceforth sanctioned by the treaty itself with direct effect" (at [30]).

In this case a person of Dutch nationality had been born and educated in Belgium. He had obtained an undergraduate degree in law from a Belgian University. That degree was sufficient qualification for admission as an avocat (solicitor). However, his application for admission to practice was rejected because Belgian law provided that only Belgian citizens could practice law (at [2]). Art 52 of the EEC Treaty (now Art 49 TFEU) provided that "freedom of establishment shall include the right to take up and pursue activities as self-employed persons... under the conditions laid down for its own nationals by the law of the country where such establishment is effected."

The Court held that the freedom of establishment became directly effective upon expiry of the transitional period, even though it was not implemented by the Community and the Member States. The Court stated:

> In laying down that freedom of establishment shall be attained at the end of the transitional period, Article 52 thus imposes an obligation to attain a precise result, the fulfilment of which had to be made easier by, but not made dependent on, the implementation of a programme of progressive measures. The fact that this progression has not been adhered to leaves the obligation itself intact beyond the end of the period provided for its fulfilment. .... It is not possible to invoke against such an effect the fact that the Council has failed to issue the Directives provided for (at [26]–[29]).

The *Reyners* case was an ideal vehicle for the ECJ to develop the doctrine of "direct effect" in relation to the right of establishment. Indeed, Reyners met all the conditions which the state of establishment imposed upon its own nationals who proposed to become avocats. Even elementary fairness suggested that Reyners should not be prevented from practising his profession.

[12.25] Vertical and Horizontal Direct Effect

The *van Gend en Loos* and *Reyners* cases show that a directly effective provision of the EU Treaty protects EU citizens against restrictive measures taken by the Member States. This is the vertical direct effect of Treaty provisions, that is, their effect between individuals and the state. However, a Treaty provision may also have a horizontal direct effect in relations between individuals. In *Belgische Radio en Televisie v SV Sabam* (127/73) [1974] ECR 51; [1974] 2 CMLR 238 the Court stated that the competition rules enshrined in Arts 85(1) and 86 (now Arts 101(1) and 102 TFEU) "tend by their very nature to produce direct effects in relations between individuals" and "create direct rights in respect of the individuals concerned which the national courts must safeguard" (at [16]).

Similarly, in *Walrave v Association Union Cycliste Internationale* (36/74) [1974] ECR 1405; [1975] 1 CMLR 320 the Court emphasised that a measure may be directly effective when it affects the relationship between individuals. The Court suggested that the right to be free from discrimination on grounds of nationality "does not only apply to the action of public authorities but extends likewise to rules of any other nature aimed at regulating in a collective manner gainful employment and the provision of services" (at [17]). The Court has since confirmed the horizontal direct effect of the prohibition of discrimination on the ground of nationality. See *Angonese v Cassa di Risparmio di Blozano SpA* (C-281/98) [2000] ECR I-4139 at [35]–[36]; [2000] 2 CMLR 1120.

[12.30] Direct Applicability Versus Direct Effect

Art 288 TFEU provides that EU regulations have a general application and are binding in their entirety and are directly applicable in all Member States. There is a distinction between "direct applicability" and "direct effect". See J A Winter, "Direct Applicability and Direct Effect: Two Distinct and Different Concepts in Community Law" (1972) 9 *Common Market Law Review* 425; Koen Lenaerts, "Constitutionalism and the Many Faces of Federalism" (1990) 38 *American Journal of Comparative Law* 205 at 210–212.

The distinction has been summarised as follows:

> The doctrine of direct applicability refers to Treaty provisions or regulations, while the doctrine of direct effect, . . . primarily applies to directives. The wider legal concept of direct effect is the basis for the distinction between the doctrine of direct applicability and direct effect. While sharing the terminology with one doctrine, the concept of direct effect is inherent to both doctrines. . . . direct effect generally relates to the fact that Community law provisions, regardless of their character as a regulation, directive or Treaty provision, contain the possibility of creating individual rights for natural and legal persons which may be protected by national courts. Therefore, provisions which are directly applicable under the doctrine of direct applicability constitute direct effect. (Christoph Henkel, "Constitutionalism of the European Union: Judicial Legislation and Political Decision-Making by the European Court of Justice" (2001) 19 *Wisconsin International Law Journal* 153 at 156–157)

Art 288 TFEU leaves open whether regulations, while directly applicable, are of direct effect. Is a Regulation capable of conferring individual rights which national courts must protect? This question was considered by the Court in *Politi Sis v Ministry for Finance* (43/71) [1971] ECR 1039; [1973] CMLR 60. The ECJ held that "[u]nder the terms of the second paragraph of Art 189 [now Art 288 TFEU] Regulations 'shall have general application' and 'shall be... directly applicable in all Member States'" and that, therefore, "by reason of their nature and their function in the system of the sources of Community law, regulations have direct effect and are as such, capable of creating individual rights which national courts must protect" (at [9]). However, a Regulation is only directly effective if the *van Gend en Loos* (26/62) [1963] ECR 1; [1963] CMLR 105 test is satisfied.

[12.35] Direct Effect of Regulations

Regulations are incorporated into the legal system of the Member States upon their enactment by the relevant EU authorities. It is not necessary for Member States to incorporate EU regulations into their domestic law in accordance with their constitutional procedures. For many years Italy adopted the practice of implementing regulations by national statutes. In *Fratelli Variola Spa v Amministrazione Italiana delle Finanze* (34/73) [1973] ECR 981 the Court held that this practice was incompatible with EEC law. The Court stated that "Member States are under an obligation not to introduce any measure which might affect the jurisdiction of the Court to pronounce on any question involving the interpretation of Community law or the validity of an act of the institutions of the Community, which means that no procedure is permissible whereby the Community nature of a legal rule is concealed from those subject to it" (at [11]).

The concept of direct applicability thus refers to the fact that no further legislative measures need be taken by the Member States or EU institutions to ensure the reception of a Regulation by the national legal order. In *Leonesio v Italian Ministry of Agriculture and Forestry* (93/71) [1972] ECR 287; [1973] CMLR 343 the Court affirmed that "Community regulations become part of the legal system applicable within the national territory, which must permit the direct effect provided for in Article 189 [now Art 288 TFEU] to operate in such a way that reliance thereon by individuals may not be frustrated by domestic provisions or practices" (at [22]).

In *Politi Sis v Ministry for Finance* (43/71) [1971] ECR 1039; [1973] CMLR 60 the Court stated that "[t]he effect of a regulation, as provided for in Article 189 [now Art 288 TFEU], is therefore to prevent the implementation of any legislative measure, even if it is enacted subsequently, which is incompatible with its provisions" (at [9]).

The Court considered the direct application of Regulations in *Antonio Munoz Y Cia SA v Frumar Ltd* (C-253/00) [2002] ECR I-7289; [2002] 3

CMLR 26 (p 734). The Court held that a trade competitor had to be able to bring proceedings to enforce a Regulation concerning quality standards in an industry, in order to ensure the "full effectiveness" of the Regulation (at [30]). The availability of such proceedings would improve the "practical working" of the Regulation (at [31]).

[12.40] Direct Effect of Directives

While Directives must be implemented by the Member States, they may also be directly effective. Member States are under an obligation to achieve a particular legal result by the date specified in the Directive. During the period before that date, the Member States may not take measures that are "liable seriously to compromise" the achievement of that result. See *Inter-Environnement Wallonie ASBL v Région Wallonne* (C-129/96) [1997] ECR I-7411 at [45]; [1998] 1 CMLR 1057; *Mangold v Helm* (C-144/04) [2005] ECR I-9981 at [67]; [2006] 1 CMLR 43 (p 1132); *VTB-VAB NV v Total Belgium NV* (C-261/07) [2009] 3 CMLR 17 (p 697) at [38]. When a Member State correctly implements the Directive, it has effect upon the nationals of that State through the national implementing legislation. But if a Member State fails to implement to the Directive, Art 288 TFEU does not preclude the direct effect of the Directive within that State.

In *Grad v Finanzamt Traunstein* (9/70) [1970] ECR 825; [1971] CMLR 1 the Court stated that while "by virtue of Article 189 [now Art 288 TFEU], regulations are directly applicable and therefore by . . . their nature capable of producing direct effects, it does not follow from this that other categories of legal measures mentioned in that article can never produce similar effects" (at [5]). The value of Directives would be greatly diminished if, when Member States had failed to implement them, individuals could not rely upon them in national courts to support their causes.

The Court has held that EU law cannot be overridden by the failure of a Member State to adopt a Directive. In *van Duyn v Home Office* (41/74) [1974] ECR 1337; [1975] 1 CMLR 1 the Court dispelled any doubts about this matter. The Court explained why Directives are capable of being directly effective:

> It would be incompatible with the binding effect attributed to a Directive by Article 189 [now Art 288 TFEU] to exclude, in principle, the possibility that the obligation which it imposes may be invoked by those concerned. In particular, where the Community authorities have, by Directive, imposed on Member-States the obligation to pursue a particular course of conduct, the useful effect of such an act would be weakened if individuals were prevented from relying on it before their national courts and if the latter were prevented from taking it into consideration as an element of Community law. Article 177 [now Art 267 TFEU], which empowers national courts to refer to the Court questions concerning the validity and interpretation of all acts of the Community institutions, without distinction, implies

> furthermore that these acts may be invoked by individuals in the national courts. It is necessary to examine, in every case, whether the nature, general scheme and wording of the provision in question are capable of having direct effects on the relations between Member-States and individuals (at [12]).

Directives do not become directly effective before the expiry of the period fixed for its implementation by Member States. However, if the Directive has not been implemented before the expiry of that period, a Member State "may not apply its internal law... which has not yet been adapted in compliance with the Directive, to a person who has complied with the requirements of the Directive". See *Pubblico Ministero v Ratti* (148/78) [1979] ECR 1629 at [24]; [1980] 1 CMLR 96.

This view was confirmed in *Becker v Finanzamt Münster-Innenstadt* (8/81) [1982] ECR 53; [1982] 1 CMLR 499:

> a Member State which has not adopted the implementing measures required by the Directive within the prescribed period may not plead, as against individuals, its own failure to perform the obligations which the Directive entails. Thus, wherever the provisions of a Directive appear, as far as their subject-matter is concerned, to be unconditional and sufficiently precise, those provisions may, in the absence of implementing measures adopted within the prescribed period, be relied upon as against any national provision which is incompatible with the Directive or in so far as the provisions define rights which individuals are able to assert against the State (at [24]–[25]).

Thus, where a provision of a national law has been retained by a Member State and a Directive is inconsistent with that national law, individuals may rely upon the Directive in the national court to avoid the effect of the national law. The continuing validity of this proposition was confirmed in *Oberkreisdirector des Kreises Borken v Handelsonderneming Moormann BV* (190/87) [1988] ECR 4689; [1990] 1 CMLR 656. The Court said:

> The third paragraph of Article 189 of the Treaty [now Art 288 TFEU] provides that Directives are binding, as to the result to be achieved, upon each Member State to which they are addressed. Article 5 of the Treaty [now Art 4(3) TEU] requires the member states to take all appropriate measures to ensure fulfilment of the obligations arising out of the Treaty or resulting from action taken by the institutions of the Community. It follows from the binding effect which the third paragraph of Article 189 ascribes to Directives and the obligations of co-operation laid down in Article 5 that the member state to which a Directive is addressed cannot evade the obligations imposed by the Directive in question.
>
> As the court has consistently held, whenever the provisions of a Directive appear, as far as the subject matter is concerned, to be unconditional and sufficiently precise, they may be relied upon against a state which has failed to implement or has not correctly implemented the Directive within the prescribed period. In such circumstances the national court must give precedence to the provisions of the Directive over those of the conflicting national legislation (at [22]–[23]).

In *Francovich v Italy* (C-6/90) [1991] ECR 5357; [1993] 2 CMLR 66 the Community provision at issue was sufficiently precise and unconditional in some but not all respects. The provision required Member States to enact legislation guaranteeing payment of unpaid wages of the employees of an insolvent employer (at [3]). The provision identified who was to benefit from that guarantee and the content of the guarantee. It was sufficiently precise and unconditional in those respects. However, the provision did not identify the person who was required to guarantee payment of the wages. It was thus not sufficiently precise to be directly effective (at [26]).

In *Marshall v Southampton and South West Hampshire Area Health Authority (No 2)* (C-271/91) [1993] ECR I-4367; [1993] 3 CMLR 293 the Court held that the right of a Member State to select among different means for attaining the objective of a Directive did not preclude the direct effect of a Directive the content of which was sufficiently precise (at [37]).

In *Impact v Minister for Agriculture and Food* (C-268/06) [2008] ECR I-2483; [2008] 2 CMLR 47 (p 1265) the Court reiterated that "whenever the provisions of a Directive appear, so far as their subject-matter is concerned, to be unconditional and sufficiently precise, they may be relied upon by individuals as against the State" (at [57]). The Directive at issue prohibited the treatment of fixed-term workers in a less favourable manner than permanent workers in relation to employment conditions unless the difference in treatment was justifiable on objective grounds (at [59]). This provision of the Directive was "unequivocal" and sufficiently precise to be invoked by individuals and applied by the national courts (at [60]). A Directive may be given direct effect even though some of the terms used within it are not defined (at [61]).

[12.45] Vertical Versus Horizontal Direct Effect of Directives

An unimplemented Directive has a solely vertical direct effect, that is, it can only be relied upon as against a Member State and its agencies. See *R v Secretary of State for Employment; Ex parte Seymour-Smith* (Case C-167/97) [1999] ECR I-623 at [39]; [1999] 2 CMLR 273. For example, a Directive normally cannot be used against a private employer because it must be implemented by the Member States. An unimplemented Directive does not apply to the "sphere of relations between individuals". See *Faccini Dori v Recreb Srl* (C-91/92) [1994] ECR I-3325 at [23]–[24]; [1994] 1 CMLR 665.

In *Marshall v Southampton and South West Hampshire Area Health Authority* (152/84) [1986] ECR 723; [1986] 1 CMLR 688 the Court confirmed that "a Directive may not of itself impose obligations on an individual and that a provision of a Directive may not be relied upon as such against such a person" (at [48]). See similarly, *Coote v Granada Hospitality Ltd* (C-185/97) [1998] ECR I-5199 at [17]; [1998] 3 CMLR 958; *Unilever Italia SpA v Central Food SpA* (C-443/98) [2000] ECR I-7535 at [50]; [2001] 1 CMLR 21 (p 566).

In *Officier van Justitie v Kolpinghuis Nijmegen BV* (80/86) [1987] ECR 3969; [1989] 2 CMLR 18 a Dutch trader was prosecuted for stocking adulterated mineral water contrary to Dutch law and an unimplemented

Directive (at [2]–[3]). The Court held that, although the court might interpret the Dutch law in the light of the wording and purpose of the Directive, the unimplemented Directive could not itself establish or aggravate the accused's criminal activity (at [14]).

Similarly, in *Criminal Proceedings Against Arcaro* (C-168/95) [1996] ECR I-4705; [1997] 1 CMLR 179 the Court held that a Directive which has not been implemented under national law cannot of its own force determine or increase the criminal liability of persons who act in a manner that is prohibited by the Directive (at [37], [42]). If a Member State has not implemented a Directive, that State cannot rely upon the Directive in legal proceedings against an individual (at [38]).

However, the creation of adverse repercussions for third party rights must be distinguished from the imposition of obligations upon an individual. The Court has held that adverse repercussions for third party rights do not prevent an individual from invoking a Directive against a Member State. See *R (on the Application of Wells) v Secretary of State for Transport, Local Government and the Regions* (C-201/02) [2004] ECR I-723 at [57]; [2004] 1 CMLR 31 (p 1027).

[12.50] Indirect Effect of Directives

This vertical-horizontal divide has been modified somewhat as a consequence of the Court's interpretation of the former Equal Treatment Directive in *Von Colson v Land Nordrhein-Westfalen* (14/83) [1984] ECR 1891; [1986] 2 CMLR 430. Art 6 of the Directive stipulated that "Member States shall introduce into their national legal systems such measures as are necessary to enable all persons who consider themselves wronged by failure to apply to them the principle of equal treatment . . . to pursue their claims by judicial process after possible recourse to other competent authorities".

Von Colson unsuccessfully applied for employment at a prison. The recruitment officials refused to appoint her, citing risks associated with working in a male-only prison (at [2]). Under the German law that purported to implement the Directive, Von Colson was only entitled to compensation in the form of travelling expenses (at [4]–[5]). The applicant argued that such compensation did not meet the requirements of Art 6 of the Directive.

The Court relied upon Article 5 of the EEC Treaty [now Art 4(3) TEU]. That Article imposes an obligation upon the Member States to take all appropriate measures to ensure fulfilment of their EU obligations. The ECJ interpreted this provision as imposing an obligation upon all authorities of the Member States, including their courts.

The Court held that "in applying the national law and in particular the provisions of a national law specifically introduced in order to implement [the Equal Treatment] Directive 76/207, national courts are required to interpret their national law in the light of the wording and the purpose of the Directive" (at [26]). In particular, German courts were obliged to interpret the implementing law so as to ensure the availability of an adequate remedy as required by Art 6 of the Equal Treatment Directive (at [28]). However, Art 6 of the Directive was not as such directly effective. The Directive was given an indirect effect.

National courts must thus interpret implementing legislation in such a way as to ensure the achievement of the objectives of the Directive. See *Coote v Granada Hospitality Ltd* (C-185/97) [1998] ECR I-5199 at [18]; [1998] 3 CMLR 958; *Pfeiffer v Deutsches Rotes Kreuz, Kreisverband Waldshut eV* (C-397/01) [2004] ECR I-8835 at [113]; [2005] 1 CMLR 44 (p 1123); *Impact v Minister for Agriculture and Food* (C-268/06) [2008] ECR I-2483 at [98]; [2008] 2 CMLR 47 (p 1265). The duty to interpret national statutes in this manner is not limited to statutes that implement a Directive. See *Faccini Dori v Recreb Srl* [1994] ECR I-3325 at [26]; [1994] 1 CMLR 665; *Silhouette International Schmied GmbH & Co KG v Hartlauer Handelsgesellschaft MBH* (C-355/96) [1998] ECR I-4799 at [36]; [1998] 2 CMLR 953.

Even national statutes enacted before the adoption of a Directive must be interpreted in conformity with the Directive. See *Marleasing SA v la Comercial Internacional de Alimentación SA* (C-106/89) [1990] ECR I-4135 at [8]; [1992] 1 CMLR 305; *Connect Austria Gesellschaft für Telekommunikation GmbH v Telekom-Control-Kommission* (C-462/99) [2003] ECR I-5197 at [38]; [2005] 5 CMLR 6 (p 302). However, this interpretational duty does not require a national court to adopt an interpretation that is *contra legem*. See *Adeneler v Ellinikos Organismos Galaktos* (C-212/04) [2006] ECR I-6057 at [110]; [2006] 3 CMLR 30 (p 867); *Impact v Minister for Agriculture and Food* (C-268/06) [2008] ECR I-2483 at [100]; [2008] 2 CMLR 47 (p 1265); *Angelidaki v Organismos Nomarkhiaki Aftodiikisi Rethimnis* (C-378/07) [2009] 3 CMLR 15 (p 571) at [199].

The importance of the doctrine of indirect effect becomes clear if one considers *Harz v Deutsche Tradax GmbH* (79/83) [1984] ECR 1921; [1986] 2 CMLR 430. An unsuccessful job applicant brought a claim under Art 6 of the former Equal Treatment Directive against a private company rather than a government. An individual cannot directly invoke a Directive against another individual. However, although the Directive cannot be applied horizontally with direct effect, it must still be interpreted by national courts in such a way that individuals are not denied the benefits of an unfulfilled or incorrectly implemented Directive (at [26]–[28]). The effect of *Harz* was to take away from the individual the onus of establishing a direct effect and to replace it with the requirement that national courts interpret their national law in the light of the Directive.

The Court has since recognised a partial direct effect of Art 6 of the former Equal Treatment Directive. In *Marshall v Southampton and South West Hampshire Area Health Authority (No 2)* (C-271/91) [1993] ECR

I-4367; [1993] 3 CMLR 293 the Court held that an individual could rely upon Art 6 against the State when it acted as an employer (at [38]).

[12.55] Direct Effect of Decisions

Decisions may also be directly effective. See *Hansa Fleisch Ernst Mundt GmbH & Co KG v Landrat des Kreises Schleswig-Flensburg* (C-156/91) [1992] ECR I-5567 at [12]–[13]; *Foselev Sud-Ouest SARL v Administration des douanes et droits indirects* (C-18/08) [2009] 1 CMLR 30 (p 827) at [11]. In *Grad v Finanzamt Traunstein* (9/70) [1970] ECR 825; [1971] CMLR 1 the Court admitted that while a Decision may have different effects from a Regulation, "this difference does not exclude the possibility that the end result, namely the right of the individual to invoke the measure before the courts, may be the same as that of a directly applicable provision of a regulation" (at [5]). A decision addressed to the Member States is binding only upon its addressees, so it cannot be relied upon in proceedings that are solely between private parties. See *Carp Snc di L Moleri e V Corsi v Ecorad Srl* (C-80/06) [2007] ECR I-4473 at [20]–[22].

[12.60] Compensation for Breaches of EU Law

In *Brasserie du Pecheur SA v Germany* (C-46/93) [1996] ECR I-1029; [1996] 1 CMLR 889 the Court acknowledged that the EU Treaties contain no express provision concerning liability for breaches of EU law by the Member States. In those circumstances it is the responsibility of the Court to formulate principles of EU law regarding such liability (at [27]).

In *Francovich v Italy* (C-6/90) [1991] ECR 5357; [1993] 2 CMLR 66 the Court held that a Member State may be obliged to pay compensation to individuals who have been harmed as a consequence of the State's failure to implement a Directive. The Court argued that "the full effectiveness of Community rules would be impaired and the protection of the rights they grant would be weakened if individuals were unable to obtain compensation when their rights are infringed by a breach of Community law for which a Member State can be held responsible" (at [33]). The Court considered that State liability for breach of EU law was inherent within the Treaty itself (at [35]).

The Court held that there is a "principle of Community law that the Member-States are obliged to pay compensation for harm caused to individuals by breaches of Community law for which they can be held responsible" (at [37]). In particular, the Court stated that a right to compensation exists when three conditions are satisfied:

(1) the objective sought by the Directive includes the creation of rights for individuals;

(2) the content of those rights is ascertainable from the provisions of the Directive itself; and
(3) there is a causal link between the violation by the State of its duty to implement the Directive and the loss sustained by the individual (at [39]–[40]).

In *Francovich* the Court held that there was an obligation to compensate where the provision breached was not directly effective. However, there is also an obligation to compensate for breach of directly effective provisions of EU law. In *Brasserie du Pecheur SA v Germany* (C-46/93) [1996] ECR I-1029; [1996] 1 CMLR 889 the Court held that the obligation to compensate individuals for breaches of EU law also applied to breaches of EU provisions that are directly effective (at [18]–[19], [23]). The doctrine of direct effect is only a "minimum guarantee" and cannot of itself ensure the complete implementation of EU law (at [20]).

The Court in *Brasserie* introduced another condition for the award of compensation. The additional condition is that "the breach must be sufficiently serious" (at [51]). In a later decision the Court argued that this additional condition was evident from the circumstances of the *Francovich* case, though it was not specifically mentioned in the Court's judgment in that case See *Dillenkofer v Germany* (C-178/94) [1996] ECR I-4845 at [23]; [1996] 3 CMLR 469.

Later cases provide guidance for when a breach will be considered to be sufficiently serious. In *R v H M Treasury; Ex parte British Telecommunications plc* (C-392/93) [1996] ECR I-1631; [1996] 2 CMLR 217 the Court held that a breach of EU law will be "sufficiently serious" where the Member State has "manifestly and gravely disregarded the limits" of its powers under EU law (at [42]). The obligation to compensate applied to breaches of EU law resulting from the incorrect implementation of a Directive by a Member State (at [40]). In this case the incorrect implementation by the Member State was based upon an interpretation that was tenable though incorrect. The interpretation was not "manifestly contrary" to the Directive (at [43]). When the Member State implemented the Directive, the ECJ had not yet issued any interpretation of the Directive (at [44]). In these circumstances the breach of EU law was not sufficiently serious to justify the payment of compensation (at [45]). See similarly, *Robins v Secretary of State for Work and Pensions* (C-278/05) [2007] ECR I-1053 at [72]–[75]; [2007] 2 CMLR 13 (p 269).

In *R v Ministry of Agriculture, Fisheries and Food; Ex parte Hedley Lomas* (C-5/94) [1996] ECR I-2553; [1996] 2 CMLR 391 the Court held that any breach of EU law may be sufficiently serious if the Member State had little or no discretion about the means by which its obligation was to be implemented (at [28]). See similarly, *Laboratoires Pharmaceutiques Bergaderm SA v Commission* (C-352/98 P) [2000] ECR I-5291 at [44]; *N v Inspecteur van de Belastingdienst Oost/kantoor Almelo* (C-470/04) [2006] ECR I-7409 at [64]; [2006] 3 CMLR 49 (p 1249); *Test Claimants in the Thin Cap Group Litigation v Commissioners of Inland Revenue* (C-524/04) [2007] ECR I-2107 at [118]; [2007] 2 CMLR 31 (p 765); *Robins v Secretary of State for Work and Pensions* (C-278/05) [2007] ECR I-1053 at [71]; [2007] 2 CMLR 13 (p 269).

In *Dillenkofer v Germany* (C-178/94) [1996] ECR I-4845; [1996] 3 CMLR 469 the Court held that failure to implement a Directive within the applicable time limit is per se a sufficiently serious breach of EU law (at [29]). This failure manifestly and gravely disregards the limits of the Member State's powers under EU law (at [26]).

In *R v Ministry of Agriculture, Fisheries and Food; Ex parte Hedley Lomas* (C-5/94) [1996] ECR I-2553; [1996] 2 CMLR 391 the Court held that in the absence of relevant EU rules Member States must provide compensation for breach of their EU obligations in accordance with their domestic law regarding liability. That domestic law must not impose less favourable conditions for obtaining compensation for breach of EU law than those applying to compensation for breach of domestic law. The domestic law regarding compensation must not make it impossible or very difficult to secure compensation (at [31]). See similarly, *Edilizia Industriale Siderurgica Srl (Edis) v Ministerio delle Finanze* (C-231/96) [1998] ECR I-4951 at [19]; [1999] 2 CMLR 995; *Roquette Frères SA v Tax Office of Pas-de-Calais* (C-88/99) [2000] ECR I-10465 at [20]–[21]; *Grundig Italiana SpA v Ministero Delle Finanze* (C-255/00) [2002] ECR I-8003 at [33]; [2003] 1 CMLR 36 (p 1065).

An individual is entitled to reimbursement of taxes levied by a Member State in breach of EU law. See *BP Soupergaz Anonimos Etairia Geniki Emporiki-Viomichaniki kai Antiprossopeion v Greece* (C-62/93) [1995] ECR I-1883 at [40]; *Test Claimants in the FII Group Litigation v Commissioners of Inland Revenue* (C-446/04) [2006] ECR I-11753 at [205]; [2007] 1 CMLR 35 (p 1021); *Test Claimants in the Thin Cap Group Litigation v Commissioners of Inland Revenue* (C-524/04) [2007] ECR I-2107 at [112]; [2007] 2 CMLR 31 (p 765).

Finally, Member States bear liability for breaches of EU law by every organ of the State, including the legislature and the judiciary. See *Brasserie du Pecheur SA v Germany* (C-46/93) [1996] ECR I-1029 at [32], [36]; [1996] 1 CMLR 889 (legislature); *Köbler v Austria* (C-224/01) [2003] ECR I-10239 at [33], [36]; [2003] 3 CMLR 28 (p 1003) (judiciary). The duty to fulfil EU legal obligations is binding upon the courts in relation to matters within their jurisdiction. See *Impact v Minister for Agriculture and Food* (C-268/06) [2008] ECR I-2483 at [41]; [2008] 2 CMLR 47 (p 1265).

See generally, Josephine Steiner, "The Limits of State Liability for Breach of European Community Law" (1998) 4 *European Public Law* 69; Georgios Anagnostaras, "The Principle of State Liability for Judicial Breaches: The Impact of European Community Law" (2001) 7 *European Public Law* 281; Bernhard Hofstötter, *Non-compliance of National Courts: Remedies in European Community Law and Beyond* (Cambridge: Cambridge

University Press, 2005); Christopher Vajda, "Liability for Breach of Community Law: A Survey of the ECJ Cases Post *Factortame*" (2006) 17 *European Business Law Review* 257; Andrea Biondi and Martin Farley, *The Right to Damages in European Law* (Alphen aan den Rijn: Kluwer Law International, 2009); Björn Beutler, "State Liability for Breaches of Community Law by National Courts: Is the Requirement of a Manifest Infringement of the Applicable Law an Insurmountable Obstacle?" (2009) 46 *Common Market Law Review* 773.

[12.65] Supremacy of EU Law Over National Law

When the Court formulated the doctrine of direct effect in *van Gend en Loos* (26/62) [1963] ECR 1; [1963] CMLR 105 it proceeded upon the basis that EEC law was supreme over the law of Member States. The supremacy question was brought squarely before the Court of Justice in the celebrated case of *Costa v ENEL* (6/64) [1964] ECR 585; [1964] CMLR 425. Costa was a shareholder of a firm that had been affected by the nationalization of electricity production and distribution. Under the nationalization law the Italian government had transferred the property of all electricity undertakings to ENEL. Costa refused to pay an electricity bill issued to him and was summoned before an Italian Court. He argued that the nationalization law violated the EEC Treaty. The Italian Constitutional Court considered that as the EEC Treaty had been ratified by an ordinary law the provisions of a later conflicting law (the nationalization law) took precedence over the Treaty.

The European Court of Justice took a different view. The ECJ emphasised the uniqueness of the EEC legal system:

> By creating a Community of unlimited duration, having its own institutions, its own personality, its own legal capacity and capacity of representation on the international plane and, more particularly, real powers stemming from a limitation of sovereignty or a transfer of powers from the States to the Community, the Member States have limited their sovereign rights, albeit within limited fields, and have thus created a body of law which binds both their nationals and themselves.
>
> The integration into the laws of each Member State of provisions which derive from the Community, and more generally the terms and the spirit of the Treaty, make it impossible for the States, as a corollary, to accord precedence to a unilateral and subsequent measure over a legal system accepted by them on a basis of reciprocity (at ECR 593–594; CMLR 455).

The Court pointed out that a Member State's right to legislate unilaterally exists only where the EEC Treaty expressly so provides. Similarly, a state may derogate from its obligations under the Treaty only in accordance with a special procedure of authorization. The ECJ argued that the express provisions of the EEC Treaty permitting a Member State to legislate unilaterally or to derogate from its obligations would be meaningless if Member States could exempt themselves from their obligations by passing a national law to that effect. The Court concluded by enunciating the supremacy principle in the following words:

> The transfer by the States from their domestic legal system to the Community legal system of the rights and obligations arising under the Treaty carries with it a permanent limitation of their sovereign rights, against which a subsequent unilateral act incompatible with the concept of the Community cannot prevail (at ECR 594; CMLR 456).

Since the *Costa* decision the Court has confirmed the supremacy of EU law over national law on many occasions. See, for example, *Consorzio Industrie Fiammiferi v Autorità Garante della Concorrenza e del Mercato* (C-198/01) [2003] ECR I-8055 at [48]; [2003] 5 CMLR 16 (p 829); *Manfredi v Lloyd Adriatico Assicurazioni SpA* (C-295/04) [2006] ECR I-6619 at [39]; [2006] 5 CMLR 17 (p 980); *Ministero dell'Industria, del Commercio e dell'Artigianato v Lucchini SpA* (C-119/05) [2007] ECR I-6199 at [61]; [2009] 1 CMLR 18 (p 501).

A Member State thus cannot justify its failure to fulfil its obligations under EU law by invoking its national law. See *Commission v Germany* (C-298/95) [1996] ECR I-6747 at [18]; *Commission v Spain* (C-298/97) [1998] ECR I-3301 at [14]; *Commission v Spain* (C-274/98) [2000] ECR I-2823 at [19]; *Commission v Belgium* (C-319/01) [2002] ECR I-10779 at [14]. A Member State may not justify its failure to implement EU law on the ground of internal difficulties of implementation. See *Commission v Greece* (C-387/97) [2000] ECR I-5047 at [69]-[70]; *Commission v France* (C-121/07) [2008] ECR I-9159 at [72].

Naturally, the supremacy of EU law applies to national administrative actions as well as legislation. A directly effective provision of the EU Treaties prevails over an inconsistent national administrative decision in a particular case. See *Ciola v Land Vorarlberg* (C-224/97) [1999] ECR I-2517 at [32]–[34]; [1999] 2 CMLR 1220. EU law also prevails over collective agreements. See *Schöning-Kougebetopoulou v Freie und Hansestadt Hamburg* (C-15/96) [1998] ECR I-47 at [35]; [1998] 1 CMLR 931; *Kutz-Bauer v Freie und Hansestadt Hamburg* (C-187/00) [2003] ECR I-2741 at [73]–[74]; [2005] 2 CMLR 35 (p 862).

[12.70] Supremacy Over National Constitutional Law

In *Internationale Handelsgesellschaft mbH v Einfuhr-und Vorratsstelle für Getreide und Futtermittel* (11/70) [1970] ECR 1125; [1972] CMLR 255 the issue was whether an EEC regulation violated fundamental rights guaranteed by the German Constitution. Internationale Handelsgesellschaft GmbH (IHG) had obtained a license for the export of a specific quantity of groats. In accordance with the requirements of the EEC regulation, IHG had lodged a deposit as a guarantee that the full quantity would be exported. IHG forfeited its deposit by failing to export the specified quantity. IHG brought an action in a German court seeking the return of the forfeited deposit on the ground that the forfeiture imposed by the regulation was contrary to several fundamental rights guaranteed by the German Constitution.

The ECJ thus had to examine whether the principle of the supremacy of Community law would apply to a conflict between a Community regulation and a national constitution. If the Court allowed the testing of a Community regulation in the light of national constitutional provisions, it would no longer be able to claim that the supremacy principle applies in all cases involving a conflict between EEC law and national law. The ECJ rejected the argument that the provisions of the German Constitution should prevail over an EEC Regulation:

> Recourse to the legal rules or concepts of national law in order to judge the validity of measures adopted by the institutions of the Community would have an adverse effect on the uniformity and efficacy of Community law. The validity of such measures can only be judged in the light of Community law. In fact, the law stemming from the treaty, an independent source of law, cannot because of its very nature be overridden by rules of national law, however framed, without being deprived of its character as Community law and without the legal basis of the Community itself being called in question. Therefore the validity of a Community measure or its effect within a Member State cannot be affected by allegations that it runs counter to either fundamental rights as formulated by the Constitution of that state or the principles of a national constitutional structure (at [3]).

In *Re Export Tax on Art Treasures (No 2)* (48/71) [1972] ECR 529; [1972] CMLR 283 the Court once again faced a conflict between the requirements of Community law and national constitutional law. An Italian tax law which imposed a tax on the export of art treasures was inconsistent with Art 16 of the EEC Treaty (now Art 28 TFEU) which imposed an obligation on Member States to "abolish between themselves customs duties on exports and charges having equivalent effect" (at [2]). Under Italian law the tax law could only be repealed by the method prescribed by the Italian Constitution (at [3]). The Court again emphasised the supremacy of Community Law as follows:

> The attainment of the objectives of the Community requires that the rules of Community law established by the Treaty itself or arising from procedures which it has instituted are fully applicable at the same time and with identical effects over the whole territory of the Community without the Member States being able to place any obstacles in the way. The grant made by Member States to the Community of rights and powers in accordance with the provisions of the Treaty involves a definitive limitation on their sovereign rights and no provisions whatsoever of national law may be invoked to override this limitation (at [8]–[9]).

The Court has continued to assert the supremacy of EU law over national constitutional law. The violation of the national constitution of a Member State by an EU measure does not affect the validity of that measure under EU law, nor does it prevent that EU measure from applying to that Member State. See *Staatsanwaltschaft Freiburg v Keller* (234/85) [1986] ECR

2897 at [7]; [1987] 1 CMLR 875; *Dow Chemical Ibérica SA v Commission* (97/87) [1989] ECR 3165 at [38]. A Member State may not invoke its national Constitution as justification for its failure to fulfil its obligations under EU law. See *Government of the French Community v Flemish Government* (C-212/06) [2008] ECR I-1683 at [57]–[58]; [2008] 2 CMLR 31 (p 859).

[12.75] Reassertion of the Supremacy of EU Law

In *Amministrazione delle Finanze dello Stato v Simmenthal SpA (No 2)* (106/77) [1978] ECR 629; [1978] 3 CMLR 263 Simmenthal had imported beef from France. Under Italian law a substantial fee was charged for veterinary and public health inspections of the imported beef. Simmenthal argued that this fee constituted an obstacle to the free movement of goods in violation of the EEC Treaty. The ECJ held that the fee was inconsistent with the Treaty (at [2]). The Italian Constitutional Court had previously decided that it alone could declare the non-application of an Italian law that contravened Community law (at [6]). An Italian judge sought a preliminary ruling from the ECJ on the question whether a national court should forthwith disregard a national law that violated EEC law without waiting for it to be declared unconstitutional by the national Constitutional Court or repealed by the national legislature (at [7]).

The ECJ reasserted the supremacy of Community law as follows:

> any recognition that national legislative measures which encroach upon the field within which the Community exercises its legislative power or which are otherwise incompatible with the provisions of Community law had any legal effect would amount to a corresponding denial of the effectiveness of obligations undertaken unconditionally and irrevocably by Member States pursuant to the treaty and would thus imperil the very foundations of the Community.... It follows from the foregoing that every national court must, in a case within its jurisdiction, apply Community law in its entirety and protect rights which the latter confers on individuals and must accordingly set aside any provision of national law which may conflict with it, whether prior or subsequent to the Community rule (at [18], [21]).

[12.80] Duty of the National Authorities

In *Simmenthal* the Court formulated the duty of a national court as follows:

> A national court which is called upon, within the limits of its jurisdiction, to apply provisions of Community law is under a duty to give full effect to those provisions, if necessary refusing of its own motion to apply any conflicting provision of national legislation, even if adopted subsequently, and it is not necessary for the court to request or await the prior setting aside of such provision by legislative or other constitutional means (at [24]).

Simmenthal concerned a conflict of national provisions and Community regulations which automatically became part of the national legal systems of the Member States. In stating the principle of the precedence of Community law, the Court did not confine itself to regulations or Treaty provisions. The principle also applied to any "directly applicable measures of the institutions". Directives or decisions which are directly effective would thus take precedence over a conflicting national law. Indeed, the precedence of Community law extends to "national legislative measures which encroach upon the field within which the Community exercises its legislative power" (at [18]). This could mean that where the European Union has introduced legislative measures in a particular field, any national legislative measures within that field may be inapplicable on the basis of a potential conflict of objective. In other words, the expression "encroach upon the field" probably goes beyond cases of direct conflict.

Art 4(3) TFEU provides that the Member States must take all appropriate measures "to ensure fulfilment of the obligations" arising out of the Treaty. Under this provision Member States must repeal a conflicting national law, not merely disapply it. In *Commission v France* (167/73) [1974] ECR 359; [1974] 2 CMLR 216 the French government argued that the national law did not constitute a violation of EEC law because officials had been directed not to apply the national provision. However, the Court considered that if the French law remained on the statute books it would create an ambiguous state of affairs which would affect people who sought to rely on EEC law (at [41]–[42]).

[12.85] Factortame Litigation

The debate over the supremacy of EC law reached a climax in the *Factortame* litigation. Under the Common Market fisheries policy each national fishing fleet was given a fishing quota. The British Government wished to ensure that all boats in its fleet could properly be regarded as British. It enacted a law restricting registration as British fishing vessels to boats owned by British nationals or British companies. A number of Spanish fishermen claimed that the British legislation violated the prohibition of discrimination on grounds of nationality and the right of establishment. The fishermen sought a suspension of the law's application pending a judicial examination of its compatibility with EC law.

In *R v Secretary of State for Transport; Ex parte Factortame Ltd (No 1)* [1990] 2 AC 85; [1989] 3 CMLR 1 the House of Lords held that an Act of Parliament will be presumed to be compatible with EC law unless and until it is declared to be incompatible (at 142). The House of Lords held that an English court had no power to order an interim stay of enforcement of a British statute pending a determination of its compatibility with the EC Treaty (at 142, 153). However, the House of Lords sought a preliminary ruling from the ECJ on the question whether there was a rule of EC law requiring interim relief in these circumstances (at 152).

In a momentous judgment, the ECJ held that where a claim is made that a British law is inconsistent with EEC law, a British judge is entitled to suspend the operation of the British law. See *R v Secretary of State for Transport; Ex parte Factortame Ltd (No 2)* (C-213/89) [1990] ECR 2433 at [20]–[21]; [1990] 3 CMLR 1. This judgment effectively modified the principle of parliamentary sovereignty which had been a cornerstone of British constitutional law. Following the ECJ's preliminary ruling, the matter came before the House of Lords again in *R v Secretary of State for Transport; Ex parte Factortame Ltd (No 2)* [1991] AC 603; [1990] 3 CMLR 375. The Law Lords granted an interim injunction to prevent the British statute from coming into operation (at 661, 676, 683).

A Declaration annexed to the TFEU reiterates the principle of the supremacy of EU law over national law. See Declaration (No 17) concerning Primacy.

[12.90] Fundamental Rights as General Principles of EU Law

The Court of Justice identifies and applies general principles of EU law. Such principles have a "general, comprehensive character" and "have constitutional status". See *Audiolux SA v Groupe Bruxelles Lambert SA* (C-101/08) [2010] Bus LR 197 at [50], [63]. Fundamental rights are among the most important general principles of EU law.

The protection of fundamental rights as general principles of EU law was foreshadowed in *Stauder v City of Ulm* (29/69) [1969] ECR 419; [1970] CMLR 112. Under a Community scheme cheap butter was provided to recipients of welfare benefits upon presentation of a coupon issued under the scheme. The German language version of the Community decision stated that the coupon had to contain the beneficiary's name. Other language versions merely stated that the coupon had to be "individualized." The applicant objected to the requirement that the coupon contain his name on the ground that it was a humiliation to have to reveal his identity. He argued that the Community decision was invalid as a violation of fundamental human rights. The ECJ held that on a proper interpretation the Community Act did not require that the recipient's name be stated on the coupon. The Court observed that when interpreted in this way the provision did "not contain any element that might jeopardise the fundamental rights of the individual contained in the general principles of the law of the Community of which the Court must ensure the observance" (at ECR 425; CMLR 119).

The automatic resolution of a conflict between the EU Treaty and a national constitution in favour of EU law carries the risk of injustice either generally or in individual cases. However, the Court seems to have been conscious of the potential for injustice that may arise from the rigid application of this principle. In *Internationale Handelsgesellschaft mbH v Einfuhr-und Vorratsstelle für Getreide und Futtermittel* (11/70) [1970] ECR 1125; [1972] CMLR 255 the Court held that a national constitutional right could not prevail against EEC law, but found that a analogous basic right under Community law restricted the power of EEC institutions.

The ECJ expressed this point as follows:

> an examination should be made as to whether or not any analogous guarantee inherent in Community law has been disregarded. In fact, respect for fundamental rights forms an integral part of the general principles of law protected by the Court of Justice. The protection of such rights, whilst inspired by the constitutional traditions common to the Member States, must be ensured within the framework of the structure and objectives of the Community. It must therefore be ascertained... whether the system of deposits has infringed rights of a fundamental nature, respect for which must be ensured in the Community legal system (at [4]).

The Court was thus able to preserve intact the principle of the supremacy of Community law, while giving indirect recognition to national constitutional values by declaring that fundamental rights are part of the general principles of law protected by the Court of Justice.

[12.95] Protection of Fundamental Rights Expanded

The protection of fundamental rights under EEC law arose again in *Nold Kohlen- und Baustoffgrosshandlung v Commission* (4/73) [1974] ECR 491; [1974] 2 CMLR 33. Under Community law a coal wholesaler could not buy Ruhr coal directly from a selling agency unless it also entered into an agreement to purchase a specified minimum quantity from the agency. Nold was a coal wholesaler. It could not satisfy this requirement and had to purchase the coal from an intermediary rather than directly from the selling agency (at [1]). Nold sought the annulment of the Community decision on the ground that it violated its fundamental rights. Nold argued that the Community decision deprived it of a property right protected by the German constitution and infringed its freedom of commercial activity (at [12]). The ECJ recognized these rights as part of the general principles of Community law:

> fundamental rights form an integral part of the general principles of law, the observance of which [the Court] ensures. In safeguarding these rights, the Court is bound to draw inspiration from constitutional traditions common to the Member States, and it cannot therefore uphold measures which are incompatible with fundamental rights recognized and protected by the constitutions of those states. Similarly, international treaties for the protection of human rights on which the Member States have collaborated or of which they are signatories, can supply guidelines which should be followed within the framework of Community law (at [13]).

The Court recognised that there were limitations upon these rights:

> If rights of ownership are protected by the constitutional laws of all the Member States and if similar guarantees are given in respect of their right freely to choose and practice their trade or profession, the rights thereby guaranteed, far from constituting unfettered prerogatives, must be viewed in the light of the social function of the property and activities protected thereunder. For this reason, rights of this nature are protected by law subject always to limitations laid down in accordance with the public interest. Within the Community legal order it likewise seems legitimate that these rights should, if necessary, be subject to certain limits justified by the overall objectives pursued by the Community, on condition that the substance of these rights is left untouched (at [14]).

The Court thereby modified the *Internationale Handelsgesellschaft* principle in several respects. First, the Court declared that it would not uphold Community measures that conflicted with the fundamental rights guaranteed by the constitutions of the Member States. Secondly, the Court acknowledged a new source for the identification of fundamental rights: the European Convention on Human Rights. Thirdly, the Court recognised that these rights were subject to the general objectives pursued by the Community.

In *Hauer v Land Rheinland-Pfalz* (44/79) [1979] ECR 3727; [1980] 3 CMLR 42 the Court considered this new limitation upon fundamental rights. A Community regulation imposed a temporary ban upon the planting of new vines. This ban prevented Hauer from planting her land as a vineyard (at [2]). She argued that the regulation violated her right to property and the freedom to pursue a trade or profession (at [4]).

The ECJ held that the right to property was a fundamental right under EEC law (at [17]). The regulation did not deprive owners of their property because they were able to sell it to others or use it for other purposes (at [19]). Such restrictions were found in all of the wine-producing Member States (at [21]). This type of restriction was considered to be legitimate in the constitutional orders of the Member States (at [22]). The Court also concluded the restriction was justified "by the objectives of general interest pursued by the Community" (at [30]). It did not infringe the substance of the right to property or the freedom to pursue trade and professional activities.

The inspiration for the Court's recognition of fundamental rights was the subject of much speculation. T C Hartley argued that the Court "was prompted by the desire to persuade the German courts to accept the supremacy of Community law even in the case of an alleged conflict with the fundamental rights provisions" of the German Constitution. He predicted that the ECJ would "never admit to applying national law as such". This explains why the Court "puts forward the notion that the Community concept of fundamental rights is merely 'inspired' by the philosophical concepts underlying the national provisions." See T C Hartley, *The Foundations of European Community Law* (6th ed, Oxford: Oxford University Press, 2007), 136.

[12.100] Broad Range of Fundamental Rights Protected

The Court's cases have recognised an extensive catalogue of fundamental rights under EU law. Among these rights are the following:

- freedom of expression: *Germany v Parliament* (C-380/03) [2006] ECR I-11573 at [154]; [2007] 2 CMLR 1 (p 1); *United Pan-Europe Communications Belgium SA v Belgium* (C-250/06) [2007] ECR I-11135 at [41]; [2008] 2 CMLR 2 (p 45);
- the principle of equal treatment: *Proceedings brought by Karlsson* (C-292/97) [2000] ECR I-2737 at [39]; *Chacón Navas v Eurest Colectividades SA* (C-13/05) [2006] ECR I-6467 at [56]; [2006] 3 CMLR 50 (p 1123);
- the right not to be discriminated against on the basis of sex: *P v S* (C-13/94) [1996] 2 CMLR 247; *Richards v Secretary of State for Work and Pensions* (C-423/04) [2006] ECR I-3585 at [23]; [2006] 2 CMLR 49 (p 1242);
- the principle of non-discrimination on the basis of age: *Mangold v Helm* (C-144/04) [2005] ECR I-9981 at [75]; [2006] 1 CMLR 43 (p 1132);
- freedom of occupation: *Nold Kohlen- und Baustoffgrosshandlung v Commission* (4/73) [1974] ECR 491 at [14]; [1974] 2 CMLR 338;
- freedom of association: *Union Royale Belge des Sociétés de Football Association ASBL v Bosman* (C-415/93) [1995] ECR I-4921 at [79]; [1996] 1 CMLR 645;
- the right to take collective action such as a strike: *International Transport Workers' Federation v Viking Line ABP* (C-438/05) [2007] ECR I-10779 at [44]; [2008] 1 CMLR 51 (p 1372); *Laval un Partneri Ltd v Svenska Byggnadsarbetareförbundet* (C-341/05) [2007] ECR I-11767 at [91]; [2008] 2 CMLR 9 (p 177);
- the right to property: *R (on the Application of ABNA Ltd) v Secretary of State for Health* (C-453/03) [2005] ECR I-10423 at [87]; [2006] 1 CMLR 48 (p 1290); *Productores de Música de España (Promusicae) v Telefónica de España SAU* [2008] ECR I-271 at [62]; [2008] 2 CMLR 17 (p 465);
- freedom of economic activity: *R (on the Application of Alliance for Natural Health) v Secretary of State for Health* (C-154/04) [2005] ECR I-6451 at [126]; [2005] 2 CMLR 61 (p 1490);
- the right to human dignity: *Netherlands v Parliament* (C-377/98) [2001] ECR I-7079 at [70]; [2001] 3 CMLR 49 (p 1173);
- the right to the protection of personal data: *Productores de Musica de España (Promusicae) v Telefonica de España SAU* (C-275/06) [2008] ECR I-271 at [63]; [2008] 2 CMLR 17 (p 465);
- the right to respect for family life: *Re Validity of Directive 2003/86: Parliament v Council* (C-540/03) [2006] ECR I-5769 at [52]; [2006] 3 CMLR 28 (p 779);

- the principle of effective judicial protection: *Kadi v Commission* (C-402/05 P) [2008] ECR I-6351 at [335]; [2008] 3 CMLR 41 (p 1207);
- the right to a fair trial: *Ordre des Barreaux Francophones et Germanophones v Conseil des Ministres* (C-305/05) [2007] ECR I-5305 at [29]; [2007] 3 CMLR 28 (p 731);
- the presumption of innocence: *Hüls AG v Commission* (C-199/92P) [1999] ECR I-4287 at [149]; [1999] 5 CMLR 1016; and
- the principle that there can be no crime or punishment without law: *Advocaten voor de Wereld VZW v Leden van de Ministerraad* (C-303/05) [2007] ECR I-3633 at [49]; [2007] 3 CMLR 1 (p 1).

Notably, the Court has held that the confidentiality of communications between lawyers and clients is protected as a general principle of EU law. The communication must have been made for the purposes of the client's defence and the lawyer must be independent of the client, that is, not an employee of the client. See *AM & S Europe Ltd v Commission* (155/79) [1982] ECR 1575 at [21]–[22]; [1982] 2 CMLR 264; *Akzo Nobel Chemicals Ltd v Commission* (T-125/03) [2007] ECR II-3523 at [77]–[78]; [2008] 4 CMLR 3 (p 97), under appeal C-550/07. See generally, Gavin Murphy, "Is It Time to Rebrand Legal Professional Privilege in EC Competition Law?" (2009) 30 *European Competition Law Review* 125.

The Court has emphasised that the right to property and freedom of economic activity are not absolute, "but must be considered in relation to their social function". See *R v Secretary of State for Health; Ex parte British American Tobacco (Investments) Ltd* (C-491/01) [2002] ECR I-11453 at [149]; [2003] 1 CMLR 14 (p 395); *Booker Aquaculture Ltd v Scottish Ministers* (C-20/00) [2003] ECR I-7411 at [68]; [2003] 3 CMLR 6 (p 133); *R (on the Application of Alliance for Natural Health) v Secretary of State for Health* (C-155/04) [2005] ECR I-6451 at [126]; [2005] 2 CMLR 61 (p 1490); *Alessandrini Srl v Commission* (C-295/03 P) [2005] ECR I-5673 at [86]; *R (on the Application of ABNA Ltd) v Secretary of State for Health* (C-453/03) [2005] ECR I-10423 at [87]; [2006] 1 CMLR 48 (p 1290); *Fabbrica italiana accumulatori motocarri Montecchio SpA v Council* (C-120/06 P) [2008] ECR I-6513 at [183].

See generally, Xavier Groussot, *General Principles of Community Law* (Groningen: Europa Law Publishing, 2006); John L Murray, "Fundamental Rights in the European Community Legal Order" (2009) 32 *Fordham International Law Journal* 531.

[12.105] Textual Basis for Fundamental Rights Protection

There is now an express basis in the founding Treaties for the fundamental rights jurisdiction of the Court of Justice. Art 6 TEU provides that fundamental rights constitute general principles of EU law. It also states that these fundamental rights have their source in the European Convention on Human Rights and the constitutional traditions common to the Member States. Under this jurisdiction the Court reviews the acts of EU institutions and the implementation of EU law by the Member States. See *Advocaten voor de Wereld VZW v Leden van de Ministerraad* (C-303/05) [2007] ECR I-3633 at [45]; [2007] 3 CMLR 1 (p 1).

The Charter of Fundamental Rights of the European Union now codifies many of the fundamental rights recognised as general principles of law by the Court. See *Charter of Fundamental Rights*, as amended at Strasbourg, 12 December 2007, OJ C 303, 14.12.2007, p 1. Since the Treaty of Lisbon the Charter has become legally binding upon the EU itself and the Member States when they implement EU law (Art 6(1) TEU; Art 51(1) Charter).

[12.110] Relationship with the European Convention on Human Rights

The Member States are all party to the European Convention on Human Rights. The ECJ has held that the Convention has "special significance" in identifying fundamental rights protected as general principles of EU law. See *ASML Netherlands BV v Semiconductor Industry Services GmbH* (C-283/05) [2006] ECR I-12041 at [26]; *Ordre des Barreaux Francophones et Germanophones v Conseil des Ministres* (C-305/05) [2007] ECR I-5305 at [29]; [2007] 3 CMLR 28 (p 731); *Re Validity of Directive 2003/86: Parliament v Council* (C-540/03) [2006] ECR I-5769 at [35]; [2006] 3 CMLR 28 (p 779); *Laserdisken ApS v Kulturministeriet* (C-479/04) [2006] ECR I-8089 at [61]; [2007] 1 CMLR 6 (p 187); *Kadi v Commission* (C-402/05 P) [2008] ECR I-6351 at [283]; [2008] 3 CMLR 41 (p 1207).

The Court of Justice frequently considers the decisions of the European Court of Human Rights as part of the process of identifying the fundamental rights protected by EU law. See *Dansk Rørindustri A/S v Commission* (C-189/02) [2005] ECR I-5425 at [70]; [2005] 5 CMLR 17 (p 796); *Re Graphite Electrodes Cartel Appeal: Commission v SGL Carbon AG* (C-301/04 P) [2006] ECR I-5915 at [43]; [2006] 5 CMLR 15 (p 877); *Ordre des Barreaux Francophones et Germanophones v Conseil des Ministres* (C-305/05) [2007] ECR I-5305 at [31]; [2007] 3 CMLR 28 (p 731).

The European Court of Human Rights provides a judicial forum for the enforcement of the individual rights and freedoms guaranteed by the European Convention. See Art 19, *Convention for the Protection of Human Rights and Fundamental Freedoms*, Rome, 4 November 1950, as amended by *Protocol No 11*, Strasbourg, 11 May 1994, 2061 UNTS 7; ETS No 155. In several cases the European Court of Human Rights has considered the liability of Member States for actions taken when they implement EU law.

In *Bosphorus Hava Yollari Turizm Ve Ticaret Anonim Sirketi v Ireland* (45036/98) ECHR 2005-VI, 42 EHRR 1 (p 1) an airplane had been impounded under an EC Regulation that gave effect to a United Nations Security Council resolution. The Court held that the Member States of the EC that were party to the European Convention bore international responsibility for any violation of the Convention resulting from the implementation of EC law (at [143]). Actions taken by an EU Member State in implementation of EU law would be justified under the Convention provided that the protection of fundamental rights under EU law was equivalent to that provided by the Convention (at [145]). If the protection was equivalent, there was a presumption that the EU Member State had not violated the Convention when it did "no more" than implement its obligations under EU law (at [146]). This presumption would be rebutted if in the specific case "the protection of Convention rights was manifestly deficient" (at [146]).

After reviewing the ECJ's case law relating to fundamental rights, the Court concluded that the protection of fundamental rights under EU law was equivalent to that under the European Convention (at [155]). There was thus a presumption that EU Member States did not violate the Convention when they implemented their obligations under EU law (at [155]). The Court held that this presumption had not been rebutted in the circumstances of this particular case (at [166]). For discussions of this case, see Alicia Hinarejos Parga, "*Bosphorus v Ireland* and the Protection of Fundamental Rights in Europe" (2006) 31 *European Law Review* 251; Steve Peers, case note (2006) 2 *European Constitutional Law Review* 443; C Eckes, "Does the European Court of Human Rights Provide Protection from the European Community? The Case of *Bosphorus Airways*" (2007) 13 *European Public Law* 68; Leonard Besselink, "The European Union and the European Convention on Human Rights. From Sovereign Immunity in *Bosphorus* to Full Scrutiny Under the Reform Treaty?" in Ineke Boerefijn and Jenny E Goldschmidt (eds), *Changing Perceptions of Sovereignty and Human Rights: Essays in Honour of Cees Flinterman* (Antwerpen: Intersentia, 2008), 295.

In *Cooperatieve Producentenorganisatie van de Nederlandse Kokkelvisserij UA v Netherlands*, No 13645/05, 20 January 2009 the Court held that this presumption applied to the procedures as well as the actions of organs of the European Union, such as the Court of Justice (p 20). See generally, Geoff Sumner, "We'll Sometimes have Strasbourg: Privileged Status of Community Law before the European Court of Human Rights" (2008) 16 *Irish Student Law Review* 127; Guy Harpaz, "The European Court of Justice and its Relations with the European Court of Human Rights: The Quest for Enhanced Reliance, Coherence and Legitimacy" (2009) 46 *Common Market Law Review* 105; Catherine Van de Heyning, case note (2009) 46 *Common Market Law Review* 2117. The Court's website is at http://www.echr.coe.int.

In the *Bosphorus* case the European Court of Human Rights held that the European Community could not be held liable under the Convention so long as it was not a party to the Convention (at [142]). However, the TEU now provides that the EU will become party to the European Convention. See Art 6(2) TEU; Protocol (No 8) to TFEU. When this occurs the European Union will thus become liable for breaches of the Convention by its institutions and other bodies. However, the accession of the EU is also contingent upon the entry into force of a Protocol amending the European Convention. The Protocol provides that the EU may accede to the Convention. See Art 59(2), Convention, as amended by *Protocol No 14, amending the Control System of the Convention*, Strasbourg, 13 May 2004, ETS No 194. The Protocol will come into force on 1 June 2010. See generally, Tobias Lock, "The ECJ and the ECtHR: The Future Relationship Between the Two European Courts" (2009) 8 *Law and Practice of International Courts and Tribunals* 375.

Apart from the European Convention on Human Rights, in identifying fundamental rights the Court takes account of the many other international treaties concerning the protection of human rights. See e.g. *Dzodzi v Belgium* (C-197/89) [1990] ECR I-3763 at [68]; *Grant v South-west Trains Ltd* (C-249/96) [1998] ECR I-621 at [44]; [1998] 1 CMLR 993 (International Covenant on Civil and Political Rights); *Re Validity of Directive 2003/86: Parliament v Council* (C-540/03) [2006] ECR I-5769 at [37]; [2006] 3 CMLR 28 (p 779); *Dynamic Medien Vertriebs GmbH v Avides Media AG* (C-244/06) [2008] ECR I-505 at [39]-[40]; [2008] 2 CMLR 23 (p 651) (Convention on the Rights of the Child). As with the European Convention, the Member States also collaborated in the adoption of these treaties or have ratified them.

[12.115] Conclusion

A "unique feature" of EU law is that provisions of the EU founding Treaties and legislation may have direct effect by granting individual rights that are enforceable in the courts of the Member States. An EU law that has a vertical direct effect applies to relations between individuals and the state. An EU law that has a horizontal direct effect applies to relations between private individuals.

Regulations are incorporated into the legal systems of the Member States upon their adoption by EU institutions. While Directives must be implemented by the Member States, they may also be directly effective. If a Member State fails to implement a Directive, it may have direct effect. A Directive has direct effect if its provisions, so far as their subject matter is concerned, are unconditional and sufficiently precise. Unimplemented Directives that do not have direct effect may have an indirect effect. National courts must interpret national legislation in conformity with the Directive, though they are not required to adopt an interpretation that is contra legem.

A Member State may be obliged to pay compensation to individuals who have been harmed as a consequence of the State's failure to implement a Directive. The breach of EU law must be "sufficiently serious" before the State may be required to compensate an individual for the breach.

The EU founding Treaties and EU legislation have supremacy over the law of the Member States, including their national constitutional law. The ECJ has ameliorated the potentially harsh consequences of the doctrine of supremacy by protecting fundamental rights as general principles of EU law. In identifying these rights the Court draws inspiration from the European Convention on Human Rights and the constitutional traditions of the Member States. The TEU now expressly provides for the fundamental rights jurisdiction of the Court of Justice.

Further Reading

A. *Direct Effect*

Becker, Florian and Angus Campbell. "The Direct Effect of European Directives – Towards the Final Act?" (2007) 13 *Columbia Journal of European Law* 401.

Colgan, Daniel. "Triangular Situations: The Coup de Gràce for the Denial of Horizontal Direct Effect of Community Directives" (2002) 8 *European Public Law* 545.

Craig, Paul. "Directives: Direct Effect, Indirect Effect and the Construction of National Legislation" (1997) 22 *European Law Review* 519.

Dashwood, Alan. "From *van Duyn* to *Mangold* via *Marshall*: Reducing Direct Effect to Absurdity?" (2007) 9 *Cambridge Yearbook of European Legal Studies* 81.

Dashwood, Alan. "*Viking* and *Laval*: Issues of Horizontal Direct Effect" (2008) 10 *Cambridge Yearbook of European Legal Studies* 525.

Deards, Elspeth. "Indirect Effect after *Webb v EMO Air Cargo (UK) Ltd*: How Must National Law Be Interpreted to Comply with a Directive?" (1996) 2 *European Public Law* 71.

Dougan, Michael. "The 'Disguised' Vertical Effects of Directives" (2000) 59 *Cambridge Law Journal* 586.

Dougan, Michael. "What is the Point of *Francovich*?" in Takis Tridimas and Paolisa Nebbia (eds), *European Union Law for the Twenty-First Century* (Oxford: Hart, 2004), I: 239.

Drake, Sara. "Twenty Years after *Von Colson*: The Impact of 'Indirect Effect' on the Protection of the Individual's Community Rights" (2005) 30 *European Law Review* 329.

Editorial. "Horizontal Direct Effect – A Law of Diminishing Coherence?" (2006) 43 *Common Market Law Review* 1.

Fletcher, Maria. "Extending 'Indirect Effect' to the Third Pillar: The Significance of *Pupino*?" (2005) 30 *European Law Review* 862.

Harlow, Carol. "*Francovich* and the Problem of the Disobedient State" (1996) 2 *European Law Journal* 199.

Lackhoff, Klaus and Harold Nyssens. "Direct Effect of Directives in Triangular Situations" (1998) 23 *European Law Review* 397.

Mastroianni, Roberto. "On the Distinction between Vertical and Horizontal Direct Effects of Community Directives – What Role for the Principle of Equality?" (1999) 5 *European Public Law* 417.

Moriarty, Brid. "Direct Effect, Indirect Effect and State Liability: An Overview" (2007) 14 *Irish Journal of European Law* 97.

Nyssens, Harold and Klaus Lackhoff. "Direct Effect of Directives in Triangular Situations" (1998) 23 *European Law Review* 397.

Prechal, Sacha. "Does Direct Effect Still Matter?" (2000) 37 *Common Market Law Review* 1047.

Prechal, Sacha. "Member State Liability and Direct Effect: What's the Difference After All?" (2006) 17 *European Business Law Review* 299.

Prinssen, Jolande and Annette Schrauwen (eds). *Direct Effect: Rethinking a Classic of EC Legal Doctrine* (Groningen: Europa Law Publishing, 2002).

Skouris, Vassilios. "Effet Utile Versus Legal Certainty: The Case-Law of the Court of Justice on the Direct Effect of Directives" (2006) 17 *European Business Law Review* 241.

Tridimas, Takis. "Black, White and Shades of Grey: Horizontality of Directives Revisited" (2002) 21 *Yearbook of European Law* 327.

B. Supremacy

Alter, Karen J. *Establishing the Supremacy of European Law: The Making of an International Rule of Law in Europe* (Oxford: Oxford University Press, 2001).

Craig, Paul. "The ECJ, National Courts and the Supremacy of Community Law" in Ingolf Pernice and Roberto Miccù (eds), *The European Constitution in the Making* (Baden-Baden: Nomos, 2003), 35, available at http://www.ecln.net.

Craig, Paul. "The Hierarchy of Norms" in Takis Tridimas and Paolisa Nebbia (eds), *European Union Law for the Twenty-First Century* (Oxford: Hart, 2004), I: 75.

Dougan, Michael. "When Worlds Collide! Competing Visions of the Relationship Between Direct Effect and Supremacy" (2007) 44 *Common Market Law Review* 931.

Kaczorowska, Alina. "The Supremacy of Community Law" (2006) 16 *Caribbean Law Review* 245.

Koch, Cornelia. "The Doctrine of Supremacy of European Community Law as a Condition Precedent for the Doctrine of Direct Effect" (2005) 9 *International Trade and Business Law Review* 201.

Lenaerts, Koen and Tim Corthaut. "Of Birds and Hedges: The Role of Primacy in Invoking Norms of EU Law" (2006) 31 *European Law Review* 287.

Rossi, Lucia Serena. "How Fundamental are Fundamental Principles? Primacy and Fundamental Rights after Lisbon" (2008) 27 *Yearbook of European Law* 65.

Chapter 13
The European Union and the World Trading System

[13.05] Introduction

The preceding chapters have described the establishment by the European Union of an internal market which comprises "an area without internal frontiers in which the free movement of goods, persons, services and capital is ensured" (Art 26(2) TFEU). It is also necessary to situate the EU within the world trading system. This necessity arises from the fact that the EU cannot operate as an isolated or self-sufficient economic grouping. The EU is bound by its membership in the World Trade Organization (hereafter "WTO"), which aims to achieve global rather than regional trade liberalization. The world trading system also includes many regional and bilateral free trade agreements. Furthermore, most EU Member States are party to the Convention on Contracts for the International Sale of Goods (CISG).

[13.10] Three-Track Trading System

There are at least three main approaches to international trade, that is, there is a "three-track trading system" See Ernest H Preeg, "The US Leadership Role in World Trade: Past, Present, and Future" (Spring 1992) 15, 2 *Washington Quarterly* 81 at 87. The first approach is the multilateral one through the WTO. See *Marrakesh Agreement establishing the World Trade Organization*, Marrakesh, 15 April 1994, 1867 UNTS 3; OJ L 336, 23.12.1994, p 3; [1995] ATS 8 p 1 (hereafter "WTO Agreement"). The WTO offers a forum for negotiations regarding multilateral trade issues (Art III(2) WTO Agreement). It also provides a mechanism for settling international trade disputes through its dispute settlement system (Art III(3) WTO Agreement).

The second track is the establishment of regional trading blocs or the adoption of regional trade arrangements. These trading blocs and regional trade arrangements aim to liberalise trade within their own geographical areas. Regional trade arrangements typically provide for the establishment

G. Moens, J. Trone, *Commercial Law of the European Union*,
Ius Gentium: Comparative Perspectives on Law and Justice 4,
DOI 10.1007/978-90-481-8774-4_13, © Springer Science+Business Media B.V. 2010

of a free trade area or for the adoption of friendship, commerce and navigation treaties.

The third approach is unilateral action. Countries may be inclined, in times of economic contraction, to take unilateral action to safeguard their export interests. Rather than relying exclusively on multilateral negotiations, many non-EU member states have also entered into bilateral free trade agreements.

[13.15] Multilateral Approach: GATT 1994

Liberalization of international trade has traditionally been achieved in multilateral negotiations organised within the framework of the General Agreement on Tariffs and Trade. This framework has been continued in a modified form under the WTO. See *General Agreement on Tariffs and Trade 1994* (hereafter "GATT 1994"), defined in Annex 1A to the WTO Agreement, 1867 UNTS 190; OJ L 336, 23.12.1994, p 20; [1995] ATS 8 p 14.

The original version of GATT was concluded in 1947. GATT 1994 is a distinct legal instrument, being the 1947 agreement as subsequently amended and as further modified by the WTO Agreement (Art II(4) WTO Agreement). GATT is dedicated to the elimination of barriers to trade. An action that is incompatible with GATT is known as a "nullification and impairment".

[13.20] Dispute Resolution System

The parties to GATT 1994 undertake to refrain from taking unilateral action in trade disputes and to submit their disputes to the WTO dispute settlement system. The procedural rules of the WTO dispute resolution system are contained in the *Understanding on Rules and Procedures governing the Settlement of Disputes* (hereafter "DSU"), which is Annex 2 to the WTO Agreement, 1869 UNTS 401; OJ L 336, 23.12.1994, p 234; [1995] ATS 8 p 375. The WTO dispute resolution system has jurisdiction over disputes concerning GATT 1994 and the specialised agreements included within the WTO Agreement, such as the Agreement on Trade-Related Aspects of Intellectual Property Rights (Art 1(1) and Appendix 1 DSU).

If not settled through consultation, conciliation or mediation (Arts 4–5 DSU), trade disputes are determined by WTO Dispute Settlement Panels (Art 6 DSU) and the Appellate Body on appeal (Art 17 DSU). All decisions ("reports") of these bodies are published in an official series of law reports, the *Dispute Settlement Reports* (Cambridge: Cambridge University Press, 1996–) (abbreviated "DSR"). They are also published in *World Trade Organization Dispute Settlement Decisions: Bernan's Annotated Reporter* (Lanham, Md: Bernan Press, c1998–). Neither of these series is widely available in libraries. WTO decisions are thus most readily accessible through the WTO website at http://www.wto.org/english/tratop_e/dispu_e/dispu_e.htm.

The Dispute Settlement Body adopts Panel and Appellate Body reports unless it decides otherwise by consensus (Arts 16, 17(14) DSU). The Dispute Settlement Body monitors the implementation of adopted reports (Art 21(6) DSU). Compensation and the suspension of concessions are available as remedies for non-implementation of an adopted report (Art 22 DSU). See generally, Sherzod Shadikhodjaev, *Retaliation in the WTO Dispute Settlement System* (Alphen aan den Rijn: Kluwer Law International, 2009); Bryan Mercurio, "Retaliatory Trade Measures in the WTO Dispute Settlement Understanding: Are there Really Alternatives?" in James C Hartigan (ed), *Trade Disputes and the Dispute Settlement Understanding of the WTO: An Interdisciplinary Assessment* (Bingley, England: Emerald, 2009), 397. Examples of WTO dispute settlement decisions concerning EU laws will be referred to throughout this chapter.

[13.25] Most-Favoured Nation

GATT 1994 is based upon four basic principles:

1. The most-favoured nation (MFN) principle (Art I).

According to this principle, whenever a Contracting Party grants a right or privilege to one of its trading partners, then that privilege or right is accorded automatically to all other trading partners. As each Contracting Party is obliged to apply to all other Contracting Parties the "most-favoured nation principle", no discrimination with regard to tariffs should exist between them.

[13.30] Non-discrimination

2. The principle of non-discrimination requires that imported and domestic products be treated equally once imported products have entered a Party's stream of commerce (Art III). Imports shall not be subjected to internal taxes or charges in excess of those applied to like domestic products (Art III(2)).

In *European Communities—Measures affecting Asbestos and Asbestos-containing Products*, Report of the Appellate Body, DS135, 12 March 2001, DSR 2001: VII, 3243; 40 ILM 1193 the WTO Appellate Body held that four criteria must be considered in determining what are "like" products. These criteria are (i) "the properties, nature and quality of the products", (ii) their end uses, (iii) the attitudes and behaviour of consumers and (iv) the tariff classification of these products (at [101]). All four criteria should be considered and an overall assessment must be made (at [109]). The physical properties of the products must be considered under the first and third criteria, including any hazards that those physical qualities may pose for human health (at [113]–[114], [122], [147]). While this decision concerned Art III(4), the same approach is applied to likeness under Art III(2).

[13.35] Gradual Reduction of Tariff Barriers

3. Gradual reduction of tariff barriers (Art II).

These reductions or tariff concessions are negotiated at "rounds" of negotiation. Successful conclusion of such "rounds" may result in Parties undertaking to refrain from levying tariffs on a stated product higher than those agreed upon during the negotiations.

[13.40] Elimination of Import Quotas

4. Elimination of import quotas (Art XI).

Parties to GATT may not maintain quantitative restrictions upon the export or import of products to or from other Parties.

[13.45] Safeguards

GATT 1994 provides that a party may suspend its obligations or withdraw a concession in relation to a product where that product is being imported into its territory in such increased quantities as to result in serious injury to domestic producers of competing products (Art XIX). A separate WTO agreement elaborates upon this provision. See *Agreement on Safeguards*, 1869 UNTS 154; OJ L 336, 23.12.1994, p 184; [1995] ATS 8 p 289. Safeguard measures may be adopted "only to the extent necessary to prevent or remedy serious injury and to facilitate adjustment" (Art 5(1)). See generally, Chad P Bown and Rachel McCulloch, "Nondiscrimination and the WTO Agreement on Safeguards" (2003) 2 *World Trade Review* 327; Alan O Sykes, *The WTO Agreement on Safeguards: A Commentary* (Oxford: Oxford University Press, 2006).

[13.50] Uniform Administration of Customs

Art X(3)(a) of GATT 1994 provides that the Contracting Parties must administer their customs laws in a "uniform, impartial and reasonable manner". The mere fact that there are differences between the penalties applicable under the national customs laws of EU members does not infringe the requirement that EU customs laws be administered in a uniform manner. See *European Communities—Selected Customs Matters*,

Report of the Appellate Body, DS315, 13 November 2006, DSR 2006: IX, 3791 at [211], [216]; 18 no 6 WTAM 3.

[13.55] Protection of Health

Art XX(b) of GATT 1994 permits Contracting Parties to adopt measures that are necessary for the protection of human life or health, even where those measures would be inconsistent with other provisions of GATT. In *European Communities—Measures affecting Asbestos and Asbestos-containing Products*, Report of the Appellate Body, DS135, 12 March 2001, DSR 2001: VII, 3243; 40 ILM 1193 a French law prohibited the importation of asbestos and products containing asbestos. The Appellate Body held that the Panel acted within its permissible discretion in holding that the French law was a measure for the protection of life or health (at [163]). The measure was also "necessary" for the protection of life or health. A WTO Member could prohibit the importation of a very risky product while permitting the use of a less risky alternative (at [168]).

[13.60] The EU and GATT

The EC was an original member of the WTO (Art XI(1) WTO Agreement). See generally, Antonis Antoniadis, "The Participation of the European Community in the World Trade Organisation: An External Look at European Union Constitution-Building" in Takis Tridimas and Paolisa Nebbia (eds), *European Union Law for the Twenty-First Century* (Oxford: Hart, 2004), I: 321.

When the EU votes at meetings of the Ministerial Conference and General Council of the WTO, it has the same number of votes as the total number of its Member States (twenty-seven). However, the total number of votes of the EU and its Member States cannot exceed the number of EU Member States: the EU itself does not have an additional vote (Art IX(1) WTO Agreement).

The GATT is concerned with tariffs and trade and thus falls within the area in which the EU has express treaty-making power by virtue of Art 207 TFEU (formerly Art 133 EC). It is thus not surprising that the Court held that "in so far as under the EEC Treaty the Community has assumed the powers previously exercised by Member States in the area governed by the General Agreement, the provisions of that agreement have the effect of binding the Community". See *International Fruit Co NV v Produktschap voor Groenten en Fruit (No 3)* (21–24/72) [1972] ECR 1219 at [18]; [1975] 2 CMLR 1.

In 1994 the European Community and each of its Member States became party to the WTO Agreement, of which GATT 1994 is a part. See 1867 UNTS

154–155. All nations that have subsequently become EU Member States have also become WTO Members. The WTO Agreement was entered into as a "mixed agreement" since some aspects of the Agreement were within the competence of the EU while others were within the competence of the Member States. See *Re Uruguay Round Treaties* (Opinion 1/94) [1994] ECR I-5267 at [34], [47], [55], [71]; [1995] 1 CMLR 205.

The EU has adopted legislation regulating the manner in which its rights under the WTO Agreement are to be exercised. See Council Regulation 3286/94 of 22 December 1994 laying down Community procedures in the field of the common commercial policy in order to ensure the exercise of the Community's rights under international trade rules, in particular those established under the auspices of the World Trade Organization (OJ L 349, 31.12.1994, p 71).

Complaints of injury caused by obstacles to trade may be made on behalf of EU industries or enterprises (Arts 3–4). The complaint is submitted to the Commission (Art 5(1)). A Member State may request that the Commission initiate the WTO dispute settlement process (Art 6(1)). The EU may adopt commercial policy measures such as suspending or withdrawing concessions, increasing customs duties or adopting quantitative restrictions (Art 12(3)). Where the adoption of commercial policy measures requires that the WTO dispute settlement process be concluded, such measures may not be adopted until that process has ended. The measures adopted shall be in accordance with the decisions adopted under the WTO dispute settlement system (Art 12(2)).

The EU has often amended its law to comply with decisions rendered under the WTO dispute resolution system. For example, in 1998 the WTO Appellate Body held that the EU legislation prohibiting growth hormones in meat violated the WTO Sanitary and Phytosanitary Measures Agreement. See *European Communities—Measures Concerning Meat and Meat Products (Hormones)*, Report of the Appellate Body, DS26, DS48, 13 February 1998, DSR 1998: I, 135. The United States and Canada were authorised to suspend trade concessions to the European Union.

The EU adopted a Directive implementing the WTO decision. See Directive 2003/74 of the European Parliament and of the Council of 22 September 2003 amending Council Directive 96/22 concerning the prohibition on the use in stockfarming of certain substances having a hormonal or thyrostatic action and of beta-agonists (OJ L 262, 14.10.2003, p 17).

The United States considered that the Directive did not properly implement the WTO decision and initiated another round of dispute resolution. The Appellate Body then decided that the United States was entitled to maintain its suspension of certain trade concessions until a decision had been reached as to whether the Directive complied with its earlier decision. See *United States—Continued Suspension of Obligations in the EC-Hormones Dispute*, Report of the Appellate Body, DS320, 16 October 2008, DSR 2008: IX–XI. The dispute is ongoing.

[13.65] GATT and Preliminary Rulings

In *Amministrazione delle Finanze dello Stato v Societa Petrolifera Italiana SpA* (267/81) [1983] ECR 801; [1984] 1 CMLR 354 the ECJ ruled that the provisions of GATT fell within its preliminary ruling jurisdiction. The Court stated:

> the provisions of GATT should, like the provisions of all other agreements binding the Community, receive uniform application throughout the Community. Any difference in the interpretation and application of provisions binding the Community as regards non-member countries would not only jeopardize the unity of the commercial policy,... but also create distortions in trade within the Community, as a result of differences in the manner in which the agreements in force between the Community and non-member countries were applied in the various Member States. It follows that the jurisdiction conferred upon the court in order to ensure the uniform interpretation of Community law must include a determination of the scope and effect of the rules of GATT within the Community (at [14]–[15]).

[13.70] Position of GATT Under EU Law

In *International Fruit Co NV v Produktschap voor Groenten en Fruit (No 3)* (21–24/72) [1972] ECR 1219; [1975] 2 CMLR 1 the Court was asked whether the provisions of GATT are directly effective in the sense that individuals may rely upon these provisions in national courts. The Court decided that although the Community is bound by GATT the indeterminate and loose language of the Agreement makes it unsuitable for the purposes of conferring direct effect. The provisions of GATT thus do not confer upon individuals rights that are enforceable in national courts. The Court held:

> This agreement which, according to its preamble, is based on the principle of negotiations undertaken on the basis of 'reciprocal and mutually advantageous arrangements' is characterized by the great flexibility of its provisions, in particular those conferring the possibility of derogation, the measures to be taken when confronted with exceptional difficulties and the settlement of conflicts between the Contracting Parties..... Those factors are sufficient to show that, when examined in such a context, Article XI of the General Agreement [elimination of quantitative restrictions] is not capable of conferring on citizens of the Community rights which they can invoke before the courts (at [21], [27]).

The Court has continued to hold that GATT does not have direct effect. See *Amministrazione delle Finanze dello Stato v Chiquita Italia SpA* (C-469/93) [1995] ECR I-4533 at [29]; *Fabbrica italiana accumulatori motocarri Montecchio SpA v Council* (C-120/06 P) [2008] ECR I-6513 at [132].

[13.75] Position of the WTO Agreement Under EU Law

In general the ECJ does not review the legality of measures adopted by EU institutions to determine their consistency with the WTO Agreement. The Court will do so only "where the Community intended to implement a particular obligation assumed in the context of the WTO, or where the Community measure refers expressly to the precise provisions of the WTO agreements". See *Portugal v Council* (C-149/96) [1999] ECR I-8395 at [47], [49]; *R v Secretary of State for Health; Ex parte British American Tobacco (Investments) Ltd* (C-491/01) [2002] ECR I-11453 at [154]–[155]; [2003] 1 CMLR 14 (p 395); *Petrotub SA v Council* (C-76/00 P) [2003] ECR I-79 at [53]–[54]; *Biret International Council SA v Council* [2003] ECR I-10497 at [52]–[53]; [2006] 1 CMLR 17 (p 436); *IKEA Wholesale Ltd v Commissioners of Customs & Excise* (C-351/04) [2007] ECR I-7723 at [29]–[30]. The ECJ has held that the courts of the Member States may not hold that EU legislation violates the WTO Agreement, even where the WTO Dispute Settlement Body has upheld a complaint regarding the legislation. See *Léon Van Parys NV v Belgisch Interventie- en Restitutiebureau* [2005] ECR I-1465 at [53]–[54].

In *Fabbrica italiana accumulatori motocarri Montecchio SpA v Council* (C-120/06 P) [2008] ECR I-6513 several companies alleged that they had suffered damage as a consequence of retaliatory action taken against the EU over its regime for the importation of bananas (at [30]–[31]). The WTO Dispute Settlement Body had decided that the importation regime violated the WTO Agreement and authorised the United States to increase customs duty upon particular EU products in retaliation for that infringement (at [22]–[23]). The ECJ held that EU law does not provide for the award of compensation for damage caused by the failure of EU institutions to fulfil Community obligations under the WTO Agreement (at [176]).

See generally, Axel Desmedt, "European Court of Justice on the Effect of WTO Agreements in the EC Legal Order" (2000) 27 *Legal Issues of Economic Integration* 93; Marc Weisberger, "The Application of *Portugal v Council*: The Banana Cases" (2002) 12 *Duke Journal of Comparative and International Law* 153; Mario Mendez, "The Impact of WTO Rulings in the Community Legal Order" (2003) 29 *European Law Review* 517; Delphine de Mey, "The Effect of WTO Dispute Settlement Rulings in the EC Legal Order: Reviewing *Van Parys v Belgische Interventie- en Restitutiebureau* (C-377/02)" (June 2005) 6, 6 *German Law Journal* 1025, http://www.germanlawjournal.com; Pieter Jan Kuijper and Marco Bronckers, "WTO Law in the European Court of Justice" (2005) 42 *Common Market Law Review* 1313; Fabrizio Di Gianni and Renato Antonini, "DSB Decisions and Direct Effect of WTO Law: Should the EC Courts be More Flexible when the Flexibility of the WTO System has Come to an End?" (2006) 40 *Journal of World Trade* 777; Marco Bronckers, "From 'Direct Effect' to 'Muted Dialogue': Recent Developments in the European Courts'

Case Law on the WTO and Beyond" (2008) 11 *Journal of International Economic Law* 885.

[13.80] WTO Agreement

The WTO Agreement provides that where there is a conflict between a provision of GATT 1994 and one of the various specialist agreements under the WTO Agreement, the specialist agreement prevails (General Interpretative Note to Annex 1A). The following sections discuss some of the specialist agreements that were adopted as part of the WTO Agreement. However, the WTO regime concerning dumping and subsidies is discussed in detail in Chapter 5, though it is based upon such specialist agreements.

[13.85] Agricultural Products

The *Agreement on Agriculture*, 1867 UNTS 410; OJ L 336, 23.12.1994, p 22; [1995] ATS 8 p 34 provides for the reduction of domestic support (Art 6) and export subsidies (Art 9). The individual commitments by each WTO Member are contained in Part IV of the Member's Schedule.

GATT 1994 applies subject to the Agreement on Agriculture (Art 21(1), Agreement on Agriculture). The WTO Appellate Body has interpreted this provision to mean that GATT 1994 applies to agricultural products, except where the Agreement on Agriculture specifically regulates the same matter. See *European Communities—Regime for the Importation, Sale and Distribution of Bananas*, Report of the Appellate Body, DS27, 25 September 1997, DSR 1997: II, 589 at [155]. The Appellate Body thus held that the Agreement on Agriculture did not authorise the EU to act inconsistently with Art XIII of GATT 1994 (non-discriminatory admission of quantitative restrictions and tariff quotas) (at [157]–[158]).

In that case the EU had allocated tariff quota shares to some WTO Members that did not have a substantial interest in exporting bananas to the EU, but not to others. The Appellate Body held that this allocation of tariff quota shares was inconsistent with Art XIII(1) of GATT 1994 since a state may not restrict importation of a product unless it restricts importation of the like product from all third countries (at [161]). In 1994 the parties to GATT 1994 granted the EU a waiver of one of its GATT obligations in relation to the Lomé Convention, a trade agreement between the EU and Asian, Caribbean and Pacific nations (at [164]). This waiver was limited to a single provision of GATT (Art 1(1)), not all of its provisions (at [168]). The waiver thus did not excuse non-compliance with Art XIII (at [180], [183], [187]). See *Fourth ACP-EEC Convention (Lomé Convention)*, Lomé, 15 December 1989, 1924 UNTS 3; 29 ILM 783; OJ L 229, 17.8.1991, p 3.

[13.90] Sanitary Measures

WTO Members may take sanitary and phytosanitary measures for the protection of human, animal or plant life or health. See Art 2(1), *Agreement on the Application of Sanitary and Phytosanitary Measures*, 1867 UNTS 493; OJ L 336, 23.12.1994, p 40; [1995] ATS 8 p 65. However, they may take such measures only to the extent necessary for those purposes (Art 2(2)). Such measures must be based upon sufficient scientific evidence (Art 2(2)). These measures may not be applied in a way that would represent a "disguised restriction" upon trade (Art 2(3)).

Sanitary and phytosanitary measures must be based upon international standards where such standards have been adopted (Art 3(1)). The intention is to promote harmonisation of such measures. Where national measures comply with international standards, they are presumed to comply with the WTO Agreement (Art 3(2)). However, WTO Members may introduce standards that are higher than the relevant international standards, provided that they have a scientific justification for so doing (Art 3(3)).

Sanitary and phytosanitary measures must be based upon an assessment of risks to human, animal or plant life or health (Art 5(1)). This assessment must take into account scientific evidence, production methods, inspection methods, ecological conditions and quarantine (Art 5(2)). In *European Communities—Measures concerning Meat and Meat Products*, Report of the Appellate Body, DS26, DS48, 13 February 1998, DSR 1998: I, 135 the Appellate Body held that these provisions do not "require a risk assessment to establish a minimum quantifiable magnitude of risk, nor do [they] exclude a priori, from the scope of a risk assessment, factors which are not susceptible of quantitative analysis by the empirical or experimental laboratory methods commonly associated with the physical sciences" (at [253(j)]). See generally, Joanne Scott, *WTO Agreement on Sanitary and Phytosanitary Measures: A Commentary* (Oxford: Oxford University Press, 2007).

[13.95] Technical Barriers

The WTO Agreement regulates technical barriers to international trade. See *Agreement on Technical Barriers to Trade*, 1868 UNTS 120; OJ L 336, 23.12.1994, p 86; [1995] ATS 8 p 114. The terms used for standardisation and conformity assessment procedures should be based upon definitions adopted by the United Nations and international standards bodies (Art 1.1).

Where relevant international standards have been adopted, Members shall use those standards as a basis for their own technical regulations (Art 2.4). In *European Communities—Trade Description of Sardines*, Report of the Appellate Body, DS231, 26 September 2002, DSR 2002: VII,

3359 the Appellate Body held that an international standard is not the basis for a national measure if the national measure contradicts the international standard (at [248], [256]–[257]). It is not necessary that these international standards were adopted by consensus (at [222], [227]).

Members need not rely upon international standards which would be "an ineffective or inappropriate means for the fulfilment of the legitimate objectives pursued" (Art 2.4). In the *Sardines Case* the Appellate Body held that these legitimate objectives include those listed in Art 2.2 of this Agreement, but are not limited to that list (at [286]). The objectives listed in Art 2.2 include national security and the protection of human, animal or plant health.

WTO Members shall accept the results of conformity assessment procedures in other member states, provided that they are satisfied that those procedures are equivalent to their own (Art 6.1). Developing countries that are WTO Members are to be given differential and more favourable treatment than that accorded to other Members (Art 12.1).

[13.100] Preshipment Inspection

Some developing countries may be permitted to apply a system of preshipment inspection, that is, "verification of the quantity, the price, . . . and/or the customs classification of goods to be exported to the territory of the user member" of the WTO. See Art 1(3), *Agreement on Preshipment Inspection*, 1868 UNTS 368; OJ L 336, 23.12.1994, p 138; [1995] ATS 8 p 205. Preshipment inspection is to be carried out in a non-discriminatory and transparent manner (Arts 2(1), 2(5), 3(1)–(2)). Price verification is to be carried out to avoid fraud (Art 2(20)).

[13.105] Rules of Origin

The Rules of Origin are the rules that determine the country of origin of goods. See Art 1(1), *Agreement on Rules of Origin*, 1868 UNTS 397; OJ L 336, 23.12.1994, p 138; [1995] ATS 8 p 215. This Agreement seeks to harmonize rules of origin applied by WTO members (Art 9(2)–(3)). Rules of origin must not be used for the achievement of trade objectives and must not restrict or distort international trade (Art 9(1)(d)).

[13.110] Import Licensing

Import licensing is the administrative procedure used as part of an import licensing system that requires the lodging of an application prior to importation. See Art 1(1), *Agreement on Import Licensing Procedures*, 1868 UNTS 436; OJ L 336, 23.12.1994, p 151; [1995] ATS 8 p 229. Import licensing procedures must be neutral in application and must be applied in a fair manner (Art 1(3)).

[13.115] Services

WTO Members are under an obligation to accord most favoured nation treatment to services from other Members. WTO Members must accord to services from another Member treatment that is no less favourable than they give to services from any other nation. See Art II(1), *General Agreement on Trade in Services (GATS)*, 1869 UNTS 183; OJ L 336, 23.12.1994, p 190; [1995] ATS 8 p 299. This Article prohibits both de facto (in fact) and de jure (by law) discrimination. See *European Communities—Regime for the Importation, Sale and Distribution of Bananas*, Report of the Appellate Body, DS27, 25 September 1997, DSR 1997: II, 589 at [233]–[234].

WTO Members must also accord services from other Members treatment that is no less favourable than that provided for in the Schedule to the Agreement (Art XVI(1)). In relation to the services set out in their national schedules, WTO Members shall accord to services from other Members treatment that is no less favourable than that it gives to its own like services (Art XVII(1)). The Agreement also provides that Members are to negotiate further liberalisation of the trade in services (Art XIX(1)). See generally, Marion Panizzon, Nicole Pohl and Pierre Sauvé (eds), *GATS and the Regulation of International Trade in Services* (Cambridge: Cambridge University Press, 2008).

[13.120] Intellectual Property

One of the most prominent elements of the WTO Agreement is the *Agreement on Trade-related Aspects of Intellectual Property Rights (TRIPS)*, 1869 UNTS 299; OJ L 336, 23.12.1994, p 214; [1995] ATS 8 p 341. WTO Members must "accord to the nationals of other Members treatment no less favourable than that it accords to its own nationals with regard to the protection of intellectual property" (Art 3(1)). If a WTO Member grants to the nationals of any other country an advantage or immunity regarding intellectual property, that advantage or immunity must be granted to the nationals of all WTO Members (Art 4).

WTO Members are required to comply with several other treaties concerning intellectual property (Arts 2(1), 9(1)). Computer programmes are to be given copyright protection as literary works (Art 10(1)). Other provisions concern trademark protection (Art 15 ff), industrial designs (Arts 25–26) and geographical indications (Art 22 ff). Inventions "in all fields of technology" are to be accorded patent protection (Art 27(1)). National compliance with these obligations regarding intellectual property is enforced through the WTO dispute resolution system (Art 64). See generally, Talia Einhorn, "The Impact of the WTO Agreement on Trips (Trade-Related Aspects of Intellectual Property Rights) on EC Law: A Challenge to Regionalism" (1998) 35 *Common Market Law Review* 1069; Peter-Tobias Stoll, Jan Busche and Katrin Arend (eds), *WTO: Trade-Related Aspects of Intellectual Property Rights* (Leiden: Martinus Nijhoff, 2008).

[13.125] Continuing Negotiations Through the WTO

Multilateral negotiations for further trade liberalisation have continued since the formation of the World Trade Organization. The Doha Round of negotiations began in November 2001. Since then further negotiations have been held each year without conclusion of a final agreement. However, consensus was achieved in relation to some contentious issues, such as medical patents and special treatment for developing nations. Agricultural tariffs and subsidies are the major remaining areas of disagreement. In July 2008 negotiations again stalled over the price level at which tariff protection of farmers in developing countries would be permitted. See "World trade deal collapses", *AM*, 30 July 2008, http://www.abc.net.au/am. In November 2008 the leaders of the G-20 major economies indicated that the Doha Round negotiations should be concluded by the end of 2008. See para 13, *Declaration of the Summit on Financial Markets and the World Economy*, Washington, 15 November 2008, available at http://www.g20.org and http://www.g8.utoronto.ca/g20. However, negotiations continued into the following year. The WTO maintains a web page devoted to the Doha Round. See http://www.wto.org/english/tratop_e/dda_e/dda_e.htm.

[13.130] Regional Free Trade Agreements

GATT 1994 allows for the establishment of regional customs unions which have free trade throughout the union along with a common external tariff structure. See Art XXIV(4)–(10); *Understanding on the Interpretation of Art XXIV*, 1867 UNTS 219; OJ L 336, 23.12.1994, p 16; [1995] ATS 8 p 25. The European Union is a good example of a customs union.

By contrast, a free trade area does not have a common external tariff structure. Free trade area protections generally only apply to goods originating within the free trade area, so rules of origin are adopted to prevent circumvention of this limitation by re-export.

NAFTA is an example of a regional free trade area. See *North American Free Trade Agreement*, Washington, Ottawa, Mexico, 8, 11, 14, 17 December 1992, 32 ILM 296, 605. Its scope encompasses all of North America: the United States, Canada and Mexico. The parties have established a free trade area (Art 101). All parties must accord to the goods of the other parties national treatment in accordance with Art III of GATT (Art 301(1)). The parties must progressively reduce tariff protection (Art 302(2)). The Agreement does not contain substantive rules regarding anti-dumping and countervailing duties. NAFTA arbitral panels thus determine whether anti-dumping and countervailing duties comply with domestic law (Ch 19). See generally, Ralph Haughwout Folsom, *NAFTA and Free Trade in the Americas in a Nutshell* (St Paul, MN: Thomson/West, 2004).

Two side agreements accompany NAFTA. These agreements provide for cooperation in relation to labour and environmental matters. See *North American Agreement on Labor Cooperation*, Mexico, Washington, Ottawa, 8, 9, 12, 14 September 1993, 32 ILM 1499; *North American Agreement on Environmental Cooperation*, Mexico, Washington, Ottawa, 8, 9, 12, 14 September 1993, 32 ILM 1480.

The website of the NAFTA Secretariat is at http://www.nafta-sec-alena.org. The decisions of arbitral panels established under NAFTA are available on that website. These decisions are reported in *International Law Reports* (Cambridge: Cambridge University Press, 1919–) and *International Legal Materials* (Washington: American Society of International Law, "1962–"). The *American Journal of International Law* (Washington: American Society of International Law, 1907–) often publishes summaries of NAFTA decisions. See generally, Patricia Isela Hansen, "Dispute Settlement in the NAFTA and Beyond" (2005) 40 *Texas International Law Journal* 417.

The ASEAN Free Trade Area is another example of a regional free trade area. See *Agreement on the Common Effective Preferential Tariff Scheme for the ASEAN Free Trade Area*, Singapore, 28 January 1992, 31 ILM 513, as amended at Bangkok, 15 December 1995, 35 ILM 1084 and on 31 January 2003. It operates as a free trade area between Members of the Association of South East Asian Nations (ASEAN). Parties are required to eliminate tariff and non-tariff barriers between Member States. The Free Trade Area operates under a Common Effective Preferential Tariff rather than a common external tariff (Arts 1(1), 2(5)). Agricultural products are excluded (Art 3). Import duties are to be eliminated (Art 4(C)). The texts of this Agreement and its amendments are available at http://www.aseansec.org. See generally, Alberta Fabbricotti, "The ASEAN Free Trade Area (AFTA) and its Compatibility with the GATT/WTO" (1999) 8 *Asian Yearbook of International Law* 37; Lok Hwee Cong, Christopher H Lim and Ng Lyn, *A Guide to Free Trade in ASEAN* (Singapore: CCH Asia, 2007).

Asia-Pacific Economic Cooperation (APEC) is composed of 21 Pacific Rim economies, including the United States, Russia, China, Japan, Australia, Canada, South Korea, Indonesia and Malaysia. The leaders of the APEC economies adopted the Bogor Declaration at their meeting on 15 November 1994. The member economies undertook that APEC would promote trade liberalisation both within and outside the APEC region. APEC would also improve trade and investment facilitation. The leaders undertook to lower tariffs in the APEC area to less than 5%. This reduction was to be achieved by the developed members by 2010, while the developing members were to achieve that goal by 2020 (paragraph 6). APEC's website is at http://www.apec.org. See generally, Ippei Yamazawa (ed), *Asia Pacific Economic Cooperation (APEC): Challenges and Tasks for the Twenty-First Century* (London: Routledge, 2000); Senate Foreign Affairs, Defence and Trade References Committee, *Australia and APEC: A Review of Asia Pacific Economic Cooperation* (2000), available at http://www.aph.gov.au/Senate/committee/FADT_CTTE/index.htm; Jürgen Rüland et al. (eds), *Asia-Pacific Economic Cooperation (APEC): The First Decade* (London: Routledge-Curzon, 2002).

There are other regional trading blocs, such as Mercosur and the Andean Community in South America. See *Treaty Establishing a Common Market (Treaty of Asuncion)*, Asunción, 26 March 1991, 30 ILM 1041; *Agreement on Andean Subregional Integration (Cartagena Agreement)*, Bogotá, 26 May 1969, 8 ILM 910. For a discussion of regional free trade agreements, see Antoni Estevadeordal, Kati Suominen and Robert Teh (eds), *Regional Rules in the Global Trading System* (Cambridge: Cambridge University Press, 2009).

[13.135] Bilateral Free Trade Agreements

There are numerous bilateral free trade agreements. For example, the United States has concluded free trade agreements with (among others) Canada, Mexico, Australia, Singapore, Bahrain, Chile, Israel, Jordan, Morocco, Oman and most of Central America. See *NAFTA* (above); *Agreement with Israel on the Establishment of a Free Trade Area*, Washington, 22 April 1985, 24 ILM 653; *Agreement with Jordan on the Establishment of a Free Trade Area*, Washington, 24 October 2000, 41 ILM 63; *US-Singapore Free Trade Agreement*, Washington, 6 May 2003, HR Doc No 108-100; *US-Chile Free Trade Agreement*, Miami, 6 June 2003, HR Doc No 108-101; *US-Morocco Free Trade Agreement*, Washington, 15 June 2004, HR Doc No 108-201; *Dominican Republic-Central America-United States Free Trade Agreement*, Washington, 5 August 2004, HR Doc 109-36; *Agreement with Bahrain on the Establishment of a Free Trade Area*, Washington, 14 September 2004, HR Doc No 109-71; *Agreement with Oman on the Establishment of a Free Trade Area*, Washington, 19 January 2006, HR Doc 109-118. Information about US bilateral free trade agreements is available at http://export.gov/fta.

Canada has free trade agreements with the United States, Mexico, Israel, Chile, Costa Rica, Peru, Colombia and Jordan. See *NAFTA* (above); *Free Trade Agreement with Israel*, Toronto, 31 July 1996, Can TS 1997 No 49; *Free Trade Agreement with Chile*, Santiago, 4 December 1996, 36 ILM 1067; Can TS 1997 No 50; *Free Trade Agreement with Costa Rica*, Ottawa, 23 April 2001; *Free Trade Agreement with Peru*, Lima, 29 May 2008; *Free*

Trade Agreement with Colombia, Lima, Peru, 21 November 2008; *Free Trade Agreement with Jordan*, Amman, 28 June 2009. The texts of these treaties are available at http://www.international.gc.ca/trade-agreements-accords-commerciaux/agr-acc/index.aspx.

Australia has entered into free trade agreements with the United States, New Zealand, Singapore and Thailand. See *Australia-New Zealand Closer Economic Relations—Trade Agreement*, Canberra, 28 March 1983, 1329 UNTS 175; [1983] ATS 2; *Singapore-Australia Free Trade Agreement*, Singapore, 17 February 2003, 2257 UNTS 103; [2003] ATS 16; *Australia-US Free Trade Agreement*, Washington, 18 May 2004, [2005] ATS 1; HR Doc No 108-199; *Australia-Thailand Free Trade Agreement*, Canberra, 5 July 2004, [2005] ATS 2; *Australia-Chile Free Trade Agreement*, Canberra, 30 July 2008, [2009] ATS 6. The texts of these treaties are available at http://www.austlii.edu.au/au/other/dfat.

In February 2009 Australia signed a free trade agreement with ASEAN and New Zealand. See *Agreement Establishing the Association of Southeast Asian Nations (ASEAN)–Australia-New Zealand Free Trade Area*, Cha-am, Thailand, 27 February 2009, [2010] ATS 1. The Agreement entered into force on 1 January 2010. Australia is currently negotiating free trade agreements with China and South Korea.

The free trade agreements entered into by Australia have many common elements. The parties generally establish a free trade area between the two countries (US Art 1(1); Thailand Art 101; Chile Art 1.1; ASEAN Ch 1 Art 2). The parties affirm their existing obligations under the WTO Agreement and other free trade agreements (US Art 1.1(2); Singapore Ch 2 Arts 7–8, Ch 7 Art 22(6), Ch 13 Art 2; Thailand Arts 206(1), 604(1), 703(1); Chile Art 1.2; ASEAN Ch 18 Art 2(1)). The Agreements define the rules of origin that determine the eligibility for a preferential tariff (US Ch 5; Singapore Ch 3; Thailand Arts 401–415; Chile Arts 4.2–4.3; ASEAN Ch 3).

Each party will accord national treatment to the goods of the other party in accordance with Art III of GATT 1994 (US Art 2.2; Singapore Ch 2 Art 2; Thailand Art 202; Chile Art 3.3; ASEAN Ch 2 Art 4). The parties agree to eliminate or reduce customs duties on originating goods (often progressively) (US Art 2.3; Singapore Ch 2 Art 3(1); Thailand Art 203; Chile Art 3.4(2), Annex 3-B; ASEAN Ch 2 Art 1). Various non-tariff measures are also prohibited, including import and export restrictions (US Art 2.9; Singapore Ch 2 Art 6; Thailand Art 209; Chile Art 3.9; ASEAN Ch 2 Art 7). Export taxes that are not also applicable to goods for domestic consumption are prohibited (US Art 2.11; Chile Art 3.11). Various export duties may be prohibited (Singapore Ch 2 Art 5).

The Agreements also regulate trade in services between the parties (US Ch 10; Singapore Ch 7; Thailand Ch 8; Chile Ch 9; ASEAN Ch 8), competition policy (US Ch 14; Singapore Ch 12; Thailand Ch 12; Chile Ch 14; ASEAN Ch 14), investment (US Ch 11; Singapore Ch 8; Thailand Ch 9; Chile Ch 10; ASEAN Ch 11), government procurement (US Ch 15; Singapore Ch 6; Thailand Ch 15; Chile Ch 15), electronic commerce (US

Ch 16; Singapore Ch 14; Thailand Ch 11; Chile Ch 16; ASEAN Ch 10) and protection of intellectual property rights (US Ch 17; Singapore Ch 13; Thailand Ch 13; Chile Ch 17; ASEAN Ch 13). Disputes are to be settled by the formation of an arbitral panel (US Art 21.7; Singapore Ch 16 Art 6; Thailand Art 1805; Chile Art 21.5; ASEAN Ch 17 Art 8).

See generally, Joint Standing Committee on Treaties, *Report 61: Australia-United States Free Trade Agreement* (2004), available at http://www.aph.gov. au/house/committee/jsct/index.htm; Jasmine Morris, "The United States-Australia Free Trade Agreement" (2006) 10 *International Trade and Business Law Review* 87; Benedict Sheehy, "Unfair Trade as Friendly Fire: The United States-Australia Free Trade Agreement" (Winter 2007) 16, 2 *Currents: International Trade Law Journal* 70; Andrew Clarke and Xiang Gao, "Bilateral Free Trade Agreements: A Comparative Analysis of the Australia-United States FTA and the Forthcoming Australia-China FTA" (2007) 30 *University of New South Wales Law Journal* 842.

New Zealand has entered into free trade agreements with Australia, China, ASEAN and Malaysia. See *Australia-New Zealand Closer Economic Relations—Trade Agreement*, Canberra, 28 March 1983, 1329 UNTS 175; [1983] ATS 2; *New Zealand-China Free Trade Agreement*, Beijing, 7 April 2008; *Agreement Establishing the Association of Southeast Asian Nations (ASEAN)–Australia-New Zealand Free Trade Area*, Hua Hin, Thailand, 27 February 2009, [2009] ATNIF 7; *Malaysia-New Zealand Free Trade Agreement*, Kuala Lumpur, 26 October 2009.

[13.140] International Sale of Goods

Most EU Member States are party to the *United Nations Convention on Contracts for the International Sale of Goods*, Vienna, 11 April 1980, 1489 UNTS 3; 19 ILM 671; [1988] ATS 32 (hereafter "CISG"). As Bruno Zeller pointed out, the "CISG has . . . become the de facto sales law in Europe". See Matthew Harvey and Michael Longo, *European Union Law: An Australian View* (Sydney: Lexis Nexis, 2008), 140. As at 28 February 2010 twenty-three of the twenty-seven EU Member States have become party to the CISG. The United Kingdom, Portugal, Ireland and Malta are not parties to the Convention. See Sally Moss, "Why the United Kingdom has not Ratified the CISG" (2005) 25 *Journal of Law and Commerce* 483.

Many common law nations are also parties to the CISG (United States, Australia, Canada, New Zealand and Singapore). India, South Africa and Malaysia are not parties. While China is a party to the CISG, it has not applied the Convention to Hong Kong. See 1489 UNTS 59; *Hannaford v Australian Farmlink Pty Ltd* [2008] FCA 1591 at [5].

The following table indicates the date on which the CISG entered into force for EU Member States and many common law jurisdictions.

State	Date of entry into force
Australia	1 April 1989 (1498 UNTS 435)
Austria	1 January 1989 (1489 UNTS 59)
Belgium	1 November 1999 (1942 UNTS 413)
Bulgaria	1 August 1991 (1568 UNTS 438)
Canada	1 May 1992 (1606 UNTS 438; extensions to remaining Provinces and Territories: 1671 UNTS 366, 1678 UNTS 428, 2217 UNTS 429)
Cyprus	1 April 2006 (2308 UNTS 154)
Czech Republic	1 January 1993 (1736 UNTS 412) (by succession)
Denmark	1 March 1990 (1523 UNTS 378)
Estonia	1 October 1994 (1733 UNTS 452)
Finland	1 January 1989 (1489 UNTS 59)
France	1 January 1988 (1489 UNTS 59)
Germany	1 January 1991 (1552 UNTS 417)
Greece	1 February 1999 (2000 UNTS 514)
Hungary	1 January 1988 (1489 UNTS 59)
Italy	1 January 1988 (1489 UNTS 59)
Latvia	1 August 1998 (1985 UNTS 491)
Lithuania	1 February 1996 (1850 UNTS 380)
Luxembourg	1 February 1998 (1963 UNTS 446)
Netherlands	1 January 1992 (1588 UNTS 528)
New Zealand	1 October 1995 (1823 UNTS 384)
Norway	1 August 1989 (1510 UNTS 499)
Poland	1 June 1996 (1865 UNTS 418)
Romania	1 June 1992 (1637 UNTS 351)
Singapore	1 March 1996 (1856 UNTS 449)
Slovak Republic	1 January 1993 (1723 UNTS 350) (by succession)
Slovenia	25 June 1991 (1761 UNTS 399) (by succession)
Spain	1 August 1991 (1569 UNTS 422)
Sweden	1 January 1989 (1489 UNTS 59)
United States	1 January 1988 (1489 UNTS 59)

Pace University School of Law maintains an extensive database of cases and commentary relating to the Convention (http://www.cisg.law.pace.edu). This superb website should be the first destination for those needing to research some aspect of the CISG.

[13.145] Domestic Implementation

Knowledge of the specific form of domestic implementation of the CISG is necessary for actually relying upon the Convention in a national legal system. Domestic implementation of the CISG may be by way of direct application, the enactment of implementing legislation or an order of execution law. In a system of direct application, treaties have the force of domestic law without the need for further legislative implementation. See John Trone, *Federal Constitutions and International Relations* (St Lucia, Qld:

University of Queensland Press, 2001), 67–69. For example, United States courts have routinely held that the CISG is self-executing, that is, it has the force of federal law without the need for implementation by Congress. See *Filanto SpA v Chilewich International Corporation* 789 F Supp 1229 at 1237 (SD NY 1992); *Delchi Carrier v Rotorex Corporation* 71 F 3d 1024 at 1027 (2d Cir 1995); *Usinor Industeel v Leeco Steel Products Inc* 209 F Supp 2d 880 at 884 (ND Ill 2002); *Caterpillar Inc v Usinor Industeel* 305 F Supp 2d 659 at 673 (ND Ill 2005).

American courts have held that the CISG creates a private right of action in US federal courts. See *Asante Technologies Inc v PMC-Sierra Inc* 164 F Supp 2d 1142 at 1147 (ND Cal 2001); *BP Oil International Ltd v Empresa Estatal Petoleos de Ecuador* 332 F 3d 333 at 336 (5th Cir 2003); *Genpharm Inc v Pliva-Lachema AS* 361 F Supp 2d 49 at 54 (ED NY 2005). The CISG thus rebuts the "background presumption" that treaties do not create private causes of action that are enforceable in national courts. See *Medellin v Texas* 552 US 491 at 506 n 3 (2008).

The Convention is also directly applied in many EU Member States, including:

- *Belgium*: Law of 4 September 1996, Belgisch Staatsblad, 7 January 1997, p 17471;
- *France*: Law 82-842 of 10 June 1982, Journal Officiel de la République Française, 11.6.1982, p 1840;
- *Luxembourg*: Law of 26 November 1996, Mémorial A, no 86 of 10.12.1996, p 2441;
- *Netherlands*: Tractatenblad 1986 no 61; and
- *Spain*: Boletín Oficial del Estado, no 26 of 20.1.1991, p 3170.

In most common law systems the CISG is implemented by the enactment of legislation. The implementing statute generally provides that the CISG has the force of law and prevails over any inconsistent national legislation. The relevant provisions of the national implementing statutes are:

- *Australia*: ss 5-6 of the following statutes: *Sale of Goods (Vienna Convention) Act* 1987 (ACT); 1986 (NSW); 1987 (NT); 1986 (Qld); 1987 (Tas); 1987 (Vic); 1986 (WA); ss 4-5 of the following statute: 1986 (SA);
- *Canada*: ss 4, 6, *International Sale of Goods Contracts Convention Act* (RS, c I-20.4); ss 2(1), 2(4), *International Conventions Implementation Act* (RSA, c I-6.8); ss 3-4, *International Sale of Goods Act* (RSBC 1996, c 236); ss 3, 5, *The International Sale of Goods Act* (CCSM, c S11); ss 4, 6, *International Sale of Goods Act* (RSNL 1990, c I-16); ss 3, 5, *International Sale of Goods Act* (RSNB, c I-12.21); ss 4, 7, *International Sale of Goods Act* (SNS 1988, c 13); ss 3, 5, *International Sale of Goods Act* (RSNWT 1988, c I-7); s 7, *International Sales Conventions Act* (SNu 2003, c 9); ss 3, 5, *International Sale of Goods Act* (RSO 1990, c I.10); ss 3, 5, *International Sale of Goods Act* (RSPEI, c I-6); s 1, *Act Respecting*

the United Nations Convention on Contracts for the International Sale of Goods (RSQ, c C-67.01); ss 4-5, *International Sale of Goods Act* (SS 1990-91, c I-10.3); ss 3, 5, *International Sale of Goods Act* (SY 1992, c 7);
- *New Zealand*: ss 4-5, *Sale of Goods (United Nations Convention) Act* 1994; and
- *Singapore*: ss 3-4, *Sale of Goods (United Nations Convention) Act* (Chapter 283A).

The CISG became part of domestic law in Germany, Austria and Italy by the enactment of order of execution laws. These laws simultaneously approved ratification of the CISG by the executive and ordered the execution of the Convention as domestic law. See John Trone, *Federal Constitutions and International Relations* (St Lucia, Qld: University of Queensland Press, 2001), 73–75. The relevant laws were as follows:

- *Austria*: Bundesgesetzblatt 96/1988, p 1530;
- *Germany*: Bundesgesetzblatt 1989 II 588; and
- *Italy*: Law No 765 of 11 December 1985.

[13.150] Application of the CISG

For reasons of space, it is only possible to give a brief outline of the CISG in this book. The Convention applies to contracts for the sale of goods between individuals or corporations whose places of business are in different countries (a) which are parties to the CISG; or (b) where under private international law the applicable law is that of a party to the CISG (Art 1(1)(a) and (b)).

Under Art 1(1)(b) the CISG may apply to a contract even where a contracting party has its place of business in a country which is not party to the Convention. A number of countries have declared that they will not be bound by Art 1(1)(b), including China (1489 UNTS 179), the Czech Republic (1560 UNTS 548), Singapore (1856 UNTS 449), the Slovak Republic (1560 UNTS 548) and the United States (1489 UNTS 180). See generally, Asa Markel, "American, English and Japanese Warranty Law Compared: Should the US Reconsider her Article 95 Declaration to the CISG?" (2009) 21 *Pace International Law Review* 163. Germany will not apply Art 1(1)(b) where the rules of private international law lead to the application of the law of a country that has declared that it will not be bound by that provision (1552 UNTS 417).

The CISG expressly provides that it does not apply to certain specific types of sale, including auction sales and goods bought for personal, family or household use, unless the seller had no actual or constructive knowledge of such use (Art 2). The parties may exclude the application of the CISG or derogate from or vary the effect of most of its provisions (Art 6).

[13.155] Formation of the Contract

Agreement (offer and acceptance) and intention to be bound are elements of a contract under the CISG. However, consideration is not a necessary element. A contract is concluded when an acceptance of an offer becomes effective under the CISG (Art 23).

An offer must be sufficiently definite and indicate an intention to be bound. In order to be sufficiently definite an offer must indicate the goods and expressly or implicitly fix or make provision for determining the price and quantity (Art 14(1)). An acceptance is a statement or other conduct by the offeree indicating assent to an offer (Art 18(1)). In themselves silence or inactivity do not constitute acceptance (Art 18(1)).

The CISG provisions regarding the formation of a contract will not apply where a contracting party has its place of business in a country which has declared that it will not be bound by these provisions (Art 92). Such declarations have been made by Denmark, Finland, Norway and Sweden. See 1489 UNTS 178–180; 1523 UNTS 378; 1510 UNTS 499.

The CISG provides that a sales contract need not be concluded in writing or evidenced by writing and is not subject to any other requirement as to form (Art 11). However, a national Statute of Frauds requirement will apply where one of the contracting parties has its place of business in a country that has declared that the CISG provisions concerning writing requirements will not apply (Art 96). Such declarations have been made by (among others) Hungary (1489 UNTS 180), Latvia (1985 UNTS 491) and Lithuania (1850 UNTS 380).

[13.160] Performance of the Contract

The buyer must pay the price for the goods (Art 53). The seller must deliver the goods and transfer property in the goods (Art 30). The seller must deliver goods which are of the quantity, quality and description required by the contract (Art 35(1)).

Goods do not conform to the contract unless they (a) are fit for the purposes for which goods of the same description would ordinarily be used; (b) are fit for any particular purpose made known to the seller at the time the contract was concluded, except where the buyer did not rely, or it was unreasonable to rely, on the seller's skill and judgment; (c) possess the qualities of goods which were provided to the buyer by the seller as a sample; and (d) are packaged in the manner usual for such goods or, if there is no usual manner, in a manner adequate to preserve and protect the goods (Art 35(2)).

If the goods do not conform to the contract and whether or not the price has already been paid, the buyer may reduce the price by the proportion that the value of the nonconforming goods at the time of the delivery bears to the value that conforming goods would have had at that time (Art 50).

The buyer must examine the goods for nonconformity within the shortest period practicable in the circumstances (Art 38(1)). The buyer loses the right to rely on any nonconformity if they do not notify the seller of the nature of the nonconformity within a reasonable time after discovery or within a reasonable period from the time when the nonconformity ought to have been discovered (Art 39(1)).

The buyer or seller may fix an additional period of time of reasonable length for performance by the other party of his or her obligations (Arts 47(1), 63(1)). The buyer or seller retains the right to claim damages for the delay by the other party, but may not resort to any remedy for breach of contract during this additional time (Arts 47(2), 63(2)).

[13.165] Breach of Contract and Remedies

A party may suspend performance of their obligations if it becomes apparent that the other party will not perform a substantial part of their obligations as a result of (a) a serious deficiency in their ability to perform or creditworthiness; or (b) their conduct in performance or preparation (Art 71(1)).

A fundamental breach of contract results in such detriment to the other party as substantially to deprive that party of what they are entitled to expect under the contract. However, a breach will not constitute a fundamental breach if the party in breach did not foresee, and a reasonable person of the same kind in the same circumstances would not have foreseen, such a result (Art 25). Non-payment is a common form of fundamental breach. See *Downs Investments Pty Ltd (in liq) v Perwaja Steel Sdn Bhd* [2002] 2 Qd R 462 at [30]–[31], [33].

If the seller fails to perform an obligation, the buyer may (a) require performance, give additional time, require that the nonconformity be remedied, avoid the contract or reduce the price; and (b) claim damages (Art 45(1)). If the buyer fails to perform an obligation, the seller may (a) require performance, give additional time, avoid the contract or make a necessary specification for the buyer; and (b) claim damages (Art 61(1)).

A contract is avoided only after a declaration to that effect by a party. Avoidance releases both parties from their contractual obligations, subject to the payment of damages (Art 81(1)). A buyer who has lost the right to declare the contract avoided retains all other remedies (Art 83).

Damages are assessed as the amount of the loss suffered as a consequence of the breach, including lost profits. Damages may not exceed the loss which the party in breach foresaw or ought to have foreseen at the time the contract was entered into as a possible consequence of the breach (Art 74). A party must take such measures as are reasonable in the circumstances to mitigate the loss resulting from the breach (Art 77).

Specific performance is determined according to domestic law. If one party is entitled to require performance of any obligation by the other party, a court is not bound to enter a judgment for specific performance unless the court would do so under its own domestic law of sales contracts (Art 28).

A party is not liable for a failure to perform their obligations due to an impediment beyond their control which they could not reasonably be expected to have avoided or overcome or to have taken into account at the time the contract was concluded (Art 79(1)).

[13.170] Conclusion

This chapter examined the international trade law context within which the EU operates. That context includes multilateral, regional and bilateral free trade agreements. Trade disputes between WTO members may be settled through the WTO dispute resolution system. GATT 1994 is based upon four basic principles: most-favoured nation, non-discrimination, gradual reduction of tariff barriers and elimination of import quotas. WTO members may take safeguard and health protection measures.

The EU was an original member of the WTO. GATT 1994 does not have direct effect in EU law. In general the ECJ does not review the legality of measures adopted by EU institutions to determine their consistency with the WTO Agreement.

Where there is a conflict between a provision of GATT 1994 and one of the specialist WTO agreements, the specialist agreement prevails. These specialist agreements concern matters such as intellectual property, agriculture, sanitary measures, technical barriers, preshipment inspection, rules of origin, import licensing and services. Examples of regional free trade agreements include the EU itself, NAFTA and ASEAN. The United States, Canada and Australia have entered into numerous bilateral free trade agreements.

The CISG is the de facto international sales law in the European Union. The Convention applies to contracts for the sale of goods between individuals or corporations whose places of business are in different countries (a) which are parties to the CISG; or (b) where under private international law the applicable law is that of a party to the CISG.

Further Reading

A. WTO Agreement

Bartels, Lorand and Federico Ortino (eds). *Regional Trade Agreements and WTO Legal System* (Oxford: Oxford University Press, 2006).

Cottier, Thomas. "Dispute Settlement in the World Trade Organization: Characteristics and Structural Implications for the European Union" (1998) 35 *Common Market Law Review* 325.

de Burca, Gráinne and Joanne Scott (eds). *The EU and the WTO: Legal and Constitutional Issues* (Oxford: Hart, 2001).

Poli, Sara. "The EC's Implementation of the WTO Ruling in the Biotech Dispute" (2007) 32 *European Law Review* 705.

Princen, Sebastiaan. "EC Compliance with WTO Law: The Interplay of Law and Politics" (2004) 15 *European Journal of International Law* 555.

Reid, Emily. "Squaring the Circle for Tomorrow's World: A Comparative Analysis of the EC and WTO Approaches to Balancing Economic and Non-economic Interests in International Trade" in Takis Tridimas and Paolisa Nebbia (eds), *European Union Law for the Twenty-First Century* (Oxford: Hart, 2004), I: 303.

Steinberg, Richard H. "Judicial Lawmaking at the WTO: Discursive, Constitutional, and Political Constraints" (2004) 98 *American Journal of International Law* 247.

Wolfrum, Rüdiger; Peter-Tobias Stoll and Karen Kaiser (eds). *WTO: Institutions and Dispute Settlement* (Leiden: Martinus Nijhoff, 2006).

WTO Analytical Index – Guide to WTO Law and Practice (2nd ed, Cambridge: Cambridge University Press, 2007). Also available in electronic format at http://www.wto.org/ English/res_e/booksp_e/analytic_index_e/analytic_index_e.htm.

B. CISG

CISG Advisory Council. "Opinion No 1: Electronic Communications Under CISG" (2003) 15 *Pace International Law Review* 453.

CISG Advisory Council. "Opinion No 2: Examination of the Goods and Notice of Non-conformity Articles 38 and 39" (2004) 16 *Pace International Law Review* 377.

CISG Advisory Council. "Opinion No 3: Parol Evidence Rule, Plain Meaning Rule, Contractual Merger Clause and the CISG" (2005) 17 *Pace International Law Review* 61.

CISG Advisory Council. "Opinion No 4: Contracts for the Sale of Goods to be Manufactured or Produced and Mixed Contracts (Article 3 CISG)" (2005) 17 *Pace International Law Review* 79.

CISG Advisory Council. "Opinion No 5: The Buyer's Right to Avoid the Contract in Case of Non-conforming Goods or Documents" [2005–2006] *Review of the Convention on Contracts for the International Sale of Goods* 233.

CISG Advisory Council. "Opinion No 6: Calculation of Damages Under CISG Article 74", available at http://www.cisgac.com.

CISG Advisory Council. "Opinion No 7: Exemption of Liability for Damages Under Article 79 of the CISG", available at http://www.cisgac.com.

CISG Advisory Council. "Opinion No 8: Calculation of Damages Under CISG Articles 75 and 76", available at http://www.cisgac.com.

CISG Advisory Council. "Opinion No 9: Consequences of Avoidance of the Contract", available at http://www.cisgac.com.

Cross, Karen Halverson. "Parol Evidence Under the CISG: The 'Homeward Trend' Reconsidered" (2007) 68 *Ohio State Law Journal* 133.

DiMatteo, Larry A. *International Sales Law: A Critical Analysis of CISG Jurisprudence* (Cambridge: Cambridge University Press, 2005).

Erauw, Johan. "CISG Articles 66–70: The Risk of Loss and Passing It" (2005) 25 *Journal of Law and Commerce* 203.

Ferrari, Franco. "Fundamental Breach of Contract Under the UN Sales Convention – 25 Years of Article 25 CISG" (2005) 25 *Journal of Law and Commerce* 489.

Flechtner, Harry M. "Funky Mussels, a Stolen Car, and Decrepit Used Shoes: Non-conforming Goods and Notice Thereof Under the United Nations Sales Convention ('CISG')" (2008) 26 *Boston University International Law Journal* 1.

Janssen, André and Olaf Meyer (eds). *CISG Methodology* (Munich: Sellier, 2009).

Korpela, Riku. "Article 74 of the United States Convention on Contracts for the International Sale of Goods" [2004–2005] *Review of the Convention on Contracts for the International Sale of Goods* 73.

Kroll, Stefan. "Selected Problems Concerning the CISG's Scope of Application" (2005) 25 *Journal of Law and Commerce* 39.

Lookofsky, Joseph M. "Consequential Damages in CISG Context" (2007) 19 *Pace International Law Review* 63.

Lookofsky, Joseph M. *Understanding the CISG* (3rd ed, Alphen aan den Rijn: Kluwer Law International, 2008).

Liu, Chengwei. "Additional Period (Nachfrist) for Late Performance: Perspectives from the CISG, UNIDROIT Principles, PECL and Case Law" [2004–2005] *Review of the Convention on Contracts for the International Sale of Goods* 3.

McQuillen, Marlyse. "The Development of a Federal CISG Common Law in US Courts: Patterns of Interpretation and Citation" (2007) 61 *University of Miami Law Review* 509.

Moens, Gabriël and Peter Gillies. *International Trade and Business: Law Policy and Ethics* (2nd ed, Abingdon, England: Routledge Cavendish, 2006), Ch 1.

Peacock, Darren. "Avoidance and the Notion of Fundamental Breach Under the CISG: An English Perspective" (2005) 8 *International Trade and Business Law Review* 95.

Quinn, James P. "The Interpretation and Application of the United Nations Convention on Contracts for the International Sale of Goods" (2005) 8 *International Trade and Business Law Review* 221.

Saidov, Djakhongir. *The Law of Damages in International Sales: The CISG and Other International Instruments* (Oxford: Hart, 2008).

Schlechtriem, Peter. "Non-material Damages – Recovery Under the CISG?" (2007) 19 *Pace International Law Review* 89.

Schlechtriem, Peter and Petra Butler. *UN Law on International Sales: The UN Convention on the International Sale of Goods* (Berlin: Springer, 2009).

Schwenzer, Ingeborg. "Avoidance of the Contract in Case of Non-conforming Goods (Article 49(1)(a) CISG)" (2005) 25 *Journal of Law and Commerce* 437.

Trone, John. "International Sales Contracts" in Clive Turner, *Australian Commercial Law* (27th ed, Sydney: Lawbook Co, 2009), Ch 15.

Ubartaite, Edita. "Application of the CISG in the United States" (2005) 7 *European Journal of Law Reform* 277.

UNCITRAL Digest of Case Law on the United Nations Convention on the International Sale of Goods (New York: United Nations, 2008), available at http://www.uncitral.org/pdf/english/clout/CISG_second_edition.pdf.

Viscasillas, M del Pilar Perales. "Modification and Termination of the Contract (Art 29 CISG)" (2005) 25 *Journal of Law and Commerce* 167.

Walker, Janet. "Agreeing to Disagree: Can We Just Have Words? CISG Article 11 and the Model Law Writing Requirement" (2005) 25 *Journal of Law and Commerce* 153.

Zeller, Bruno. "The Black Hole: Where are the Four Corners of the CISG?" (2002) 7 *International Trade and Business Law Review* 251.

Zeller, Bruno. *CISG and the Unification of International Trade Law* (New York: Routledge-Cavendish, 2007).

Appendix A
Problem Questions

Note: This Appendix contains a number of problem questions that may be of assistance to lecturers and students. The majority of these questions concern the most important areas of EU law, such as the free movement of persons and goods, direct effect and judicial review by the Court of Justice. Not all chapters are represented by questions.

Question 1 (Chapters 1, 12)

In 2012, the EU adopts Directive 2012/125 imposing an obligation upon Member States to enact national legislation that provides for wheelchair access to government-owned buildings and buildings that are owned or occupied by companies that employ at least 250 people.

The Member States are required to implement this Directive by 1 December 2013. Spain enacts an implementing law on 1 July 2013. This law provides that companies which employ at least 200 people must provide wheelchair access to any buildings that they own or occupy. However, the Spanish law does not cover government-owned buildings. The reason for this omission lies in the fact that Spain has embarked upon an ambitious public building program. The new government buildings, which are expected to be completed between 2012 and 2032, will satisfy the most stringent architectural standards and will obviously provide wheelchair access. It was thus deemed unnecessary to extend the law to government-owned buildings.

In February 2014 Ana Espinosa, who is the National Secretary of the Spanish Council for the Disabled, is dismissed by the Spanish Taxation Department for criticizing the continued absence of access ramps at the government-owned Taxation Building.

Answer the following questions:

1. What is a Directive?
2. Describe the legislative process involved in an Art 294 TFEU procedure. Indicate whether Art 294 may be used by the Council to adopt Directive 2012/125; and

G. Moens, J. Trone, *Commercial Law of the European Union*,
Ius Gentium: Comparative Perspectives on Law and Justice 4,
DOI 10.1007/978-90-481-8774-4,

3. Ana seeks your advice as to whether she has a remedy under EU law against her employers and what can be done to enforce the Directive in Spain.

Question 2 (Chapter 2)

In February 2012 the United Kingdom legislature enacts the *Sale of Beer (Health and Safety) Act* 2012. Section 15 of the Act provides that in the United Kingdom beer may only be sold in licensed liquor shops. However, in municipalities where there is no liquor shop beer may be marketed in licensed pharmacies. Section 18 provides that importers of beer, operating in other EU countries, can only purchase British beer from either licensed liquor shops or licensed pharmacies in the United Kingdom.

Karl Gutt is a German importer of British beer. He takes the view that the United Kingdom legislation constitutes a quantitative restriction on imports. In particular, he argues that the legislation prevents him from buying beer directly from its British producer. In his opinion, this limitation significantly increases the price at which he could possibly buy British beer, making importation of beer from the United Kingdom into Germany an uneconomical proposition. Karl initiates legal action in a United Kingdom court, seeking to establish the incompatibility of the British law with Art 34 TFEU.

During the proceedings, the legal representatives of the British government argue that the legislative requirement that beer be exclusively sold in licensed liquor shops or licensed pharmacies does not adversely affect the rights of German importers to obtain British beer products for resale in Germany and therefore does not constitute a quantitative restriction upon imports. The British government also argues that even if the legislation constitutes a quantitative restriction, the statute is justified under Art 36 TFEU because it is necessary and appropriate to protect the health and life of beer drinkers. Karl claims that the legislation violates Art 34 TFEU because it exceeds what is necessary to achieve the aims of protecting the health and life of consumers of beer.

The United Kingdom court refers to the European Court of Justice the issue of the compatibility of the legislation with Art 34 TFEU. Is the ECJ likely to hold that the *Sale of Beer (Health and Safety) Act* 2012 violates Art 34 TFEU?

Question 3 (Chapters 2, 11)

The United Kingdom is concerned about the proliferation on its territory of fake foreign-sourced jewellery. In order to combat this problem, the UK Parliament enacts the *Control of Fake (Foreign) Jewellery Act* 2011.

Section 2 of the Act defines jewellery as "articles made of precious metal or rolled precious metal or of base metal, including polished or plated articles suitable for setting". Section 11 of the Act requires that imported jewellery, including jewellery imported from other Member States of the European Union, bear a designation of origin or, alternatively, the word "foreign". In enacting Section 11, the legislator hopes to encourage purchasers of jewellery to focus on the origin of the goods and to reduce the importation of fake foreign-sourced jewellery.

Ralph Baker is a London-based importer and vendor of jewellery from Romania. He complains to the National British Jewellery Council, which licenses jewellery vendors in the UK and regulates the profession of jewellers. The Council refers the case to the European Court of Justice for a preliminary ruling.

The legal representatives of the UK government contend that the legislation is the only effective way in which the sale of fake foreign-sourced jewellery can be combated. They also point out that since the implementation of the impugned law sales of fake jewellery have substantially decreased.

Independently of Ralph's action, the European Commission initiates an action in the ECJ, claiming that the UK legislation violates EU law because it lowers the value of an imported product, in particular by causing a reduction in its intrinsic value.

Answer the following questions:

1. Does the *Control of Fake (Foreign) Jewellery Act* 2011 constitute a measure having an effect equivalent to a quantitative restriction on imports under Art 34 TFEU?
2. If the Act constitutes a quantitative restriction on imports, does the Act violate Art 34 TFEU?
3. If the Act violates Art 34 TFEU, could the Act be saved by Art 36 TFEU?
4. What form of action is involved in the Commission's approach to the ECJ? Identify the relevant Articles of the TFEU.

Question 4 (Chapter 2)

The German Parliament adopts a law pertaining to pharmaceutical products supplied only upon prescription. Art 14 of the law prohibits a pharmacist from substituting any other product for a product specifically named in the prescription. Art 14 is compatible with the Code of Ethics adopted by the German Society of Pharmacists.

Hence, once a product has been prescribed by its proprietary name, only the product bearing that name may be supplied by the pharmacist. Art 14 applies to imported (inter-State) and locally-produced medicines. The rule also applies to parallel imports. As a consequence of the enactment of Art 14, parallel imports of proprietary medicinal products bearing a brand name different from that of the product previously authorized in Germany have practically ceased.

Answer the following questions:

1. Is Art 14 a measure having an equivalent effect under Art 34 TFEU?
2. Is Art 14 compatible with Art 34 TFEU?
3. Is Art 14 justified under Art 36 TFEU?

Question 5 (Chapter 2)

Chocolaterie Belge SA is a major Belgian producer of fine chocolates. It sends a shipment of chocolates to its distributor in the United Kingdom, but the shipment is refused entry at the port of Dover. The reasons given by the customs authority for refusing entry are:

First: the chocolate boxes are not labelled in English. There is a UK legislative requirement that all foodstuffs imported into the United Kingdom must be labelled in English;

Second: the chocolates are packed in carton boxes and therefore do not satisfy United Kingdom consumer protection standards, which require chocolates to be packed only in metal containers; and

Third: the Belgian chocolates contain additives which are not allowed in chocolates marketed and sold in the United Kingdom.

Chocolaterie Belge SA have also been told by Cotes plc, a supermarket chain to whom it had hoped to sell large quantities of chocolates, that they will not be stocking the Belgian product, as part of their "We are backing British confectionary" campaign.

In light of these facts, advise Chocolaterie Belge SA as to its rights, if any, under EU law.

Question 6 (Chapters 2, 12)

In 2012, London is plagued by demonstrations sparked by the spiralling cost of beer. At the time of the demonstrations, beer generally costs £20.00 a pint in London pubs. This price applies to both locally produced beer and beer imported from other EU Member States.

The Beer Promotion Party (BPP) wins the election that is held in February 2013. The new Parliament adopts the *Beer Relief (Fair Pricing) Act* 2013. The legislation treats locally produced beer (ie beer produced in the United Kingdom) and imported beer (including beer produced in other EU countries) differently. Beer manufactured in the UK is subject to a price freeze applied as of 1 April 2013. Section 17 of the Act stipulates that the price of imported (inter-State) beer is to be fixed at the level of the price charged by producers to retailers in the EU State of production.

The Beer Prices Surveillance Authority (BPSA) administers the legislation. The Director of the Authority considers applications by producers of local and imported beers for an increase in the selling prices of their beers. In the exercise of this function, the Director is constrained only by s 27 of the Act, which states that the Director "shall take into consideration the profitability of breweries established in the UK and the public interest".

The implementation of the legislation places inter-State producers in a situation in which they are compelled either to accept for their exported beers a retail price which corresponds to the level prevailing in the EU State of origin or to forego the opportunity of selling their products in the UK market.

Joseph Blunt is an importer of beer. He imports the highly acclaimed "Manneken" beer that is produced by a small brewery in Brussels, Belgium. Its producer sells the "Manneken" beer to Belgian retailers for €10.00.

Blunt initiates legal proceedings in an English court in order to test the validity of the *Beer Relief (Fair Pricing) Act* 2013. In particular, he argues that the legislation constitutes a quantitative restriction on imports or is a measure having an equivalent effect since it is no longer profitable for him to import "Manneken" beer from Belgium. Blunt alleges that the *Beer Relief (Fair Pricing) Act* 2013 violates Art 34 TFEU. The English court suspends the application of the Act and refers the question of the compatibility of the UK law with the TFEU to the European Court of Justice (ECJ).

During the hearing in the ECJ, the legal representatives of the UK government contend that the legislation is aimed at combating inflation. They also point out that since the implementation of the impugned law, demonstrations disrupting law and order in the UK have ceased.

Answer the following questions:

1. Is an English court entitled to suspend the application of the *Beer Relief (Fair Pricing) Act* 2013 on the ground that it is potentially incompatible with Art 34 TFEU, even though an incompatibility has not yet been established by the European Court of Justice?
2. Is the *Beer Relief (Fair Pricing) Act* 2003 compatible with Art 34 TFEU?

Question 7 (Chapter 3)

In November 2012 Eva, a German national, moves to Brussels, Belgium to take up a part-time post as a music teacher in the Belgian Academy for Music. Her job is not permanent and she is paid a lower rate than Belgian nationals doing the same work. When she complains about her treatment she is informed that her job is within the "Belgian public service".

In February 2013, Eva's American husband, Andrew, and their son, Phillip, join her in Brussels. Andrew was a dock worker in New York before his arrival in Brussels. He is unable to find suitable work in Brussels. He considers that the flat he is sharing with Eva and Phillip is too small. His failure to find a job and the accommodation problems place strain on the marriage. Andrew goes to the Belgian port city of Antwerp in order to seek work and to look for a bigger flat for his family. However, the Belgian immigration authorities suspect that the marriage has irretrievably broken down and order his immediate deportation to the United States.

Phillip is convicted of vandalism and is ordered by a local magistrate to do 150 hours of community service. The Belgian Minister of the Interior orders his deportation after the service has been completed. In addition, a deportation order which does not state any reasons is issued against Eva.

Advise Eva, Andrew and Phillip of their rights, if any, under EU law.

Question 8 (Chapter 3)

In 2008 the University of Chicago conferred upon Dr Carolin Muller the degree of doctor of medicine. In 2011, she successfully passed examinations at the University of Munich, Germany, which entitled her to a specialist diploma in cancer treatment. Dr Muller is an American citizen. She wished to work in Germany as a medical doctor. To that end, she repeatedly sought registration with the National League of German Doctors, membership of which was necessary in order to practise medicine in Germany. However, on each occasion the National League refused to grant her authorization to practise medicine in Germany on the ground that, in accordance with German law, her American degree did not entitle her to practise medicine in Germany. Dr Muller then decided to seek a preliminary ruling from the European Court of Justice in order to test the compatibility of this decision with the TFEU.

Answer the following questions:

1. Is Dr Muller entitled as a matter of law to a preliminary ruling by the ECJ?
2. Is Dr Muller a "worker" under European Union Law? What is the relevance of this question in the EU legal system?
3. Provide legal advice to Dr Muller as to what she would have to do in order to be admitted as a medical practitioner in Germany.

Question 9 (Chapter 3)

A French woman, Dominique Paganon, enters the UK and applies for a residence permit. Four months later her application is refused and she is ordered to leave the country on the ground that she is a sex worker.

Prostitution is not as such illegal in the United Kingdom, although various activities connected with prostitution constitute criminal offences. Dominique files a complaint against the government in the Decency Tribunal. This Tribunal has been established in order to enforce standards of personal behaviour in the United Kingdom. The Tribunal seeks a preliminary ruling from the European Court of Justice.

Would it be possible for the United Kingdom to rely on Art 45(3) TFEU for the purpose of expelling Dominique? In particular, if prostitution does not constitute a criminal offence under the law of the United Kingdom, can the UK government nevertheless resort to the public policy exception of Art 45(3)?

Question 10 (Chapters 3, 11)

Ermanno Zacco, an Italian citizen, works as a self-employed plumber in Milan, Italy. He hopes to establish himself as a plumber in Germany because plumbers earn much more in Germany than in Italy. He travels to Berlin, Germany on 8 July 2011. Soon after his arrival he is employed by the Interior Ministry as a member of the Ministry's plumbing unit.

He is paid €20 per hour even though his five colleagues in the unit are paid €25. All of his colleagues are German citizens. Ermanno complains about his lower pay but is told that his job is not equal to the job performed by the German plumbers. This is because his poor knowledge of German prevents him from seeking the allocation of challenging plumbing assignments.

Ermanno is retrenched on 15 June 2013 because the German Government orders the Ministry to reduce the number of its staff members. Ermanno is also told that his position is a "public service" position which is exempted from the application of the principle of the free movement for workers by Art 45(4) TFEU.

Ermanno feels that he has been discriminated against. He brings a case for reinstatement before the German Anti-Discrimination Board (ADB). However, the Board refuses to consider his complaint because it considers that his position in the Ministry comes within the exception in Art 45(4) TFEU.

Undeterred by this setback, Ermanno applies to the German Plumbing Registration Board (GPRB) for registration as a self-employed plumber. The relevant German legislation requires that self-employed plumbers must be members of the GPRB.

By a letter dated 3 August 2013 the Board indicates that it is not likely to approve his application on the grounds that (i) he does not possess a German Plumbing Certificate and (ii) he has failed his German-language examination, success in which is necessary for registration with the Board.

Nevertheless, the President of the Board decides to seek a preliminary ruling from the European Court of Justice in order to ascertain whether Art 45 TFEU and Council Regulation 1612/68 give Ermanno an enforceable right to registration. Note that under German law the Board's decision cannot be appealed to a higher German court or tribunal.

Answer the following questions:

1. Is the German Plumbing Registration Board (GPRB) a "tribunal" under Art 267 TFEU?
2. If the GPRB is a "tribunal" under Art 267 TFEU, what questions are likely to be asked of the ECJ?
3. Is Ermanno entitled to a preliminary ruling by the ECJ?
4. What is the purpose of the Art 267 TFEU preliminary ruling action?
5. Is Ermanno a "worker" under European Union Law? What is the relevance of this question in the EU legal system?
6. What legal advice would you provide to Ermanno regarding his chances of being registered with the GPRB? In particular, discuss whether Ermanno's position is a "public service" position that comes within the exception in Art 45(4) TFEU.

Question 11 (Chapters 1, 3)

Claude Brol is a 22-year old French citizen who had worked as a postal employee in Paris. He arrives in London, United Kingdom on 3 July 2012, seeking employment. Approximately 1 year after his arrival in the UK, Claude is robbed and severely beaten by hoodlums. Claude is refused criminal injuries compensation by the UK authorities because of his nationality. Claude challenges the validity of this refusal, citing Art 21(2) of the Charter of Fundamental Rights of the European Union. That Article provides that "[w]ithin the scope of application of the Treaties and without prejudice to any of their specific provisions, any discrimination on grounds of nationality shall be prohibited." Subsequently, the UK authorities describe him as a "trouble maker" and deport him to France. Eventually, the matter reaches the European Court of Justice by way of a preliminary reference.

Answer the following questions:

1. Is Claude's reliance on Art 21(2) of the Charter of Fundamental Rights likely to be successful? Explain the position both before and after the entry into force of the Treaty of Lisbon.
2. What other EU law could he rely upon in order to secure compensation for the robbery and beating?
3. Is Claude a "worker" under EU law? What is the relevance of this question in the EU legal system?

4. What would Claude have to do in order to ensure that he can stay in the UK?
5. If Claude were granted the right to stay in the UK, what would be his rights in the UK as a citizen of the European Union?
6. Assume that Claude is not deported to France, but instead is appointed as a postal employee by the British Postal Service. Would it be possible for the Postal Service to sack Claude, after his appointment, on the ground that his knowledge of the English language is insufficient? Would the Postal Service be able to sack Claude on the ground that a postal employee is a British public servant?

Question 12 (Chapter 5)

On 18 September 2010 France enters into a bilateral treaty with the United States regarding environment protection. The treaty provides for the adoption and co-ordination of American and French measures aimed at fighting the pollution of the Atlantic Ocean. The Council had previously adopted Regulation 345/2005 on the protection of the environment. Art 16(7) of the Regulation provides for the imposition of heavy penalties upon sea carriers that discharge chemical products into the Atlantic Ocean. Explain the doctrine of parallelism with reference to these facts.

Question 13 (Chapter 10)

Ursula and Karl are employed by the German Clothing Factory, a private employer in Hamburg. Ursula is a sales manager and Karl is a plumber. Karl's rate of pay is €25 per hour, whereas Ursula is paid only €9 per hour. In addition, Karl is provided with a vehicle to enable him to get to the factory in comfort. All sales managers in the company are female and all plumbers are males.

Ursula considers that her work is of equal value to Karl's work. When Ursula complains to the management about her low pay, she is told that:

1. There are very few good plumbers and, if the company finds a good plumber, that person should be paid very good wages; and
2. There is an oversupply of sales managers; the economic law of supply and demand dictates that sales managers will accept low wages to retain employment.

One year after Ursula complained to the management, the German Clothing Factory experiences financial difficulties. The factory retrenches a number of workers, all of whom are sales managers, including Ursula. Advise Ursula as to whether she has any remedy under EU law.

Question 14 (Chapter 10)

Liz works part-time for a manufacturer of women's clothing in Hamburg, Germany. The pay for full-time work is the same for male and female workers. However, the hourly rate for part-time work is substantially lower than the hourly rate for full-time work. The part-time employees are all women.

The clothing manufacturer justifies the difference between the full-time and part-time rates on the ground that the administrative costs associated with part-time (and casual) employees are significantly higher than those for full-time workers. Is the difference in remuneration between part-time and full-time work contrary to Art 157 TFEU, where the class of part-time employees is comprised entirely of women?

Question 15 (Chapters 3, 11)

Eugenio Ciampi, an Italian citizen, is a graduate of the Notre Dame Law School, Indiana, where he obtained his Juris Doctor (JD) degree in 2005. After working for a few years in various American law firms, he decides to pursue a law degree at the University of Florence, Italy. Eugenio hopes to become a prominent Italian lawyer in an international law firm in Rome. In 2010, after completing the required Italian legal studies, he registers as an *Avvocato* (legal practitioner or attorney).

In 2011 he meets Maria Kloppenburg, a German citizen residing in Berlin. After a short period of courting, Maria and Eugenio marry in Berlin and decide to settle permanently in that city. Eugenio now wants to become a German *Rechtsanwalt* (legal practitioner or attorney). He applies to the German Bar Registration Board for registration as a *Rechtsanwalt*. By letter of 3 August 2012 the Board rejects his application on the ground that he does not satisfy the conditions laid down in the relevant German laws, because his American and Italian law degrees and admissions to practice do not entitle him to practice law in Germany. However, the President of the Board also decides to seek a preliminary ruling from the European Court of Justice in order to test the compatibility of the Board's decision with the TFEU.

Answer the following questions:

1. Is the German Bar Registration Board a "tribunal" under Art 267 TFEU?
2. Assuming that the German Bar Registration Board is a "tribunal" within Art 267 TFEU, what questions should be asked of the ECJ?
3. Is Eugenio entitled as a matter of law to a preliminary ruling by the ECJ?
4. Is Eugenio a "worker" under European Union Law? What is the relevance of this question in the EU legal system?
5. What is the purpose of the Art 267 preliminary ruling action?

6. Could this case have been initiated by Eugenio in the EU General Court, or is the ECJ the only European Court authorized to hear the case?
7. Advise Eugenio regarding his prospects of being admitted to the legal profession in Germany as a *Rechtsanwalt*.

Question 16 (Chapter 12)

In 2012 the Council of the European Union adopts Directive 2012/207 imposing an obligation upon Member States to enact national legislation which provides for the same retirement age for male and female workers. Member States are expected to adopt the national implementing legislation by 1 January 2014. Portugal fails to implement the Directive before the deadline for implementation. The relevant Portuguese legislation mandates a compulsory retirement age of 55 years for female electricity workers and 60 years for male electricity workers.

Maria de Oliveira is employed by the Portuguese Electrical Company (PEC), which is a statutory government-owned corporation responsible for developing and maintaining the electricity distribution network in Portugal. It also has a monopoly over the supply of electricity. Upon reaching her 55th birthday Maria is compulsorily retired in May 2014. Maria wishes to rely on the Directive against her employer before Portuguese courts in order to continue working for PEC.

Answer the following questions:

1. Describe the principle of "direct effect" and its importance to EU Law.
2. Is Directive 2012/207 "directly effective"?
3. Does Maria have a remedy under EU law against her employer (PEC), and what can be done to enforce the Directive in Portugal?
4. Would Maria have a remedy under EU law if PEC had been privatized?

Question 17 (Chapter 12)

On 15 September 2010 the EU adopts Directive 2010/136. The Directive imposes an obligation upon Member States to adopt domestic legislation requiring all processed food products to be labelled in English as well as in the language(s) of the producing Member State. This requirement applies regardless of whether the Member States produce the food products for export or for local consumption. The Directive further requires EU Member States to adopt implementing legislation by 1 August 2012.

The government of France claims that the Directive is "insensitive" to the maintenance of France's cultural identity. The French government refuses to implement the Directive and embraces a policy of benign neglect. The government defiantly refers to Art 2 of the French Constitution which provides that French is the official language of France. The French Parliament enacts a law which requires that all processed food products produced in France be labelled only in French.

Karen Osborne produces processed carrots in France for export to the United Kingdom. Karen decides to adhere to the EU Directive and labels her processed food products in both English and French. She is prosecuted for violating the French law.

Answer the following questions:

1. Does Directive 2010/136 have direct effect? What test is used to determine the direct effect of Directives?
2. Is France liable for its intentional failure to implement Directive 2010/136? In particular, could France be required to compensate Karen for its failure to implement the Directive?
3. What principles have been formulated by the European Court of Justice regarding failure by a Member State to implement a Directive?
4. Would France be able to rely upon its national Constitution for the purpose of refusing to implement the Directive?

Question 18 (Chapters 10, 12)

In 2011 the Council adopted Directive 2011/315 imposing upon Member States an obligation to adopt national legislation providing for the payment of a government pension to all male and female workers who retire at age 60 and whose total assets are less than €200,000.

Member States were expected to adopt national implementing legislation before 31 December 2012. Greece failed to implement the Directive before the stipulated date. The existing Greek legislation provides that a government pension will only be paid to female workers who retire at age 65 and male workers who retire at age 68.

Amelia Demetriou is employed by the Greek Electrical Company (GEC), which is a statutory government-owned corporation responsible for developing and maintaining the electricity distribution network in Greece. It also has a monopoly on the supply of electricity.

Upon reaching her 60th birthday Amelia resigns her position at GEC and applies for a government pension. Her total assets at the time of resignation are less than €100,000. Her application is rejected because she has not reached the age of 65. Amelia wishes to rely on the Directive and initiates a legal action in a Greek court against the Greek government.

Answer the following questions:

1. Describe the principle of "direct effect" and its importance in EU Law. Discuss the principle of the supremacy of EU law in this context.

2. Does Directive 2011/315 have direct effect?
3. Does Amelia have any remedies under EU law against Greece for its failure to implement the Directive, and what can be done to enforce the Directive in Greece?
4. Is the Greek pension scheme that discriminates between male and female workers on the ground of age compatible with Art 157(1) TFEU according to which "[e]ach Member State shall ensure that the principle of equal pay for male and female workers for equal work or work of equal value is applied"?
5. Would Amelia have a remedy under EU law if GEC had been privatized?

Question 19 (Chapter 13)

James Townsend is a United States manufacturer of a computer software program called "Anglialingua", which is designed to assist non-English speaking background students in learning the English language. Josephine Chiraque is a French distributor of educational materials. Her head office is in Paris, France. Townsend meets Chiraque in London, United Kingdom, during a conference entitled the "Teaching of English as a Second Language". In conversations with Chiraque, Townsend describes his computer software program in glowing terms and states that it has already been successfully marketed and used in Germany.

Chiraque orally agrees to purchase 1,000 packages of "Anglialingua" at US $300 each. Townsend undertakes to ship the packages to Paris upon his return to the United States. Chiraque agrees to pay for the packages by letter of credit upon receipt of the appropriate shipping documents.

After returning to Paris Chiraque contacts a German importer of "Anglialingua" to ascertain the usefulness of the program. The German importer tells Chiraque that "Anglialingua" has not been well received in Germany because the program does not work and is overpriced. Chiraque, who did not actually see "Anglialingua" in operation, becomes very concerned that "Anglialingua" may not actually be suitable for French high school students.

Answer the following questions:

1. Does the transaction have a sufficient connection with States that have ratified the Convention on Contracts for the International Sale of Goods (CISG) so that its provisions will govern the contract?
2. Has a valid contract for the international sale of goods been formed? Does it matter that the contract is not in writing?
3. If a valid contract for the international sale of goods has been formed, under what circumstances would Chiraque be able to avoid the contract?

4. If Chiraque refuses to accept the packages, is Townsend likely to receive specific performance? Should he request specific performance in a French court?
5. What are Townsend's options at law? In particular, discuss the other remedies, if any, which are available to the seller under the CISG.

Question 20 (Chapter 13)

Andrew Munday is an English manufacturer whose place of business is in Surrey, United Kingdom. Silvio Capodimonte uses printing machines as part of his business located in Naples, Italy. Andrew receives a request from Silvio to manufacture three ink rolls of standard thickness and 2,450 mm in length. The printing machines cannot be operated without the ink rolls. The ink rolls are to be installed by Andrew's mechanics into Silvio's printing machines. In the printing industry standard thickness is regarded as 40 mm, but some older models and some specialized rolls have a thickness of 42 mm.

The request arrives in Surrey on 6 January 2012. On 10 January 2012 Andrew replies that he "can possibly manufacture the ink rolls at č25,000 each by 20 April 2012". Silvio responds on 8 February 2012. Silvio asks what the price of the ink rolls would be if they were to be delivered to Silvio's place of business in Naples and installed into his printing presses. Andrew replies by return mail advising that the three ink rolls, including delivery and installation, would cost č27,000. Andrew also indicates that the ink rolls will be sent to Naples in the week beginning on 23 April 2012 because an assembly team will be in Italy at that time.

On 1 March 2012 Silvio advises that he accepts Andrew's offer. However, in his purported acceptance he indicates that the goods must arrive in Italy on 5 April 2012 at the latest. Silvio has received a very lucrative printing job which he will lose if the ink rolls arrive later than 5 April 2012.

The ink rolls arrive in Naples on 26 April 2012. Upon inspection, Silvio discovers that the thickness of the ink rolls is correct but one of the rolls is 2,300 mm long. He sends an email to Andrew indicating that the rolls did not arrive on time and that one of the rolls is not long enough. He also advises Andrew that he cancels the contract and that the ink rolls are available for collection by Andrew.

Andrew seeks your advice regarding the following questions:

1. Has a contract for the international sale of goods been formed? If so, what are the terms of the contract?
2. What is the substantive law applicable to the contract?
3. Is Silvio entitled to avoid the contract under the Convention on Contracts for the International Sale of Goods?
4. What are the legal obligations of Andrew and Silvio once the contract is avoided?

Question 21 (Chapter 13)

Daniel Bates is a business person whose place of business is in Trafalgar Square, London. He operates a Hot Chocolate Café. For that purpose, he contacts a manufacturer of hot chocolate machines, Chocolade Fabrik (CF). The place of business of CF is located in Dresden, Germany.

A purchase order is placed during a telephone conversation between Bates and Gerhard Münzer, the CEO of CF. When placing the order, Mr Bates specifically indicates to Mr Münzer that the machine should be able to make a cup of hot chocolate in 60 s. Mr Münzer confirms that CF has a machine suitable for this purpose, namely the "Choco60", which costs €15,900 uninstalled.

During the conversation Mr Münzer mentions that it is CF's policy to inform purchasers that arbitration is CF's preferred method of dispute resolution and that German law is the law applicable to the contract. Daniel responds by saying that he is not familiar with arbitration and that he prefers mediation as a method of dispute resolution. However, he points out that he does not anticipate that disputes will occur. The chocolate machine is duly delivered on 30 August 2011.

When Daniel opens café on 3 September 2011, he discovers that the machine needs 180 s to produce a cup of hot chocolate. For nearly 2 years after the sale, Daniel does not complain to CF about this slowness because business has been brisk. But by Easter 2013, demand for the chocolate drink has substantially reduced. To make matters worse, on 15 May 2013 Daniel is seriously burned by hot steam emitted by the machine when he tries to accelerate the process of producing a hot cup of chocolate. Daniel is dismayed and wishes to avoid the contract.

Answer the following questions:

1. Has a contract for the international sale of goods been formed? Does it matter that the contract is not in writing? Is the disagreement about the appropriate method of dispute resolution a relevant issue?
2. If a contract for the international sale of goods has been formed, what substantive law will be applicable to the contract?
3. Is the chocolate machine fit for the particular purpose made known to the seller? Discuss the conformity requirements under the United Nations Convention on Contracts for the International Sale of Goods (CISG).
4. What remedies are available to Daniel for non-conformity of goods under the CISG?
5. Does the CISG apply to the wounds sustained by Daniel while operating the machine?
6. Under what circumstances would it be possible for Daniel to avoid the contract under the CISG?
7. What are the consequences of avoidance under the CISG?

Appendix B
Table of Equivalence: EEC Treaty Version – Treaty of Amsterdam Version

Reproduced from OJ C 340, 10.11.1997, pp 85–91.

Treaty on European Union

(*) New Article introduced by the Treaty of Amsterdam.
(**) New Title introduced by the Treaty of Amsterdam.
(***) Title restructured by the Treaty of Amsterdam.
Previous numbering // New numbering
TITLE I // TITLE I

Article A // Article 1
Article B // Article 2
Article C // Article 3
Article D // Article 4
Article E // Article 5
Article F // Article 6
Article F.1 (*) // Article 7

TITLE II // TITLE II

Article G // Article 8

TITLE III // TITLE III

Article H // Article 9

TITLE IV // TITLE IV

Article I // Article 10

TITLE V (***) // TITLE V

Article J.1 // Article 11
Article J.2 // Article 12
Article J.3 // Article 13
Article J.4 // Article 14
Article J.5 // Article 15
Article J.6 // Article 16
Article J.7 // Article 17
Article J.8 // Article 18
Article J.9 // Article 19
Article J.10 // Article 20
Article J.11 // Article 21
Article J.12 // Article 22
Article J.13 // Article 23
Article J.14 // Article 24
Article J.15 // Article 25
Article J.16 // Article 26
Article J.17 // Article 27
Article J.18 // Article 28

TITLE VI (***) // TITLE VI

Article K.1 // Article 29
Article K.2 // Article 30
Article K.3 // Article 31
Article K.4 // Article 32
Article K.5 // Article 33
Article K.6 // Article 34
Article K.7 // Article 35
Article K.8 // Article 36
Article K.9 // Article 37
Article K.10 // Article 38
Article K.11 // Article 39
Article K.12 // Article 40
Article K.13 // Article 41
Article K.14 // Article 42

TITLE VIa (**) // TITLE VII

Article K.15 (*) // Article 43
Article K.16 (*) // Article 44
Article K.17 (*) // Article 45

TITLE VII // TITLE VIII

Article L // Article 46

Article M // Article 47
Article N // Article 48
Article O // Article 49
Article P // Article 50
Article Q // Article 51
Article R // Article 52
Article S // Article 53

Treaty Establishing the European Community

(*) New Article introduced by the Treaty of Amsterdam.
(**) New Title introduced by the Treaty of Amsterdam.
(***) Chapter 1 restructured by the Treaty of Amsterdam.

Previous numbering // New numbering

PART ONE // PART ONE

Article 1 // Article 1
Article 2 // Article 2
Article 3 // Article 3
Article 3a // Article 4
Article 3b // Article 5
Article 3c (*) // Article 6
Article 4 // Article 7
Article 4a // Article 8
Article 4b // Article 9
Article 5 // Article 10
Article 5a (*) // Article 11
Article 6 // Article 12
Article 6a (*) // Article 13
Article 7 (repealed) // -
Article 7a // Article 14
Article 7b (repealed) // -
Article 7c // Article 15
Article 7d (*) // Article 16

PART TWO // PART TWO

Article 8 // Article 17
Article 8a // Article 18
Article 8b // Article 19
Article 8c // Article 20

Article 8d // Article 21
Article 8e // Article 22

PART THREE // PART THREE

TITLE I // TITLE I

Article 9 // Article 23
Article 10 // Article 24
Article 11 (repealed) // -

CHAPTER 1 // CHAPTER 1

Section 1 (deleted) // -

Article 12 // Article 25
Article 13 (repealed) // -
Article 14 (repealed) // -
Article 15 (repealed) // -
Article 16 (repealed // -
Article 17 (repealed) // -

Section 2 (deleted) // -

Article 18 (repealed) // -
Article 19 (repealed) // -
Article 20 (repealed) // -
Article 21 (repealed) // -
Article 22 (repealed) // -
Article 23 (repealed) // -
Article 24 (repealed) // -
Article 25 (repealed) // -
Article 26 (repealed) // -
Article 27 (repealed) // -
Article 28 // Article 26
Article 29 // Article 27

CHAPTER 2 // CHAPTER 2

Article 30 // Article 28
Article 31 (repealed) // -
Article 32 (repealed) // -
Article 33 (repealed) // -
Article 34 // Article 29
Article 35 (repealed) // -

Article 36 // Article 30
Article 37 // Article 31

TITLE II // TITLE II

Article 38 // Article 32
Article 39 // Article 33
Article 40 // Article 34
Article 41 // Article 35
Article 42 // Article 36
Article 43 // Article 37
Article 44 (repealed) // -
Article 45 (repealed) // -
Article 46 // Article 38
Article 47 (repealed) // -

TITLE III // TITLE III

CHAPTER 1 // CHAPTER 1

Article 48 // Article 39
Article 49 // Article 40
Article 50 // Article 41
Article 51 // Article 42

CHAPTER 2 // CHAPTER 2

Article 52 // Article 43
Article 53 (repealed) // -
Article 54 // Article 44
Article 55 // Article 45
Article 56 // Article 46
Article 57 // Article 47
Article 58 // Article 48

CHAPTER 3 // CHAPTER 3

Article 59 // Article 49
Article 60 // Article 50
Article 61 // Article 51
Article 62 (repealed) // -
Article 63 // Article 52
Article 64 // Article 53
Article 65 // Article 54
Article 66 // Article 55

CHAPTER 4 // CHAPTER 4

Article 67 (repealed) // -
Article 68 (repealed) // -
Article 69 (repealed) // -
Article 70 (repealed) // -
Article 71 (repealed) // -
Article 72 (repealed) // -
Article 73 (repealed) // -
Article 73a (repealed) // -
Article 73b // Article 56
Article 73c // Article 57
Article 73d // Article 58
Article 73e (repealed) // -
Article 73f // Article 59
Article 73g // Article 60
Article 73h (repealed) // -

TITLE IIIa (**) // TITLE IV

Article 73i (*) // Article 61
Article 73j (*) // Article 62
Article 73k (*) // Article 63
Article 73l (*) // Article 64
Article 73m (*) // Article 65
Article 73n (*) // Article 66
Article 73o (*) // Article 67
Article 73p (*) // Article 68
Article 73q (*) // Article 69

TITLE IV // TITLE V

Article 74 // Article 70
Article 75 // Article 71
Article 76 // Article 72
Article 77 // Article 73
Article 78 // Article 74
Article 79 // Article 75
Article 80 // Article 76
Article 81 // Article 77
Article 82 // Article 78
Article 83 // Article 79
Article 84 // Article 80

TITLE V // TITLE VI

CHAPTER 1 // CHAPTER 1

SECTION 1 // SECTION 1

Article 85 // Article 81
Article 86 // Article 82
Article 87 // Article 83
Article 88 // Article 84
Article 89 // Article 85
Article 90 // Article 86

Section 2 (deleted) // -

Article 91 (repealed) // -

SECTION 3 // SECTION 2

Article 92 // Article 87
Article 93 // Article 88
Article 94 // Article 89

CHAPTER 2 // CHAPTER 2

Article 95 // Article 90
Article 96 // Article 91
Article 97 (repealed) // -
Article 98 // Article 92
Article 99 // Article 93

CHAPTER 3 // CHAPTER 3

Article 100 // Article 94
Article 100a // Article 95
Article 100b (repealed) // -
Article 100c (repealed) // -
Article 100d (repealed) // -
Article 101 // Article 96
Article 102 // Article 97

TITLE VI // TITLE VII

CHAPTER 1 // CHAPTER 1

Article 102a // Article 98
Article 103 // Article 99

Article 103a // Article 100
Article 104 // Article 101
Article 104a // Article 102
Article 104b // Article 103
Article 104c // Article 104

CHAPTER 2 // CHAPTER 2

Article 105 // Article 105
Article 105a // Article 106
Article 106 // Article 107
Article 107 // Article 108
Article 108 // Article 109
Article 108a // Article 110
Article 109 // Article 111

CHAPTER 3 // CHAPTER 3

Article 109a // Article 112
Article 109b // Article 113
Article 109c // Article 114
Article 109d // Article 115

CHAPTER 4 // CHAPTER 4

Article 109e // Article 116
Article 109f // Article 117
Article 109g // Article 118
Article 109h // Article 119
Article 109i // Article 120
Article 109j // Article 121
Article 109k // Article 122
Article 109l // Article 123
Article 109m // Article 124

TITLE VIa (**) // TITLE VIII

Article 109n (*) // Article 125
Article 109o (*) // Article 126
Article 109p (*) // Article 127
Article 109q (*) // Article 128
Article 109r (*) // Article 129
Article 109s (*) // Article 130

TITLE VII // TITLE IX

Article 110 // Article 131
Article 111 (repealed) // -
Article 112 // Article 132
Article 113 // Article 133
Article 114 (repealed) // -
Article 115 // Article 134

TITLE VIIa (**) // TITLE X

Article 116 (*) // Article 135

TITLE VIII // TITLE XI

CHAPTER 1 (***) // CHAPTER 1

Article 117 // Article 136
Article 118 // Article 137
Article 118a // Article 138
Article 118b // Article 139
Article 118c // Article 140
Article 119 // Article 141
Article 119a // Article 142
Article 120 // Article 143
Article 121 // Article 144
Article 122 // Article 145

CHAPTER 2 // CHAPTER 2

Article 123 // Article 146
Article 124 // Article 147
Article 125 // Article 148

CHAPTER 3 // CHAPTER 3

Article 126 // Article 149
Article 127 // Article 150

TITLE IX // TITLE XII

Article 128 // Article 151

TITLE X // TITLE XIII

Article 129 // Article 152

TITLE XI // TITLE XIV

Article 129a // Article 153

TITLE XII // TITLE XV

Article 129b // Article 154
Article 129c // Article 155
Article 129d // Article 156

TITLE XIII // TITLE XVI

Article 130 // Article 157

TITLE XIV // TITLE XVII

Article 130a // Article 158
Article 130b // Article 159
Article 130c // Article 160
Article 130d // Article 161
Article 130e // Article 162

TITLE XV // TITLE XVIII

Article 130f // Article 163
Article 130g // Article 164
Article 130h // Article 165
Article 130i // Article 166
Article 130j // Article 167
Article 130k // Article 168
Article 130l // Article 169
Article 130m // Article 170
Article 130n // Article 171
Article 130o // Article 172
Article 130p // Article 173
Article 130q (repealed) // -

TITLE XVI // TITLE XIX

Article 130r // Article 174
Article 130s // Article 175
Article 130t // Article 176

TITLE XVII // TITLE XX

Article 130u // Article 177
Article 130v // Article 178
Article 130w // Article 179
Article 130x // Article 180
Article 130y // Article 181

PART FOUR // PART FOUR

Article 131 // Article 182
Article 132 // Article 183
Article 133 // Article 184
Article 134 // Article 185
Article 135 // Article 186
Article 136 // Article 187
Article 136a // Article 188

PART FIVE // PART FIVE

TITLE I // TITLE I

CHAPTER 1 // CHAPTER 1

SECTION 1 // SECTION 1

Article 137 // Article 189
Article 138 // Article 190
Article 138a // Article 191
Article 138b // Article 192
Article 138c // Article 193
Article 138d // Article 194
Article 138e // Article 195
Article 139 // Article 196
Article 140 // Article 197
Article 141 // Article 198
Article 142 // Article 199
Article 143 // Article 200
Article 144 // Article 201

SECTION 2 // SECTION 2

Article 145 // Article 202
Article 146 // Article 203
Article 147 // Article 204
Article 148 // Article 205
Article 149 (repealed) // -

Article 150 // Article 206
Article 151 // Article 207
Article 152 // Article 208
Article 153 // Article 209
Article 154 // Article 210

SECTION 3 // SECTION 3

Article 155 // Article 211
Article 156 // Article 212
Article 157 // Article 213
Article 158 // Article 214
Article 159 // Article 215
Article 160 // Article 216
Article 161 // Article 217
Article 162 // Article 218
Article 163 // Article 219

SECTION 4 // SECTION 4

Article 164 // Article 220
Article 165 // Article 221
Article 166 // Article 222
Article 167 // Article 223
Article 168 // Article 224
Article 168 a // Article 225
Article 169 // Article 226
Article 170 // Article 227
Article 171 // Article 228
Article 172 // Article 229
Article 173 // Article 230
Article 174 // Article 231
Article 175 // Article 232
Article 176 // Article 233
Article 177 // Article 234
Article 178 // Article 235
Article 179 // Article 236
Article 180 // Article 237
Article 181 // Article 238
Article 182 // Article 239
Article 183 // Article 240
Article 184 // Article 241
Article 185 // Article 242
Article 186 // Article 243
Article 187 // Article 244

Article 188 // Article 245

SECTION 5 // SECTION 5

Article 188a // Article 246
Article 188b // Article 247
Article 188c // Article 248

CHAPTER 2 // CHAPTER 2

Article 189 // Article 249
Article 189a // Article 250
Article 189b // Article 251
Article 189c // Article 252
Article 190 // Article 253
Article 191 // Article 254
Article 191a (*) // Article 255
Article 192 // Article 256

CHAPTER 3 // CHAPTER 3

Article 193 // Article 257
Article 194 // Article 258
Article 195 // Article 259
Article 196 // Article 260
Article 197 // Article 261
Article 198 // Article 262

CHAPTER 4 // CHAPTER 4

Article 198a // Article 263
Article 198b // Article 264
Article 198c // Article 265

CHAPTER 5 // CHAPTER 5

Article 198d // Article 266
Article 198e // Article 267

TITLE II // TITLE II

Article 199 // Article 268
Article 200 (repealed) // -
Article 201 // Article 269
Article 201a // Article 270

Article 202 // Article 271
Article 203 // Article 272
Article 204 // Article 273
Article 205 // Article 274
Article 205a // Article 275
Article 206 // Article 276
Article 206a (repealed) // -
Article 207 // Article 277
Article 208 // Article 278
Article 209 // Article 279
Article 209a // Article 280

PART SIX // PART SIX

Article 210 // Article 281
Article 211 // Article 282
Article 212 (*) // Article 283
Article 213 // Article 284
Article 213a (*) // Article 285
Article 213b (*) // Article 286
Article 214 // Article 287
Article 215 // Article 288
Article 216 // Article 289
Article 217 // Article 290
Article 218 (*) // Article 291
Article 219 // Article 292
Article 220 // Article 293
Article 221 // Article 294
Article 222 // Article 295
Article 223 // Article 296
Article 224 // Article 297
Article 225 // Article 298
Article 226 (repealed) // -
Article 227 // Article 299
Article 228 // Article 300
Article 228a // Article 301
Article 229 // Article 302
Article 230 // Article 303
Article 231 // Article 304
Article 232 // Article 305
Article 233 // Article 306
Article 234 // Article 307
Article 235 // Article 308
Article 236 (*) // Article 309
Article 237 (repealed) // -

Article 238 // Article 310
Article 239 // Article 311
Article 240 // Article 312
Article 241 (repealed) // -
Article 242 (repealed) // -
Article 243 (repealed) // -
Article 244 (repealed) // -
Article 245 (repealed) // -
Article 246 (repealed) // -

FINAL PROVISIONS // FINAL PROVISIONS

Article 247 // Article 313
Article 248 // Article 314

Appendix C
Table of Equivalence: Treaty of Amsterdam Version – Treaty of Lisbon Version

Reproduced from OJ C 115, 9.5.2008, pp 361–388.

Table C.1 TABLES OF EQUIVALENCES[1]

Treaty on European Union

Old numbering of the Treaty on European Union	**New numbering of the Treaty on European Union**
Title I—Common Provisions	Title I—Common Provisions
Article 1	Article 1
	Article 2
Article 2	Article 3
Article 3 (repealed)(1)	
	Article 4
	Article 5 (2)
Article 4 (repealed) (3)	
Article 5 (repealed) (4)	
Article 6	Article 6
Article 7	Article 7
	Article 8
Title II—Provisions Amending the Treaty Establishing the European Economic Community with a View to Establishing the European Community	Title II—Provisions on Democratic Principles
Article 8 (repealed) (5)	Article 9
	Article 10 (6)
	Article 11
	Article 12
Title III—Provisions Amending the Treaty Establishing the European Coal and Steel Community	Title III—Provisions on the Institutions

(1) Replaced, in substance, by Article 7 of the Treaty on the Functioning of the European Union (TFEU) and by Articles 13(1) and 21, paragraph 3, second subparagraph of the Treaty on European Union (TEU).
(2) Replaces Article 5 of the Treaty establishing the European Community (TEC).
(3) Replaced, in substance, by Article 15.
(4) Replaced, in substance, by Article 13, paragraph 2.
(5) Article 8 TEU, which was in force until the entry into force of the Treaty of Lisbon (hereinafter "current"), amended the TEC. Those amendments are incorporated into the latter Treaty and Article 8 is repealed. Its number is used to insert a new provision.
(6) Paragraph 4 replaces, in substance, the first subparagraph of Article 191 TEC.

[1] Tables of equivalences as referred to in Article 5 of the Treaty of Lisbon. The original centre column, which set out the intermediate numbering as used in that Treaty, has been omitted.

Table C.1 (continued)

Treaty on European Union

Old numbering of the Treaty on European Union	New numbering of the Treaty on European Union
Article 9 (repealed) (7)	Article 13
	Article 14 (8)
	Article 15 (9)
	Article 16 (10)
	Article 17 (11)
	Article 18
	Article 19 (12)
Title IV—Provisions Amending the Treaty Establishing the European Atomic Energy Community	Title IV—Provisions on Enhanced Cooperation
Article 10 (repealed) (13)	Article 20 (14)
Articles 27a–e (replaced)	
Articles 40–40b (replaced)	
Articles 43–45 (replaced)	
Title V—Provisions on a Common Foreign and Security Policy	Title V—General Provisions on the Union's External Action and Specific Provisions on the Common Foreign and Security Policy

(7) The current Article 9 TEU amended the Treaty establishing the European Coal and Steel Community. This latter expired on 23 July 2002. Article 9 is repealed and the number thereof is used to insert another provision.

(8) – Paragraphs 1 and 2 replace, in substance, Article 189 TEC;
- paragraphs 1–3 replace, in substance, paragraphs 1–3 of Article 190 TEC;
- paragraph 1 replaces, in substance, the first subparagraph of Article 192 TEC;
- paragraph 4 replaces, in substance, the first subparagraph of Article 197 TEC.

(9) Replaces, in substance, Article 4.

(10) – Paragraph 1 replaces, in substance, the first and second indents of Article 202 TEC;
- paragraphs 2 and 9 replace, in substance, Article 203 TEC;
- paragraphs 4 and 5 replace, in substance, paragraphs 2 and 4 of Article 205 TEC.

(11) – Paragraph 1 replaces, in substance, Article 211 TEC;
- paragraphs 3 and 7 replace, in substance, Article 214 TEC.
- paragraph 6 replaces, in substance, paragraphs 1, 3 and 4 of Article 217 TEC.

(12) – Replaces, in substance, Article 220 TEC.
- the second subparagraph of paragraph 2 replaces, in substance, the first subparagraph of Article 221 TEC.

(13) The current Article 10 TEU amended the Treaty establishing the European Atomic Energy Community. Those amendments are incorporated into the Treaty of Lisbon. Article 10 is repealed and the number thereof is used to insert another provision.

(14) Also replaces Articles 11 and 11a TEC.

Table C.1 (continued)

Treaty on European Union

Old numbering of the Treaty on European Union	New numbering of the Treaty on European Union
	Chapter 1—General Provisions on the Union's External Action
	Article 21
	Article 22
	Chapter 2—Specific Provisions on the Common Foreign and Security Policy
	Section 1—Common Provisions
	Article 23
Article 11	Article 24
Article 12	Article 25
Article 13	Article 26
	Article 27
Article 14	Article 28
Article 15	Article 29
Article 22 (moved)	Article 30
Article 23 (moved)	Article 31
Article 16	Article 32
Article 17 (moved)	*Article 42*
Article 18	Article 33
Article 19	Article 34
Article 20	Article 35
Article 21	Article 36
Article 22 (moved)	*Article 30*
Article 23 (moved)	*Article 31*
Article 24	Article 37
Article 25	Article 38
	Article 39
Article 47 *(moved)*	Article 40
Article 26 (repealed)	
Article 27 (repealed)	
Article 27*a* (replaced) (15)	*Article 20*
Article 27*b* (replaced) (15)	*Article 20*
Article 27*c* (replaced) (15)	*Article 20*
Article 27*d* (replaced) (15)	*Article 20*
Article 27*e* (replaced) (15)	*Article 20*
Article 28	Article 41
	Section 2—Provisions on the Common Security and Defence Policy
Article 17 (moved)	Article 42
	Article 43
	Article 44
	Article 45
	Article 46

(15) The current Articles 27*a*–*e*, on enhanced cooperation, are also replaced by Articles 326–334 TFEU.

Table C.1 (continued)

Treaty on European Union

Old numbering of the Treaty on European Union	New numbering of the Treaty on European Union
Title VI—Provisions on Police and Judicial Cooperation in Criminal Matters (repealed) [16]	
Article 29 (replaced) [17]	
Article 30 (replaced) [18]	
Article 31 (replaced) [19]	
Article 32 (replaced) [20]	
Article 33 (replaced) [21]	
Article 34 (repealed)	
Article 35 (repealed)	
Article 36 (replaced) [22]	
Article 37 (replaced)	
Article 38 (repealed)	
Article 39 (repealed)	
Article 40 (replaced) [23]	*Article 20*
Article 40 A (replaced) [23]	*Article 20*
Article 40 B (replaced) [23]	*Article 20*
Article 41 (repealed)	
Article 42 (repealed)	
Title VII—Provisions on Enhanced Cooperation (replaced) ([24])	Title IV—Provisions on Enhanced Cooperation
Article 43 (replaced) [24]	*Article 20*
Article 43 A (replaced) [24]	*Article 20*
Article 43 B (replaced) [24]	*Article 20*
Article 44 (replaced) [24]	*Article 20*
Article 44 A (replaced) [24]	*Article 20*
Article 45 (replaced) [24]	*Article 20*
Titre VIII—Final Provisions	Title VI—Final Provisions
Article 46 (repealed)	
	Article 47
Article 47 (replaced)	*Article 40*

[16] The current provisions of Title VI of the TEU, on police and judicial cooperation in criminal matters, are replaced by the provisions of Chapters 1, 5 and 5 of Title IV of Part Three of the TFEU.
[17] Replaced by Article 67 TFEU.
[18] Replaced by Articles 87 and 88 TFEU.
[19] Replaced by Articles 82, 83 and 85 TFEU.
[20] Replaced by Article 89 TFEU.
[21] Replaced by Article 72 TFEU.
[22] Replaced by Article 71 TFEU.
[23] The current Articles 40–40 B TEU, on enhanced cooperation, are also replaced by Articles 326–334 TFEU.
[24] The current Articles 43–45 and Title VII of the TEU, on enhanced cooperation, are also replaced by Articles 326–334 TFEU.

Table C.1 (continued)

Treaty on European Union

Old numbering of the Treaty on European Union	New numbering of the Treaty on European Union
Article 48	Article 48
Article 49	Article 49
	Article 50
	Article 51
	Article 52
Article 50 (repealed)	
Article 51	Article 53
Article 52	Article 54
Article 53	Article 55

Treaty on the Functioning of the European Union

Old numbering of the Treaty establishing the European Community	New numbering of the Treaty on the Functioning of the European Union
Part One—PRINCIPLES	Part One—PRINCIPLES
Article 1 (repealed)	
	Article 1
Article 2 (repealed) (25)	
	Title I—Categories and Areas of Union Competence
	Article 2
	Article 3
	Article 4
	Article 5
	Article 6
	Title II—Provisions Having General Application
	Article 7
Article 3, paragraph 1 (repealed) (26)	
Article 3, paragraph 2	Article 8
Article 4 (moved)	*Article 119*
Article 5 (replaced) (27)	
	Article 9
	Article 10
Article 6	Article 11
Article 153, paragraph 2 (moved)	Article 12
	Article 13 (28)

(25) Replaced, in substance, by Article 3 TEU.
(26) Replaced, in substance, by Articles 3–6 TFEU.
(27) Replaced, in substance, by Article 5 TEU.
(28) Insertion of the operative part of the protocol on protection and welfare of animals.

Table C.1 (continued)

Treaty on the Functioning of the European Union

Old numbering of the Treaty establishing the European Community	New numbering of the Treaty on the Functioning of the European Union
Article 7 (repealed) [29]	
Article 8 (repealed) [30]	
Article 9 (repealed)	
Article 10 (repealed) [31]	
Article 11 (replaced) [32]	*Articles 326–334*
Article 11a (replaced) [32]	*Articles 326–334*
Article 12 (repealed)	*Article 18*
Article 13 (moved)	*Article 19*
Article 14 (moved)	*Article 26*
Article 15 (moved)	*Article 27*
Article 16	Article 14
Article 255 (moved)	Article 15
Article 286 (moved)	Article 16
	Article 17
Part Two—Citizenship of the Union	Part Two—Non-discrimination and Citizenship of the Union
Article 12 (moved)	Article 18
Article 13 (moved)	Article 19
Article 17	Article 20
Article 18	Article 21
Article 19	Article 22
Article 20	Article 23
Article 21	Article 24
Article 22	Article 25
Part Three—Community Policies	Part Three—Policies and Internal Actions of the Union
	Title I—The Internal Market
Article 14 (moved)	Article 26
Article 15 (moved)	Article 27
Title I—Free Movement of Goods	Title II—Free Movement of Goods
Article 23	Article 28
Article 24	Article 29
Chapter 1—The Customs Union	Chapter 1—The Customs Union
Article 25	Article 30
Article 26	Article 31
Article 27	Article 32
Part Three, Title X, Customs Cooperation (moved)	Chapter 2—Customs Cooperation
Article 135 (moved)	Article 33
Chapter 2—Prohibition of Quantitative Restrictions Between Member States	Chapter 3—Prohibition of Quantitative Restrictions Between Member States

(29) Replaced, in substance, by Article 13 TEU.
(30) Replaced, in substance, by Article 13 TEU and Article 282, paragraph 1, TFEU.
(31) Replaced, in substance, by Article 4, paragraph 3, TEU.
(32) Also replaced by Article 20 TEU.

Table C.1 (continued)

Treaty on the Functioning of the European Union

Old numbering of the Treaty establishing the European Community	New numbering of the Treaty on the Functioning of the European Union
Article 28	Article 34
Article 29	Article 35
Article 30	Article 36
Article 31	Article 37
Title II—Agriculture	Title III—Agriculture and Fisheries
Article 32	Article 38
Article 33	Article 39
Article 34	Article 40
Article 35	Article 41
Article 36	Article 42
Article 37	Article 43
Article 38	Article 44
Title III—Free Movement of Persons, Services and Capital	Title IV—Free Movement of Persons, Services and Capital
Chapter 1—Workers	Chapter 1—Workers
Article 39	Article 45
Article 40	Article 46
Article 41	Article 47
Article 42	Article 48
Chapter 2—Right of Establishment	Chapter 2—Right of Establishment
Article 43	Article 49
Article 44	Article 50
Article 45	Article 51
Article 46	Article 52
Article 47	Article 53
Article 48	Article 54
Article 294 (moved)	Article 55
Chapter 3—Services	Chapter 3—Services
Article 49	Article 56
Article 50	Article 57
Article 51	Article 58
Article 52	Article 59
Article 53	Article 60
Article 54	Article 61
Article 55	Article 62
Chapter 4—Capital and Payments	Chapter 4—Capital and Payments
Article 56	Article 63
Article 57	Article 64
Article 58	Article 65
Article 59	Article 66
Article 60 (moved)	*Article 75*
Title IV—Visas, Asylum, Immigration and Other Policies Related to Free Movement of Persons	Title V—Area of Freedom, Security and Justice
	Chapter 1—General Provisions

Table C.1 (continued)

Treaty on the Functioning of the European Union

Old numbering of the Treaty establishing the European Community	**New numbering of the Treaty on the Functioning of the European Union**
Article 61	Article 67 [33]
	Article 68
	Article 69
	Article 70
	Article 71 [34]
Article 64, paragraph 1 (replaced)	Article 72 [35]
	Article 73
Article 66 (replaced)	Article 74
Article 60 (moved)	Article 75
	Article 76
	Chapter 2—Policies on Border Checks, Asylum and Immigration
Article 62	Article 77
Article 63, points 1 et 2, and Article 64, paragraph 2 [36]	Article 78
Article 63, points 3 and 4	Article 79
	Article 80
Article 64, paragraph 1 (replaced)	*Article 72*
	Chapter 3—Judicial Cooperation in Civil Matters
Article 65	Article 81
Article 66 (replaced)	*Article 74*
Article 67 (repealed)	
Article 68 (repealed)	
Article 69 (repealed)	
	Chapter 4—Judicial Cooperation in Criminal Matters
	Article 82 [37]
	Article 83 [37]
	Article 84
	Article 85 [37]
	Article 86
	Chapter 5—Police Cooperation
	Article 87 [38]
	Article 88 [38]
	Article 89 [39]

(33) Also replaces the current Article 29 TEU.
(34) Also replaces the current Article 36 TEU.
(35) Also replaces the current Article 33 TEU.
(36) Points 1 and 2 of Article 63 EC are replaced by paragraphs 1 and 2 of Article 78 TFEU, and paragraph 2 of Article 64 is replaced by paragraph 3 of Article 78 TFEU.
(37) Replaces the current Article 31 TEU.
(38) Replaces the current Article 30 TEU.
(39) Replaces the current Article 32 TEU.

Table C.1 (continued)

Treaty on the Functioning of the European Union

Old numbering of the Treaty establishing the European Community	New numbering of the Treaty on the Functioning of the European Union
Title V—Transport	Title VI—Transport
Article 70	Article 90
Article 71	Article 91
Article 72	Article 92
Article 73	Article 93
Article 74	Article 94
Article 75	Article 95
Article 76	Article 96
Article 77	Article 97
Article 78	Article 98
Article 79	Article 99
Article 80	Article 100
Title VI—Common Rules on Competition, Taxation and Approximation of Laws	Title VII—Common Rules on Competition, Taxation and Approximation of Laws
Chapter 1—Rules on Competition	Chapter 1—Rules on Competition
Section 1—Rules Applying to Undertakings	Section 1—Rules Applying to Undertakings
Article 81	Article 101
Article 82	Article 102
Article 83	Article 103
Article 84	Article 104
Article 85	Article 105
Article 86	Article 106
Section 2—Aids Granted by States	Section 2—Aids Granted by States
Article 87	Article 107
Article 88	Article 108
Article 89	Article 109
Chapter 2—Tax Provisions	Chapter 2—Tax Provisions
Article 90	Article 110
Article 91	Article 111
Article 92	Article 112
Article 93	Article 113
Chapter 3—Approximation of Laws	Chapter 3—Approximation of Laws
Article 95 (moved)	Article 114
Article 94 (moved)	Article 115
Article 96	Article 116
Article 97	Article 117
	Article 118
Title VII—Economic and Monetary Policy	Title VIII—Economic and Monetary Policy
Article 4 (moved)	Article 119
Chapter 1—Economic Policy	Chapter 1—Economic Policy
Article 98	Article 120
Article 99	Article 121

Table C.1 (continued)

Treaty on the Functioning of the European Union

Old numbering of the Treaty establishing the European Community	New numbering of the Treaty on the Functioning of the European Union
Article 100	Article 122
Article 101	Article 123
Article 102	Article 124
Article 103	Article 125
Article 104	Article 126
Chapter 2—Monetary Policy	Chapter 2—Monetary Policy
Article 105	Article 127
Article 106	Article 128
Article 107	Article 129
Article 108	Article 130
Article 109	Article 131
Article 110	Article 132
Article 111, paragraphs 1–3 and 5 (moved)	*Article 219*
Article 111, paragraph 4 (moved)	*Article 138*
	Article 133
Chapter 3—Institutional Provisions	Chapter 3—Institutional Provisions
Article 112 (moved)	*Article 283*
Article 113 (moved)	*Article 284*
Article 114	Article 134
Article 115	Article 135
	Chapter 4—Provisions specific to Member States whose currency is the euro
	Article 136
	Article 137
Article 111, paragraph 4 (moved)	Article 138
Chapter 4—Transitional Provisions	Chapter 5—Transitional Provisions
Article 116 (repealed)	
	Article 139
Article 117, paragraphs 1, 2, sixth indent, and 3–9 (repealed)	
Article 117, paragraph 2, first five indents (moved)	*Article 141, paragraph 2*
Article 121, paragraph 1 (moved)	Article 140 [(40)]
Article 122, paragraph 2, second sentence (moved)	
Article 123, paragraph 5 (moved)	
Article 118 (repealed)	

(40) – Article 140, paragraph 1 takes over the wording of paragraph 1 of Article 121.
– Article 140, paragraph 2 takes over the second sentence of paragraph 2 of Article 122.
– Article 140, paragraph 3 takes over paragraph 5 of Article 123.

Table C.1 (continued)

Treaty on the Functioning of the European Union

Old numbering of the Treaty establishing the European Community	New numbering of the Treaty on the Functioning of the European Union
Article 123, paragraph 3 (moved)	Article 141 [(41)]
Article 117, paragraph 2, first five indents (moved)	
Article 124, paragraph 1 (moved)	Article 142
Article 119	Article 143
Article 120	Article 144
Article 121, paragraph 1 (moved)	*Article 140, paragraph 1*
Article 121, paragraph 2–4 (repealed)	
Article 122, paragraphs 1, 2, first sentence, 3, 4, 5 and 6 (repealed)	
Article 122, paragraph 2, second sentence (moved)	*Article 140, paragraph 2, first subparagraph*
Article 123, paragraphs 1, 2 and 4 (repealed)	
Article 123, paragraph 3 (moved)	*Article 141, paragraph 1*
Article 123, paragraph 5 (moved)	*Article 140, paragraph 3*
Article 124, paragraph 1 (moved)	*Article 142*
Article 124, paragraph 2 (repealed)	
Title VIII—Employment	Title IX—Employment
Article 125	Article 145
Article 126	Article 146
Article 127	Article 147
Article 128	Article 148
Article 129	Article 149
Article 130	Article 150
Title IX—Common Commercial Policy (moved)	*Part Five, Title II, Common Commercial Policy*
Article 131 (moved)	*Article 206*
Article 132 (repealed)	
Article 133 (moved)	*Article 207*
Article 134 (repealed)	
Title X—Customs Cooperation (moved)	*Part Three, Title II, Chapter 2, Customs Cooperation*
Article 135 (moved)	*Article 33*
Title XI—Social Policy, Education, Vocational Training and Youth	Title X—Social Policy
Chapter 1—Social Provisions (repealed)	
Article 136	Article 151
	Article 152
Article 137	Article 153
Article 138	Article 154
Article 139	Article 155

(41) – Article 141, paragraph 1 takes over paragraph 3 of Article 123.
– Article 141, paragraph 2 takes over the first five indents of paragraph 2 of Article 117.

Table C.1 (continued)

Treaty on the Functioning of the European Union

Old numbering of the Treaty establishing the European Community	**New numbering of the Treaty on the Functioning of the European Union**
Article 140	Article 156
Article 141	Article 157
Article 142	Article 158
Article 143	Article 159
Article 144	Article 160
Article 145	Article 161
Chapter 2—The European Social Fund	Title XI—The European Social Fund
Article 146	Article 162
Article 147	Article 163
Article 148	Article 164
Chapter 3—Education, Vocational Training and Youth	Title XII—Education, Vocational Training, Youth and Sport
Article 149	Article 165
Article 150	Article 166
Title XII—Culture	Title XIII—Culture
Article 151	Article 167
Title XIII—Public Health	Title XIV—Public Health
Article 152	Article 168
Title XIV—Consumer Protection	Title XV—Consumer Protection
Article 153, paragraphs 1, 3, 4 and 5	Article 169
Article 153, paragraph 2 (moved)	*Article 12*
Title XV—Trans-European Networks	Title XVI—Trans-European Networks
Article 154	Article 170
Article 155	Article 171
Article 156	Article 172
Title XVI—Industry	Title XVII—Industry
Article 157	Article 173
Title XVII—Economic and Social Cohesion	Title XVIII—Economic, Social and Territorial Cohesion
Article 158	Article 174
Article 159	Article 175
Article 160	Article 176
Article 161	Article 177
Article 162	Article 178
Title XVIII—Research and Technological Development	Title XIX—Research and Technological Development and Space
Article 163	Article 179
Article 164	Article 180
Article 165	Article 181
Article 166	Article 182
Article 167	Article 183
Article 168	Article 184
Article 169	Article 185
Article 170	Article 186
Article 171	Article 187
Article 172	Article 188
	Article 189

Table C.1 (continued)

Treaty on the Functioning of the European Union

Old numbering of the Treaty establishing the European Community	**New numbering of the Treaty on the Functioning of the European Union**
Article 173	Article 190
Title XIX—Environment	Title XX—Environment
Article 174	Article 191
Article 175	Article 192
Article 176	Article 193
	Title XXI—Energy
	Article 194
	Title XXII—Tourism
	Article 195
	Title XXIII—Civil Protection
	Article 196
	Title XXIV—Administrative Cooperation
	Article 197
Title XX—Development Cooperation (moved)	*Part Five, Title III, Chapter 1, Development Cooperation*
Article 177 (moved)	*Article 208*
Article 178 (repealed) [(42)]	
Article 179 (moved)	*Article 209*
Article 180 (moved)	*Article 210*
Article 181 (moved)	*Article 211*
Title XXI—Economic, Financial and Technical Cooperation with Third Countries (moved)	*Part Five, Title III, Chapter 2, Economic, Financial and Technical Cooperation with Third Countries*
Article 181*a* (moved)	*Article 212*
PART FOUR—Association of the Overseas Countries and Territories	PART FOUR—Association of the Overseas Countries and Territories
Article 182	Article 198
Article 183	Article 199
Article 184	Article 200
Article 185	Article 201
Article 186	Article 202
Article 187	Article 203
Article 188	Article 204
	Part Five—External Action by the Union
	Title I—General Provisions on the Union's External Action
	Article 205
Part Three, Title IX, Common Commercial Policy (moved)	Title II—Common Commercial Policy
Article 131 (moved)	Article 206
Article 133 (moved)	Article 207
	Title III—Cooperation with Third Countries and Humanitarian Aid
Part Three, Tile XX, Development Cooperation (moved)	Chapter 1—Development Cooperation

(42) Replaced, in substance, by the second sentence of the second subparagraph of paragraph 1 of Article 208 TFUE.

Table C.1 (continued)

Treaty on the Functioning of the European Union

Old numbering of the Treaty establishing the European Community	New numbering of the Treaty on the Functioning of the European Union
Article 177 (moved)	Article 208 (43)
Article 179 (moved)	Article 209
Article 180 (moved)	Article 210
Article 181 (moved)	Article 211
Part Three, Title XXI, Economic, Financial and Technical Cooperation with Third Countries (moved)	Chapter 2—Economic, Financial and Technical Cooperation with Third Countries
Article 181a (moved)	Article 212
	Article 213
	Chapter 3—Humanitarian Aid
	Article 214
	Title IV—Restrictive Measures
Article 301 (replaced)	Article 215
	Title V—International Agreements
	Article 216
Article 310 (moved)	Article 217
Article 300 (replaced)	Article 218
Article 111, paragraphs 1–3 and 5 (moved)	Article 219
	Title VI—The Union's Relations with International Organisations and Third Countries and the Union Delegations
Articles 302–304 (replaced)	Article 220
	Article 221
	Title VII—Solidarity Clause
	Article 222
Part Five—Institutions of the Community	Part Six—Institutional and Financial Provisions
Title I—Institutional Provisions	Title I—Institutional Provisions
Chapter 1—The Institutions	Chapter 1—The Institutions
Section 1—The European Parliament	Section 1—The European Parliament
Article 189 (repealed) (44)	
Article 190, paragraphs 1–3 (repealed) (45)	
Article 190, paragraphs 4 and 5	Article 223
Article 191, first paragraph (repealed) (46)	
Article 191, second paragraph	Article 224
Article 192, first paragraph (repealed) (47)	
Article 192, second paragraph	Article 225
Article 193	Article 226
Article 194	Article 227

(43) The second sentence of the second subparagraph of paragraph 1 replaces, in substance, Article 178 TEC.
(44) Replaced, in substance, by Article 14, paragraphs 1 and 2, TEU.
(45) Replaced, in substance, by Article 14, paragraphs 1–3, TEU.
(46) Replaced, in substance, by Article 11, paragraph 4, TEU.
(47) Replaced, in substance, by Article 14, paragraph 1, TEU.

Table C.1 (continued)

Treaty on the Functioning of the European Union

Old numbering of the Treaty establishing the European Community	**New numbering of the Treaty on the Functioning of the European Union**
Article 195	Article 228
Article 196	Article 229
Article 197, first paragraph (repealed) (48)	
Article 197, second, third and fourth paragraphs	Article 230
Article 198	Article 231
Article 199	Article 232
Article 200	Article 233
Article 201	Article 234
	Section 2—The European Council
	Article 235
	Article 236
Section 2—The Council	Section 3—The Council
Article 202 (repealed) (49)	
Article 203 (repealed) (50)	
Article 204	Article 237
Article 205, paragraphs 2 and 4 (repealed) (51)	
Article 205, paragraphs 1 and 3	Article 238
Article 206	Article 239
Article 207	Article 240
Article 208	Article 241
Article 209	Article 242
Article 210	Article 243
Section 3—The Commission	Section 4—The Commission
Article 211 (repealed) (52)	
	Article 244
Article 212 (moved)	*Article 249, paragraph 2*
Article 213	Article 245
Article 214 (repealed) (53)	
Article 215	Article 246
Article 216	Article 247
Article 217, paragraphs 1, 3 and 4 (repealed) (54)	
Article 217, paragraph 2	Article 248
Article 218, paragraph 1 (repealed) (55)	

(48) Replaced, in substance, by Article 14, paragraph 4, TEU.
(49) Replaced, in substance, by Article 16, paragraph 1, TEU and by Articles 290 and 291 TFEU.
(50) Replaced, in substance, by Article 16, paragraphs 2 and 9 TEU.
(51) Replaced, in substance, by Article 16, paragraphs 4 and 5 TEU.
(52) Replaced, in substance, by Article 17, paragraph 1 TEU.
(53) Replaced, in substance, by Article 17, paragraphs 3 and 7 TEU.
(54) Replaced, in substance, by Article 17, paragraph 6, TEU.
(55) Replaced, in substance, by Article 295 TFEU.

Table C.1 (continued)

Treaty on the Functioning of the European Union

Old numbering of the Treaty establishing the European Community	New numbering of the Treaty on the Functioning of the European Union
Article 218, paragraph 2	Article 249
Article 219	Article 250
Section 4—The Court of Justice	Section 5—The Court of Justice of the European Union
Article 220 (repealed) (56)	
Article 221, first paragraph (repealed) (57)	
Article 221, second and third paragraphs	Article 251
Article 222	Article 252
Article 223	Article 253
Article 224 (58)	Article 254
	Article 255
Article 225	Article 256
Article 225a	Article 257
Article 226	Article 258
Article 227	Article 259
Article 228	Article 260
Article 229	Article 261
Article 229a	Article 262
Article 230	Article 263
Article 231	Article 264
Article 232	Article 265
Article 233	Article 266
Article 234	Article 267
Article 235	Article 268
	Article 269
Article 236	Article 270
Article 237	Article 271
Article 238	Article 272
Article 239	Article 273
Article 240	Article 274
	Article 275
	Article 276
Article 241	Article 277
Article 242	Article 278
Article 243	Article 279
Article 244	Article 280
Article 245	Article 281
	Section 6—The European Central Bank
	Article 282
Article 112 (moved)	Article 283
Article 113 (moved)	Article 284
Section 5—The Court of Auditors	Section 7—The Court of Auditors

(56) Replaced, in substance, by Article 19 TEU.
(57) Replaced, in substance, by Article 19, paragraph 2, first subparagraph, of the TEU.
(58) The first sentence of the first subparagraph is replaced, in substance, by Article 19, paragraph 2, second subparagraph of the TEU.

Table C.1 (continued)

Treaty on the Functioning of the European Union

Old numbering of the Treaty establishing the European Community	New numbering of the Treaty on the Functioning of the European Union
Article 246	Article 285
Article 247	Article 286
Article 248	Article 287
Chapter 2—Provisions Common to Several Institutions	Chapter 2—Legal Acts of the Union, Adoption Procedures and Other Provisions
	Section 1—The Legal Acts of the Union
Article 249	Article 288
	Article 289
	Article 290 (59)
	Article 291 (59)
	Article 292
	Section 2—Procedures for the Adoption of Acts and Other Provisions
Article 250	Article 293
Article 251	Article 294
Article 252 (repealed)	
	Article 295
Article 253	Article 296
Article 254	Article 297
	Article 298
Article 255 (moved)	*Article 15*
Article 256	Article 299
	Chapter 3—The Union's Advisory Bodies
	Article 300
Chapter 3—The Economic and Social Committee	Section 1—The Economic and Social Committee
Article 257 (repealed) (60)	
Article 258, first, second and fourth paragraphs	Article 301
Article 258, third paragraph (repealed) (61)	
Article 259	Article 302
Article 260	Article 303
Article 261 (repealed)	
Article 262	Article 304
Chapter 4—The Committee of the Regions	Section 2—The Committee of the Regions
Article 263, first and fifth paragraphs (repealed) (62)	
Article 263, second to fourth paragraphs	Article 305
Article 264	Article 306
Article 265	Article 307

(59) Replaces, in substance, the third indent of Article 202 TEC.
(60) Replaced, in substance, by Article 300, paragraph 2 of the TFEU.
(61) Replaced, in substance, by Article 300, paragraph 4 of the TFEU.
(62) Replaced, in substance, by Article 300, paragraphs 3 and 4, TFEU.

Table C.1 (continued)

Treaty on the Functioning of the European Union

Old numbering of the Treaty establishing the European Community	New numbering of the Treaty on the Functioning of the European Union
Chapter 5—The European Investment Bank	Chapter 4—The European Investment Bank
Article 266	Article 308
Article 267	Article 309
Title II—Financial Provisions	Title II—Financial Provisions
Article 268	Article 310
	Chapter 1—The Union's Own Resources
Article 269	Article 311
Article 270 (repealed) [63]	
	Chapter 2—The Multiannual Financial Framework
	Article 312
	Chapter 3—The Union's Annual Budget
Article 272, paragraph 1 (moved)	Article 313
Article 271 (moved)	*Article 316*
Article 272, paragraph 1 (moved)	*Article 313*
Article 272, paragraphs 2–10	Article 314
Article 273	Article 315
Article 271 (moved)	Article 316
	Chapter 4—Implementation of the Budget and Discharge
Article 274	Article 317
Article 275	Article 318
Article 276	Article 319
	Chapter 5—Common Provisions
Article 277	Article 320
Article 278	Article 321
Article 279	Article 322
	Article 323
	Article 324
	Chapter 6—Combating Fraud
Article 280	Article 325
	Title III—Enhanced Cooperation
Articles 11 and 11a (replaced)	Article 326 [64]
Articles 11 and 11a (replaced)	Article 327 [64]
Articles 11 and 11a (replaced)	Article 328 [64]
Articles 11 and 11a (replaced)	Article 329 [64]
Articles 11 and 11a (replaced)	Article 330 [64]
Articles 11 and 11a (replaced)	Article 331 [64]
Articles 11 and 11a (replaced)	Article 332 [64]
Articles 11 and 11a (replaced)	Article 333 [64]
Articles 11 and 11a (replaced)	Article 334 [64]

(63) Replaced, in substance, by Article 310, paragraph 4, TFEU.
(64) Also replaces the current Articles 27*a*–*e*, 40–40*b*, and 43–45 TEU.

Table C.1 (continued)

Treaty on the Functioning of the European Union

Old numbering of the Treaty establishing the European Community	New numbering of the Treaty on the Functioning of the European Union
Part Six—General and Final Provisions	Part Seven—General and Final Provisions
Article 281 (repealed) [(65)]	
Article 282	Article 335
Article 283	Article 336
Article 284	Article 337
Article 285	Article 338
Article 286 (replaced)	*Article 16*
Article 287	Article 339
Article 288	Article 340
Article 289	Article 341
Article 290	Article 342
Article 291	Article 343
Article 292	Article 344
Article 293 (repealed)	
Article 294 (moved)	*Article 55*
Article 295	Article 345
Article 296	Article 346
Article 297	Article 347
Article 298	Article 348
Article 299, paragraph 1 (repealed) [(66)]	
Article 299, paragraph 2, second, third and fourth subparagraphs	Article 349
Article 299, paragraph 2, first subparagraph, and paragraphs 3–6 (moved)	*Article 355*
Article 300 (replaced)	*Article 218*
Article 301 (replaced)	*Article 215*
Article 302 (replaced)	*Article 220*
Article 303 (replaced)	*Article 220*
Article 304 (replaced)	*Article 220*
Article 305 (repealed)	
Article 306	Article 350
Article 307	Article 351
Article 308	Article 352
	Article 353
Article 309	Article 354
Article 310 (moved)	*Article 217*
Article 311 (repealed) [(67)]	
Article 299, paragraph 2, first subparagraph, and paragraphs 3 to 6 (moved)	Article 355

[(65)] Replaced, in substance, by Article 47 TEU.
[(66)] Replaced, in substance, by Article 52 TEU.
[(67)] Replaced, in substance by Article 51 TEU.

Table C.1 (continued)

Treaty on the Functioning of the European Union

Old numbering of the Treaty establishing the European Community	New numbering of the Treaty on the Functioning of the European Union
Article 312	Article 356
Final Provisions	
Article 313	Article 357
	Article 358
Article 314 (repealed) [(68)]	

(68) Replaced, in substance by Article 55 TEU.

Index

NOTE: The Locators in Square Brackets refer to section numbers.

A

Access to EU Information, [1.155]

Accessions to EU, [1.20]

Admission to EU, [1.100]

Advertising Restrictions, [2.70], [10.170]

Advocates-General, [11.120]–[11.35]

Affirmative Action, [10.85]–[10.95]

Agriculture Agreement (WTO), [13.85]

Alcohol, Excise upon, [7.50]

Amendments to Founding Treaties, [1.25]–[1.55]

Anti-Dumping Duties, [5.165]

APEC, [13.130]

Arbitration

Convention, [7.70]

International Commercial, [3.256]

ASEAN

Free Trade Agreement with Australia, [13.135]

Free Trade Area, [13.130]

Audi Alteram Partem, [11.135]

Australia

Bilateral Free Trade Agreements, [13.135]

Relations with EU, [1.65]

B

Banking, [4.45]

Beer Cans Case, [2.110]

Biotechnological Inventions, [9.105]

Board Appointments, [4.15], [4.30]

Budget Deficits of Member States, [1.15]

Budget of EU, [1.100]

Byrd Amendment, [1.60]

C

Cable Transmission, [9.95]

Canada

Bilateral Free Trade Agreements, [13.135]

Relations with EU, [1.70]

Capital

Taxation of, [7.45]

See also Free Movement of Capital

Censorship Classification, [2.80]

Charges with an Equivalent Effect, [2.10]

Charitable Donations, [4.10], [4.15], [4.30]

Charter of Fundamental Rights, [1.40], [10.30]

CISG

Acceptance, [13.155]

Additional Time for Performance, [13.160]

Application of, [13.150]

Breach of Contract, [13.165]

Common Law Nations, party to, [13.140]

Conformity to Contract, [13.160]

Damages, [13.165]

Domestic Implementation, [13.145]

EU Member States, party to, [13.140]

Formation of Contract, [13.155]

Frustration of Contract, [13.165]

Fundamental Breach, [13.165]

Intention to be Bound, [13.155]

Offers, [13.155]

Performance of Contract, [13.160]

Private International Law, [13.150]

Remedies for Breach of Contract, [13.165]

Specific Performance, [13.165]

Suspension of Performance, [13.165]
Writing, [13.155]
Citizenship, EU, [1.15]
Co-decision, [1.30], [1.35], [1.45], [1.100]
Colour as Trade Mark, [9.120]
Comitology, [1.90]
Committee of Permanent Representatives, [1.95]
Committee of the Regions, [1.120]
Common Commercial Policy, [5.06]–[5.10]
Common Customs Tariff, [2.15]
Common Policies, [1.15]
Common Rules on Imports and Exports, [5.31]
Community Customs Code, [2.15]
Community Designs, [9.160]
Community Trade Marks, [9.150]
Companies
Company Law, [3.145]
European Company, [3.145]
Freedom of Establishment, [3.70], [3.80]–[3.85], [3.130]
Merger Control, [6.150]–[6.155]
Comparative Advertising, [9.130], [10.170]
Comparative Tables for Founding Treaties, [1.55], Appendices B–C
Compensation for Breaches of EU Law, [12.60]
Competition Law
Abuse of a Dominant Position, [6.105]–[6.150]
Abuse, Concept of, [6.115]
Agreement, Concept of, [6.45]
Agriculture, [6.170]
Associations of Undertakings, [6.35]
Block Exemptions, [6.95], [6.160]
Collective Dominant Position, [6.110]
Competence of EU, [6.05], [6.195]
'Competition' Defined, [6.65]
Concerted Practices, [6.100]
Declarations of Inapplicability, [6.90]
De Minimis Effect, [6.80]
Direct Effect, [6.10], [12.25]
'Dominant Position' Defined, [6.110]
Economic Activity, [6.25]
Economic Entity Approach, [6.40]
Effect upon Trade, [6.75], [6.140]
Effects Theory, [6.40]
Enforcement, [6.190]–[6.235]
Exclusive Purchasing Agreements, [6.60]
Exemptions, [6.90]–[6.95], [6.145], [6.160], [9.70]
Fines, [6.205], [6.230], [6.235]
Governmental Measures, [6.05]
Horizontal Agreements, [6.15]
Indispensability, [6.115]
Industrial and Commercial Property, Exercise of, [6.135], [9.60]–[9.70]
Judicial Review of Competition Law Decisions, [6.205], [6.215]
Justification for Limitations, [6.85]
Licences for Industrial and Commercial Property, [6.135]
Limitation Periods, [6.210]
Merger Control, [6.150]–[6.155]
National Competition Authorities, [6.225]–[6.230]
Non-Member States, Cooperation with, [6.235]
Object of the Agreement, [6.65]
Predatory Pricing, [6.115]
Prevention, Restriction or Distortion, [6.70]
Private Arrangements, [6.05]
Prohibited Agreements, [6.55]–[6.60]
Public Bodies, [6.25]
Public Procurement, [8.95]
Relevant Market, [6.130]
Services of General Economic Interest, [6.185]
Single Economic Unit, [6.30], [8.95]
Special Responsibility of Dominant Undertakings, [6.120]
State Aid, [6.160]
Subsidiaries, [6.40]
Substantial Part of the Internal Market, [6.125]
Tacit Approval, [6.45]
'Trade' Defined, [6.75]
Transportation, [6.175]
Undertaking, Concept of, [6.25]
Undertakings Situated Outside EU, [6.40]
Undertakings with Exclusive Rights, [6.180]
Undistorted Competition, [6.05]
Unilateral Acts, [6.50]
Vertical Agreements, [6.15]
Voidness of Prohibited Agreements, [6.20]
Voluntary Conduct, [6.05]
Compulsory Licences, [9.40]
Computer Programs, [9.90]

Concurrent Jurisdiction of EU and Member States, [1.130]
Constitution of Europe, [1.45]
Constitutional Law, National, [12.70]–[12.75]
Constructed Normal Value, [5.60]–[5.75]
Consumer Credit, [4.10], [10.200]
Consumer Protection
  Advertising, [10.170]
  Aggressive Practices, [10.160]
  Air Passengers, [10.210]
  Comparative Advertising, [10.170]
  Conformity of Goods to Contract, [10.165]
  Consumer Credit, [10.200]
  Contractual Terms, [10.175]
  Distance Contracts, [10.190]
  Doorstep Selling, [10.195]
  Exception to Freedom of Establishment, [3.115]
  Exception to Freedom of Movement of Goods, [2.110]
  Exception to Freedom to Provide Services, [3.185]
  Guarantees, [10.165]
  Health Claims, [10.185]
  Health Protection, [10.220]
  Implementation by Member States, [10.225]
  Injunctions, [10.225]
  Misleading Advertising, [10.170]
  Misleading Practices, [10.160]
  Product Labelling, [2.135], [10.185]
  Product Liability, [10.215]
  Product Safety, [10.220]
  Proposed Reforms, [10.155]
  Rail Passengers, [10.210]
  Sale of Consumer Goods, [10.165]
  Subliminal Advertising, [10.170]
  Timeshare Contracts, [10.205]
  Tobacco Advertising, [10.170]
  Unfair Commercial Practices, [10.160]
  Unfair Contractual Terms, [10.175]
  Unit Pricing, [10.180]
  Withdrawal from Contracts, [10.190]–[10.205]
Contracts, *see* CISG; Consumer Protection; Public Procurement
Convention on the Future of Europe, [1.50]
Convention on the International Sale of Goods, *see* CISG
Coordination of Economic Policies, [2.95]
Copyright, *see* Industrial and Commercial Property
Coreper, [1.95]
Council, [1.95]
Council of Europe, [1.15]
Countervailing Duties, [5.165]
Court of Auditors, [1.110]
Court of First Instance, *see* General Court
Court of Justice, *see* European Court of Justice
Credit Institutions, [4.45]
Cross-border Credit Transfers, [4.45]
Cross-border Mediation, [3.255]
Currency Export Restrictions, [4.15]
Customs Code, Community, [2.15]
Customs Duties, [2.10], [7.10], [7.20]
Customs Union, [1.15], [2.10], [13.130]

D

Databases, [9.95]
Data Protection, [10.140]–[10.150]
Decisions, [1.150], [11.120], [12.55]
Defrenne Case, [10.20]
Designations of Origin, *see* Industrial and Commercial Property
Designs, *see* Industrial and Commercial Property
Direct Effect
  Decisions, [12.55]
  Direct Applicability, [12.30]
  Directives, [12.40]–[12.50]
  Directives with Direct Effect, Particular, [10.145]
  European Economic Area law, [2.150]
  GATT 1994 [13.70]
  Horizontal Direct Effect, [3.15], [3.150], [10.20], [12.25], [12.45], [12.55]
  Indirect Effect, [12.50]
  International Agreements, [5.15]
  Interpretation of National Legislation, [12.50]
  Regulations, [12.30]–[12.35]
  Test for Direct Effect, [12.15]
  Treaty Provisions, [12.20]
  Treaty Provisions with Direct Effect, Particular, [2.90], [3.15], [3.150], [3.265], [4.05], [6.10], [8.90], [10.20], [12.20], [12.25]
  Van Gend en Loos Case, [12.10]
  Vertical Direct Effect, [10.20], [12.25], [12.45]
Direct Investments, [4.10]

Direct Taxation, [7.55]–[7.85]
Directives, [1.150], [12.40]–[12.50]
Discrimination
  Age Discrimination, [10.110]
  Burden of Proof, [10.60]
  Compensation, [10.60]
  Direct Discrimination, [10.60]
  Disability Discrimination, [10.115]
  Enforcement, [10.60]
  Equal Opportunities Directive, [10.60]
  Equal Treatment Directive, [10.100]
  Indirect Discrimination, [10.60]
  Public Contracts, [8.40]
  Racial Discrimination, [10.105]
  Sexual Orientation Discrimination, [10.120]
  See also Discrimination, Sex; Nationality
Discrimination, Sex
  Affirmative Action, [10.85]–[10.95]
  Defined, [10.15]
  Fundamental Right Against, [10.15]
  Maternity Leave, [10.80]
  Occupational Requirements, [10.65]
  Pregnant Workers, [10.75]
  'Sex' Defined, [10.55]
  Sexual Harassment, [10.60]
  Sexual Orientation, [10.55]
  Supply of Goods and Services, [10.70]
  See also Equal Pay for Equal Work
Disposable Beer Cans Case, [2.110]
Distinctive Character (Trade Marks), [9.125]
Distribution of Powers between EU and Member States, [1.130]
Doha Round, [13.125]
Domestic Law, Effect of EU Law upon, *see* Direct Effect; Supremacy of EU Law over National Law
Dumping
  Anti-dumping Duties, [5.165]
  Community Industry, [5.140]
  Community Interest, [5.145]
  Comparison of Export Price and Normal Value, [5.85]
  Constructed Normal Value, [5.60]–[5.75]
  Defined, [5.50]
  Definitive Duty, [5.175]
  Division of Market within EU, [5.140]
  Dumping Margin, [5.90]
  Duties, Anti-dumping, [5.165]
  Duties Apply Prospectively, [5.180]
  Duties, Judicial Review of, [5.200]
  Duties, Refund of, [5.190]
  Duties, Review by Council, [5.195]
  EU Legislation, [5.45]
  Export Price, [5.80]
  Investigation of Complaints, [5.150]–[5.155]
  Material Injury, [5.11]–[5.130]
  Normal Value, [5.55]
  Provisional Duty, [5.170]
  Related Producers, [5.140]
  Safeguard Measures, [5.31]
  Surveillance Measures, [5.31]
  Termination of Investigation and Proceedings, [5.155]
  Threat of Injury, [5.135]

E
Electronic Commerce and Communications, [3.235]
Electronic Signatures, [2.135]
Enhanced Cooperation between Member States, [1.145]
Environmental Protection
  Disposable Beer Cans Case, [2.110]
  Environmental Tax, [2.10]
  Free Movement of Goods, Exception to, [2.110]
Equal Pay for Equal Work
  Defrenne Case, [10.20]
  Directives, [10.45]
  Generally, [10.10]
  Indirect Discrimination, [10.30]–[10.35]
  Job Classification Schemes, [10.50]
  Pay, [10.40]
  Piece Work, [10.10]
  Same Establishment, [10.25]
Equivalent Effect
  Charges with an, [2.10]
  Measures with an, [2.35]–[2.85]
Euro, [1.15]
European Atomic Energy Community, [1.20]
European Central Bank, [1.115]
European Coal and Steel Community, [1.20]
European Commission, [1.90]
European Committee for Electrotechnical Standardization, [2.140]
European Committee for Standardization, [2.140]
European Council, [1.105]

European Constitution, [1.45]
European Convention on Human Rights, [12.110]
European Court of Human Rights, [12.110]
European Court of Justice
  Action for Annulment, [11.85]
  Action for Failure to Act, [11.110]
  Action for Failure to Fulfil a Treaty Obligation, [11.115]
  Acts of the Institutions, [11.145]
  Advocates-General, [11.120]–[11.35]
  Composition, [11.10]
  Court of First Instance: *see* General Court
  'Court or Tribunal' [11.130]
  Direct and Individual Concern, [5.200], [11.85]
  Dissenting Judgments, [11.20]
  General Court, [11.40]
  Grounds of Review, [11.106]
  Independence of Judges, [11.15]
  Indirect Actions, [11.120]
  Interim Measures, [11.85]
  Interpretation, Methods of, [11.45]–[11.70]
  Invalidity, Temporal Effect of, [11.85]
  Judgments, [11.20]
  Judicial Review of Anti-Dumping and Countervailing Duties, [5.200]
  Judicial Review of Competition Law Decisions, [6.205], [6.215]
  Judicial Review of International Agreements, [5.15]
  Jurisdiction, generally, [11.75]
  Lump Sum or Penalty, [11.115]
  Misuse of Power, [11.106]
  National Courts, Role regarding Preliminary Rulings, [11.135]
  Obligatory References, [11.140]
  Policy-Making, [11.150]–[11.155]
  Preliminary Rulings, [11.125]–[11.150], [13.65]
  Presumption of Validity, [11.125]
  Reviewable Act, [11.90]–[11.105]
  Severance, [11.85]
  Temporal Effect of Decisions, [11.85], [11.150]–[11.155]
European Data Protection Supervisor, [1.125]
European Economic Area Agreement, [2.150]
European Economic Community, [1.20]
European Economic and Social Committee, [1.120]
European Free Trade Area, [1.70], [2.150]
European Ombudsman, [1.125]
European Parliament, [1.100]
European Patent Convention, [9.105]
European Patent Office, [9.105]
European System of Central Banks, [1.115]
European Telecommunications Institute, [2.140]
European Union
  Accessions, [1.20]
  Competence, Competition Law, [6.05], [6.195]
  Competence, Exclusive, [1.130]
  Competence, Intellectual Property, [9.05]
  Finance through Own Resources, [7.40]
  Historical Development, [1.20]–[1.55]
  Membership, [1.05]
Excessive Budget Deficits, [1.15]
Excise Duties, [7.50]
Exclusive Competences of EU, [1.130]
Exhaustion of Rights, [9.25]–[9.50], [9.135]
Export Price, [5.80]

F

Factortame Case, [12.80]
Financial Interests of Member States, [4.30]
Fiscal Barriers, Removal of, *see* Taxation Barriers to Trade, Removal of
Fiscal Supervision, Effectiveness of, [4.30]
Flexibility Clause, [1.130]
Foodstuffs Advertising, [2.135]
Foreign Direct Investment, [4.15]
Foreign Relations of EU
  Australia, [1.65]
  Canada, [1.70]
  New Zealand, [1.75]
  South Africa, [1.80]
  United States, [1.60]
Founding Treaties
  Amendments to, [1.25]–[1.55]
  Comparative Tables for, [1.55], Appendices B–C
  Generally, [1.15]
  Historical Development, [1.20]–[1.55]
Framework Decisions, [1.50]

Freedom of Establishment
Abuse of, [3.130]
Application of Protection, [3.95]
Branches, [3.85]
Collective Action Limitation, [3.130]
Companies, [3.70], [3.80]–[3.85], [3.130]
Consumer Protection Limitation, [3.115]
Crime Prevention Limitation, [3.120]
Discrimination, [3.90]
Freedom to Provide Services, Relationship with, [3.150]
Individuals, [3.70]–[3.75]
Industrial Action Limitation, [3.130]
Internal to a Member State, [3.95]
Lawyers, [3.75]
Limitations, [3.100]–[3.135]
Official Authority, [3.15]
Professionals, [3.75]
Public Policy Exception, [3.110]
Purpose, [3.70]
Service Providers, [3.140]
Subsidiaries, [3.85]
Tax Avoidance Prevention Limitation, [3.125]
Freedom of Information, [1.155]
Freedom of Movement of Capital
Comparable Situations, [4.20]
Existing Restrictions, [4.30]
Freedom to Provide Services, Relationship with, [3.150]
Justifications for Restrictive Measures, [4.20]
'Movement of Capital' Defined, [4.10]
Overriding Requirements, [4.25]
Proportionality, [4.30]
Protective Measures, [4.35]
Purely Internal Movements, [4.10]
Restrictions on Free Movement of Capital, [4.15]
Step back, [4.30]
Taxation Laws, [4.20]
Third States, [4.05], [4.30]
Freedom of Movement and Residence
Border Posts between Member States Removed, [3.265], [3.290]
Deportation, [3.275]
Direct Effect, [3.265]
Entry, Right of, [3.275]
External Borders, [3.290]
Expulsion, [3.285]
Internal to a Member State, [3.265]
Non-EU Citizens, [3.295]
Residence, Right of, [3.280]
Restrictions upon, [3.285]
Schengen Agreement, [3.290]
Secondary Legislation, [3.270]–[3.280]
Travel to Another Member State, [3.270]
Freedom of Movement of Goods
Distinctly Applicable Measures, [2.105]
'Goods' Defined, [2.10]
Harmonisation of Treaty Exceptions, [2.100], [2.135]
Indistinctly Applicable Measures, [2.105]
Measures with an Equivalent Effect, [2.35]–[2.85]
Necessity Principle, [2.120]
Private Action Threatening Interstate Trade, [2.130]
Proportionality, [2.125]
Rule of Reason, [2.105]–[2.110]
Technical Standards, [2.140]
Treaty Exceptions, [2.100]
Freedom of Movement of Workers
Application of Protection, [3.15]
Direct Effect, [3.15]
Discrimination, [3.40]
Internal to a Member State, [3.15]
Low Income Workers, [3.30]
Obstacles, [3.45]
Public Policy, [3.55]
Public Service Employment, [3.60]
Residence, Right of, [3.35]
Secondary Legislation, [3.65]
Social and Tax Advantages, [3.65]
Treaty Provisions, [3.10]
'Worker' Defined, [3.20]–[3.30]
Freedom to Provide Services
Consumer Protection Limitation, [3.185]
Cross-border Mediation, [3.255]
Direct Effect, [3.150]
Discrimination, [3.170]
Electronic Commerce and Communications, [3.235]
Freedom of Establishment, Relationship with, [3.150]
Freedom of Establishment of Service Providers, [3.140]
Freedom of Movement of Capital, Relationship with, [3.150]
Fundamental Rights Limitation, [3.190]

Horizontal Effect, [3.150]
Insurance Services, [3.245]
Investment Services, [3.245]
Internal to a Member State, [3.150]
Lawyers, [3.205]
Limitations, [3.180]–[3.190]
Mediation, Cross-border, [3.255]
Non-EU Citizens, [3.260]
Obstacles, [3.175]
Payment Services, [3.250]
Postal Services, [3.240]
Professional Services, [3.205]
Public Policy Exception, [3.180]
Recipient's Right to Travel to State of Service Provider, [3.165]
Scope of Protection, [3.165]
Secondary Legislation, [3.195]–[3.255]
'Services' Defined, [2.10], [3.155]–[3.160]
Services in the Internal Market, [3.200]
Transport Services, [3.210]–[3.230]
Treaty Provisions, [3.150]
Free Trade Agreements
Bilateral, [13.135]
EFTA, [1.70], [2.150]
EU-South Africa, [1.80]
Regional Agreements, [13.130]
Fundamental Freedoms, Four, [1.15]
Fundamental Rights in EU Law
Charter of Fundamental Rights, [1.40], [10.30]
European Convention on Human Rights, [12.110]
Free Movement of Goods, Exception to, [2.110]
General Principles of EU Law, [12.90]–[12.110]
Textual Basis for, [12.105]

G
GATT 1994
Anti-Dumping Duties, [5.40]
Countervailing Duties, [5.40]
Direct Effect, [13.70]
Dumping, [5.40]
Generally, [13.15]
EU Membership, [13.60]
Health Protection, [13.55]
Import Quotas, Elimination of, [13.40]
Like Products, [13.30]
Most-favoured Nation, [13.25]
Non-discrimination, [13.30]
Position under EU Law, [13.70]–[13.75]
Preliminary Rulings, [13.65]
Regional Free Trade Agreements, [13.130]
Relationship with Specialist Agreements, [13.80], [13.85]
Review of the Legality of Measures, [13.75]
Subsidies, [5.40], [5.100]
Tariff Barriers, Gradual Reduction of, [13.35]
General Agreement on Tariffs and Trade 1994, *see* GATT 1994
General Court, [11.40]
General Principles of EU Law, [12.90]–[12.110]
Geneva Act, [9.160]
Geographical Indications, *see* Industrial and Commercial Property
Goods
defined, [2.10]
See also Free Movement of Goods
Government Contracts, *see* Public Procurement
Graphical Representation (Trade Marks), [9.120]

H
Hague Agreement, [9.160]
Harmonisation
Direct Taxation, [7.55]–[7.80]
Indirect Taxation, [7.35]
Treaty Exceptions to Free Movement of Goods, [2.100], [2.135]
Health, Protection of
Food Safety, [10.220]
Free Movement of Goods, [2.100]
GATT 1994 [13.55]
Health Claims, [10.185]
Hong Kong
CISG, Non-application to, [13.140]
Relations with EU, [1.81]
Human Rights, *see* Fundamental Rights in EU Law

I
Import Authorisation, [2.40]
Import Licensing Procedures Agreement (WTO), [13.110]
India
Relations with EU, [1.81]
Indications of Origin, [2.65]
Indirect Taxation, [7.25], [7.35]

Individuals, Taxation of, [7.80]
Industrial and Commercial Property
Competition Law, [6.135], [9.60]–[9.70]
Copyright, [9.30], [9.80]–[9.100]
Counterfeit Measures, [9.185]
Deception of Consumers, [9.55]
Defined, [9.15]
Designations of Origin, [9.175]
Designs, [9.160]
Enforcement Measures, [9.180]
Exhaustion of Rights, [9.25]–[9.50], [9.135]
Free Movement of Goods, Exception to, [2.100], [9.05]–[9.55]
Geographical Indications, [9.175]
International Treaties, [9.100]–[9.105], [9.155]
Licences and Competition Law, [6.135]
National Law, [9.10]
Packaging, [9.20], [9.45], [9.135]
Patents, [9.35]–[9.40], [9.105]
Pirated Goods, [9.185]
Plant Variety Rights, [9.165]
Property Ownership Systems, [9.75]
Semi-conductors, [9.170]
Trade marks, [9.45], [9.110]–[9.155]
Information Society, [9.85], [10.145]
Inheritances, [4.10], [4.15]
Insider Dealing, [4.50]
Insurance, [3.245], [4.55]
Intellectual Property
TRIPs Agreement, [13.120]
See also Industrial and Commercial Property
Interest for Late Payment, [2.135]
Interest and Royalties Directive, [7.75]
Interim Measures, [11.85]
Internal Market, [1.15], [4.05], [7.05]
Internal Taxation, [7.15]–[7.30]
International Agreements, *see* Treaty-making by EU
International Commercial Arbitration, [3.256]
International Electrotechnical Association, [2.140]
International Law
Role in Interpretation of Legislation, [11.45]
International Organisation for Standardization, [2.140]
International Registration of Marks, [9.155]
International Sale of Goods, *see* CISG
International Trade, *see* World Trade
International Union for the Protection of New Varieties of Plants, [9.165]
Internet
Data Protection, [10.150]
Intellectual Property, [9.85]
Interpretation of Legislation
Contextual Interpretation, [11.60]
Generally, [11.45]
Historical Interpretation, [11.55]
International Law, Role of, [11.45]
Language Versions, Different, [11.70]
Literal Interpretation, [11.50]
Teleological Interpretation, [11.65]
Invalidity, Temporal Effect of, [11.85]
Investment Services, [3.245], [4.50]

J

Judicial Review by ECJ, *see* European Court of Justice

L

Labeling Rules, [2.60]
Labour Law
Charter of Fundamental Rights, [10.130]
Competition Law, [6.85]
Transfer of Undertakings, Protection of Workers' Rights, [10.125]
Vocational Training, [10.135]
Worker Participation in Management of European Companies, [3.145]
Late Payment in Commercial Transactions, [2.135]
Law Reports
Commission Decisions, [6.220]
ECJ Cases, [1.110]
EFTA Cases, [2.150]
EPO Cases, [9.105]
NAFTA Panel Decisions, [13.130]
WTO Dispute Settlement Cases, [13.20]
Legislation, EU
Interpretation *see* Interpretation of Legislation
Public Availability of EU Legal Acts, [1.155]
Reasons for Legislation, [1.150]
Types, [1.150]
Legislative Procedure in Parliament, [1.100]

Lending Rights, [9.80]
Licensing Agreements, [9.140]
Life Assurance, [4.55]
Lomé Convention, [13.85]
Luxury Goods, [9.140]

M
Maastricht Treaty, [1.30]
Madrid Protocol, [9.155]
Malaysia
  Relations with EU, [1.81]
Market Manipulation, [4.50]
Maximum Prices, [2.55]
Measures with an Equivalent Effect
  Advertising Restrictions, [2.70]
  Censorship Classification, [2.80]
  Direct Effect, [2.90]
  Generally, [2.35]
  Import Authorisation, [2.40]
  Indications of Origin, [2.65]
  Labeling Rules, [2.60]
  Maximum Prices, [2.55]
  Origin, Indications of, [2.65]
  Packaging Rules, [2.60]
  Prize Competitions, Prohibition of, [2.75]
  Product Description Rules, [2.60]
  Production Quotas, [2.45]
  Sunday Closing Laws, [2.80]
  Transport Restrictions, [2.50]
Mediation, Cross-border, [3.255]
Member States
  Accessions to EU, [1.20]
  Admission to EU, [1.100]
  Budget Deficits, [1.15]
  Distribution of Powers between the EU and Member States, [1.130]
  Enhanced Cooperation between, [1.145]
  Financial Interests of, [4.30]
  Historical Development, [1.20]–[1.55]
  Membership of EU, [1.05]
  National Law, Effect of EU Law upon: *see* Direct Effect, Supremacy of EU Law over
National Law
  Property Ownership Systems, [9.75]
  Retained Competences, [1.130]
  Secession of, [1.145]
  Treaty-making power, [5.30]
Mergers Directive, [7.60]
Minority Shareholders, [4.30]
Misuse of Power, [11.106]
Monetary Union, [1.15], [4.35]
Money Laundering, [4.40]
Mutual Acceptance of Goods, [2.145]
Mutual Recognition Agreements, [1.60]–[1.75]

N
National Courts, Role regarding Preliminary Rulings, [11.135]
National Law, Effect of EU Law upon, *see* Direct Effect; Supremacy of EU Law over National Law
Nationality
  Free Movement of Capital, [4.15]
  Non-Discrimination on Ground of, [3.300]
  Public Procurement, [8.85]
Necessity Principle regarding Free Movement of Goods, [2.120]
New Zealand
  Relations with EU, [1.75]
Normal Value, [5.55]
North American Free Trade Agreement, [13.130]

O
Odour as Trade Mark, [9.120]
Office for Harmonisation in the Internal Market, [9.150], [9.160]
Official Journal of the European Union, [1.155], [5.150], [5.155], [6.220], [9.175]
Ombudsman, [1.125]
Opinions, [1.150]
Ordinary Legislative Procedure in Parliament, [1.100]
Origin
  Indications of, [2.65]
  Rules of, [2.20], [13.105]

P
Packaging Rules, [2.60]
Parent/Subsidiary Directive, [7.65]
Paris Convention, [9.105]
Patent Cooperation Treaty, [9.105]
Patents, *see* Industrial and Commercial Property
Payment Services, [3.250]
Personal Data, [10.140]–[10.150]
Pillar System, [1.30], [1.50]–[1.55]
Plant Variety Rights, *see* Industrial and Commercial Property
Policy-Making, Judicial, [11.150]–[11.155]

Political Institutions of EU, [1.05]–[1.160]
Postal Services, [3.240]
Preliminary Rulings, [11.125]–[11.150], [13.65]
Preshipment Inspection Agreement (WTO), [13.100]
Presumption of Validity, [11.125]
Prior Authorisation System, [4.30]
Privacy
  Data Protection, [10.140]–[10.150]
Private Action Threatening Interstate Trade, [2.130]
Private International Law
  CISG, [13.150]
Prize Competitions, Prohibition of, [2.75]
Product Description Rules, [2.60]
Production Quotas, [2.45]
Professional Services, [3.205]
Proportionality
  Free Movement of Capital, [4.30]
  Free Movement of Goods, [2.125]
  Generally, [1.140]
Public Availability of EU Legal Acts, [1.155]
Public Contracts, *see* Public Procurement
Public Health
  Exception to Free Movement of Goods, [2.100]
Public Morality
  Exception to Free Movement of Goods, [2.100]
Public Procurement
  Annex II A Services, [8.35]
  Annex II B Services, [8.65]
  Award of Public Contracts, [8.60]
  Competition Law, [8.95]
  Defence and Security Contracts, [8.75]
  Enforcement of Procurement Rules, [8.80]
  Excluded Sectors, [8.75]
  Exclusions from Directive, [8.15], [8.85]
  Non-discrimination Obligations, [8.40]
  Procedure for Award of Public Contracts, [8.45]
  'Public Contracts' Defined, [8.30]
  Publicity of Contracting Opportunities, [8.55]
  Qualification and Disqualification of Bidders, [8.70]
  Quantitative Restrictions, [8.90]
  Technical Specifications, [8.45]
  Threshold Amounts, [8.25]
  Types of Government Contracts, [8.05]
  WTO Agreement, [8.100]

Q

Qualified Majority Voting, [1.95]
Quantitative Restrictions between Member States, [2.30], [8.90]

R

Real Estate, [4.10]
Reasons for Legislation, [1.150]
Recommendations, [1.150]
Regional Free Trade Agreements, *see* Free Trade Agreements
Regulations, [1.150], [12.30]–[12.35]
Relations with EU
  Australia, [1.65]
  Canada, [1.70]
  New Zealand, [1.75]
  South Africa, [1.80]
  United States, [1.60]
Rental Rights, [9.80]
Resale Royalty for Artworks, [9.80]
Restriction of Selling Arrangements, [2.115]
Retained Competences of Member States, [1.130]
Retention of Title Clauses, [2.135]
Revocation of Trade Marks, [9.140]
Right to be Heard, [11.135]
Rules of Origin
  Goods, [2.20]
  WTO Agreement, [13.105]
Rule of Reason, [2.105]–[2.110]

S

Safeguards
  EEA, [2.150]
  WTO Safeguard Agreement, [13.45]
Sale of Goods, *see* CISG; Consumer Protection
Sanctions, [5.10]
Sanitary Measures Agreement (WTO), [13.90]
Satellite Broadcasting, [9.95]
Schengen Agreement, [3.290]
Secession of Member States, [1.145]
Securities, [4.50]
Semi-conductors, [9.170]
Services Agreement (WTO), [13.115]
Severance, [11.85]
Sex Discrimination, *see* Discrimination, Sex

Shared Jurisdiction, [1.130]
Singapore
  Relations with EU, [1.81]
Single European Act, [1.25]
Sound as Trade Mark, [9.120]
South Africa
  Relations with EU, [1.80]
Subsidiarity, [1.135]
Subsidies
  Amount of the Subsidy, [5.110]
  Community Industry, [5.140]
  Community Interest, [5.145]
  Countervailable Subsidies, [5.105]
  Countervailing Duties, [5.165]
  Defined, [5.100]
  Definitive Duty, [5.175]
  Division of Market within EU, [5.140]
  Duties Apply Generally, [5.185]
  Duties Apply Prospectively, [5.180]
  Duties, Countervailing, [5.165]
  Duties, Judicial Review of, [5.200]
  Duties, Refund of, [5.190]
  Duties, Review by Council, [5.195]
  EU Legislation, [5.95]
  Investigation of Complaints, [5.150]–[5.155]
  Material Injury, [5.115]–[5.130]
  Provisional Duty, [5.170]
  Related Producers, [5.140]
  Termination of Investigation and Proceeding, [5.155]
  Threat of Injury, [5.135]
  Undertakings, [5.160]
Sunday Closing Laws, [2.80]
Supremacy of EU Law over National Law
  Administrative Action, [12.65]
  Collective Agreements, [12.65]
  Constitutional Law, National, [12.70]–[12.75]
  Duty of the National Authorities, [12.80]
  Factortame Case, [12.80]
  Generally, [12.65]
  Invocation of National Law as Excuse for Noncompliance, [12.65]
  Suspension of National Statute, [12.80]

T
Taxation
  Barriers to Trade: *see* Taxation Barriers to Trade, Removal of
  Capital, [7.45]
  Companies, [7.55]–[7.75]
  Excise Duties, [7.50]
  Free Movement of Capital, [4.20]
  Indirect Taxation, [7.25], [7.35], [7.55]
  Individuals, [7.80]
  Internal Taxation, [7.15]–[7.30]
  Value Added Taxes, [7.40]
Taxation Barriers to Trade, Removal of
  Arbitration Convention, [7.70]
  Customs Duties Prohibited, [7.10], [7.20]
  Direct Taxation, [7.55]
  Excise Duties, [7.50]
  Indirect Taxation, [7.25], [7.35]
  Interest and Royalties Directive, [7.75]
  Internal Taxation, [7.15]–[7.30]
  Mergers Directive, [7.60]
  Parent/Subsidiary Directive, [7.65]
  Similar Domestic Products, [7.30]
  Substitutability of Products, [7.30]
  Value Added Taxes, [7.40]
Technical Barriers Agreement (WTO), [13.95]
Technical Standards, [2.140]
Technological Protection Measures, [9.85]
Temporal Effect of ECJ Decisions, [11.85], [11.150]–[11.155]
Term of Copyright Protection, [9.80]
Terrorist Financing, [4.35]
Tobacco
  Advertising, [10.170]
  Excise upon, [7.50]
  Marketing, [1.140]
Trade marks, *see* Industrial and Commercial Property
Transportation Services
  Air, [3.220], [10.210]
  Competition Law, [6.175]
  Inland Waterways, [3.225]
  Maritime, [3.225]
  Rail, [3.215], [10.210]
  Restrictions, [2.50]
  Road, [3.230]
Treaty of Amsterdam, [1.35]
Treaty Exceptions to Free Movement of Goods, [2.100]
Treaty of Lisbon, [1.55]
Treaty of Maastricht, [1.30]
Treaty of Nice, [1.45]
Treaty of Rome, [1.20]
Treaty-making by EU
  Direct Effect, [5.15]
  Express Powers, [5.20]–[5.25]
  Generally, [5.15]

Implied Powers, [5.25]–[5.30]
International Personality of EU, [5.20]
Judicial Review, [5.15]
Member States, Power of, [5.30]
Mixed Agreements, [9.100], [13.60]
Procedure for Conclusion, [5.15]
TRIPs Agreement, [13.120]

U
Union Treaty, [1.30]
United States
Bilateral Free Trade Agreements, [13.135]
Relations with EU, [1.60]
UPOV Convention, [9.165]
Uruguay Round, *see* World Trade Organization

V
Value Added Taxes, [7.40]
Van Gend en Loos Case, [12.10]
Vienna Sales Convention, *see* CISG

W
Wine, [9.175]
World Intellectual Property Organization, [9.100], [9.155]
World Trade
Regional Free Trade Agreements, [13.130]
Three Track Trading System, [13.10]
See also World Trade Organization
World Trade Organization
Agriculture Agreement, [13.85]
Amendments to Comply with WTO Rulings, [13.60]
Customs, Uniform Administration of, [13.50]
Dispute Settlement, [1.60]–[1.75], [13.20]
Doha Round, [13.125]
Dumping, [5.40], [5.90]
EU Membership, [13.60]
EU Rights, Exercise of, [13.60]
Import Licensing Procedures Agreement, [13.110]
Import Quotas, Elimination of, [13.40]
Intellectual Property Agreement, [13.120]
Most-favoured Nation, [13.25]
Non-discrimination, [13.30]
Preshipment Inspection Agreement, [13.100]
Public Procurement Agreement, [8.100]
Rules of Origin Agreement, [13.105]
Safeguards Agreement, [13.45]
Sanitary Measures Agreement, [13.90]
Services Agreement, [13.115]
Subsidies, [5.40], [5.100]
Tariff Barriers, Gradual Reduction of, [13.35]
Technical Barriers Agreement, [13.95]
TRIPs Agreement, [13.120]

Breinigsville, PA USA
10 May 2010

237600BV00001B/4/P

9 789048 187737